Sociology: An Introduction

About the Author

Christopher Bates Doob has been teaching Introductory Sociology as well as courses in Social Problems, The Family, Social Change, and The City in Western Civilization for twenty years. He is currently professor of sociology at Southern Connecticut State University. He has been a Senior Research Scientist for the New York State Department of Mental Hygiene. He also served as a consultant to the Roper Organization in New York City.

In addition to *Sociology: An Introduction*, Dr. Doob has written *The Open Covenant: Social Change in Contemporary Society* published by Praeger Publishers in 1987. Currently he is completing a core text on American racism titled *Racism: An American Cauldron*. He has also begun a study of the relationship between ideology and small-group behavior.

Dr. Doob received his bachelor's and master's degrees in sociology from Oberlin College and his Ph.D. in sociology from Cornell University.

Sociology: An Introduction

THIRD EDITION

Christopher Bates Doob
Southern Connecticut State University

HOLT, RINEHART AND WINSTON, INC.

Fort Worth   Chicago   San Francisco   Philadelphia
Montreal   Toronto   London   Sydney   Tokyo

Publisher:	Ted Buchholz
Acquisitions Editor:	Christopher P. Klein
Developmental Editor:	Meera Dash
Senior Project Editor:	Dawn Youngblood
Production Manager:	Kathleen Ferguson
Art & Design Supervisor:	John Ritland
Text Designer:	Tom Dawson/DUO Design
Cover Illustration:	Masato Nishimura

LIBRARY OF CONGRESS CATALOGING-IN-PUBLICATION DATA

Doob, Christopher Bates.
     Sociology: an introduction/Christopher Bates Doob. -- 3rd ed.
         p.   cm.
     Includes bibliographical references.
     1. Sociology   I. Title.
HM51.D645   1991
301--dc20
                                91-31236
                                CIP

ISBN: 0-03-047004-8

Address Editorial Correspondence To: 301 Commerce Street, Suite 3700, Fort Worth, TX 76102

Address Orders To: 6277 Sea Harbor Drive, Orlando, FL 32887
                1-800-782-4479, or 1-800-433-0001 (in Florida)

Printed in the United States of America

1 2 3 4   069   9 8 7 6 5 4 3 2 1

Holt, Rinehart and Winston, Inc.
The Dryden Press
Saunders College Publishing

Permissions acknowledgments and other credits appear on pages 561 – 563.

Once again, to Eveline Bates (Doob)
and Leonard William Doob who,
besides being my parents, have always
been my best teachers.

Preface

As I write the preface to the third edition of this text, spring is starting. The season seems appropriate because, like spring, a new edition represents a renewal. While no human activity can match the magnificence of the yearly appearance of new grass, leaves, and flowers, the process of putting together a text edition is both interesting and complex.

Colleagues teaching introductory sociology, editors at Holt, Rinehart and Winston, and students have all participated, and their comments have been invaluable. Those involved with the third edition have proposed a number of specific changes, but there has been general support for the basic structure established in the second edition. The following features are new:

A systematic effort is made at various points in the text to illustrate the uniqueness of the sociological perspective, using *Habits of the Heart,* the study of American society written by Robert Bellah and his associates, and a variety of other sources. Such topics as changing American values and the prospects for upward mobility are examined.

In-text references link particular discussions to important concepts introduced earlier in the text, thereby providing valuable conceptual linkages between material in different chapters.

Nine new feature sections offer up-to-date analyses of such topics as Gorbachev's leadership, drugs in America, and the abortion controversy.

About 300 in-text references to new studies and other recent sources help keep the text current in content.

Numerous updates or replacements of tables and figures also contribute to the book's up-to-date coverage.

From the second edition, the text has retained the following features:

A streamlined, 17-chapter format permits comprehensive coverage comfortably within a semester.

A built-in study guide, updated for this edition, enables students to review the material they have just learned.

Five updated "Research in Sociology" sections provide concrete illustrations of what sociological research involves. These sections have been removed from the study guides and placed within the actual chapters.

Organization

I remain convinced that a fairly traditional organization is the best for an introductory text. Thus the five parts of the original edition have been retained. Part One examines the particular features, contributions, and theories that distinguish the sociological point of view and surveys the major methods and problems of doing research. Part Two launches into the variety of influences, conditions, and pressures that help make individuals part of the larger social environment. Part Three examines the nature of inequalities in modern society and the processes that affect specific minorities in the United States. Part Four brings the student to the next level of complexity in social arrangements by surveying a range of social institutions, how (and how well) they meet the collective needs of American society, and how and why they are changing. The final section of the text examines the forces and issues that have affected and often changed each level of our social order, from relationships between institutions to small-group interactions.

Once again, the text has seventeen chapters. Many instructors who have used the book indicated that they are comfortable with its length. They have also confirmed that the best way to economize is in the coverage of social institutions. Thus the institutions are presented in combination chapters, which illustrate the respective relationships between religion and education, the political and economic institutions, and science and medicine.

Style of Presentation

Many introductory sociology students, even potential majors, have little background in the social sciences and even less familiarity with the way scientists and academicians think. For this reason textbooks that make assumptions about the students' reach can easily slip beyond their grasp. In spite of a subject matter than is inherently interesting and relevant, student motivation can quickly subside when there are too many hurdles to learning. Students need to feel successful about understanding and interpreting what they read. This means that a text must spell out the implications of the material presented in straightforward language, interrelate facts and ideas so that they make sense together, and anchor concepts and theories within familiar experiences and events.

To help the student experience success — and, I hope, excitement — in learning about sociology, I have tried to provide the following:

Careful attention to vocabulary and sentence length, consistent presentation of basic terminology, and a personalized, informal style that speaks with, instead of at, the student.

An orderly presentation of topics, moving — especially in Part Four — from large-scale theoretical and substantive issues to small-group and individual experiences.

A special emphasis on contemporary issues and examples with which students already have some familiarity and personal interest.

Careful integration of all visual supplements to the text — figures, charts, tables, and photographs — through well-developed in-text references, explanations, and captions.

Coverage that is comprehensive — all the major topics, research, and trends — without being overly detailed.

A balanced presentation of the major theories with careful attention to both their contributions and their limitations.

Up-to-date statistical information drawn from government and survey data with special care given to explaining the relevance of these facts and figures to the issues and trends under discussion. Topics analyzed include the fear of AIDS, the effectiveness of public education, the willingness to protect environmental health, and the best means to resolve the American drug problem.

Throughout the preparation of the third edition, there has been a relentless effort to supply new source material — new studies and statistics, in particular.

Special Aids To Teaching and Learning

It is easy to fill a text with a range of pedagogical devices. In fact, it is sometimes difficult to know when to stop. I have, however, carefully put together a variety of aids that I felt would work together in the scope of an introductory text and genuinely enhance the effectiveness of teaching and learning.

Built-in Study Guide

Study-guide materials appear in sections after each chapter in the text, so that students have immediate, economical access to features that can aid their review of the material. The sections contain:

LEARNING OBJECTIVES A list of major issues outlines the basic material that must be learned within the chapter.

SUMMARIES   Numbered sets of paragraphs at the end of each chapter provide a framework for review and help reinforce learning.

KEY TERMS   Concepts are highlighted in bold-face type and defined in the text proper and then regrouped alphabetically and redefined in an end-of-chapter list for easy reference and review. For further assistance an alphabetized glossary containing all the concepts in the Key Terms sections appears at the end of the text.

TESTS   True-false, multiple-choice, and essay tests offer opportunities to determine how well students have assimilated the material. At the end of the study-guide sections, answers to the true-false questions and the multiple-choice questions are provided.

SUGGESTED READINGS   Each chapter of the study guide contains an average of ten incisively annotated readings drawn from a variety of categories: novels, essays, case studies, articles, critiques, theoretical analyses, biographical and autobiographical accounts, practical guides, historical and cross-cultural documents, and literature surveys.

ADDITIONAL ASSIGNMENTS   Independent projects involve reorganization of material in the chapter or some kind of simple study. Instructors can assign these projects to give students a chance to apply the knowledge gained from the chapter.

"Research in Sociology" Sections

I believe that one of the most difficult tasks teachers of introductory sociology must face is conveying a concrete sense of the challenges and problems involved in doing sociological research.

To make this task easier, the text contains five sections that examine sociological research into the topics of culture, sexual behavior, rape, charisma, and prison riots. It is my intention that these "Research in Sociology" sections reexamine throughout the text many of the methodological issues discussed in Chapter 2, and, most importantly, that they bring sociological research to life for the student.

Other Feature Sections

Three other types of featured sections provide recent illustrations of many issues and topics discussed in the text. Two are found in each chapter, introduced within the body of the chapter.

Social Applications

These sections emphasize the use of sociological skills and analysis of social issues. They include such subjects as drugs in America, the vicious cycle of poverty, and the earthquake in California in 1989.

Cross-Cultural Perspectives

These inserts offer an invaluable counterperspective to issues and trends in American society by examining such topics as the development of Gorbachev's leadership, the relationship between blacks and whites in South Africa, and demonstrations by Chinese students.

American Controversies

These featured sections provide opposing positions on such issues as sociologists' preferences for particular theories, affirmative action for minority groups, and abortion. As students evaluate, discuss, and debate these issues, the stimulation they receive will undoubtedly produce insights into the related social processes.

Supplements to the Text

No text can address all the particular needs of each student and instructor, and so the quality of the supplementary materials is nearly as important as the text itself. The following supplements provide a comprehensive and easy-to-use package of materials suitable for different paces and styles of teaching, geared to both the motivational and learning needs of various students.

Instructor's Manual and Test Bank

Prepared by Robert Alexander, North Hehnepin Community College.

Each chapter of the Instructor's Manual portion contains a chapter synopsis, teaching objectives, a list of key concepts and terms, lecture ideas with references, topics for class participation and debate, and an annotated list of films and videos. The manual also includes advice in using the built-in study guide and other features of the text. The test bank portion contains one hundred multiple-choice, true-false, and short-answer questions per chapter, designed in part to test students' ability to apply information from the text.

Computerized Test Base

The test questions from the *Instructor's Manual and Test Bank* are offered in a software program known as *ExaMaster*™. Instructors using *Sociology: An Introduction* can obtain the program on floppy diskettes for use with IBM, Apple II, and MacIntosh microcomputers. *ExaMaster*™, a straightforward, versatile, and powerful computer program, is capable of randomly generating tests within parameters specified by the instructor and of permitting instructors to create and edit their own tests.

Test Compilation

The publisher also provides a customized test construction service, known as *RequesTest*™, for instructors using *Sociology: An Introduction*. Exams can be generated within forty-eight hours and dispatched by either mail or facsimile machine.

Computerized Study Guide

The built-in study guide is available in an interactive software program known as *ExamTutor*™. *ExamTutor*™ enables students to review randomly selected questions, customize a study to cover one or more chapters, and perform other helpful functions.

Interactive Computer Program

Users of this book will also be able to obtain *Social Scene,* an interactive computer program specifically designed for sociology students. This program lets students put their newfound knowledge to work in surveying data analyses and manipulating data sets drawn from the General Social Survey (GSS).

Overhead Transparencies

Classroom lectures will be enhanced with this collection of fifty, full-color transparencies. All contain information to supplement (not duplicate) sociological material in the textbook.

Sociology Videos

Holt, Rinehart and Winston will offer videos to accompany the third edition of *Sociology: An Introduction*. These videos apply sociological concepts to everyday situations.

Acknowledgments

Once again the professionals at Holt, Rinehart and Winston have served this project well. It has been a pleasure to work with Meera Dash, who was both skillful and thorough in overseeing the complicated process of producing the manuscript. As Senior Project Editor, Dawn Youngblood deftly and quickly directed the preparation of the manuscript. I am also indebted to John Ritland, Art and Design Supervisor, and Kathleen Ferguson, Production Manager. Finally I am grateful for the fine work done by Kathleen Nevils Bunnell, copy editor, and Greg Meadors, photo researcher.

Reviewers are essential for this type of project. They have provided several general insights and many specific evaluations and commentaries that have proved nothing less than invaluable. I simply don't know what I would have done without them. For this edition the reviewers were Robert Alexander, North Hennepin Community College; Paul Brasky, Ulster Community College; Lois Easterday, Onondaga Community College;

Laura Hartman, University of Texas at Austin; Margaret Park Haun, St. Louis Community College at Florissant Valley; Clinton McCurdy Lipsey, Tennessee State University; Vicki Pate, Fayetteville Technical Community College; Richard Phillips, Kalamazoo Valley Community College; Stephanie Shanks-Meile, Indiana University Northwest, Stephan Spitzer, University of Minnesota at Minneapolis, Metaleen Thomas, Caldwell Community College; and Robert Thompson, Minot State University.

Once more the contribution of Teresa E. M. Caraballal, with whom I discussed (and sometimes debated) every significant change, was enormous. Her presence also made the writing process much more enjoyable and meaningful.

Recognizing how interesting and valuable input can be, I encourage any instructor or student with a comment or question about this book to write me at the address below. I promise to answer all letters.

Chris Doob
Sociology Department
Southern Connecticut State University
501 Crescent Street
New Haven, CT 06515

Brief Contents

Detailed Contents

Detailed Contents

Part IV
The Institutions of American Society   325

Feature Contents

Social Applications

Cross-Cultural Perspectives

American Controversies

Research in Sociology

Sociology: An Introduction

PART

The Contribution of Sociology

1
Introduction

2
Doing Research in Sociology

1
INTRODUCTION

The Sociological Perspective

The Development of Sociology

Karl Marx
Émile Durkheim
Max Weber
American Sociology

Contemporary Sociological Theories

Conflict Theory
Structural-Functional Theory
Symbolic-Theory Interaction
Choosing and Using Theories

Study Guide

At fifteen Willie Bosket killed two people in the New York subway and was sent to prison. Several years later he was released, but soon he was back in custody for assault and arson. In prison since 1984, Bosket has set fire to his cell seven times, attacked guards nine times, and attempted numerous escapes. Then, in 1987, while being interviewed by a reporter writing his life story, Bosket stabbed a guard, seriously wounding him. "It was so senseless and stupid," the reporter explained. "He didn't even know the guard."

Bosket said, "I laugh at this system because there ain't a damn thing that it can do to me except to deal with the monster it has created" (Butterfield, 1989).

Is Bosket's claim about his development correct? Evidence indicates that Bosket grew up in a social world with distinctly negative overtones. His mother was loving but passive, and when Bosket asked about his father, whom he had never met, she would say, "He's a bad man, and you're just like him." In school teachers couldn't control the young boy, and Bosket was brought to Bellevue Hospital for observation, and then, at the age of nine, his mother sent him to a reformatory. Psychological tests indicated that he was "precocious, warm, and empathetic" and needed strong support and guidance from adults to attain an above-average intellectual and creative potential.

A judge, disregarding the advice, sent Bosket to a maximum security reformatory for boys, where most inmates had committed murder, rape, and armed robbery. Sylvia Honig, a social worker who has known Bosket since he was twelve, is convinced that those years were crucial: He was hardly ever disciplined, allowed to cut classes, and was even permitted to go to town with female staff members and get drunk. Bosket became increasingly aggressive and violent, hitting one boy with a poker in the eye, sodomizing another in the shower, and driving a truck into a social worker. Still, in 1977, at the age of fourteen, Bosket was released from the reformatory. Within a year he had committed a long list of crimes, including the subway murders.

What's ahead for Willie Bosket? Since the latest stabbing, Bosket is being kept in isolation. Even Honig, his only confidant and friend, has stopped visiting him, indicating that the more monstrous the social world in which Bosket must live, the more monstrous he becomes. She believes that he will soon try to kill either someone else or himself. Bosket told her, "If they kill me, then I can rest forever" (Butterfield, 1989: B5).

How does this account make you feel? Perhaps you are angry and believe that because of the atrocities Bosket has committed, the best course of action would be to execute him. On the other hand, you might be struck by the fact that because of the circumstances described, a capable human being's positive potential has been squandered and that as a result, he—the victim of social mismanagement—has become a destructive force. Or, perhaps you are simply confused.

If you are even somewhat confused, don't feel too bad. Sociologists have dedicated their lives to studying social issues, and they recognize that both an effective sociological analysis of these issues and solutions to those presenting social problems are usually complex and debatable. Throughout this book we discuss a range of social issues. We hope that at the end of the course you will understand more about the tools for analyzing them as well as the issues themselves.

Let's start with some basic ideas. As Willie Bosket's story shows, people are affected by their social world. Sociology centers on the belief that a scientific analysis of these social forces is one of the most effective ways to understand human behavior. To restate this, **sociology** is the scientific study of human behavior in groups and of the social forces that influence that behavior.

In the first section of this chapter, we look at the group settings of human behavior and describe the scientific nature of sociology. Our focus then shifts to a discussion of early sociologists who have contributed significantly to the developme of sociological thought. In the final section, w survey the three most prominent contemporary theories of sociology.

The Sociological Perspective

The sociological perspective emphasizes that people's thoughts and actions are strongly influenced by the groups to which they belong, as well as by other impinging social factors, such as values, beliefs, practices, and institutions. Of course, individuals often have the opportunity to choose between or among alternative courses of thought and action. They are not entirely independent beings, however. From birth until death, individuals are imbedded within and influenced by groups and larger structures. Groups are often small and immediate, for example, families and friends. Larger structures, called *institutions* and discussed in Chapter 4, "Groups," can be enormous and remote—the economy and government, for instance.

Think about what you have just read, because it is fundamental to understanding what sociology involves. The basic idea of the sociological perspective is that people's behavior is affected by the groups and other social forces with which they come in contact. The fact is that many Americans*—and perhaps you are one of them —resist this idea, feeling that individuals control their destiny. Certainly sociologists do not deny individuals' ability to affect what happens to them, but more than most Americans, they emphasize the impact of group forces on their behavior. The concept of the sociological perspective is so important that it will be consistently emphasized throughout this book.

The ways groups influence their members can be surprising, even for sociologists. In the late 1930s, for example, a young sociologist named William Foote Whyte was conducting a lengthy study of a group of young men in Boston. One evening Whyte and a number of the men went bowling. Before the game started, some of the group leaders predicted that they would score higher than the other men, and, as a close associate of the leaders, Whyte was included in the prediction. At first Whyte paid little attention, because such an outcome made little sense. Why, for example, should Frank Bonnelli, the best athlete in the entire group, finish well down the list? Why did Frank himself say that he did not expect to score well, not when he was "playing with fellows I know like that bunch" (Whyte, 1955: 318)?

After some thought Whyte realized that he was observing the influence of a group upon each of these men. The expectations and support of the group leadership strongly affected each man's bowling scores, regardless of his ability. Even Whyte himself was affected. That evening he felt strong group support, and as he stepped up to bowl, he was entirely confident that he would hit the pins at which he aimed. He had never felt that way before. Whyte later wrote, "It was a strange feeling, as if something larger than myself was controlling the ball as I went through my swing and released it toward the pins" (Whyte, 1955: 319). When the bowling was over, Whyte checked the scores. He was pleased to discover that the predicted order of finish was almost entirely correct. Whyte now had evidence to support his idea that the group did indeed influence its individual members.

Besides studying how groups influence their members, sociologists also analyze how social conditions influence the development of group memberships. Sociologists Maureen T. Hallinan and Richard A. Williams (1989) examined high-school students' friendships. Were blacks and whites more likely to have friends within their own or the other race? "Easy," you might quickly answer. "The same race." That's correct, but how much more likely were they to choose members of their own race? The study of 58,000 sophomores and seniors from more than 1000 public and pri-

* Throughout this book "American" is used to refer to citizens of the United States. While the citizens of other countries in both North and South America might object to the choice, it has been popularly used, and other designations prove wordy and clumsy.

In many racially integrated classrooms, informal patterns of segregation are developed and maintained.

vate schools found that, when asked to list their three closest friends, same-race friendships were cited six times as frequently as interracial friendships and that other factors like class size and racial composition had only a modest impact on this outcome.

Other results of the study indicated that school systems which place students into tracks according to academic achievement tend to discourage interracial friendships, since whites' more privileged backgrounds make it more likely that they enter higher-level tracks than blacks. On the other hand, evidence indicated that school programs encouraging interracial respect and self-esteem pro-

moted interracial friendships. At the end of their article, the sociologists suggested that these last two findings suggested recommendations to increase interracial friendships: First, minimize or eliminate tracks based on achievement levels, and, second, develop classroom policies that decrease status differences and give all students a chance to achieve high self-esteem.

These examples illustrate the meaning of the sociological perspective. The following Social Application provides a prominent sociologist's analysis of why this perspective is both important and useful.

SOCIAL APPLICATION

C. Wright Mills on Private Troubles and Public Issues

When should the sociological perspective be applied to individuals' problems? In his book *The Sociological Imagination* (1959), C. Wright

Mills offered a clear answer: when the problem ceases to be what he called "a personal trouble" and becomes "a public issue."

Consider the topic of unemployment. If a small number of men and women are unemployed, that is their "personal trouble." We can examine their character and skills and probably find deficiencies that make them incapable of holding a job. However, if over 6.7 million people representing over 5.4 percent of the labor force are unemployed—the situation in the United States in 1988—then sociological analysis produces a different conclusion. Such a high unemployment rate represents a "public issue." Sociologists, economists, and other analysts cannot focus only on individuals and their inadequacies to understand why so many people are unemployed. They must examine the American economic system and assess the various reasons why such a substantial percentage of Americans are unable to find jobs.

Consider another topic. If a few American couples seek divorce, we might conclude that these individuals are suffering from personal trouble. Perhaps they lack the skills and motivation necessary to make a marriage succeed. However, current statistics—about one-half of first marriages formed in the past decade will end in divorce—reveal an unprecedentedly high divorce rate. Sociologists must analyze a number of relatively new social conditions to understand why such a high rate of divorce now exists.

Mills realized that in times of rapid social changes, most people find it difficult to look beyond personal troubles to the public issues that affect them and people they know. He emphasized, however, that the more capable one becomes in using the sociological imagination, the more insight one develops into many problems in one's own life and the more effectively one will be able to deal with them.

After more than two decades of being a sociologist, I am deeply impressed by the contribution the sociological perspective makes. Using it doesn't make life idyllically simple, but it does help people understand more fully the problems in their personal, professional, or political life. That's a huge step, because once one understands a problem, the possibility of confronting and resolving it is greatly increased.

Source: C. Wright Mills. *The Sociological Imagination*. New York: Oxford University Press. 1959.

Like Whyte and Hallinan and Williams, sociological investigators do not simply declare their beliefs indisputable truth—they do research to determine whether those beliefs are correct. Their investigations are rooted in the scientific method. It is this method that distinguishes the sociological perspective from a "commonsense" interpretation of the world.

A **science** is a systematic effort to develop general principles about a particular subject matter, based on actual observations and stated in a form that can be tested by any competent person. Sciences are usually divided into two main branches: the **natural sciences**—older sciences such as astronomy, chemistry, physics, and biology that study the physical world—and the **social sciences**—the sciences that focus on various aspects of human behavior. Besides sociology, the social sciences include anthropology, economics, history, political science, and psychology.

Like their colleagues in the natural sciences, sociologists systematically use testable observations to develop general principles about their subject matter. Human beings are their subject matter; however, study of human beings poses some special problems. Unlike rats, rocks, or molecules, people are self-aware and capable of changing their behavior when they decide to. In fact, individuals sometimes alter their behavior abruptly when they know they are being observed. Furthermore, sociologists face much sharper limitations on what they can do to their subjects than do chemists, physicists, and biologists. As we see in Chapter 2, "Doing Research in Sociology," the great value placed on human beings means that researchers are compelled to consider subjects' rights and well-being.

How did such fascinating study of human beings begin? As for all sciences, the sociological perspective suggests that certain social conditions encouraged the birth of this field.

8

The Development of Sociology

The growth of science contributed to the development of sociology. In 1687 Isaac Newton, an Englishman, published his famous *Mathematical Principles of Natural Philosophy* about the laws of motion and the law of gravity. He concluded that the universe was logical and operated itself and was not, as had been believed for centuries, under divine influence. During the next century, leading French intellectuals came to accept the idea that science and reason, not religion, should shape their thinking.

Then, beginning with its revolution in 1789, France went through a series of radical political upheavals. Meanwhile the Industrial Revolution was drastically changing the economic and social structure of French society. Thus it is hardly surprising that many nineteenth-century social philosophers with a distinctly scientific bent, such as Auguste Comte (1798–1857), placed a strong emphasis on the need to reestablish order in the developing industrial society. Comte, whom many sociologists consider the founder of sociology, coined the word *sociology* and developed a useful distinction between what he called "social dynamics" (social change) and "social statics" (social order or stability). However, the work of three other nineteenth-century European social thinkers — Karl Marx, Émile Durkheim, and Max Weber — has left a more significant impact on modern sociology.

Karl Marx

Karl Marx (1818–1883) was born in the Rhineland district of Germany. The young Marx attended local schools and then went to the University of Bonn and later the University of Berlin, where he associated with a group of socialist philosophers whose ideas influenced his later writings. In 1841 Marx received a doctorate from the University of Jena (also in Germany) but was unable to obtain a university post because of his political connections. Instead he took a position with a socialist newspaper. When the paper was closed down by the authorities in 1843, he moved to Paris, where he became acquainted with some of the leading French socialists. While in Paris,

Marx also met Friedrich Engels (1820–1895), with whom he frequently collaborated throughout the rest of his life. Engels, the son of a wealthy textile manufacturer, often provided financial support for Marx and his family when no other source of income was available. Marx was expelled from France in 1845 because of his socialist activities. Later returning to Germany, he was deported once again, and when he returned to France, he received the same treatment. In 1849 Marx and his family moved to London, where he spent the rest of his life.

Marx was not a sociologist, and yet his ideas have had a significant impact on sociology in several ways. First, throughout his work he emphasized the importance of economic factors in determining social life. In particular, he stressed that the capitalist economic system is responsible for the injustices and inequalities of the modern social-class structure. As we see in the upcoming discussion of sociological theories, many modern sociologists are sympathetic to this conclusion.

Another of Marx's key ideas was that systems of belief and thought are the products of the era in which they occur. This position asserts that even cultural and religious ideas are products of economic and social conditions and that, as these conditions change, so do the ideas. Once again, many contemporary sociologists back the Marxist position.

A third main idea that has emerged from Marx's writings is the concept of work alienation — that modern workers have lost control over their work routines as well as what happens to the products of their labor. A century after Marx wrote on the subject of work alienation, sociologists continue to explore and refine this concept.

Émile Durkheim

Émile Durkheim (1858–1917) was born in Lorraine, on the northeastern border of France. The son of a rabbi, Durkheim received his basic education in France and then studied economics, folklore, and cultural anthropology in Germany. In 1887 he returned to France as a professor of sociology at the University of Bordeaux, where he taught the first sociology course offered at a French university. In 1896 he founded *Année Sociologique,* which was for years the leading journal of sociological thought and research in France. In 1902 he joined the faculty of the University of Paris.

In response to France's disastrous defeat in the Franco-Prussian War and the chaotic era that followed this defeat, Durkheim, like Comte, developed an overriding concern for social order. He believed that the scientific study of society could provide a sense of how to establish and maintain social order in modern industrial societies. Durkheim believed that one way to learn about social order was to study a situation in which order appeared to be absent—suicide. Durkheim's book *Suicide,* published in 1897, was a careful investigation of suicide rates in various European countries. It was also the first prominent study conducted by a sociologist.

Durkheim's project had two goals. First, he intended to refute the various popular theories that tried to explain the differences in group suicide rates in terms of racial, genetic, climatic, or geographical factors. Second, he wanted to develop a theoretical approach that would better explain the suicide rates in different places. Durkheim's findings supported his first goal. His data clearly invalidated the old theories about suicide rates. The evidence also suggested a new theory—that suicide was produced by three basic social conditions. One condition was the individual's lack of group support. Durkheim's investigation showed that single people were more likely than married people to commit suicide and that married individuals with children were even less likely to kill themselves. A second condition promoting suicide, according to Durkheim, was the disruption of social life. He found that depression, revolution, war, or even sudden prosperity within a society can increase that society's suicide rate. Finally, Durkheim suggested that in some preindustrial societies, as well as in some modern armies, people would be called on to commit suicide for the common good. In Japan, for example, the practice of hara-kiri—ritual suicide traditionally committed by nobility when they felt they had performed a dishonorable act—assured that the family and community would be spared disgrace.

A century later *Suicide* remains a significant contribution to the field because it was the first

effective attempt to test sociological theories by conducting scientific research. In addition, Durkheim demonstrated that suicide, which is an individual act, can be explained by sociocultural factors. Thus the study both justifies and illustrates the usefulness of the sociological perspective.

Max Weber

Max Weber (1864–1920) was a member of a wealthy German family. As a young man, Weber received training in law and economics. He earned a doctorate in law from the University of Berlin in 1889 and joined the bar a short time later. In 1891 he became a member of the law faculty of the University of Berlin, and in the following years Weber earned several full-time appointments at leading German universities. Over the course of his life, Weber published a large number of books and essays. He also traveled widely, including a visit to the United States.

No sociologist has had a more profound impact on the field of sociology than Max Weber. His contributions to sociological thought will be apparent throughout this book. The areas of study to which he made extensive contributions include bureaucracy and formal organization, religion, political authority systems and political organization, caste and class, economic activity, and the city.

One of Weber's most significant contributions was the **principle of *verstehen*** (understanding), which describes an effort to grasp the relationship between individuals' feelings and thoughts, and their actions. To Weber the principle of *verstehen* involved a three-step process: First, a sociologist observing a situation tries to imagine the emotions people are feeling. Second, that observer attempts to figure out the participants' motives. Third, the sociologist's explanation of any activity that occurs includes his or her interpretation of the participants' feelings and motives.

Consider the following illustration. A young man and a young woman are walking arm in arm while chatting loudly and smiling at each other. Suddenly the young woman says, "I don't want to climb mountains for my vacation." The young man stops walking, pulls his arm away from hers, jams his hands into his pockets, and without a word turns and walks stiffly and quickly in the direction from which they had come. A sociologist who employs the principle of *verstehen* might conclude that the young man is angry with the woman's statement; his motive is to communicate that anger; therefore he acts in a way that shows her that he is angry.

The principle of *verstehen* was an important contribution to sociology because it helped "humanize" the field by emphasizing that people's feelings and motives, and not just their behavior, must be studied.

American Sociology

Although Durkheim, Marx, Weber, and other Europeans made the initial contributions to sociology, the field has been most widely accepted in the United States. Social problems arising in the early twentieth century encouraged the growth of sociology in this country. Rapid industrialization and urbanization made poverty, violence, crime, and vice painfully apparent in American cities. Like their European predecessors, the early American sociologists believed that an effective study of society could promote an understanding of major social problems and their solutions.

In 1892 Albion W. Small (1854–1926) became the head of a newly formed department of sociology at the University of Chicago. He retained this position until 1925. During that era the department was the unchallenged leader in American sociology. Until 1930, in fact, the University of Chicago produced more Ph.Ds in sociology than all other American sociology departments combined. Among them was Lester F. Ward (1841–1913), another important early American sociologist. Like Comte, Ward believed that the discovery of the basic principles of social behavior could lead to effective social reform. In the 1920s Robert Ezra Park (1864–1944), a former journalist, organized an ambitious research program at the University of Chicago designed to promote the understanding and the elimination of such major urban problems as juvenile delinquency, crime, divorce, and social disorganization.

From the 1940s through the 1960s, leadership in sociology spread from Chicago to such academic institutions as Harvard, Columbia, and Michigan. The focus of sociology also shifted. The dominant concerns were no longer specific social problems but rather the development of theory and advances in research techniques. Talcott Parsons (1902–1979)—the most significant figure in the discipline from the early 1940s until the late 1960s—emphasized the need to develop a systematic general theory of social action. He believed that until such a theory was constructed, the empirical research conducted by sociologists would lack overall coherence and that sociology would never become a mature science. Robert Merton (b. 1910), a student of Parsons, has also emphasized that the growth of sociology can occur effectively only if theory and research promote each other's development.

In the late 1960s, antiwar and civil-rights protests resurrected the former concern with social problems. During the 1970s and 1980s, however, there was no single dominant figure or issue in sociology. Traditional topics such as the family, race relations, and the cities are still being studied, and such social issues as gender roles, the plight of elderly people, environmental problems, energy, nuclear power and weaponry, peace, and homelessness have started to receive extensive attention. A journalist interviewing sociologists at the annual American Sociological Association convention in 1988 found a division of opinion about sociologists' involvement in such a wide range of subjects. Some applauded it, believing that it showed the openness of a discipline that encourages its members to raise a wealth of important, interesting questions about how society functions. Others were less optimistic, however, contending that the current state of affairs points to "an aimless drift," where individuals and groups pursue special interests with limited or no concern about their contribution to the growth of the field (Bernstein, 1988).

In his presidential address at the same convention, Herbert Gans indicated that if sociologists wish to increase their currently modest impact on the American public, then they must take certain decisive steps: (1) Pursue research topics that provide people with useful knowledge about subjects central to their well-being—such as the family, the economy, and health; (2) recruit and encourage what Gans called "public sociologists," who are members of the discipline especially capable of presenting sociological analysis clearly and forcefully; (3) revitalize social criticism of issues and problems of concern to both members of the public and sociologists themselves, and offer solutions based on analysis of all competent informational sources (Gans, 1989).

Contemporary Sociological Theories

A **sociological theory** is a combination of observations and insights that offers a systematic explanation of social life. All people make use of informal theories about social behavior. Parents and educators, for instance, support different ideas about proper child-rearing. The old saying "Spare the rod and spoil the child" is one informal theory about this topic. Americans also have different theories about the best strategy to maintain world peace. One of them favors the development of increasingly powerful nuclear weapons that will make the Soviet Union avoid nuclear war for fear of massive retaliation. Opponents of nuclear weaponry consider this theory insane, and emphasize that a continuing nuclear-weapons build-up increases the possibility of accidental nuclear war. They offer a contrasting theory that proposes bilateral nuclear disarmament as the best way to prevent such a war.

A major difference between the theories constructed by practicing sociologists and those developed by the majority of the public is that sociologists, like other scientists, are expected to subject their theories to continuous scrutiny and testing. They conduct extensive research to determine whether or not their theories provide effective explanations of social behavior, and they carefully examine other studies published in professional journals and books to further evaluate relevant sociological theories.

Sociologists have produced a wealth of fine theories. In this section we focus on three important theories that sociologists continue to examine and reevaluate: conflict theory, structural-functional theory, and symbolic interaction. Each of these theories focuses on a different set of factors considered central to explaining human behavior. Table 1.1 summarizes these three theories.

Conflict Theory

Conflict theorists argue that groups are inevitably organized to compete against one another. Change is a continuous element in this theory. Karl Marx's perspective on class conflict is the foundation upon which modern conflict theory has been built. Marx observed that each of the major industrial societies of his day maintained a system of capitalism, in which a ruling class controlled the means by which goods were produced and constantly sought to extend its wealth and power. For the working class, Marx argued, the economic and working conditions would steadily worsen. Yet out of this desperate situation, workers would be able to seize the opportunity to produce a dramatic change in their lives. Eventually they would recognize that they shared a common plight — because of the oppressions imposed by the ruling class, their one hope for a better life was to organize themselves and overthrow their oppressors. According to Marxist theory, the defeat of the ruling class and the economic system it

Table 1.1
Three Contemporary Sociological Theories

THEORY	KEY CONCEPTS OR IDEAS
Conflict theory	Definition of conflict theory; Marx's perspective on class conflict; Mills's concept of the power elite
Structural-functional theory	Definitions of structural-functional theory; Merton's manifest function, latent function, manifest dysfunction, and latent dysfunction
Symbolic-theory interaction	Definitions of symbolic interaction and symbol; Blumer's analysis of the nature of symbolic interaction

controls would create extensive change because economic systems significantly affect all other elements within any society. In the major capitalist countries, Marx's predictions about revolution have not come to pass, and yet many of his ideas have influenced modern sociologists.

Some American sociologists have developed conflict perspectives that share Marx's focus on the centrality of both conflict and the role of the ruling class. For example, in *The Power Elite* (1956), C. Wright Mills argued that an upper-class group of politicians, business people, and military leaders effectively controls American society and gives top priority to their own political, economic, and military interests while subordinating those of the general citizenry. Chapter 9, "Social Stratification," and Chapter 14, "The Political and Economic Institutions," use Mills's application of conflict theory. In *Class and Class Conflict in Industrial Society (1959)*, Ralf Dahrendorf also used a conflict approach, and, like Mills he considered the scarce commodity of power the focus of conflict. Dahrendorf examined the conditions that promote and diffuse conflict. Although he concluded that the more violent manifestations of conflict can be toned down, to him conflict seemed inevitable in society. Conflict, he argued, always produces change, and since conflict would be continuous, societies are in constant flux.

In brief, **conflict theory** contends that the struggle for power and wealth in society should be the central concern of sociology. Many people are restricted or controlled by limits placed on them by the powerful, and this restriction creates or at least encourages conflict. In turn, conflict generates change. According to this theory, there is never enough wealth and power to satisfy everyone within a given society. Those who have the wealth and power—the chief beneficiaries of the existing system—will attempt to control the general citizenry in order to protect their own privilege. The wealthy, for instance, will contribute heavily to the campaigns of politicians who support legislation to protect the economic interests of the wealthy.

People with limited power often engage in conflict in order to reduce or remove restrictions placed on them by the powerful; they are seeking to obtain a full share of the benefits the society can provide. Conflicts sometimes involve physical violence, sometimes not. Arguments, debates, legal suits, picketings, and strikes are generally nonviolent activities, but they all involve conflict.

Since the late 1960s, many groups of people—in particular, racial and ethnic minorities, and women—have begun resisting the restrictions traditionally placed on them. These groups have initiated the long and difficult process of changing social arrangements that have denied them equal opportunities to seek wealth, power, and prestige in American society. Since the goals of these groups require the pursuit of scarce resources, conflict is usually one consequence of their efforts. Sometimes such conflict has been violent, as in the killings of black leaders and other activists during the 1960s, but more often it has been nonviolent, as in the lobbying for or against legalized abortion.

A major contribution of conflict theory is that it has encouraged sociologists to recognize the great significance that wealth and power play in people's lives and then to analyze the impact of these

Even though most conflict theorists probably would applaud the fact that General Colin L. Powell was sworn in as the first black Chairman of the Joint Chiefs of Staff, they would predict that his appointment is not a signal that the power elite's policies will change.

two factors in detail. For instance, Michael Patrick Allen and Philip Broyles (1989) examined the presidential campaign contributions made by 100 wealthy families, each of which was worth $100 million in 1972, the last year the size of campaign contributions was unrestricted. Recall what you read a moment ago—C. Wright Mills's contention that the power elite is composed of a select group of people who try to control society so that the lion's share of wealth and power stays in their hands. With such a perspective in mind, one might suspect that all very wealthy individuals would contribute heavily to one or both presidential candidates, believing that this would be the way to influence the president to execute their preferred economic and political policies. Was that the case in 1972? No! The researchers learned that about half these wealthy family members contributed little or nothing, while others, especially individuals who were very visible to the public, tended to contribute heavily. The current significance of this study is that it demonstrates that using the conflict perspective, sociological researchers now look beyond broad, unsupported conclusions about wealth and power and assess the impact these factors have on people in modern society.

The conflict perspective makes an important contribution to sociological analysis by focusing on issues of struggle and change. This theory, however, tends to ignore some aspects of society. In particular, it fails to take into account the topics of cooperation and stability addressed by the structural-functional perspective.

Structural-Functional Theory

The American work world contains more than 20,000 types of jobs. People in each kind of job tend to be interdependent with those in many other work roles. Nurses, for instance, provide direct care for sick or injured people, act as administrators in hospitals, and in some cases train student nurses. In turn, they depend on other workers for food, clothes, transportation, communication, entertainment, and many other needs. Another example is farmers, who supply meat, poultry, vegetables, fruit, and dairy products to the American consumers; they too depend on other occupational groups to meet their needs in a range of areas.

The interdependence of different categories of American workers illustrates **structural-functional theory.** This theory suggests that groups in interaction tend to influence and adjust to one another in a fairly stable, conflict-free pattern.

In the examples above—nurses and farmers—the groups in interaction are the various occupational groups. According to this theory, these groups are mutually supportive and interdependent, and each group contributes to the overall stability of the society. The focus of this type of theory is the concept of **function**—an adjustive or stabilizing consequence produced by an item, individual, or group and affecting a particular group or society. For example, the functions performed by nurses help restore the sick and injured workers in various occupational categories to health (an "adjustive consequence"). Nurses, in short, function to maintain the stability of the American occupational system, according to structural-functional theory.

Robert Merton (1968) developed some important refinements of the structural-functional theory. He defined a **manifest function** as a function that is intended and openly recognized by members of the group producing it. A **latent function** is a function that is not intended and that often goes unrecognized by members of the group producing it. A **dysfunction** is a disruptive or destabilizing consequence produced by an item, individual, or group and affecting a particular group or society. A dysfunction can be manifest or latent. The following discussion uses computer technology to illustrate the four types of functions and dysfunctions.

One manifest function of the computer is its ability to contribute directly to the effective performance of different types of workers. Computers can do such things as keep business accounts, retrieve the police records of criminal suspects, provide doctors with detailed information about drugs and diseases, and offer research sociologists lists of all published studies about a given topic. The manifest functions provided by computers have had a decisive effect on the structure of the American work force. It is apparent, for example, that many businesses are much more ef-

A manifest function of computers is that with them office workers can store and retrieve information much more efficiently than they can without them.

ficient and prosperous because of their effective use of computers.

Less obvious, however, are the latent functions of computers. Some companies are starting to place computer terminals in employees' homes and letting them work there. With such an arrangement, couples are able to maintain closer, more satisfying relationships. Children can develop a better understanding of their parents' work activities than they generally have been able to do in the past. In addition, if employees are permitted to perform most or all of their work tasks at home, it becomes less likely that they need to move every time they change jobs. As a result many families might be able to develop more stable community relationships than they have at present (Toffler, 1981). All of these observations illustrate some latent functions of computers. In other words computers can have indirect effects that were not intended by those who first developed them.

Computers have also caused certain problems or dysfunctions. For example, they eliminate many work tasks that people have traditionally performed. The elimination or phasing out of certain job holders, such as filing clerks, research assistants, and factory workers, represents a manifest dysfunction for the people in those job categories.

Like many, perhaps most, new forms of technology, computers have sometimes contributed to problems that their owners and advocates never anticipated. In other words they created latent dysfunctions. For example, ingenious but dishonest individuals have learned to engage in so-called computer crimes. Stanley Mark Rifkin, a computer analyst in Los Angeles, used a computer to trick the machines at the Security Pacific National Bank into giving him $10 million. While free on bail for that crime, he was arrested for using a computer to try to steal $50 million from the Union Bank (Friedrich, 1983: 22).

Another latent dysfunction of computers could provide disastrous results for the entire planet: American nuclear weaponry is linked to computerized warning systems that could malfunction, leading to a nuclear war. Jonathan Schell (1982) wrote:

> On three occasions in the last couple of years, American nuclear forces were placed on the early stages of alert: twice because of the malfunctioning of a computer chip in the North American Air Defense Command's warning system and once when a test tape depicting a missile attack was inadvertently inserted in the system. The greatest danger in computer-generated misinformation and other mechanical errors may be that one error might start a chain reaction of escalating responses between command centers, leading, eventually, to an attack.
>
> (Schell, 1982: 27)

These examples suggest that the structural-functional theory makes a distinct contribution to sociological thought by emphasizing the functions and dysfunctions that promote cooperation and stability within societies. The most profound limitation of this theory, according to critics, is its failure to examine systematically conflict and change in social relations.

The following American Controversy analyzes why one prominent sociologist supported structural-functionalism and another conflict theory. The discussion suggests the possibility that the supporters of these two theories might differ in more than their theoretical preferences.

AMERICAN CONTROVERSY

Why Sociologists Prefer Particular Theories

The approaches of structural-functionalism and conflict theory differ significantly. Sociologists often have a strong preference for one theory or the other. Why is that?

Two prominent sociologists provide excellent illustrations. Why, for example, did Talcott Parsons support structural-functional theory? Why did C. Wright Mills adopt a conflict perspective?

Sociologist Alvin Gouldner argued that one specific condition in Parsons's upbringing most strongly supported his preference for a theory that downplayed conflict and change — his year of birth, 1902. Actually year of birth seems to combine with several other factors. For example, Parsons grew up in an upper-middle-class family during an era of affluence. He attended Amherst Col-

lege in Massachusetts and later Heidelberg University in Germany. He was a faculty member at Harvard University before the stock market crash of 1929 signaled the beginning of the Great Depression. Distant from Parsons's own life, then, were the poverty, misery, and inequality that encouraged other sociologists to embrace conflict theory.

C. Wright Mills grew up in a different time and place, however. Roughly sixteen years younger than Parsons, he was only a college student during the 1930s. In those depression years, brutal economic conditions encouraged sociologists to launch strong criticisms of American society. Furthermore Mills did not leave his native state of Texas until he was twenty-one. Mills himself believed that growing up out-

side of major urban centers made it easier for him to become a critic of the political and economic activity that was concentrated in those cities. Thus some factors in Mills's background seem to have encouraged him to become a conflict theorist.

The protests of the 1960s convinced many sociologists that the structural-functional perspective did not effectively analyze the conflict and change that were widespread at that time. During that era conflict theory gained support.

What about the 1990s? As you examine modern society, which theory seems to provide a more effective analysis? In your response you might include references to important political and economic issues in the news. It is often difficult to analyze personal reasons for reaching a particular conclusion but, nonetheless, try to explain why you prefer one of the two theories. In other words try to determine which fac-

tors in your own background encourage you to support one of these perspectives instead of the other. You might find it interesting to discuss

with other students your respective preferences and the reasons for those preferences.

Sources: Alvin Gouldner. *The Coming Crisis of Western Sociology.* New York: Equinox Books. 1970; Irving Louis Horowitz (ed.). *The New Sociology.* New York: Oxford University Press. 1964.

Symbolic-Interaction Theory

Julie and her husband are at a party. Julie wants to make a point to her husband but does not want to cause a scene. Her words emerge in little more than a whisper. "Frank," she begins, "your treatment of me has been intolerable ever since we arrived. You're going to have to stop it." Julie says the word *stop* slowly and emphatically. She has not raised her voice, but Frank has received her message.

This example illustrates a type of social analysis that is the focus of a theory known as symbolic interaction. **Symbolic-interaction theory** emphasizes the importance of symbolic communication — the use of gestures and, above all, language — in the development of the individual, group, and society. Human beings are unique in their capacity to use symbolic communication. Knowledge of what a symbol is will help to clarify the significance of this form of communication.

A **symbol** is an object or event whose meaning is fixed not by the nature of the item to which it is attached but by the agreement of the people who use it in communication. For example, words such as *book* or *shoe* are symbols. We use those words because people who speak the English language have agreed to associate the particular word with the particular object; there is nothing inherent in the objects themselves requiring the choices that have been made. Moreover, by using words people communicate with one another in a way that otherwise would be impossible.

The symbolic-interaction theory appreciates the subtlety of human communication. Julie knew that if she said the word *stop* slowly and emphatically, Frank would grasp the meaning she wanted to convey. The supporters of this theory also emphasize that communication is not entirely verbal.

Gestures and body language also play an important part.

Sociologists who favor the symbolic-interaction approach tend to focus on the more minute, personal aspects of social interaction occurring in small groups. Frequently this theory is used to analyze situations involving socialization, where people, often children or young people, are learning the rudiments of their culture. Chapter 5, "Social Interaction," further discusses symbolic interaction, including analysis of ethnomethodology and dramaturgic sociology, which are both versions of symbolic interaction. In three other chapters, varieties of symbolic interaction are examined. Although the practice has been to apply this theory to small-group situations, some proponents have argued that all human behavior involves symbolic communication, and thus no inherent reason restricts symbolic interaction from analyzing the larger topics that structural-functionalism and conflict theory have traditionally monopolized (Lyman, 1988).

One of the major proponents of symbolic interaction was Herbert Blumer. According to Blumer, the symbolic quality of social interaction centers on the meanings individuals ascribe to other people and things. These meanings do not simply exist in the social world but derive from people's judgments in the course of their daily experience; a major contributor to these meanings is contact with other people. Sometimes as individuals interpret their experience, however, meanings change. Whether meanings change or remain the same, they affect people's behavior (Blumer, 1969: 2–10).

Let's consider an example involving Matt Winters, a professional baseball player. At the age of eighteen, Winters went to Oneonta, New York, to play minor-league baseball. In the following eleven years, Winters played in nine minor-league cities and for three baseball organizations. In 1986 Winters was released by the New York Yankees' organization and found himself without a job in baseball. He could have quit professional baseball, but he didn't. "I considered quitting, but working in a factory isn't the same as playing baseball," he said. The quotation raises two distinct points related to symbolic interaction. First, it suggests that the meaning Winters gave to baseball did not exist independently in the social world but had developed out of his dual experiences of playing baseball and working in a factory (a frozen-food factory during the winter). Second, the way the statement is phrased implies that an important part of what baseball meant to Winters was the social interaction with other ball players. Consistent with this second point is the fact that many professional athletes in different sports indicate that what makes it particularly difficult to

retire is that they believe that never again will they experience such intense bonds of friendship

Appreciating how significant the meaning of baseball was to him, Winters contacted the Kansas City Royals' organization and was told that they had an opening at Memphis, their AA affiliate (occupying the second of three levels within the minor-league system). At this point Winters needed to evaluate the situation, interpreting what had happened to him in the recent past and what he should try to achieve in the immediate future. As Blumer indicated, sometimes meanings are changed or revised, and that appeared to be the case here. The meaning of baseball itself did not change—Winters had consistently valued it highly. What had changed was the meaning given to his activity within baseball. The previous four years he had belonged to a AAA affiliate, the highest level within the minor leagues. He had always assumed that a successful player, one who eventu-

Professional baseball players recognize that for them the game is a job. Thus, if they are going to be successful, extensive practice must be part of the daily routine.

ally made it to the major leagues, was consistently promoted. Was another interpretation reasonable? Could he accept a demotion and still ultimately make it to the big leagues? Winters's assessment of the situation was that since baseball meant so much to him, he needed to risk this unappealing course of action. He said, "It was a step backward, but I had to take a step backward to take a step forward." Thus the interpretation Winters made in the situation determined his behavior.

The decision paid off. After two-and-a-half years in the Royals' AA and AAA affiliates, Winters was brought to the parent club. In his first eleven times at bat, he got four hits — a promising beginning (Chass, 1989).

Choosing and Using Theories

The previous discussion of contemporary sociological theories suggests that there is no such thing as the "best" sociological theory. As the American Controversy earlier in this chapter observes, background factors can determine the theoretical approach a sociologist prefers. One individual might feel most comfortable studying what appear to be the inevitable sources of conflict, while another chooses to focus on how social groups provide support and continuity within society. Thus no theory is inherently correct or incorrect. In some situations a particular theory is more appropriate or is well-matched with a sociologist's personal tastes. Within the field of sociology and even within individual sociology departments, people recognize that their colleagues differ in their theoretical preferences. Sometimes disagreements are sharp and well publicized. Often, however, preferences for different theories lead to useful discussions and debates. One quality all sociological theories share is their unrelenting emphasis on the sociological perspective.

Now that you have read about the theories, you might find that you too have a preference. To help determine your preference, you might look back at Table 1.1, which lists the major features of each theory, and use the table to help evaluate them. Does one theory make the most sense to you? In other words does one of the three seem most consistent with your own outlook on the social world? On the other hand, does one theory seem particularly distasteful? Discuss what seem to be the respective strengths and weaknesses of the different theories with classmates or friends.

STUDY GUIDE

Learning Objectives

After studying this chapter, you should be able to:

1. Define sociology.
2. Discuss the sociological perspective.
3. Define science, distinguish between natural sciences and social sciences, and discuss a problem that sociology faces in the scientific study of human beings.
4. Describe the social conditions of the era in which sociology originated and identify Auguste Comte's contributions to the field.
5. Summarize the contributions to sociology of Karl Marx, Émile Durkheim, and Max Weber.
6. Discuss the twentieth-century development of American sociology.
7. Define sociological theory, and compare and contrast it with informal theory.
8. Define conflict theory, structural-functional theory, and symbolic-interaction theory; provide examples of each; and discuss their respective strengths and weaknesses.
9. Explain why there is no one "best" sociological theory.

Summary

1. Sociology is the scientific study of human behavior in groups and of the social forces that influence that behavior.

2. The sociological perspective emphasizes that people's thoughts and actions are strongly influenced by the groups to which they belong, as well as by other impinging social factors, such as values, beliefs, practices, and institutions. Sociology is a science, but it has two distinct disadvantages when compared to the natural sciences: It is a much newer discipline, and its subject matter — human beings — poses special problems.

3. Auguste Comte coined the word *sociology* and founded the field. Marx, Durkheim, and Weber also made major contributions to the development of sociology in Europe. In the United States, the University of Chicago was the first center of sociology. Then, in the 1940s, the most prominent departments developed at Harvard, Columbia, and Michigan. During these years Talcott Parsons and Robert Merton had the strongest influence on the discipline. In the 1970s and 1980s, there were no single dominant figures or issues in sociology.

4. A sociological theory is a combination of observations and insights that offers a systematic explanation about social life. Conflict theory contends that the struggle for power and wealth in society should be the central sociological concern.

In contrast, structural-functional theory suggests that groups in interaction tend to influence and adjust to one another in a fairly stable, conflict-free pattern.

Symbolic interaction is a theory emphasizing the importance of symbolic communication — gestures and, above all, language — in the development of the individual, group, and society.

There is no such thing as the "best" sociological theory. A sociologist uses a particular perspective because it seems most appropriate for a particular analysis or because it matches his or her personal tastes.

Key Terms

conflict theory   a theory contending that the struggle for power and wealth in society should be the central concern of sociology

dysfunction   a disruptive or destabilizing consequence produced by an item, individual, or group and affecting a particular group or society

function   an adjustive or stabilizing consequence produced by an item, individual, or group and affecting a particular group or society

latent function   a function that is not intended and that often goes unrecognized by members of the group producing it

manifest function   a function that is intended and openly recognized by members of the group producing it

natural sciences   older sciences such as astronomy, biology, chemistry, and physics that study the physical world

principle of *verstehen*   Max Weber's concept that involves an effort to grasp the relationship between individuals' feelings and thoughts, and their actions

science   a systematic effort to develop general principles about a particular subject matter, based on actual observations and stated in a form that can be tested by any competent person

social sciences   the sciences that focus on various aspects of human behavior

sociological theory   a combination of observations and insights that offers a systematic explanation of social life

sociology   the scientific study of human behavior in groups and of the social forces that influence that behavior

structural-functional theory   a theory suggesting that groups in interaction tend to influence and adjust to one another in a fairly stable, conflict-free pattern

symbol   an object or event whose meaning is

fixed not by the nature of the item to which it is attached but by the agreement of the people who use it in communication

symbolic-interaction theory   a theory that emphasizes the importance of symbolic communication — the use of gestures and, above all, language — in the development of the individual, group, and society

---

Tests

True – false Test

_____   1. William Foote Whyte's study of young men in Boston suggests that the expectations and support of the group, especially its leaders, influence individual members.

_____   2. Maureen T. Hallinan and Richard A. Williams's study of high-school students' friendships concluded that same-race friendships are about twice as common as interracial friendships.

_____   3. Sociology is less advanced as a scientific discipline than the natural sciences.

_____   4. Durkheim found that in some preindustrial societies, as well as in some modern armies, people will be called upon to commit suicide for the common good.

_____   5. The principle of *verstehen* has helped to humanize sociology.

_____   6. From the 1940s through the 1960s, the University of Chicago dominated the field of sociology.

_____   7. Conflict theory asserts that conflict inevitably leads to violence.

_____   8. The elimination or phasing out of workers when computers are used is an example of a latent function for those workers.

_____   9. Symbolic-interaction theory never analyzes face-to-face social situations.

_____   10. Symbolic interaction is concerned with the meanings individuals give to other people and things.

Multiple-choice Test

_____   1. The sociological perspective:
   a. indicates that people are seldom influenced by the groups to which they belong.
   b. can be used to explain the bowling performances of the young men described in Whyte's study conducted in Boston in the 1930s.
   c. is not relevant to Hallinan and Williams's study of friendships.
   d. a and b

_____   2. Which of the following is a natural science?
   a. biology
   b. economics
   c. history
   d. sociology

_____   3. In which of the following ways does sociology differ from the natural sciences?
   a. Its subject matter (human beings) is easier to study than the subject matter in the natural sciences.

b. Sociologists are less limited in what they can do to their subjects than their colleagues in the natural sciences.
c. Sociologists study human subjects who are self-aware and can alter their behavior when they choose.
d. a and c

_____ 4. Karl Marx's theory was based in part on which of the following ideas?
a. The socialist economic system is responsible for injustice and inequality in the modern social-class structure.
b. Systems of belief and thought are independent of the era in which they occur.
c. Modern workers have more control over their work routines than did preindustrial workers.
d. Economic conditions determine what happens in the social world.

_____ 5. Durkheim's study of suicide theorized that suicide was produced by three basic social conditions. Which of the following is NOT one of these basic conditions?
a. the disruption of social life
b. the individual's lack of group support
c. certain distinct personality characteristics
d. the individual's call to commit suicide for the common good

_____ 6. The principle of *verstehen* is a three-step process. Which of the following actions is NOT part of the process?
a. The sociologist tries to figure out the participants' motives.
b. The observer tries to imagine the emotions people are feeling.
c. The sociologist makes recommendations to improve the situation.
d. The observer's explanation includes an interpretation of the participants' feelings and motives.

_____ 7. According to conflict theory, the central sociological concern should be:
a. the legal system.
b. politicians' bid for election.
c. physical violence.
d. the struggle for wealth and power.

_____ 8. According to structural-functional theory, a function that is intended and openly recognized by members of the group producing it is called:
a. a manifest function.
b. a latent function.
c. a manifest dysfunction.
d. a latent dysfunction.

_____ 9. Computer crime is described in the text as an example of:
a. conflict theory.
b. social dynamics.
c. a latent dysfunction.
d. a manifest dysfunction.

_____ 10. Symbolic-interaction theory:
a. cannot be used to analyze large groups.
b. emphasizes that the meanings of things and people are obtained in interaction with others.
c. is identical to conflict theory in most respects.
d. emphasizes that the meanings individuals give to people and things seldom affect behavior.

Essay Test

For each essay carefully choose your words so that you capture and develop the basic idea or ideas in question. Make an effort to stay on the topic at hand and provide as much detail as possible. When you have finished, turn to the relevant section in the book and compare your answer with the material there.

1. Discuss the sociological perspective, giving an example that demonstrates its usefulness.
2. Summarize the contributions to early sociology of Marx, Durkheim, and Weber.
3. Define sociological theory. Give an example of an informal theory of social behavior and indicate how such a theory differs from the sociological type.
4. What is conflict theory? Discuss a social situation in which this perspective seems particularly relevant.
5. Define structural-functional theory. Describe situations that demonstrate the workings of a manifest function, a latent function, a manifest dysfunction, and a latent dysfunction.
6. Define symbolic-interaction theory. Describe a group context that illustrates the symbolic-interaction process.
7. Discuss in detail the theory you like best.

Suggested Readings

Bart, Pauline, and Linda Frankel. 1986. *The Student Sociologist's Handbook.* New York: Random House. Fourth edition. A source of valuable information for the beginning sociology student about writing a sociology paper, doing library research, examining periodical literature, following guides to research and resource material, and using computers in sociological work.

Cuzzort, R. P., and E. W. King. 1989. *Twentieth Century Social Thought.* Fort Worth: Holt, Rinehart and Winston. Fourth edition. Nicely written, effective coverage of the works of classic and modern sociological theorists.

Finsterbusch, Kurt (ed.). 1991. *Sociology 91/92.* Guilford, CT: Dushkin Publishing Group. An array of articles from magazines and popular journals supplying supplementary material for most topics covered in an introductory-sociology course.

Finsterbusch, Kurt, and George McKenna. 1986. *Taking Sides: Clashing Views on Controversial Social Issues.* Guilford, CT: Dushkin Publishing Group. Fourth edition. An examination of a "pro" and "con" position on twenty different topics that are of interest to sociologists. These issues include the benefit of sociology to society, the contribution of the women's movement, the effective way to prevent nuclear war, the state of the economy, and prospects for prosperity and freedom in the future.

Kennedy, Robert E., Jr. 1986. *Life Choices: Applying Sociology.* New York: Holt, Rinehart and Winston. An examination of the social context in which today's young people are making basic life choices. Using statistical data and sociological analysis, the author demonstrates to college students how sociological thinking can be used in their own lives.

Mills, C. Wright. 1959. *The Sociological Imagination.* New York: Oxford University Press. A conflict-perspective analysis of American society that makes some thought-provoking proposals about the role that ought to be played by modern sociologists.

Smelser, Neil J. (ed.). 1989. *Handbook of Sociology.* Newbury Park, CA: Sage Publications. Twenty-two chapters written by sociological specialists, providing detailed, updated information about nearly all the major topics covered in most introductory-sociology courses.

Theodorson, George A., and Achilles G. Theodorson. 1969. *A Modern Dictionary of Sociology.* New York: Thomas Y. Crowell Company. Concise definitions of an extensive list of sociological concepts.

Additional Assignments

1. Take a topic of interest to you that deals with human behavior—for example, the effects of war, male–female differences, or violent crime. After learning about the subject through books, magazines, and other sources, write about the social forces that produce this behavior and also the effects that this particular activity has upon different groups in American society. Share your report with other students and obtain their reactions to your conclusions.
2. Consider a current social problem—for example, unemployment, civil rights, family tensions. Indicate why this problem has occurred and continues to occur, using the three major sociological theories—structural-functional, conflict, and symbolic-interaction theory. Does any theory seem more or less effective than the others for explaining the behavior? Does any theory do more to suggest actions that might solve the problem?

Answers to Objective Test Questions

True–false Test

1. t	4. t	7. f	9. f
2. f	5. t	8. f	10. t
3. t	6. f		

Multiple-choice Test

1. b	4. d	7. d	9. c
2. a	5. c	8. a	10. b
3. c	6. c		

2
DOING RESEARCH IN SOCIOLOGY

The Scientific Approach of Sociological Research

Scientific Principles
Stages in the Research Process

Types of Research Design

Surveys
Experiments
Observation Studies
Secondary Analysis

Issues in Sociological Research

Objectivity in the Research Process
Ethics in the Researcher's Role

Study Guide

William Darrow, Research Sociologist at the Centers for Disease Control, indicated that "Much has been learned in the five years since the first cases of AIDS were reported" (Berg, 1986). Darrow studied patients afflicted with Acquired Immune Deficiency Syndrome (AIDS) to learn how their sexual practices spread the disease, and his findings have served as the foundation for the development of AIDS education and prevention programs. Carole Campbell, another sociologist, has started to study prostitutes to determine whether they are a means by which the virus is transmitted to the general populace from high-risk groups like bisexual men and drug users. Important issues in this research concern the prevalence of AIDS among prostitutes, the extent to which the disease is obtained from sexual contact with bisexuals or drug users, and the determination of whether or not prostitutes are altering their sexual practices (such as by requiring customers to use condoms).

The other major body of sociological research on AIDS involves studies seeking means of effective behavior modification. From an investigation of 133 gay men who did not have the virus, sociologists Karolynn Siegel and Laurie Bauman found that men whose reports of their sexual behavior indicated that they were at high risk continuously underestimated that risk. A major strategy these men employed was the denial of their own anxiety. Siegel emphasized that to eliminate their high-risk behavior, people's anxiety must be high enough to motivate different sexual patterns but not so high that denial of anxiety would occur. In other research on AIDS victims, Samuel Friedman has studied intravenous drug users. He has concluded that because addicts' time, attention, and money are largely controlled by their addiction, they generally have fewer resources than others to learn about preventative measures. Programs to educate addicts on AIDS prevention have been developed in Holland and New York City, and Friedman indicated that the mass media and public health programs should be enlisted to support such efforts (Berg, 1986).

The National Institute for Drug Abuse has provided grants in six cities to social researchers seeking to develop among intravenous drug users strategies that will curtail or modify their risk of contracting and spreading AIDS (Berg, 1988). With growing concern for the spread of AIDS beyond current high-risk groups, sociologists have started to study the relationship between AIDS and the general public in order to develop strategies to restrict the disease's spread (*Footnotes*, 1989).

When most people examine social research, they concentrate on the results and show little or no concern about how those results are obtained. Perhaps that is most emphatically the case when the issue under investigation is a life-threatening subject like AIDS: People wonder how the information obtained by the research can be used to alleviate the impact of the disease. Sociologists and other scientists evaluating AIDS research, however, must be concerned about how the study was done. If it were done badly, they realize, then the results will be invalidated and individuals setting up programs or establishing policies based on that information might be significantly misguided. Thus the conduct of social research, which this chapter examines, can be very important.

Sociologists speak of **methodology,** the set of principles and procedures that guides sociological research. The effective use of methodology permits sociologists to do research that produces systematic, convincing results.

This chapter is fundamental. The substance of sociology comes from articles, monographs, and books that present research findings. Such research, however, is impossible without specific principles and procedures. We discuss them in this chapter. The first section focuses on sociology as a science, including the stages in the research process. Then the four principal types of social research are analyzed. The final section examines two significant issues involving the researcher's role.

The Scientific Approach of Sociological Research

In medieval Europe there was a popular belief that the devastating epidemics that occasionally swept across the continent were caused by gases or mists originating somewhere in the East. Medical research has discredited this theory, establishing that a variety of microorganisms were responsible for these diseases. In another case, however, folk wisdom proved correct. In the late eighteenth century, Edward Jenner investigated English peasants' claims that people who had contracted cowpox, a relatively mild disease, would be immune to smallpox. After determining that the peasants' claim was accurate, Jenner developed a vaccine that used cowpox bacteria to immunize people against smallpox, one of the most potent diseases ever suffered by humanity.

Scientific Principles

Scientists seek the truth systematically. To understand the process requires knowledge of a number of basic concepts, which, like the letters in the alphabet, might be dull but must be understood if you wish to become "literate" as a researcher. A central concern in this process is **causation,** a situation in which one variable can produce the occurrence of another. A **variable** is a factor that has two or more categories or measurable conditions. Common sociological variables are social class (e.g., working class, middle class), political affiliation (e.g., Democrat, Republican), and sex (male, female). An **independent variable** is a variable that influences another variable — the dependent variable. Thus the **dependent variable** is a variable that is the consequence of some cause. In sociological research dependent variables are frequently attitudes and activities.

Sociologists agree that causation is present if three conditions are met (Cole, 1980). First, causation can only occur if the independent variable exists before the dependent variable. For example, people's political affiliation, which exists when they enter the polls, often strongly influences their voting behavior. In other words the affiliation — the independent variable — exists *before* the voting behavior — the dependent variable. Second, if causation exists, then change in the independent variable affects the dependent variable. Thus if causation occurs, then Democrats and Republicans would generally vote for different candidates. Finally, causation cannot be established until researchers have ruled out the influence of other possible independent variables. Their method is to analyze the effect of each possible independent variable on the dependent variable, while keeping constant all other possible independent variables. To establish the impact of political affiliation as an independent variable, for example, researchers would need to make certain that their Republicans and Democrats were matched on such factors as age, sex, race, education, and occupation.

Sociologists recognize that in the situations they study, causation is difficult to determine. It is seldom possible to specify that a or b is the sole independent variable influencing c. Sociologists generally must settle for a **correlation** — that is, a statistical description of the relationship between variables. A positive correlation of $+1.0$ indicates the strongest possible statistical relationship. It means that an increase in an independent variable is associated with a corresponding increase in the dependent variable. A negative correlation of -1.0 is a perfect inverse relationship. It means that an increase in the independent variable is associated with a corresponding decrease in the dependent variable. A correlation of 0 indicates no relationship at all between the two variables.

Correlations almost always fall somewhere between the two extremes. For example, sociologists undertaking the hypothetical study just mentioned might find a correlation of $-.72$ between class size and the amount of discussion. Thus as classes become larger, class discussion tends to decrease. One more point: By squaring a correlation, a researcher can determine how much of the total variation in the dependent variable is associated with the independent variable. If we square the figure of $-.72$, we obtain a value of nearly $.52$. That figure signifies that class size accounts for about 52 percent of the variation in the amount of class participation. Other independent variables, such as the professor's style and the subject matter of the course, account for the other 48 percent of the variation.

Stages in the Research Process

The following analysis considers the major activities of sociologists in the course of their research. The stages are presented here in an ideal, logical pattern, that does not necessarily summarize the sequence of events in an actual study.

It should also be emphasized that sociological theory has a powerful effect on researchers while they work, from the choice of topic to the reporting of their findings. Sociologists are likely to be influenced by the ways different theories encourage them to analyze the social world. They also tend to keep in mind the possibility that their findings can contribute to existing theories, either supporting certain theoretical positions or suggesting new ones.

1. *Choosing a Topic.* Several factors are likely to determine a sociologist's choice of a topic to study. The factors include the researcher's personal interest in the topic, its current popularity, the potential contribution such a study would make to sociological literature, and the availability of government or private funding for research in that area.

   Realizing that there is a widely held belief, especially among critics of the welfare system, that women on welfare have an above-average number of children, sociologist Mark R. Rank (1989) did research to find out whether this claim was actually true.

2. *Reviewing the Literature.* As sociologists start a research project, they are aware that others have done work that may help them. It is likely that a theory or set of theories can help map out the questions their studies should attempt to answer. In addition, previous investigations might provide researchers with some specific aids for their own study.

For example, in his literature review, Rank found no competent investigations that compared the number of children produced by women on welfare with the number of children produced by women in the general population. Thus he realized that his study would provide unique information.

3. *Formulating a Hypothesis.* Researchers are looking for answers to questions. To guide their searches, they present their expectations in a form that permits them to be researched. A **hypothesis** is a scientifically researchable suggestion about the relationship between two or more variables. Most sociological studies are devised to test hypotheses—that is, to find out whether or not they are true. Thus hypotheses are central to the development of sociological investigations. Hypotheses contain both independent and dependent variables.

   Rank's study tested the following hypothesis: Women on welfare tend to have more children than women in the general population. In this instance the independent variable is source of support—welfare or some other source; the dependent variable is the number of children.

4. *Picking the Research Design.* In order to do research, sociologists must choose a method. (We discuss the four major methods of social research in the following section.) A researcher's preference for one particular method might help determine the choice. In many situations, however, the particular hypotheses to be tested will require a certain type of design.

   Certainly Rank could have engaged in original research to obtain the information he sought. However, the relevant data were already available in state and federal records, to which Rank was able to obtain access. As we see later in this chapter, this type of research design is called secondary analysis. In addition, to gather in-depth information not available from these sources, Rank conducted interviews with fifty welfare families.

5. *Gathering the Data.* Data are the substance of a study. Thus even though collecting and recording data sometimes strike those who perform the tasks as tedious work, it is essential that they do these jobs conscientiously. Researchers for large sociological projects often hire graduate students, undergraduates, or other people to conduct interviews. In training interviewers, team leaders must help their workers develop the requisite skills. In addition, they must convince them that conscientious job performance is essential for effective completion of the study.

Research often provides valuable insights about people from varied backgrounds. A face-to-face interview with this woman, who lives on welfare in public housing in New Haven, Connecticut, is likely to reveal significant information about the difficult, demanding world in which she lives.

Rank's data on welfare women came from two sources in Wisconsin — welfare records for welfare recipients and Department of Health and Social Services information for nonwelfare subjects — and also U.S. Bureau of the Census information for the national population of women.

6. *Analyzing the Data.* Sociologists examine their data to find out whether the information supports the hypotheses or whether new hypotheses need to be developed to account for the data. Frequently sociological theories, as well as related, research can help complete the analysis.

Rank's central finding was that in 1980, women in the prime child-bearing years (18 to 44) had about 46 children per 1000 women, while women in the general Wisconsin population had about 75 children per 1000 women and those in the general U.S. population had 71 children. Thus the hypothesis Rank proposed was rejected. According to this

One of the benefits of large studies is that the participants can engage in brainstorming sessions throughout the research process. From reviewing the literature to producing a report, many heads often produce more insight and understanding than one person working alone.

study, women on welfare have fewer, not more children than the general population.

7. *Producing a Report.* Organizations that sponsor studies require researchers to write a report summarizing their findings. In addition to fulfilling such a formal requirement, researchers belong to a scientific community, and they realize that a monograph or an article in a professional journal is an effective way to make their peers aware of their research results. Sociologists are likely to emphasize implications that their findings have for sociological theory when they write up their studies. Furthermore they probably discuss the directions that future research could take.

Having obtained the results of his study, Rank wrote an article, which was published in the *American Sociological Review,* one of the most distinguished, widely read sociological journals. Many sociologists subscribe to this journal and are likely to read the article and evaluate its contribution. In particular, those doing research on related issues will find it a useful source in their own review of the literature.

Figure 2.1 summarizes the stages of the research process.

Figure 2.1
Stages in the Research Process

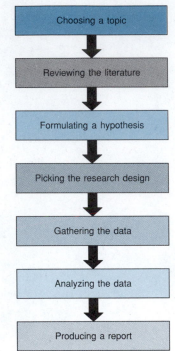

The stages of the research process tend to follow each other in this order. Other sequences are possible, but researchers find that this arrangement is the most convenient.

When a sociologist's peers read a report of findings, they consider validity. **Validity** is the condition in which a research item accurately measures what it claims to measure. For example, a group of workers might express satisfaction with their work to a researcher, but is this investigator obtaining valid information? Perhaps not. The workers' statements might reflect their knowledge of a false rumor indicating that the investigator will pass on all dissatisfactions to their boss, who then plans to fire any discontented employees.

Besides considering validity, sociologists assessing their peers' work are concerned with reliability. **Reliability** is consistency in measurement. Researchers want to know whether a research item produces a similar result when it is used as a mea-

surement in one situation and then used again in another. Is what the ruler designates an inch in the first instance the same as what the ruler designates an inch in the second case? Does such consistency in measurement get produced with a researcher's designation of social class? In the example used to illustrate validity, evidence in favor of reliability would be obtained if the researcher conducted the same study in a different setting with people of similar background, and those individuals expressed a comparable level of job satisfaction to those interviewed in the original study.

Types of Research Design

Even though sociological research generally passes through the same sequence of stages, the research process can vary considerably. One major reason is that the different research methods pose particular demands and challenges. We explore

these differences in the upcoming discussion of the four major techniques of social research currently used by modern sociologists — surveys, experiments, observation studies, and secondary analysis.

Surveys

A **survey** is a research technique that uses carefully constructed questions to obtain a variety of facts about people's thoughts and behavior. One type of survey is an **interview** — a set of questions that are delivered face-to-face or over the telephone. The other type of survey is a **questionnaire,** in which a respondent writes the answers to a list of questions. The questions contained in a survey can either be closed-ended, requiring responses that fall into two or more categories provided by the researcher, or open-ended, permitting respondents to speak or write whatever they want. Surveys are administered in a variety of natural settings, such as in homes, offices, restaurants, and even on park benches or beaches.

Researchers conduct surveys by taking a sample from a population. A **population** is the entire category of people possessing the characteristics that interest a researcher undertaking a particular study — for example, the female students at a certain college, male blue-collar workers in a midwestern city, or the entire American electorate. A **sample** is a limited number of individuals chosen from a population for the purpose of conducting research. Researchers often use a **random sample,** which is a sample drawn from a population by a process that assures that every individual in that population has an equal probability of being included.

Why do sociologists bother with random sampling? The reason is that the information this technique elicits is more likely to produce a sample with members whose characteristics are representative of the overall population than is a nonrandom sample. And why is it important to have a representative sample? If the informants in a random sample are representative of the population, then whatever conclusions researchers reach about the sample will apply to the entire population.

To illustrate the utility of random sampling, we might consider the surveys conducted before presidential elections — presidential polls. The naïve observer might suspect that the best way to predict the outcome of a national election is to sample as many people as possible. In 1936, for example, the staff of the *Literary Digest,* a prominent magazine, used this approach. These researchers mailed out about 10 million postcard ballots, obtaining their list of respondents from telephone directories and auto-registration records. The results of their survey indicated that Alfred Landon, the Republican candidate, would win easily, with about 56 percent of the vote.

The *Literary Digest* poll was proved dramatically wrong when Franklin Roosevelt, the Democratic candidate, obtained 56 percent of the popular vote and carried forty-six of the forty-eight states. The problem with the *Literary Digest* poll was that it drew its sample only from people who had cars and telephones. In other words its sample consisted of relatively affluent people in the 1930s — and the affluent tend to vote Republican. There was, in short, a distortion, or bias, built into the *Literary Digest*'s sampling procedure. A young pollster named George Gallup, however, used a random sample to predict that Roosevelt would win the election, and he also predicted the precise outcome of the *Literary Digest* poll. Gallup's triumph in 1936 helped convince the American public that with a random sample of about 2000 people, pollsters could usually make accurate predictions about the outcome of presidential elections (Gallup, 1972).

Undoubtedly you are aware of many other modern uses of surveys. Television, radio, newspapers, and magazines frequently report the results of public-opinion polls on a range of subjects. Big businesses conduct surveys in order to learn how consumers or potential consumers react to their products. Political candidates or parties sponsor survey research in order to determine politicians' popularity or the electorate's dominant needs and interests. The principal difference between sociological surveys and other surveys is that the sociological variety involves more extensive analysis of patterns and relationships in the social world. Ishmael Okraku's (1987) survey of attitudes toward multigenerational residence is a case in point.

A Study of Attitudes toward Multigenerational Residence

Independence, self-reliance, and privacy are values prized by many Americans, and having one's own residence is a means of maintaining these values. So, one might expect, most Americans would be highly critical of multigenerational

*According to the Okraku study of multigenerational residence,
about half of the respondents surveyed accepted the idea that
elderly parents live with their adult children. As this scene suggests,
senior citizens can be integrated effectively into family activity.*

residence, in which elderly parents live with their adult children. But is this true?

Ishmael Okraku (1987), a sociologist, found little published material about people's attitudes toward multigenerational residence. He obtained data from the National Opinion Research Center, which conducts large annual surveys using samples representative of the adult noninstitutionalized population of the United States. In six of the eleven years between 1973 and 1983, including those two years, the survey asked respondents whether they considered multigenerational households a good idea. Okraku obtained the results of these six surveys, which used interviews.

Of those who answered the question (about 99 percent), 36 percent indicated unconditional acceptance (it is a good idea), while an additional 15 percent expressed conditional support (it depends). Thus over half the respondents (51 percent) gave at least a partial endorsement to the idea of multigenerational residence. The 15 percent of the sample that suggested conditional support was a remarkably high figure, Okraku indicated. Because the question had been phrased to elicit general sentiment, respondents had to take the initiative when providing a conditional response. Most of the time, subjects take little initia-

tive when interviewed, and those who do seldom provide a consistent pattern. Obviously many people felt strongly about the conditional factor in this instance.

Another basic finding was that people's support for multigenerational housing increased over time. In 1973, 42 percent of the overall sample expressed approval of the practice, and in each successive survey the figure rose, reaching 58 percent in 1983. The data were broken into six age groups, and over time each group became more positive about multigenerational residence. The younger the age category, however, the more supportive of the practice. For instance, among those born between 1944 and 1953, 62 percent were positive about multigenerational housing in 1983, while only 39 percent of those born between 1904 and 1913 expressed that opinion.

Okraku concluded that the respondents' fairly strong support for multigenerational housing and the increase of support over time do not mean that people are changing their values about residential independence. In a social world in which the number of aging people has increased and in which the many difficulties elderly people must face have received increasing attention, it is becoming widely recognized that multigenerational housing represents a viable if not ideal solution. The elderly themselves are the least supportive of this conclusion, but they too have gradually begun to accept it.

Commentary

A major strength of surveys is that they are a quick means of gathering information about large populations. In the surveys analyzed by Okraku, those who collected the data used random-sampling techniques to obtain an accurate idea of how adult Americans feel about multigenerational residence.

A disadvantage of surveys is that they do not directly measure what people have done but only what they say they have done or would do. No assurance emerges from Okraku's study that all the age groups' behavior would be consistent with their attitudes. In particular, such an inconsistency between attitudes and behavior might develop for young people who expressed the desire to bring elderly parents into their households but who also had little concrete sense of how difficult this course of action could turn out to be.

Experiments

An **experiment** is a research technique in which the investigator manipulates conditions so that the effects produced by one independent variable can be isolated and observed. Experimenters seek to establish causal connections. The most basic procedure is to select two groups of respondents whose social characteristics are similar, duplicate to the extent possible the conditions affecting the two groups, and then introduce the expected independent (experimental) variable to one group (the experimental group) and not to the other (the control group). Experiments can be conducted either in laboratories or in natural settings.

A well-known study of aggression conducted by Albert Bandura and his colleagues (1963) illustrates the basic experimental model. In Bandura's study a number of children who had basically simi-

lar social characteristics were randomly divided into two groups. Both groups were placed in a room that contained a large plastic doll, a punching-bag toy. In the experimental group, the children observed an adult hammering the doll, and when the adult stopped doing it, the children started to hammer the doll themselves. In the control group, in which no adult had hammered the doll, the children were much less likely to do it themselves. Since the only difference between the two groups had been the presence of the experimental variable in one group and its absence in the other, the researchers were in a strong position to assert that the presence of the experimental variable — the adult's hammering of the toy — caused the greater amount of children's hammering in the experimental group (Bandura et al., 1963).

Sometimes experimenters decide that circumstances do not require a control group — that with two groups of subjects possessing similar backgrounds exposed to two or more experimental variables, any behavioral differences that the subjects could exhibit are very likely to result from the different experimental variables. The following study offers such an illustration.

Experiment on Work Roles and Perceptions

Americans can become quite heated about the topic of personal worth. "How dare you even suggest that some people in this country are better than others?" a citizen might ask angrily.

Ronald Humphrey (1985) studied this emotional subject. In an experiment he hypothesized that people who are in high positions in organizational structures and who do high-level tasks will be more favorably regarded than individuals of equal ability who have lower positions and are performing lower-levels tasks.

Humphrey used college students as his subjects — 100 students in twenty experimental groups. Within each experimental group, three individuals were randomly assigned to be clerks and two to be managers. Because the members of each group had not previously known each other, there seemed no reason to suspect that before the introduction of the experimental variable, there would have been a tendency for some individuals to receive a higher evaluation than others. So there appeared to be no necessity to use a control group.

After they were assigned to be clerks or managers, the subjects were taken to an "office" where they were seated and told that the study was designed to determine how people work together in an office setting. Then the experimenter went from one subject to another explaining in a loud voice what each individual was expected to do— low-skill, repetitive jobs for the clerks and more challenging and interesting tasks for the managers. For the next two hours, the members of the groups performed their respective activities. At the end of the two-hour period, the subjects were given a brief set of questions in which they were asked to rate themselves and the others on a variety of traits, such as leadership, intelligence, assertiveness, supportiveness, warmth, and humor. The results were generally consistent with Humphrey's hypothesis: Both clerks and managers rated managers more favorably. This pattern emerged even though the students were aware of the random assignment to the two groups and thus knew that there was no reason to believe that the managers actually possessed more desirable traits than the clerks did. Humphrey concluded that the manner in which organizations are set up—in this case with clerks having lower status and performing lower-status tasks than managers —will strongly affect participants' evaluations of each other.

Commentary

Both of the experiments we have discussed indicate a distinct strength of the experimental method—the likelihood of establishing a causal link. The researcher sets up an experiment that seeks to eliminate the influence of other independent variables. If this influence is effectively removed, then the dependent variable—the manner in which the subjects respond—can be attributed to the influence of the experimental variable. In Humphrey's experiment the independent variable was the random assignment of people to be either clerks or managers; the dependent variable was the subjects' evaluations of clerks and managers. Because of the random assignment of individuals, other independent variables were

ruled out—there was no reason besides the assignment to be a clerk or manager that appeared to influence the ratings individuals received. Thus when the managers actually did receive higher ratings, only the independent variable—assignment to either the manager or clerk group—seemed to remain as a possible cause. A causal connection was established. By contrast, surveys do not employ procedures that rigorously test the isolated impact of an independent variable.

Experiments, however, also have weaknesses. One issue is the problem of whether or not they are realistic. Would Humphrey's results have been produced in "the real world"? One possibility is that in an actual office, clerks and managers would have more extensive information about one another. This knowledge might affect their respective perceptions and perhaps offset the tendency for individuals to be evaluated primarily on the basis of the positions they hold and the work they do. Another criticism of many experiments involves an ethical issue—Is it right to engage in deception in the course of doing research? Does the end, which in this case is the investigator's quest for information, justify the means, the use of deceit? In Humphrey's study the subjects were told that the experimenter was attempting to determine how people work together in an office setting. This was a minor deception. As we see at the end of this chapter, in the section about research ethics, sometimes experimenters engage in much larger deceptions.

Observation Studies

To some people it might seem a bit strange that individuals can do research simply by observing others. "All right," an individual might say, "I can understand that conducting surveys and experiments is hard work. But just people watching?!" Actually that can be hard work. It is true that sociologists who conduct observation studies do not enter the research situation with a carefully developed survey or experiment, but they must be prepared to be active investigators, who conscientiously observe their research subjects over a fairly lengthy period of time (months, sometimes even years), analyze what they observe, and relate their conclusions to concepts and theory in their field.

There are two types of observation research. Some studies use **nonparticipant observation,** a method of observation in which an investigator examines a group process without taking part in the group activities. In many instances, however, researchers believe that they will obtain a more detailed knowledge of their topic if they use **participant observation,** a method of observation in which an investigator becomes involved in the activities of the group being studied.

Participant-Observation Study of Peer-Group Development

Between 1969 and 1970, I conducted a year-long participant-observation study of the development of peer groups among adolescent Puerto Rican males (Doob, 1970). The principal finding was that the young men's peer groups reflected their family of origin in two significant respects: shared interests and activities, and range of contacts. For instance, respondents who came from families that shared many interests and activities and participated in large social networks tended to belong to peer groups with these same two traits.

During the study I lived on the block where the research was focused, and I spent considerable time observing, talking to, and playing a variety of sports with the boys who were the research subjects. A tape recorder was my constant companion, and I took extensive notes.

What these observations produced was detailed, often subtle information about the process by which family patterns become peer patterns. One striking example was how one thirteen-year-old boy, whose father and mother shared few interests and activities, was being slowly but relentlessly pressured to give up peer contacts to become his mother's frequent companion. The result? The boy was steadily withdrawing into a fantasy life featuring a half-dozen television cartoon characters. In contrast, I had ample opportunity to observe the process by which a local eighteen-year-old became involved in a peer group composed of ambitious, hard-working students, whose activities, interests, and contacts were much like those of his family and were systematically encouraged by his parents.

Could this richly detailed information have been obtained with any other research technique? I doubt it.

Commentary

The research section at the end of Chapter 3, "Culture," discusses the use of participant observation for studying culture. The strength illustrated by such a study of peer-group development is demonstrated there once again: The researcher has the opportunity to obtain detailed information about individuals and groups over time in a natural setting. Neither surveys nor experiments obtain the same rich detail available to the participant-observation investigator, who spends a fairly lengthy period of time studying a small number of subjects.

On the other hand, because of the lengthy involvement with their subjects, observation researchers, particularly participant observers, risk the possibility of emotional involvement—attraction, dislike, or some other distinct reaction—that will distort their observations. Did my personal feelings about the research subjects affect my analysis of their activities? This was often a major concern, which I tried to relieve by comparing my assessments of individuals and groups to those of other outsiders with some social-research training. Observation studies have another weakness: They usually involve a single or a small number of group situations. As we have observed, sociological inquiries are seeking to uncover patterns and generalizations. Researchers who study a single or small number of cases might encounter distinct or unusual characteristics in the situations they are studying, and these qualities might encourage the investigators to produce misleading or downright incorrect generalizations. I wondered, for instance, whether the particularly heavy drug trafficking on the block where I focused my study had a distinct impact on local behavior, producing peer-group activity for the block's adolescent boys that was significantly different from the peer-group activity on other blocks in the locale.

No matter what research technique they employ, sociologists often use tables as a means of presenting their data. The following Social Application is a lesson in how to read a table.

SOCIAL APPLICATION

Reading a Table

 Anyone studying sociology needs to read tables. In this exercise carefully follow the sequence of steps, concentrating on each step as you reach it.

1. *Examine the title, which indicates the topic to be analyzed.* Many people plunge into tables and other reading matter without even a glance at the title, which is a succinct summary of the information the writer is supplying. In Table 2.1 the topic is sources of satisfaction and enjoyment. The data in this table appear in percentage form.

Sometimes tables present the numbers of people instead of percentages.

2. *Read captions and footnotes.* It is probably even easier to disregard captions, footnotes, and source notes than the titles of tables, since their placement is less prominent. Such omissions are often crucial, however. The caption, for example, is likely to offer a brief substantive statement about the data. In Table 2.1 the caption supplies the precise wording of the question. Footnotes are likely to supply such facts as the source of the data

and the means by which the information was obtained. In both cases the reader learns something about the quality of the research. As our discussion on surveys indicated, a national random sample of 2000 men and women offers an accurate representation of the entire adult American population on a given question. The Roper Organization is a well-established commercial survey firm.

3. *Identify the variables.* When researchers devise tables, they frequently put the independent variable across the top and

---

Table 2.1

[Title] **People's Sources of Satisfaction and Enjoyment**[1]

[Data labels] SOURCES OF SATISFACTION AND ENJOYMENT	[Independent variable] EDUCATION LEVEL		
	COLLEGE GRADUATE	HIGH-SCHOOL GRADUATE	LESS-THAN-HIGH-SCHOOL GRADUATE
[Dependent variables]			
Television	33%	50%	65%
Music	34	33	23
Reading books, magazines, newspapers	34	29	19
Work	31	22	13
Radio	16	22	27
Physical exercise	20	14	9

[1][Footnote] The data presented here were obtained from 2000 men and women 18 years of age and over. The sample was obtained nationwide, and a complicated sampling procedure insured the randomness of the respondents chosen. Interviews were conducted face-to-face in the respondents' homes.

[Source note] Source: Adapted from the Roper Organization. *Roper Reports.* May 1981.

[Caption] *The following message was on a card that was shown to respondents. "Here are some things most people experience in their daily lives. Of course, they may all be important, but which three or four of those things do you find give you the most personal satisfaction or enjoyment day in and day out?"*

then arrange the dependent variable or variables along the left-hand side. Sociologists are likely to assume this arrangement exists when they first examine a table. However, anyone reading a table must be aware that for emphasis or convenience researchers may reverse the pattern. Table 2.1 maintains the convention. The independent variable—level of education—is horizontal, and the dependent variables—the sources of satisfaction and enjoyment—appear vertically.

4. *Study the labels to understand the data in the table.* Researchers call each vertical list of data a *column* and each horizontal list a *row.* Read the labels for each column and row and try to set them firmly in mind. You will need to consider both column and row headings simultaneously when you read the table. The variable across the top—education—has three breakdowns: college graduate, high-school graduate, and less-than-high-school graduate. Thus in Table

2.1 there are three columns of data. A set of six dependent variables— television, music, reading, work, radio, and physical exercise—runs down the side. Six rows of data are thus shown.

5. *Analyze the information presented in the table.* In a table that presents the independent variable across the top, you should examine the column headings to see whether the various categories of the independent variable establish distinct patterns in relation to the categories listed down the left side. The accompanying table does indicate some distinct differences among the respondents with different levels of education. For instance, the higher the education, the less likely television is a major source of satisfaction and enjoyment—the specific figures are 33 percent for college graduates, 50 percent for high-school graduates, and 65 percent for less-than-high-school graduates. On the other hand, the higher the education, the more likely that people will feel that

reading books, magazines, and newspapers is a major source of satisfaction and enjoyment—34 percent for college graduates, 29 percent for high-school graduates, and 19 percent for less-than-high-school graduates.

6. *Consider how further analysis can expand the central conclusions.* As you study the table, you will perceive that the greater the education, the more likely that people find satisfaction and enjoyment in active pastimes—reading (mental activity), work, and physical exercise— and less in the passive amusements of television and radio. Additional research could investigate a number of issues. It would be interesting to know, for example, what independent variables besides education operate in the process of choosing one's pastimes. It is possible, for instance, that people's family background and their friends' characteristics might help determine their preferences for active or passive sources of satisfaction and enjoyment.

Secondary Analysis

Sometimes researchers undertake **secondary analysis,** a study using data banks available to researchers but produced by other individuals and organizations for their own purposes. The United States Bureau of the Census, for example, obtains large quantities of data that sociologists frequently use as secondary sources. In some cases researchers find that they can use earlier studies as sources of data. Other secondary sources include diaries, letters, court records, biographies, autobiographies, and novels. Ishmael Okraku's study of multigenerational residence, which obtained its data from six large nationwide samples, is an example of secondary analysis.

Secondary sources may provide a researcher with the only information about a particular

Table 2.2
Types of Research Design

TYPE	VARIETIES	STRENGTHS	WEAKNESSES
Surveys	Telephone or face-to-face interviews, question-naires	A great deal of information can be gathered easily and efficiently	Possibility of distorted findings since data involve people's words and not their actions
Experiments	Laboratory or field experiments	Distinct possibility of establishing a causal link	Possible artificial influence of experimenters operating in a laboratory setting; ethical issues associated with experimenters' deception
Observation studies	Nonparticipant observation, participant observation	Detailed observations of groups over time in a natural setting	Danger of emotional involvement and loss of objectivity; problem of generalizing from a single case
Secondary analysis	Earlier studies, diaries, court records, biographies, novels	Procurement of data in situations where the use of other methods is impracticable	The diverse limitations imposed by researchers not gathering data themselves: e.g., inability of secondary sources to answer some questions of particular significance to the study at hand

topic. Unless he had had a time machine to transport him back to the last third of the nineteenth century, Richard Sennett (1974) could not have gathered direct information about Chicago families between the years 1872 and 1890. He had to rely on a variety of secondary sources—census material, novels, and historical analyses, in particular.

Using these materials, Sennett was able to learn a great deal about nineteenth-century families. For example, the census data demonstrated that in the majority of cases, husbands were at least five-to-ten years older than their wives. The researcher wondered why such a gap existed. The census material offered no information on this point, but Sennett was able to find a clue in another source from the nineteenth century. A novel about a middle-class Chicago household of the 1880s suggested that a young doctor would not get married until he was sufficiently well established to maintain his family at a comfortable material level. Sennett's study illustrates that sociologists can often use secondary sources to gather a great deal of information on a subject that cannot be studied by other sociological research techniques.

Secondary sources can serve as future resources. One researcher wrote, "The best of this information should be preserved, not only so that contemporary colleagues may use it, but also so that we leave a legacy for posterity describing what we were like, we of a particular period and place" (Card, 1988).

Table 2.2 summarizes the four types of research design discussed in this section.

Issues in Sociological Research

We now turn to some general issues in research that pose major challenges to sociologists and other social scientists. Each of the issues discussed involves controversy. In some instances, such as the question of objectivity in the research process, debate occurs primarily among social scientists; in other cases the disputes tend to pit social researchers against individuals outside of social science, such as law-enforcement officials or government bureaucrats.

Objectivity in the Research Process

Objectivity is the ability to evaluate reality without using personal opinions and biases. Researchers try to maintain objectivity in their work —that is, to report the facts in the situations that they study without reflecting their personal feelings. If two investigators conducted the same piece of research independently of each other and produced the same or almost the same findings, then we would have strong reason to believe that they had achieved objectivity.

Loss of objectivity can occur for several reasons. Some research areas might provoke intense personal feelings in entire groups of investigators. As an extreme case, it would be unreasonable to expect a black or Jewish sociologist to do an objective study of the Ku Klux Klan, a group that has had a history of brutally terrorizing both ethnic groups, especially blacks. Furthermore the majority of American sociologists are white, middle-class, and politically liberal, and each of these qualities could be a source of bias in a research situation.

Another reason for the loss of objectivity is a researcher's commitment to a fixed theoretical or ideological position. Researchers sometimes approach their studies not as open-minded observers but as individuals selectively seeking evidence for a particular position.

A third factor is the researcher's relations with his or her respondents. During a participant-observation study, for example, an investigator might develop such a close relationship with research subjects that he or she might begin to accept the subjects' definitions of critical situations —their analyses of community events, their assessments of the "good people" and the "bad people," and more. Such a situation can seriously endanger the objectivity of a project.

Several steps can be taken, however, to avoid the loss of objectivity. First, recognizing that both their topics and their techniques are affected by their own values, sociologists can attempt to carefully analyze how their values apply to their studies. Once they have determined the impact of their values, they are probably less likely to let personal inclinations undermine the objectivity of their investigations. Second, sociologists might seek the assistance of colleagues who can visit the research site and make independent assessments of the people under study. The colleagues' assessments, though based on brief observations, might provide the investigators with clues to whether or not they are losing their objectivity.

A researcher's objectivity can also be assessed by another person's follow-up investigation. After reading a report about a particular study, a second sociologist might want to evaluate the accuracy of the findings. He or she will conduct a **replication** —a repetition or near-repetition of an earlier study to determine the accuracy of its findings.

The loss of objectivity can occur in any social scientific study. As the following Cross-Cultural Perspective indicates, even famous social researchers can be vulnerable to this criticism.

Margaret Mead in Samoa: Objectivity in Participant-Observation Research

Objectivity is a priority in research, but sometimes investigators fail in this regard. This example illustrates some of the conditions that might undermine objectivity.

In 1925 Margaret Mead, a twenty-three-year-old anthropologist, arrived in Samoa. After nine months of research, she produced a book that became the first anthropological bestseller, *Coming of Age in Samoa.* Nearly sixty years later, after her death, a New Zealand anthropologist named Derek Freeman completed *Margaret Mead and Samoa,* a book stating that Mead's participant-observation study lacked objectivity and that its conclusions were largely incorrect.

Before Mead left for Samoa, she had been a graduate student of the anthropologist Franz Boas. At the time Boas was deeply involved in the debate about whether human development is primarily the result of biological influence or of cultural influence. According to Freeman, Boas wholeheartedly supported the latter idea, and, to bolster the cultural position, he sought evidence to counter his opponents' contention that the turmoil of adolescence was a biological necessity. In Samoa Mead hoped to find a culture free of adolescent stress, and this discovery would have given Boas valu-

able ammunition in his debate with the biological determinists. Freeman contended that Boas was pleased with the study that Mead planned to undertake. Freeman wrote, "In Margaret Mead there was at hand a spirited young cultural determinist ideally suited to the project he had in mind" (Freeman, 1983: 60).

If Freeman is correct, then Mead's objectivity was already seriously tarnished even before she left the United States. Independent support for Freeman's claim does exist. Robin Fox, an English anthropologist, indicated that Mead characterized the relationship of Boas with his graduate students in the following fashion: "He told us what to look for and we went and found it" (Leo, 1983: 69).

Freeman concluded that because Mead's research lacked objectivity, she produced blatantly inaccurate findings. In *Coming of Age in Samoa,* Mead described a culture in which people had a pleasant, relaxed attitude toward sex. Before marriage, she contended, adolescents could engage in free lovemaking, and marriage itself was not a major hindrance to free love. Mead's overall sense of the Samoans was that they were an amiable, relaxed, and peaceful people. Freeman disagreed with her on both points. His more recent study concluded that

Samoan adolescents were subjected to authoritarian control. The adults did not encourage youthful sex; in fact, they explicitly prohibited it. In addition, he found them not amiable and peaceful but competitive, jealous, and frequently violent. While Mead reported that forcible rape was unknown to the Samoans, Freeman offered data indicating that the incidence of forcible rape was high, twice that of the United States and twenty times that of England. He claimed that all Mead had needed to do to learn about the frequency of rape among the Samoans was to read the local newspaper, which regularly reported rape cases during her stay.

Freeman claimed throughout his book that biological factors have as much impact in the shaping of human development as cultural factors do. Freeman's critics, however, contended that, like Mead, he has forsaken objectivity in an effort to convey an ideological position. Bradd Shore, another anthropologist who has done field work in Samoa, suggested that the Samoans fall somewhere between the Mead and Freeman characterizations. They are neither as amiable and peaceful as Mead described nor as competitive and violent as Freeman claimed.

The Mead–Freeman confrontation is not the first situation in which anthropologists have studied the same culture and produced different findings. Because the loss of objectivity is a distinct danger in their studies, anthropological researchers have found an increasing number of ways to control their biases. Often they use independently developed psychological tests as a non-subjective means of assessing respondents' thought and behavioral patterns. Census data and statistical analysis can serve the same purpose. Team research can permit anthropologists to examine a wider range of groups and activities than a single investigator could. In addition, this approach provides team members with an opportunity to evaluate one another's objectivity and to attempt to correct any individual's biases that might distort their findings.

Sources: Derek Freeman. *Margaret Mead and Samoa*. Cambridge, MA: Harvard University Press. 1983; John Leo. "Bursting the South Sea Bubble." *Time*. V. 121. February 14, 1983, pp. 68–70; Eliot Marshall. "A Controversy on Samoa Comes of Age." *Science*. V. 219. March 1983, pp. 1042–1045; John Noble Wilford. "Customs Check: Leave Your Ideological Baggage Behind." *New York Times*. February 6, 1983. Section 4, p. 8.

Ethics in the Researcher's Role

All sociologists agree that research must be conducted in an ethically sound manner. Exactly what the ethical limits should be, however, is often a topic for debate. In this section we consider three possible areas in which ethical problems can arise — issues of confidentiality, inflicting mental suffering, and use of findings.

Problem of Confidentiality

Different aspects exist to the issue of confidentiality. Occasionally sociologists publish data that prove embarrassing or irritating to subjects who believe that their confidentiality has been violated. On the other hand, sociologists like Mario Brajuha sometimes find themselves acting to protect informants' confidentiality.

In 1982 Mario Brajuha, a graduate student in sociology at the State University of New York at Stony Brook, began his dissertation research, a participant-observation study of a restaurant, where he was employed as a waiter. Brajuha had collected about 700 pages of notes when a suspicious fire destroyed the restaurant.

A few days later, local police and fire investigators contacted Brajuha, demanding the release of his records. Brajuha refused, saying that this move would violate the confidentiality he had promised his subjects. The Assistant Attorney General threatened to have Brajuha jailed for contempt. On the day that he was expected to surrender his records, Brajuha appeared before the judge presiding over the case. Upon examination of Brajuha's records, the judge agreed that the researcher's claim that people would be embarrassed if his records were revealed was realistic. Nonetheless, the judge eventually ruled that Brajuha should surrender his notes. The pressure on Brajuha increased when the Federal District Attorney issued a subpoena for the research records. Attorneys for both sides presented their cases to a federal judge, who ruled that serious scholars must be permitted the same confidentiality as journalists. At the same time, the Brajuha case was sent back to the lower court for additional information. One unanswered question was whether or not as a graduate student, Brajuha could claim to be a serious scholar.

This question was never answered in court. Following a reorganization of the Federal District Attorney's Office, there was an out-of-court settlement in which Brajuha supplied federal investigators with some carefully edited information from his notes. Because of the settlement, this case did not establish a legal precedent (Hallowell, 1985). For those who know about it, however, it is a testimony of one young sociologist's commitment to high ethical research standards.

The issue of confidentiality is also relevant to AIDS research. As in Brajuha's study, social scientists are vulnerable to subpoenas from law-enforcement officials, who might feel that the investigators have access to information about hard-drug use or other illegal activity. Researchers studying AIDS can apply to the Public Health Service for certificates of confidentiality that will provide immunity from subpoena (Melton and Gray, 1988).

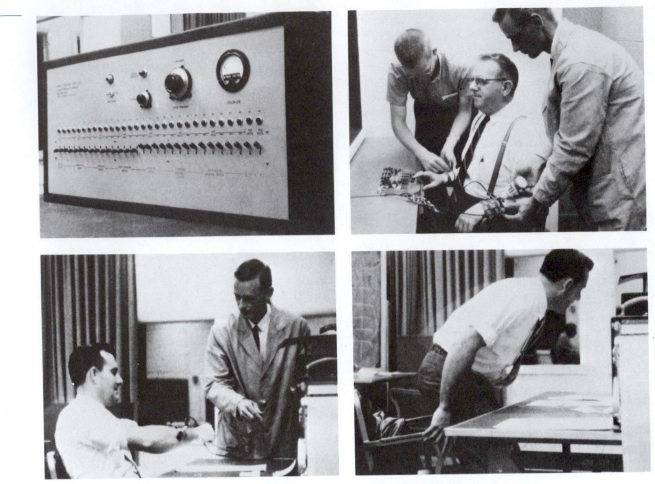

In the above series of photos taken from the film Obedience *by Stanley Milgram, one can see the "shock machine," the "victim" (seated, upper right), the researcher (in white lab coat), and the subject (bottom photos).*

Problem of Inflicting Mental Suffering on Research Subjects

When research subjects are manipulated, painful self-revelations are sometimes produced. Stanley Milgram (1963), a psychologist, did a series of experimental studies in which his subjects believed that they were applying a sequence of increasingly powerful shocks to other subjects in a learning experiment. Milgram's elaborate "shock machine" did not actually administer any shocks to the supposed victims, who had been instructed by the researcher to express surprise, pain, and sometimes even pleas for mercy after the subject pushed one of the shock buttons. Yet for the purposes of the experiments, which focused on the subjects' willingness to obey an authority figure (the experimenter), it was essential that the people who pushed the buttons on the machine believed that it was producing real shocks. The following exchange illustrates how a typical subject responded to this experimental situation.

The subject began the experiment calmly but became increasingly nervous as he proceeded. After believing that he had administered a 180-volt shock, this man pivoted in his chair and addressed the experimenter in an agitated voice.

Subject: I can't stand it. I'm not going to kill that man in there. You hear him hollering?
Experimenter: As I told you before, the shocks may be painful, but—

(Milgram, 1974: 73)

As the voltage increased, the subject became even more agitated.

> *Subject:* What if he's dead in there? . . . I mean, he told me he can't stand the shock, sir. I don't mean to be rude, but I think you should look in on him. All you have to do is look in on him. All you have to do is look in the door. I don't get no answer, no noise. Something might have happened to the gentleman in there, sir.
> *Experimenter:* We must continue. Go on, please.
>
> (Milgram, 1974: 76)

The subject did go on, pushing the voltage buttons until the experimenter finally indicated that the exercise was over.

Milgram (1963) explained that before subjects left, a "friendly reconciliation" occurred between them and their imagined victims. Furthermore the experimenter made a distinct effort to reduce any tensions that had arisen during the experiment. But could he actually succeed in this regard? One critic was very doubtful. She noted that Milgrim himself conceded that the reaction produced in subjects was "traumatic to a degree . . . nearly unprecedented in sociopsychological experiments," and so "his casual assurance that these tensions were dissipated before the subject left the laboratory is unconvincing" (Baumrind, 1964: 422).

In spite of such problems, some psychologists and sociologists have defended Milgram's research. Several have pointed out that his experiments revealed startling, important findings about people's tendencies to obey authority figures. But does the importance of the findings justify the emotional disruption that many subjects suffered? If researchers accept that the ends justify the means, then they have taken a frightening ethical position.

Use of Findings

At the beginning of the twentieth century, social scientists considered mental retardation the most serious problem in the United States. Policymakers were warned that unless retarded individuals were prevented from reproducing, mental retardation would assume frighteningly larger proportions and that significantly more crime, prostitution, alcoholism, poverty, and delinquency would accompany the increase.

Two developments in the field of psychology promoted that concern. The first was fragmentary research concluding that mental retardation is inherited; the second was the adaptation of Alfred Binet's intelligence test to classify mentally handicapped individuals. In the early 1920s, a prominent researcher gave IQ tests to delinquents, criminals, members of ethnic and racial minorities, and prostitutes and found that many received low scores. Instead of considering that most of these people lacked the cultural background to do well on such tests, the investigator simply concluded that low scores were attributable to genetic inferiority. Impressed by these findings, a host of prominent social scientists advocated the institutionalization and involuntary sterilization of mentally handicapped people. Between 1910 and 1923, such types of institutionalization more than doubled, and twenty-six states passed sterilization laws.

By the 1930s new research caused some scientists to question the wisdom of the earlier policies, and gradually the policies began to change, but institutionalization of mentally handicapped people capable of functioning in the social world has continued to the present. This historical case illustrates that in areas of sensitive research, findings need to be applied with great care and a sense of social responsibility (Sieber and Stanley, 1988).

STUDY GUIDE

Learning Objectives

After studying this chapter, you should be able to:

1. Define methodology and explain its importance in scientific research.
2. Define causation, distinguish between an independent variable and a dependent variable, and identify the conditions necessary for causation.

3. Define correlation, indicating its relationship to causation and distinguishing between positive and negative correlations.
4. List the stages in the research process, describing the sociologist's task at each stage.
5. Define hypothesis and explain the contribution that hypotheses make in the research process.
6. Distinguish among the following concepts — population, sample, and random sample — and explain the importance of random sampling in sociological research.
7. Define and discuss the four major types of research design — surveys, experiments, observation studies, and secondary analysis — and evaluate the strengths and weaknesses of the first three types.
8. Define objectivity, explain its importance in scientific research, identify factors that may hinder objectivity, and indicate how the loss of objectivity may be prevented.
9. Identify and discuss ethical issues involved in sociological research.

Summary

1. Methodology is the set of principles and procedures that guides sociological research.

2. The stages of the research process include choosing a topic, reviewing the literature, formulating a hypothesis, picking the research design, gathering the data, analyzing the data, and producing a report.

3. The four main types of sociological research design are surveys, experiments, observation studies, and secondary analysis. A survey uses carefully constructed questions to obtain large amounts of information about people's thoughts and behavior. The two principal types of surveys are interviews and questionnaires. An advantage of surveys is that they permit researchers to gather a great deal of information easily. A disadvantage is that they measure people's anticipated or reported behavior and not their actual behavior, and sometimes inconsistency occurs.

In an experiment the investigator manipulates conditions so that the effects of one variable can be observed while other variables are held constant. An advantage of experiments is that they can indicate a causal link. They also have weaknesses. Critics question whether experimental results would materialize in the "real world." Another criticism involves an ethical issue —

whether it is right to deceive subjects in the course of research.

The two types of observation research are participant observation and nonparticipant observation. Participant observation, in particular, offers the special opportunity to study individuals and groups over time in a natural setting. On the other hand, participant observers can lose their emotional detachment, and such a loss might impede a full and balanced understanding of the group process under investigation.

Secondary analysis involves the use of sources available to researchers but produced by other individuals and organizations for their own purposes. The United States Bureau of the Census obtains large quantities of data that can serve as the principal or exclusive source for sociological research.

4. Researchers are expected to be objective. A number of factors influence their success in this regard.

Research has raised serious ethical questions. Issues arising in major social-scientific studies involve confidentiality, the problem of inflicting mental suffering on research subjects, and the use of findings.

Key Terms

causation   a situation in which one variable can produce the occurrence of another

correlation   a statistical description of the relationship between variables

dependent variable   a variable that is the consequence of some cause

experiment   a research technique in which the investigator manipulates conditions so that the effects produced by one independent variable can be isolated and observed

hypothesis a scientifically researchable suggestion about the relationship between two or more variables

independent variable a variable that influences another variable—the dependent variable

interview a type of survey composed of questions that are delivered face-to-face or over the telephone

methodology the set of principles and procedures that guides sociological research

nonparticipant observation a method of observation in which an investigator examines a group process without taking part in the group activities

objectivity the ability to evaluate reality without using personal opinions and biases

participant observation a method of observation in which an investigator becomes involved in the activities of the group being studied

population the entire category of people possessing the characteristics that interest a researcher undertaking a particular study

questionnaire a type of survey in which a respondent writes the answers to a list of questions

random sample a sample drawn from a population by a process that assures that every individual in that population has an equal probability of being included

reliability consistency in measurement

replication a repetition or near-repetition of an earlier study to determine the accuracy of its findings

sample a limited number of individuals chosen from a population for the purpose of conducting research

secondary analysis a study using data banks available to researchers but produced by other individuals and organizations for their own purposes

survey a research technique that uses carefully constructed questions to obtain a variety of facts about people's thoughts and behavior

validity the condition in which a research item accurately measures what it claims to measure

variable a factor that has two or more categories or measurable conditions

---

Tests

True–false Test

_____ 1. In sociological research, dependent variables are frequently attitudes and activities.

_____ 2. A correlation of "0" indicates no relationship at all between two variables.

_____ 3. Surveys usually use samples instead of populations.

_____ 4. Ishmael Okraku's study of multigenerational housing indicated that a strength of surveys is that they demonstrate the relationship between people's claims and their actions.

_____ 5. In Ronald Humphrey's experiment, he used real clerks and managers to play their respective roles.

_____ 6. The loss of objectivity is less likely to occur in an observation study than in an experiment or survey.

_____ 7. Sociologists often use data produced by the United States Bureau of the Census as a secondary source.

_____ 8. Certificates of confidentiality have never provided social researchers with protection from legal prosecution.

_____ 9. Stanley Milgram's experiments support the ethically dangerous principle that the ends justify the means.

_____ 10. Research about mentally handicapped people early in the twentieth century immediately produced progressive policies making the lives of these individuals more rewarding.

Multiple-choice Test

_____ 1. Scientists' central concern is:
   a. causation.
   b. the systematic pursuit of the truth.
   c. the effective use of random samples.
   d. correlation.

_____ 2. Causation cannot be established until researchers have *ruled out* the:
   a. existence of other possible dependent variables.
   b. influence of other possible independent variables.
   c. possibility that the independent variable existed before the dependent variable.
   d. inverse relationship between variables.

_____ 3. "The higher people's social class, the fewer children they have" is an example of a:
   a. theory.
   b. correlation.
   c. hypothesis.
   d. logical pattern.

_____ 4. Organizations that sponsor research specifically demand that the researchers:
   a. gather data.
   b. analyze their findings.
   c. summarize their findings in a report.
   d. demonstrate the importance of their findings for sociological theory.

_____ 5. The *Literary Digest* poll of 1936 demonstrated that:
   a. random samples don't work.
   b. biases in sampling can produce disastrous research results.
   c. very large samples are necessary for predicting elections.
   d. several other types of samples work as well as random samples.

_____ 6. In Albert Bandura's experiment with a punching-bag toy:
   a. there was no independent variable.
   b. there were no children in the experimental group.
   c. the adult's hammering of the toy occurred in the control group.
   d. the adult's hammering of the toy occurred in the experimental group.

_____ 7. Participant-observation studies:
   a. make it possible to observe individuals and groups over time in a natural setting.
   b. are usually done with surveys.
   c. require a set of no fewer than six hypotheses.
   d. use a control group.

_____ 8. Richard Sennett needed information on Chicago families for the period from 1872 to 1890. Information of this sort must now be obtained from:
   a. experimental design.
   b. primary sources.

      c. secondary sources.
      d. nonparticipant observation.

———— 9. The loss of objectivity may occur because:
      a. some researchers are not intellectually equipped for the studies they do.
      b. some topics provoke intense feelings in entire groups of investigators.
      c. researchers do not have a fixed theoretical or ideological position.
      d. investigators are too detached from their subjects.

———— 10. Milgram's "shock-machine" studies focused social scientists' attention on the ethical issue of:
      a. confidentiality.
      b. painful self-revelation.
      c. validity.
      d. replication.

Essay Test

1. Describe the stages in the research process, indicating the major activity occurring at each stage.
2. What is a survey? Indicate a major strength and a major weakness of this approach.
3. Define experiment and indicate how the experimental process works. What are an important strength and an important weakness of this technique?
4. Write about observation studies, defining participant observation and pointing out a significant strength and a significant weakness of this research form.
5. What are secondary sources? Under what conditions might a sociologist decide to use them?
6. Define objectivity and discuss conditions that can undermine it during research. What steps can researchers take to avoid the loss of objectivity?
7. Discuss two areas in which ethical problems can arise in the course of social-scientific studies.

Suggested Readings

Bailey, Kenneth D. 1982. *Methods of Social Research.* New York: The Free Press. Second edition. A comprehensive introduction to sociological research methods, including four chapters on the details of constructing surveys.

Barnes, J. A. 1980. *Who Should Know What?* New York: Cambridge University Press. A thought-provoking discussion of the ethical dilemmas that social scientists must confront during research.

Converse, Jean M. 1987. *Survey Research in the United States: Roots and Emergence 1890 – 1960.* Berkeley, CA: University of California Press. A detailed history of the development of surveys, featuring analyses of such major issues as sampling and the wording of questions.

Hammond, Phillip E. (ed.). 1964. *Sociologists at Work.* New York: Basic Books. Sociologists involved in eleven methodologically varied studies candidly analyzing their research experiences in detail. These accounts offer a concrete discussion of issues and problems that can arise at different steps in the research process.

Huff, Darrell. 1954. *How to Lie with Statistics.* New York: W. W. Norton and Company. A revealing, entertaining discussion of the problems and limitations of statistical material.

48   Singleton, Royce, Jr., et al. 1988. *Approaches to Social Research.* New York: Oxford University Press. A thorough, effectively organized, well-written introduction to the principles and practice of social research.

Sociological Abstracts. A report issued five times a year and containing summaries of the latest articles and books in sociology.

Webb, Eugene J., Donald T. Campbell, Richard D. Schwartz, and Lee Sechrest. 1966. *Unobtrusive Measures.* Chicago: Rand McNally. A discussion of a large variety of ingenious ways in which social researchers can gather information about individuals and group members through nonparticipant observation.

Additional Assignments

1. Assume that you have been hired to study a problem of job satisfaction and dissatisfaction where you work. You have recently developed the following hypothesis: The better the workers are paid, the greater their job satisfaction. In your library find articles and books on job satisfaction, and use these sources for developing a study to test this hypothesis. Are you able to discuss effectively all the stages in the research process? (Hint: *Sociological Abstracts* and *Psychological Abstracts* will help you find articles.)
2. In a newspaper or magazine find a questionnaire or a self-test. Make a list of the variables asked about, such as age, sex, level of education, and occupation. What is the questionnaire trying to determine? Sort the variables into two categories—independent and dependent variables. Now using these variables, construct what seem to be reasonable hypotheses about the subject in the questionnaire.

Answers to Objective Test Questions

True–false Test

1. t	4. f	7. t	9. t
2. t	5. f	8. f	10. f
3. t	6. f		

Multiple-choice Test

1. b	4. c	7. a	9. b
2. b	5. b	8. c	10. b
3. c	6. d		

PART II

The Individual in Society

3
CULTURE

Components of Culture

Beliefs
Technology
Norms
Values
Language

We and They: Cultural Diversity and Conflict

Diversity and Conflict within Cultures
A Look at Other Cultures

American Culture

Traditional American Values
Changing American Values

Research in Sociology: The Participant-Observation Study of Culture

Study Guide

Is it obvious that everyone walks the same way? Perhaps it seems obvious, but actually it is not true. A recent study of human locomotion in 160 societies (Devine, 1985) revealed that many early Western observers entering non-Western societies immediately noticed that the people displayed manners of walking that were different from their own. The researcher wrote, "Whether they describe the novel walk or trot . . . as graceful, poised, noble, peculiar, stilted, or ungainly is secondary to the fact that they were so conscious of a difference that they almost always felt compelled to comment on it" (Devine, 1985: 553).

Travelers' written accounts also show that non-Western people were often aware that their styles of locomotion were very different from Westerners'. In one journal a visitor to a South Pacific island indicated that the local people found Europeans' gait so humorously awkward that they would burst into uncontrolled laughter.

A cultural item—in this case, style of walking—does not simply materialize. Distinct factors encourage its development. Were we to study a variety of cultures, we would be likely to find suggestions about the development of cultures' walking or running styles indicated by apparent connections between their styles and the traditional activities performed within particular cultures. Even though modern cultures are complex, careful analysis can produce an understanding of their development, patterns, and contributions.

Culture consists of all the humanmade products associated with a society. Basically two types of cultural products exist—the material and the nonmaterial. Material products consist of the physical objects people make and use—ranging in size from laboratory-developed microorganisms to skyscrapers and in complexity from the crudest stone or wood tools and weapons to the most sophisticated computers. Nonmaterial products are intangible. However, these nonmaterial products are the foundations of culture, providing information essential for interpersonal behavior and for the development of material culture. Beliefs, technology, norms, values, and language are important types of nonmaterial culture that we discuss in this chapter.

Culture is one of the most basic yet profound realities of people's lives. Culture provides them with a shared framework to guide them as they solve their everyday problems. If this statement seems abstract to you, try applying it to yourself. Imagine that you are sitting alone, just thinking. Note that the process of thought involves language and that language is a shared component of culture. You feel hungry. You might think that hunger is simply a biological urge, but a person's sense of hunger is inevitably affected by cultural standards. Perhaps you find yourself looking at your watch wondering if it is "time" to be hungry. Many, perhaps most, Americans are geared to three meals a day at fairly fixed times. However, people in other cultures often follow different arrangements; and, of course, differences also exist in food preferences. Americans would probably find their culturally prescribed sense of hunger rapidly receding if they were offered a few staples of some different cultures—such delicacies as lice, lizards, snakes, ants, worms, animal eyes or brains, wasps, and beetles.

Perhaps you take culture for granted, but, like air, which you might also take for granted, culture plays a fundamental part in your life. Consider politics. Americans frequently complain about the corruption and ineffectiveness of their politicians. As a kind of impotent protest, many people often fail to vote. Most of us seem to accept our existing political system most of the time with relatively little thought. But imagine how you would respond if the political leadership suddenly declared that you could never vote again and that as an ordinary citizen you could never participate at all in the political process—as often is the case in many nations.

A distinction needs to be made between "culture" and "society." Culture involves the humanmade products associated with a group, and **society** consists of the interacting people who share a

The activities in which the members of different cultures engage influence walking styles. We Westerners seldom carry heavy objects for long distances. If we did, many of us would probably alter our current walking style to make the impact of weight less burdensome.

culture. The two concepts are closely interrelated. A culture cannot exist without a society to implement it, and a society cannot exist unless a culture provides guidelines for its activities. In one sense culture is like a game plan developed by a coach for an athletic team, which represents society. The team needs the game plan to guide the strategy for its upcoming contest. However, without the players to put it into action, the game plan is no more than an idea. Thus people and the groups that they form are components of a society; in order to interact, these individuals and groups require the guidance of their culture. Given the close relationship between the terms *culture* and *society,* it is not surprising that they are often used interchangeably. Yet you must realize that a distinction between the two can be made.

One additional point: Are you familiar with the following use of "culture?" Someone says, "She's a really cultured person." Or another person contends, "He ain't got no culture." In these instances "culture" means classy, polished, or stylish—in short, a quality of someone a "cut" above the average. We are not concerned with this meaning of "culture." Whether we are classy or not, all of us have culture.

In this chapter we will examine the components of culture, the diversity and unity of culture, and American culture.

Components of Culture

Since the arrival of modern humanity, culture has developed very rapidly. About 40,000 years ago, human beings started wearing clothes, constructing shelters, and learning to survive in climates ranging from the tropical to the subarctic. About 4000 years ago, the domestication of animals and the cultivation of crop plants became widespread, producing a profound effect on human life. People no longer needed to move constantly from place to place in search of big game. With improved production of crops and animals, the environment could support increasingly larger populations, permitting a growing number of people to move into specialized occupations. Towns and cities started to develop. About 200 years ago, the Industrial Revolution began, eventually producing worldwide communication systems, effective mass transportation, and a vast assortment of technological advances.

Throughout human history technological changes have affected the content of culture. That trend continues in modern times, as we see in the next section. We examine the following components of culture: beliefs, technology, norms, values, and language.

Beliefs

A **belief** is a statement about reality that people accept as true. Beliefs are based on observation, logic, tradition, other people's opinions, or faith. Thus we can speak about scientific and nonscientific beliefs.

People who share a culture do not necessarily share beliefs. When asked which political party's members would more effectively handle the country's most important problem (which was not specified), 40 percent of a random sample of adult Americans indicated the Democrats, 29 percent the Republicans, and the rest were undecided (Popkin, 1988).

Age often affects beliefs. One would be hard pressed to find any adult Americans who believe in Santa Claus, but many children do. As Table 3.1 indicates, a national poll concluded that 87 percent of American children aged three to ten believe in Santa Claus. While few differences were found between boys and girls, whites and blacks, or Protestants and Catholics, the children's age

Table 3.1
American Children's Belief in Santa Claus

ALL CHILDREN	AGES 3–5	AGES 6–8	AGES 9–10
87%	96%	88%	69%

Source: *New York Times Poll.* December 24, 1985.

As children become older, they are less likely to believe in Santa Claus.

As children grow older, they are less inclined to believe in Santa Claus. These children, who are about seven years old, probably have some doubts about the jolly old gent's existence.

was highly correlated with belief. The older the children, the less likely they believed in Santa. The survey demonstrated that older children were more inclined to see logical reasons not to believe in Santa. For instance, Sara Oates, aged eight, pointed out, "A bike can't come down a chimney" (Rimer, 1985).

Beliefs can produce deadly effects. For nineteenth-century Americans, the doctrine of Manifest Destiny reflected the belief that the Europeans and their descendants were the properly dominant race in North America. They were supposed to be the guardians of American Indians, the land, and other natural resources. This popular nineteenth-century belief was a rationalization for the settlers' violent takeover of Native-American lands and for a pattern of violating treaties once they were signed.

Beliefs supply the framework for people's perceptions. Many Americans believe that people are generally untrustworthy, that only locks, bolts, and bars can protect personal property. Thus it surprised a newsman accompanying President Nixon's tour to China in 1972 to find that his camera was still sitting on the bus seat where he had forgotten it. Americans abroad can also encounter foreigners' beliefs about the United States. To the poor people of many African, Asian, and Latin American countries, all people from the United States seem fabulously wealthy. These poor would find it difficult to believe that poverty, malnutrition, and hunger exist in the United States. Furthermore the widespread exposure of American television programming has contributed to a glamorous, violent image of the country. To many foreigners the United States is simply the land of *Dallas, Dynasty, Knots Landing, Wiseguy,* and *L.A. Law.*

Technology

Technology is any repeated operation that people use to manipulate the environment to achieve some practical goals. Technology ranges in complexity from such simple activities as the construction of crude digging tools or weapons to the production of the most sophisticated, modern computers. Perhaps it is the technology of modern cultures that most dramatically sets them off from earlier cultures. Since Mark Twain wrote *A Connecticut Yankee in King Arthur's Court* in 1889, many writers and filmmakers have dramatized the tremendous power and influence that time travelers could exercise if they could move backward to ancient cultures. One can argue that such a "step backward in time" was, in effect, made by European explorers and settlers when they used advanced weaponry, communication forms, and means of transportation to subdue or annihilate the native inhabitants of five continents.

Technology profoundly affects people's everyday lives in various ways, such as compelling the development of new occupations. A hundred years ago none of the following occupations existed: radiologist, astronaut, computer programmer, professional race-car driver, or deep-sea diver. These occupations could not exist because the respective technologies that make them possible had not yet been invented. Technology can also influence existing occupations. Today a doctor's job is often simplified by modern equipment. Does the leg have a fracture or the brain contain a tumor? X-rays and brain scans can provide definitive answers that could not be obtained in the past.

In the last several decades, rapid technological advances have facilitated a host of sophisticated innovations. At the Media Lab at Massachusetts Institute of Technology, a team has developed a computer model called "Conversational Desktop," which is supposed to imitate a good secretary. It speaks in a natural-sounding woman's voice, can answer a variety of questions, can determine from a speaker's location whether or not a question or statement is directed toward it, can exchange a sequence of messages with another computer, and can accurately assess whether or not a caller is sufficiently important to interrupt its owner in a meeting (Brand, 1987: 51–55). Reading about Conversational Desktop, you might wonder whether the human occupation of secretary will still exist in twenty or thirty years.

Norms

For a moment imagine that you are small enough to fit into an anthill or a beehive. Standing out of the flow of traffic, you would observe thousands of insects unerringly moving about their tasks, each a tiny cog in a complicated organizational structure. Such behavior is a magnificent testimony to the finely tuned genetic programming of these little organisms. Human beings, however, function very differently from ants and bees. People are primarily directed or controlled not by instinctive genetic guidelines but by learned norms.

A **norm** is a standard of desirable behavior. Norms are the rules people are expected to follow in their relations with each other. Norms not only provide guidelines dictating appropriate behavior in a given situation but also supply people with expectations of how others will respond to their actions. Norms often vary widely from society to society. In many respects English and American cultures are similar, and yet numerous normative differences exist—for example, the English drive on the left-hand side of the street and they always hold their forks in the left hand while eating. Norms also change over time. In the early twentieth century, for example, bathing suits were ridiculously modest by current standards. Skimpy modern models would have been viewed with horror.

Norms are often situational—that is, they are associated with certain positions and not with others. It is considered appropriate to express problems and fears to therapists but not to bank tellers, whose embarrassment or irritation would indicate that they expect only "small talk" when transacting bank business. During a football game, the players are supposed to block and tackle each other, but they are penalized for continuing such action after the whistle has been blown to stop play. In some situations people find it difficult to forsake previously relevant norms after they have become inappropriate or even criminal. After returning to the United States, some Vietnam veterans found it difficult or impossible to forsake their violent lifestyles and either got into trouble with the law or signed on as mercenaries in foreign wars. In all societies most people follow important norms, but individuals violate some of them. Chapter 8, "Deviance," explores norm-violating behavior.

Sociologists make some basic distinctions about norms. The following classifications are simplifications of reality, developed to demonstrate specific qualities of norms. Keep in mind that actual

Very different norms can co-exist within the same society. The wet suit, surfboard, and "laid back" lifestyle contrast sharply with the norms of the Amish (Mennonites) who, as suggested by their "plain folk" clothing, continue to try to maintain their traditional standards within our rapidly changing American society.

norms often fail to fit neatly into one category or the other.

Folkways and mores. **Folkways** are norms that specify the way things are customarily done; they are concerned with standards of behavior that are socially approved but not considered morally significant. Folkways leave room for eccentric or harmless behavior, and violation seldom leads to punishment. Picking one's nose in public or arguing loudly with one's spouse at a party would be considered violations of folkways.

Violations of mores are much more serious. Child abuse, forcible rape, torture, murder, and cannibalism are prominent examples of violations of mores. **Mores** (pronounced "morays") are norms people consider vital; they are embedded in what members of a society believe to be morality. Unlike folkways, mores involve clear-cut distinctions between right and wrong. Punishment for the violation of mores will range from avoidance and ridicule to imprisonment and death.

All mores and some folkways are supported by **laws,** which are norms recorded by political authorities and supported by police or other enforcement officials. Most mores violations are crimes, and American society has a large body of criminal law, which is discussed in Chapter 8, "Deviance." Examples of folkways transgressions for which laws exist include parking violations, littering, and public drunkenness.

Explicit and implicit norms. Within a culture some norms are **explicit,** out in the open. Explicit norms are learned formally. For example, parents tell their children, "Don't speak with your mouth full, Sally" or "Stop that, Frank! Don't hit your sister." Because explicit norms are formally learned, almost everyone can explain them. Other norms are **implicit,** not normally discussed and not easily stated. Often these norms are most easily identified when violated. In many American households, parents enforce an implicit norm about nudity. The family members are not supposed to see each other naked. In most families this norm is probably never stated, but the children learn it when Mom or Dad hurriedly turns around or closes the bedroom so as not to be seen unclothed.

Ideal norms and real norms. **Ideal norms** are standards requiring strict obedience to the guidelines provided. In everyday life, however, some "slippage" occurs because the standards are often too lofty, impractical, or demanding. As a result **real norms** emerge: adjusted standards that reflect the practical conditions of living. Small deviations from norms are expected, even tolerated, but limits to the deviations are set.

People often fail to achieve ideal norms, even where they want to. For example, let us suppose that every day in the park a man sees a particular woman whom he would like to meet. He has watched numerous movies and TV skits that suggest how this should be done: He should simply go up to her and start talking or should contrive some means for meeting her, such as an apparently accidental collision in front of the grocery store. But he lacks the courage for such a ploy and constantly scolds himself for falling short of the ideal norm.

When people find it unpleasant or awkward to acknowledge that their response falls short of an ideal norm, they are likely to offer rationalizations to explain why they are not responsible for the violation of the ideal norm. The Hindu religion prohibits Indian farmers from killing cattle. Through the centuries farmers have developed means of avoiding direct slaughter. For example, to "kill" unwanted calves, owners place a triangular wooden yoke around the calves' necks so that when they try to nurse they jab the cow's udder and get kicked to death. Farmers then rationalize that the cows, not they, were responsible for the calves' deaths (Harris, 1974: 28).

Values

Fierceness is very important to the Yanomamö of the South American jungle. When a Yanomamö wife has been caught in an affair with another man, the value of fierceness is reflected in universally endorsed club fights. In these duels one man holds a ten-foot club, steadies himself by leaning on the club, and then exposes his head for a blow from the opponent's club. After that the positions are reversed. The majority of duels end up as free-for-alls, with everyone clubbing everyone else. Fatalities sometimes result but not very often because the headmen of the different groups stand by with bows drawn ready to kill anyone who delivers an intentionally lethal blow. The scalps of the older men often contain as many as a dozen enormous, angry scars, which are fully displayed on the possessors' proudly shaved heads (Chagnon, 1977). Around the planet Americans are considered aggressive and prone to violence. They are amateurs, however, compared to the Yanomamö, who strongly emphasize the values of fierceness and violence.

As this illustration suggests, values vary from one culture to another, but all cultures have them. A **value** is a general conviction about what is good or bad, right or wrong, appropriate or inappropriate. Values are abstract, stating broad behavioral

preferences, while norms guide behavior in specific situations. Americans tend to embrace the value of patriotism. Norms associated with patriotism specify that adult citizens should vote and that they should stand up, face the flag, and sing when the national anthem is played in public. Values concern what people regard as good or desirable, while beliefs focus on what they consider true and factual. The members of a family or community attend regular religious services and donate heavily to their religious organization; a prominent value in their lives is the importance of religion. A significant belief for these same people involves the existence of God.

Values are important because they influence the content of norms. If a culture such as the Yanomamö values fierceness and violence, its norms will provide such opportunities as club fights to permit members to demonstrate fierceness and engage in violence.

While values influence the development of norms, the "fit" between the two is not always a neat, one-to-one relationship. By definition values are abstract and norms are specific. Thus it is not surprising that different norms can be derived from a given value. The American emphasis on competition is a case in point. One high-school football coach might tell his players that they should do anything to win. "The other team is the enemy out there," he explains. "They're trying to stop you from winning, and you've got to punish them for that." He teaches his players a number of illegal moves that can knock opponents out of action and yet are difficult for a referee to detect. By contrast, another coach tells the team "play to win, but I expect you to stay within the rules and give your best effort. This game is just a small part of life, and I expect you guys to play hard but also with character."

Language

Alice and Bill are an elderly couple with an elderly dog. They tell people that their dog is just like a member of the family. "He listens to everything I say," Bill reports, "and I can tell by the look in his eye if he agrees with me." Alice concurs. "Ralph is nothing short of brilliant," she explains. "He must understand what I say, because he seems to know what I plan to do almost

Among the Yanomamö, for whom fierceness is an important value, disputes about extramarital affairs are often settled with fights using these long clubs.

before I've made the decision myself." Undoubtedly Ralph is very sensitive to his owners' wishes and plans, but is he actually using language?

Ralph is responding to signs. A **sign** is an object or event that stands for something else. Many signs provide a fixed interpretation. The smell of smoke suggests that a fire is in the vicinity; the taste of a particular beverage indicates that it is coffee. Ralph's capacity to interpret signs is aided by hearing and a sense of smell that are well developed. Thus no matter how quietly Bill or Alice opens the refrigerator door, Ralph will dash to the kitchen, hoping for a snack.

Although Ralph can detect certain signs, he has a limited capacity to understand symbols. A **symbol** is a sign with a meaning that is not fixed by the nature of the item to which it is attached but by the agreement of the people who use it to communicate. In American culture a wave of the hand stands for "hello" or "good-bye," a whistle blown by a referee means "stop," and the color black represents mourning.

A **language** is a system of symbolic communication that uses words, which are sound patterns that have standardized meanings. Like all symbols, words for items are not choices fixed by the nature of the items themselves. The four-legged piece of furniture on which a teacher writes papers and letters is called a *desk,* but no inherent quality of the object requires it to be so labeled. The desk could just as easily be called a *glump.* In this case the word is *desk* because the members of English-speaking cultures recognize and accept the word to represent the particular object. Language has two prominent traits as a communications system. First, there is its symbolic quality, which we have just discussed. Second, the symbols of language are combined in ways prescribed by a set of norms called *grammar* — for instance, the grammatical norm of word order. Thus "Marilyn smiled at Frank" has a different meaning from "Frank smiled at Marilyn."

We have considered some of the qualities of language. How should we describe its purpose?

The Social Construction of Reality

Basically language supplies meaning to cultures in a couple of ways. First, language can be used to accumulate human experience. When animals die, everything they have learned from experience perishes with them. But language lets human beings develop a history. Through written or oral accounts, people can gain access to knowledge and experience that have come before. No matter how intelligent human beings might be, without language each generation would possess no greater advantage over its ancestors than do geese, rabbits, or donkeys over their predecessors.

Second, language organizes our perception of the world. We can use language to refer to the past ("I went yesterday"), the present ("I am going now"), or the future ("I will go next week"). Language permits us to speak about single cases ("It was hot yesterday") or make general statements ("Summers are always hot around here"). Without language we would not be able to interpret the evidence of our own senses, and with language we are capable of describing subtle thoughts and perceptions.

The last point raises an interesting question. Do the people of all cultures see the world the same way, or do their respective languages organize their perceptions in different ways? The **linguistic-relativity hypothesis** contends that the unique grammatical forms of a language actually shape the thoughts and perceptions of its users (Sapir, 1921, 1929; Whorf, 1956). According to this conception, therefore, language is much more than just another element of culture.

The issue of time provides an example. Americans and other Westerners tend to think of time as something that can be broken into segments — years, days, hours, minutes, and seconds — and used for one's purposes. "Time is money," says a businessperson in the typical American tradition. Someone asks a friend to stay and talk. "Can't," the other replies. "I haven't got the time." To Americans time is scarce, elusive, and, therefore, precious. In contrast, the Hopi Indians have no words for "time," "late," "day," "hour," and "minute." They live in the present, emphasizing that all forms of life are working on their own time schedules and that things simply happen when they happen and will take as long as they take (Whorf, 1956). Inevitably these different orientations to time have created conflicts between the Hopi and their white neighbors. For instance, Hopi who were expected to show up for appointments at certain hours or to make mortgage payments by specific dates simply did not understand the system of time measurement the whites used and often would not show up at all or would be outrageously late by whites' standards. Table 3.2 shows how a grammatical difference between En-

Table 3.2
The English and Spanish Use of the Pronoun "You":
An Illustration of the Linguistic-Relativity Hypothesis

	SPANISH USE OF "YOU"[1]	
ENGLISH USE OF "YOU"	"TU" (INFORMAL)	"USTED" (FORMAL)
For all people, regardless of the type of relationship or age	Family members Friends Children and adolescents God Animals	Individuals with whom formal relations exist (one's doctor, teacher, or plumber)

[1] Usage varies to some extent from one Spanish-speaking counry to another. Furthermore there is a distinct tendency for younger people to use the informal form more readily.

The use of the two "you" forms in Spanish affects people's perceptions and behavior. Young people know that they are considered adults when strangers begin using the formal form when addressing them. On the other hand, when adults start addressing each other with the familiar form, they have crossed the boundary from acquaintance to friend. The fact that modern English has only the single "you" form means that similar perceptions are not built into the language.

Table 3.3
Culture

COMPONENT	BRIEF DEFINITION	EXAMPLES
1. Belief	1. A statement about reality that people accept as true	1. "The earth is round."
2. Technology	2. Any repeated operation people use to manipulate the environment for practical goals	2. A wooden club or a computer
3. Norm	3. Standard of desirable behavior	
a. Folkways	a. Norms that specify the way things are customarily done	a. Norms about public nose-picking or street littering
b. Mores	b. Norms people consider vital	b. Norms about murder and rape
c. Laws	c. Norms that are officially recorded and supported by political authorities	c. Laws about murder, rape, or street littering
4. Value	4. A general conviction about what is good or bad, right or wrong, appropriate, or inappropriate	4. Equality or a sense of racial superiority
5. Language	5. A system of symbolic communication using words, which are sound patterns that have standardized meanings	5. English, Spanish, and Hottentot

glish and Spanish illustrates the linguistic-relativity hypothesis.

The more involved the members of a culture are with a particular activity or thing, the more detailed their language becomes. Arabs have hundreds of words to describe camels and camel equipment, and, in many societies where grazing animals are a prominent feature, there is a variety of terms for different textures of hay. Americans do the same thing with cars, distinguishing a number of types—station wagons, sports cars, compacts, subcompacts, and sedans—as well as companies and finally models produced by a given company: Buick's Riviera, Electra, LeSabre, Regal, Skylark, and other models.

These examples suggest that some relationship exists between language and people's thoughts and perceptions. However, the examples do not necessarily confirm the linguistic-relativity hypothesis, which indicates that language shapes thought and perception. Which is it? Does language shape people's view of reality, or is it really the other way around? The problem is somewhat like the old question: Which came first—the chicken or the egg? Such issues simply cannot be resolved by research. What seems most probable is that language develops as a means of enabling people to describe and explain their experiences. Then, once a particular language has evolved, it shapes the world view of those brought up with its usage.

Thus moderate support for the linguistic-relativity hypothesis seems justified: Language does appear to influence certain perceptions and thoughts. This relationship is apparent in everyday life. For example, consider the function of a word like "un-American." Such a term establishes a clear boundary, indicating that any outlook or activity not traditionally American is traitorous. In particular, it is "un-American" to be "soft" on "Commies." These terms rigidly outline the idea that Americans are good and that they, the "Commies," are bad. Such uses of the language predispose many Americans to accept indiscriminately all negative evaluations of the Soviet Union, Eastern Europe, and China and to ignore or at least to tolerate the U.S. government's support of anti-communist dictatorships, the injustices of the U.S. economic system, and the enormous financial emphasis the government places on defense. Furthermore research continues to offer support for the linguistic-relativity hypothesis; for instance, one study discovered that Chinese-speaking informants and English-speaking informants possessed significant, language-related differences in their perceptions and memory (Hoffman, Lau, and Johnson, 1986).

Table 3.3 summarizes the components of culture presented in this section.

From the previous discussion, you have learned that all cultures contain the same basic components. In fact, anthropologists have discovered that cultures always have a fairly large number of **cultural universals** — traits believed to exist in all cultures. George Murdock (1965) listed over sixty cultural universals, including cooking, family,

feasting, folklore, funeral rites, gift giving, greeting forms, housing, incest taboos, laws, medicine, music, sport, toilet training, and toolmaking.

A major reason that cultural universals develop is the need to resolve the issues that all human beings face in the common effort to survive and, whenever possible, to enjoy life. Thus new members must be reared; guidelines for behavior must be developed; goods and services must be produced and distributed; sick people must receive care; individuals must be given opportunities to escape the daily "grind."

We and They: Cultural Diversity and Conflict

While cultural universals do exist, there is a great deal of variety in the ways different societies carry out a given universal. For instance, Americans often greet each other informally, while the Baganda of the East-African country of Uganda exchange a standardized set of questions and answers.

This section focuses on cultural differences. Within a given culture, groups often make a "we – they" distinction — an emphasis on being culturally separate from and superior to other groups. That same distinction can also occur when the members of different cultures make contact.

Diversity and Conflict within Cultures

So far we have discussed culture as if all its elements were shared equally by everyone within the society. This is not always the case. In most societies subcultures exist.

Subcultures and Countercultures

A **subculture** is the culture of a specific segment of people within a society, differing from the dominant culture in some significant respects, such as in certain norms and values or in language. When do sociologists determine that a particular segment of the population possesses its own subculture, and when do they decide that people merely have a number of relatively unimportant differences with the dominant culture? Frankly this distinction is hard to make with actual cases. As we

saw in the discussion about types of norms, concepts do simplify reality. We can learn from studying concepts but must realize that reality is usually more complicated than they suggest.

In modern, industrialized societies, many subcultures exist. They are based on such factors as occupation, racial and ethnic status, disadvantaged condition (such as being blind, deaf, or mentally handicapped), or deviant or previously deviant lifestyle (such as being a criminal, a drug addict, an alcoholic, a former criminal, a former drug addict, or a former alcoholic).

Subcultures are usually useful for their members because they provide emotional and social support and help them to cope with their life situations. Typically an American with a strong ethnic affiliation might say, "I was born in this country, raised here, and most of the time I feel like an American. But also, deep down, I'm Greek. And when I'm back in Baltimore having a Greek meal, surrounded by family and friends and speaking Greek, then I'm really home." Or a former drug addict might explain, "After going through this drug program, I'm convinced that the only people who should work with junkies are ex-junkies. After all, we've been through the whole thing ourselves. We know all the tricks, and so they won't pull anything with us."

Subcultures are generally supportive for their members, but let us consider whether they are beneficial for the society as a whole. One might argue that a society that allows subcultures to develop extensively — that, in essence, lets people "do their own thing" — gives those people a chance to feel self-fulfilled. Furthermore members of such tolerated groups would probably be unlikely to rebel because they are permitted to live much as they like. However, sometimes rebellion may seem to be the only way that members of a subculture can accomplish their most cherished goals.

A case in point involves the escalation of the protests of the 1960s. In the early years of the decade, some middle-class white students formed a subculture that worked with Southern blacks to promote the racial integration of buses, restaurants, and other public facilities. Others actively sought nuclear disarmament. The number of students involved in this protest-oriented subculture was fairly small, and their tactics were nonviolent.

By the late 1960s, however, the situation had changed. Small but determined groups of primarily young people, both on college campuses and elsewhere, began to take a variety of measures to oppose dominant American economic and political policies. Members of the different protest groups made speeches, wrote pamphlets and articles, and participated in sit-ins and building take-overs. These and other actions were supposed to dramatize to the American public the need to oppose the Vietnam War, the capitalist economic system, civil-rights injustices, and also local economic and political abuse.

The protest groups in this example were a counterculture. A **counterculture** is a subculture whose members consciously and often proudly reject some of the most important cultural standards of the mainstream society. Countercultures require extensive, sometimes full-time, commitment of members' time and energy and tend to have relatively few members. Under certain conditions, particularly during major protests on college campuses, countercultural groups have received larger, subcultural support.

The countercultural activity of the 1960s created considerable disruption and conflict, and one might argue that it was harmful to the society as a whole. However, as a legacy of those protests, a number of previously unquestioned social, economic, and political conditions have been challenged, and new perspectives and, in some cases, laws have been introduced. Civil-rights legislation was passed to attack prejudice and discrimination in education, housing, jobs, public accommodations, and voter registration in the South. Legislation also established new programs to relieve the

Countercultural members resist the values and beliefs within the dominant culture. But some forms of resistance are more acceptable than others. In the spring of 1969, a few student protesters at Cornell University emerged from a building occupation carrying guns. There was widespread surprise and shock, and photos like this one were displayed on the front pages of newspapers across the country.

effects of poverty. In addition, the protests against the Vietnam War contributed to the Nixon Administration's withdrawal of troops from Vietnam.

In the 1980s some public figures began sharply criticizing the drug abuse and sexual behavior that sometimes accompanied countercultural activity in the 1960s. It needs to be appreciated that the freedoms advocated by members of the 1960s countercultural groups have not been a pure blessing. Self-indulgent, confused behavior was often intermingled with activities that have produced significant progressive trends (Gitlin and Rosen, 1987). Instead of simply condemning or praising this era as a whole, sociologically oriented citizens of the 1990s need to study what happened and assess the distinct effects of that era on the present culture.

A Look at Other Cultures

Americans are often surprised and sometimes confused when they are introduced to some common practices of other cultures. In a number of societies, children may watch their parents engage in acts of sexual intercourse. In one culture all males must perform explicit homosexual acts before adopting heterosexual roles in adulthood. In another society all males at puberty go through a ritual in which the penis is cut to the urethra and sliced the entire length of the organ. Are these people "crazy"? No, they simply have cultural patterns that differ from those of Americans.

Observing such practices, Americans might experience **culture shock,** the psychological and social maladjustment many people suffer when they visit or live in another society. A study of Americans living in England found that in spite of the similarities between the two cultures, many of the subjects experienced culture shock, especially those whose test results indicated poor mental health (Weissman and Furnham, 1987).

When people of one culture assess the standards and practices in another, two distinct possibilities exist. One alternative is that people view the customs of the other culture as inferior; the second possibility is that they simply consider them different. Let us examine both possibilities.

Ethnocentrism

Ethnocentrism is the automatic tendency to evaluate other cultures by the standards of one's own. Ethnocentric people consider their own culture superior.

Many people spend their entire lives without ever leaving their own culture. It is hardly surprising that such people tend to view their particular cultural standards as the only acceptable way to live. Consider Laura Bohannon's experience. Bohannon (1975), an anthropologist, attempted to tell the story of Shakespeare's *Hamlet* to a group of old men of the Tiv tribe in Nigeria. It was her chance, she felt, to make *Hamlet* "universally intelligible." However, she failed because the story aroused the old men's ethnocentrism, and they constantly interrupted Bohannon to emphasize that the cultural practices she was describing were unacceptable. For instance:

The elders could not understand why Hamlet was upset when his mother remarried quickly. After all, if she had not done so, there would have been no man to hoe the land.

The old men could not accept the claim that a ghost appeared before Hamlet and spoke to him. They explained to Bohannon that no such things as ghosts exist. It was an omen, but omens, the men contended, cannot talk.

Furthermore it was not appropriate for Hamlet to avenge his father's death. Since the killer was a generation older than he, the task should have been performed by an older man.

Like the members of many other cultures, the Tiv elders were ethnocentric because they had been immersed in their own cultural tradition from infancy, with little exposure to any other.

An additional factor helps explain the occurrence of ethnocentrism: It can be functional for those who practice it. First, ethnocentrism can establish and sustain group loyalties, especially under stressful conditions. Warfare would be a case in point. If soldiers are going to fight well, they should believe that their cause is just, and ethnocentric slogans and inspirationally titled policies promote such a belief. For instance, World War I was sold as "the war to end all wars" and "the war to make the world safe for democracy." In World War II, Americans and their allies believed that they were fighting for the "Four Freedoms" — freedom of speech and expression, freedom of worship, freedom from want, and freedom from fear. These slogans were first presented to Americans by President Roosevelt in the course of his message to Congress in January 1941, shortly after the United States entered the war. During the Korean War, ethnocentric passions centered on "stopping the spread of the Red menace," and the policy designed to accomplish this task was called "containment." In the Vietnam War era, the target of the most prominent slogan was not the enemy but antiwar protesters. "America, your country, love it or leave it" was an outright demand that people be ethnocentric.

Ethnocentrism has another function: to help an already dominant group maintain its position of superiority. In many American cities of the 1830s, Protestant groups distributed large amounts of strongly anti-Catholic literature. The most notorious of these publications was Maria Monk's *Awful Disclosures,* an account of atrocities experienced by a young woman in a Catholic convent. The book was eventually exposed as the work of anti-Catholic propagandists; yet it went into twenty

An ethnocentric American might say that the office is no place to exercise. Chinese citizens, however, would point out that practicing Tai Chi before work not only helps people feel good physically but also creates a sense of participation in harmonious group activity.

printings and sold over 300,000 copies. Anti-Catholic ethnocentrism contributed to the development of a movement of native-born Protestant Americans who strongly resented the masses of newly arrived Irish immigrants. This anti-Catholic movement developed because the Protestant workers feared competition over jobs with the Irish, because they saw Catholicism as a threat to established values, and because they wished to maintain the northern European homogeneity of the nation's large cities (Shannon, 1966: 41 – 43).

We have seen that the Tiv of Nigeria and Americans often engage in ethnocentric behavior. The following Cross-Cultural Perspective illustrates ethnocentrism among the French and the Chinese.

CROSS-CULTURAL PERSPECTIVE

Making Wine Together: The French and Chinese Encounter Each Other's Ethnocentrism

It seems reasonable to assume that the more closely people from very different cultural traditions must interact, the more likely it becomes that ethnocentrism will surface. Certainly the history of a cooperative wine-producing effort between the French and the Chinese seems to be a case in point.

The joint venture began optimistically. A French company, Remy Martin Ltd., that is internationally known for its cognac, decided to develop an Oriental wine for Chinese restaurants in both Asia and Europe. The French firm provided $270,000 worth of winery equipment and its experience in the business. The Chinese supplied water, workers, electricity, a factory, and land in exchange for 62 percent of the profit from sales.

Problems started almost immediately. The French wanted the Chinese farmers, who grew their grapes chiefly for eating, to upgrade the quality of their crop. The Remy winegrowers were astonished to learn that the art of grape cultivation had not advanced much beyond the Middle Ages in China. For one thing the farmers covered their vines with paper bags to protect them from insects, and as a result the grapes never matured in the sun — a stage essential if they are to be a high quality. In addition, the farmers often brought their grapes to market a full day after harvesting, well past the point of freshness.

Guillaume d'Avout, Remy Martin's managing director for Far East operations, expressed the French opinion of Chinese grape farming, "Their methods were, how should I say, primitive. We had to tell them that we wouldn't accept damaged grapes or grapes that weren't fresh enough to make a wine for export on the world market."

Ju Lifan, a Chinese winery official, offered this response. "The French were so picky, you just couldn't satisfy them. They wouldn't buy grapes unless they had 18 percent sugar content. We had never heard of such a thing" (Weisskopf, 1982: 6).

The French began getting their way by offering more money for top-quality grapes. This situation created another problem. Because the French had to pay more than they had originally planned for grapes, the cost of the wine rose. The French wanted to keep the cost of the wine as low as possible. Pricing, of course, is one factor in a customer's decision to buy a product. As socialists, however, the Chinese showed little concern for competitive pricing and cost cutting.

The Chinese and the French also differed on another economic issue — how many workers to employ. D'Avout contended that the Chinese had "a natural tendency" to increase the number of workers as much as possible and that they were not nearly as efficiency-minded as the French.

Overall there was a sharp, often bitter clash between cultural styles. The French considered their Chinese workers much too casual. One Remy official complained that the first lesson was "to teach them not to spit in the winery." The Chinese, on the other hand, found the French too highstrung. One Chinese winemaker said, "When the electricity fails, they fly into a rage."

In spite of the operational problems, a history of success was established. Between 1980 and 1987, wine production increased tenfold, and the company has won quality titles four times in China and twice at international fairs. The original contract was extended from eleven to twenty-one years. Thus the evidence to date suggests that in spite of early differences, the participants triumphed over ethnocentrism.

Sources: Michael Weisskopf. "French Wine Venture in China in a Ferment." *International Herald Tribune.* June 1, 1982, p. 6; Xinhua News Service. "Joint Wine Venture Extends Contract." June 1987.

Cultural Relativism

When people are ethnocentric, they view other cultures as inferior. On the other hand, if they practice cultural relativism, they see them as just different. **Cultural relativism** is the principle that a culture should be evaluated by its own standards and not by those of any other culture. A custom is not good or bad or right or wrong, in and of itself. The cultural-relativistic point of view requires that any element of a culture be evaluated in relation to the entire culture. People who adopt this point of view recognize that while the lifestyle in another culture might make no sense at first, a careful study will reveal a distinct, understandable pattern.

The fact that Indian Hindus are often desperately poor and yet refuse to eat beef, while cows wander where they wish, dumbfounds many Americans. Marvin Harris, an anthropologist, noted that during lectures students would often ask for an explanation:

"But what about all those cows the hungry peasants in India refuse to eat?" The picture of a ragged farmer starving to death alongside a big fat cow conveys a reassuring sense of mystery to Western observers. In countless learned and popular allusions, it confirms our deepest conviction about how people with inscrutable Oriental minds ought to act.

(Harris, 1974: 11)

Harris studied the relationship between cows and the Hindu culture. Indeed, he did find out that in the Hindu religion the cow is the symbol of all living creatures and that there is no greater sin than killing one.

Harris also uncovered other important information. He found out that cows generally give about 500 pounds of milk a year — an important, sometimes critical part of the family diet. In addition, the cows' manure is the only fertilizer that poor farmers can afford, and, when dried, it also serves as a primary cooking fuel. Furthermore the possibility exists that a cow can give birth to a male calf that, when castrated, will develop into an ox, the scarce, highly prized animal used by Indian farmers for dry-field plowing. Certainly Hindus' religion requires them to revere cattle, but a careful analysis of the culture shows that some very practical reasons reinforce their conviction that cattle should not be killed.

Are there situations in which social researchers and other outside observers of a culture find that cultural relativism no longer serves as a productive tool for analysis? One distinct possibility is that very difficult economic or political circumstances can undermine cultural standards so that the members of a culture begin thinking and acting in ways that are significantly different from their cultural tradition. For instance, I would argue that severe poverty in Germany following World War I made German citizens responsive to Hitler's effort to rally citizens in support of an effort to return the country to past prominence and glory. The positive, often fervent response to Hitler included widespread willingness to support the persecution and organized murder of millions of European citizens. The willingness to kill innocent people is not apparent in an analysis of traditional German culture; it seems to have been the result of unusual, culture-disrupting circumstances. The same argument applies to the Ik, discussed in the Cross-Cultural Perspective in Chapter 6, "Socialization." Their traditional culture and lifestyle were destroyed by colonial officials, and one symptom of this destruction was that parents readily abandoned their children. Before colonial control was imposed, adults in this culture had treated any children as their own, making extensive efforts to nurture and support them.

American Culture

As our focus shifts from the contacts between different cultures to the analysis of American culture, your first reaction might be to suspect that cultural variation and conflict will be much less prominent issues. But do not forget our discussion of counterculture! American culture has always included conflicting elements, and that tendency is especially clear in this era of rapidly changing values.

Traditional American Values

Robin Williams, Jr. (1970: 452–500), an American sociologist, has produced a well-known analysis of American values. Williams has described fifteen values, which have been evident in American culture. These values include freedom, achievement and success, progress, equality, democracy, humanitarian goals, and racism and other themes of group superiority.

Some studies suggest that a number of these values are more strongly emphasized in American culture than in most other cultures. For instance, on individual freedom, researchers found that individuals and groups involved in commercial-development projects in cities faced far less government regulation in the United States than in Japan or Italy (Molotch and Vicari, 1988). Research supports the conclusion that an emphasis on achievement and success is particularly strong in American culture. In the United States, men in higher occupational positions reported greater self-confidence than other men, while in Poland, where the emphasis on achievement and success is probably weaker, men in higher occupational positions actually expressed lower levels of self-confidence than other men (Slomczynski et al.,

In a culture in which the value of competition is strongly emphasized, winning a major sporting event creates great excitement for both athletes and fans. This scene, which occurred in the fall of 1989, shows three members of the Oakland Athletics celebrating after winning the American League pennant. Later Oakland defeated the San Francisco Giants in the World Series.

1981). In addition, in a study on the ideal qualities respondents associated with the performance of their gender roles, a researcher learned that compared to their counterparts in six European countries, young American women and men were more likely to emphasize assertiveness and ambi-

tion as part of the gender-role ideal—qualities that generally are associated with an emphasis on achievement and success (Block, 1973).

The last two studies indicate that Americans are unusually emphatic about the individual's role in achievement and success. In *Blaming the Victim,* William Ryan (1976) concluded that Americans are also inclined to focus on the individual's contribution when failure occurs—for example, he or she is poor, does badly in school, has illegitimate children. While sociologists are not suggesting that individuals be freed of all responsibility for their actions, they consistently emphasize the sociological perspective, that is, social forces—parents, teachers, friends, available professional help, and various impersonal resources such as books, computers, and other educational aids—play a crucial role in helping to determine who succeeds and who fails.

In a society that emphasizes achievement and success, people are likely to be very competitive. The following American Controversy presents two positions about competition and encourages you to think about and evaluate them.

Changing American Values

How have American values changed in recent years? Many people believe that over the past decade the country has become more conservative. Is this actually true? Some evidence supports this conclusion.

For more than twenty years, data from 200,000 freshmen at 300 colleges and universities around the United States have been obtained annually. Money-oriented, conservative trends were more dominant among freshmen in 1987 than they were two decades earlier. For example, when asked whether it is important or essential to be very well-off financially, 41 percent of the 1968 sample responded affirmatively while the 1987 figure was nearly double, 76 percent. In that span of time, those who wanted a business career increased from 11 to 26 percent of the sample. On the other hand, when asked whether it was important or essential to develop a philosophy of life, 83 percent replied affirmatively in the socially conscious year of 1968; in 1987 the percentage had plummeted to 39. When evaluating the statement that an individual can do little to change society, 32

AMERICAN CONTROVERSY

Competition in American Society

Whether it is in sports, business, or school, Americans stress the importance of defeating the competition. Their language is filled with expressions that make this point. "In business it's kill-or-be-killed," an urban professional observes. "Honey," his wife replies, "it's a dog-eat-dog world out there." Talking to his sister on the telephone, Betty's father says: "Yes, Judy, we're so proud of our little girl. Year after year she's at the top of her class!" An emphasis on competition exists in American society, but is it desirable?

Those who strongly emphasize competition are likely to say that an emphasis on it is "the American way" —separating winners from losers in head-to-head competition. The proponents of competition will often contend that the process is character-building. They will argue that in the course of competition, individuals will be encouraged to do better; as the well-known phrase goes, they will "strive for excellence." Sport, many backers of competition will argue, is so popular in the United States because it is a theater in which competition appears in a pure form. Football, in particular, is competition with an especially crude yet deeply appealing style, where magnificent physical specimens use both brawn and brains to try to defeat each other in a nearly no-holds-barred situation of team-to-team combat.

The opponents of an emphasis on competition might accept part of the last point. While they would probably concede the impact of spectator sports in the United States, they would be critical of this type of impact. There's no need to glorify violent competition, they would argue. With limited emphasis on it, children can grow up to be intelligent, skilled, and sensitive to the needs of others. The opponents of competition might even cite research indicating that in experimentation involving physical skills, an emphasis on competition lowered performance level (Baumeister, 1984). Furthermore people deemphasizing competition would be likely to point out that what often appears to be open competition is not. One individual or organization starts with the advantage of better education, an emotionally health- ier upbringing, more extensive work experience, or a tax break from the government. Those speaking on behalf of competition, the critics will contend, are the people most likely to have a lion's share of the advantages.

What do you think? Do you strongly favor one position or the other? Or do you find yourself somewhere in the middle, supporting competition under some circumstances and not others?

Evaluate and discuss the following statement: In many competitive circumstances, it is possible to avoid a focus on competition by, instead, striving to do one's best. While discussing the issue of competition, try to understand more fully the position of those who think differently from you. Attempt to figure out what were the circumstances that led to your respective positions on the issue. One way to analyze the topic would be to reverse positions with someone whose stance is different from your own. See if you can state that individual's outlook convincingly to him or her, and then have that person try to perform the same task.

Source: Roy F. Baumeister. "Choking under Pressure: Self-Consciousness and Paradoxical Effects of Incentives on Skillful Performance." *Journal of Personality and Social Psychology.* V. 46. March 1984, pp. 610–620.

70

Table 3.4
Young Americans' Changing Values

IMPORTANT OR ESSENTIAL TO BE WELL-OFF FINANCIALLY

	1968	1987
All	41%	76%
Male	51	80
Female	27	72

PLAN TO ENTER BUSINESS

	1968	1987
All	11%	26%
Male	18	28
Female	3	24

IMPORTANT OR ESSENTIAL TO DEVELOP A PHILOSOPHY OF LIFE

	1968	1987
All	83%	39%
Male	79	40
Female	87	39

Source: Adapted from Richard G. Braungart and Margaret M. Braungart. "From Yippies to Yuppies: Twenty Years of Freshman Attitudes." *Public Opinion.* V. 11. September/October 1988, pp. 53–56.

percent of the sample in 1968 and 37 percent in 1985 somewhat or strongly agreed. (Braungart and Braungart, 1988) Table 3.4 gives further details of several of these survey items.

These data are certainly significant, suggesting a current conservative trend in American values. But let us become less abstract. In *Habits of the Heart: Individualism and Commitment in American Life,* Robert Bellah and his associates (1986) provided the following interesting example of a current American's inability to analyze accurately the relationship of his values to modern social forces. By the way—this important study, which effectively demonstrates the sociological perspective, will be used a number of times throughout this book.

The authors told about Howard Newton, who owns a Chrysler dealership in Suffolk, Massachusetts. Newton has always believed that it is possible to be self-reliant, earn a good livelihood, and,

at the same time, make a substantial contribution to his community. Until recent years Newton felt that he had been successful in all regards and that the Chrysler Corporation, with which his father had started the dealership a half-century earlier, had always been both financially successful and honorable. In 1981, however, a dramatic twist occurred. Facing bankruptcy, the Chrysler Corporation sought a large loan from the federal government. Appearing before the Suffolk Rotary Club, Newton, the strong proponent of self-reliance, began by pulling a little American flag out of his pocket. He waved it in front of his audience and then gave an impassioned speech explaining that Chrysler was forced to this desperate, undesirable step by unions' unreasonable demands and by the impact of frequent recalls initiated by consumer spokesman Ralph Nader and other "do-gooders." Newton's fellow club members responded with polite if unenthusiastic applause.

The Rotary Club members seemed to appreciate that their speaker was letting Chrysler off the hook rather easily. Newton continued to believe doggedly that his values should be rooted in community life—that he could control his own destiny by maintaining effective, honorable relations with people in his community and with others, like the representatives of the Chrysler Corporation. Bellah and his associates pointed out, however, that the social forces of the modern world have become considerably more complicated than that. In Howard Newton's case, the ineffective business policies of an international corporation—Chrysler—and a changing international economy together produced major impacts that cannot be altered at the community level (Bellah et al., 1986: 172–176). If you want to understand the world in which you live, you too must use the sociological perspective to examine your values and beliefs and consider the distinct possibility that on occasion you are also operating with oversimplified, outdated standards.

The following section is the first of this book's five detailed discussions of research. Each one of these analyses provides readers an opportunity to see how in the course of their studies, social researchers address important methodological issues introduced in Chapter 2, "Doing Research in Sociology". In this case the topic is research using the participant-observation technique to study culture.

The Participant-Observation Study of Culture

The participant-observation studies, which we examined in Chapter 2, "Doing Research in Sociology," have represented an effective technique to uncover the subtlety and complexity of individual cultures. Certainly this type of research has produced more accurate information about cultures than the earliest efforts to understand them.

To modern Americans it is clear that to understand cultures one must conduct research—careful research. One hundred fifty years ago, however, such a conclusion was not obvious. In that era scholars were more inclined to read and reflect and then produce abstract conclusions. It was the era of "armchair anthropology," and one of the best-known scholars of that time was Lewis Henry Morgan. Morgan and other "armchair anthropologists" often provided interesting, logical analyses. However, the problem was that they were not scientific; little or no supportive research had been done.

Early in the twentieth century, the anthropological approach changed. It was at this time that one of the most renowned participant-observation studies of culture was done by Bronislaw Malinowski, in the Trobriand Islands of New Guinea in the South Pacific. At first Malin-

owski found the research difficult. He had few guidelines on how to conduct this kind of research. Furthermore he was an outsider, he did not speak the language, and there were no other Europeans around. Malinowski wrote, "I had periods of despondency, when I buried myself in the reading of novels, as a man might take to drink in a fit of tropical depression and boredom" (Malinowski, 1922: 4). Certainly Malinowski was implying that "armchair" anthropology would have been easier. In the end, however, his persistence paid off. Malinowski was able to develop several procedures for conducting participant-observation research: to have research goals set clearly in mind; to isolate oneself from members of one's own culture by immersing oneself in the local culture; and to develop techniques for obtaining thorough information about the entire culture.

Besides helping to refine the participant-observation technique, Malinowski uncovered some significant information about the Trobriand Island culture. Particularly interesting were his conclusions about magic. Malinowski learned that magic played an important part in the tribespeople's daily lives. They believed that magical rites and spells would insure the success of

gardening and fishing throughout the society. Thus this research helped reject what was then a widely held but erroneous view that magic is used only for such personal and vicious purposes as causing harm to enemies.

Sociologists' Use of Participant Observation

Eventually sociologists began to adopt the participant-observation technique. Their use, however, tended to occur in modern cultures, which generally are much more complex and diversified than those studied by anthropologists. As a result sociologists have not studied entire cultures but focused on subcultures. Perhaps the best known of all such sociological investigations has been William Foote Whyte's *Street Corner Society,* discussed in Chapter 1, "Introduction." Like Malinowski, Whyte had a problem of entry into the community he studied—Cornerville, an Italian-American slum district of Boston. On a friend's advice, he tried going to a bar and buying drinks for a woman; this, he had been told, was an effective way of obtaining a woman's life story. For his effort, however, he almost got himself thrown down a flight of stairs. Finally Whyte met a local young man known as

Doc, who became interested in the study and promised to do everything he could to advance the research.

The book that Whyte eventually wrote included important new observations about American slum communities. Just as early anthropologists made unsupported generalizations about culture, some social scientists of Whyte's era produced undocumented statements about the culture and structure of slum communities. In particular, they believed that slums were completely disorganized. Whyte's three-year study compelled him to disagree:

Cornerville's problem is not lack of organization but failure of its own social organiza-

tion to mesh with the structure of the society around it. This accounts for the development of the local political and racket organizations and also for the loyalty people bear toward their . . . [ethnic group] and toward Italy.

(Whyte, 1955: 273)

Whyte documented this point at length, showing that in spite of their involvement in local organizations, most of the young people he studied failed to succeed in the larger society.

Through the years sociologists have continued to use the participant-observation technique to clarify the workings of subcultures. In the late 1950s, Blanche Geer found that only three days of research during the orienta-

tion of freshmen at the University of Kansas gave her and her co-workers new, revealing information about them. Geer wrote:

Before entering the field, I thought of them as irresponsible children. But as I listened to their voices, learned their language, witnessed gesture and expression, and accumulated the bits of information about them which bring people alive and make their problems real, I achieved a form of empathy with them and became their advocate.

(Geer, 1964: 341)

Geer suddenly found herself immersed in her subjects' lives; she obtained information about college-student subculture, which she was able to pass on to her readers.

These two sociologists are conducting participant-observation research in East Harlem, New York City. Sometimes, as in this case, participant observers obtain information from informal interviews, but usually they just accompany their subjects, observing what they say and do.

Participant-observation research has also revealed details about other subcultures. William Waegel examined the police subculture and the use of deadly force. As he began the study, Waegel realized that previous research had uncovered a number of factors linked to police violence: the level of violent crime in a community, occupational stress suffered by police, and the influence of the work environment. But in the tradition of participant-observation research, Waegel believed that an effective understanding of the situation would emerge only with intensive investigation of how the relevant actors — in this case the police — behaved in the research context. Thus he focused on the beliefs in the police subculture that rationalize the use of deadly force. One belief centered around the following idea: "I'd rather be judged by twelve than carried out by six." The argument is that police work is filled with danger and anxiety; some-

times a police officer's split-second decision to shoot will make the difference between living and dying. Another belief justifying force could be summed up with this statement: "What's another dead animal?" Widespread racism in American society is a factor contributing to this belief. In addition, this position is often supported by the pleas of victims or victims' relatives to avenge a crime.

Waegel's study points to the special contribution that participant-observation investigations can make to the understanding of culture. Cultures are often filled with subtle conflicts and inconsistencies. It is difficult to sort out the complexities. Surveys might provide some information, but often the subtleties are best revealed by painstaking, detailed observation. Waegel, for example, spent ten months as a participant observer in a police department, observing officers and interviewing them about shooting incidents and their use of firearms.

Conclusion

These studies have produced important information about cultures that was not previously known. But are the results of these investigations unquestionably correct? Certainly not! As we saw in Chapter 2, one of the principal difficulties with participant-observation research is the problem of generalizing from a single case. Could Malinowski claim that in all technologically simple societies magic would be used in just the same way that it was in the Trobriand Islands? Could Waegel be certain that police personnel in another city would rationalize the use of deadly force in precisely the manner that his informants had? In both situations the answer is no. That does not detract from the significance of these studies, however. They produced powerful ideas that later researchers could investigate.

Sources: Blanche Geer. "First Days in the Field." In Phillip E. Hammond (ed.), *Sociologists at Work.* New York: Basic Books. 1964, pp. 322–345; Bronislaw Malinowski. *Argonauts of the Western Pacific.* London: Routledge and Kegan Paul Ltd. 1922; Lewis H. Morgan. *Ancient Society.* Cambridge, MA: Belknap Press. 1964. Originally published in 1877; William B. Waegel. "How Police Justify the Use of Deadly Force." *Social Problems.* V. 32. December 1984, pp. 144–155; William Foote Whyte. *Street Corner Society.* Chicago: University of Chicago Press. Revised edition. 1955.

STUDY GUIDE
Learning Objectives

After studying this chapter, you should be able to:

1. Define culture and describe its importance in human life.
2. Define the major components of culture — beliefs, technology, norms, values, and language — and discuss their respective activities.

3. Examine the different types of norms, defining and discussing folkways, mores, and laws; explicit norms and implicit norms; and ideal norms and real norms.
4. Distinguish between sign and symbol, define language, and explain how language supplies meaning to culture.
5. Define and illustrate the linguistic-relativity hypothesis.
6. Define subculture and counterculture, providing examples of each.
7. Distinguish between ethnocentrism and cultural relativism and explain two functions of ethnocentrism.
8. List several traditional American values and summarize research comparing Americans' values with those of individuals in other cultures.
9. Discuss young Americans' changing values, indicating why the changes are occurring and what new commitments are emerging.

Summary

1. Culture consists of all the humanmade products associated with a society. The products of culture include material products and nonmaterial products.

2. The different components of a culture — beliefs, technology, norms, values, and language — are all products of their respective cultural traditions, and each, in turn, also affects the culture from which it develops.

3. Within cultures and between cultures, distinctive differences often exist, and sometimes these differences produce conflict. In modern societies various subcultures arise based on such factors as occupation, racial and ethnic status, disadvantaged condition, and deviant or previously deviant lifestyle. Some subcultures, namely countercultures, reject many of the standards of the mainstream society. As the members of one culture contact those of another, ethnocentrism fre-

quently develops. Although the members of all cultures are ethnocentric, the practice is most dominant in isolated societies. To offset ethnocentrism, one can use a cultural-relativistic approach to other cultures.

4. Sociologists have extensively studied American values. Robin Williams, Jr., has described fifteen value orientations that have been prominently displayed by American culture. Studies have suggested that the values of achievement and success are more apparent in American culture than in most other cultures.

Young Americans' values have changed during the past ten to twenty years, becoming more money-oriented and conservative. To start changing society, young people might begin by learning more about Americans' relationship to their values and beliefs.

Key Terms

belief   a statement about reality that people accept as true

counterculture   a subculture whose members consciously and often proudly reject some of the most important cultural standards of the mainstream society

cultural relativism   the principle that a culture should be evaluated by its own standards and not by those of any other culture

cultural universals   traits believed to exist in all cultures

culture   all the humanmade products associated with a society

culture shock   the psychological and social

maladjustment many people suffer when they visit or live in another culture

ethnocentrism the automatic tendency to evaluate other cultures by the standards of one's own

explicit norm a standard that is out in the open

folkway a norm that specifies the way things are customarily done; folkways are concerned with standards of behavior that are socially approved but not considered morally significant

ideal norm a standard requiring strict obedience to the guidelines provided

implicit norm a standard that normally is not discussed and is not easily stated

language a system of symbolic communication that uses words, which are sound patterns that have standardized meanings

law a norm that is recorded by political authorities and supported by police or other enforcement officials

linguistic-relativity hypothesis the contention that the unique grammatical forms of a language actually shape the thoughts and perceptions of its users

mores norms people consider vital

norm a standard of desirable behavior; norms are the rules people are expected to follow in their relations with each other

real norm an adjusted standard reflecting the practical conditions of living

sign an object or event that stands for something else

society the interacting people who share a culture

subculture the culture of a specific segment of people within a society, differing from the dominant culture in some significant respects

symbol a sign with a meaning not fixed by the nature of the item to which it is attached but by the agreement of the people who use it to communicate

technology any repeated operation people use to manipulate the environment to achieve some practical goals

value a general conviction about what is good or bad, right or wrong, appropriate or inappropriate

Tests

True–false Test

———— 1. Society cannot exist without culture, but culture exists independent of society.

———— 2. People who share a given culture can disagree about some beliefs.

———— 3. In modern societies real norms and ideal norms tend to be identical.

———— 4. Values are important because they influence the content of norms.

———— 5. The smell of smoke signifies the presence of fire; in this case smoke is a sign but not a symbol.

———— 6. Evidence suggests that Americans no longer experience culture shock.

———— 7. Bohannon's experience in trying to bring Shakespeare's *Hamlet* to the Tiv tribe suggests that this universal story actually eliminated ethnocentrism.

———— 8. People who take a cultural-relativistic perspective believe that the lifestyles of other cultures have understandable patterns.

———— 9. A recent study has concluded that the levels of self-confidence expressed by American and Polish men in high-status jobs are strikingly similar.

———— 10. When modern sociologists have used the participant-observation technique to study cultures, they have tended to focus on subcultures rather than entire cultures.

Multiple-choice Test

_____   1. Material culture includes:
  a. beliefs.
  b. physical objects people make and use.
  c. values.
  d. b and c

_____   2. Which of the following is NOT a component of culture?
  a. language
  b. value
  c. technology
  d. group

_____   3. Which statement about technology is NOT true?
  a. It has profound effects on people's everyday lives.
  b. It can contribute significantly to the development of new occupations.
  c. It cannot be dysfunctional for specific groups.
  d. It involves manipulation of the environment.

_____   4. Which of the following is (are) true about folkways?
  a. They specify the way things are customarily done.
  b. They are considered to be morally significant.
  c. Violation always leads to punishment.
  d. All of the above

_____   5. The idea of adjustment of a standard to practical conditions of living is found in which one of the following concepts?
  a. explicit norm
  b. implicit norm
  c. real norm
  d. ideal norm

_____   6. Values:
  a. are abstract, stating broad behavioral preferences.
  b. are becoming rare in modern societies.
  c. have little or no relationship with norms.
  d. are a type of material culture.

_____   7. The linguistic-relativity hypothesis:
  a. does not apply to modern languages.
  b. indicates that some ethnic groups have a greater inborn tendency to use complex language forms than other ethnic groups.
  c. has been used to explain body language but not spoken language.
  d. contends that the unique grammatical forms of a language actually shape the thoughts and perceptions of its users.

_____   8. The members of a certain occupational group develop a common set of beliefs, values, and activities that are different in significant respects from those in the general culture. These people share a(n):
  a. counterculture.
  b. subculture.
  c. cultural-relativistic approach.
  d. ethnocentric outlook.

———— 9. Ethnocentrism can be functional for those who practice it because it:
    a. encourages people to become more tolerant.
    b. helps dominant groups retain positions of superiority.
    c. establishes how much influence different mores maintain.
    d. helps make explicit norms more implicit.

———— 10. According to the discussion in this chapter:
    a. modern Americans' values are remarkably similar to the values of people in other industrialized nations.
    b. traditional values no longer affect modern Americans.
    c. all Americans consider an emphasis on competition highly desirable.
    d. people who want to change American society might begin by learning about people's relationships to their values and beliefs.

Essay Test

1. What is culture? Why does culture have a profound impact on people's lives?
2. Discuss five cultural components, indicating how each affects social activity.
3. Define the different types of norms and illustrate each type.
4. Discuss the linguistic-relativity hypothesis, giving examples that demonstrate its usefulness.
5. Define the concepts of subculture and counterculture, emphasizing their impact on societies.
6. Define ethnocentrism and cultural relativism and give examples of each.
7. How do young Americans' values differ from those of young people twenty years ago? What is a first step one might take toward changing people's values? Discuss.

Suggested Readings

American Anthropologist. Official journal of the American Anthropological Association published four times a year and containing up-to-date articles and research reports about culture.

Bellah, Robert N., Richard Madsen, William M. Sullivan, Ann Swidler, and Steven M. Tipton. 1986. *Habits of the Heart: Individualism and Commitment in American Life.* New York: Harper & Row. A provocative study of past and present American values, to be incorporated a number of times through this textbook.

Curry, Timothy, and Robert M. Jiobu. 1984. *Sports: A Social Perspective.* Englewood Cliffs, NJ: Prentice-Hall. An interesting, readable text on sport, an important but often analytically neglected aspect of American culture. The book includes effective discussions on cultural sources of competition and deviance in the sporting world.

Gitlin, Todd. 1987. *The Sixties: Years of Hope, Days of Rage.* New York: Bantam Books. A detailed, scholarly, but also partially autobiographical account of the 1960s protests by a sociologist who participated extensively in those activities.

Harris, Marvin. 1974. *Cows, Pigs, Wars and Witches.* New York: Random House. A captivating series of essays demonstrating how to apply the concept of cultural relativism to a variety of cultural situations where Americans' ethnocentrism is likely to be aroused.

Howard, Michael C. 1989. *Contemporary Cultural Anthropology.* Glenview, IL: Scott, Foresman and Company. Third edition. A one-semester core text covering the field of cultural anthropology and developing most of the topics discussed in the first two main sections of this chapter.

Kohn, Alfie. 1986. *No Contest.* Boston: Houghton Mifflin. A detailed, highly critical analysis of the impact of competition on American society. Most provocative is the final chapter, which contains suggestions for deemphasizing and eventually eliminating competition from modern life.

Slater, Philip. 1976. *The Pursuit of Loneliness.* Boston: Beacon Press. Revised edition. A critical examination of American value conflicts: the longing for engagement, dependence, and community that is often frustrated by emphasis on individualism and competition. The family, the political structure, and the economy are examined.

Williams, Robin M., Jr. 1970. *American Society: A Sociological Interpretation.* New York: Random House. Third edition. A well-known analysis of American culture and society containing a comprehensive classification and examination of American values.

Additional Assignments

1. Select some aspect of federal government activity, such as military spending, foreign aid, relations with the Soviet Union, welfare programming, or civil rights. Read the editorial pages of a major daily newspaper for two or three weeks and then list the expressed values you find related to our topic. Can you conclude that there is a consistent set of values presented in the editorials?
2. Choose a holiday celebrated in American culture, such as Halloween, Easter, Passover, Christmas, Thanksgiving, or the Fourth of July. List the norms frequently associated with celebrating the holiday. Do the "norms of celebration" suggest any value conflicts? Find information in the library about the origins of the holiday. Which value(s) seem(s) to have inspired its development?

Answers to Objective Test Questions

True – false Test

1. f	4. t	7. f	9. f
2. t	5. t	8. t	10. t
3. f	6. f		

Multiple-choice Test

1. b	4. a	7. d	9. b
2. d	5. c	8. b	10. d
3. c	6. a		

4
GROUPS

Types of Groups

Primary and Secondary Groups
In-Groups and Out-Groups
Membership and Reference Groups
Formal Organizations and Bureaucracies
Communities

Institutions

Humanization of Group Activity

Study Guide

Imagine spending six months in a spacecraft! The view is incredible — 270 miles down to earth and a sunset or sunrise every ninety minutes. But you can't leave the spacecraft, which is the size of a moderate-sized motor home, and you must live with the same companion or companions during the entire time. Valery Ryumin, who was on a pair of two-man Soviet missions, pointed out in his diary that people on long spaceflights have been compelled to solve problems together: "taking into account the feelings of the other. Here we are totally alone. Each uttered word assumes added importance. One must bear in mind — constantly — the other's good and bad sides, anticipate his thinking, the ramifications of a wrong utterance blown out of proportion" (Bluth, 1985: 31). Ryumin added that after two spaceflights he completely understood the writer O. Henry's claim that a sure way to produce a murder is to lock two men in a small cabin for two months.

While no murders have occurred in space, there has been evidence of hostility and stress. Evidence to date suggests that the longer the flight, the more likely incompatibilities will appear. Cosmonaut Ivan Lenov has concluded that "it is impossible to insure good compatibility on a long flight." One of the sources of tension in long spaceflights is that the individual is with the same crew all the time. Normally people's lives fluctuate between work and play, and in the latter — at home with the family, for instance — one can relax and feel that he or she is not being judged. In a spacecraft, however, one's colleague(s) is (are) always close by; the individual can never entirely escape the formality of the work situation. This source of tension is compounded by the fact that in spaceflight there is constant danger; one can never relax and entirely get away from work.

In one respect, perhaps, the American crews have had an advantage over their Soviet counterparts. The Soviets maintain two-person crews for long spaceflights, while Americans have used three people. Research on small groups has demonstrated that an odd-numbered membership means that when decision making occurs, tension-producing deadlocks of numerically equal factions will be avoided. Evidence to date suggests Americans with their crews of three have had fewer interpersonal problems than the Soviets with their crews of two.

Whether people are in space or simply on earth, much of their time is spent in groups, and what happens in the groups to which we belong profoundly affects our lives. A **group** consists of two or more interacting people who share certain expectations and goals. When people share group membership, there is a feeling of unity, a set of common goals, a number of collective norms, and a direct or indirect communication among the members based on their common rights and obligations.

Everyone participates in groups. Families and school classes are groups. So are army units, baseball teams, corporate boards of directors, debating organizations, and exotic dance troops. It would

be easy to move through the alphabet and provide a long list of groups to which people belong.

We can distinguish groups from two closely related clusters of people — aggregates and categories. An **aggregate** consists of two or more people who share physical space but lack the interaction maintained by group members. Aggregates can sometimes become groups. For example, a number of people might be waiting for a bus. Since they are not interacting, they do not constitute a group. However, a group might form if an approaching person fainted and several individuals rushed forward to provide assistance. A **social category** consists of a number of people who have one or more social characteristics in common, such as age, sex, marital status, income, or race. Members of a category sometimes have common values, interests, or grievances that can provide a foundation for the development of such groups as women's rights organizations, taxpayers' associations, and ethnic support groups.

Ever since you were born, you have been involved in group activity. Most likely this awareness started in the family, where even in infancy you began to have some sense of how you would fit in. You probably learned what behavior would please a parent or older sibling and what behavior would displease such people. Very quickly others' body language and words made it clear when you could get away with imposing your own will in a situation involving family or peers. As you have grown older, you have extended your range of group involvement. It should be easy to name a number of groups to which you belong—for instance, your family, a group of close friends, the classroom portion of this introductory sociology course, some extracurricular club or team, and an organization for which you work. It is also likely that within a year or two years, some of your group affiliations will change, and since all people are strongly influenced by the groups to which they belong, you also will change.

The group is the most basic unit of sociological analysis. In this chapter we first analyze several important types of groups. Then we look briefly at institutions, large systems that contain groups and fulfill the basic needs of citizens within a society. The chapter concludes with an assessment of some of the prominent problems facing Americans in everyday group activity.

Types of Groups

The group is one of the most significant concepts in sociology, and sociologists have designated many varieties. Primary and secondary groups, in- versus out-groups, membership and reference groups, formal organizations and bureaucracies, and communities are among the most prominent types. The first three types of groups involve the **micro-order**—the structure and activity of small groups.

Primary and Secondary Groups

The terms *primary group* and *secondary group* are not widely known in U.S. society, but we are all aware of their significance in the everyday social world. For instance, a woman comes home from work and says to her husband, "It was awful, Ted. The boss called me into his office and just spilled his guts—all the problems he's having with his wife and children. Then he started to cry. I was so embarrassed." She pauses to draw a deep breath. "This was a man I've been on formal terms with for five years. The most intimate thing I knew about him was that he'd get really excited over last year's marketing reports. And now this . . . " Obviously the woman's boss had violated an implicit norm that had kept their relationship formal to that time. Here is another example. Jack and Judy are graduate students giving a party for a dozen of their friends. At first Jack enjoys himself but soon perceives that an uneasiness fills the room. It's too quiet. Eventually he realizes that the problem is Judy. She's still wrapped up in her research project and can't talk about anything else. He walks up to her, angrily pulls her aside, and whispers in her ear, "Dammit, Judy, will you lighten up? These are our friends, not your colleagues. There's a time and place for everything!"

As members of both primary and secondary groups, we all learn what is appropriate behavior in each group setting. Generally speaking, primary group behavior is more personal and less specialized than secondary group behavior. Let's examine both types.

Primary Groups

A **primary group** is a group in which relationships are usually stable over long periods of time, members are able to expose many facets of their personality, and a strong sense of affection and identity (a "we feeling") develops (Cooley, 1962: 23). Primary groups are small, permitting face-to-face contact. The family is the most important primary group. Other primary groups to which many Americans belong include peer groups, neighborhood circles, social clubs, and informal groups within complex organizations, such as cliques within factories or offices. Research and analysis of primary groups have extended from early in the twentieth century to recent years (Scott and Scott, 1981).

PRIMARY-GROUP NORMS At times primary-group norms are consistent with the standards that exist elsewhere in society, and at times they are not. Consider the issue of disciplining children within the family. In preindustrial societies most family norms were widely shared. Modern societies are less consistent in this respect, however. Many modern parents are permissive, putting few limitations on their children's behavior and seldom punishing them when they break existing family rules. Children whose families have lenient primary-group norms are likely to have a difficult and confusing time if they encounter teachers who set exacting limits on their behavior.

Within a given type of primary group, members' relationships can vary distinctly. A study of families found that in father–child dyads (two-person groups), interaction patterns involving such issues as vocal exchange and child compliance were similar to the patterns involving both parents and the child, while the patterns created in mother–child dyads differed from the other two group situations. The researchers suspected that since mothers spend more time with their children, they are able to develop unique relational patterns that do not appear in other social contexts (Liddell, Henzi, and Drew, 1987).

Since primary groups involve extensive, intimate relations, their members have ample opportunity to observe each other and assess the group's norms. "You know, Mommy," a little girl says. "Every time I talk about the money for dancing lessons, Daddy starts wrinkling his nose and sniffing. Then he hardly talks to me for the next couple of hours." With no more than a facial expression or a few words, primary-group members can let each other know whether their behavior is desirable or undesirable. Frequently people in these groups conform to each other's expectations because they value their membership and do not want to risk losing it.

SOLIDARITY AND PRIMARY-GROUP MEMBERSHIP Willie Stargell, a star of the Pittsburgh Pirates for two decades, was being inter-

Primary-group members engage in various activities together. This couple is simultaneously taking care of their daughter and buying a car.

viewed at the beginning of his last season. It had been a marvelous experience, Stargell said, much more exciting than he ever could have imagined. He was asked what he would miss the most. Stargell smiled. "The guys," he said. They had lived together through the long baseball seasons, struggled, and finally had won the World Series. The primary-group quality of that team was demonstrated by the fact that the members called themselves "the family."

Common activity often seems to be a principal basis of primary groups. A study of undergraduate psychology majors revealed that friends were more similar in their activities than in their attitudes and were more accurate in estimating friends' activity preferences than their attitudes. Attitudes tended to be as dissimilar between friends as they were between strangers, but activity preferences were distinctly more similar between friends than between strangers (Werner and Parmelee, 1979).

Primary groups also emerge in the course of activity — warfare, for instance. Most of us probably have seen the vintage World War II films that portray the fighting men as motivated primarily by patriotism and a fervent belief in "the American way." In contrast, research has shown that during war American soldiers are primarily motivated by loyalty to their buddies. For instance, a soldier wounded while fighting in Sicily commented:

> You know the men in your outfit. You have to be loyal to them. . . . They depend on each other — wouldn't do anything to let the rest of them down. They'd rather be killed than do that. They begin to think the world of each other. It's the main thing that keeps a guy from going haywire.
>
> (Stouffer et al., 1949: 136)

Captain John Early, a veteran of Vietnam and a former mercenary, called the association between men in combat "a love relationship." He emphasized the importance of this relationship among professional soldiers. "And you'll find that people who pursue combat . . . are there because they're friends, the same people show up in . . . wars time and again" (quoted in Dyer, 1985: 104).

In secondary groups, to which we now turn, such strong personal commitments are less common.

Secondary Groups

A **secondary group** is a group of people who cooperate with each other for distinct, practical reasons and generally maintain few, if any, strong emotional ties within the group. Face-to-face contact between secondary-group members is normally limited, with the individuals relating to each other exclusively on the basis of specific roles they are playing — secretary and boss, student and teacher, or senator and constituents. However,

In military units, which are secondary groups, strong primary groups are likely to develop because of the members' critical dependence on each other. In this photo taken during the Vietnam War, soldiers are carrying a wounded buddy, who was shot in the leg by a sniper.

primary relations sometimes arise within secondary groups. The members of a college class or of a work team are initially secondary group members, but in the course of their activity together, they may develop genuine friendships.

Primary groups involve a more intimate kind of relationship than do secondary groups. In a secondary group, the strong emotions that normally accompany primary-group relations can impede effective decision making. For example, presidents and their advisers have sometimes made very poor decisions on crucial issues because of the emphasis on cohesiveness and unanimity (primary-group feelings) that have crept into their secondary group. In 1961 John Kennedy had just been elected president, and his immediate advisers were convinced that with Kennedy leading the country "the world was plastic and the future unlimited" (Janis, 1972: 36). They believed, in short, that with Kennedy in command anything could be accomplished. There was a powerful sense of united purpose, a "we feeling" shared by the circle of advisers around the President. Some of these advisers, however, had personal misgivings about the administration's plan to overthrow the Castro regime in Cuba. Like Kennedy these advisers feared having a communist government so close to their own shores, but they questioned whether the president's plan to invade Cuba would work. However, because of the strong "we feeling" that filled this secondary group, their misgivings were mildly expressed or not expressed at all. When the Bay of Pigs invasion occurred, it was a humiliating failure for Kennedy and his administration.

One experiment emphasized that the "we feeling" within a group leads to the rejection of individual members' opinions when they disagree with the majority. In discussions of political candidates, it was learned that when individuals offered descriptions that were unfavorable toward the most popular candidates, the participants tended not to examine the new, critical material; the initially favored candidates retained stronger support than other candidates (Stasser and Titus, 1985).

In spite of the fact that primary-group feeling can hamper secondary-group relations, people sometimes regret the absence. Early in Thomas Mann's novel *Confessions of Felix Krull, Confidence Man,* Krull was traveling to Paris. During the trip he watched the conductor—how each time he punched a ticket he remained silent and emotionless. The repeated scene reminded Krull of "the standoffishness, amounting almost to lack of interest, which one human being, especially an official, feels compelled to manifest toward his fellows" (Mann, 1955: 119). Krull noted the wedding ring on the man's finger and realized that he had a wife and children. Krull, in turn, had a private life that was hidden from the conductor. None of this was supposed to be revealed, however. Their relationship should remain focused on the conductor's inspection of Krull's ticket. The arrangement struck Krull as unnatural, and yet to abandon the impersonal system, he realized, would create confusion and embarrassment. While Krull was analyzing secondary-group relations, the conductor returned, examined the ticket once again, and perhaps inspired by Krull's youth noted that he was bound for Paris. Krull replied cordially, and a brief conversation developed. At the end they wished each other luck, and Krull asked the conductor to convey his regards to the man's wife and children. The conductor replied, " 'Yes, thanks—well, what do you know!' He laughed in embarrassment, mixing his words up oddly, and hastened to leave. But on his way out he tripped over a nonexistent obstacle, so completely had this human touch upset him" (Mann, 1955: 120).

In-Groups and Out-Groups

Even some nonhuman species establish group boundaries. For instance, among wolves, when a family wants to designate its territory, the members mark it off with a trail of urine (Mowat, 1965: 60). Human beings can be just as explicit about boundaries, marking them with such things as family names, passports, team uniforms, or employee membership cards.

The idea of group boundaries is central to the distinction between in-groups and out-groups. An **in-group** is any group characterized by a strong sense of identification and loyalty and by the exclusion of nonmembers. An **out-group** is composed of people who do not belong to an in-group, outsiders who are viewed with hostility and even contempt by the in-group members

Sometimes a conflict between an in-group and an out-group draws support outside the country in which it occurs. In 1989 university students in the People's Republic of China protested their government's refusal to promote democratic practices. Many students at American colleges and universities rallied in public support of the Chinese students.

(Summer, 1906: 12–13). Research on these concepts still continues (Ng and Cram, 1988).

In-group/out-group hostility occurs frequently in small groups. The struggle for scarce resources is one way to produce it. Muzafer Sherif and Carolyn Sherif (1956), two social psychologists, studied friction and competition between two groups of twelve-year-old boys, with a dozen to a group. The Sherifs conducted experiments in which the members of each group were required to cooperate with one another in order to win a tournament of competitive games. The competition was keen because the boys on each team had been promised a four-bladed jackknife if they won, and these knives were highly valued. Competition soon led to bad feelings between the two groups, however, and cheers like "2-4-6-8, who do we appreciate" deteriorated to "2-4-6-8, who do we appreci*hate*." Throughout the experiment hostility between the two groups remained at a high level, and retaliatory acts occurred on both sides.

As this material suggests, situations to which the concepts *in-group* and *out-group* apply are situations in which people's feelings are strong and often conflicting. The following American Controversy provides an opportunity to address this emotional issue personally.

AMERICAN CONTROVERSY

In-Group Membership: Healthy or Unhealthy?

 Americans vary considerably in their feelings about in-groups and out-groups. Let's consider a number of different issues.

To begin, there are people who are strongly inclined to designate their own in-group superior. For instance, members of the American Nazi Party or of the Ku Klux Klan believe in what they call "racial superiority;" they claim that members of certain racial groups are superior to members of other racial groups. Whites, primarily whites of northern European backgrounds, are considered the in-group, and blacks, Asians, and Jews are members of the out-group. This kind of in-group/out-group distinction is particularly inflexible because there is nothing people can do to move from the in-group to the out-group: They are locked in by superficial biological characteristics. While our society officially discourages using racial characteristics as a way of making an in-group/out-group distinction, such activity continues to be widespread.

Other uses of in-groups and out-groups are generally considered more acceptable — claims of patriotism, for example. Historically politicians, business leaders, and others have suggested that the United States is the greatest country in the world. In both times of war and peace, it has been widely claimed that anyone who opposes the interests of the United States is misguided at best and downright evil at worst.

In the past few decades, however, this outlook has begun to change. At the time of the Vietnam War, a large number of Americans took the position that their government was making a mistake — a tragic mistake — by involving itself in a war

with a little country in southeast Asia. Slogans were the order of the day as youthful opponents of the war shouted, "Hell no! We won't go!" From the perspective offered by the in-group/out-group distinction, these protesters were turning their backs on traditionally patriotic (in-group) standards which demanded that all young men be willing to serve and die for their country in its wars. Traditional patriots were horrified by such a stance, and often their reply was: "America, your country, love it or leave it!" In other words, as in-group members, traditional patriots were telling the anti-war protesters that either they played by the rules of the in-group or got out — left the country and joined the (communist) out-group.

Perhaps the contemporary issue that most significantly challenges a conventional distinction between in-groups and out-groups is the topic of nuclear weaponry. From 1983 to 1988, about three-quarters of Americans favored a bilateral (Soviet and American) freeze on nuclear weaponry. This figure suggests that the majority of Americans recognize that, in a nuclear war, a winner is unlikely and that they want to take steps to avoid such a confrontation. The traditional military situation in

which one country can clearly dominate another is replaced by an advanced technological condition by which a military clash produces only losers. Such a position represents a challenge to the long-time, popular in-group conviction that the United States is unbeatable in any war. Furthermore an awareness of the great danger accompanying nuclear war has forced Americans to recognize that in this case the long unchallenged hostility between the in-group and the out-group could precipitate catastrophe for all.

Now comes the chance to discuss and argue a little. Get together with a group of your friends or fellow students and examine the following questions:

1. Are you a member of any in-groups? What are they? What are their positions about their respective out-groups?

2. Do you approve of patriotic in-groups? Does the present presidential administration effectively express your patriotic views? Discuss.

3. What effect, if any, does the issue of nuclear weaponry have upon traditional American perceptions of the Soviets as an out-group?

Source: Richard Karmen Gilbert. "The Dynamics of Inaction: Psychological Factors Inhibiting Arms Control Activism." *American Psychologist*. V. 43. October 1988, pp. 755–764.

Membership and Reference Groups

Cal and George are sitting in the lounge an hour before their fraternity party is supposed to begin. Cal begins enthusiastically:

"Boy, I love this place!"
"You mean the frat house?"
"Yeah, I feel awfully lucky to be a member of Alpha Beta Alpha. I just like everything about the place — the way the guys talk and dress, the kinds of things they like to do for fun . . ."
"I think you're nuts." George stands up and starts pacing nervously. "I've had it with *all* of them. I think they're a bunch of jerks. In fact, I'm thinking of getting out next semester."

For George the fraternity is a mere **membership group** — a group to which an individual belongs. Cal's feelings are very different. For him the fraternity is not only a membership group, but it is also a **reference group** — a group whose standards a person uses to help shape his or her own values, beliefs, and behavior. The previous illustration suggests that the way people regard a particular group will affect their attitudes toward and behavior within that group. Research has offered some support for these conclusions (Granberg et al., 1981). Studies have determined that reference groups affect people's behavior in a variety of areas, including younger siblings' behavioral style (Abramovitch et al., 1986), adolescents' drug problems (Barrett, Simpson, and Lehman, 1988), and early adolescents' likelihood of smoking (Mosbach and Leventhal, 1988).

It is important to recognize that a group can be a reference group even if an individual does not belong to it. **Anticipatory socialization** is the acceptance of a group's standards preparatory to becoming a member of the group. When little children talk and behave like older children, they are preparing themselves for their later roles. Adolescents, college students, and older adults engage in similar, if more sophisticated, behavior. Anticipatory socialization can provide benefits for individuals. Research conducted during World War II suggested that privates who accepted the formal army standards valued by officers were more likely to be promoted than were privates who did not accept those standards (Merton, 1968: 319).

Theodore Newcomb and his colleagues (Newcomb et al., 1967) analyzed the attitudes and beliefs of women at Vermont's Bennington College in a well-known investigation of reference-group behavior. The original research, which occurred in the 1930s, took place over a four-year period so that Newcomb could study changes in his subjects' attitudes and beliefs during their college careers. He found that most of the freshmen reflected their well-to-do parents' conservative views on political and economic issues. As they moved through college, however, the women tended to adopt the much more liberal attitudes of their teachers. The faculty members served as a reference group for the students. The teachers did not deliberately try to change their students' values, but they did "think of their students . . . as having led overprotected lives, and they included among their teaching responsibilities that of introducing students to the rest of the world" (Newcomb et al., 1967: 4). A sizable minority of the students resisted the teachers' liberal values. These students tended to be relatively isolated at college, very dependent on their parents, or rebellious toward prevailing community values. In a follow-up study, Newcomb and his

A reference group establishes values and norms for guiding its members' activities. When women become cadets at West Point, they are expected to meet the behavioral standards required of the male cadets.

Figure 4.1
**Shared Outlooks of Group Members
in the Micro-Order**

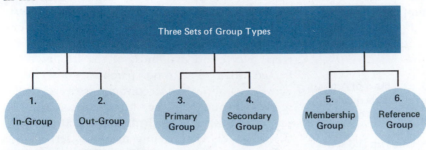

In this figure, the members of each group type share a common outlook. Thus, if we consider the groups in the numerical order shown, we see the following patterns: (1) a feeling of exclusiveness; (2) a feeling of exclusion; (3) a "we" feeling; (4) cooperation for distinct, practical reasons; (5) a recognition of belonging to a group; (6) a willingness to accept the influence of group standards to shape one's own values, beliefs, and behavior.

associates (1967) learned that the women who were liberals when they left college in the late 1930s were still liberal in 1960, while those who were conservative in the 1930s were usually still conservative over twenty years later. This research suggests that the impact of reference groups on a person's standards can persist over long periods of time.

Figure 4.1 represents the different kinds of groups that are found in the micro-order. Formal organizations and bureaucracies tend to be larger.

Formal Organizations and Bureaucracies

Throughout our lives all of us are in regular contact with schools, hospitals, courts, corporations, and government agencies. These are **formal organizations,** groups characterized by formally stated rules, clearly defined members' roles, and distinct objectives. As formal organizations become larger and more complex, they need **bureaucracies**—formal organizations' administrative sections that have the task of controlling their operation. Students, for example, are part of the formal organization of a school, but they are not part of its bureaucracy because they have no administrative duties.

Bureaucracies often evoke a negative image in people's minds. In its least negative form, a stereotype of bureaucracy includes masses of paperwork,

inefficiency, and taut nerves. More negatively individuals might visualize mental patients or prison inmates incarcerated for years, perhaps for decades, because of some "bureaucratic slip-up," or Adolph Eichmann claiming that he was a guiltless cog in the Nazi bureaucracy when he "just followed orders" to execute millions of Jewish concentration camp victims.

Bureaucracies existed in preindustrial times— in ancient Egypt, China, and Rome, for instance —and the impressive monuments and buildings those ancient civilizations produced are in part a result of the organized use of labor and materials that their bureaucracies helped promote. With its highly practical emphasis on maximizing profit, the Industrial Revolution encouraged business leaders to establish large-scale bureaucratic structures that used workers efficiently and gave business owners increased control over both their employees and the work process. Eventually bureaucratic procedures developed in public institutions, such as government, education, the penal system, and facilities for the mentally handicapped people.

As bureaucracies became prominent in modern societies, Max Weber produced what is now considered the classic analysis of this type of structure.

Weber's Analysis of Bureaucracies

Weber developed an ideal-type model of bureaucracy. An **ideal type** is a simplified description of some phenomenon based on an analysis of concrete examples, emphasizing those characteristics that best help us to understand its essential nature. Weber analyzed bureaucracies as the most efficient means of structuring employees' time and energy. His ideal-type model emphasized the following points (Gerth and Mills, 1946: 196–198).

Specialization. Within a bureaucracy it is most efficient to have each worker specialize in a task, thus becoming an expert in its performance. When faculty members at a college or university have questions concerning their salaries, they call the payroll office and speak to the person in charge of the faculty payroll, the specialist on this subject within the college bureaucracy.

Formal qualifications for bureaucratic roles. The members of bureaucracies are hired on the basis of merit, not favoritism; they have the appropriate educational credentials, experience, or both. Much of the training for bureaucratic positions, of course, occurs before a person actually enters an organization. However, within many large-scale bureaucracies, training for medium-status roles is common today. Personnel are often expected to complete intensive training programs that may vary in length from a few days to many months and are sometimes carried on at special centers built by the organization. American Telephone and Telegraph, several fast-food chains, and many of the major insurance companies have developed such centers. Successful completion of these programs makes employees eligible for higher salaries and promotion. In addition, graduates are provided with certificates that resemble diplomas and are meant to increase the sense of personal pride resulting from affiliation with their organization.

Full-time employment. In modern bureaucracies the amount of work that must be completed generally requires that staff members be hired on a full-time basis. During formally prescribed hours, they are expected to be on the job devoting their time and energies to their tasks. How employees spend their time when they are off the job is not the concern of the bureaucracy; a clear distinction is drawn between work and personal lives.

Impersonality. Officials remain impersonal with their clients, treating them as "cases" and not as individuals. They adopt the same formality in their relations with fellow staff members. As a result personal preferences and biases are excluded from the work process and are unlikely to affect the decisions bureaucratic officials must make.

Files, providing written documentations of precedents.

The decisions of a bureaucratic staff are based on precedent, and so in order to make decisions, they must be sure that all prior actions of the bureaucracy are recorded and retained indefinitely for reference. Specialists receive the task of organizing and updating these files. Since Weber's era computers, microfilm, and other types of modern technology have greatly increased the efficiency with which these records can be maintained.

Hierarchy of authority. Within bureaucracies people receive orders or directives from their superiors and are directly accountable to them. Majors give orders to captains in the army, just as deans issue commands to departmental chairpersons in colleges and universities. In both situations the "chain of command" is a distinct, efficient means for the transmission of orders and information.

Elaborate formal norms. There are clear-cut rules governing all possible contingencies. These rules tend to remain stable over time and must be learned by employees of the organization. Try to imagine what a bureaucracy would be like without such an emphasis on rules. Consider, for instance, college registration. For many students and college administrators, this is a difficult, time-consuming period at the beginning of each semester. If there were no rules covering such matters as reimbursement of funds, numerical limitations on class size, or prerequisites for entry into certain courses, administrators would need to deliberate on each case as it arose, making the long lines students sometimes must face during registration seem, in contrast, very short.

As we have noted, Weber's description of bureaucracy offers a simplified version of its structure and activities — an ideal type. Modern analysts of bureaucracies have continued to use Weber's ideas in their own work (Grey, 1988; Sjoberg, Vaughan, and Williams, 1984; Warren, 1988). At the same time, researchers recognize that bureaucracies contain some important characteristics he did not consider.

Informal Structure of Bureaucracies

"Things are not always what they appear to be." This well-known saying can apply to Weber's analysis of bureaucracies. He suggested that bureaucracies are formal structures, with clearly designated lines of authority and fully specified rules. In any particular organization, however, one individual frequently exercises much more influence in reality than does another occupying a compara-

Figure 4.2
Informal Activities of a Bureaucracy: Commentary on Weber's Model
Partial organizational chart. When the informal activities of a hypothetical computer company are examined, exception can arise to each of the points contained in Weber's model of bureaucracies.

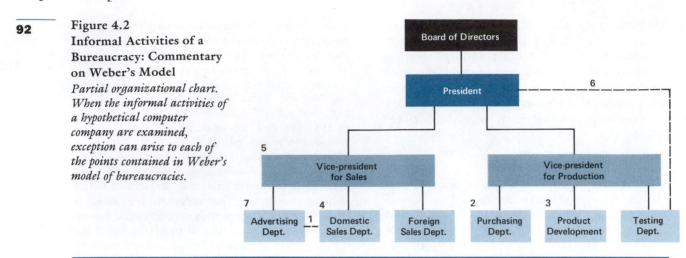

WEBER'S CHARACTERISTICS	INFORMAL ACTIVITIES IN THE COMPUTER COMPANY PROVIDING EXCEPTIONS TO WEBER'S MODEL
1. *Specialization*	1. Booming domestic sales necessitates a temporary shift to sales of one-third of the advertising specialists.
2. *Formal qualifications*	2. The manager of the purchasing department has advanced rapidly because he is an expert at "playing politics;" in fact, he has very little experience in the area of purchasing.
3. *Full-time employment*	3. A twenty-year-old computer whiz is paid a full time salary for part-time work.
4. *Impersonality*	4. Some customers receive distinctly preferential treatment. It is well known that a number of mayors received huge discounts on high-priced models in exchange for their cities signing large contracts with the company.
5. *Written documentation of precedents*	5. The vice-president for sales has been so busy directing the hiring and training of sales staff that he has not kept records on the procedures he has used.
6. *Hierarchy of authority*	6. The president, who has a strong background in product resting, frequently bypasses the production vice-president to give orders to the testing department.
7. *Elaborate formal norms*	7. Members of the advertising department recognize that some of the rules relating to their duties are more important than others. Many members of this department, for example, break an ofice rule about taking office supplies for personal use.

ble position in the formal organizational structure. Similarly workers frequently recognize that some rules are much more important than others, despite the fact that in the organizational handbook all rules appear equally important. As Figure 4.2 suggests, the informal organization within a bureaucracy frequently decreases the significance of the formal structure. Cliques, grapevines, and informal power alliances are among the factors contributing to this outcome.

An important set of studies demonstrating the impact of the informal structure within bureaucracies was conducted at the Hawthorne plant of the Western Electric Company in Illinois (Roethlisberger and Dickson, 1939). One of the principal Hawthorne studies was completed by some observers sitting in a room with fourteen workers wiring telephone equipment. The researchers learned that the workers had developed group norms often in opposition to the official norms established by management. For instance, if someone worked more quickly than the standard, fellow workers designated that person a "ratebuster," while someone who worked more slowly than the norm was called a "chiseler." The punishment for minor violations, such as working quickly, was often "binging"—hitting the offender on the upper arm—or ridicule. The worst violation of the informal group norms occurred when a worker "squealed" on fellow workers to the foreman. In this case the punishment was exclusion; the other workers simply pretended that the person did not exist.

Informal group norms defined "a fair day's work" as less than the amount of production desired by management. In order to conform to group norms, the fastest members simply stopped working earlier than did the others. These workers seemed to realize that voluntary restriction of output was useful for the group as a whole since increased production would probably have encouraged the company to initiate layoffs. In addition, if the workers had increased their production level, cutthroat competition and massive disruption of the group might well have occurred. The informal norms restricting productivity prevented the occurrence of both possibilities (Blau and Scott, 1963: 92–93).

Besides his failure to analyze the informal workings of bureaucracies, Weber also overlooked their weaknesses.

Weaknesses of Bureaucracies

Weber's ideal type of bureaucracy emphasizes the positive contributions this type of structure can make. However, bureaucracies can also produce negative outcomes for some of the people in contact with them (Burns, 1980).

Efficiency is one of the most obvious assets of bureaucracy, but placing an excessive emphasis on it can violate humanitarian standards. For example, in public mental hospitals, the laundering process is easier if patients are issued institutional clothes. This procedure eliminates the necessity of individually marking each piece of clothing and returning it to its owner. The emphasis on efficiency, however, overlooks the fact that wearing one's own clothes can be very meaningful, provid-

ing continuity with one's previous life and perhaps helping combat mental illness.

On the other hand, bureaucracies can be inefficient. This attribute has provoked a number of satirical analyses, including the Peter Principle, which contends that within bureaucracies officials continue to rise until they reach a level at which they are incompetent. If people do their jobs well, they are promoted; only when they do their jobs badly do they stop advancing, and there they remain. According to the author, Lawrence Peter, the only reason bureaucracies function at all is because at any given time a certain number of individuals have not yet reached their level of incompetence (Peter and Hull, 1969).

Another possible weakness of bureaucracies is their frequent focus on self-perpetuation. Staff members are likely to stress the importance of their group operation, whether or not they are providing a demonstrably useful service; the obvious collective motive is that members' jobs are their source of livelihood. Government agencies are particularly notorious for maintaining long-term survival. A study of the Environmental Protection Agency's enforcement of clean-air standards indicated that officials invariably acted to promote the agency's survival. At times this meant restraining clean-air enforcement in order to avoid budget reductions, while at other times an aggressive stance was intended to show politicians and the public that the agency had a crucial role in cleaning up the nation's air (Wood, 1988).

Communications problems can also be a weakness of bureaucracies. Within the construction industry, for example, managers used to hold meetings over a cup of coffee at the work site. However, these organizations have grown larger and more complex, and their different activities have become more separate. One observer wrote:

On our present job, our engineer–managers are paper-oriented. . . Their working styles consist of spending days and weeks studying details on plans or researching specifications before they are ready to help our people who are doing construction work. Many or most consider neat files more important than getting involved in meeting deadlines, making decisions which might be risky, and taking abuse for failures or mistakes.

(Applebaum, 1982: 231)

One of the weaknesses of bureaucracies is that what represents efficient practice for bureaucratic officials often promotes highly inefficient situations for clients.

This statement suggests that the growth of bureaucracies isolates managers and encourages a more aloof, less communicative style than they generally maintained when the structures were smaller.

An additional weakness of bureaucracies is that they encourage the development of a type of personality widely regarded as abnormal. The **bureaucratic personality** emphasizes rules and procedures and tends to lose track of organizational goals (Merton, 1968). This type of person enforces "rules for rules' sake." Most of us have probably encountered such an approach when dealing with certain bureaucratic personnel: The college official who never "bends" the rules to help students; the Motor Vehicles Department clerk who makes a host of trivial corrections on a car registration application; or the hospital administrator who will not admit a patient, even one in considerable discomfort, until the proper forms

are completed in triplicate. On the other hand, some evidence suggests that in reality bureaucratic personalities are not common in modern bureaucracies. For example, Melvin Kohn (1971) studied a sample of more than 3000 men engaged in a wide variety of civilian occupations. He discovered that men working in bureaucracies more readily think for themselves, are more open to new experiences, place greater emphasis on self-direction, and maintain more responsible moral standards than do nonbureaucratic personnel. Kohn suggested that the fact that bureaucratic organizations often hire people with higher educational qualifications than those found in many other types of jobs helps to explain the differences.

We have seen that bureaucracies often have dysfunctional tendencies, but is the modern picture primarily negative? The following Cross-Cultural Perspective provides one response to this question.

CROSS-CULTURAL PERSPECTIVE

The Human Factor in Bureaucracies: The Japanese Case

 William Ouchi (1981), a management specialist, developed Theory Z, a model for organizing bureaucracies that is based on Japanese management practices and emphasizes long-term planning, decision making by consensus, and the development of intense loyalty between workers and management. Ouchi has contended that Theory Z can help many American firms with serious problems of high employee turnover, declining productivity, and profound worker alienation. Some American corporations, such as IBM, Proctor and Gamble, and Hewlett-Packard, now use Theory Z techniques.

The theory commands attention because Japanese production has become legendary in Western societies. Between 1975 and 1981, the annual sale of Japanese cars in the United States rose from 800,000 to 1.9 million; today Japanese products control 23 percent of the American car market. Japanese cameras, radios, televisions, microwave ovens, and motorcycles have also proven popular in the United States and other Western nations. In recent years, admittedly, the Japanese economy has fallen on hard times, and some of the practices discussed in this section have had to be restricted. Yet these bureaucratic practices are still worthy of Americans' attention.

The central idea of Theory Z is the importance of establishing a powerful bond between workers and their firms. Japanese managers take a number of steps to maintain and strengthen this bond. Among them:

1. *Lifetime employment.* Over 35 percent of the Japanese work force is covered by this practice, which requires sacrifice by all company employees when recession or other problems threaten layoffs. Instead of dismissing workers, management will cut everyone's paychecks, including its own, or will defer payment of the large, twice-yearly bonuses all employees normally receive.
2. *Evaluation and promotion policies.* Many Japanese companies provide promotions as infrequently as once every ten years. Yet since all employees receive the same treatment, no one must fear falling behind.
3. *Nonspecialized careers.* Unlike American managers, who generally specialize in one area of company business (e.g., sales, finance, or production), Japanese executives regularly move from one corporate department to another and eventually become experts in the entire structure and activities of their firms.
4. *Collective decision making.* Compared with American executives, who are often expected to act quickly and decisively and to accept the consequences of their individual decisions, Japanese management makes major decisions by means of a collective compromise process that may involve sixty to eighty people. The Japanese call this process of establishing consensus *nemawashi* (root building). In the same way that a gardener carefully wraps all the roots of a tree together before planting it, Japanese business leaders must bring together all the members of a company before finalizing a decision. This process may be tedious, but when it is completed everyone is likely to feel committed to the collective goal.

Because the Japanese approach to business differs from that of the United States, one might suspect that it would be ineffective in the United States. It has, however, been fairly successful in some cases. In a Sony plant in San Diego, which employs 1800 workers, 700,000 color television sets were produced in 1981, a level of productivity that approaches the one achieved in the Japanese plants. The Japanese factory manager said, "Americans are as quality conscious as the Japanese. But the question has been how to motivate them." Managers have tried to build strong ties with workers, expecting that they will then reciprocate. During the recession of 1973 to 1975, when television sales dropped and production plummeted, no one was fired. Workers stayed busy with plant maintenance and other chores. In fact, since the plant opened in 1972, no workers have been laid off. This personnel policy has been a success. Several attempts to unionize the work force have been defeated by margins as high as three to one. A parts dispatcher who was a former member of the Retail Clerks Union explained, "Union pay was better, and the benefits were probably better. But basically I'm more satisfied here."

Sony has not forced Japanese customs on its American workers. The use of lemon-colored smocks for assembly-line workers is optional, and most of the employees prefer jeans and running shoes. An attempt to establish an exercise period similar to those common in the Japanese plants was dropped when managers saw that it was not popular.

Inevitably differences in customs cause some misunderstandings. American workers often interpret the Japanese system of managing by consensus as reflecting an inability to make decisions. One employee complained, "There is a lot of indecision. No managers will ever say do this or do that."

In general, however, most of the workers like the Japanese management style and do not feel that it is particularly foreign. An American supervisor said, "A long time ago, Americans used to be more people-oriented, the way the Japanese are. It just got lost somewhere along the way" (Coutu, 1981). The Japanese approach to employee–management relations appears to contain some valuable lessons for Americans.

Sources: Christopher Byron. "How Japan Does It." *Time.* V. 117. March 30, 1981, pp. 54–60; D. L. Coutu. "Consensus in San Diego." *Time.* V. 117. March 30, 1981, p. 58; William Ouchi. *Theory Z: How American Business Can Meet the Japanese Challenge.* Reading, MA: Addison-Wesley. 1981; Takahiro Suzuki. "A Hollow Future for Japan?" *Futurist.* V. 22. May/June 1988, p. 33.

Communities

As the young man reached the center of the park, his dog ran up to an elderly man sitting on a bench. "Here. I've got something for him," the old man said. Stiffly he reached into his pocket and took out a cookie.

"I'm sure she'll like it."
"You know, these days many people your age don't have enough time to stop and talk."
"Well, I guess I rush around too, but I'm not in that bad a hurry. Besides I'm living right over there on Court Street, and I'm interested in the community."
"The community." The old man nodded and smiled as if the phrase were the punchline to a quiet joke. "This ain't no community no more. Back in the thirties, back then it was a community. People of all ages used to be out on the street till midnight. There'd be vendors selling food and drinks. Back then you could sit in the park and watch the whole show. It was better than a Jimmy Cagney thriller." He paused to look at a man walking by. "Do you know him?"

"I don't think so."
The old man nudged his listener with an elbow. "You should. That's Barry Garcia. He's got that little factory over on Sweet Street. Right now he's paying twenty-five workers, but he's moving out to Shortland Hills into a large, new plant. That guy's really going places, and Barry's from right here — the community." He nodded proudly.

Like this man many Americans yearn for a sense of community they once knew or perhaps they know only from hearsay, and at the same time they respond positively to the very social conditions — the emphasis on individual achievement and on industrial development — that have undermined communities in the United States and other Western countries. For many Americans it has been difficult to come to grips with their changing communities.

Some modern urban residents are deeply involved in community activities. This photo shows residents of Cincinnati's Over the Rhine district cleaning up a debris-filled lot in preparation for a neighborhood garden.

To begin, a **community** is a settlement of people living in a specific geographical area and maintaining a system of interrelationships that satisfies many of the people's physical and social needs. Because of the interrelationship among its inhabitants, a community is normally a source of group identification.

Early in the twentieth century, Robert Ezra Park and other members of the Chicago School of sociology undertook an extensive set of community studies that helped transform sociology from an "armchair" discipline into an empirical science. Park, a former newspaper reporter, retained his sharp curiosity for facts; when he became a professor at the University of Chicago, he outlined an extensive program of research into the sociology of the community. Park emphasized that sociologists studying communities should analyze them as social systems, characterized by shared attitudes toward morality, business, the law, politics, and the future of the area (Krause, 1980).

Currently sociologists find that communities in the traditional sense are an unusual, even rare item. In *Habits of the Heart,* Robert Bellah and his coauthors (1986) made a distinction between communities and lifestyle enclaves. While defining community in much the same way as we have, they distinguished it from a *lifestyle enclave,* a group of people who emphasize similarities in private life, especially similarities involving leisure and consumption patterns. Lifestyle enclaves are narrower than communities in two respects. Instead of including all residents within a locale, they are composed of selected individuals; in addition, instead of encouraging their members to relate to each other in diverse ways, lifestyle enclaves involve highly focused, shared interests. Frequently, these sociologists argued, when people use the word *community* in specific contexts — referring to the youth community, the Hispanic community, or the gay community — their conception of community closely resembles the idea of lifestyle enclave (Bellah et al., 1986: 72 – 75).

Certainly many investigations that are considered to be community studies focus on the fact that the interrelatedness of supposed community members is minimal. For example, research on over 9000 randomly selected households in fifty-nine residential communities found that when citizens feel vulnerable to crime or perceive police services as ineffective, their likelihood of purchasing weapons for protection increases (Smith and Uchida, 1988). A study of farm communities concluded that farmers tend to consider relations with their neighbors as exchanges, and thus if neighbors are so crippled financially that they show no prospects of reciprocating favors, then future relations are broken off (Wright and Rosenblatt, 1987).

Table 4.1 supports the same trend, indicating that over time people have become less enthusiastic about participation in community action.

Table 4.1
Students' Participation in Community Action

ESSENTIAL OR VERY IMPORTANT TO PARTICIPATE IN COMMUNITY ACTION		
	1970	1987
All	29%	20%
Male	27	18
Female	32	22

Source: Richard G. Braungart and Margaret M. Braungart. "From Yippies to Yuppies: Twenty Years of Freshman Attitudes." *Public Opinion.* V. 11. September/October 1988, pp. 53–56.

These data come from an annually conducted national study of college freshmen. Over a seventeen-year time span, the subjects' desire to participate in community action declined 9 percent.

Institutions

We have just examined the principal types of groups sociologists distinguish. All groups are visible to the naked eye; they exist in a concrete sense. The same claim, however, cannot be made about institutions, even though they contain a visible element — groups.

An **institution** is a system of statuses, roles, groups, and behavioral patterns that satisfies a basic human need and is necessary for the survival of a society. Industrial societies always contain a well-developed set of institutions, while preindustrial societies often have limited or no development in many institutional areas. Institutions are part of the **macro-order** — the large-scale structures and activities that exist within societies and even between one society and another.

The chapters in the third part of this book examine major institutions. The family is an institution that supplies a host of functions, including sexual regulation, reproduction, child rearing, and the provision of food, shelter, and emotional support. Religion develops group cohesion (a common sense of purpose), maintains social control, and provides an ethical design for living. Education serves a variety of purposes, including the transmission of culture, the teaching of knowledge and skills, and the sorting of students into vocational and college-preparatory programs. The political institution maintains social order and exerts change in the legal structure, while the economic institution controls the production, distribution, and consumption of goods and services. Medicine is concerned with the prevention and treatment of disease and the treatment of injury, and science supplies systematic knowledge that can be used to produce progress in a variety of technological and social areas. Institutions not discussed in the third part of the text include the military, which can either attack the enemies of a society or defend against them, and sport, which provides recreation, exercise, and entertainment.

Institutions tend to be relatively stable because members of society, especially those who are wealthy and powerful, generally do not feel that social change supports their interests. Consider the political institution. For almost the entire history of the United States, there have been only two political parties in most elections. The majority of the citizens, especially influential people, find that their political interests are well enough represented by the principal parties that they are not motivated to support third parties. Thus third parties have almost always lacked the wealth and influence to launch successful political campaigns, even at the local level.

Institutions do not change readily, but when they do, they are likely to alter one or more other institutions. The reason is that the institutions are intimately tied to one another. Changes in the economic institution, for instance, can affect families. In an agricultural society, children generally represent a source of wealth for their parents — more hands to work the land. However, in an industrial society, in which people live off wages, children represent an economic liability. It makes sense, therefore, to restrict the number of children. This appears to be one important reason that families in industrial societies are smaller than families in agricultural societies.

Across time and space, the form of a particular institution and the kind of activities it produces will often vary considerably. Recreation and sport, for instance, have changed over time in U.S. society. In the first permanent American villages, the Puritans opposed play, games, and sport for two reasons. First, they emphasized that it was a full-time task simply to survive — to wrest a living from the wilderness and to protect themselves from the Indians. Second, religious rules prohibited leisure, branding such activities as idle and wasteful. But as the frontier moved westward, religious restrictions weakened. Gambling on horse races, cock fights, fist fighting, wrestling, and rifle shooting were popular activities. In the taverns, drinking, cards, billiards, bowling, and rifle and pistol shooting provided both competition and entertainment (Leonard, 1980: 23–24). As the country grew, leisure also expanded. Industrialization, transportation growth, and the expansion of mass media all contributed. Eventually leisure and spectator sport became big business.

Other societies often have institutions very different from those in the United States. Americans have a variety of spectator sports but none like the following examples. In Merida, in western Spain, the people once walled off an enormous plain to a height of four feet, creating a small lake on which ships could engage in simulated naval battles. In less technologically advanced societies, citizens use natural structures as settings for spectator sports. In a remote island of the New Hebrides, the entire community would gather at the bottom of a cliff to watch young male villagers throw themselves headlong toward the cliff floor, confident that the vine ropes attached to their heels would bring them to a halt just before they smashed into the rocks (Michener, 1976: 11–12).

Humanization of Group Activity

On July 3, 1988, the commander of an American Navy warship mistook an Iranian passenger plane for an Iranian F-14 fighter, fired two surface-to-air missiles at the plane, and killed 290 civilians. Admiral William J. Crowe, Jr., Chairman of the Joint Chiefs of Staff, said that he regretted the loss of life but that "the commanding officer had a very heavy obligation to protect his ship, his people" (Halloran, 1988: A1). This incident emphasizes what we have seen in several sections of this chapter, especially in the discussions of bureaucracies and communities — that modern group activity is aggressive, self-centered, and not especially humane.

Sociologist Philip Slater (1976) contended that Americans must choose between an emphasis on community, in which the wish to live in trust and cooperation in a collective setting is the chief concern, and a focus on competition, in which the advancement of the individual at the expense of others is given top priority. American culture, Slater noted, did not invent competition, but he claimed that, compared to most other societies, the United States is extraordinarily competitive.

And yet it should be remembered that a desire for community was very strong in many of the earliest American settlements — in particular, among the Puritans. Just before landing in Salem harbor in 1630, John Winthrop, the governor of the colony, gave a famous speech describing the "city upon a hill" that he and his fellow Puritans intended to found. He said, "We must delight in each other, make others' condition our own, rejoice together, mourn together, labor and suffer together, always having before our eyes our community as members of the same body." In *Habits of the Heart,* Bellah and his coauthors noted that the Puritans' fundamental criterion of success was "the creation of a community in which a genuinely ethical and spiritual life could be lived" (Bellah et al., 1986: 28–29).

Can individuals find evidence of this legacy today? Perhaps most people don't think of big business truly supporting a sense of cooperation and community or showing significant concern for anything but increase in profits, but cases of corporate responsibility and good citizenship exist. Merck & Company, for example, provides without cost a drug that treats one of the leading causes of blindness in the developing world. Du Pont has voluntarily stopped producing several chlorofluorocarbons in order to alleviate harmful depletion of the ozone layer. The Monsanto Company promised to cut its hazardous air emissions by 90 percent by 1992 even though the organization was already in compliance with federal clean-air standards. Dow Chemical cooperated with the Sierra Club to reduce hazardous-waste production (Pagan, 1989). Some people view these corporate efforts suspiciously, feeling that they are a fairly cheap way to purchase public good will. However, even if some truth to such a claim exists, these early activities are setting a precedent for such cooperative ventures in the future.

Students too can become active in community life. Sociologist Elliot Krause (1980) pleaded, "Join your community! Now, not later!" He urged his students to go out and get to know their town or city, mapping out the landmarks and the different districts. In addition, he suggested that students should read their community newspaper in order to discover what issues are presently controversial. Then, Krause said, they should join action groups whose values and tactics they could endorse. At the very least, such participation can help the individual feel less like a robot.

STUDY GUIDE

Learning Objectives

After studying this chapter, you should be able to:

1. Define group and distinguish among group, aggregate, and social category.
2. Compare and contrast primary groups and secondary groups.
3. Define in-groups and out-groups and indicate circumstances encouraging their development.
4. Distinguish between membership and reference groups and define anticipatory socialization.
5. Define formal organization, bureaucracy, and ideal type and discuss Weber's analysis of bureaucracies.
6. Describe informal activities within bureaucracies.
7. Identify weaknesses of bureaucracies.
8. Define community and discuss modern communities and lifestyle enclaves.
9. Define institution and describe the activities of the major institutions.
10. Indicate major problems of group life in modern society and suggest how these problems might be solved.

Summary

1. A group consists of two or more interacting people who share certain expectations and goals. Groups can be distinguished from aggregates and social categories, which are related concepts.

2. Sociologists have defined many different types of groups. Primary groups entail stable, long-lasting relationships, permitting members to exercise many facets of their personality and to develop strong ties of affect and identity. By contrast, secondary groups are composed of people who join a group for distinct, practical reasons and generally maintain few, if any, strong emotional ties.

Other significant concepts are in-groups and out-groups. An in-group is any group characterized by a strong sense of identification and loyalty and by the exclusion of nonmembers. The out-group consists of people who do not belong to the in-group and who are viewed with hostility and even contempt by in-group members.

Reference groups, groups that a person uses to help shape his or her own values, beliefs, and behavior, are influential in the socialization of people. The concept of anticipatory socialization suggests that groups can serve as reference groups, even if people do not belong to them.

Another significant type of group is the bureaucracy—a formal organization's administrative section that has the task of controlling its operation. Max Weber analyzed the bureaucracy as an ideal type, indicating the bureaucratic features that make it the most efficient structure for using employees' time and energy within an organizational structure. Later sociological analysis modified Weber's conclusions, identifying the informal group activities within bureaucracies and weaknesses of bureaucracies.

The community is a settlement of people living in a specific geographical area and maintaining a system of interrelationships that satisfies many of the people's physical and social needs.

3. An institution is a system of statuses, roles, groups, and behavioral patterns that satisfies a basic human need and is necessary for the survival of a society. Institutions include the family, religion, education, the political order, the economy, medicine, science, the military, and sports.

4. In an industrial age, people often find themselves confronting two opposing demands—one pulling them toward efficiency and achievement and the other toward intimacy and community. People can take decisive steps to offset the impersonal tendencies of modern life.

Key Terms

aggregate   two or more people who share physical space but lack the interaction maintained by group members

anticipatory socialization   the acceptance of a group's standards preparatory to becoming a member of the group

bureaucracy   a formal organization's administrative section that has the task of controlling its operation

bureaucratic personality   a type of personality that emphasizes rules and procedures and tends to lose track of organizational goals

community   a settlement of people living in a specific geographical area and maintaining a system of interrelationships that satisfies many of the people's physical and social needs

formal organization   a group characterized by formally stated rules, clearly defined members' roles, and distinct objectives

group   two or more interacting people who share certain expectations and goals

ideal type   a simplified description of some phenomenon based on an analysis of concrete examples, emphasizing characteristics that best help us to understand its essential nature

in-group   any group characterized by a strong sense of identification and loyalty and by the exclusion of nonmembers

institution   a system of statuses, roles, groups, and behavioral patterns that satisfies a basic human need and is necessary for the survival of a society

macro-order   the large-scale structures and activities that exist within societies and even between one society and another

membership group   a group to which an individual belongs

micro-order   the structure and activity of small groups

out-group   people who do not belong to an in-group, outsiders who are viewed with hostility and even contempt by the in-group members

primary group   a group in which relationships are usually stable over long periods of time, members are able to expose many facets of their personality, and a strong sense of affection and identity develops

reference group   a group whose standards a person uses to help shape his or her own values, beliefs, and behavior

secondary group   a group of people who cooperate with each other for specific, practical reasons, and generally maintain few, if any, strong emotional ties within the group

social category   a number of people who have one or more social characteristics in common

Tests

True–false Test

_____T_____   1. The family is a major primary group.

_____F_____   2. After World War II, American soldiers' primary groups failed to develop a sense of loyalty among their members.

_____T_____   3. This chapter argues that the strong emotions that normally accompany primary-group relations can hamper effective decision making in secondary groups.

_____   4. Anticipatory socialization occurs only when people already belong to a reference group.

_____   5. Theodore Newcomb's study of college women's political attitudes and values over time indicated that teachers' influence had little or no lasting effect on attitudes and values.

_____   6. Bureaucracies do not exist separately from formal organizations.

_____   7. An ideal type emphasizes those characteristics of a phenomenon that best help us to understand its essential nature.

_____   8. In analyzing bureaucracies, Weber produced major insights about their informal structure.

_____   9. Lifestyle enclaves are closely knit, traditional communities, such as those which existed in preindustrial America.

_____ 10. Industrial societies always have a set of well-developed institutions, while preindustrial societies often have limited or no development in many institutional areas.

Multiple-choice Test

_____   1. A number of people who have one or more social characteristics in common, such as age, sex, or race, would be a(n):
   a. group.
   b. aggregate.
   c. social category. ✓
   d. secondary group.

_____   2. Compared to a primary group, a secondary group tends:
   a. to have less face-to-face contact.
   b. to have more of a "we feeling."
   c. to be inferior.
   d. to involve a more intimate kind of relationship.

_____   3. When a person accepts a group's standards preparatory to becoming a member of the group, this behavior is called:
   a. a membership group.
   b. aggregate behavior.
   c. anticipatory socialization.
   d. an ideal type.

_____ 4. Which statement is true of bureaucracies?
  a. They have existed for less than a century.
  b. They are informal organizations.
  c. They do not exist in economic or political structures.
  d. They are found in large formal organizations.

_____ 5. Which of the following characteristics is included in Weber's analysis of bureaucracies?
  a. an informal system of authority
  b. hiring based on formal qualifications
  c. a blending of work and personal lives
  d. self-perpetuation as a goal

_____ 6. Which of these factors is an important weakness of bureaucracies?
  a. an excessive emphasis on efficiency
  b. the discouragement of the bureaucratic personality
  c. specialization
  d. unwritten traditions

_____ 7. Communities:
  a. have not been studied by sociologists in recent decades.
  b. no longer contain lifestyle enclaves.
  c. are now revitalized in most large cities, according to a recent study.
  d. have been studied by sociologists since early in the twentieth century.

_____ 8. Which of the following statements is true of institutions?
  a. In some societies many institutions simply exist without any apparent functions.
  b. They tend to be unstable.
  c. Their structure and activities tend to be very similar across time and space.
  d. When they change, they tend to affect other institutions.

_____ 9. Institutions are part of the:
  a. micro-order.
  b. macro-order. ✓
  c. aggregate structure.
  d. bureaucratic ideal type.

_____ 10. Solutions to the problems of modern group life discussed in the text include:
  a. participating in community activities.
  b. joining a major corporation and working for its success.
  c. learning new ways to succeed in competitive situations.
  d. a and c

Essay Test

1. Define the following concepts and give an example of each: group, aggregate, and social category.
2. Evaluate the following statement: Primary groups and secondary groups serve the same purposes for people.
3. Describe two situations presented in the text illustrating how in-group/out-group hostility is produced.
4. Distinguish between formal organizations and bureaucracies and summarize Weber's analysis of bureaucracies. Then examine the informal structure and weaknesses of bureaucracies, indicating why this material represents a criticism of Weber's work.
5. Define community and discuss modern sociologists' conclusions about communities.

Suggested Readings

Blau, Peter, and Marshall W. Meyer. 1971. *Bureaucracy in Modern Society.* New York: Random House. Second edition. An examination of the theory of bureaucracy and the activities, functions, and dys-functions of modern bureaucratic organizations.

Fischer, Frank, and Carmen Sirianni (eds.). 1984. *Critical Studies in Organization and Bureaucracy.* Philadelphia: Temple University Press. Twenty-eight articles on organizations and bureaucracies, including classic analyses by Marx, Weber, and others; assessments of individuals' adaptations to limited power in the organizational context; and examinations of efforts to establish and maintain democratic organizations.

Gerth, Hans H., and C. Wright Mills (eds.). 1946. *From Max Weber.* New York: Oxford University Press. A well-known collection containing an informative biography of Max Weber and compelling excerpts from his major works, including a chapter devoted to his analysis of bureaucracies.

Kanter, Rosabeth Moss. 1977. *Men and Women of the Corporation.* New York: Basic Books. Case-study research explaining why sexism persists in modern American corporations.

Scott, W. Richard. 1987. *Organizations: Rational, Natural, and Open Systems.* Englewood Cliffs, NJ: Prentice-Hall. Second edition. A thorough, well-organized introduction to the topic of formal organi-zations with effective integration of relevant concepts and theories.

Shkilnyk, Anastasia M. 1985. *A Poison Stronger than Love: The Destruction of an Ojibwa Community.* New Haven: Yale University Press. The moving account of how a forced move to a reservation and industrial waste in the local river combined to destroy a Native-American community.

Warren, Roland L., and Larry Lyon (eds.). 1988. *New Perspectives on the American Community.* Belmont, CA: Wadsworth. Fifth edition. The latest edition of a successful book of readings containing both classical perspectives and studies on the community and a substantial up-to-date list of contemporary contributions.

Additional Assignments

1. Interview three people, preferably of different ages, who have been residents of your community for at least five years. Ask them what significant changes they have seen in their community, why they consider these changes significant, and whether they feel optimistic or pessimistic about the impact of the community changes. Then seek information about your community in a local newspaper. (*Hint:* At the end of the year, many newspapers contain sections reviewing the year's events.) Did your respondents highlight the same changes as those discussed in the newspaper? Does what you learned about your own community correspond with information in the text? Discuss.

2. Keep a diary for a week that logs (a) your formal activities at work and school and (b) your social activities. At the end of each week, use your diary to answer the following questions:
    a. How much involvement occurred in primary groups and in secondary groups? Was one type of involvement more rewarding than the other? Explain.
    b. Did you experience any in-group/out-group tensions or hostilities? From which sources?
    c. Did you obtain significant support from any reference group(s)?
    d. Did your contact with bureaucracies suggest that they are efficient, inefficient, or both?
    e. How often did you feel your activities were affected or controlled by others? Explain.

Answers to Objective Test Questions

True – false Test

1. t
2. f
3. t
4. f
5. f
6. t
7. t
8. f
9. f
10. t

Multiple-choice Test

1. c
2. a
3. c
4. d
5. b
6. a
7. d
8. d
9. b
10. a

5
SOCIAL INTERACTION

Theories of Social Interaction

Symbolic Interaction
Ethnomethodology
Dramaturgic Sociology

The Structuring of Social Interaction

Status and Role
Leadership
Conformity
Decision Making

The Disruption of Patterns of Social Interaction

Study Guide

The general managers, who build basketball teams in the National Basketball Association, are astute judges of talent, and yet judging talent is not all that is required. They also need to be amateur sociologists, anticipating what the loss of a current player or the addition of a new player will mean for the team's chemistry.

As Al Bianchi, the successful general manager of the New York Knicks, observed:

> The word chemistry has come into vogue in recent years, but it has always been important. It seems almost ludicrous that you have to worry about chemistry these days when guys are being paid millions to play basketball. Who wouldn't be happy doing that? But some guys aren't. And yes, there are certain players I would not draft or trade for, largely because of their reputation.

> *(Brown, 1989: Section 8, p. 4)*

In the spring of 1989, the Detroit Pistons made a controversial trade, sending Adrian Dantley, a high-scoring forward to Dallas in exchange for Mark Aguirre, another high-scoring forward. Both men were fine players; the question, as Bianchi observed, was whether they would be able to fit in with their new teams, getting along with team mates and effectively contributing their talents to win ball games. Aguirre was especially questionable — the leading scorer at Dallas but at odds with his team mates and coaches. In addition, he'd be going to a team with two players to whom he would be expected to subordinate his talents. At the time of the trade, Detroit had the best record in professional basketball. Had the front office badly misjudged the situation?

Three months later the answer was clear. Detroit completed the regular season with the best record in professional basketball and won four play-off rounds, sweeping four games from the former champion Los Angeles Lakers in the finals. Obviously Aguirre's acquisition had not hurt the team.

Whether it is the issue of a basketball player relating to new team mates or a greeting as two people pass each other on the street, human contacts involve **social interaction** — the basic process through which two or more people use language and gestures to affect each other's thoughts, expectations, and behavior. Through social interaction people obtain the knowledge and skills that make them functioning members of society. Social interaction is essential for all organized life.

No social activity could take place in the political, educational, religious, economic, or familial structures without the process.

In this chapter we explore social interaction. The first section examines three important theories in this area. Next we consider the major components of social interaction. The chapter concludes with an analysis of what happens when patterns of social interaction are disrupted.

Theories of Social Interaction

This section examines three theoretical perspectives that help explain social interaction and social relationships: symbolic interaction, ethnomethodology, and dramaturgic sociology.

Symbolic Interaction

Symbolic-interaction theory emphasizes the importance of symbolic communication —

gestures and, above all, language—in the development of the individual, group, and society. A large body of research related to this theory has been produced. For instance, studies using this perspective have included investigations about the image of the self presented in North Yemeni wedding ceremonies (Caton, 1985), the effect of spouses' evaluations on research subjects' sense of self (Schafer and Keith, 1985), the development of norms relating to justice (Stolte, 1987), and the impact of the conception of social-interaction patterns on agricultural production in Ifugao society (Brosius, 1988).

As we read in Chapter 1, "Introduction," a major proponent of symbolic interaction was Herbert Blumer (1969), who emphasized that the nature of the theory could be summarized in the following manner. Blumer observed that the symbolic quality of social interaction centers on the meanings individuals give to people and things. The meanings do not simply exist in the social world but derive from people's judgments in the course of their daily experience; a major contributor to these meanings is contact with other people. Sometimes as individuals interpret their experience, meanings change. Whether meanings change or remain the same, they affect people's behavior. Figure 5.1 illustrates responses and meanings associated with some symbols.

We continue this analysis, using as illustration a discussion of fathers' changing roles. Blumer noted that one of the basic elements in symbolic interaction is the nature of the objects with which people must interact. These objects are three types—physical objects such as chairs or trees, social objects such as parents or friends, and abstract objects such as ideas or philosophical principles. People's conceptions of the significant objects in their environment can differ vastly and are shaped by the interpretations developed in interaction with others. For instance, a progressive father was expertly changing his baby's diaper on a park bench. While he was laboring, an older gentleman, who clearly had a different conception of fatherhood, stopped to watch. As the father slipped the plastic bag containing the diaper into a small pack, the gentleman said with a slight accent, "In my country I have never seen such a thing." The father smiled and replied, "Welcome to America" (Fort, 1989: 79).

Symbolic interaction also perceives the individual as an acting organism. In Chapter 6, "Social-

Figure 5.1
A Comparison of Signs and Symbols

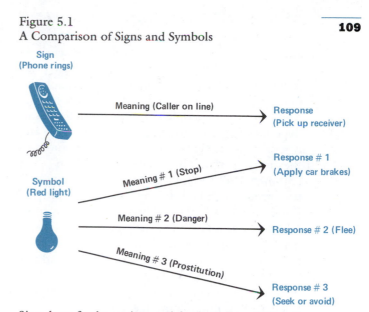

Signs have fixed meanings and fixed responses. When the telephone rings, people know that a caller is on the line, and they will generally pick up the receiver. Symbols, however, have neither fixed meanings nor fixed responses. A red light, for instance, can mean to stop one's car at an intersection, to recognize danger when a jammed valve is creating a buildup of pressure that will soon produce an explosion within a furnace, or to realize that one has entered a so-called "red-light district," where houses of prostitution are located. As the figure indicates, each meaning of a symbol requires a particular response.

Like the man pictured here, many modern fathers are more actively involved in their children's upbringing than fathers tended to be in the past.

ization," the summary of George Herbert Mead's version of symbolic interaction develops this idea, and so, at this time, we only need to discuss the point briefly. Blumer observed that most other social theories consider people the passive objects of others' behavior; by contrast, symbolic interaction emphasizes people's ability to function as independent entities in the social world — to analyze significant events in their own lives and note the impact that these events have on them (Blumer, 1969: 14). Frequently other individuals and groups can help in this assessment process. For over a decade, Mark Podolner has been counseling individual fathers and groups of fathers, helping them to understand that in most cases they were raised to repress their feelings and that for both themselves and their children it would be beneficial if they could express their feelings openly. Podolner helps his clients understand what he believes are the destructive effects of this repression on both the men themselves and their children. For instance, he explains that because boys are largely raised by women and yet are expected to use fathers as role models, they often become insecure as adults and seek to oppress women, feeling their mothers had too much control over them.

Once individuals have analyzed the impact of events on their lives, they take action. According to Blumer, the factors people take into account include their goals, the means to achieve those goals, their self-image, and the likely result of the course of action (Blumer, 1969: 15). A substantial number of modern fathers have embarked on a course of action where, as Podolner phrased it, their goal is "to become the father they wish they had." These men realize that they have not been brought up to be emotionally expressive, and so their self-image includes the recognition that they are likely to experience an inner struggle as they attempt to give emotional support to and receive it from their children. They appreciate, however, that the likely result of such a course of action will be release from a chain of emotional repression that has existed for generations, with significant improvement in the emotional lives of all directly involved (Fort, 1989: 80–82).

Ethnomethodology

Two mothers are sipping coffee and talking. One turns to the other and says, "Carrie, I don't know what it is. You seem to have such an effortless time with your children."

"It's really pretty straightforward, Lucy," the other replies. "I have a set of simple rules, and come hell or high water I stick to them. The kids and I really understand each other."

Carrie seems to have some grasp of the ethnomethodological perspective. **Ethnomethodology** is the study of the sometimes recognized but often unrecognized social order — the set of underlying shared norms and expectations that promote harmony in most everyday social interactions. That "often unrecognized social order," you might realize, suggests that ethnomethodology is concerned more with implicit than with explicit norms; both types of norms were discussed in Chapter 3, "Culture." If the distinction is not clear, you can find the discussion of these concepts on p. 57.

While one can consider ethnomethodology a form of symbolic interaction, this approach focuses on the process by which the social order develops and not on social interaction itself. In contrast to symbolic interaction, ethnomethodology has received limited attention in sociology. Nonetheless its perspective interests many sociologists, as exchange of viewpoints about the quality of the current research suggests (Bruce and Wallis, 1983; Sharrock and Watson, 1984).

Harold Garfinkel, a leading proponent of ethnomethodology, summarized the special contributions he feels the theory can make to sociology (Garfinkel, 1988). Garfinkel's studies emphasized that an effective way of grasping the significance of shared norms and expectations is to violate them. As people express their irritation, anger, or confusion in response to the violation, the functions performed by the underlying norms will become apparent.

In one informal study, Garfinkel (1967) asked undergraduate students to create informal experiments that would reveal the "seen-but-unnoticed" set of shared understandings that existed in their families. Members were horrified. The students' reports were filled with accounts of anger, astonishment, bewilderment, anxiety, and embarrassment. Parents demanded explanations. What was wrong? Was the student sick? Had he or she flunked a test at school? Garfinkel wrote, "One student acutely embarrassed his mother in front of her friends by asking if she minded if he had a snack from the refrigerator. 'Mind if you have a little snack? You've been eating little snacks around here for years without asking me. What's gotten into you?' " (Garfinkel, 1967: 47–48).

Eventually the students told their families what had been happening. Most were neither amused nor intrigued by the study. To them the underlying social order was not a subject of interest. The aroused emotions of family members demonstrated, however, that they became acutely concerned when there was a disruption of the established patterns.

Garfinkel's studies all involved contrived experimental situations. Under natural circumstances people may also find themselves facing challenges to the existing social order that reveal its unstated but nonetheless great significance. In the winter of 1846, the Donner Party, a group of travelers heading westward, was trapped by a blizzard in the Sierra Mountains. Slowly the party began starving to death. Just before he died, F. W. Graves urged his weeping, grief-stricken daughters to take any measure possible to keep themselves alive. With his last breaths, Graves insisted that the living use his flesh to sustain themselves. Soon the deed was done. An historian provided the following account, "The men finally mustered up courage to approach the dead. With averted eyes and trembling hand, pieces of flesh were severed from the inanimate forms and laid upon the coals. It was the very refinement of torture to taste such food, yet those who tasted lived." But eating human flesh was not the only horror of the situation. The historian explained:

> Although no person partook of kindred flesh, sights were often witnessed that were blood curdling. Mrs. Foster . . . fairly worshipped her brother Lemuel. Has human pen power to express the shock of horror this sister received when she saw her brother's heart thrust through with a stick, and boiling upon the coals?
>
> (McGlashan, 1879: 69–70)

It is obvious that cannibalism represents a serious violation of cultural standards. However, why this is true is not immediately self-evident. After all, few if any of us receive parental advice urging us to refrain from eating human flesh. However, we do encounter an unrelenting if often implicit emphasis on the spiritual value of human beings. To eat people is to unspeakably violate underlying normative standards: to reduce human beings to

something repulsively material. The woman who saw her brother's heart roasted and eaten was witnessing a prime symbol of love and emotion turned into mere food. Thus the survivors of the Donner Party faced a gruesome dilemma on the issue of social order. They could die, clearly violating the social order. On the other hand, they could stay alive by eating human flesh—an act that invariably defiled the social order by reducing human beings to nothing more than a source of protein.

Dramaturgic Sociology

Wearing sunglasses, Marilyn Monroe could usually appear in public without being recognized. One day she was walking down a city street with a close friend. Marilyn turned to the friend and asked, "Do you want to see me be her?" At first the friend didn't understand the question. Then she saw that something was happening, something difficult to explain. It was as though a light bulb were being turned on—an inner adjustment was occurring—and suddenly the people around began to notice that the world's most famous actress was in their midst (American Broadcasting Company, 1988).

As this illustration suggests, social interaction involves people playing parts. **Dramaturgic sociology** is a theoretical approach that analyzes social interaction as if the participants were actors in a play. Sociologists sometimes use this theory to analyze social activities; for example, a journal article examining the former wife's role at her former husband's funeral concluded that in this context standard dramaturgic-sociological concepts needed to be refined for application to this unusual, emotionally charged situation (Riedmann, 1988). Erving Goffman (1959), the creator of dramaturgic sociology, suggested that actors perform their parts, follow the script most of the time, and improvise whenever the script is unclear. People's daily performances are generally given in distinct settings. Rooms, furniture, food and drink, and so forth constitute props, the physical context of social interaction. Furthermore, as in an actual play, the setting tends to be immobile, and often the interaction cannot begin until the actors reach the setting. Even if all the people scheduled to participate in a meeting happened to meet by chance on the street a few minutes before the meeting was due to begin, they would proba-

Dramaturgic sociology emphasizes that life is a play in which people provide performances. This doctor seems to appreciate that during a consultation an effective performance involves not only the transmission of information to a patient but also the manner by which the doctor transmits that information.

bly not conduct their business right there. Customary procedures, as well as efficiency, would likely dictate that they head for the conference room.

Many performances are straightforward. Garage mechanics fix cars, and dentists take care of teeth. Salespeople in clothing stores sell dresses, suits, shirts, socks, and underwear. Sometimes, however, Goffman emphasized, people's performances are deceptive, involving a form of activity that remains concealed from the public because of its incompatibility with a respectable, honest image. For instance, there is the cigar store or barber shop owner who secretly runs a bookie joint, or workers who routinely rob their employers by stealing tools, reselling food and other supplies, or traveling on company time. Another type of deceptive performance involves the concealment of errors and mistakes, a practice that provides the impression of infallibility so important in many performances. There is a well-known saying that doctors bury their mistakes. One of the discomforting features of a malpractice suit is its

clear implication that doctors are distinctly not infallible.

Frontstage versus Backstage

Like a theater performance, social interaction may be thought to have a frontstage and a backstage. The **frontstage** is the physical area or region where people present a performance. On the frontstage people are expected to maintain certain behavioral standards toward those with whom they interact: their audience. These standards fall roughly into two categories. One category involves the treatment of the audience; Goffman designates these standards as *matters of politeness.* Waiters or waitresses are supposed to be pleasant, respectful, and attentive when they wait on customers. The second category concerns performers' behavior when they are within visual or hearing range of the audience but not necessarily in direct communication; Goffman uses the term *decorum* here. Often people within a given social context fail to appreciate the significance of standards of decorum until someone violates them. Most people would readily accept the necessity of being quiet during a funeral service. The fact that this quiet signifies respect for the deceased and his or her family would strike those present forcefully only if someone entered the service speaking in a loud, boisterous manner.

Unlike the frontstage, the backstage lies outside the audience's view. The **backstage** is the physical area or region where people construct the illusions and impressions they will use in a performance. Frequently the frontstage and backstage lie close to each other. This arrangement permits the performer to receive assistance from backstage if necessary and also allows him or her to spend brief periods of rest and relaxation in the back region, where members of the audience are unlikely to intrude. A waiter, for instance, passes through a swinging door into the kitchen, picks up "props" — the food and drink for customers — and then returns to the dining hall, which is the frontstage. In many restaurants, including the fanciest, it is essential that the audience — the customers — be kept out of the backstage, where they would probably discover conditions and practices that could destroy their appetites. The British author George Orwell, who worked in the kitchens of many French restaurants, observed that most kitchens were insufferably dirty. The cook, he conceded,

> is an artist, but his art is not cleanliness. To a certain extent he is even dirty because he is an artist, for food, to look smart, needs dirty treatment. When a steak, for instance, is brought up for the head cook's inspection, he does not handle it with a fork. He picks it up in his fingers and slaps it down, runs his thumb around the dish and licks it to taste the gravy, runs it round and licks again, then steps back and contemplates the piece of meat like an artist, judging a picture, then presses it lovingly into place with his fat, pink fingers, every one of which he has licked a hundred times that morning.
>
> (Orwell, 1959: 59)

Orwell believed that the less expensive the restaurant, the less thorough the cook's care and thus the more hygienic the preparation of food.

As people move from backstage to frontstage, they engage in **impression management:** the attempt to control others' evaluations by presenting themselves in the most favorable light. In some instances impression management is relatively easy, especially when the actor can anticipate others' reactions and can visualize a way to behave that will be mutually acceptable to everyone involved. However, in other situations the appropriate style of presentation is not readily apparent or is difficult to execute. Sometimes performers must be simultaneously concerned with impression management and with the effective maintenance of valued relationships. For instance, chief surgeons are likely to make joking comments if subordinates commit minor mistakes during operations. Such observations reflect well on the surgeons — clearly they retain a distinct yet re-

Table 5.1
Three Theories of Social Interaction

THEORY	VIEW OF HUMAN BEHAVIOR	EXAMPLE
Symbolic Interaction	The meanings individuals give people and things determine human behavior and are learned in interaction with others.	The significance some modern men give to the father role can be learned from a variety of sources, including individual or group counseling.
Ethnomethodology	An often unrecognized social order underlies everyday social activity.	Through informal research Garfinkel's students discovered some shared understandings that existed in their families.
Dramaturgic Sociology	The participants in social interaction behave like actors in a play.	When interviewed for a job, an effective candidate will engage in impression management.

laxed control over their team—and at the same time they ease the tension among team members anticipating punishment for their mistakes (Goffman, 1961: 122).

We have examined three perspectives on social interaction. None of these three theories can claim to be inherently superior to the others. Sometimes one perspective might seem more effective for analyzing a given social interaction. Often a sociologist chooses a particular approach because he or she simply favors it, feeling that the issues it emphasizes are more interesting and thought-provoking than those raised by the other perspectives. Table 5.1 compares the three theories of social interaction.

The Structuring of Social Interaction

The theoretical perspectives discussed in the previous section indicate that social interaction uses symbolic communication, that it contains an underlying social order, and that social interaction can be analyzed like the action of a play. In each case the theory reveals certain patterns that occur in social interaction. If we examine such concepts as status and role, leadership, conformity, and decision making, other patterns will become apparent, and our understanding of social interaction will increase.

Status and Role

Imagine that two twenty-year-old women—Jan and Jill—meet at a bus station. Both are on the way home from college for the spring break, and soon they are talking about their school experience. Jan has been studying over fifty hours a week ever since her freshman year. "It's the only way I can keep a high average," she explains. Jill, in contrast, is relaxed about her grades and spends a lot of time socializing, drinking, and going to parties. "We're certainly having a very different time at college," Jan says.

These two women occupy a common status: that of college student. A **status** is a position that indicates where a person fits into a group or society and how he or she should relate to others in the structure. Any particular status stands in a definite relationship to other statuses because of the rights and obligations associated with it. As college students both Jan and Jill have the right to take courses for credit, and they are expected to pay for their schooling and to complete their assignments.

Whereas both Jan and Jill occupy the status of student, they perform the role of student differently. A **role** is a set of expected behaviors associated with a particular status. Several roles may be "attached" to one status. An individual occupying the status of student may emphasize academic performance; extracurricular activities, such as student government, clubs, and athletics; or social life, particularly parties and friendships. As Figure 5.2 indicates, Jan and Jill visualize the student status very differently. Jan concentrates on the academic role, while Jill's chief concern is the partying role.

Figure 5.2
Statuses and Roles

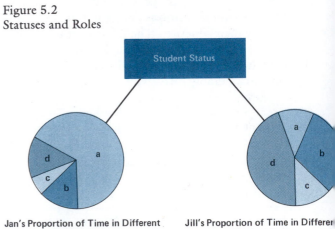

Jan's Proportion of Time in Different Student Roles

Jill's Proportion of Time in Differen Student Roles

"a" represents time doing schoolwork (studying, attending classes, speakin to professors, etc.).
"b" is time at work to pay for schooling and basic expenses.
"c" stands for extra-curricular activities (school clubs, athletic teams, etc.
"d" represents social activities.

These two students differ profoundly in their interpretation of their student status. Knowledge of their respective priorities permits som predictions about role strains. Jill, for instance, would be much more likely to interrupt studying to socialize with her friends. The resolutions to role conflicts would be difficult to predict without more knowledge of the women. For instance, how would a conscientious student like Jan respond to the pressing needs of a sic relative at exam time?

In modern societies people play many roles, and often two roles played by an individual will clash. **Role strain** is an incompatibility between two or more roles associated with the same status. For example, students experience role strain when they must decide whether to study for a test or go to a party.

Role conflict refers to incompatibility between two or more roles associated with different statuses. For instance, a certain man has the statuses of husband and businessman. In the role of husband, he recognizes that he should be concerned about his wife's happiness — he knows that she is attached to the town they live in — and thus as a husband the man wants to remain in town. In the role of businessman, however, he receives an offer for a better paying, more prestigious job with a company in another state, and so, as a businessman, he wants to leave town. Therefore this man's two role expectations are in direct conflict, and the decision on what to do will mean that either as a husband or as a businessman he will fail to meet the expectation.

In the past twenty years, a large body of research has developed on one topic involving role conflicts. What is the topic? Keep in mind that a rapid growth in social research tends to reflect events within the society. Have you got the answer?

The topic is the role conflicts faced by current adults, who must meet the often conflicting demands on their time and energy made by family members and work obligations. Many studies focus on role conflicts of working women with children (for instance, Beutell and O'Hare, 1987; Burden, 1986; McLaughlin et al. 1988), but some investigations examine the role conflicts both women and men face in reconciling the demands of family and job (for example, Farber, 1988; Kelly and Voydanoff, 1985; Wiley, 1987).

Besides the problems produced by role strain and role conflict, people can end up in situations where they are compelled to fill roles they do not want to perform. As the following Social Application indicates, such a circumstance can encourage disruptive behavior.

SOCIAL APPLICATION

The Evacuation of 400 Mental Patients

We have just discussed statuses and roles. We have considered the fact that often individuals in the same status will perform a role differently. In addition, we should note that changing circumstances sometimes encourage or even compel people to alter the way they perform their roles. In this Social Application, we will see how these two conclusions about roles apply to a situation in which patients were evacuated from one mental hospital to another and then later returned to the original hospital.

During the autumn of 1968, in the capacity of participant-observation researcher, I accompanied a group of mental-health personnel and 400 mental patients from a state-run mental hospital in Benedict, New York, near New York City, to a facility in Holzlein, New York, 400 miles away, directly south of Buffalo. The patients were moved in anticipation of a strike of nonprofessional staff workers. Two weeks later, when it was clear that there would be no strike, the patients were returned to the original hospital. In both cases the stage was the same — a train — but the attendants and the mood of many of the patients differed on the two trips. As a result the role performances were distinctly different.

On the trip to Holzlein Hospital, the attendants had been flown in from the receiving facility. Most of these people came from the town of Holzlein. There was a waiting list of people who wanted to become attendants at the hospital. The workers with whom I spoke valued their jobs, especially those working in units for the rehabilitation of long-term patients. The flight to New York City and the chance to take a tour of the city were a boost to the morale of the Holzlein attendants. Many had never been so far from home before. The train trip to Holzlein took about nine hours, and the attendants were kept busy, feeding the patients, providing medication, and helping the less agile to the bathroom. Yet even though they worked hard, most kept a positive frame of mind. The older attendants seemed pleased to see the younger, less experienced members of their units working efficiently.

During this trip I was able to spend several hours walking through the cars and talking with the attendants and the patients. None of the patients seemed openly negative about being moved, and some were distinctly positive. The following comment from a young male patient was almost joyful. "This is great! I've been in Benedict for five years, and I've never been more than about thirty miles from the city. I'm really enjoying myself!"

Two weeks later the trip back to Benedict was an entirely different matter. This time the attendants came from Benedict, and they were quite unlike their counterparts on the trip out. The Benedict staff members were residents of the New York City area. In contrast to the Holzlein attendants, they seemed to take little pride in their jobs; the position of nonprofessional mental-health worker offers relatively low pay and prestige in a major metropolitan context. During an orientation

meeting shortly before the return trip, there were indications that difficulties would develop. Several times a speaker had to rap on the table to quiet the attendants. One individual, in particular, had been drinking heavily and made loud, hostile comments throughout the meeting.

Once the train had departed, it became clear that the Benedict attendants would not perform their roles in the same pleasant, disciplined manner as their Holzlein counterparts. The Benedict attendants frequently visited friends in other cars, leaving their patients unsupervised. They also slept and drank while on duty. The care they provided patients was minimal and often hostile. Some attendants played manipulative games with the patients. At one point, for instance, the attendants were distributing soup. As each patient's name was called, he rose from his seat and came forward. One man, anticipating that he would be called next, started to stand up. An attendant shouted: "Hey, you son-of-a-bitch, get your fat ass down 'til I call you!" Then about five seconds later: "Now come up!"

In addition to the Benedict attendants' behavior, the patients' role performances helped make the return trip substantially different. Many of the patients enjoyed their two weeks at the Holzlein hospital. The atmosphere there was relatively relaxed and pleasant. A number of

the Benedict patients had formed new and meaningful ties with Holzlein patients, and they did not want to leave. Some patients who had been optimistic and hopeful on the trip out were sullen or depressed on the way back. Several who had spoken with me at length on the way out refused to say a word to me on the return trip. With their attendants frequently asleep, drunk, or absent, many of the patients were free to roam as they chose. And many did, sometimes moving from one car to the next. To make matters worse, the train had to detour around a derailment, and the return trip took nearly fifteen hours compared to scarcely nine on the way out.

Both trips were under the leadership of the same nurse, who had been dispatched from the headquarters of the Department of Mental Hygiene in Albany. On the trip out he had proudly explained his system of "loose centralization"—he would remain in a central car from which he would issue orders to attendants who would direct operations in the individual cars. On the return trip, this man's confidence visibly faded. He spoke less, appeared tense, and kept looking at his watch. When one of his associates burst into the car shouting that two attendants three cars back were making love—and this was scarcely an exaggeration—the beleaguered nurse threw his arms in the air and sighed loudly. Obviously "loose centralization" was not working well on the return trip.

Years later I'm still struck with how very different the two trips were. The two principal reasons for the difference seem related to the topic of roles: The two sets of attendants had entirely dissimilar conceptions of their roles; in addition, because of their attendants' neglect and hostility, as well as other depressing conditions about the return trip, many patients performed their role quite differently on the way back.

Source: Christopher Bates Doob. "An Evacuation of 400 Mental Patients: Implications for Continuity and Change." *Journal of Health and Social Behavior.* V. 10. September 1969, pp. 218–224.

Leadership

A man pridefully watches his son playing with a group of children in his backyard. His wife walks over, and he puts his arm around her. "That kid of ours, Judy, is giving orders like a shop foreman. He's one heck of a leader. You know what I think? I think some day Pete's going to be elected president." Like many people, Pete's father apparently believes that leadership is simply the ability to issue commands. As we see in this section, research has indicated that leadership is more complicated than that.

Leadership is the exercise of influence or authority within a group by one or more members. The study of leaders and their effectiveness has been part of an ongoing sociological investigation of the problem-solving activities of groups (Frost, Fiedler, and Anderson, 1983; Smircich and Morgan, 1982). Since early in the twentieth century, researchers have recognized that activities seem to follow a systematic pattern or, at any rate, that problem solving might be simplified if they did. In spite of this early interest, a thorough effort to map out small-group activities did not begin until after World War II. In the late 1940s, Robert Bales and his associates (Bales, 1953; Bales and Strodtbeck, 1968) set out to analyze all the basic types of interpersonal relations that occur in small groups. Studies in the late 1980s investigated the development of leadership styles (Bryman et al., 1988), the mysterious bond between leaders and followers (de Vries, 1988), and women's expectations of female and male leadership effectiveness (Russell, Rush, and Herd, 1988).

Bales studied twenty-two small groups involved in a wide variety of tasks, and he identified twelve types of communication that occurred in these groups. Six of these types are **instrumental,** intended to promote the pursuit of group goals. The other six types of communication are **expressive,** concerned with emotional or social issues. Expressive communications frequently are meant to restore the harmony disrupted in the pursuit of group goals. If a group is to function effectively, the competent performance of both types of tasks is essential. Laboratory studies indicate, however, that a single person seldom provides both expressive and instrumental leadership in a group (Bales and Slater, 1955). The skills required of each type of leader are different, and furthermore the considerable time and energy that must be devoted to providing one type of leadership often precludes actively pursuing the other type of leadership.

Small-group researchers have also assessed the consequences of different styles of leadership. One investigator studied the behavior of groups of boys subjected to three different adult leadership styles. **Authoritarian leaders** controlled all aspects of group activity yet stayed somewhat aloof from the group. **Democratic leaders** permitted group members to determine many policies and took an active role in discussions. In contrast, **laissez-faire leaders** did not take an active role and left group members free to reach their own individual or group decisions. The research showed that:

Authoritarian leadership tended to be ineffective because the group members became bogged down in internal conflicts.

Democratic leadership proved to be efficient. The quality of work in democratically led groups was better than that performed by groups with authoritarian leadership, and work motivation was stronger in a democratically led group than in an authoritarian setting. In addition, originality was more common, and greater group-mindedness and friendliness prevailed.

Under laissez-faire leadership, the group members did less work, and the quality of the work accomplished was poorer than was the case in democratic contexts. More time was spent playing.

In any particular situation, a number of factors are likely to influence the effectiveness of a particular style of leadership. Among the relevant factors are:

The followers' opinion of the leader. If group members like and trust the leader, then compliance is more likely.

The amount of power invested in the leadership position. If a leader has indisputable power in a group situation, then followers are likely to obey that person, whether or not he or she is popular in their eyes.

The task involved. If the task is an activity that seems understandable and reasonable to the participants,

then they will probably try to accomplish it (Fiedler, 1967).

If all three factors are positive, then leadership is likely to be effective. If a popular, respected army captain receives an order from the general calling for a practice maneuver that the company has performed many times, the captain is likely to obtain the whole-hearted support of the troops. On the other hand, if an untrustworthy business executive who, according to rumors, is likely to be dismissed undertakes a vague project that none of the associates understands, the executive probably will not receive much support from subordinates.

An interesting problem involves the challenge

As the group therapy session below indicates, some group settings encourage role performances that are emotional and spontaneous, while in others, such as this business meeting, members' role performances are more structured and controlled emotionally and most likely follow a formal agenda.

of supplying leadership to groups that are largely self-managed. A study of self-managed work groups within a production plant has indicated that there is a fine line between overdirection and underdirection. So-called *unleaders* tend to be most effective when they have well-developed social skills and act as counselors or communication facilitators. Frequently such people refuse to provide answers themselves; instead they ask reflective questions, throwing the burden of decision-making back on the group itself (Manz and Sims, 1984).

The following Cross-Cultural Perspective takes a sociological perspective on a prominent leader's rise to prominence.

CROSS-CULTURAL PERSPECTIVE

The Development of Gorbachev's Leadership

Why does an individual become an important world leader? In the case of Mikhail Gorbachev, it is tempting to believe that his extraordinary personal qualities vaulted him to Soviet and world prominence. But is it that simple? Let's consider.

Mr. Gorbachev has been the General Secretary of the Communist Party in the Soviet Union for several years. As the Soviet leader, he has initiated a major program of planned reform involving all major aspects of living, especially the economic realm. But the biggest changes seem to have been occurring in the political and cultural arenas. In what had been one of the world's most secretive countries, people are starting to express their desires and grievances. Internationally Gorbachev has traveled to many nations, including the United States. The results have been improved relations and concrete steps toward de-escalation of the arms race.

Using the sociological perspective, you might observe that in the Soviet Union, pre-

vailing social conditions favored a new type of leadership. Under Leonid Brezhnev, Gorbachev's predecessor, the economy had stagnated; little technological development was occurring, and in the cost, quality, and availability of consumer products, the Soviet Union had lost considerable ground to Western nations. In addition, artistic and creative output was low-quality, with many leading artists either repressed or exiled. Meanwhile a growing, young, middle-class group was much better educated than their parents and becoming increasingly frustrated by the decline in opportunities to improve their economic and social status.

Social conditions in Soviet society encouraged Gorbachev's rise to power and the innovative policies he introduced, but the man's personal qualities have also helped. Unlike some other general secretaries, Gorbachev has the ability to draw other party members to him and then provide them with guidance. One social scien-

tist wrote, "Among his close supporters and aides he has been able to create in this very short period of time an aura of exceptionality, of charisma" (Bialer, 1988: 417).

Gorbachev's personal style helps produce a very positive reaction. He has been the first Soviet leader since Lenin to speak, not read, his speeches. As a speaker he is both exciting and convincing. He is also adept at informal exchanges, telling jokes and impressing people by appearing to be genuinely interested in their work and their lives.

While visiting New York City in December 1988, Gorbachev demonstrated his well-known ability to work a crowd. With a knack for the dramatic, he ordered his limousine driver to screech to a halt on Broadway. Beneath a huge neon Coca-Cola advertisement, the Soviet leader raised his arms in a victory salute. As the Gorbachev party drove through the city, huge crowds of people struggled to see the man who in just a few years has become the world's most celebrated politician.

What twists and turns Gorbachev's leadership will take in the years ahead is, of course, unforeseeable. One point seems clear, however —that social conditions in the Soviet Union and elsewhere, as well as the man's unusual personality, will affect the outcome.

Sources: Seweryn Bialer. "Gorbachev's Program of Change: Sources, Significance, Prospects." *Political Science Quarterly.* V. 103. Fall 1988, pp. 403–460; Maureen Dowd. "The Star Is a Smash in the Street Scenes." *New York Times.* December 8, 1988, p. A1+; David Holloway. "Gorbachev's New Thinking." *Foreign Affairs.* V. 68. No. 1, 1989, pp. 66–81; George Soros. "The Gorbachev Prospect." *New York Review of Books.* V. 36. June 1, 1989, pp. 16–18+.

Conformity

Conformity is an individual's behavior in line with the relevant social norms. Society could not survive without considerable conformity, and yet excessive conformity suggests mindlessness, an inability to think and act on one's own. In Hans Christian Andersen's fairy tale "The Emperor's New Clothes," all the subjects watching the king were excessive conformists, acting in line with the official norm that their ruler was wearing beautiful new clothes, even though he was actually naked. Finally a little girl commented loudly that the king was wearing nothing. As soon as the little girl had spoken, her father said, "Just hear what the innocent says." Quickly the word spread through the crowd of conformists that the king was indeed naked.

A wide range of research has been conducted on the topic of conformity. Studies have examined the relationship between low self-esteem and conformity (Hurley and Meminger, 1987), the association between men's sexual orientation and their boyhood gender conformity (Hockenberry and Billingham, 1987), and the relationship between shame and conformity (Scheff, 1988). Solomon Asch's experiments are among the best known investigations of conformity.

The Asch Experiments

Some years ago Asch (1963), a social psychologist, devised an experiment to explore how group pressure affects judgment. The original study featured a control group and an experimental group. In the control situation, people sat in a room without talking and examined two set of cards. As Figure 5.3 indicates, there was one line on the card on the left, and the card on the right held three lines, only one of which exactly matched the length of the line on the first card. Each person recorded the number of the line on the second card that seemed to be the same length as the line on the first card. Altogether there were twelve sets of cards, and in each case there was one obvious match between the single line on the first card and the three lines on the second. Virtually no mistakes were made, indicating that normally people had no difficulty accomplishing this task.

In the experimental group, there were eight men. Seven of them were confederates, who had met previously with the experimenter, who had instructed them to respond at certain points with unanimous, incorrect judgments. The eighth person, the actual subject, who confronted this unanimous majority, was the real focus. Asch wrote, "He faced, possibly for the first time in his life, a situation in which a group unanimously contradicted the evidence of his senses" (Asch, 1963: 179).

Figure 5.3
A Sample Comparison of Lines in the Asch Experiment

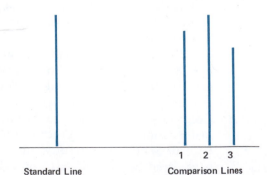

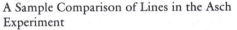

Control subjects made correct matchings over 99 percent of the time. Experimental subjects conformed to incorrect matchings one-third of the time when faced with the unanimous incorrect matchings of seven confederates. (Source: Solomon E. Asch. Social Psychology. Englewood Cliffs, NJ: Prentice-Hall. 1952, p. 452.)

The results from the experimental group were very different from those that emerged from the control group. In the experimental context, a third of the total number of matchings made by the subject were factually incorrect, conforming to the prearranged stated judgment of the confederates.

Variations in the experimental setup produced different results. When there were two subjects, the incidence of conformity to the group opinion dropped sharply. If, however, this "true partner" suddenly stopped giving accurate answers and sided with the majority, then the incidence of conformity rose to 28.5 percent, nearly as high as in the original experiment. Asch also varied the group size of confederates. When there was only one person who had been instructed to give incorrect answers, conforming responses by the subjects practically disappeared. With two confederates 12.8 percent of the naive subjects' responses were conforming. Conformity rose to the one-third level when there was a majority of three opposing the subject. Larger groups of confederates (four, eight, and sixteen) did not significantly increase the level of conformity.

Subsequent experiments have tried to refine Asch's results. For instance, in experiments similar to those conducted by Asch, Jennings and George (1984) sought to determine the extent to which the distortion of judgment produced by group influence was conscious or unconscious. They found that conscious distortion of judgment occurred four to five times more frequently than unconscious distortion. Since the research subjects were aware of their incorrect judgments, it can be assumed that they felt that it was more important to support the group judgment than to be correct.

While some people are probably disturbed by the mindlessness often accompanying conformity, conforming behavior generally does not arouse strong reactions until cases are revealed in which people felt compelled to obey orders to commit brutal acts. If a person is already inclined to commit such acts, then the support of authority figures simply makes such behavior easier, as the following illustration suggests. In January 1942, Adolph Eichmann, head of the Jewish Office in the German Secret Police (Gestapo), met with a group of top-level Nazi civil servants to coordinate efforts to the Final Solution, Hitler's plan to exterminate the Jews of Europe. Eichmann still

In extreme form conformity is frightening and dangerous. The deputies of the German Reichstag saluting in unison Hitler's arrival represents a vivid illustration of such a phenomenon.

122 had some doubts about "such a bloody solution through violence," but when he observed this group of elite civil servants competing against one another to take the initiative in the genocidal effort, he felt freed of guilt. As Eichmann told the court at his trial in Jerusalem, he not only obeyed orders but also was following the new law of the land (Berkowitz, 1980: 316–317). We well might wonder whether the members of modern societies can eventually eliminate the conditions producing Eichmanns.

Decision Making

There is an old saying that two heads are better than one. This proverb is certainly valid if the "two heads" are trying to make a decision that can be based on factual knowledge. For instance, a team of people do better at a crossword puzzle than a single individual. Similarly a clinic that employs a variety of medical specialists is likely to be better equipped than a single physician to diagnose and treat a wide range of illnesses.

In other situations it is less clear whether an individual or a group will make better decisions. One researcher first asked individual subjects to reach decisions on hypothetical problems and then combined the individuals into groups and instructed them to reach group decisions. The latter decisions often displayed a "risky shift," a move toward a more daring course of action (Stoner, 1961). One reason this occurred is that a group decision diffuses responsibility among the members, particularly if the decision turns out to be bad.

The vast literature on the topic includes studies analyzing the impact on decision making of rationality (Cohen and Jaffray, 1988), work values (Ravlin and Meglino, 1987), and shared responsibility and goal interdependence (Tjosvold, 1988). A number of factors affect group decision making. Among them are:

Members' personality characteristics. More extroverted, dominant, and socially aggressive people are likely to control discussion and generally will have the lion's share of influence on the decisions reached.

Prior commitments. People who join a group with a particular solution in mind usually will argue forcibly in favor of their position and will firmly oppose alternative decisions.

Group composition. The more varied the available perspectives on a problem, the more likely that a high-quality solution will emerge. When group members encompass a diversity of personalities, leadership abilities, and points of view, their decisions are generally more creative and innovative than those that emerge from groups whose members have similar characteristics. However, different viewpoints can create strain, and when group members become openly antagonistic, they cannot fully capitalize on their diversity. The tendency of many secondary groups to emphasize their "we feeling" and deemphasize members' differences of opinion is examined in Chapter 4, "Groups," p. 86.

Interpersonal relationships. Positive feelings among group members increase people's sense of security, making them more willing to risk unusual solutions. By contrast, group members' loss of positive feelings about each other tends to block or distort their communication (Hoffman, 1979).

Is it possible to train individuals, particularly specialists in some field, to make more effective decisions than they would make without training? Such so-called *gaming* was first done with simulated military situations and has been adopted by some major corporations. Lincoln Bloomfield, the father of modern military gaming, explained, "You're trying out a strategy or a tactic before you're committed to it, or you're looking for alternatives you may have missed or discarded. . ." (Schofield, 1989: 8).

Decision-making specialists differ about whether the gaming process sufficiently sharpens professionals' skills for uncovering crucial but easily overlooked questions to justify the cost. Clearly whether or not to engage in gaming is itself a difficult decision.

The Disruption of Patterns of Social Interaction

In the last two sections, we examined theories and concepts that demonstrate how the social-interaction process works. These analyses have emphasized the central role that social interaction plays in human relations. Further support for that conclusion becomes apparent if we examine situations where there is a breakdown in the normal social-interaction patterns. The absence of such patterns will suggest their importance in maintaining people's sense of well-being.

Frequently people experience stress when isolated. Research indicates that there are several stages isolated people are likely to pass through (Schachter, 1959). In the beginning these people often experience full-blown anxiety attacks that increase with time and then decrease sharply in many cases. As the sense of isolation diminishes, there is apathy or even withdrawal and detachment. Finally the isolated individual may dream, fantasize, or even hallucinate about other people.

Many human beings are highly adaptive in a solitary condition. A small number of hearty individuals have sailed alone around the world, in small boats, apparently without suffering significant psychological damage. Admiral Richard Byrd, an experienced polar explorer, spent the winter of 1933 completely alone in his camp in Antarctica. Such people have been able to withstand their isolation because they have had activities to keep busy. Individuals in situations of forced isolation seem to do better when they invent tasks for themselves, such as solving puzzles, reciting poetry, or performing exercises.

Patterns of social interaction are also disrupted when communities disintegrate because of such factors as disasters, widespread ill health, extensive poverty, and rapid technological change. Various alternatives confront people. They can leave, rebuilding their lives elsewhere; they can stay, deciding that in spite of the disruptions, the possibility of rebuilding their community and reestablishing effective patterns of social interaction definitely exists; or they can stay because they no longer possess the will to take active steps on their own behalf.

Totalitarian governments can also disrupt patterns of social interaction. During the Nazi period, nonparticipants and victims reacted in a number of ways to the events of the era. Many average citizens were shocked by the persecution, mass torture, and murder of millions of Jews and other victims of the Third Reich. Both during and after World War II, many Germans found that the most expedient course of action was to avoid talking and, if possible, thinking about this dreaded subject. In some cases people's ability to avoid the topic was so well developed that they were simply unable to maintain their concentration whenever the subject arose in conversation (Hughes, 1968).

Under Hitler's rule life had become a nightmare for Jews. They were deprived of all civil rights, including the right to retain personal property, to be employed, to practice a profession, or to enter restaurants, cafés, bathing beaches, or public parks. They could expect to receive the foulest, most vicious insults or to suffer arrest. In Vienna many Jews spoke of committing suicide with no more emotion than discussing an hour's journey by train. Sometimes killing themselves seemed easier than living in a situation in which normal social-interaction patterns had been shattered (Gedye, 1939).

Within Nazi concentration camps, inmates made significant adjustments in their outlook and behavior. Bruno Bettelheim, a psychologist and survivor of a Nazi concentration camp, noted that prisoners had made the ultimate surrender to camp life as soon as they accepted the Gestapo guards' values as their own and imitated their behavior. Many old prisoners would mistreat and even torture newcomers, appropriate any available patches of Gestapo uniforms and sew them on their own, and adopt guards' anti-Semitic sentiments, even if they were Jewish themselves (Bettelheim, 1958).

Yet even in concentration camps, some opportunities arose to elevate people's spirits, making them feel better about themselves and about the circumstances in which they lived. Viktor Frankl, a psychiatrist, was interned in a Nazi concentration camp during World War II. At a moment when the situation was particularly desperate and the prisoners' morale especially low, the power in the compound went out. The block warden called on Frankl to provide some psychological counseling. Cold, hungry, irritable, and tired as he was,

124

Frankl nonetheless realized that if he failed to say something helpful, many men were likely to commit suicide. Therefore he started by explaining that their situation was far from the most terrible imaginable. As long as they remained alive, health, family, happiness, professional standing, and social position could be restored. He told his companions that human life never ceases to have meaning and that it includes suffering, privation, and death. Frankl also spoke about sacrifice and its meaning. In the course of his speech, he established intense social interaction with his listeners that reminded them that love, hope, and other positive qualities had not disappeared from the earth. Frankl wrote, "When the electric bulb flared up again, I saw the miserable figures of my friends limping toward me to thank me with tears in their eyes" (Frankl, 1959: 84).

AIDS or another lethal disease, homelessness, divorce, or death of a loved one — these are common disruptive events in current Americans' lives. The sociological perspective can be applied to each of them. One can examine the social and nonsocial factors that have produced the disruptive situation, analyze the sequence of events that occur as the individual or group confronts the problem, and speculate about people's adaptation after the crisis has passed.

STUDY GUIDE

Learning Objectives

After studying this chapter, you should be able to:

1. Define social interaction and discuss its significance in people's lives.
2. Discuss symbolic interaction, ethnomethodology, and dramaturgic sociology, defining each theory and offering clear, detailed examples of all three.
3. Define status and role, distinguishing between the two concepts by using clear illustrations.
4. Discuss role strain and role conflict, clarifying their differences and providing an example of each.
5. Define leadership, examine the leadership styles of authoritarian, democratic, and laissez-faire leaders, and identify the factors determining leadership effectiveness.
6. Analyze conformity, defining the concept and summarizing the major findings of the Asch experiments.
7. Examine the factors that affect group decision making.
8. Indicate how social-interaction patterns may become disrupted and how people may react or adapt to such disruption.

Summary

1. Social interaction is the basic process through which two or more people use language and gestures to affect each other's thoughts, expectations, and behavior. Social interaction provides the foundation of people's development.

2. Theories of social interaction include symbolic interaction, ethnomethodology, and dramaturgic sociology. Symbolic interaction is a theory that emphasizes the importance of symbolic communication — gestures and, above all, language — in the development of the individual, group, and society. To understand symbolic interaction, researchers must study the meanings of social interaction.

Ethnomethodology is the study of the sometimes recognized, often unrecognized social order. Harold Garfinkel's informal experiments have supplied the pioneer research in this theoretical area.

Dramaturgic sociology is a theoretical approach that analyzes interaction as if the participants were actors in a play. The actors perform their parts, follow the script if possible, and improvise whenever the script is unclear or nonexistent. Dramaturgic sociology emphasizes that like a theater performance, social interaction involves a frontstage and a backstage. Performers also engage in impression management—an attempt to control others' evaluations by presenting themselves in the most favorable manner.

3. Concepts that play a significant part in social interaction include status and role, leadership, conformity, and decision making. A status is a position that indicates where a person fits into a group or society and how that person should relate to others in the structure. A role is a set of expected behaviors associated with a particular status. Role strains and role conflicts also influence group activities.

Leadership is another important component of the social-interaction process. Studies of leadership demonstrate that two broad sets of leadership tasks exist: the instrumental and the expressive; and that different kinds of leadership develop: the democratic, authoritarian, and laissez-faire varieties.

In examining social interaction, some researchers have studied conformity, an individual's behavior in line with the relevant social norms. The well-known Asch experiments have demonstrated how group pressure affects judgment.

Decision making is another prominent social-interaction process. Factors affecting group decision making include members' personality characteristics, their prior commitments, the group composition, and members' interpersonal relations.

4. Disruption of social-interaction patterns can profoundly affect people's lives. When people are experiencing the stress of being alone or of surviving within a totalitarian setting, their behavior will demonstrate a number of different adjustments.

Key Terms

authoritarian leader   a leader who controls all aspects of group activity yet stays somewhat aloof from the group

backstage   the physical area or region where people construct the illusions and impressions they will use in a performance

conformity   an individual's behavior in line with the relevant social norms

democratic leader   a leader who permits group members to determine many policies and take an active role in discussion

dramaturgic sociology   a theoretical approach that analyzes social interaction as if the participants were actors in a play

ethnomethodology   the study of the sometimes recognized, often unrecognized social order, the set of underlying shared norms and expectations that promote harmony in most everyday social interactions

expressive   concerned with emotional or social issues

frontstage   the physical area or region where people present a performance

impression management   the attempt to control others' evaluations by presenting oneself in the most favorable light

instrumental   intended to promote the pursuit of group goals

laissez-faire leader   a leader who does not take an active role in group discussions, leaving group members free to reach individual or group decisions

leadership   the exercise of influence or authority within a group by one or more members

role   a set of expected behaviors associated with a particular status

role conflict   an incompatibility between two or more roles associated with different statuses

role strain   an incompatibility between two or more roles associated with the same status

social interaction   the basic process through which two or more people use language and gestures to affect each other's thoughts, expectations, and behavior

status   a position that indicates where a person fits into a group or society and how that person should relate to others in the structure

symbolic-interaction theory   a theory that emphasizes the importance of symbolic communication—gestures and, above all, language—in the development of the individual, group, and society

Tests

True – false Test

_____   1. Researchers using the symbolic-interaction theory are concerned with the meanings individuals give to people and things.

_____   2. Garfinkel's ethnomethodological study of his students' families showed that to most family members the underlying social order was not a very interesting subject.

_____   3. According to the dramaturgic-sociological perspective, frontstage and backstage often lie close together, allowing performers to receive assistance from backstage.

_____   4. Several statuses may be "attached" to one role.

_____   5. In a role-conflict situation, the fulfillment of one role expectation means that another role expectation will not be met.

_____   6. In recent years there has been almost no research done on role conflicts.

_____   7. Instrumental leaders are concerned with emotional or social issues.

_____   8. Mikhail Gorbachev's rise to leadership can be entirely attributed to his extraordinary personal qualities.

_____   9. In the Asch experiments that explored how group pressure affects judgment, the behavior in the experimental group was sometimes very different from the behavior in the control group.

_____ 10. Bruno Bettelheim reported that prisoners had made their final adjustment to Nazi concentration camps when they accepted Gestapo guards' values as their own and imitated the guards' behavior.

Multiple-choice Test

_____   1. According to the discussion of the changing father role:
   a. most men find it easy to be open emotionally.
   b. some men want to try to become the father they wish they had.
   c. group counseling cannot change men's conception of the father role.
   d. a and b

_____   2. The Donner party described in this chapter faced a challenge to the social order when its members had to choose between death or survival by committing:
   a. war atrocities.
   b. cannibalism.
   c. violations against animals they worshiped.
   d. incest.

_____ 3. Using a dramaturgic-sociological perspective, Goffman suggested that the performances people give are:
   a. independent of the social setting.
   b. only done in the backstage.
   c. always done without impression management.
   d. sometimes based on deception.

_____ 4. An incompatibility between two or more roles associated with the *same* status is a:
   a. role conflict.
   b. role strain.
   c. anticipatory status.
   d. conformity conflict.

_____ 5. Bales and Slater studied communication in task-oriented groups. They found that:
   a. instrumental and expressive leadership skills are similar.
   b. the typical leader has well-developed instrumental and expressive skills.
   c. only very nervous people have instrumental skills.
   d. both sets of skills are necessary for a group to function effectively.

_____ 6. According to this chapter, all but one of the following conditions contributes to a leader's effectiveness. Which factor is NOT included?
   a. the leader's power
   b. followers' opinion of the leader
   c. the leader's attractiveness
   d. the task involved

_____ 7. Jennings and George's experiments that sought to refine Asch's research on conformity found that:
   a. surprisingly, Asch's results were incorrect.
   b. conscious distortion of judgment occurred four to five times more frequently than unconscious distortion.
   c. unconscious distortion of judgment occurred four to five times more frequently than conscious distortion.
   d. Americans are much less likely to conform than people in other countries.

_____ 8. Group decision making is affected by:
   a. members' prior commitments.
   b. backstage activities.
   c. the influence of control groups.
   d. role strain.

_____ 9. Gaming:
   a. was first performed in simulated military situations.
   b. is now approved by all decision-making specialists.
   c. can only be used for recreational activities.
   d. b and c

_____ 10. Viktor Frankl, a psychiatrist, was interned in a Nazi concentration camp. He assisted prisoners by:
   a. helping them escape.
   b. helping them commit suicide.
   c. reminding them of positive qualities still existing on earth.
   d. obtaining permission to turn off lights and make horrors less visible.

Essay Test

1. List and discuss two theories of social interaction, providing definitions of each and your own examples (*not* those in this chapter) representing the major issues and concepts of each theory.
2. Define status and role, drawing a clear distinction between the two terms. Write about a social situation that demonstrates the meanings of the two concepts. Use this same situation to illustrate the meanings of role conflict and role strain.
3. Define leadership and also three different leadership styles. Discuss the leadership style in two groups in which you participate. Are the styles effective in both cases? Explain.
4. Define conformity and discuss in detail the findings of the Asch experiments.
5. Discuss how people are likely to respond to the disruption of social-interaction patterns within their communities.

Suggested Readings

Blumer, Herbert. 1969. *Symbolic Interactionism: Perspective and Method*. Englewood Cliffs, NJ: Prentice-Hall. A thorough, thoughtful, if somewhat abstract introduction to symbolic interaction by an authority on the subject. The opening essay is particularly informative.

Caughey, John L. 1984. *Imaginary Social Worlds: A Cultural Approach*. Lincoln: University of Nebraska Press. An innovative, interesting book discussing and analyzing the intimate relationship between imaginary social worlds (as represented, for instance, by television, in dreams, and in psychotic experiences) and the real social world.

Erikson, Kai. 1976. *Everything in Its Path: Destruction of Community in the Buffalo Creek Flood*. New York: Simon and Schuster. A nicely written, well-documented account of what happened to the interaction patterns of a tightly knit mining community when it was ravaged by a flood.

Garfinkel, Harold. 1967. *Studies in Ethnomethodology*. Englewood Cliffs, NJ: Prentice-Hall. A set of eight challenging articles outlining Garfinkel's informal studies of the social order underlying all social interactions.

Goffman, Erving. 1959. *The Presentation of Self in Everyday Life*. Garden City, NY: Doubleday. An introduction to some of the intricacies and subtleties of social interaction. Goffman discusses the devices people use to influence others' perceptions of them. The illustrative material is colorful, wide-ranging, and thought-provoking.

Golding, William. 1954. *Lord of the Flies*. New York: Coward-McCann. A classic novel describing how a group of boys gradually deteriorates into savagery following an airplane crash. Group decision making, leadership, and the influence of groups on individuals are important themes throughout the account.

Hare, A. Paul. 1982. *Creativity in Small Groups*. Beverly Hills, CA: Sage Publications. A clearly written, well-organized presentation of important processes, concepts, and theories involving the social interaction of small groups.

Janis, Irving L. 1972. *Victims of Groupthink*. Boston: Houghton Mifflin. Use of case studies of the Bay of Pigs invasion, the escalation of the Vietnam War, the Cuban missile crisis, and other important international confrontations to illustrate the process by which top governmental leaders make both foolish and effective decisions.

Orwell, George. 1959. *Down and Out in Paris and London*. New York: Berkeley Medallion Books. Originally published in 1933. The youthful adventures of the well-known writer when he was cleaning pots in Paris restaurants and living as a tramp in England. The book reads like a gripping novel and is filled with insights about social-interaction patterns.

Worchel, Stephen, J. Cooper, and George R. Goethals. 1988. *Understanding Social Psychology*. Belmont, CA: Wadsworth. A comprehensive textbook introducing students to sociology's sister discipline and examining in detail the major concepts presented in this chapter.

Additional Assignments

1. Select a place to eat — a fast-food restaurant, a student cafeteria, or a fairly expensive restaurant. As you eat, make mental notes (to be recorded as soon as you leave) regarding the physical layout, behavior of patrons, interaction of patrons and waiters and waitresses, or other important features of the setting. When you are alone, try to visualize the activity as if you were going to write and produce a play. Would social interaction flow more smoothly if any of the actions, settings, or props were changed? Did you detect any failures in impression management? Did any actions occur in the frontstage that more appropriately should have occurred backstage? Compare your findings with those obtained by other students.

2. Among people you like and trust (such as friends, family members, or roommates), violate a fairly minor social norm. Note people's immediate reactions. After the violation behave as though you had done nothing wrong or unusual, and observe others' reactions for the next few minutes. Do they seem to be encouraging you to maintain conforming behavioral patterns? Complete this informal experiment by explaining what you have done and what sociologists seek to learn from such research. How did you feel during the experiment? Did this experience give you insight into the Garfinkel and Asch studies presented in the text?

Answers to Objective Test Questions

True–false Test

1. t	4. f	7. f	9. t
2. t	5. t	8. f	10. t
3. t	6. f		

Multiple-choice Test

1. b	4. b	7. b	9. a
2. b	5. d	8. a	10. c
3. d	6. c		

6
SOCIALIZATION

The Origin of Human Development

The Results of Deprived Socialization

Theories of Socialization

Sociological Theories of Socialization
Psychological Theories of Socialization
Comparisons of the Four Theories

Sources of Socialization

The Family
Mass Media
Peers
Schools and Day-care Centers
Additional Agents of Socialization
Total Institutions

Tough Times: Transitions in the Socialization Process

Adolescence
Job Loss
Divorce
Death of Spouse
Conclusion

Study Guide

The account began on a low note. Dibs was a five-year-old problem child attending a private school in New York City. Some of the teachers thought he was mentally handicapped. Certainly his behavior was unusual. Most of the time, he crawled around the edge of the room, sucking his thumb or chewing on his hand and lying rigid on the floor when anyone tried to involve him in school activity. After two years the teachers decided that something had to be done about Dibs. Parents were complaining about him, particularly on occasions when he scratched or bit children who came too close to him. Virginia Axline (1968), a clinical psychologist who specialized in working with children, was called in at this point. Dr. Axline was asked to meet with Dibs and his mother and then to offer suggestions. Interviewing Dibs's mother, Dr. Axline soon learned that she had been putting tremendous pressure on her son to achieve since early infancy. His response had been to withdraw.

The first time Dibs went to visit Dr. Axline, he spent a long time just standing in the middle of the play-therapy room. Finally he walked slowly across the room and then moved along the walls. He passed from one toy to another, tentatively touching them. Then he began calling the toys by name — dog, cat, rabbit. He turned to the dolls and the doll house. He looked at the house and said over and over, "No lock doors. No lock doors. No lock doors." There was desperation in Dibs's voice. He kept playing with the doll house, eventually finding that the walls could be removed. "No like walls. Dibs no like walls." And in the playroom Dibs started taking down the emotional walls that had been built around him.

Every Thursday at 3 P.M., Dibs and Dr. Axline met for an hour. At each session Dibs's awareness that he was free to do as he wished increased. Never before had he been so free, and from one meeting to the next Dibs became more talkative and active. Dr. Axline's part was important. She was there to respond to Dibs in the free and open atmosphere of the play-therapy room, to let him know by her unspoken approval that what he was doing, and thus he, himself, was acceptable to her.

With Dr. Axline's help, Dibs was undergoing **socialization,** the process by which a person becomes a social being, learning the necessary cultural content and behavior to become a member of a group or society. Socialization is most apparent in childhood when the basic elements of culture are learned, but the process continues throughout people's lifetimes as they change their group affiliations and thus must learn new ways of thinking and acting.

You are in many ways a product of socialization. For one thing you have been significantly influenced by your parents. Perhaps you do not even recognize the extent to which you have adopted their beliefs, values, and behavioral patterns as your own, but if you analyze your family life, you will recognize that both the many things you were taught and the patterns you observed in your family influenced the development of your standards and behavior. For this reason you are probably different from your friends or classmates. You get angry faster or perhaps slower, you drink more or perhaps less, or you study many more hours or perhaps fewer. You can recognize that others have also contributed to your socialization: friends, neighbors, and teachers. Furthermore socialization continues throughout the entire life span. Perhaps you have older parents, grandparents, or other elderly acquaintances, and you can observe the extent to which modern values and lifestyle and perhaps retirement have affected them. In American society people often pride themselves on being independent and self-reliant, but we are social animals, and we require socialization in order to function competently in group situations.

In examining socialization, this chapter is concerned with the process of the individual's growth in the social world. The following section assesses the factors that determine human development. Next we consider the effects of deprived childhood socialization, followed by a summary of four important theories of socialization. Our fourth topic concerns sources of socialization, and the chapter closes with a look at certain common socialization experiences people find difficult.

The Origin of Human Development

In the film *Trading Places,* two wealthy brothers have a bet. One wagers that if they use their influence to manipulate a number of circumstances, a certain successful businessman will become a criminal, and a particular poor, uneducated con man will become a successful businessman. The other brother disagrees, believing that no matter what the circumstances, "breeding" will prevent the two men from trading places. The first brother wins the bet. His perspective on human development has been more prominent in our society, where achievement receives more emphasis than heredity. However, for over a century, controversy has raged on the issue of nature versus nurture: Are human beings the product of their **nature** (their inborn biological characteristics or heredity), their **nurture** (their socialization), or some combination of both?

The "nature" position dominated the thinking of most scholars in the nineteenth century. For example, the renowned biologist Charles Darwin emphasized *natural selection*—the view that in the struggle for space, food, and shelter, the most adaptable members of a species will live, and the less adaptable will perish. In sociologist Herbert Spencer's words, this is the principle of "the survival of the fittest." This principle proved useful to many elitist nineteenth-century political and economic leaders. They could justify their positions of dominance by arguing that the fact that they held such exalted posts was merely an indication of their natural superiority. Such people would say that there was nothing wrong with exploiting the poor in the United States and elsewhere in the world. They would say that individuals' poverty and deprivation were clear indications of innate inferiority, and, like beasts of burden, inferior human beings should be exploited.

Some social scientists who shared the heredity-oriented approach began to focus their analysis on **instincts**—unalterable behavior complexes that parents transmit genetically to their children. In the late nineteenth century, psychologists started to compile lists of what they believed to be human instincts and went on to attribute many behavioral patterns to them. Thus warfare was supposedly the result of an "aggressive" instinct, capitalism of an "acquisitive" instinct, and society of a "herding" instinct. These simplistic analyses overlooked the massive evidence suggesting that such types of behavior are principally learned. If these behaviors were instinctual, then they would occur in all societies, and they do not. Societies exist where most people are nonaggressive and nonacquisitive, and under certain circumstances people will voluntarily isolate themselves.

By the early twentieth century, the "nature" perspective had begun to lose support. Ivan Pavlov, a Russian physiologist, proved that he could train or condition dogs to exhibit an involuntary response, such as salivation, when they heard the ringing of a bell. The writings of John B. Watson, an American psychologist, emphasized the same general conclusion: Nurture is the most important factor in human development. According to Watson (1924), children can be turned into anything—doctors, lawyers, artists, beggars, or thieves—depending on how they are raised. The well-known contemporary psychologist B. F. Skinner (1972) made a similar point, claiming that such environmental influences as parental approval and social custom lead us to want to do certain things.

In the past two decades, a new school of thought emphasizing the importance of heredity has emerged. Proponents of **sociobiology** argue that through the evolutionary process, human beings have acquired tendencies that determine much of their behavior. Edward Wilson (1978), a zoologist, has claimed that among human beings, behaviors such as aggression, selfishness, territoriality, and the tendency to form dominance hierarchies are both innate and universal. Accord-

134

ing to Wilson and other sociobiologists, government officials planning public policy should take into account certain alleged inflexible tendencies in human nature.

Many sociologists have sharply criticized sociobiology, arguing that little supportive evidence has been presented in defense of this perspective and that unlike sociologists, sociobiologists pay almost no attention to the effects of social, political, and economic factors on the societies about which they generalize. However, social scientists have produced both essays (Davies, 1987; Kemper, 1987) and studies (Mulder, 1987; Rushton and Nicholson, 1988) that offer support for a modified sociobiological position. Thus these specialists argue that human behavior will be enhanced if both genetic and cultural factors are examined.

The Results of Deprived Socialization

Both nature and nurture affect human development, but the sociological perspective decidedly emphasizes nurture. The present section implicitly supports the nurture position, which suggests that from early infancy an intimate relationship between child and caretaker establishes a child's sense of well-being and permits the child to develop the social and intellectual skills necessary for effective participation in society. When children are deprived of such relationships, their development is seriously affected.

Three decades ago Harry Harlow and his associates at the University of Wisconsin conducted research on the effects of extreme isolation on young rhesus monkeys (Harlow and Harlow, 1962; Harlow and Zimmerman, 1959). Harlow found that the monkeys isolated in his labs showed behavior similar to that of human psychotics: They were afraid of and hostile toward other monkeys, and, in general, they acted sluggish and reclusive. In one experiment Harlow built two artificial "mothers." One was built of wire mesh and dispensed milk, while the other, which was similar in size and shape, was made from a terrycloth bath towel and offered the comfort of soft contact but not milk. During the 165-day period that the infant monkeys spent with both "mothers," they showed a marked preference for the cloth substitute, spending an average of sixteen hours per day clutching the cloth figure compared to one and a half hours on the wire mesh. Apparently the need for contact with a soft object proved more compelling than the need to reduce hunger.

Of course, researchers cannot devise experiments where children are purposefully deprived of nurture. One investigator, however, discovered a situation in which caretakers for children were very scarce. René Spitz (1945) conducted a study that compared infants raised by their own mothers with infants of the same age raised in an orphanage. The first group of children had extensive social involvement with their mothers, while the orphans were kept isolated in small cubicles, with no human contact beyond feeding, clothing changes, and doctoring. After eighteen months the two groups showed dramatic differences. One third of the orphans were dead, and the remainder were physically, intellectually, and emotionally handicapped. The children raised by their mothers were physically and mentally healthy.

Kingsley Davis's (1948) case studies of two isolated girls provide further evidence for the harmful effects of depriving children of conventional socialization. The first girl, an illegitimate, unwanted child named Anna, had been kept isolated in an upstairs room for nearly six years. When Anna was discovered, her clothing and bedding were filthy, and she had received no instruction or friendly attention whatsoever. She could not walk, talk, feed herself, or do anything that showed intelligence. She was emaciated, with skeletonlike arms and legs and a bloated stomach. Anna made considerable progress after she was discovered. She learned to follow directions, to string beads, to identify a few colors, and to build with blocks. Eventually she also learned to talk (though in phrases and not full sentences), to wash her hands, and to brush her teeth. Anna died before she was eleven, but the progress she made demonstrates that it is possible to teach many things to a child totally isolated during the first six years of life. At her death Anna's social and cognitive development was equivalent to that of a nor-

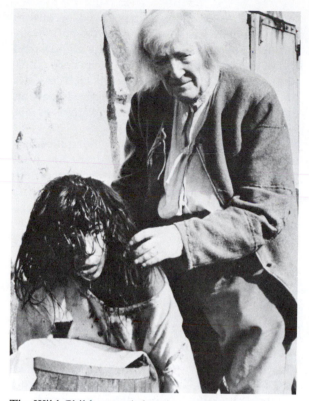

The Wild Child, *a movie based on an historical account first published in 1800, describes an extreme case of social deprivation. The wild boy had no attachments to other humans (he didn't even seem interested in the company of those who captured him), and displayed the behavior of the animals with whom he had shared the forest for years—getting food, sleeping, and running from predators. Like other such stories, this one raises questions about the degree to which our social environment molds us and essentially "creates" our humanity, as well as the degree to which we, unlike other animals, inherit the capacity to respond to socialization.*

mal two- or three-year-old. The possibility that Anna was mentally handicapped might have prevented more extensive progress.

Davis's other case study involved a girl named Isabelle, who also was found at about the age of six. Her mother was a deaf-mute, and the two of them had spent most of their time together in a dark room. They communicated by gestures, not by speech. Because of lack of sunshine and poor diet, Isabelle was in poor health. At first she seemed incapable of forming relationships, and it was not clear whether or not she was deaf. When it

was established that she could hear, specialists started working with her. People first believed she was feebleminded, but, under a program of skillful guidance, she began to show signs of a rapidly expanding intelligence. A little more than two months after speaking her first words, Isabelle started making sentences. Nine months later she could read and write quite well, add to ten, and retell a story after hearing it. Seven months later she had a vocabulary of between 1500 and 2000 words and was asking complicated questions. By the age of eight-and-a-half, she had reached a normal level of knowledge, covering in two years the development that usually requires six. The case of Isabelle suggests that, with conscientious and skillful effort, specialists can overcome the deficiencies produced by highly deprived socialization.

The Spitz research and the Davis case studies show the devastating effect of isolation on children. These are extreme situations, and yet one might wonder whether some negative impact is apparent in less extreme situations.

Without doubt the answer is affirmative. A study of abused toddlers concluded that some impact of the abuse they had received was revealed when other children cried. Toddlers from nonabusive households responded with interest, empathy, or sadness when their agemates were distressed. By contrast, toddlers from abusing homes reacted to agemates' crying with physical attacks on the distressed children, fear, or anger. For instance, Thomas, an abused one-year-old, was playing when he heard a child crying in the distance. The researchers wrote:

> Suddenly, Thomas becomes a statue. His smile fades and his face takes on a look of distress also. He sits very still, his hand frozen in the air. His back is straight, and he becomes more and more tense as the crying continues. The fingers on his hand slowly extend a bit. . . . The [distant] crying diminishes. Suddenly, Thomas is back to normal, calm, mumbling and playing in the sand.

> (Main and George, 1985: 410)

Children's socialization affects their behavior in a variety of ways, and those who have been abused are more likely to respond stressfully to other children's pain and stress. One of the more frightening aspects of such a situation is the legacy it can produce; it is very possible that an adult with

Thomas's background will also respond more harshly and abusively than most people to stressful situations.

A related topic is sexual abuse of children. How widespread it occurs is unknown; however, it is more frequent than many specialists realize. For instance, when a mental-health treatment center started to give assistance to sexually abused children, the social-work clinicians expected to receive about three referrals each month; the first month they obtained fifteen referrals, and by the sixth month, sexual abuse accounted for 40 percent of their cases. Child victims of sexual abuse frequently feel stigmatized, filled with shame and guilt, and consider themselves "damaged goods;"

they also consider themselves betrayed, because in their view parents failed to protect them; finally they feel powerless, subjected to the all-powerful will of another who has treated them vilely. Clinicians widely consider the impact of such episodes traumatic, producing a lasting negative impact on the individuals' mental health (Patten et al., 1989).

We have seen the effects that deprived socialization can have on individual children. But what happens if all the children within a society experience highly deprived socialization? The following Cross-Cultural Perspective considers such a situation.

CROSS-CULTURAL PERSPECTIVE

Socialization among a People Driven Mad: The Case of the Ik

Colin Turnbull (1979), an anthropologist, studied the Ik (pronounced "eek"), who live in a mountainous region of the central African nation of Uganda. The details of the Ik case make it clear that the deprived socialization experienced by Ik children was one result of living in what had become a drastically deprived society.

Before World War II, the Ik were nomadic hunters and gatherers. Traditionally Ik children regarded all adults living in the same village as parents and all other children as brothers and sisters. During prosperous times such a social arrangement meant that a village was in effect one large family. But then disaster struck. Following World War II, much of the Ik's traditional land was turned into a national park, and the Ik were forbidden to hunt and gather there. The tribespeople were forced to

settle on barren and arid land. In the United States, victims of disasters generally receive relief from the government and from the local community. In addition, family members usually pull together in such circumstances, helping each other as much as possible. By contrast, the Ik received no outside help, nor do they possess family or other group structures to provide support.

In this situation the socialization process has deteriorated rapidly. At the age of three, children are normally thrown out of the home by their parents. These children survive by forming "age bands," with each child seeking others close to his or her age for protection against older children. However, these alliances are temporary. Each child eventually turns on the ones with whom he or she has become closest, and the fragile bond they

called friendship is ended. Three or four such friendships will be formed and then broken. At that point the child is twelve or thirteen and has learned the wisdom of acting on his or her own, while acknowledging it is occasionally profitable to associate temporarily with others.

Only the strongest and craftiest children survive. Turnbull wrote that a young girl named Adupa, unable to accept her parents' rejection, kept coming back for food and shelter, but they laughed and drove her away each time. Adupa kept going back to them, and finally they did let her stay, leaving the hut themselves and shutting the door so tightly that the half-starved little girl could not open it. Turnbull learned later that that was how Adupa died.

Grown children treat their parents in the same spirit.

When Turnbull departed, he left a sack of ground corn-meal with the police for an old man. The cornmeal was enough to last the old man for months, and Turnbull promised to send money for more when the sack was fin-ished. However, the anthro-pologist had underestimated the old man's son. Within two days the son had per-suaded the police that it would save them a lot of bother if he looked after the cornmeal for his father. Later Turnbull heard that the old man had died of starvation within two weeks.

Novelists and filmmakers often try to shock their audi-ences, devising horrifying scenes that show human beings' capacities to hurt or to destroy each other. But what could be more horrify-ing than the true case of the Ik, which demonstrates that under certain social condi-tions parents will completely reject their youthful chil-dren, leaving them to die?

Source: Colin M. Turnbull. "The Mountain People." In Phillip Whitten (ed.), *Readings in Sociology: Contemporary Perspectives*. New York: Harper & Row. Second edition. 1979, pp. 19–26.

Theories of Socialization

The **self** is one's perception of his or her own person, which forms as a result of other people's response in the course of socialization. In the last section, we noted that institutionalized children often possess a confused sense of self, and children who grow up as isolated as Anna and Isabelle seem to have an undeveloped sense of self.

This section examines four theories that analyze the growth of the self. Two of the theories were developed by sociologists and two by psycholo-gists.

Sociological Theories of Socialization

Charles Horton Cooley's and George Herbert Mead's theories have distinct differences, but on one point they agree — that the self is the product of a learning process that occurs in interaction with others. Both theories, in short, are distinctly sociological.

Cooley and the Looking-Glass Self

A child of scarcely eighteen months toddles toward her parents, smiles, and then dives to the floor. The parents clap their hands and roar with laughter. The little girl perceives that her parents see her as cute and funny and that they heartily approve of her action. She feels happy and proud and begins to think of herself as a funny person and will repeat her performance or some version of it in the future.

This situation illustrates a concept Charles Hor-ton Cooley (1864–1929) called the **looking-glass self:** Our understanding of what sort of per-son we are is based on how we think we appear to others. Cooley wrote, "We always imagine, and in imagining share, the judgments of the other mind" (Cooley, 1964: 185).

According to Cooley, there are three steps in the development of the looking-glass self:

1. Our perception of how we appear to another person.
2. Our estimate of the judgment the other person makes about us.
3. Some emotional feeling about this judgment, such as pride or shame. Looking back, you can see that the little girl in the previous example experienced these three steps.

Of course, one person does not have direct con-tact with another's thoughts or feelings; an indi-vidual only makes guesses from other people's re-sponses. Faulty communication or confusion sometimes happens: A disapproving expression might be mistaken for an approving smile; or a person may receive mixed messages from different people. The diving child's mother might applaud, while her father registers stony disapproval. The child is not certain whether or not she should do funny things in the future. If such mixed messages continue, she is not likely to develop a clear sense of whether or not she is a funny person. Children who grow up with a constant supply of mixed messages are likely to become adults who are con-fused and unsure of themselves.

The looking-glass self develops in many social contexts, including the classroom. Whether or not this child feels comfortable performing before classmates in the future is likely to be influenced by their reaction to this performance.

Mead's Conception of the Development of Self

George Herbert Mead (1863–1931) accepted the idea of the looking-glass self theory. However, he believed that the development of the self-concept is the product of more than people's perceptions of others' reactions to them (Mead, 1930). According to Mead, the socialized individual has learned to read complicated social situations before taking whatever actions are judged the most appropriate.

Mead visualized the development of the self as a three-stage process:

1. The preparatory stage occurs in early childhood. In the course of their second and third years, children imitate others' behavior. They copy the way that their parents or older siblings hold a spoon, do a dance step, or make an obscene gesture. Children do learn some useful skills through imitation but discover little about how roles work.
2. Children enter the play stage at the age of four or five. **Play** is the process of taking the role of specific individuals and thereby starting to learn the rights and obligations that particular roles entail. Mead wrote, "A child plays at being a mother, at being a teacher, at being a

policeman; that is, it is taking different roles" (Mead, 1934: 150). At this stage children's role performances begin to give them an understanding of their significance. These performances are definitely "play," however, in the sense that children are not committed to these roles and are able to make up the rules as they proceed.

3. The final stage is the game stage. According to Mead, a **game** is a group activity in which each participant's role requires interaction with two or more individuals. In order to take part in games, a person must have a **generalized other**—an image of the role expectations for all the game participants with whom a person must interact. Mead noted, "The fundamental difference between play and the game is that in the latter the child must have the attitude of all the others involved in that game" (Mead, 1934: 153–154). Unlike the play stage, the game stage is serious business. Children are expected to commit themselves to the roles they perform, and, to perform effectively, they must learn the rules governing all participants' behavior. Not following the rules can lead to a sense of personal failure.

An actual game provides an illustration. In baseball, for instance, the infielders must be aware of not only their own role expectations but also those of their fellow infielders. The first baseman must realize that without a runner on base, he must take the throw on a ground ball to the shortstop. With a runner on first base, the first baseman knows that the shortstop's throw will go to the second baseman, who then will throw to first.

The concept of game also applies to social situations. Let us imagine, for example, that Jackie is having problems with her boyfriend. She wants to discuss the situation with her friend Angela, and so she gives her a call. They agree to meet an hour later at the college cafeteria. Angela arrives, however, with her younger sister Peggy. "Mom had to go shopping," Angela says apologetically, "and she asked me to bring Peggy along." Peggy is ten years old, always curious, and is likely to pass on any information she hears to her mother, who in turn will tell Jackie's mother. In this situation the Meadian game includes the following facts: Both Jackie and Angela are aware of how Peggy is likely to act in this situation, and each knows that the other is aware. Thus the two young women engage in a careful conversation, avoiding references to certain issues: that Jackie frequently spends the night with her boyfriend, that most of their friends drink liquor and use drugs, and that Jackie has seriously considered dropping out of school. They also convey some information with facial expressions and gestures when Peggy is not looking. As they are leaving, Jackie whispers to Angela, "Ma's pretty understanding about my personal life. She really tries not to ask too many questions. She knows she'll just get upset and that I'll end up doing what I want anyway."

The two young women understand how the generalized other applies here. They know what behavior to expect from Peggy, their mothers, and each other. With this knowledge they perform their roles smoothly in this Meadian game. The skills demonstrated by Jackie and Angela involve a level of social sophistication that far exceeds what is necessary to develop a looking-glass self.

Psychological Theories of Socialization

In general, psychologists are more inclined than sociologists to focus on individuals and their experiences and less on the group contexts affecting people. This difference is apparent when Sigmund Freud's and Jean Piaget's theories are compared to Cooley's and Mead's. These two psychological theories have had a profound impact on scholars in diverse fields concerned with socialization.

Freudian Theory of Socialization

Sigmund Freud (1856–1939), certainly one of the most prominent theorists in psychology, described the different impulses to which we are subjected. All of us experience impulses pulling us in different directions: Our wish to have another piece of pie conflicts with concern for our waistline; the wish to sleep through an early morning class clashes with concern that the material covered in lecture will be featured on the next test.

Freud (1952) contended that socialization is a process that requires people to sacrifice personal impulses and desires for the common good. Without such a sacrifice, society would disintegrate as people pursued their most selfish goals. According to Freud, the energy inherent in these impulses

and desires is redirected along socially acceptable paths by the socialization process. As you read about this theory, recognize that the struggles Freud analyzed can also be considered either role strains or role conflicts discussed in Chapter 5, "Social Interaction." Do you recall the distinction between the two terms? If not, you might look up the terms on p. 115.

Freud identified three distinct parts of the personality that exist as concepts, not in a physical form. One part is the **id,** which is unconscious, primitive, and constantly pleasure-seeking. The second part is the **superego,** which has internalized standards of right and wrong, a conscience. Parental influence is strong in the development of the superego, but other authority figures such as teachers or the police also affect its development. Struggle between the superego and id is not inevitable, but Freud suggested that in modern life almost continuous warfare will occur between them. In short, there is an ongoing conflict between basic impulses produced by the id and standards of society supplied by the superego. Generally the superego tries to force the id to modify or renounce its urges or at least to postpone them. The final part of the personality is the ego. The **ego** is Freud's conception of the self. It must cope with pressures from three often contradictory forces: the outside world, the id, and the superego.

In everyday life one can easily visualize the

The demands of modern people's superegos are diverse. In recent years an increasing proportion of Americans have accepted the idea that they should engage in strenuous exercise in order to appear physically fit.

140

struggle among the three parts of the personality Freud described. Suppose that a student has an important test scheduled the next day. That evening, however, a party will take place at a friend's apartment. The party promises to be a lot of fun — plenty to drink and eat — and many of the student's friends will be there. The id urges, "There's only one way to handle a party like this one — go early and stay late!" The superego takes the opposite tack. It argues, "This test could make or break your grade. You must study all evening and then turn in early. Parties are for weekends, after all." The ego is forced to evaluate both arguments. Which decision will be reached? The party? Studying? Perhaps the ego will compromise: Study most of the evening, then spend two hours at the party, and have only one or two drinks. From a Freudian point of view, the decision reached will reflect the relative abilities of the id and the superego to "convince" the ego.

Piaget's Theory of Cognitive Development

Jean Piaget (1896–1980) was a Swiss psychologist and a leading expert on children's thought processes. Piaget's work has complemented Mead's analysis, with the latter focusing on the child's growing understanding of social relations and Piaget emphasizing **cognitive ability** — the capacity to use perception, thought, memory, and other mental processes to acquire knowledge. Piaget (1970) contended that a child's cognitive ability develops through four principal stages. These stages are age-related because the brain must develop physically over time in order to allow certain types of cognitive processes to occur and because passage into a given stage requires a successful experience in the preceding one. Indeed people are generally aware that cognitive abilities are age-related. We would be shocked to hear a six-month-old infant speaking in full sentences or an eight-year-old discussing the theory of relativity or symbolic interaction. The four stages cover the time period from birth to the age of fifteen.

1. *The sensorimotor stage.* This phase involves the first two years of life. During these years infants learn to coordinate sensory experiences (such as seeing objects) with motor activities (such as touching objects). Infants discover that if they reach for bright-colored objects, like mobiles or rattles, they can touch, grasp, or even jiggle them. They are starting to distinguish themselves from the surrounding environment, an ability an infant does not possess for the first three or four months of life. Eventually infants develop **object permanence,** the childhood recognition that specific objects still exist after they are removed from one's line of vision. A child of four months might play with a toy but will not seem to notice when it is taken away. However, a child of nine months will start looking for the same toy if removed. The older child has developed object permanence, recognizing that the toy has an existence independent of his or her own perception.

2. *The preoperational stage.* This phase is named from the fact that a child between two and seven years old does not yet fully understand certain basic concepts one must grasp in order to function effectively in the everyday world. These concepts include weight, volume, speed, and cause and effect. Children's abilities at this stage can be deceptive, sometimes dangerously so. For instance, a babysitter is with Jamie, a four-year-old, in the child's yard. "I'm thirsty," Jamie says. "I'd like a glass of milk." The sitter stands up, and as he heads for the kitchen door he says, "Now you stay right here, Jamie. I don't want you going into the street." Just to check, he might add, "Now tell me what you're supposed to do, Jamie." The little girl will be able to explain — she seems to understand danger — but in reality she does not yet comprehend the speed of cars, nor does she grasp the process of cause and effect (that is, that if hit she will be injured or killed). Thus even though she has understood her babysitter's words, she is too young to grasp their significance, namely the personal danger that speeding cars represent.

3. *The concrete operational stage.* This phase involves children approximately seven to eleven years of age, and, in the course of it, they master the cognitive skills necessary for everyday life. They come to understand measurement, speed, weight, time, and cause and effect. Unlike younger children they are able to appreciate other people's outlooks and, as Mead suggested, to coordinate other people's viewpoints and actions with their own. Children at the concrete operational stage, however, lack the ability to think abstractly.

4. *The formal operational stage.* Children's responses to the following set of sentences

display the difference between the concrete operational and the formal operational stages:

(1) All children like spinach.
(2) Boys are children.
(3) Therefore boys like spinach.

Younger children, especially if they do not like spinach, will focus on the content of the syllogism, while adolescents are much more likely to examine the argument because they are impressed by its logical form (Phillips, 1969). This stage occurs from ages eleven to fifteen. Children develop the ability to think abstractly, to manipulate concepts not linked to experience in the immediate environment. In the formal operational stage, children are beginning to explore the vast capacities of the mind, and education is a prominent vehicle for these explorations.

Piaget's theory has some interesting implications for education. Because expanded cognitive abilities are the result of both the physical maturation of the brain and intellectual experiences, it would be difficult and counterproductive to force children to think abstractly before they are intellectually ready. On the other hand, once they have developed their full intellectual capacities, there is no reason to move slowly. A child of fourteen has completed the formal operational phase, suggesting that most high-school students are fully capable of the same sort of abstract thinking college students must perform.

Comparisons of the Four Theories

The four theories of socialization we have discussed all recognize the changing nature of the self. Three of the theories contend that social interaction determines the development of the self, while Piaget's theory claims that brain maturation

Table 6.1
Four Prominent Theories of Socialization

THEORIST	PRINCIPAL CONCEPT(S)	CENTRAL IDEA(S)	INDIVIDUAL'S RELATIONSHIP TO SOCIETY
Charles Cooley	Looking-glass self	People's sense of self is based on how they imagine they appear to others.	Continuous effort to adjust one's behavior to one's perception of others' desires and expectations
George Mead	Play, generalized other, and game	The development of the self is a three-stage process, where each stage represents a more sophisticated understanding of the world.	The necessity to understand the generalized other for each game in which one participates
Sigmund Freud	Id, ego, and superego	There is an ongoing conflict between a person's primitive impulses and societal controls, with the ego (self) serving as negotiator.	Requirement that the ego places heavy restraints on the id in line with the demands of the superego
Jean Piaget	Cognitive abilities	The acquisition of knowledge is a four-stage process occurring in childhood and featuring a particular set of mental operations at each stage.	Expectation that at each stage a child meets socially approved cognitive demands, such as in school performance

is the major source. Furthermore each theory has its own particular focus. Cooley's approach concludes that a person's perceptions of how other people evaluate his or her behavior determines the content of the self. Mead's analysis accepts Cooley's central point but emphasizes that the development of the self requires an understanding of how roles work. Unlike the two sociological theories, the Freudian perspective suggests that there is a conflict-laden relationship between the individual and society in the on-going struggle between the id and superego. Finally Piaget's theoretical contribution involves an entirely different aspect of socialization, focusing on children's development of cognitive abilities and not on their increasing understanding of social relations. Table 6.1. compares these four theories.

Sources of Socialization

The focus now shifts from an examination of theories that analyze the entire process of socialization to a discussion of specific influences in the process—key sources of socialization. In fact, one of these sources, the family, has already received some attention in the previous section.

The Family

Children are born into families, and it is within the family context that they obtain their first exposure to the values, norms, beliefs, and knowledge characteristic of their society. Research has shown that parents significantly affect their children's outlook on such wide-ranging issues as gender-role identity (Costos, 1986), alcohol and drug abuse (Halebsky, 1987), achievement (Metcalf and Gaier, 1987), and aggression (Weidner et al., 1988). Furthermore the socialization experience within the family continues for many years. Most American children live with their parents until they are in their late teens, and many continue living with them much longer. As the Cooley and Mead theories emphasize, parents and other family members have a tremendous impact on children. Sometimes family influences involving distinctive patterns of facial and bodily expression or behavioral patterns are readily apparent. In other cases these traits are not obvious, and yet the parental influence remains equally pervasive.

Americans usually think of childhood as a distinct period of time in people's lives, but such a conception has not always been accepted. Let's examine how it has changed.

The Changing Conception of Childhood

During the Middle Ages, children were treated as little adults. Parents had no distinct perception of themselves as people involved in child rearing, and the family was generally thought of as an institution for the transmission of a name and inheritance. Between the thirteenth and the seventeenth centuries, this outlook gradually changed. Religious groups began to take an increasingly important part in the education of children, and the members of these groups started to emphasize that parents were the guardians of their children's souls. From the seventeenth through the nineteenth centuries, parents' growing involvement showed itself in increasingly stricter codes of discipline. This trend became particularly apparent in the early nineteenth century when the Industrial Revolution encouraged a sharp role distinction between men and women, forcing many wives to remain in the home where they were expected to concentrate much of their energy on rearing their children. By the end of the nineteenth century, the combined forces of the family and the school had firmly established the conception of childhood (Ariès, 1962).

With the existence of childhood confirmed, people have disagreed about which child-rearing patterns are appropriate. Before the 1920s a restrictive approach to parenting generally prevailed. There was a widespread belief that it was critical to maximize children's obedience to the social norms. Most parents felt that the use of punishments and rewards was the best means of securing this obedience. During the 1920s the increasing acceptance of the ideas of Sigmund

Many modern parents believe that childhood should be a period of time in which their children learn from varied experiences. Having family members collectively plan their vacation would illustrate this child-rearing philosophy.

Freud, educator John Dewey, and others led to an almost complete reversal of the earlier approach. Parents became aware that children have their own individual perceptions and needs and that bad experiences suffered in childhood can produce psychological damage that will carry into adulthood. Different opinions regarding discipline also have become apparent. Some critics of the student protest of the 1960s, for example, suggested that a major cause of the unrest was the supposedly overly permissive child rearing typical of the post-World-War-II era.

People often contend that a particular approach to rearing children is best. However, many social scientists argue that there is no single "right approach." Americans are inclined to believe that infants are inherently helpless and must establish strong emotional bonds with their caretakers. The ethnocentrism within many Americans arises when they learn that traditional Japanese mothers believed that their young children were uncivilized creatures whose emotions needed to be soothed and tamed—quite the opposite of the American approach. It further strains Americans' capacity for cultural relativism to discover that many Indian mothers in the highlands of Guate-

mala believe that their children's day of birth will determine their dispositions and, therefore, make no effort to shape their personalities. However, in all three of these societies, most children grow up to be relatively well-adjusted, productive adults; research indicates that children do not need exposure to a particular set of socialization patterns to develop properly. Beyond basic care and feeding, there appear to be no universal needs among children. One psychologist has concluded, "To ask what a child needs is to pose half a question. We must always specify the demands the community will make upon the adolescent and young adult" (Kagan, 1983: 411). Thus the child rearing of American children will prepare them for American society, not for traditional Japanese or Guatemalan societies.

Mass Media

The **mass media** are the instruments of communication that reach a large audience without any personal contact between the senders and the receivers. Books, records, newspapers, magazines, television, radio, and movies are the most promi-

Figure 6.1
Media Use in the Last Twenty-Four Hours

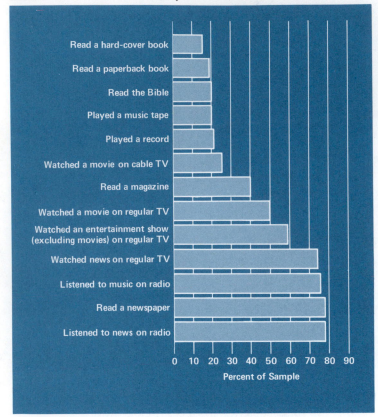

Americans make extensive use of the mass media. With the exception of reading the newspaper, they are more likely to watch TV or listen to the radio than they are to read. (Source: Roper Organization. Roper Reports. *April 1982.)*

nent mass media. Figure 6.1, based on national survey data, indicates how extensively Americans employ various types of media information during the typical day.

As Figure 6.1 implies, of any of the mass media, television probably has the most extensive impact on Americans; four of the categories in this figure involve television. One study indicated that by the age of eighteen, the average American child will have spent more time watching television than performing any other waking activity (Liebert and Poulos, 1972). Since 1950 the amount of time Americans have spent watching television has steadily increased. In 1983 American households with televisions averaged seven hours, two minutes of TV time, an increase of fourteen minutes from the previous year (*U.S. News and World Report,* February 6, 1984).

Television and other commercial media are profit-oriented. Television networks and local channels, radio stations, newspapers, and magazines sell time or space to advertisers, whose investment proves worthwhile only if a large audience pays attention to the medium. A team of experts noted, "The purchase of a 30-second spot on CBS or a page in *Time* is a meaningless act — and a poor business decision — unless there are audiences involved. In reality, advertisers buy the audience, which is a byproduct in the mass communication process" (Hiebert, Ungurait, and Bohn, 1974: 39). Television programming involves vast sums of money, and thus competition for the audience is intense. The producers of most major network shows attempt to develop programs that will "hook" the viewers, reel them in like fish. The central concern, then, is audience appeal; any consideration of artistic merit is distinctly secondary.

One of the most effective ways to hook an audience is with violent activity. It has been estimated that an average American child will see more than 13,000 killings on television by age fifteen. There is twice as much violence in American television as there is in British programming. Yet it is difficult to assess the effects of television violence. A rigorous study of the relationship between violent programming and violent behavior has determined that previous research claiming a relationship is inconclusive (Baron and Reiss, 1985). Still certain developments appear possible: that audiences that have had extensive contact with violence in the mass media are relatively likely to perform violent acts in situations in which they expect to be rewarded for such behavior or when they encounter a situation similar to the one presented by the media (National Commission on the Causes and Prevention of Violence, 1969).

Suicide is also violence, directed against oneself. A study in California found that shortly after television-news accounts of suicide, the suicide rate would jump, especially among adolescents (Phillips and Carstensen, 1988).

The following Social Application considers one of the perplexing current issues of the mass media — the freedom of the press.

SOCIAL APPLICATION

What about Freedom of the Press?

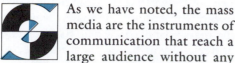

As we have noted, the mass media are the instruments of communication that reach a large audience without any personal contact between the senders and receivers. The lack of personal contact, however, does not prevent people from having strong feelings about the press — newspapers, magazines, TV, and radio — and their personnel. In our society, viewpoints about the freedom of the press are diversified. Many Americans believe that media personnel have too much freedom. Nationwide surveys conducted by the National Opinion Research Center in the middle 1970s and again in the middle 1980s indicate that the percentage of Americans with a great deal of confidence in the press dropped during that decade from 29 to 14. Furthermore a majority of Americans would favor repealing the First-Amendment clause guaranteeing freedom of the press. Commenting on this information, Joseph Kopec, a public-relations specialist, suggested that the American public perceives the press as arrogant, unnecessarily intrusive, and as distant from the everyday struggles of average citizens as big business or big government. Kopec proposed ways for press officials to reform this situation: policing themselves; using whatever means necessary to correct errors

and establish credibility with the public; and reestablishing contact with the people, holding meetings where reporters and editors can candidly communicate with local citizens.

Other observers of the press, however, would suggest that Kopec's reforms are insufficient. The problem, some critics observe, is that the mass media are a prime portion of the corporate world. Michael Parenti noted that just ten major companies control fifty-nine major magazines (including *Time* and *Newsweek*), fifty-eight important newspapers (including the *New York Times* and the *Washington Post*), the three major TV and radio networks, thirty-four TV stations, 201 cable systems, and twenty record companies. The owners of the major media have diversified business involvements, and they emphatically do not see it as in their interest to examine big-business activities in depth, especially when those businesses have significant problems. Thus an investigation of the media coverage of a major oil spill at Santa Barbara in 1969 showed that the local news media, which were not owned by large corporations, were about equally likely to provide coverage to environmental groups and oil companies. In sharp contrast the nonlocal press, which was considerably more likely to

be controlled by large corporations, generally excluded the environmental groups, giving six times as much coverage to the oil companies.

Is the central issue in freedom of the press simply a question of power and influence? Do powerful corporations control mass media in line with their interests? While some apparently believe this is the basic question, others don't. Leo Szilard, a Hungarian-born scientist and writer who lived in the United States, contended that Americans are subtly socialized to censure themselves. In a short story, he described the process by which a brilliant dolphin was taught the workings of modern societies. What he learned about American society was often complicated and perplexing.

> Thus, on one occasion, Pi Omega Ro [the dolphin] asked whether it would be correct to assume that Americans were free to say what they think, because they did not think what they were not free to say. On another occasion, he asked whether it would be correct to say that in America honest politicians were men who were unable to fool others without first fooling themselves.
>
> *(Szilard, 1961: 42–43)*

Herbert Marcuse, a philosopher, agreed with Szilard's dolphin, indicating that even members of the press will monitor and control themselves. Why do members of the press respond this way? The reason, Marcuse claimed, is because they are all playing the same game: They want to become rich and successful and revel in the good life, glorifying in material wealth. The press is no different from any other sector of American society in this respect. Thus mass media are not a particularly significant factor shaping Americans' perceptions and views. "The preconditioning does not start with the mass production of radio and television and with the centralization of their control. The people enter this stage as preconditioned receptacles of long standing" (Marcuse, 1964: 8).

So what do you think? Do we have freedom of the press? And if your answer is wholly or partially negative, what do you believe is the source of the restriction?

Sources: Joseph A. Kopec. "The Big Chill." *Vital Speeches.* V. 50. June 1, 1984, pp. 528–530; Herbert Marcuse. *The One-Dimensional Man.* Boston: Beacon Press. 1964; Harvey Molotch and Marilyn Lester. "Accidental News: The Great Oil Spill As Local Occurrence and National Event." *American Journal of Sociology.* September 1975, pp. 235–260; Michael Parenti. "The Moneyed Media." *Economic Notes.* V. 51. October 1983, pp. 7–12; Leo Szilard. *The Voice of the Dolphins and Other Stories.* New York: Simon and Schuster. 1961.

Peers

In a scene from the film *Diner,* one young man was complaining that since he was getting married, all the good times would be over. His male companion, whom everyone regarded as knowledgeable about sexuality, suddenly looked strangely at the other young man. Then he smiled confidently and said, "You're a virgin." The other, acutely embarrassed, admitted that his friend was "technically" correct.

Research indicates that American males are likely to face strong peer pressure to become sexually experienced and that virgins are sometimes made to believe that they are not demonstrating proper masculinity and that something must be wrong with them (Kirkendall, 1968).

Sex is hardly the only activity over which peers exert influence. Articles have shown that peers influence such issues as problem solving (Azmitia, 1988), fear of success (Balkin, 1987), and drug and alcohol use (Barrett, Simpson, and Lehman, 1988). The fact that young people of school age spend an average of twice as much time with their peers as they do with parents, and that they like that arrangement, underlines the significance of teenage peer groups (Bronfenbrenner, 1970).

Whether we applaud or condemn the influence of young people's peer groups, we might wonder why they have become so important. The sociological perspective, which neither applauds nor condemns that influence, examines the social world in which modern young people live and observes that in a highly complex industrial society, the family turns over many of its primary functions, such as moral training, to the schools. Within the school, however, a close, emotional relationship is unlikely to develop between adolescent students and their teachers. Thus students must look to their own age group for much of their emotional support and guidance (Coleman, 1961).

Schools and Day-care Centers

The first day of school is an important moment sociologically. When they enter school, children encounter for the first time a significant source of socialization outside the bounds of the family. In school, children receive formal knowledge from teachers and from books but also much more. In some of their courses, they are likely to obtain more distinct emphasis on patriotism than is normally provided at home. In addition, children in school will learn how to behave in group settings. They learn to sit quietly and to obey teachers providing instructions, whether the instructions make sense or not. Children are also encouraged to compete, to attempt to produce higher quality work than do their classmates. A body of criticism has developed concerning the regimentation that occurs in the early school years. One writer, for instance, suggested that kindergarten is "an academic boot camp," in which the system of routines and orders prepares young children for blind

Table 6.2
Public Schools As a Socialization Agent

GRADE FOR THE PUBLIC SCHOOLS

	NATIONAL SAMPLE	PUBLIC-SCHOOL PARENTS
A	3%	3%
B	20	22
C	48	52
D	13	12
F	3	2
Don't know	13	9

WILLINGNESS TO PAY MORE TAXES TO RAISE EDUCATIONAL STANDARDS

	NATIONAL SAMPLE	PUBLIC-SCHOOL PARENTS	NO CHILDREN IN SCHOOL
Yes	64%	73%	61%
No	29	23	31
Don't know	7	4	8

Source: Alex M. Gallup and Stanley M. Elam. "The 20th Annual Gallup Poll of the Public's Attitudes toward Public Schools." *Phi Delta Kappan.* V. 69. 1988, pp. 33–46.

While Americans do not feel that public schools have done a particularly good job, the majority recognize that their role is sufficiently important that they are willing to pay more for their improvement.

obedience over the next dozen years of schooling and also within the large-scale occupational bureaucracies of current society (Gracey, 1977).

Parents, educators, politicians, and others are well aware that schools are a critical means of socialization in modern society, but most Americans do not feel that public schools are doing their job well. When asked to give the nation's public schools a grade, 3 percent of the respondents in a national survey gave an "A," 20 percent "B," 48 percent "C," 13 percent "D," 3 percent "F," and 13 percent didn't know. For public-school parents, the percentages were slightly more favorable. Considering these fairly low scores, the survey team asked the respondents whether they would be willing to pay more taxes to help raise American educational standards. Overall 64 percent of the sample responded affirmatively, with 73 percent of public-school parents saying yes (Gallup and Elam, 1988). Table 6.2 shows the data.

For working parents of preschool children, day care is often necessary. The issue of day care has produced a great deal of controversy and confusion. One basis for confusion is that interested parties, including researchers, can focus on different basic questions. One topic is whether or not day care is harmful for children, and distinctly different outlooks exist here. A recent study concluded that once in kindergarten, children who had been in day-care centers and those who had been in family care showed no significant differences in adaptive behavior, communication skills, daily living abilities, and motor skills (Moore, Snow, and Poteat, 1988). On the other hand, a pair of prominent sociologists indicated that separation from intimate family ties and the rapid turnover of personnel that occurs in many day-care programs might have a negative impact on children's development (Berger and Berger, 1984: 155).

We could consider a different basic topic. Instead of focusing on harm to children, we might ask what conditions produce children's most effective development. One investigation of ele-

Figure 6.2
Agents of Socializaton

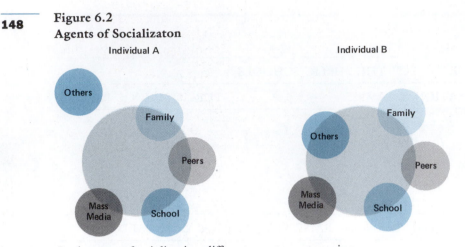

In the course of socialization, different agents exert varying degrees of influence. For Individual A the family and peers were especially significant. In contrast, Individual B received much less influence from these two agents. In this case the school, particularly two teachers, and others—a couple that owned a local small business—were the most influential.

mentary-school students who had been in both day care and family care concluded that the children who had the most effectively developed social and academic skills had received high-quality care, with limited turnover of personnel (Howes, 1988). Obviously day-care programs can supply these qualities, but children are more likely to obtain this combination from family members. However, family care is an option that many parents do not pursue, either because they can not afford it, because they conclude that the career sacrifice required, most frequently for women, is too great, because they believe day care is more beneficial for children, or because of a combination of factors.

Additional Agents of Socialization

Parents, the media, teachers, and peers are important sources, or agents, of socialization. But are there others as well? Several types come to mind.

Institutional "caretakers." Staff members provide significant socialization for orphans, juvenile delinquents, and mentally and physically handicapped children. However, the fact that these staff members are frequently overworked generally means that the quality of socialization they can provide would be considered quite inadequate by most people.

Social workers. Individuals of various ages often receive help from such organizations as child-abuse centers; programs for the elderly; centers for the treatment of drug abuse, alcoholism, or gambling; and social-welfare departments. In some cases a kindly, insightful staff person (or the opposite—a cold, uncaring individual) can have an impact seemingly out of proportion to the time and energy spent with the person needing help.

Sometimes people will encounter individuals whose guidance or example may lead them to decisions about their best future course of action. For example, a charming, articulate professor or physician may inspire a young woman or man to prepare for the same profession. Or, in a different vein, a pleasant, kindly representative of the Unification Church ("Moonies") may offer what seems to be a message of hope to a confused, unhappy young man or woman who relinquishes control over his or her destiny in exchange for the promise of happiness and fulfillment.

Figure 6.2 represents the possible impact of different agents of socialization on two individuals.

Total Institutions

Unlike the other socialization agents discussed in this section, total institutions are concerned with resocialization. A **total institution** is a place of residence where inhabitants experience nearly complete restriction of their physical freedom in order to be effectively resocialized into a radically new identity and behavioral pattern. Frequently such barriers as locked doors, high walls, water, cliffs, or barbed wire are used to prevent unrestricted contacts with outsiders. Psychiatric hospitals, prisons, monasteries, boarding schools, and some army camps are examples.

Inhabitants' resocialization in closed institutions is a two-step procedure: The old identity must be stripped away and replaced with a new one. This change begins with a **mortification process,** a series of degradations and humiliations of inhabitants that are systematically carried out by staff members of total institutions. The mortification process begins the moment an individual enters the total institution. Erving Goffman wrote:

> We very generally find staff employing what are called admission procedures, such as taking a life history, photographing, weighing, fingerprinting, assigning numbers, searching, listing personal possessions for storage, undressing, bathing, disinfecting, haircutting, issuing institutional clothing, instructing as to rules, and assigning to quarters.
>
> (Goffman, 1961: 16)

Obviously the mortification process in a psychiatric hospital will be different from the one in a boarding school. In both cases, however, significant portions of inmates' former identities are systematically stripped away by admissions procedures and other new, often deeply disturbing

The mortification process strips away people's identities as a first step toward attempting to resocialize them to useful social roles. We can wonder whether the process will succeed with these men, whose convictions for criminal violations led to their placement in a "shock" camp in New York.

situations they must experience. As the mortification process continues, inmates are gradually exposed to the **privilege system,** a framework for inmates' resocialization. The three parts of the privilege system are the "house rules," norms that indicate the main requirements of inmate conduct; punishments for breaking the rules; and rewards or privileges provided in exchange for obedience to staff. Goffman noted:

> The building of a world around these minor privileges is perhaps the most important feature of inmate culture, and yet it is something that cannot easily be appreciated by an outsider, even one who has previously lived through the experience himself. This concern with privileges sometimes leads to generous sharing; it almost always leads to a willingness to beg for such things as cigarettes, candy, and newspapers.
>
> (Goffman, 1961: 50)

Does the resocialization that occurs within closed institutions prepare people to function effectively in the greater society? While the question is so general that neither "yes" nor "no" would be an adequate answer, a negative response often seems more appropriate. The American prison system, in particular, has been largely ineffective in this respect. In fact, two experts in criminal justice acknowledged this conclusion when they suggested that in the future, prisons might be reserved for only dangerous individuals. Others might be treated at community-based correctional centers and reintegrated, as rapidly as possible, into society as useful citizens (Montgomery and MacDougall, 1986).

Total institutions have also failed in the mental-health field. Articles indicate that in Greece (Mavreas, 1987), the United States (Mechanic, 1987), and Italy (Pirella, 1987), mental hospitals have generally proved ineffective and that new, much more effective mental-health programs that truly rehabilitate people need to be devised and implemented.

It seems likely that one of the major impediments to improving or replacing mental hospitals and prisons is the likelihood that the major motivation is not individuals' resocialization: The dominant motivation is summarized by "the toilet assumption," the idea that for many modern policymakers and citizens, the principal concern when distasteful problems occur is to get rid of them — flush them as one does feces — and then they disappear, in this case out of public view into mental hospitals and prisons. Out-of-sight means out-of-mind (Slater, 1976: 15–16). The problem is that if this principle determines the course of action when people's lives are involved, those lives will be destroyed.

Tough Times: Transitions in the Socialization Process

In the last two sections, we have learned something about how socialization works. Most of the time the process runs smoothly. However, when people make major transitions in their lives, they must undergo socialization, and at these times they can have difficulties learning or accepting the new cultural standards or modes of behavior. Adolescence, job loss, divorce, and the death of a spouse are significant "tough times."

Adolescence

Several years ago in Hartford, Connecticut, a fifteen-year-old girl named Kathy stood on the steps of a church and slashed her arms with a knife. A taunting crowd gathered, and she continued, eventually fainting in a pool of her own blood, but surviving. Later, when asked why she tried to kill herself, Kathy explained that it was because she realized how confused and unhappy her family life was. An investigation revealed that her life had been unstable, involving shifts from one foster home to another as well as occasional stays in institutionalized settings (Papirno, 1976). This girl's socialization had been inadequate, and it is easy to understand why she possessed an unclear, undeveloped sense of self.

Far less disruptive upbringings than Kathy's can lead to confusion and hopelessness for adolescents. These psychological conditions, along with the wish to impress peers and lack of experience in effectively judging risks, have made young people much more reckless than any other age group. The federal government and private foundations have begun a new program of teenage study, which has been driven by "a chilling fact: adolescents are the only age group in which mortality has risen since 1960. Three-quarters of adolescent deaths are caused by accidents, homicide and suicide, all of which indicate a lethal propensity for risk-taking" (Goleman, 1987: C1).

Numerous investigations document the fact that adolescence is a confusing time. For instance, Offer (1969) studied fourteen- to eighteen-year-olds, and his subjects and their parents generally agreed that the greatest turmoil occurred between ages twelve to fourteen. Research conducted by Simmons, Rosenberg, and Rosenberg (1973) of nearly 2000 urban school children in grades three through twelve found that the most disturbed sense of self developed among early adolescents. Compared with the other children, these early adolescents tended to be more self-conscious, less stable in their self-image, less positive in their self-esteem, and less confident about the evaluations of them maintained by parents, teachers, and peers of the same sex. The researchers suggested that the move from the relatively protected, personalized atmosphere of the junior-high school to the more impersonal environment of the high school contributed significantly to their informants' disturbed sense of self.

Elements in middle-class socialization sometimes compound adolescents' confusion and uncertainty. Middle-class adolescents commonly grow up in households in which their fathers are so dedicated to occupational success that they spend little time with their families, thereby producing limited interaction with their children. As a result middle-class adolescents often become skeptical about the pursuit of material success and uncertain about their occupational future. Yet, because of parental emphasis on success, they are likely to have "vague yearnings for recognition and fame" (Flacks, 1979: 30).

Another source of adolescent confusion in modern cultures is the failure to provide youths with a clear indication of their status. In preindustrial cultures a rite of passage is normally provided, a formal ceremony initiating both boys and girls into adulthood. Such ceremonies contribute to young people's socialization, giving them strong assurance that their status has truly changed and that in the future people will regard them differently. No such assurance is provided to teenagers in modern societies. In the United States, boys and girls gradually emerge from childhood into adolescence, putting away childish things and taking up adult activities — drinking, drugs, sex, and more mature types of entertainment forms — but not yet assuming full adult responsibilities. When does one actually become an adult? We have no generally accepted way of marking the transition. Adolescence in America can be considered a "big waiting room" (Davison and Davison, 1979).

A study of depressed adolescents suggested that young women and young men respond differently to the pressures and tensions of this "tough time." Troubled young women tended to become fixated on their physical appearance, to suffer the loss of appetite and weight, and to feel dissatisfied, while the depressed young men were likely to withdraw from work and social activities, to lose sleep, and to become easily irritated (Baron and Joly, 1988).

Thus adolescence can be a difficult, confusing period. Sometimes young people feel overwhelmed by their problems; yet they often lack the motivation and skills to discuss them. Can anything be done to encourage disclosures? Research has indicated that adolescents were more encouraged to discuss their problems if the conversation started off with such easily approached topics as music or hobbies than if it began with an analysis of such emotionally demanding subjects as unhappy or happy moments in their lives. Furthermore disclosure of personal problems was more extensive in group than in individual interviews. In the former context, adolescents used each other as models; once one individual disclosed his or her problems, others felt encouraged to do so too (Mills, 1983).

Job Loss

Most people value their jobs, and this is revealed when they lose them. Research has concluded that loss of job produces such reactions as a diminished self-esteem and sense of well-being, increased anxiety and depression, and more physical illness (Iversen and Sabroe, 1988; Kessler, Turner, and House, 1988; Payne, 1988; Wilhelm and Ridley, 1988).

Powell and Driscoll (1979) studied seventy-five

152 male scientists and engineers who lost their jobs. The subjects averaged forty-one years of age, had a mean of sixteen years of education, and had experienced 9.5 months of unemployment. As they were gradually socialized to the unemployed status, these men generally passed through four stages that involved the learning of new values and norms.

Stage I: Period of relaxation and relief. In most cases the men were aware of the layoffs in advance, and they were relieved when they finally took place. There was a sense of being "between jobs," and while most of the men made a definite effort to look for work, they tended to treat this period like a vacation at home, spending time with their families, sleeping late, and reading or tinkering in their workshops.

Stage II: Period of concerted effort. After about twenty-five days, the men usually felt rested and sometimes also bored. At this point they generally initiated a systematic effort to find new work, using such well-established strategies as calling friends, sending out résumés in response to ads, and going to job-placement centers. This phase averaged about three months, but the length varied considerably depending on such factors as the individual's ability to sustain his morale in the face of repeated rejection letters from potential employers, the amount of savings or other financial resources available to tide over

People who lose their jobs suffer the loss of both the tangible and intangible rewards of work. This photo shows unemployed steelworkers waiting in line at a food bank.

the family, and the extent to which the wife provided moral support and handled the secretarial chores that accompany job seeking. During this stage the men often avoided others who were unemployed. "I'm not like them," one engineer said. "They are out of a job. I am waiting for an offer from Corning Glass."

Stage III: Period of uncertainty and doubt. At this point the men had been unemployed longer than they had ever been before. After repeated unsuccessful encounters with the job market, their optimism began to erode. During this stage many men lost a clear sense of their occupational competence, often starting to feel that they were losing to younger men in the job competition or that their own knowledge and skills had become obsolete. Depression and rage often set in, with the rage frequently directed inward because there was no suitable external object on which to vent it. Toward the end of this period, a decline in job-hunting activity took place. The men made comments like the following: "I've stopped using certain approaches like sending out résumés. I push a little harder only when an opportunity comes up."

Stage IV: Period of cynicism. The transition to this stage was fairly smooth. The intervals between efforts to secure a job became longer and longer. The researchers concluded that a man was socialized to the status of unemployed person when he went two months without personally contacting a potential employer or job counselor. At this time many of the men in the study started to lose the conviction that they were in control of their occupational lives. The following statement was typical. "No matter what I do it just doesn't make any difference. It's just a throw of the dice, whether I'll get the job or not." A strong sense of powerlessness and pessimism appeared. "Why go in for an interview?" a physicist asked. "I'll never get past the secretary anyway." This cynicism seemed to be a way of avoiding a confrontation with the reality that a return to work would require a major change in lifestyle—in particular, that any jobs the men would be able to obtain would pay much less than the ones they had had previously. Once in this stage, men were likely to spend more time at home and to associate less with friends. While financial limitations played a part in this change, the major reason seemed to be a deliberate avoidance of people whose lifestyle now differed sharply from their own. With their husbands out of work, wives frequently sought full-time employment, and husbands assumed a more active role on the domestic front. Further developments would depend on changes in the job market and on the willingness of the man to accept a more modest position than the one he had previously held.

Divorce

Do you think that divorce tends to be a difficult experience? A study of stressful life events ranked the relative impact of forty-three issues. The death of one's spouse was placed first, and divorce was second. A pair of researchers, however, have asserted that these findings have actually minimized the impact of divorce. They concluded that the impact of divorce is "often much more disruptive, both immediately and in the long term, than losing one's spouse" (Counts and Sacks, 1985: 151). It appears to be easier for divorced people if they feel less committed to the former spouse. The more positive an individual's feelings toward the former spouse, the greater that person's distress (Berman, 1988).

Paul Bohannon (1970) suggested that divorce is especially difficult because it encompasses six different dimensions simultaneously and because American society does not yet possess effective means of helping people cope with these experiences. What Bohannon has called the "six stations of divorce" include:

1. *The emotional divorce.* The spouses withhold emotion from each other—they grow apart—because their trust in and attraction for each other has ended.
2. *The economic divorce.* When the household is broken up, an economic settlement is necessary, separating the shared assets into two portions.
3. *The legal divorce.* In the courts the formal termination of the marriage takes place, along with bestowal of the right to remarry.
4. *The coparental divorce.* Decisions are made about such issues as the custody of the children, visitation rights, each parent's financial and child-rearing responsibilities, and so forth.
5. *The community divorce.* Changes occur in the way friends and acquaintances react to the former couple when they learn about the divorce. Like property, friends too are often divided, becoming "her friends" or "his friends."
6. *The psychic divorce.* When marriage partners break up, an uncoupling occurs, and the sense of self alters. Each spouse must fully realize that he or she is no longer part of a couple. Once again the person is single, and for many this is a shock.

Divorces are normally unsettling; remarriages can be also, especially when children are involved. In such cases the socialization of the stepparent includes learning how to build a relationship with his or her spouse's children. At present our society lacks clear standards on how stepparents should treat their spouses' children. Even the terms to use are unclear. What do children call their parents' new spouses—"Dad," "Mom," or do they refer to them by their first names? One obvious problem is that the missing biological parent is likely to resent the new spouse being called "Dad" or "Mom:" It symbolizes a seizure of the parental role (Cherlin, 1983). Additional questions arise: For instance, does the new spouse have a parent's full rights and obligations—the right to use discipline on the children or the obligation to become a full partner in the lengthy list of tasks that accompany parenthood?

Death of Spouse

Research has indicated that elderly citizens who had lost a spouse in the past two months were more likely to report a newly developed or worsened illness, greater use of medication, and generally poor health than a comparison group of elderly citizens who had not suffered such a loss (Thompson et al., 1984). On the other hand, a large study that followed subjects' lives over a ten-year period found that widowed people showed little or no differences from married individuals in self-rated health, daily activities, social-network size, openness to new experiences, psychological well-being, and depression (McCrae and Costa, 1988). Thus while it is undeniable that people suffer when a spouse dies, most of them fully recover.

People inevitably undergo a period of adjustment after the loss of their spouse. This socialization experience is often referred to as **grief work:** the process by which people attempt to establish a new identity after the death of a loved one. Grief work involves several stages. First, numbness and disbelief dominate. In the beginning surviving spouses often cannot accept the fact that their husbands or wives have actually died. This stage frequently continues for several weeks beyond the funeral. Second, longing for the lost spouse becomes obsessive. Constant crying, psychosomatic symptoms, such as headaches and insomnia, feelings of guilt about failing to prevent the spouse's death, hostility toward doctors, and other strong emotional reactions occur at this time. Third, depression is likely; sadness and loneliness become incapacitating. The surviving spouse no longer follows his or her normal routine and often expresses no motivation to keep living. Finally recovery occurs. The surviving husband or wife recognizes that, with adjustments, life can continue. When people reach this point, they have completed the grief work (Hiltz, 1980; Hultsch and Deutsch, 1981).

Because American women average about seven more years of life than do American men and also tend to be younger than their husbands, wives generally survive longer. At any given point in time, in fact, there are about five times more American widows than widowers. Studies on women suggest that several factors determine how difficult they will find the acceptance of the new role. One consideration involves the circumstances of the husband's death. If there is a long illness, then the wife has some opportunity to prepare for her new role. On the other hand, if death arrives unexpectedly, then she finds herself thrust suddenly into the widow's role despite being utterly unprepared to meet the psychological, economic, and social problems looming before her; the impact of this factor is increased if the woman has little general sense of control over life events. A related condition is the character of the relationship between the husband and wife. A wife who was dependent upon her husband to make decisions and to handle practical matters is in a more difficult situation than is a wife who has taken a more active part in family affairs. Another factor is the woman's marital role orientation. Research indicates that women who have given their highest priority to the wife role have more difficulty accepting the death of their husbands and assuming the widow role than do those who have emphasized the mother role as their strongest priority (Loether, 1975; Stroebe, Stroebe, and Domittner, 1988).

Perhaps the most significant factor, however, becomes the widow's social network. If a widow is greatly distressed one month after her husband's death, the most frequently associated condition is the absence of support from friends. Besides friends, family members, neighbors, service agencies supplying help in transportation, housekeeping, legal aid, and sick care, psychotherapy groups, and mutual self-help groups can contribute to widows' support systems (Lopata, 1988; Marmar et al., 1988; Vachon and Stylianos, 1988).

Losing one's spouse is difficult, and yet, according to one team of researchers, "the majority, it appears, see themselves stronger for having undergone the experience. We do them a disservice if we insist on focusing upon potential pathology associated with this transition period" (Thomas, DiGiulio, and Sheehan, 1988: 238).

Conclusion

In discussing the loss of a spouse, we have seen that in spite of the pain and stress involved, widowed people generally recover. Critical to their recovery is the support of social networks, and seeking support from these networks often requires individuals to act differently than in the past.

An instructive conclusion seems to emerge here: As the sociological perspective emphasizes, people are influenced by surrounding social forces, but, as in the case of widowed individuals, modern Americans face options and thus can make some choice about what forces should influence them.

Might it be possible for a variety of modern Americans to do something similar — resocialize themselves to some degree to more productive, cooperative patterns? A pair of researchers suggested that Americans could learn a great deal from people in developing nations. For instance, the people in Papua, New Guinea, have a conception of land sharing that is different from the prevailing standard in the Western world: People have specific rights to the same piece of land; one individual has the fishing rights, another the living rights, a third the ceremonial rights, and so forth (Ellis and Ellis, 1989).

This is simply an illustration of how different cultural standards might be instructive. The crucial idea is that maybe our lives could be made more tranquil, safer, and, in some ways, more productive if we sought to socialize ourselves to new, cooperative cultural standards.

STUDY GUIDE

Learning Objectives

After studying this chapter, you should be able to:

1. Define socialization and discuss its importance for human life.
2. Discuss the interplay of nature and nurture in human development.
3. Describe the effects on human development of deprived socialization in childhood.
4. Discuss in detail Cooley's, Mead's, Freud's, and Piaget's theories of socialization.
5. Examine the family as an agent of socialization, indicating how conceptions of childhood have changed over time.
6. Discuss mass media, peers, and schools and day-care centers as sources of socialization.
7. Define total institution and describe the two-step process of inmate resocialization.
8. Analyze the following "tough times," major transitions in the socialization process: adolescence, job loss, divorce, and death of spouse.

Summary

1. Socialization is the process by which a person becomes a social being, learning the necessary cultural content and behavior to become a member of a group or society. The most fundamental socialization occurs in childhood, but the process continues throughout people's lifetimes.

2. Sociologists address the question of whether human beings are the product of their nature (their innate biological characteristics or heredity) or their nurture (their socialization). While recognizing the significance of the nature issue, sociologists emphasize the importance of nurture or socialization.

3. When children grow up in very isolated circumstances or are the victims of deprived socialization, their sense of self is likely to be underdeveloped, confused, or unusual in some other respect. Studies of isolated infant monkeys, isolated children, and abused children have demonstrated these patterns of development.

4. Several well-known theories analyze the development of the self: Cooley's "looking-glass self" and George Herbert Mead's discussion of "play" and "game" indicate how the self develops as a result of interaction with others. Freudian theory divides the self into three parts, with one of the parts — the ego — acting as a mediator between the conflicting demands of the other two. Jean Piaget's theory of cognitive abilities involves four age-graded stages, where progressive knowledge builds on the experience obtained in the previous stage or stages. The four theories of socialization we have examined all recognize the changing nature of the self.

5. Sources of socialization include the family, mass media, the school and day care, and peers. The family is a prominent source of socialization because within it children receive their first exposure to the cultural standards of their society. The conception of childhood and appropriate child-rearing practice varies in different eras and social settings. The mass media, especially television, are also a modern agent of socialization for people. The influence of television in the area of violent programming is a source of widespread concern. The school is another prominent socialization force. The content of children's schooling often arouses controversy. Day care for small children is also a controversial issue. With so many mothers working, however, the continuance of day care in the future seems inevitable. Peers are another agent of socialization. In industrialized societies peer groups appear to have assumed some of the socialization functions performed by the family in the past. Besides the previous agents of socialization, a variety of others can be important influences on individuals. Inhabitants in total institutions experience resocialization, with the

mortification process and the privilege system contributing to that outcome.

6. In the course of their lives, people encounter certain "tough times," transitional periods when new standards and new activities affect them. Some of these periods are occasioned by adolescence, job loss, divorce, or the death of a spouse. Adolescence is a difficult, confusing time period because it involves a shift from childhood to adult roles. Job loss can be a disturbing experience. People who suffer it can pass through four stages that involve a gradual socialization to their unemployed status. Divorce also involves a significant readjustment. Bohannon described six levels on which divorce occurs. The loss of a spouse also produces new socialization experiences. Learning to live without one's spouse can be described as a four-step process.

Key Terms

cognitive ability   the capacity to use perception, thought, memory, and other mental processes to acquire knowledge

ego   Sigmund Freud's conception of the self that must cope with pressures from three often contradictory forces

game   according to George Herbert Mead, a group activity in which each participant's role requires interaction with two or more individuals

generalized other   an image of the role expectations for all the game participants with whom a person must interact

grief work   the process by which people attempt to establish a new identity after the death of a loved one

id   according to Sigmund Freud, the part of the personality that is unconscious, primitive, and constantly pleasure-seeking

instincts   unalterable behavior complexes that parents transmit genetically to their children

looking-glass self   according to Charles Cooley, our understanding of what sort of person we are is based on how we imagine we appear to other people

mass media   the instruments of communication that reach a large audience without any personal contact between the senders and the receivers

mortification process   a series of degradations and humiliations of inhabitants systematically carried out by staff members of total institutions

nature   inborn biological characteristics or heredity

nurture   socialization

object permanence   according to Jean Piaget, the childhood recognition that specific objects still exist after they are removed from one's line of vision

play   according to George Herbert Mead, the process of taking the role of specific individuals and thereby starting to learn the rights and obligations that particular roles entail

privilege system   a framework for inmates' resocialization

self   one's perception of his or her own person, formed as a result of other people's response in the course of socialization

socialization   the process by which a person becomes a social being, learning the necessary cultural content and behavior to become a member of a group or society

sociobiology   a field in which the proponents contend that through the evolutionary process, human beings have acquired tendencies that determine much of their behavior

superego   according to Sigmund Freud, the part of the personality that has internalized standards of right and wrong, a conscience

total institution   a place of residence where inhabitants experience nearly complete restriction of their physical freedom in order to be effectively resocialized into a radically new identity and behavioral pattern

Tests

True – false Test

_____ 1. Socialization continues throughout the entire life-span.

_____ 2. Sociobiologists argue that the tendency to form dominance hierarchies among human beings is neither innate nor universal.

_____ 3. Cooley and Mead both believed that the self is the product of a learning process that occurs in interaction with others.

_____ 4. Piaget's theory is concerned with children's increasing understanding of social relations.

_____ 5. During the Middle Ages, children were treated as little adults.

_____ 6. A rigorous study of the relationship between violent television programming and violent behavior has determined that violent programming is definitely the main reason many people engage in violence.

_____ 7. One of the reasons why confusion and controversy about day care occur is because interested parties, including social researchers, sometimes focus on different issues.

_____ 8. The resocialization of patients in mental hospitals has been surprisingly effective.

_____ 9. Grief work is a type of socialization.

_____ 10. In a given year, there are about equal numbers of widows and widowers in the United States.

Multiple-choice Test

_____ 1. Darwin's idea of "natural selection" is consistent with the idea of:
   a. nurture.
   b. the id.
   c. instinct.
   d. survival of the fittest. ✓

_____ 2. Cooley's concept of the looking-glass self:
   a. was rejected by George Herbert Mead.
   b. involves an image of the role expectations for all the game participants with whom a person must interact.
   c. suggests that our understanding of what sort of person we are is based on how we imagine we appear to other people.
   d. is closely related to Freud's concept of the superego.

_____ 3. All but one of the following are stages in the development of the self as described by Mead. Which is NOT a stage?
   a. play
   b. game
   c. generalized
   d. preparatory

4. In Freud's theory of the self, the internalized standards of right and wrong (conscience) exist in the:
   a. superego.
   b. id.
   c. ego.
   d. instinct.

5. In Piaget's theory of cognitive development, the ability to think abstractly occurs in which stage?
   a. concrete operational
   b. formal operational
   c. sensorimotor
   d. preoperational

6. On the topic of child rearing, it now seems apparent that:
   a. children in all societies should be reared the same way.
   b. beyond basic care and feeding, there are no universal needs among children.
   c. Americans have developed the best approach to child rearing for all societies.
   d. non-Westerners rear their children more effectively than Westerners do.

7. The federal government and private foundations have begun a new program of adolescent study because of:
   a. the steady increase over time in the teenage death rate.
   b. the recent rise in adolescents' drug use.
   c. the AIDS epidemic.
   d. growing concern for teenagers' alcohol consumption.

8. Powell and Driscoll studied scientists and engineers who had lost their jobs. Depression and rage occurred during which stage of response to job loss?
   a. period of relaxation and relief
   b. period of concerted effort
   c. period of uncertainty and doubt
   d. period of cynicism

9. Which of the following is a common problem of remarriage?
   a. lack of clear standards for stepparent's treatment of spouse's children
   b. less value attached by society to second marriages
   c. lack of strong parental support for second marriages
   d. absence of formal rituals to legitimate second marriages

10. It is easier for widows to accept their new roles if:
    a. the husband died suddenly.
    b. the woman gave highest priority to the wife role.
    c. the wife had been dependent on her husband to make decisions and handle practical matters.
    d. the widow is imbedded in a supportive social network.

Essay Test

1. Define socialization. Why is this process important?
2. Distinguish nature and nurture and discuss the development of the "nature" position, including sociologists' reaction to it.

3. How does deprived socialization affect young children? Discuss the different issues raised in the section on this topic.
4. What is the self? Describe Cooley's, Mead's, Freud's, and Piaget's analyses of the self. Indicate significant similarities and differences between and among the theories.
5. Discuss the impact of three important sources of socialization on American college students.
6. Describe three difficult transitions that can occur in the socialization process, referring to relevant concepts and studies.

Suggested Readings

Axline, Virginia. 1968. *Dibs: In Search of Self.* New York: Ballantine Books. A vivid account of a withdrawn child's effort to clarify his sense of self with the aid of a highly skilled therapist.

Erikson, Eric. 1964. *Childhood and Society.* New York: W. W. Norton and Company. Revised edition. A theoretical analysis of socialization and the development of the self. The book contains an eight-stage developmental process through which modern people pass.

Goodman, Paul. 1960. *Growing Up Absurd.* New York: Vintage. A sociologist's uncompromisingly critical account of the frustrations and confusion that all children face growing up in American society where, according to Goodman, useless, destructive, and above all absurd standards and activities are dominant.

Honess, Terry, and Krysia Yardley (eds.). 1987. *Self and Identity: Perspectives across the Life Span.* London: Routledge & Kegan Paul. Articles by twenty-nine social scientists (sociologists, psychologists, and psychiatrists) on the development of the self during infancy, childhood, adolescence, and adulthood.

Intintoli, Michael James. 1984. *Taking Soaps Seriously: The World of "Guiding Light."* New York: Praeger. A study of the process by which a soap is put together. The author emphasizes that the soap's morality and domesticity themes are dictated by Proctor and Gamble, the show's owner and chief sponsor.

Kagan, Jerome. 1984. *The Nature of the Child.* New York: Basic Books. A noted psychologist's highly readable analysis of what is known about children. A wealth of cross-cultural references are included. Frequently traditional theory and research is challenged.

Kamerman, Jack B. 1988. *Death in the Midst of Life: Social and Cultural Influences on Death, Grief, and Mourning.* Englewood Cliffs, NJ: Prentice-Hall. A nicely written text using a symbolic-interaction perspective to examine a variety of topics involving dying and death.

Roth, Henry. 1932. *Call It Sleep.* New York: Cooper Square Publishers. A novel sensitively describing the fear, confusion, and loneliness encountered by a young Jewish immigrant boy living in early twentieth-century New York City.

Spock, Benjamin, and Michael B. Rothenberg. 1985. *Dr. Spock's Baby and Child Care.* New York: Pocket Books. Sixth edition. A book originally published in 1945, which continues to be the country's leading guide to parents seeking practical knowledge about how to care for their children.

Zelizer, Viviana A. 1985. *Pricing the Priceless Child: The Changing Social Value of Children.* New York: Basic Books. An interesting book showing how the conception of children has shifted from perceiving them in economic terms to perceiving them within a moral framework.

Additional Assignments

1. In the course of an ordinary day at school or work, observe the behavior of someone (without being noticed), noting how often and under what circumstances this person seems to alter his or her behavior in order to fit in with others' expectations. Alternatively you might make mental notes on your own behavior, recording your own behavioral changes when you are with other people. Discuss your findings with other class members. How do your observations fit with Cooley's and Mead's theories? How do your findings fit with Goffman's theory (dramaturgic sociology) discussed in Chapter 5?

2. Make a list of the different agents of socialization with whom you have been in close contact today. Then ask yourself which of these agents of socialization you would consult regarding the following issues: problems with school, difficulties in interpersonal relations (such as your love life), career choices, self-improvement goals, and the need to release strong emotions (such as love, hate, or fear). What does this exercise suggest about the varied influences of different agents of socialization? Would you have made the same consultations five years ago?

Answers to Objective Test Questions

True–false Test

1. t	4. f	7. t	9. t
2. f	5. t	8. f	10. f
3. t	6. f		

Multiple-choice Test

1. d	4. a	7. a	9. a
2. c	5. b	8. c	10. d
3. c	6. b		

7
GENDER ROLES AND SEXUALITY

Gender-Role Development

Biological Differences between the Sexes
Cultural Differences between the Genders
The Biosocial Position

Theories

The Structural-Functional Theory of Gender Roles
The Conflict Theory of Gender Roles
The Symbolic-Interaction Theory of Gender Roles

Sexual Behavior

Premarital Sex
Marital Sex
Extramarital Sex

Homosexuality

Homosexuality and Modern Society

American Gender Roles in the Years Ahead

Research in Sociology: Research on Sexuality and Its Acceptance: Reflections of Changing Values

Study Guide

Recently Bill Orr, who is married to the governor of Nebraska, was cashing a check at a local bank. The teller recognized the name, became flustered, and asked, "Aren't you the wife of the governor?" Embarrassed she sputtered, "No, what I meant to say is, 'Aren't you Mr. Kay Orr?'"

Mr. Orr, an insurance executive as well as the husband of Nebraska's first woman governor, said he generally takes such situations in stride, though he sometimes feels a slight identity crisis. "But that's O.K.," he added. "I'm a liberated guy."

To emphasize this point, Mr. Orr announced that he would soon publish his first book—a cookbook containing his own recipes, as well as those of other Nebraska men, including Tom Osborne, the football coach at the University of Nebraska, and Johnny Carson, who was born in the state. The cover shows Mr. Orr wearing a tuxedo and clutching a football while leaning over a table loaded with food. The proceeds will be used to renovate the governor's mansion.

"Whether he knows it or not, Orr also has been writing another sort of book," an editorial in the *Lincoln Journal* declared, praising his wit and good humor. "This one is about how the state's First Man should act."

Bill Orr has received considerable kidding from friends, and he has responded good-humoredly. "It's my nature to laugh," he said. "There's nothing to be embarrassed about here. I'm just as proud as I can be about my wife" (Schmidt, 1988: A14).

A sociological analysis of the preceding discussion requires the use of three concepts—sex, gender, and gender role. All women or all men share the same **sex.** A variety of animal forms, including human beings, are divided into the biological categories of male and female.

Distinctions of gender, however, are not as fixed. **Gender** consists of the general behavioral standards that distinguish males and females in a given culture. In the United States, women and men have traditionally been expected to dress and to behave quite differently. Gender is a status, specifying for both women and men their culturally supported rights and obligations. In the late twentieth century, the definition of female gender has been reevaluated as the traditional expectation that women should be subordinate to men in all social activities has come under strong attack.

Some **gender roles**—sets of specific behavioral patterns associated with either the female or male gender—are still more conventionally filled by the members of one sex than by members of the other sex. While women have steadily moved into a variety of prestigious, influential jobs, most governorships continue to be held by men. Thus the official role performed by the governor's spouse has largely been filled by women, and a "First Man" is unusual. As Bill Orr's example indicates, modern times have brought changing roles for men as well as for women.

It is noteworthy that until the past decade the concept *sex role* was used instead of the term *gender role*. The switch has occurred as people have increasingly recognized that the ability of women and men to perform roles effectively is usually determined by sociocultural factors, including socialization, not by the fact that one has been born a male or female (Berger and Berger, 1984: 54–59).

As you read this chapter, you might consider how issues involving gender roles apply to you. You might evaluate the different ways parents, peers, and others have shaped your conception of yourself as a male or female, as well as the various gender roles you have played. It might be interesting to analyze the extent to which you have accepted traditional female or male roles.

You undoubtedly realize the prominent part that gender and gender roles play in everyday life. For example, the addition of a person of the opposite sex to an all-female or all-male group will often have a more marked effect on the conversation than will the addition of an individual of the same sex. In a sense an intruder has appeared. To

The addition of a person of the opposite sex to an all-female or all-male group can have a more noticeable effect on conversation and behavior than the addition of a person of the same sex.

some extent, one might argue, men and women form separate subcultures. Furthermore it is likely that you are aware that your gender-role behavior substantially differs from what was conventional in your parents' generation. What would you emphasize? Freer, more relaxed sex? Greater leeway in the realm of gender-role definitions? Better communication between the sexes? Or is some or all of this nothing but hogwash?

The following section considers the biological and cultural bases for differentiating people into female and male gender roles. Then the discussion shifts to the leading theoretical perspectives on gender roles. The next topic is sexuality in premarital, marital, and extramarital situations. Fourth, we consider homosexuality, a subject on which ignorance, tension, and antipathy are widespread in U.S. society. Then we look briefly at the future of American gender roles. The chapter also contains a Research in Sociology section about research on sexuality.

Gender-Role Development

What kind of factors account for gender-role development? Biological? Cultural? A combination of both? Let us consider.

Biological Differences between the Sexes

Sigmund Freud believed that "anatomy determines destiny." Critics correctly note that this stance has been used to justify keeping women subordinated to men in the work place and at home. What are the facts, however? How much does the physical reality of being male or female influence a person's attitudes and behavior? In order to address this question, we must start by examining the importance of chromosomes and hormones in shaping human activity.

The Differentiation between Male and Female

The differentiation—the development of differences—between males and females is fundamental, depending on whether or not a Y chromosome was present at the zygote (single-cell) stage of development. About half of all human sperm cells contain a Y chromosome, and the other half an X chromosome. The human egg always includes one X chromosome. If a Y-bearing sperm unites with the egg, then an XY sex-chromosome pattern is produced and a male results. An X-bearing sperm uniting with the egg creates an XX pattern and a female. The single-celled zygote divides, then divides again and again, and at adulthood a person has at least 100 trillion cells, each of which contains either an XX or an XY sex-chromosome pattern.

About six weeks after conception, the fetal sex chromosomes direct the formation of either testicles (from the XY pattern) or ovaries (from the XX pattern). In turn, the embryonic testicles or ovaries start producing male or female sex hormones (androgen and estrogen), which mold the originally undifferentiated reproductive tissues into either female or male genitals and internal reproductive systems. The hormones also influence the brain centers, controlling such adult reproductive functions as ovulation, menstruation, and erection. The second obvious effect of sex hormones occurs at puberty, with a sharp increase in hormone production creating sexual maturation.

*Evidence of Biological Factors in
Sexual Differentiation*

Men and women experience different physiological processes related to reproduction — such as the menstrual cycle in women and the erection of the penis in men — and so the controlling brain centers must also be different. Research, in addition, is finding further evidence of differences in men's and women's brains. Research on epileptics, who have had portions of the brain removed to control seizures, has led to some interesting findings. Men lose verbal skills after surgery on the left half of their brains and spatial abilities after damage to the right half. Women, on the other hand, lose both verbal and spatial skills, no matter which half of their brains has been damaged. This suggests that women's verbal and spatial abilities are duplicated on both sides of the brain, while men seem to have the speech center located on the

left and the locus of spatial skills on the right side of the brain. The implications of the research are noteworthy. Because the halves of women's brains are less specialized, it might be simpler for them to perform tasks combining the two skills — for instance, attempting to understand someone's behavior on the basis of both facial expression and words. On the other hand, the structure of men's brains may make it easier for them to do a verbal task and a spatial task at the same time, such as simultaneously reading a map and talking (Goleman, 1978).

Cultural Differences between the Genders

It seems indisputable that biological factors play a significant part in the development of gender roles. However, the sociological perspective compels one to recognize also the significant contribution of culture. Even before a child is born, people's expectations about what is appropriate male or female behavior begin to appear. Late in pregnancy a parent might say, "The baby's kicking a lot. It must be a boy." During infancy mothers tend to look at and talk to female infants more than to males and to respond to girls more quickly when they cry. As toddlers, girls are encouraged to spend more time touching their mothers and staying close to them than are boys.

Different treatment for girls and boys intensifies at about the age of two, when parents are able to use children's rapidly expanding language ability to mold their behavior. There are "girl" toys (dolls and dollhouses) and "boy" toys (trucks, airplanes, and rubber balls). Many two-year-old boys who would prefer dolls are steered away from them and warned not to become "sissies." By the age of five or six, children's preferences are relatively stabilized. Young children's appearance and dress also normally conform to our cultural norms of femininity and masculinity. For example, a girl's hair is expected to be carefully combed and decorated. She will be clothed in dresses, encouraged to play with her mother's jewelry and makeup, and warned to stay clean, to keep her underpants always covered, and to be restrained, cute, and coy. Boys, on the other hand, are permitted and even encouraged to participate in physically active games and sports, to get as dirty

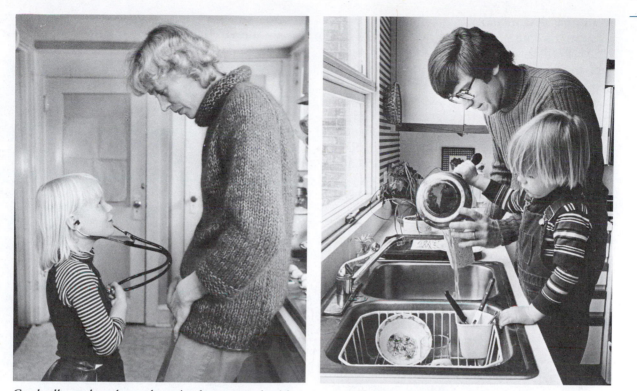

Gradually gender roles are becoming less sex-typed, with some men taking a more active role in the performance of domestic tasks.

as they wish in the process, and to be generally noisy, aggressive, and even combative (Scarpitti and Andersen, 1989: 255–259).

As we noted in Chapter 6, "Socialization," children internalize their parents' conceptions of appropriate behavior. When asked how boys and girls differ, children explain that boys are noisy, dirty, and active, while girls are quiet, clean, gentle, and inclined to cry. Men, they indicate, become protectors, adventurers, laborers, and decision makers, while women engage in cooking, sewing, and child rearing (Gagnon and Greenblatt, 1978).

A study of hermaphrodites (people with genitals part male and part female) supports the cultural basis for sex differentiation. Matched pairs were employed, with each pair involving two people similar in chromosome pattern (both had either an XX or XY pattern) and in personal characteristics (such as age, income, and education). One, however, had been raised a female and the other male. In each case the hermaphrodite who was a

chromosomal male but had been raised a female was typically "feminine" behaviorally, while the hermaphrodite who was a chromosomal female but was reared as a male acted typically "masculine" (Money and Ehrhardt, 1972). Researchers examined the case histories of twenty-four male-assigned hermaphrodites and found that while twenty of the twenty-four accepted the assigned gender and also did not engage in bisexual or homosexual activity, such personal difficulties as suicidal depression, drug and alcohol addiction, and marital failure were widespread (Money and Norman, 1987).

Cross-Cultural Evidence

A look at gender roles in different societies suggests that certain sex-linked tasks seem to be partly rooted in the biological differences between females and males. On the other hand, the fact that gender-role standards can vary from one culture to another demonstrates that cultural factors are also extremely important.

ANTHROPOLOGICAL RESEARCH   Joel Arnoff and William Crano (1975; Crano and Arnoff, 1978) studied data drawn from cultures carefully picked to represent six broad geographical areas encompassing the planet. Their findings suggest that generalizations about typical male or female behavior must be carefully made. They note that food production (hunting, gathering, fishing, animal husbandry, and agriculture) has frequently been considered a male-dominated, instrumental task, but their evidence indicates that, in reality, women often participate. Furthermore in spite of widespread belief to the contrary, women do not dominate child rearing in all cases. In the 186 societies they studied, the investigators found that women invariably were responsible for most of the child rearing during infancy (the first nine months). As Figure 7.1 indicates, mothers were the principal or almost exclusive caretakers of infants in over 90 percent of the societies. However, in early childhood (aged nine months to four or five years), no societies confined most care responsibilities to the mother. In 32 percent of the cultures studied, most or practically all of the young child's time was spent apart from the mother. Fathers were excluded or nearly excluded from child rearing in only 16 percent of the societies, and in 55 percent fathers maintained a frequent or regular relationship with their children.

A study that examined data from 117 societies indicated that the ratio of women to men affects women's gender role. When an undersupply of women exists, a higher proportion of women marry and have children, while women's literacy rate and extent of labor-force participation are relatively low. The irony is that when scarcity of women means a high value placed on them, their life options are more restricted than when they are more plentiful and are considered less valuable (South and Trent, 1988).

The following Cross-Cultural Perspective demonstrates that, in spite of some biologically influenced gender-role tendencies, societies can develop highly varied gender-role patterns.

Evidence from Modern Societies

Jeanne Block (1973) studied gender-role stereotypes in six countries — Norway, Sweden, Den-

Figure 7.1

Cross-Cultural Comparison of Mothers' and Fathers' Contribution to Child-Rearing[1]

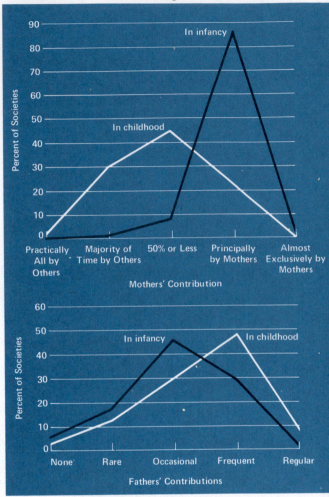

[1] A total of 186 societies were included in the study, with data on 141 societies in the infancy phase and 122 in the childhood phase.

While across societies mothers make a distinctly more substantial contribution to child-rearing than fathers, men nonetheless do provide significant assistance in many societies. (Source: Adapted from Joel Arnoff and William D. Crano. "A Cross-Cultural Study of Expressive and Instrumental Role Complementarity in the Family." American Sociological Review. V. 43. 1978, pp. 466–467.)

mark, Finland, England, and the United States. She found that male and female college students shared similar images of ideal male and female behavior in these six Western, technologically advanced societies. Adjectives that described the ideal man included the following: practical, as-

CROSS-CULTURAL PERSPECTIVE

Gender Roles among the Arapesh and the Tchambuli

Margaret Mead (1963), an anthropologist, studied several preindustrial societies located within a hundred miles of each other on islands in the South Pacific. Her analysis of socialization practices characteristic of two cultures provides some indication of why the Arapesh of both sexes were gentle and strongly concerned with each other's emotional needs and why the Tchambuli women tended to fill their culture's principal breadwinner roles, while Tchambuli men customarily spent the entire day insulting each other and laboring over their appearance. The larger implication of Mead's research is that gender roles are highly flexible, primarily developing from prevailing socialization patterns.

Among the Arapesh both mothers and fathers participated equally in child rearing. Fathers tended to show as little embarrassment as mothers in disposing of infants' feces and as much patience teaching young children to eat from spoons too large for their small mouths. Throughout Arapesh society it was recognized that men played a prominent role in child rearing. If an observer were to comment that a middle-aged man was good-looking, people would reply: "Good-looking? Ye-e-s. But you should have seen him before he bore all those children" (Mead, 1963: 39).

According to the Arapesh standards, a young child's crying was "a tragedy to be avoided at any cost." The most trying period of time in child rearing occurred at about the age of three when children were too old to be comforted by breast feeding and yet too young to explain why they were weeping. The best way to ensure that infants maintained their sense of well-being, the Arapesh believed, was to provide the continuous comfort of human voices and skin contact. Thus when a mother was working in the garden, she would bring along a young child to hold her infant instead of laying it on the ground.

Arapesh children were not pressured to grow up quickly. Their socialization was informal and easy, and attentive adults and older children were always around to help.

Among the Tchambuli Mead found that boys were raised by hard-working mothers who nursed them "generously but nonchalantly" while busily weaving reeds into baskets. There were always women present, willing to attend to a boy's needs while they worked. Mead wrote, "If his father's other wife failed to feed him as generously as his mother, his mother needed only to make the light reproach: "Are children so plentiful that you should neglect them?" (Mead, 1963: 248) Like the Arapesh children, Tchambuli boys were raised indulgently. Their childhood days were spent tumbling around the floors of the great dwelling houses where the mothers worked. After being weaned, they were fed delicacies, such as sugar cane, whenever they cried.

Significant change happened, however, somewhere between the ages of eight and twelve, when boys were subjected to the ritual of scarification required of all males approaching manhood. The boy was held squirming and howling on a rock, while a maternal uncle and an expert scarifier cut patterns on his back. Then he was painted with oil and turmeric (a spice) and kept in seclusion for as long as three months until his father decided that the best moment for the ceremonial washing of the child's body had arrived; the boy's immense discomfort was never considered. When the ritual washing was completed, the child's seclusion ended. He was given an elaborately woven belt, shell ornaments, and other decorative items to carry around with him.

Tchambuli men did not trust each other. As a boy grew into manhood, his father and elder brothers watched him jealously to make certain that he made no advances toward their wives.

Mead wrote little about the

socialization of Tchambuli girls. Apparently they were simply raised to identify with their mothers, to become the workers and breadwinners. Among women there was always an emphasis on "comradeship, efficient, happy work enlivened by continuous brisk banter and chatter" (Mead, 1963: 252). While the women worked and chatted, the men labored over their appearance, their flute playing, and dancing and were always prepared to reply

to caustic comments and insults from jealous rivals.

Mead's body of research has received a fair amount of criticism. Recall our discussion in the Cross-Cultural Perspective in Chapter 2. In 1983 Derek Freeman claimed that Mead's well-known book *Coming of Age in Samoa* was a distorted analysis of the lives of Samoan adolescent girls. It is also possible that Mead's studies of the Arapesh and Tchambuli contain some

exaggerated conclusions. Nonetheless it is probable that the gender roles of people in both societies differ sharply from those that Americans typically associate with women and men.

Certainly Mead's data emphasize an important theme in this chapter: In spite of biologically influenced gender-role tendencies for both women and men, societies can produce highly diversified gender-role patterns.

Source: Margaret Mead. *Sex and Temperament in Three Primitive Societies*. New York: William Morrow and Company. 1963.

sertive, dominating, competitive, self-controlled, and rational. For females the list contained such adjectives as affectionate, impulsive, generous, sympathetic, perceptive, sensitive, and shy. American men placed the most emphasis on males being "macho," while American women described their ideal female as being more "masculine" than did women from the other societies. Furthermore in several respects, American child-rearing values differed sharply from those of the other five societies. Americans placed especially strong emphasis on early and clear differentiation of male and female gender roles and also stressed competitive achievement, while putting relatively little emphasis on the control of male aggression.

In such socialist nations as the Soviet Union and the People's Republic of China, both sexes are expected to participate actively in the labor force. Compared to women in the United States and other Western countries, Soviet women seem to have more educational and occupational opportunities. This appearance, however, is somewhat deceiving. While it is true that the majority of physicians in the Soviet Union are women, medicine as a profession provides much lower prestige and pay in the Soviet Union than in the United States. In medicine and in other job areas as well, women are generally excluded from high-level positions (Smith, 1976). Before the advent of socialism,

Chinese women were clearly subordinate to men. Some were forced to bind their feet, crippling them and making it impossible to walk. Women were also beaten, physically abused, and treated as servants. Since the Chinese Revolution in 1949, women have received increased educational and occupational opportunities. However, few women attain higher levels of education, and few hold managerial positions or prestigious governmental posts (Stacey, 1975).

The Biosocial Position

As we have seen, some uncertainty currently exists on the issue of whether sex-linked abilities and psychological attributes are principally biologically or culturally determined. In Chapter 6, "Socialization," we noted that the field of sociobiology has developed as a response to the nature–nurture debate on whether human beings are the product of their inborn biological characteristics, their socialization, or both. The **biosocial position** is a recently developed perspective that acknowledges the significance of both biology and social experience in the development of gender roles and that emphasizes their interplay, contending that the independent significance of each factor is impossible to assess since they never exist in isolation from each other. This position suggests that biological factors determine a few limits and lead to a number of predispositions but that culture generally has the "final say" about development.

Sorting out the relative significance of biological and cultural factors is difficult. Some current studies, for instance, indicate that the bonding between mother and newborn child is more biological than previously realized. The ability of mothers of two-day-old infants to pick out their baby's teeshirt from others' by smelling it or to identify their babies blindfolded after only one encounter with them is believed to be biological in nature (Segell, 1989).

In her presidential address to the American Sociological Association several years ago, Alice Rossi suggested that in order to understand gender-role issues most effectively "it is my firm conviction, and conclusion, that the goals we seek are best approached through an integrated biosocial science" (Rossi, 1984: 15).

Theories

There is no doubt that biological factors affect the development of gender roles. However, the three theories discussed in this section—the structural-functional, the conflict, and the symbolic-interaction theories of gender roles—focus on social influences.

The Structural-Functional Theory of Gender Roles

Parsons and Bales's (1955) analysis supports the traditional outlook on gender roles, suggesting that men and women should exhibit distinct, task-related gender roles. Such a sharp distinction between women's and men's roles no longer exists in our society, and, as the upcoming discussion of conflict theory indicates, this traditional distinction has been sharply criticized for over two decades. Nonetheless this theory remains important, because the different patterns for males and females described by Parsons and Bales still serve as the cultural groundwork for current gender-role relations.

A central concept in the structural-functional theory of gender roles is **identification,** a process by which an individual incorporates another person's values, standards, and expectations into his or her own behavior and sense of self. Parsons and Bales contended that, as infants, children of both sexes identify with their mothers. As they become older, girls continue that identification, but boys are encouraged to start finding male role models. Therefore boys turn toward their fathers as a model for identification. The fact that girls identify with their mothers is apparent from their patterns of play. According to Parsons and Bales, little girls tend to play with dolls and to play "house." They quickly become directed toward domestic chores like those done by their mothers. Little boys, on the other hand, are more inclined to play with trains, cars, and airplanes and to act out masculine roles such as fireman and soldier (Parsons and Bales, 1955: 100).

Parsons and Bales also suggested that the basic gender-role patterns formed in childhood extend into adulthood. As girls grow up, they concentrate on domestic roles, and marriage becomes their primary concern. A woman establishes her basic social status by competently performing the roles of wife and mother. For a man, Parsons and Bales wrote, the carry-over of the breadwinner role from childhood to adulthood "is so clear as to need relatively little comment." Boys are brought up with an emphasis on attaining knowledge, and, as they progress through school, growing importance is placed on preparing for an occupation (Parsons and Bales, 1955: 127–128).

Parsons and Bales (1955) claimed that the nuclear family, composed of husband, wife, and children, obtains positive functions from these distinctive male and female gender roles. Role complementarity develops. The wife stays at home and cooks, cleans, raises the children, and seeks to maintain the family's emotional health and stability. The husband, in turn, is the breadwinner. In short, "he is in the first instance giver-of-care or pleasure, and secondarily the giver of love, whereas the wife is primarily the giver of love and secondarily the giver of care or pleasure" (Parsons and Bales, 1955: 151). Parsons and Bales recognized that any given social structure, such as the nuclear family, can vary in its form and function in different societies. However, they believed that the nuclear family will operate efficiently only if there is a sex-linked division of labor within it, with men chiefly performing the breadwinner and women the domestic roles.

The Conflict Theory of Gender Roles

The development of the modern women's movement has helped produce a growing sense that women should have a right of equal access to educational and occupational opportunities and a corresponding distaste or even repugnance for traditionally defined men's and women's roles. At present, therefore, it is understandable that many Americans feel that Parsons and Bales's analysis represents little more than a defense of the status quo and that a different approach, a conflict perspective, is necessary.

In her book *Sexual Politics,* Kate Millett (1970) emphasized that men traditionally have dominated women in all institutions and activities. The conflict perspective on gender roles makes the same point. Randall Collins (1971; 1974) concluded that gender inequality, like any other inequality, involves a conflict for scarce resources between a dominant group (males) and a subordinate group (females). In order for men to have superior political, social, and economic status, women must have inferior status in all respects.

According to conflict theorists, a relationship between economic and sexual inequality frequently exists. In their five-part classification of marriage types in American society, Letha Scanzoni and John Scanzoni (1988: 244–266) developed this relationship. In early America, the Scanzonis indicated, the owner–property pattern was the prevailing type. The husband was the owner, and the wife was his property. He earned a living, provided protection, had little or no domestic responsibilities, ruled the family as he chose, beating his wife if he considered it would keep her in line, and engaged in sex strictly for his own pleasure. The wife was in charge of domestic duties that fully occupied her from dawn to dusk. If the wife felt oppressed, there was little to do: No alternative means of support existed.

In the eighteenth century, factory work began, and the head–complement pattern started. At first women could earn no more than a third or half a man's wages, but now a married woman had an option. Conceivably she could leave an unwanted husband and support herself and her children. During this time the husband's control began to weaken: Decision making and sexual behavior became slightly more collaborative; men started to participate more in domestic activities. In the head–complement pattern, the wife has still been focused on domestic activity and has been primarily concerned with pleasing her husband, but blind obedience has no longer been the order of the day.

The senior partner–junior partner pattern is a third development, with many modern marriages switching between this and the previous type as women with children move in and out of the work force. With the wife contributing income, she now becomes a partner, albeit a junior one; her earning power gives her a stronger voice in the couple's decision making. In this type of marriage, each partner has the right to receive and the expectation to give prized marital rewards involving sex, empathy, and companionship.

The equal partner–equal partner pattern involves spouses who are both working full-time, earning approximately the same income, and maintaining equal rights, including equal emphasis on both partners' occupational achievement. This type of marriage represents a flat rejection of Parsons's idea of role complementarity: It is not desirable or useful to have women and men make distinctly different contributions; both should emphasize career advancement, and, if children are involved, the spouses have equal responsibility for their care. One test of whether a marriage is truly the equal-partner variety is to determine whether the couple is as likely to move for a wife's new job as for a husband's. Many spouses pursuing this type of marriage engage in commuter marriage, spending weekdays near their jobs and then getting together on weekends.

The final marriage type is wife as senior partner.

and the loss of potential female talent for an array of occupations. An up-to-date structural-functional perspective allows for women's greater involvement in occupations and men's increased participation in domestic tasks. On the other hand, conflict theorists, though critical of traditional gender roles, recognize that these roles were often highly functional in the past. Furthermore both schools agree that gender roles are based primarily on cultural, not biological, factors.

The Symbolic-Interaction Theory of Gender Roles

Theories, such as that of Parsons and Bales which emphasize children's imitation of their parents and parents' reinforcement of their children's appropriate behavior, tend to focus on children's passivity and downplay the children's active participation.

According to George Herbert Mead (1934), young children learn to act out the roles of significant people in their lives — in particular, parents. As the children do so, they slowly begin to understand what these roles really involve. Their developing conceptions of the roles of Mommy, Daddy, or other significant individuals will differ depending on whether or not the model plays his or her gender role in a traditional or a nontraditional manner.

As children grow older, Mead observed, they gradually begin to understand that the roles they have learned to play are not necessarily and exclusively bound to specific individuals. Children begin to recognize that the expectations are associated with the roles themselves and also that the roles are interconnected. When children understand this, they have started to realize that norms guide the behavior of all participants in social situations. At this point children grasp the fact that not only must they know what behavior to perform in a particular interaction, but they also must be aware of whether or not their actions are roughly in line with the attitudes and expectations of others. A little boy who plays with dolls at home will probably stop playing with them at a day-care center if caretakers and male peers verbally or nonverbally suggest to him that his behavior is inappropriate. A little girl accustomed to playing with fire engines, trucks, and other traditionally

As wives make a more significant contribution to family income, some husbands tend to become more actively involved in domestic life.

For various reasons, such as husband's loss of job or illness or a couple's preference for a role reversal from a more conventional arrangement, the wife becomes the chief or sole provider. With increasing opportunities for women, it seems likely that a greater proportion of couples than in the past will find themselves in a situation in which a wife's greater skills or aspirations will be acknowledged by the couple and their marriage will become the reverse of either the senior partner – junior partner or head – complement variety.

While structural-functional and conflict theorists are sharply opposed to each other, some points of agreement do exist. Many structural-functional theorists recognize that extreme gender inequalities are no longer functional in the modern world — such inequalities lead to discontent, conflict,

174

male toys will be likely to do the same if she en-counters decisive disapproval.

Kohlberg (1966) concluded that children's conceptions of the appropriate behavior in female and male gender roles derive from what they have seen, heard, and been told. These observations are a distortion of reality because they consider only features children perceive, such as hairstyles, clothing, and facial expressions. Frequently children's judgments are oversimplified. A case in point would be a four-your-old girl who insists that girls can become nurses but not doctors, even though her mother is a doctor.

According to Kohlberg, children face two problems in learning and adopting appropriate gender-role behavior. First, they must be able to distinguish between behavior appropriate for boys and that appropriate for girls. Second, they must have a clear sense of their own sexual identity in order to know which kind of behavior they ought to display. Neither children's understanding of what constitutes "masculine" or "feminine" behavior nor their own sexual identity is always clear. A boy of four, for instance, is able to distinguish boys from girls, but he may simply lump all men and women into the category "adult." Until he can separate men from women and identify

with the former, he will be unable to develop a full understanding of what constitutes appropriate masculine behavior based on observing the kinds of things done by men as opposed to those done by women.

Modern research suggests that the development of people's gender-role perceptions is a complicated, subtle process. For instance, a study of college students concluded that while subjects frequently made use of simplified gender-role generalizations (stereotypes) for males and females, these stereotypes tended to be discarded as more information about the individuals in question was provided (Deaux and Lewis, 1984). Over time traditional gender-role stereotypes can change. A study of two groups of female college students indicated that the traditional gender-role stereotype of women as passive had been replaced with the expectation that they should be assertive. On the other hand, the traditional view that women should be concerned with having and caring for children was still supported (England, 1988).

In summary, the structural-functional theory of gender roles assumes a traditional stance, emphasizing distinct, task-related gender roles for males and females. Conflict theory opposes that tradi-

Table 7.1
Theoretical Perspectives on Gender Roles

	STRUCTURAL-FUNCTIONAL THEORY	CONFLICT THEORY	SYMBOLIC-INTERACTION THEORY
Prominent features of gender roles	Domestic roles for women; breadwinner roles for men	Distinct cross-cultural tendency for men's roles to provide higher political, social, and economic status than those of women	Children's gradual understanding of gender-role expectations, with behavior modeled after the expectations
Major source of gender-role development	Identification with parent of the same sex	Economic inequality between women and men	Children's conception of appropriate gender-role behavior based on their interaction with parents and other influential individuals
Support for changing gender roles	Not a consideration	Emphasis on its necessity	Acknowledgment of the distinct possibility

tional arrangement, contending that women have generally suffered inferior political, social, and economic status. The symbolic-interaction theory does not support the position expressed by either of the other two theories but focuses on the process by which children develop their conceptions of gender roles. A study about the relationship between gender and power concluded that theories of gender role tend to be oversimplified analyses, and that undoubtedly the best approach is to combine their respective strengths in a single, integrated theory (Molm, 1986). Table 7.1 summarizes the three theories discussed in this section.

Sexual Behavior

As the conflict perspective on gender roles emphasizes, women have traditionally been treated differently and been given fewer opportunities than men. Since sexual activity is one aspect of gender roles, it is not surprising that unequal standards for the sexes have developed.

For many Americans, especially young Americans, it is difficult to realize how much sexual standards have changed in this country. Were we able to go back 300 years, we would find most people settled in rural communities, where life was simple and hard, and religion often played a prominent role in shaping people's self-images and behavior. Young men might quite openly "sow some wild oats" with various women, including prostitutes, but in that owner–property era, a young woman had to be discreet about sexual encounters if she wanted to escape being branded a "bad girl."

The slow, arduous evolution toward sexual equality must be linked to a number of factors. In the nineteenth and early twentieth centuries, the cities grew, and people were freed from the formal and informal controls of small-town life; religion with its frequent emphasis on one's purity became less influential; in large numbers young people began to seek higher education and participation in the job world, and they became less inclined to live with their parents. All of these factors helped young people develop a sense of freedom and autonomy lacking a century earlier, and increased sexual experimentation was an inevitable result.

Yet in the 1950s and early 1960s, the sexual lives of most American college students were sedate by current standards. As the structural-functional theory of gender roles (produced in 1955) indicated, young women, including college students, were supposed to be preparing to become wives and mothers. College was an ideal place to meet a future husband and to court him, but most young women accepted the dominant norms, returning to their dormitories before curfew and, in many cases, "saving themselves" for their wedding night or at least until they believed they had located the man who would share that night with them. In the middle 1960s, civil-rights and anti-war protests became common student phenomena. Many of them condemned the parental generation for maintaining a corrupted, controlled way of living, and the remedy, the young people said, was to eliminate the old standards, including the outdated sexual standards, and live freely. At the end of the protest years, the development of the modern women's movement basically supported this position. Women, the proponents said, should not be restricted by traditions that set tight limits on women and let men do as they chose. Equality was the order of the day, and women should be as free as men to engage in sexual activity. Furthermore in the past two decades, films and television have been influenced by the changing standards, becoming much more explicit about sexual discussion and activity. For many adults over forty who grew up in an era when the idea that two people were about to make love was conveyed by a discreet fade-out, X-rated films continue to be surprising, even shocking.

As we see in the next section, Americans continue to encounter struggles in the sexual realm.

Premarital Sex

In the past twenty-five years, two patterns involving premarital sexual behavior have been apparent: First, females continue to be more likely than males to perceive sex in a context of love and marriage—to be less inclined to accept sex for sex's sake. Second, considerable change is occurring in the sexual realm, with females' attitudes and behavior gradually changing toward those of males.

Male – Female Differences in Outlook on Sexuality

A cross-cultural study of adolescent sexual behavior concluded that in 186 societies boys tend to have more sexual freedom than girls (Barry and Schlegel, 1984). In our society boys and girls typically hold different attitudes toward sexuality. With the implicit, if not explicit, approval of parents, teachers, and other adults, boys are frequently encouraged to experiment with sex, talk about it, and joke about it. Girls, on the other hand, are taught to avoid such easy familiarity with sexuality. They learn that sexual activity is not supposed to be an act in its own right, that it is supposed to occur for the sake of love and the creation of children.

Given this, it is not surprising that male and female sex-related behavior is often different. Male adolescents, for instance, often treat sexual contacts with females as a means of building social status in their peer groups. They talk about "scoring," "how far one can get," or "hitting a home run." The emphasis is on sexual access—a highly goal-oriented approach that sometimes resembles closing a business deal in a competitive setting more than an expression of love. Young women, by contrast, are more likely to focus on the emotional element, emphasizing the affection they feel and demonstrations of fondness or love on the male's part (Gagnon and Simon, 1973).

Since men's approach to sexuality is more opportunistic than that of women, it is reasonable to expect that males will tend to lose their virginity at an earlier age than will females. A national sample of nearly 1200 undergraduates from twelve American colleges and universities found a higher percentage of nonvirginal men than women in each college year. Among freshmen 36 percent of the men were nonvirgins compared with 19 percent of the women. Among seniors the respective percentages were 68 and 44. Women are more likely than men to develop a strong emotional tie with their first sexual partner. In the study just cited, the researchers found that 59 percent of the women planned to marry their first sexual partner

following their first sexual experience, while a much lower 14 percent of men had the same intention (Simon, Berger, and Gagnon, 1972). Later research on college students has produced supportive findings. In assessing the significance of the relationship as a factor in reaching a decision about whether or not to engage in sexual intercourse, female virgins were more inclined than male virgins to weigh the relationship factor heavily (Christopher and Cate, 1985).

Changing Patterns of Sexuality

While to some extent men and women still hold somewhat different sexual attitudes and behavior, changes are occurring. Ira Reiss (1960) suggested that patterns of premarital sexual behavior may be divided into four categories: abstinence, the double standard, permissiveness with affection, and permissiveness without affection. **Abstinence** means total restraint from sex. The **double standard** asserts that men may engage in premarital sex but women may not. The two standards have traditionally coexisted, with abstinence the official norm, while the double standard was widely practiced. In recent years, however, young people have come to accept two different standards. The **permissiveness with affection** position argues that men and women who love each other and have a stable relationship have the right to express their feelings sexually. Those who endorse **permissiveness without affection** contend that women and men should feel free to have sexual relations whether or not there is commitment or affection between them. Emphasis here is on sexual pleasure. While all four standards of sexual behavior were found in a sampling of couples from four colleges in the Boston area (Peplau, Rubin, and Hill, 1977), a subsequent investigation has emphasized that college students' behavior has become increasingly consistent with an equal standard for sexual conduct—in short, the restriction or even elimination of the double standard (Keller, Elliot, and Gunberg, 1982).

When you think about premarital sex, you undoubtedly have young people and not elderly individuals in mind. A study of 200 healthy 80- to 102-year-olds examined sexual activity among this primarily unmarried set of subjects. The most common activity was touching and caressing

Table 7.2 Americans' Attitudes toward Premarital Sex		
YES, IS WRONG	NO, IS NOT WRONG	NO OPINION
38%	52%	10%

Source: George H. Gallup, Jr. *Gallup Poll.* April 12, 1985.

without sexual intercourse, then masturbation, and finally intercourse (Bretschneider and McCoy, 1988).

Table 7.2 indicates that in 1985 more than a majority—52 percent of a representative sample of adult Americans—felt that premarital sex is not wrong. Americans' changing attitudes on the subject are revealed by comparative responses in earlier years: In 1973, 43 percent indicated premarital sex was not wrong, and, in 1969, just as sexual standards were becoming more flexible, the figure was only 21 percent (George Gallup Jr., *Gallup Poll,* April 1985).

For young Americans sexual activity has often involved tension and fear, but, since the early 1980s, a new reason for concern has appeared. The following Social Application describes this concern.

SOCIAL APPLICATION

Sex and AIDS: A Major Problem for Young People

For the first several years of the AIDS epidemic, most Americans were convinced that the disease would almost exclusively be contracted by gay males and intravenous drug users. Now it is widely recognized that AIDS has reached the general populace and that anyone who engages in sexual activity with a partner who has not been sexually exclusive for many years could be exposed to the disease. Americans' concern is reflected by the fact that in an international survey in which the citizens of thirty-four countries were asked what was the most urgent health problem, only Brazil, where 79 percent of the sample picked AIDS, exceeded the U.S. sample's 68-percent choice of that disease (George Gallup, Jr., *Gallup Poll,* June 1988).

The danger is widely recognized, but unfortunately those most likely to be affected—young people—are least likely to be cautious. Recall that in the discussion of adolescence in Chapter 6, "Socialization," we noted that for several reasons young people are more inclined than other age categories to take risks. Furthermore *not* preparing for sexual activity has been long recognized as a rationalization for doing it—"I just got swept along; it's not as though we planned it." In the AIDS era, the problem with such an approach is that it is dangerous. It is indisputable that risk of infection increases with the number of sexual partners and that, aside from abstinence, the best protection is using a condom.

While it is widely accepted that condom use is wise, the burning question is this: How can a prospective partner most effectively confront the issue? Men are often reluctant to use them, and women frequently find it difficult to show initiative in sexual situations. One practical approach is not to rush into bed with each other, taking some time as the relationship develops to discuss past sexual histories and how best to develop the relationship so that both partners can feel comfortable and enjoy themselves.

Support has grown for use of public-service announcements on television and radio and in magazines about protecting oneself from obtaining AIDS through sexual activity. The problem with such announcements is that they tend to be puritanical, either promoting abstinence or trying to frighten young people into "safe sex" that is made to seem clinical and joyless. According to Suzanne Moore in the British magazine *New Statesman,* American announcements tend to

178

be more puritanical than the European ones, but no country to date features public-service statements that tune in effectively to the youth subculture. One possibility is to follow the British gay-community lead, producing ads, posters, films, and books emphasizing that sex with condoms is exciting as well as necessary. Unless that is done, Moore concluded, "men won't get into them and women won't make sure they do" (Moore, 1988: 24).

Sources: George Gallup, Jr. *Gallup Poll.* June 1988; Suzanne Moore. "Condom Culture." *New Statesman.* V. 115. February 19, 1988, pp. 24–25; Marian Segal. "AIDS Education." In Ollie Pocs (ed.), *Marriage and Family 89/90.* 1989. Guilford, CT: Dushkin, pp. 229–233; Michael Shernoff. "Integrating Safer-Sex Counseling into Social Work Practice." *Social Casework.* V. 69. June 1988, pp. 334–339.

Marital Sex

Modern married couples tend to engage in sex frequently, and wives play a significant part in the initiation of sexual activity. A study revealed that in the 1970s husbands and wives in five different age categories estimated higher rates of sexual frequency than did their counterparts in the 1940s (Hunt, 1983). Table 7.3 points out that modern married couples' frequency of sex tends to be high. A recent investigation indicated that 51 percent of husbands and only 12 percent of wives said they were more likely than their spouses to initiate sexual activity. However, 33 percent of husbands and 40 percent of wives suggested that the initiation of sex was equally likely to come from either partner (Blumstein and Schwartz, 1983: 207).

Some research suggests that people with certain social characteristics are more likely to experience uninhibited, mutually pleasurable sexual activity than those without them. For women, age and social class seem to be two significant considerations. When women are younger and come from middle-class or upper-middle-class backgrounds, they are likely to have been socialized to believe that sex should be a pleasurable experience for women as well as for men. Social class is also a factor for the couple as a unit. Because of their more extensive educational background, middle-class spouses are likely to communicate their needs to each other more effectively than their working-class counterparts, and effective communication often enhances sexual relations (Bell and Lobsenz, 1977; Rainwater, 1972; Rubin, 1983).

A number of agents of socialization currently influence marital couples' sexual attitudes and behavior. Peers, the mass media, and sex-therapy clinics have been particularly influential. The following quotation shows how peers and the media combined to affect the sexual activity of a twenty-six-year-old mechanic and his wife. He explained:

Table 7.3
Married Couples' Sexual Frequency

	YEARS TOGETHER		
	0–2	2–10	10+
Sex once a month or less	6%	6%	15%
Sex between once a month and once a week	11	21	22
Sex between one and three times a week	38	46	45
Sex three times a week or more	45	27	18

Source: Adapted from Philip Blumstein and Pepper Schwartz. *American Couples.* New York: William Morrow and Company. 1983, p. 196.

The results of this study, which involved over 3600 married couples, indicated that the longer couples are together, the less frequently they have sex. However, this table also suggests that the majority of married couples, no matter how long they have been together, tend to have sex frequently.

My wife works, and at lunchtime she and all the girls talk about things, and she comes home one time and tells me she hears there's nothing like pornography for a turn-on. So I go along with it; I go out and buy an armful of stuff—mostly picture magazines—and bring it home. First, it embarrasses her, but then she gets to see it differently, and to like some of the things she sees. Same way with a stag film I borrowed and brought home to show her. Personally, I think it's good and wholesome; it stimulates and opens the mind.

(Hunt, 1983: 226)

The widespread availability of contraceptive devices has been another important influence on marital sexuality. In particular, the pill, the IUD (intrauterine device), and the vasectomy have freed couples from the fear of unwanted pregnancy and permitted new spontaneity and joy to enter marital sex.

Finally the women's liberation movement has also affected married couples' sex lives. The effect has been two-fold. First, the movement has encouraged women to forsake passivity and to take a more active part in all aspects of living, including sex. Second, many women have openly struggled to gain more power in their marriages, and the struggle has often extended to the bedroom. Some husbands who strongly support a tradition of male sexual dominance are unable to cope with wives' sexual assertiveness. It appears that one symptom of this failure has been an increase in the incidence of impotence (Hunt, 1983).

Many married people have heavy demands on their time and energy, and these can affect the quality and frequency of marital sex. When both spouses are dedicated to career advancement (Reynolds, 1989) or have had a child or children recently (Rubenstein, 1989), couple's sexual activity can be sharply reduced.

Extramarital Sex

What factors encourage people to engage in extramarital sex? One determinant seems to be residential location. Research has concluded that large communities are more permissive toward extramarital sex than small ones. It appears that increases in population are accompanied by a diversity of subcultures, supporting and encouraging tolerance toward a variety of lifestyles (Weis and Jurich, 1985). Another study discovered several factors that seem to be associated with permissive attitudes toward extramarital sex. These include the person's level of marital satisfaction and the individual's perceived sense of freedom to associate with members of the opposite sex. Most significantly related to permissive attitudes, however, was a respondent's willingness to share highly personal and private feelings with someone besides the spouse (Saunders and Edwards, 1984). It's an interesting, thought-provoking conclusion—a point that seems to imply the great importance of effective communication in marriage if one wishes the marriage to survive.

Let's move from attitudes to behavior. An investigation of upper-middle-class business and professional men concluded that those who were alienated (had lost their youthful idealism and felt powerless and isolated) were more inclined to initiate extramarital involvements than those who were not alienated (Whitehurst, 1972). Sometimes the affairs are with so-called "office wives," executive secretaries or other female office personnel with whom the man works closely. The following quotation suggests the special closeness that can develop on the job. A forty-year-old woman, a scientist's assistant, said:

> We do have an advantage over the wives at home. If I help him draft a proposal that comes through with flying colors, I can really feel overjoyed at our mutual success, can feel that I have been a real part of it. But if the proposal falls through, I'm the one closest to his disappointment and I find deep comfort myself in my efforts to comfort him.
>
> (Cuber and Harroff, 1972: 117)

It is a relationship that can be destructive, however, for participants, especially unmarried women. Interviewing sixty-five single women who had been involved with married men, Laurel Richardson (1988) hypothesized that the peculiar circumstances of these relationships—the man's need to keep the affair hidden, constraint on his time, and the distinct sense that the situation would not last—and not the women's personality characteristics were primarily responsible for the subjects' tendency to develop an intense, idealized feeling about both the man and the relationship. The couple generally became a passionate, secretive "we," cherishing their limited time together and seeking to enjoy it to the fullest. Frequently they would develop rituals, such as writing each other at the same time each day and thereby producing the sense, as one woman said, that "we were really together."

The problem, Richardson found, was that the secrecy that was required often caused the woman to withdraw from her friends and family. One respondent said, "I gave up my family, my identity, my culture, the theatre, the arts . . . my therapist." Subjects indicated that often they became dependent on the man, doing such things as "lying on the couch on a Sunday afternoon drinking gin, crying, and waiting for him to call" (Richardson, 1988: 216). While one might agree with Richardson's hypothesis that structural conditions encourage single women and married men to develop a secretive, highly idealized relationship, one can also consider the possibility that only a selected segment of women would be willing to tolerate such oppressive circumstances for a long period of time.

In this section we have seen that Americans'

sexual outlooks and behavior have been changing. While the amount of premarital and marital sexual activity is increasing, there are also indications that many Americans are trying to improve the quality of sexual intercourse, making it a more pleasurable and meaningful aspect of their relationships. There is, in short, a trend to develop a more relaxed, open-minded approach toward sexual relations between men and women. Does this trend include attitudes toward homosexuality?

Homosexuality

Since the late 1960s, many gay Americans have decided that their interests will be best served if they seek to change the political, economic, and social injustices they have suffered. Gay people's public actions to produce these changes have received extensive media coverage. Yet homosexuality remains a mysterious, confusing subject for most Americans. In fact, even social workers and other clinicians providing therapy to gay people generally lack a clear definition of homosexuality (Berger, 1983).

Untruths about the subject abound. One is that homosexuals come from conflict-ridden families. Evidence from a study of over 320 gay men and women concluded that two-thirds perceived their relationships with their fathers as either satisfactory or extremely satisfactory, and three-quarters felt that they maintained either a satisfactory or extremely satisfactory relationship with their mothers (Robinson, Skeen, Hobson, and Herrman, 1982). It is also widely believed that homosexuality is an indication of serious psychological disturbance. While recent research comparing heterosexuals and homosexuals found some differences — for instance, that gay men were more expressive than heterosexual men and lesbian women more goal-oriented than heterosexual women — findings indicated no differences in psychological adjustment (Kurdek, 1988).

In addition, many people believe that homosexuality is particularly communicable to children in contact with adult gays. A preliminary study disputes this claim, suggesting that children with gay parents almost invariably prefer the toys, games, clothing, and activities typical of their own sex

and as they become older report sexual fantasies or activities that are heterosexually oriented (Green, 1978). Finally it is often felt that homosexuals, whether male or female, assume either an "active" or "passive" role in sexual relations. The evidence indicates, however, that gays of both sexes commonly alternate between active and passive roles (Saghir and Robins, 1971).

"Straight" people's outlook on gays is often influenced by the fact that their observations of homosexuals are largely confined to the more obvious. The majority of gays lead unremarkable lives except for their sexual orientation, which often remains a well-kept secret from most people. In colleges, for example, large numbers of gay students never reveal their sexual preference to campus friends and even roommates, although a "coming out" trend has become more popular since the late 1960s.

In a study of sixty-five male and forty-seven female cohabiting gay couples, Lawrence Kurdek (1988) reached the following conclusions. First, the research showed that there were some differences between the female and male gay couples. Compared to the males, the lesbian couples reported higher relationship satisfaction, greater liking of the partner, stronger motivation for being in the relationship, more trust, and more shared decision making.

Second, Kurdek found that for both male and female respondents, the length of the relationship seemed to be an important factor. Those couples who had been together six or more years tended to show greater relationship satisfaction, more liking and love of the partner, and a higher level of trust than those who had been together for a shorter period of time. Third, the couples of both sexes in this study tended to be more similar to than different from each other in such social characteristics as age, social-class background, religion, and race. In spite of the limitations in how and where gay couples can meet, homosexual partner selection follows the heterosexual pattern of choosing partners with similar characteristics that we see in Chapter 12, "Family and Alternative Lifestyles."

Finally Kurdek sought to isolate factors that predicted relationship quality. He found that high motivation to be in the relationship, trust in one's partner, satisfaction with the social support the relationship provided, shared decision making, and limited belief that disagreements would hurt the relationship were good predictive factors of relationship quality. As an illustration of the last point, a member of a lesbian couple referring to her partner explained, "It took her a long time to learn to get overtly angry with me. She is getting better at locating her feelings. . . . I am always afraid that she is going to slip into this kind of apathy. And if I don't keep on top of things, we are just going to be this bored married couple" (Blumstein and Schwartz, 1983: 488).

Homosexuality and Modern Society

What are the conditions that produce homosexuality? The biological evidence is not yet decisive. One specialist concluded that while no data gathered from human subjects have shown that hormonal development determines that a person becomes either homosexual or heterosexual, it is possible that hormonal changes, including stress-related changes, in a pregnant woman's bloodstream can have a masculinizing or feminizing impact on the unborn child (Money, 1987). Evidence in the social realm seems clearer. Research has not found any distinct differences between the family backgrounds of homosexuals and heterosexuals (Siegelman, 1974).

There are some indications that experiencing homosexuality as a normal, pleasurable activity encourages its acceptance. A study of seventy-six preindustrial societies concluded that forty-nine of them (64 percent) accepted some form of homosexual activity as normal behavior. Among the Siwans of Africa, for instance, men who did not engage in homosexuality were considered peculiar. The Keraki of New Guinea believed that boys would not grow up healthy and well adjusted unless adult men practiced anal intercourse on them. Among the Mbundu and Nama of Africa, women were expected to perform mutual masturbation, using an artificial penis (Ford and Beach, 1951).

In U.S. society experience also seems to be a determining factor. One researcher who studied lesbians concluded that in an examination of the sources of lesbianism "one factor stands out as having more . . . weight than others. This is the importance of the first sexual experience and whether it is pleasurable and positive with a woman or discomforting and negative with a man" (Rosen, 1974: 70). If, indeed, this finding is maintained by further research, it will be a powerful indication of how single episodes can significantly affect people's gender-role socialization.

While pleasurable experience seems to encourage people to become gay, homosexuals' lives are often difficult because of the severe economic and social sanctions they experience. Recognizing gays' adjustment problems, many expert observers have urged that criminal penalties should not be imposed on adults voluntarily engaging in homosexual activity in private. In 1961 Illinois was the first state to repeal its statutes against homosexual acts between consenting adults in private, and seven other states took similar action during the 1970s. A number of towns and cities

Table 7.4
Americans' Outlook on Gays

LEGALIZATION OF HOMOSEXUALITY			
	YES	NO	NO OPINION
1985	44%	47%	9%
1982	45	39	16
1977	43	43	14

HOW AIDS HAS AFFECTED ATTITUDES TOWARD HOMOSEXUALITY			
		NO	NO
BETTER	WORSE	DIFFERENCE	OPINION
1985 2%	37%	59%	2%

Source: George H. Gallup, Jr. *Gallup Poll.* November 11, 1985.

have experienced bitter struggles over gay civil rights, including debates over whether or not gays should be allowed to teach in the public schools.

Can fear and hostility toward homosexuals be lessened? An experiment found that when two female and two male homosexual students ran a three-hour class session providing biographical sketches and answering questions, 82 percent of the students who interacted with them expressed low to moderate discomfort with gays. On the other hand, in another class where the students' characteristics were similar but no session occurred, 61 percent of the students indicated high discomfort with gays (Lance, 1987).

At present the greatest threat to gays comes from a nonhuman source — AIDS. It is likely that in the past decade, the high incidence of AIDS among gay males has frightened many heterosexual Americans, making them feel more negative about homosexuality. When about 200,000 college freshmen were asked whether homosexual relations should be prohibited, more than half — 53 percent — answered affirmatively, up eight percentage points from eleven years earlier (Braungart and Braungart, 1988). Table 7.4, on page 181, which addresses two issues on Americans' attitudes toward gays, includes this topic.

American Gender Roles in the Years Ahead

If we use the sociological perspective to look back over the major topics of this chapter, we see that in each case behavioral standards have altered, providing more rights and opportunities for certain groups. Traditionally gender roles were sharply divided, with men working and women caring for the family and home. Sexual behavior, especially for women, was supposed to be restricted to marriage. Finally homosexuality was considered misguided, perhaps even evil, and homosexuals were to be avoided.

Now a steadily increasing proportion of women are rejecting traditional limitations and seeking the educational and occupational opportunities once largely restricted to men. Sexual standards and behavior have altered, with the rejection of the double standard and support for the two permissiveness standards receiving widespread support. In addition, many Americans consider the pursuit of a gay lifestyle legitimate. Even with the negative impact produced by the relatively high incidence of AIDS among male homosexuals, the survey cited in Table 7.4 indicated that nearly half the public would be willing to legalize homosexuality.

Nonetheless liberalized attitudes on these issues does not mean that participants' struggles are eliminated. Consider modern women's role. The survey data presented in Table 7.5 indicate that in 1985 about 72 percent of married women wanted to be married and have children and that over half of those women (38 percent) also wanted a full-

time job. Is this possible? According to Betty Friedan (1981), the most effective way to accomplish both goals is to have wives and husbands cooperate. Friedan reported that many equality-minded women are consciously and effectively implementing two ideologies often believed contradictory. One is the woman-as-individual ideology, often involving careers pursued part-time or on

Table 7.5
Women's Views of the Ideal Lifestyle

	1975	1980	1985
Married with children	76%	74%	72%
With full-time job	32	33	38
With no full-time job	44	41	34
Married with no children	9	10	9
With full-time job	6	6	6
With no full-time job	3	4	3
Unmarried with full-time job	9	8	9
Not sure	6	8	10
(Total)	100%	100%	100%

Source: George H. Gallup, Jr. *Gallup Poll.* May 1, 1985.

Over a ten-year period, women's view of the ideal lifestyle has remained fairly stable. The most noteworthy change, perhaps, is the increased proportion that want to be married with both children and a full-time job — a jump from 32 percent in 1975 to 38 percent in 1985.

different shifts from their husband's; the other is the woman-serving-her-family ideology, ideally supported by husbands willing to assume much more extensive domestic roles than they did in the past.

Both women and men might benefit from such an approach. Research suggests that the **androgynous** person, who possesses a definite blend of both traditionally masculine and traditionally feminine traits, is usually more emotionally healthy and better adjusted than someone strongly masculine or feminine (Bem, 1975).

Such people can make special contributions in many situations. If an androgynous person were the chairperson of a college committee or a business meeting, she or he would be concerned about the effective accomplishment of the goals at hand — such as the evaluation of colleagues for promotion or the planning of a marketing campaign — but would also be tuned into the participants' emotional needs and would take the time and trouble to make certain they were met as adequately as possible.

Using the sociological perspective, we can ask ourselves whether or not current social conditions encourage androgyny. One study suggests some distinct support. When asked to describe the ideal man and the ideal woman, both American men and women generally agree on similar lists of traits for both sexes. In all four cases, "able to love" led the list, and "stands up for beliefs" and "self-confident" scored in the top five characteristics (Tavris, 1984). One implication of this study is that the emerging androgynous pattern has most emphatically borrowed from both the traditional female standard — "able to love" — and also from the traditional male stance — "stands up for beliefs" and "self-confident."

Besides data on values, research has offered other evidence of social conditions promoting androgyny. One study using industrial-psychology undergraduates to act out the manager role concluded that successful performance of this role required an androgynous style: Typical masculine directive behavior often appealed to superiors and enhanced their sense of the manager's effectiveness; on the other hand, subordinates generally preferred an emotionally supportive environment, which traditionally has been women's responsibility (Cann and Siegfield, 1987).

As managerial positions increasingly are filled by women, it will be interesting to observe whether or not female managers are more inclined to be androgynous than are their male counterparts.

Do these two studies represent significant trends for the future, or are they off the mark? What do you think?

The following section, on sexuality research, offers specific information about an important subject examined earlier in this chapter.

Research on Sexuality and Its Acceptance: Reflections of Changing Values

 For the past half-century, research on sexuality has always been surrounded with controversy. What is notable is that the substance of that controversy has changed as dominant values have changed. In the 1930s and 1940s, the focus of people's opposition was simply the existence of research on sexuality. Nowadays the opposition revolves around very different issues.

Confronting Resistance to Research on Sexuality

Before 1938 there were nineteen published studies of human sexuality. Most of them used only (written) questionnaires — not nearly as satisfactory a method as interviews to encourage people to expose the intimate details of their sexual lives. Furthermore none of the investigations were extensive enough to obtain a detailed sexual life history. Alfred Kinsey's research was a departure in both respects. Kinsey and his associates conducted detailed interviews of both American men and women. Each interview contained a minimum of 350 questions and as many as

521. In the 1990s it probably seems commonplace to undertake a detailed study of human sexuality. In the 1930s and 1940s, however, such a study was unprecedented. Kinsey was widely criticized for starting his investigations, and yet most of his research subjects cooperated when interviewed. Why?

One reason was the highly organized nature of the interview. At the beginning the researcher (Kinsey himself or one of his carefully chosen assistants) would painstakingly explain the value of the individual's contribution and emphasize the fact that everything said in the interview would remain completely confidential. Then the actual interview would begin. The early questions were nonthreatening: the person's age, place of birth, religion, education, and other such matters. For fifteen or twenty minutes, the subjects answered questions that had nothing to do with sex. In fact, even when the interviewer switched to sex, the questions were easy and unthreatening: about early knowledge of the subject. By the time the questions on adult sexual feelings and ac-

tivities were reached, many people were quite relaxed. However, others were not; in fact, some people stayed tense throughout. Interviewers did what they could to alleviate this condition. If an individual seemed especially nervous, the interviewer might switch momentarily to another subject and then back to the first topic, hoping that this time the individual would be more relaxed.

Overall Kinsey and his associates were successful in obtaining cooperation. However, Kinsey did not feel that it was wise to use a random-sampling technique, because he believed that even a modest refusal rate would invalidate any claims that the sample accurately reflected the adult American population. Instead Kinsey chose to interview a variety of different groups — the teachers in a certain school, the employees of a factory, or whatever. As the research progressed, Kinsey became increasingly determined to obtain 100 percent of each chosen group. So while he could not claim to have a random sample, at least he was able to state that once a group was picked to be in-

William Masters and Virginia Johnson not only are a renowned team of researchers on human sexuality, but they also are husband and wife.

cluded in the study, all or nearly all its members had been interviewed.

The following situation illustrates the value Kinsey placed on this approach. A magazine sent a questionnaire to its college-student readers and sought information about their sex lives. Only twenty percent of those contacted filled out the questionnaire and returned it. Kinsey was asked to comment on the limited response. He wrote:

If you are getting something like 20 per cent response, you are left completely in the dark as to the 80 per cent of the persons who fail to answer the questionnaire. This is very different from our 100 per cent sampling, where we get the histories of everybody in a group.

(Pomeroy, 1982: 225)

Kinsey's two massive volumes on the sex lives of American women and men were well received. In fact, it was the favorable response to Kinsey's second book—on the sex lives of American women—that encouraged William Masters, a gynecologist, to launch his own studies of sexuality. Masters's plan was to do an exhaustive physiological study of human sexual activity. In order to perform this research, Masters and his associates needed to observe and take physiological measures of research subjects engaged

in masturbation and sexual intercourse. Masters originally became interested in this research in the late 1930s. At the time a well-known authority on the biology of sex supported the research in principle but urged Masters to follow three rules to insure that both experts and the public would take his work seriously: Wait until he was forty before starting; earn a scientific reputation in a medical specialty; and obtain the sponsorship of a major medical school or university. Masters conscientiously followed his mentor's suggestions. He became a gynecologist, affiliating himself with Washington University School of Medicine and publishing twenty-five papers in his specialty. Furthermore he did not start his study of sexuality until the age of thirty-eight, thus waiting nearly as long as his advisor suggested.

Current Controversy in Research on Sexuality

Since the late 1960s, Americans' sexual attitudes and behavior have been liberalizing, and so there has been little opposition to the idea of conducting research on sexuality. Disagreements and debates have erupted around more specific issues. As we noted at several points in Chapter 2, "Doing Research in Sociology," social researchers have a variety of motives for conducting studies. Controversy can develop when the researchers' motives conflict with those of others who have a stake in the investigation.

In the middle 1970s, difficult economic times encouraged government officials to look for ways of saving money. In the spirit of those times, Senator William Proxmire of Wisconsin began to issue his tongue-in-cheek "Golden Fleece Awards" — a monthly acknowledgment of what he considered a particularly effective effort to waste taxpayers' money. One month the award went to a study of romantic love. The senator wrote, "I believe that 200 million Americans want to leave some things in life a mystery, and right at the top of the things we don't want to know is why a man falls in love with a woman and vice

versa" (Rubin, 1980: 284). Perhaps one can understand Proxmire's position. Still, it is not the position taken by researchers interested in love and sexuality. They believe that their task is to obtain information about their subjects and that often this information will be interesting, revealing, and even prove useful in helping improve people's lives.

When sociologist Morton Hunt undertook a major study of American sexuality in the 1970s, his outlook was utterly different from Proxmire's. He wanted to discard mystery and ignorance and reveal dominant trends in sexuality. He believed that a revelation of modern trends could supply important, practical information about couple relationships. Hunt stated:

Lacking a major census of American sexual behavior, we have had no good way to judge whether that behavior has changed radically or merely come out in the open; whether such changes as have taken place are affecting only a highly visible minority or the largely unseen majority; whether the increase in freedom, whatever its scope, has strengthened love relationships and marriage among the sexually liberated or weakened them; whether sexual liberation is bringing the liberated greater satisfaction or only a frenetic quest for stronger sensations and new kicks; and whether America is becoming a dissolute and degenerate nation or a sensuous and healthy one.

(Hunt, 1974: 15)

Feminists have raised a different set of criticisms of research on sexuality. A number of feminists have contended that like all or most elements in American society, this body of research has been male-dominated and male-oriented. For instance, Carole Vance attended an important conference on human sexuality given at a major center for research on sexuality and concluded that while prominent researchers spoke in favor of openness and general tolerance, the conference was structured to maintain male dominance, heterosexuality, the preeminence of a highly traditional nuclear family, with little or no tolerance for alternative perceptions and lifestyles.

Martha Vicinus made a related point. She argued that the conceptualization of sexuality continues to be viewed in male terms — what she has called "the energy-control (or hydraulic) model."

Sex is always something to be released or controlled; . . . Sexual modernists, such as Alfred Kinsey and more recently Masters and Johnson, have continued to describe sex as a force seeking release. The male bias of the energy-control model reflects both the gender of the major theoreticians and the unchanging assumption of a male-dominated society.

(Vicinus, 1982: 136–137)

Vicinus goes on to explain that a number of analysts of sexuality have been starting to examine the subject using other models, where they reject sexuality as an autonomous force and examine it as a product of social and historical forces.

Researchers on homosexuality have also challenged traditional standards, indicating that the dominant Western tendency to draw a sharp distinction between heterosexuals and homosexuals has discouraged investigators from studying and learning from other cultural contexts where distinctly different norms for sexual preference apply.

The feminist and gay criticisms represent a thought-provoking commentary or research on human sexuality. In the years ahead, it will be interesting to observe whether studies are able to incorporate these insights, thereby making a significant contribution to this body of research.

Sources: Philip Blumstein and Pepper Schwartz. *American Couples.* New York: William Morrow and Company. 1983; Edward M. Brecher. *The Sex Researchers.* Boston: Little, Brown and Company. 1969; Morton Hunt. *Sexual Behavior in the 1970s.* Chicago: Playboy Press. 1974; Wardell B. Pomeroy. *Dr. Kinsey and the Institute for Sex Research.* New Haven, CT: Yale University Press. 1982. Revised edition; Will Roscoe. "Making History: The Challenge of Gay and Lesbian Studies." *Journal of Homosexuality.* V. 15. 1988, pp. 1–40; Zick Rubin. "The Love Research." In Arlene Skolnick and Jerome H. Skolnick (eds.), *Family in Transition.* Boston: Little, Brown and Company. 1980. Third edition, pp. 279–285; Carole S. Vance. "Gender Systems, Ideology, and Sex Research." In Ann Snitow et al., *Powers of Desire: The Politics of Sexuality.* New York: Monthly Review Press. 1983, pp. 371–384; Martha Vicinus. "Sexuality and Power: A Review of Current Work in the History of Sexuality." *Feminist Studies.* V. 8. Spring 1982, pp. 133–156.

STUDY GUIDE

Learning Objectives

After studying this chapter, you should be able to:

1. Define sex, gender, and gender roles.
2. Discuss the influence of biological and cultural (including cross-cultural) factors on gender-role development.
3. Summarize the biosocial position.
4. Examine the structural-functional, conflict, and symbolic-interaction theories of gender roles.
5. Describe the traditional patterns of premarital sexuality and indicate how and why these patterns are changing.
6. Discuss marital couples' sexual attitudes and behavior and identify the factors influencing marital sexuality.
7. Summarize trends in extramarital sex.
8. Analyze homosexuality, discussing untruths about the subject, factual information about gay couples, and conditions producing this sexual preference.
9. Discuss the changes that seem to be occurring in Americans' gender-role outlooks.

Summary

1. Sex is the division of a variety of animal forms, including human beings, into the biological categories of male and female. Gender consists of the general behavioral standards that distinguish males from females in a given culture. A gender role is a set of specific behavioral patterns associated with either the female or male gender.

2. Sex differentiation is determined by both biological and cultural factors. Whether a fertilized egg develops into a male or female depends

on whether or not a Y chromosome was contained in the human sperm cell. Besides chromosomes the sex hormones — androgen and estrogen — seem to influence sex differentiation, producing somewhat different male and female brain structures and behavioral patterns.

Culture is an important factor determining gender differentiation. From birth our cultural standards of treatment for girl and boy babies are different, and these cultural standards are sufficiently powerful to insure that hermaphroditic children will effectively adopt the gender role in which they are raised. Cross-cultural evidence further endorses the impact of culture on gender-role development. Most likely biology and culture both influence gender differentiation, and, therefore, a biosocial position seems to be a sensible outlook.

3. One theory on gender roles is the structural-functional theory. Parsons and Bales took a traditional view, arguing that men and women have distinct task-oriented gender roles — men at work and women in the home. The conflict theory emphasizes the inequalities in the traditional arrangement, contending that economic inequality promotes sexual inequality. The symbolic-interaction theory of gender roles focuses on the development of gender roles. Kohlberg contended that sex-typed behavior is a set of ever-changing rules children compile from what they see, hear, and are told.

4. The discussion of sexual behavior divides the topic into three parts: premarital sex, marital sex, and extramarital sex. In the premarital area, men demonstrate a more detached approach to premarital sex than women. However, studies indicate that women's approach to premarital sexual activity is becoming more like that of men.

A number of factors presently support more uninhibited and pleasurable sex for married couples. Age, social-class background, socialization agents, effective contraception, and the women's liberation movement are significant influences.

Extramarital relations are encouraged by various conditions, including residential location and the diffuseness of intimacy. The peculiar conditions that accompany extramarital relations between some unmarried women and married men cause the women to idealize both the man and the relationship.

5. Myths and confusion about homosexuality abound in American society, and research, such as a recent study on male and female gay couples, can help eliminate widespread ignorance. Like gender-role activity generally, homosexuality is the product of a combination of biological and social factors, with the latter considerably more important than the former.

6. The future of American gender roles is difficult to predict. It seems likely, however, that in the years ahead an androgynous standard will become increasingly prominent.

Key Terms

abstinence total restraint from sex

androgynous possessing a definite blend of both traditionally masculine and traditionally feminine traits

biosocial position a recently developed perspective that acknowledges the significance of both biology and social experience in the development of gender roles and that emphasizes their interplay, contending that the independent significance of each factor is impossible to assess since they never exist in isolation from each other

double standard a position asserting that men may engage in premarital sex but women may not

gender the general behavioral standards that distinguish males and females in a given culture

gender role a set of specific behavioral patterns associated with either the female or male gender

identification a process by which an individual incorporates another person's values, standards, and expectations into his or her own behavior and sense of self

permissiveness with affection a standard arguing that men and women who love each other and have a stable relationship have the right to express their feelings sexually

permissiveness without affection a position contending that women and men should feel free to have sexual relations whether or not there is commitment or affection between them

sex the division of a variety of animals forms, including human beings, into the biological categories of male and female

---

Tests

True – false Test

_____ 1. In recent years the term *sex roles* has started to replace the term *gender roles*.

_____ 2. Women's and men's brains have identical locations for both speech and spatial centers.

_____ 3. Jeanne Block's study indicated that Americans more strongly emphasize gender-role differentiation and competitive achievement than the respondents from five other technologically advanced nations.

_____ 4. A recent study of 117 societies concluded that in societies where women are underrepresented, women's life options are more limited than when their proportion is larger.

_____ 5. Randall Collins's conflict perspective on gender roles focuses on a struggle for scarce resources between a dominant group (males) and a subordinate group (females).

_____ 6. Structural-functionalists believe that gender roles are determined by biological factors, while conflict theorists contend that they are produced by cultural factors.

_____ 7. The symbolic-interaction theory of gender roles has concluded that children's conceptions of appropriate gender roles are a distortion of reality because they consider only what they have seen, heard, and been told.

_____ 8. Women's sexual attitudes and behavior are becoming less like men's.

_____ 9. In her study of extramarital affairs, Laurel Richardson concluded that the special circumstances under which these relationships occurred were primarily responsible for the woman's tendency to idealize the man and the relationship.

_____ 10. Feminists and researchers of homosexuality are enthusiastic about the approaches to studies on sexuality used by such widely recognized investigators as Alfred Kinsey and William Masters.

Multiple-choice Test

_____ 1. General behavioral standards that distinguish males from females in a given culture are referred to as:
   a. biosocial roles.
   b. sex roles.
   c. gender roles.
   d. gender.

_____ 2. Crano and Arnoff examined data from cultures in six broad geographical areas and found that:
   a. most traditional generalizations about female and male behavior are true.
   b. men dominate food production in all societies.

c. women often participate extensively in food production.
d. fathers are excluded from child care in most societies.

_____ 3. The biosocial position:
   a. concludes that anatomy determines destiny.
   b. presumes that biology produces some limits and predispositions but that culture has the "final say."
   c. has been officially rejected by the American Sociological Association, though a few researchers support it.
   d. rejects all cross-cultural research.

_____ 4. According to Letha Scanzoni and John Scanzoni, when both spouses work full-time:
   a. an equal partner–equal partner pattern must develop.
   b. an owner–property pattern is likely to occur.
   c. an equal partner–equal partner pattern is possible but not certain.
   d. the wife has a smaller role in important family decisions than if she were a full-time homemaker.

_____ 5. Lawrence Kohlberg identified problems in learning and adopting appropriate gender-role behavior. Which of the following did he include?
   a. distinguishing which behavior is appropriate for boys and which is appropriate for girls
   b. separating adult from child behavior
   c. awareness of social context of behavior for both youthful and elderly roles
   d. understanding task-related gender roles

_____ 6. Emphasis on sexual pleasure for both partners is found in which of the following patterns of premarital sexual behavior?
   a. permissiveness with affection
   b. permissiveness without affection
   c. double standard
   d. abstinence

_____ 7. Compared with those who oppose extramarital sex, those who are permissive toward it are:
   a. more likely to be from rural than urban areas.
   b. more likely to be satisfied with their marriages.
   c. less likely to discuss intimate issues with someone besides their spouse.
   d. more likely to be from urban than rural areas.

_____ 8. Studies of homosexuality have provided evidence that:
   a. gays come from conflict-ridden homes.
   b. homosexuality is not particularly communicable to children in contact with adult gays.
   c. homosexuals typically adopt either an active or a passive sexual role.
   d. a and b

_____ 9. In his study of gay couples, Lawrence Kurdek found that:
   a. his subjects were much more likely than heterosexuals to find partners with different social characteristics.
   b. lesbians who believed disagreements were harmful for couples had vibrant, long-lasting relationships.
   c. female and male couples were similar in some respects.
   d. the length of time the two people had been together indicated nothing important about the relationship.

———— 10. Androgynous women and men:
   a. are likely to operate well in many managerial positions.
   b. tend to focus their time and energy on bisexuality.
   c. tend to be weak in task performance.
   d. have unusual chromosome patterns.

Essay Test

1. Define sex, gender, and gender role. What do you believe is the most significant gender-role issue today in society?
2. If females and males received identical treatment in American society, would their outlooks and behavior be the same? Discuss, drawing from material in the section on gender-role development.
3. Summarize the structural-functional, conflict, and symbolic-interaction theories of gender roles. What point(s) would you extract from each theory in constructing a general theory of gender roles?
4. Has Americans' sexual behavior changed in the past twenty years? Discuss, drawing from material in the section on sexual behavior.
5. Summarize three myths about homosexuality. What are three conclusions from Kurdek's study of gay couples?
6. Discuss possible changes in gender-role activity in the years ahead.

Suggested Readings

Bell, Alan, and Martin Weinberg. 1978. *Homosexualities: A Study of Diversity among Men and Women.* New York: Simon and Schuster. A study of almost 1000 male and female homosexuals and nearly 500 heterosexuals in the San Francisco area, contrasting gay and straight attitudes, behavior, and problems.

Benderly, Beryl Lieff. 1987. *The Myth of Two Minds: What Gender Means and Doesn't Mean.* Garden City, NY: Doubleday. A well-written introduction to the vast material about the biological and cultural influences on gender development.

Block, Jeanne H. 1984. *Sex Role Identity and Ego Development.* San Francisco: Jossey-Bass. A book containing Block's major articles and papers. Collectively they provide a great deal of information and insight about female and male development.

Blumstein, Philip, and Pepper Schwartz. 1983. *American Couples.* New York: William Morrow and Company. A sociological study based on over 12,000 surveys and 300 interviews with married, heterosexual cohabitational, and gay couples. The book focuses on the issues of money, work, and sex.

Maccoby, Eleanor Emmons, and Carol Nagy Jacklin. 1974. *The Psychology of Sex Differences.* Palo Alto, CA: Stanford University Press. A painstaking review of hundreds of studies of the psychological similarities and differences between males and females.

Masters, William, and Virginia Johnson. 1975. *The Pleasure Bond: A New Look at Sexuality and Commitment.* Boston: Little, Brown and Company. An easy-to-read, nontechnical discussion of human sexuality based on a massive experimental research program conducted by these two prominent investigators.

Troiden, Richard R. 1988. *Gay and Lesbian Identity: A Sociological Analysis.* Dix Hills, NJ: General Hall. A text providing a detailed summary of the research on homosexual identity development.

Twain, Mark. 1962. *Adventures of Huckleberry Finn.* Boston: Houghton Mifflin Company. A marvelously funny novel describing the off-beat gender-role socialization of a nineteenth-century boy who seemed to thrive on getting himself and his friends into trouble.

Additional Assignments

1. Take one of the following topics — androgyny, extramarital sex, homosexuality, or premarital sex — and develop an explanation of why it occurs, using these three theories of gender roles: structural-functionalism, conflict theory, and symbolic interaction. Use print, films, radio and television programming, and information in the text to provide support for each of the theoretical analyses of the topic. Is any theory clearly superior or inferior in its explanation?

2. Watch an hour of rock videos, if available, or select television shows that are likely to contain more than one setting where gender roles are displayed. Keep a tally on the frequencies with which females and males present themselves as either sex or love objects and also the frequencies with which females and males present members of the opposite sex as either sex or love objects. If the information is available, analyze gay males and lesbians in a similar manner. Do any patterns in media portrayals of gender-role relationships emerge? Discuss the significance of these portrayals.

Answers to Objective Test Questions

True – false Test

1. f	4. t	7. t	9. t
2. f	5. t	8. f	10. f
3. t	6. f		

Multiple-choice Test

1. d	4. c	7. d	9. c
2. c	5. a	8. b	10. a
3. b	6. b		

8
DEVIANCE

Sociological Theories of Deviance

The Anomie Theory
Differential-Association Theory
Conflict Theory
Labeling Theory

Crime

Limitations of Criminal Statistics
Types of Crime
Who Commits Crime?

The Social Control of Deviance

Informal Social Control
Formal Social Control: The Criminal-Justice System

Research in Sociology: Research on Rape: A Progressive Struggle

Study Guide

At a news conference, Representative Daniel Crane (a Republican from Illinois) spoke with tears in his eyes. "I've broken the law of God, and I can only ask for God's forgiveness, my wife's forgiveness and my friends'" (Alter, 1983: 16).

Crane and fellow House member Gerry Studds (a Democrat from Massachusetts) had just been censured in the House of Representatives for having sexual relations with House pages, Crane with a seventeen-year-old female in 1980 and Studds with a seventeen-year-old male in 1973. The punishment of censure required the two congressmen to stand before their colleagues while the Speaker of the House read a brief censure resolution. The House Ethics Committee had recommended that the two congressmen be given the mildest possible punishment—a reprimand, which would not have required public criticism. The majority of the House, however, voted against the milder punishment. "The idea of a reprimand was not strong enough for the American people," said Representative Bill Alexander, Democrat of Arkansas. "After all, these guys molested minors. I was out in my district over the weekend and I was overwhelmed. The reaction was brutal" (Roberts, 1983: B22).

The reaction of people in Representative Studds's district was mixed but primarily sympathetic. Representative Crane, on the other hand, had campaigned against moral laxity, presenting himself as a staunch supporter of traditional value, and this scandal hardly endorsed that image.

Clearly both congressmen had engaged in deviant behavior. What is deviance? Sociologist Albert Cohen suggested that it includes "knavery, skullduggery, cheating, unfairness, crime, sneakiness, malingering, cutting corners, immorality, dishonesty, betrayal, graft, corruption, wickedness, and sin . . ." (Cohen, 1966: 1). But simply listing types of deviant activities, colorful though they may be, does not indicate precisely what qualifies them as deviant. I offer the following definition. **Deviance** is any behavior that violates social norms considered sufficiently significant that the majority of a group or society responds negatively. The word *deviance* conveys the strong feeling that the people who engage in this behavior—the *deviants*—are different or even inferior and generally set apart from the rest of us.

Because social groups determine whether a thought or action qualifies as deviant, it should be apparent that what is considered deviant behavior will vary widely across space and time. Perhaps one of the reasons Representative Daniel Crane's affair with a House page created such a negative reaction in his district was that many of the citizens were traditional, believing that extramarital sex is wicked behavior that will destroy the precious family unit. Representative Studds, on the other hand, came from a socially and politically more liberal district, where the voters were more inclined to focus on his work record and to ignore his personal life.

Three hundred years ago, however, Studds's district was part of the newly established Commonwealth of Massachusetts, where Puritan settlers had just founded a colony of fervently religious people who wanted to free themselves from the decadence and corruption they believed were sweeping across Europe. Those caught engaging in sexual activity outside marriage would have been imprisoned, exiled, branded, or even put to death for engaging in activities that are currently commonplace.

Deviance is a broad and interesting topic. In American society such legal activities as alcoholism, compulsive gambling, lying, radical political behavior, the refusal to bathe regularly, the sale or purchase of pornography, and transvestism are widely considered deviant. In the following section, we examine some of the most useful sociological theories of deviance, followed by a discussion of crime. The chapter continues with an examination of the social control of deviance. The final topic involves a discussion of research on rape.

Admittedly the chapter strongly emphasizes crime and offers relatively little material on non-criminal deviant behavior. The reason, unfortunately, is that with the space limitations of an introductory text, it is important to pay considerable attention to a subject that creates extensive concern and fear for most Americans, including students.

Sociological Theories of Deviance

Over the past half-century, a rich body of theory involving deviance, especially criminality, has developed. The following four theories are among the most prominent.

The Anomie Theory

Anomie is the confusing situation produced when norms are either absent or conflicting. Societies that experience widespread anomie risk disintegration because their members no longer possess guidelines for achieving common purposes. The individual members often feel isolated and disoriented.

Robert Merton (1968) used the concept *anomie* more specifically, suggesting that it is a discrepancy between a socially approved goal and the availability of means to achieve that goal. Merton indicated that the attainment of wealth has been a strongly emphasized goal all Americans have been encouraged to seek. However, he also noted that many strivers for wealth and success, especially members of minority groups, have found the channels to achievement relatively closed. Either these individuals have lacked easy access to the culturally acceptable means to attain wealth or, primarily because of their socialization, they have not possessed the appropriate personality qualities that would have allowed them to become achievers.

Merton described five courses of action or adaptations to being in such a condition of blocked opportunity. Only in the case of conformity does the individual continue to accept both the pursuit of culturally prescribed goals and to feel favorable toward using solely legitimate means. The other four adaptations are regarded as deviant. They involve the nonacceptance of legitimate means, goals, or both. Table 8.1 summarizes Merton's theory.

1. **Conformity.** This is a nondeviant adaptation. Individuals pursue legitimate goals and use the culturally accepted means to achieve them, even though it is likely they will not attain

---

Table 8.1
The Five Modes of Adaptation in Merton's Anomie Theory

MODES OF ADAPTATION	CULTURALLY APPROVED GOALS	CULTURALLY APPROVED MEANS
Conformity	Accepts	Accepts
Innovation	Accepts	Rejects
Ritualism	Rejects	Accepts
Retreatism	Rejects	Rejects
Rebellion	Seeks to create new goals	Seeks to create new means

Source: Adapted from Robert K. Merton. *Social Theory and Social Structure*. New York: Free Press. 1968. Third edition, p. 194.

When people are blocked from culturally approved activities to obtain wealth, they pursue one of five adaptations. Either they endorse conformity, accepting the culturally approved means and goals, even though it is unlikely they will obtain their goals, or they pursue one of four deviant adaptations, rejecting either the culturally approved means, the culturally approved goals, or both the culturally approved means and goals, or seeking to create new means and goals.

those goals. In the 1920s a young black person who went to college with the hope of eventually becoming a wealthy professional was pursuing a culturally legitimate means to a legitimate goal. However, with the widespread discrimination that existed, it was unlikely the goal would have been achieved.

2. **Innovation.** This common deviant adaptation develops when a person seeks legitimate goals but is blocked from effectively using culturally accepted means to achieve them. If the drive to become wealthy cannot be satisfied through legitimate means, then some people turn elsewhere. For instance, some poor but ambitious members of economically deprived ethnic groups have turned to organized crime. There has been a definite pattern of ethnic succession in this activity. In the nineteenth century, organized crime was initially dominated by the Irish, followed by Jews and then Italians. Blacks and Puerto Ricans are the latest in line. As each ethnic group has found conventional channels of success becoming increasingly available to them, they move gradually out of the underworld (Bell, 1962: 148).

Organized criminals are not the only success-oriented people who display innovative behavior. Merton observed that most great American fortunes were accumulated at least in part by techniques generally considered culturally illegitimate and even illegal. The respect most Americans show toward those who have accumulated such wealth indicates that the goal itself—the achievement of wealth—generally is considered more important than the legitimacy of the means by which it is achieved (Merton, 1968: 195–203).

3. **Ritualism.** This pattern occurs when culturally prescribed success goals are no longer actively sought, but the legitimate means for achieving those goals are conscientiously pursued. The ritualist avoids the dangers and possible frustrations of open competition and simply follows safe and easy routines of living and working. The ritualist qualifies as deviant because he or she fails to address goals that are strongly supported within the society. Merton mentioned a number of well-known clichés that apply to the ritualist—"I'm not sticking my neck out," "I'm playing it safe," and "Don't aim high and you won't be disappointed." As a prime example of ritualism, Merton cited the "zealously conformist bureaucrat" (Merton, 1968: 203–205). Such a person accepts the organization's goals or rules as personal goals or rules and is characterized by an unquestioning allegiance to the organization.

4. **Retreatism.** A person is a retreatist if he or she neither pursues the culturally prescribed goal of success nor uses the means for achieving this goal because of limited opportunities or a sense of personal inadequacy. Among the types of deviants who may be regarded as retreatists are "psychotics, . . . outcasts, vagrants, vagabonds, tramps, chronic drunkards, and drug addicts" (Merton, 1968: 207). In short, retreatists are dropouts, and they are frequently condemned by many people because of their inability or unwillingness to lead normal, productive lives.

5. **Rebellion.** The deviant adaptation of rebellion happens when an individual decides that the existing society imposes barriers preventing the achievement of success goals. Therefore that individual strikes out against the society, seeking to change its goals and also the existing means for achieving them. According to Merton (1968: 210), people who engage in rebellion withdraw their allegiance from the existing society and develop "a new myth." This myth or set of beliefs claims that the source of frustration lies in the organizational and cultural patterns of the present society. Thus the myth proposes new cultural arrangements that do not display the problems emphasized by the people involved in the rebellion. In the past fifteen years, women, blacks, students, welfare recipients, antiwar activists, antinuclear protestors, work groups, and environmentalists have been prominent groups initiating social movements that support rebellious activity.

Commentary

A major contribution of the anomie perspective is that it allows us to interpret a wide variety of deviant behavior by means of a single theory. As one writer noted, the scheme includes such diverse deviant personality types "as Cubists, alcoholics, lone-wolf inventors, religious martyrs, executives, and beggars" (Hunt, 1961: 59). Furthermore this theory contributes significantly to an understanding of deviance by taking a distinctly sociological perspective: It indicates that social forces play an important role in encouraging people to behave in a deviant manner and opposes the widely held belief that all responsibility for deviant acts should be placed on the individuals in question.

On the other hand, Merton's analysis has been sharply criticized. Some individuals have claimed that the scheme provides no more than a general idea of how anomie can contribute to deviance; the precise process by which people learn deviance, including the motivation to learn deviance, needs to be mapped out much more thoroughly and systematically (Agnew, 1985; Messner, 1988). Merton (1976: 32) himself admitted that his theory addresses only selected issues as it analyzes sources of deviance and contributes nothing about how people learn to be deviant. That task is left to other theories, in particular the differential-association perspective.

Differential-Association Theory

What is the process by which criminal behavior is learned? Edwin Sutherland's theory of differential association addresses this issue. Essentially this perspective emphasized that people's behavior is largely determined by the company they keep. The concept of reference group, which is discussed in Chapter 4, "Groups," on p. 89 and p. 90, is closely related to this theory. The following four steps summarize the differential-association process.

1. Criminal behavior, like behavior generally, is learned in interaction with others, mostly in intimate groups.
2. Learning criminal behavior consists of acquiring both criminal techniques and the motives, drives, and attitudes appropriate for criminal behavior.
3. A person becomes a criminal "because of an excess of definitions favorable to violation of law over definitions unfavorable to violation of law." Therefore someone is likely to become a criminal if that person's values and the values of the individuals who have the greatest influence over him or her more strongly support criminal than support noncriminal activity.
4. A person's criminal associations can vary in certain respects. In particular, the frequency, length, and intensity of these contacts will help determine the impact of these associations on the individual (Sutherland and Cressey, 1978: 80–83).

The differential-association theory can be applied to diverse forms of criminal and delinquent behavior. For example, a detailed study indicated that in Nazi Germany many doctors joined the Nazi party, enthusiastically promoting Hitler's program for racial "purity" by mudering Jews, handicapped children, psychiatric patients, and other designated undesirables with a variety of techniques (Proctor, 1988). Thus these doctors encountered an excess of definitions favorable to widespread murder of supposed undesirables over those unfavorable to such a course of action.

Ironically one of the latent dysfunctions of prisons is that they provide a learning context for budding criminals. Young, fairly inexperienced people arrive in prison, and from the more experienced inmates they may obtain critical information for a successful criminal career. In the mid-1970s, a young man was sent to a minimim-security federal prison, where he served a short sentence for selling marijuana. In prison he learned the intricacies of the system — using small airplanes, for example, to smuggle hundreds of pounds of marijuana into the country at a time. While still in prison, he realized that the same approach could be used with cocaine, and upon release he began setting up such a system and soon became one of the most successful drug traffickers (Massing, 1989).

During the first half of this century, juvenile gangs were often the context in which young men could learn the values, skills, and motivation necessary for a criminal career in association with others (Shaw and McKay, 1942; Thrasher, 1926). The minority and ghetto gangs of recent years have been less clearly linked to criminal life. If these gangs have had one distinguishing factor, it has been that they provide an excess of definitions favoring violence as a means of self-glorification and status achievement in a situation where the gang members are usually characterized by limited social ability and training, excessive aggression, and a desire to retaliate against others and against the society in general. As one gang member graphically stated, "A knife or a gun makes you feel ten feet tall" (Haskell and Yablonsky, 1974: 525).

Commentary

Critics of the differential-association perspective have charged that some of the terminology of the theory is vague, making verification through research difficult. For example, it is not entirely

Gang membership may provide a supportive context for attributes such as toughness and daring as well as an "excess of definitions" favoring violence as a means of achieving status within the gang, if not in the larger world.

clear how the phrase "excess of definitions favorable to violation of law over definitions unfavorable to violation of law" can be tested (Sutherland and Cressey, 1978: 83–92).

On the other hand, differential-association theory has made a significant contribution: It emphasizes the fact that the development of criminal behavior can be understood only by examining the particular needs and values that specific criminal groups provide to their members.

Conflict Theory

In 1973 Ian Taylor, Paul Walton, and Jock Young produced a book called *The New Criminology*. While their analysis offered little that was actually new, it did give increased prominence to the social-critic role of criminologists, noting the failure of modern society to promote a truly just social-justice system. The book applied Marxist thinking to the analysis of criminal justice, emphasizing that complete social freedom for most citizens is severely limited by the fact that laws are enacted and maintained by people at the upper socioeconomic levels — the ruling class — whose intention is to keep those who are not wealthy and powerful in their place (Taylor, Walton, and Young; 1973).

Proponents of conflict theory offer somewhat varied explanations of why the situation they describe has arisen in modern societies. Chambliss and Seidman (1971) contended that such a condition will occur in any complex society that has a multilevel class system. On the other hand, Richard Quinney (1974) argued that Western capitalism is the prime source of these inequities.

Quinney's (1975: 37–41) version of the conflict theory of deviance has focused on "the social reality of crime." He described four conditions that help explain both the high U.S. crime rate and the prevailing system of criminal justice. First, the ruling class defines as criminal those behaviors that threaten its existence. Second, the elite uses these definitions of criminal behavior to protect its own interests. Third, because of the limited life chances available to them, members of the subordinate classes are virtually compelled to engage in the sorts of behaviors defined as criminal. Finally the ruling class develops an ideology that explains criminal behavior and that, in effect, downgrades the subordinate classes or groups, which are said to contain a disproportionate number of dangerous people.

Commentary

Conflict theory suggests that those defined as criminals are generally members of subordinate classes; this suggestion is an oversimplification. Consider the crimes of the prominent politicians, business people, and labor leaders who have been indicted in the post-Watergate years.

Conflict theory has also been criticized for its failure to describe the causes of deviant behavior. However, the theory makes no claim to do so; it pursues a specific task. The theory attempts to explain why certain standards for criminal behavior are established and not others. For instance, why are homosexuality, excessive drinking, the habitual use of powerful prescription drugs, and uncontrolled gambling frequently considered deviant but not classified as criminal? According to the conflict perspective, the reason is that it is not in the interests of the ruling class to establish a criminal definition for these activities.

Labeling Theory

Labeling theory is a form of symbolic interaction, and, because it falls within this theoretical tradition, the perspective is centrally concerned with interaction between deviants and conformists. In addition, since the interaction is symbolic, labeling theory is concerned with the meanings the participants derive from each other's actions and reactions. Labeling theory emphasizes that behavior itself does not distinguish deviants from nondeviants. Instead the distinction is provided by the actions of the conforming members of society. These members interpret certain behavior as deviant and then apply the deviant label to individuals. Like conflict theory, the labeling perspective does not seek the causes of deviance but raises such questions as who applies the deviant label to whom and what are the consequences for the people labeled.

Labeling theory emphasizes that labels are applied by people powerful enough to impose their standards on society—for instance, police, judges, prison guards, and psychiatrists. Those labeled include criminals, juvenile delinquents, drug addicts, alcoholics, prostitutes, homosexuals, mental patients, and retarded people (Thio, 1978: 56–58). Recent studies have examined the rationalizations heroin addicts use to minimize the self-rejection of being labeled an addict (Covington, 1984), police and mental-health officials' impact on the development of juveniles' deviant self-images (Palamara, 1986), and the process by which self-labeling leads to seeking help for mental illness (Thoits, 1985).

If labeling theory were concerned only with the issue of who imposes labels on whom, then it would be closely related to conflict theory. However, labeling theory also examines another important issue: the consequences of being labeled deviant.

Consequences of Labeling

The labeling process can be divided into two stages, primary deviance and secondary deviance (Lemert, 1951: 75–76). With **primary deviance** individuals violate a social rule but are not labeled and so do not see themselves as deviant. **Secondary deviance** is violation of a social norm in which authorities label individuals deviants and those individuals accept the status of deviant. The label fits. "Yes," the person admits, "I am an alcoholic," or "I did commit a crime by embezzling the company funds."

Why does primary deviance tend to become secondary deviance? Edwin Lemert (1951: 77) suggested that there is a process of interaction between the person and various forces of social control. Primary deviance is followed by the imposition of social penalties. Additional primary deviance happens, followed by stronger penalties and rejections. Further hostilities and resentment occur, perhaps with a hostile focus on those penalizing. The community now takes formal action, labeling the individual as a deviant. Eventually the person accepts the deviant role and incorporates an awareness of being deviant into his or her life pattern. At this point secondary deviance has taken place.

In a study of two groups of white, male, high-school students, William Chambliss (1973) demonstrated the selective nature of the labeling process. Both groups were frequently involved in delinquent acts—truancy, drinking, petty theft, vandalism, and (for one group) wild driving. The members of one group, however, were never arrested, while the members of the other were in constant difficulty with the police. The boys who were never in trouble—in the study they were called the "Saints"—came from respectable families. They had established good, sometimes excellent reputations in school; tended to have good grades; and were careful "to cover their tracks" so that they would not be caught following their misdeeds. If confronted by the police, the Saints were polite and apologetic, and, if necessary, their parents would intervene on their behalf. These boys engaged in primary deviance but carefully avoided run-ins with the authorities. In other words they escaped the labeling process that would have led them to see themselves as deviants.

The other group, whose members were called the "Roughnecks" in the study, came from much lower-status families. The Roughnecks had poor reputations and grades in school; they were less likely to have cars than the Saints, and so if they got into trouble they were less easily able to escape the situation. Being without cars also encouraged the Roughnecks to stay in the center of town where everyone, including teachers and the police, could see them. Unlike the Saints the Roughnecks appeared hostile and disdainful if confronted by the police. Also the parents of the Roughnecks, feeling powerless, were unlikely to intervene with the police on behalf of their children. In short, various social forces in the community propelled the Roughnecks toward secondary deviance.

It proved difficult to make an accurate comparison of the relative severity of the deviance engaged in by members of the two groups. The Saints took part in a greater number of deviant acts and may have caused greater damage with their drunken driving. The Roughnecks were much more inclined toward physical violence. From the point of view of the community, however, the comparison was easy. Selective perception operated. As the products of upper-middle-class families, the Saints were perceived to be "good;" the lower-class Roughnecks were seen as "bad." The police frequently took action against the Roughnecks and never against the Saints, setting the secondary deviance process in motion for the Roughnecks.

Commentary

There are several limitations to the labeling perspective. First, this theory applies only to a relatively small range of deviant behavior. The majority of the people who take part in deviance are never caught or labeled. This generalization applies to types of deviance as diverse as stealing, homosexuality, extramarital sex, marijuana use,

Table 8.2
Four Sociological Theories of Deviance

THE THEORY	ITS BASIC QUESTION	THE ANSWER
Anomie theory	1. What are the social conditions that produce deviance?	1. Limited access to culturally approved goals, the means to achieve them, or both
Differential-association theory	2. How do people learn deviant norms, values, and behavior?	2. By the influence of the company they keep
Conflict theory	3. What is the primary motivation behind a society's definitions of deviance and crime?	3. The definitions project wealthy and powerful people's needs and interests
Labeling theory	4. What happens to a person who is labeled deviant?	4. Subjection to a two-part process that is likely to produce a deviant career

drunken driving, and crimes committed by business people or politicians. Second, sociologists who employ the labeling perspective tend to focus primarily on the lower-class people who are relatively easily labeled and to ignore middle- and upper-class individuals who have considerable ability to resist labeling. This situation seems unavoidable. After all, the labeling process is initiated by middle- and upper-class people in positions of authority, and these people are not likely to permit themselves or their children to be labeled deviants (Thio, 1978), as the Chambliss study on high-school boys illustrates. Furthermore in recent articles, sociologists have indicated that the concepts in this theory are "murky" and

thus difficult to test in studies (Dotter and Roebuck, 1988: Tittle, 1988). Under precisely what circumstances, for instance, has an individual crossed the line from primary to secondary deviance?

Despite such limitations labeling theory does contribute substantially to our understanding of many kinds of deviant activity. In particular, the theory emphasizes that a force other than the deviant act itself—namely, the reactions of others—frequently contributes to the development of deviance (Clinard, 1974: 25–27).

Table 8.2 summarizes all four theories of deviance.

Crime

In the previous section, we encountered a number of references to crime. The majority of crimes are, in fact, generally regarded as deviant activities—for instance, murder, rape, assault, robbery, burglary, embezzlement, and a host of others. On the other hand, some people who talk to themselves in public or who do not bathe would qualify as deviant but not criminal in U.S. society. In addition, some technically illegal behaviors are often not regarded as deviant. There is widespread violation of some outdated laws, such as restrictions against premarital sexual relations or Sunday sports. Criminal laws generally reflect the prevailing standards of deviant behavior, and when those standards change, the laws are likely to be altered or disregarded.

Crime is simply an act that violates criminal law. Punishment for crime is provided by the criminal-justice system of a society. Behavior is likely to be defined as criminal when it is too disruptive to be permitted and cannot be controlled by informal means.

In this section we examine the limitations of criminal statistics, the different types of crime, and criminals' characteristics.

Limitations of Criminal Statistics

Official crime statistics drawn throughout the United States are reported in the FBI's annual

Uniform Crime Report. Serious biases exist in these data, and we examine four sources of these biases.

From Complaints to Official Statistics

One of law-enforcement officials' chief tasks is to respond to people's complaints. The officer must decide whether or not to file a formal report of the complaint, thereby making it a crime known to police. One study indicated that the major variable affecting the reporting and recording of a crime is its perceived seriousness—most important is the victim's perception and less significant is the officer's view. Unlike earlier research this investigation found that offenders' and victims' personal characteristics seem to have a minor impact on reporting and recording crimes (Gove et al., 1985). Besides perceived seriousness affecting reporting, some crimes pose particular problems in this regard. Arson is probably underreported, because before a report of arson can be made, it must be established that a fire has been "willfully or maliciously set," and that can be difficult to determine (Jackson, 1988).

Issues Involving the Victim's Willingness to Cooperate

Other factors also strongly affect the official crime statistics. The victim's willingness to cooperate is often significant. It is unlikely that rape will be made known to the police and that an arrest will be made unless the victim reports the crime and cooperates with the investigation. Between 1978 and 1987, the number of rapes known to the police increased by 35 percent (U.S. Bureau of the Census, *Statistical Abstract of the United States: 1989.* No. 277). While it is likely that the actual amount of rape increased during that period, there undoubtedly was also an increase in the victims' willingness to cooperate with an investigation. A couple of factors have supported this trend. Some women's groups have argued that a war against rapists should be declared — "We shall win back the night" — and many police departments have supported this campaign. In addition, the findings of a recent study suggested another factor — when a large city's police department improved its procedures for dealing with rape victims, the reporting of rape increased (Le-Beau, 1988).

Administrative Distortions

Sometimes crime rates appear to increase because a police force has become more professionalized. For example, in 1950, under pressure from the FBI, the New York City Police Department changed its system of reporting crime — in one year the city's reported robbery rate increased 400 percent and the burglary rate rose 1300 percent.

Furthermore law-enforcement officials or politicians — in an effort to serve their own purposes — sometimes deliberately alter statistics in order to "prove" that there has been an increase or decrease in crime. For instance, the FBI reported that of the people arrested and then released by the courts in 1963, 92 percent were rearrested within six years. Careful investigation revealed, however, that the FBI did not include all people released in 1963 in this study. Seventy-six percent of the records involving people in that category were conveniently lost, and apparently most of these people were not rearrested. J. Edgar Hoover, then the Director of the FBI, wanted to show that the courts were too lenient with offenders. He, therefore, distorted FBI crime statistics in order to support that conclusion (Hans Zeisel, cited in Reid, 1982: 50 – 51).

Absence of White-Collar Crime

Later in this chapter, we discuss white-collar crime, which is committed by people of higher socioeconomic status in the course of their business activities. This type of crime is omitted from the annual *Uniform Crime Report,* thus significantly underrepresenting crimes committed by high-income individuals, whose arrests are much more likely to occur with this type of crime than in other criminal activities.

Types of Crime

The people who commit different types of crime are likely to vary in their background characteristics, lifestyles, and subcultures. However, all are probably affected by some of the social forces referred to in the theories we have examined. Many are, in Merton's terminology, innovators: seeking wealth through crime because legitimate access to its pursuit has been blocked. Furthermore, as differential-association theory indicates, most lawbreakers are exposed to criminal reference groups, providing an excess of definitions favorable to violation of the law. And in line with conflict theory, most criminals engage in behavior that influential citizens have — to their advantage — designated as criminal. Finally many lawbreakers experience the process of being labeled as criminals and, especially if sent to prison, enter the phase of secondary deviance.

Crime against Persons and Property

The crime statistics presented in the FBI's *Uniform Crime Reports* are divided into two categories, Part-I offenses and Part-II offenses. Part-II offenses are less serious crimes, such as drunkenness, fraud, prostitution and commercialized vice, and disorderly conduct. Part-I offenses are further divided into two subcategories: (1) violent crimes, namely murder, negligent manslaughter, rape, robbery, and aggravated assault; and (2) property crimes, specifically burglary, larceny (theft), motor-vehicle theft, and arson. The *Uniform Crime Reports* focus on these two sets of offenses because they have distinctly uniform definitions throughout the states and because they occur frequently enough to be statistically significant.

VIOLENT CRIME In the past decade, at least one member of about 6 percent of all households has been raped, robbed, or assaulted each year. In 1987 a violent crime known to the police took place every twenty-one seconds on the average. An aggravated assault occurred every thirty-seven seconds, a robbery every sixty-one seconds, a rape every six minutes, and a murder every twenty-six minutes. In 1987 there were nearly 1.5 million violent crimes out of the nearly 13.5 million total Part-I crimes known to the police, with violent crime representing 11 percent of that total. However, law-enforcement officials place special emphasis on violent crime, arresting suspects in 31.9 percent of the known violent crimes, compared to 14.8 percent of the suspects in property crimes (U.S. Bureau of the Census, *Statistical Abstract of the United States: 1989.* No. 277 and No. 293).

Many Americans today fear being murdered. Americans often think of murderers as deranged people like the Son of Sam, Charles Manson, the Zodiac Killer, the Boston Strangler, or Jack the Ripper, who strike quickly and entirely unexpectedly, murdering and sometimes raping victims they have never met. Of course, such murders are often well publicized. However, these murders make up only a small proportion of the total. Most murders occur after social interaction between the murderer and the victim. In a substantial number of cases, the victim precipitated the violence, perhaps by striking the first blow or by attempting to use a deadly weapon. Furthermore most people who kill lack apparent psychotic tendencies.

Murders, in fact, tend to occur in the course of ordinary behavior. A recently developed theory— the "routine activities" approach—suggests that most murders are committed in the midst of people's everyday routines, which tend to vary ac-

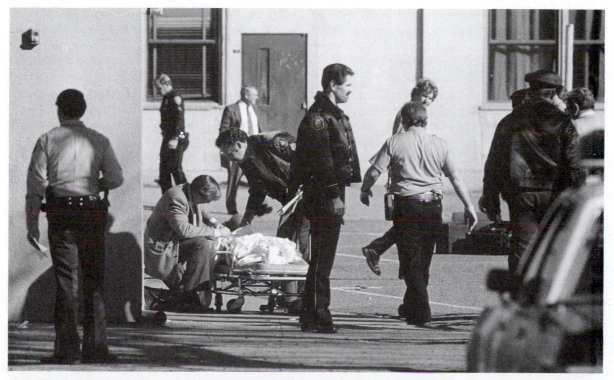

A small percentage of murders are highly publicized killings, such as those at Cleveland Elementary School in Stockton, California, in 1989. A gunman shot and killed five students and wounded more than thirty others, including the child on the stretcher pictured here.

cording to such personal characteristics as age, sex, race, marital status, and employment status. For example, since the very young and the very old are more likely to have their routine activities centered in the home than are other people, these two age categories are more likely to be murdered at home than are others (Messner and Tardiff, 1985).

Studies suggest that men kill and are killed four to five times more frequently than women; that there is no actual season for murder but that December, July, and August are the most common months; that murders are most likely to occur in large cities; that most murders take place on weekends, particularly on Saturday night between 8 PM and 2 AM; and that in nearly two-thirds of all murders, either the victim or the offender (or both) has been drinking (Cheatwood, 1988; Wolfgang, 1967).

In a national survey, 79 percent of the sample indicated support for the death penalty, and only 16 percent opposed it (George Gallup, Jr., *Gallup Report,* January 1989). While people can have different motives for supporting the death penalty, including the desire to punish — "a life for a life" — the issue that has received considerable attention from sociologists has been whether or not the use of the death penalty has a deterrent effect, stopping individuals who are tempted to commit murder from actually doing it. For many years sociologists have pointed out that while this is a difficult or impossible question to answer with certainty, many murders occur under the influence of alcohol, drugs, or passion, and the offenders simply are not thinking clearly enough to consider the possibility that they might be executed for their crime. A study found that since many states restored capital punishment in the early 1970s, there has been no apparent decline in murder rates. The roots of killing and violence in America can be traced most prominently to social and economic inequalities, racism, and family disorganization, the study concluded (Peterson and Bailey, 1988). Thus the sociological perspective suggests that the most effective way to reduce the death rate is not to execute murderers but to relieve the economic and social conditions that increase the likelihood that people will engage in violence and killing.

Unfortunately rape is widespread in the United States. At some colleges, security has been increased and members of fraternities and other men's groups volunteer to escort women home at night.

Violent sex-offenders generally do not consider themselves criminals, though they recognize themselves as "different." Except in the sexual realm, their behavior is usually conventional, and they often have no previous criminal records. Repressed sexuality frequently appears in case studies, but its source is generally unclear (Gibbons, 1977: 389–391). When asked why they engaged in rape, a group of 114 convicted rapists referred to revenge or punishment (with the victim substituting in the rapist's mind for the actual object of his anger), a means of access to unwilling or inaccessible women, or a bonus in a burglary or robbery (Scully and Marolla, 1985).

In the past twenty years, some women's groups have strongly protested the general availability of pornographic magazines, films, and album covers, claiming that these materials blatantly encourage men to see women as objects for exploitation. Efforts to legislate against pornography are now underway. In major cities around the country, supporters of such legislation have worn buttons that make statements like: "Women against Pornography: It's About Time" (McCarthy, 1981). As the research section at the end of the chapter indicates, the modern women's movement has also helped produce a steadily growing body of research on rape.

CRIME AGAINST PROPERTY People who know little about correctional institutions might assume they are filled to overflowing with murderers and rapists. Actually, of the nearly 1.5 million individuals under some form of correctional supervision, by far the greatest number are held for offenses against property. In short, the prisoners have stolen or damaged something that belongs to someone else. Property crimes are much more common than violent crimes. In fact, a property crime known to the police occurs in the United States every 2.6 seconds, more frequently than most of us blink. About one in twenty Americans is the victim of a property crime each year (U.S. Bureau of the Census, *Statistical Abstract of the United States: 1989.* No. 5 and No. 277).

Between 1976 and 1987, the amount of crime known to the police increased by 19 percent (U.S.

Bureau of the Census, *Statistical Abstract of the United States: 1989.* No. 277). Part of the increase resulted not from an actual increase in crime but rather from improved procedures for collecting and reporting crime statistics. Furthermore during this period, the population of young people was increasing substantially, and the members of this group are especially likely to commit property crimes. In 1987 people under twenty-five accounted for 59 percent of larcenies, 73 percent of motor-vehicle thefts, and 70 percent of burglaries (U.S. Bureau of the Census, *Statistical Abstract of the United States: 1989.* No. 293). Finally some current social conditions seem to promote increasing rates of property crime. Americans are living in a "ripoff society," one critic asserted. He suggested that impersonal urban conditions, the cost of adequate security in businesses and homes, the ability of the mass media — especially television — to stimulate an intense desire for worldly goods, and the lessening impact of organized religion have all encouraged an increase in property crime (Bacon, 1979).

In addition, use of computers has permitted a new type of property crime — "computer crime." Anyone with a small computer and a modem (a device costing approximately $100 that converts a computer's digital pulses into electromagnetic waves that can be transmitted over a phone line) can employ a relatively easy trial-and-error procedure to hook into thousands of business and military computers. Some experts estimate that computer criminals use such methods to steal as much as $300 million per year. One prominent computer scientist suggested that the low level of security at many computer centers is "like leaving the keys in the ignition of an unlocked car" (Broad, 1983: 1). It is now widely acknowledged that the most sophisticated computer systems cannot be protected from penetrators who have high-level skill, knowledge, and resources.

One of the unusual aspects of computer crime is that since widespread use of computers is recent, the formation of criminal laws in relation to them is also recent. It appears that mass-media personnel have played a major role in the development of computer law. These people decided that computer abuse was a newsworthy issue, and thus they provided the public detailed accounts of instances in which individuals used computers to embezzle large sums of money or to break into strategic information systems. By showing that such abuses were quite frequent, mass-media personnel both contributed to the public's sense of threat and encouraged widespread support for the development of criminal laws related to computer abuse (Hollinger and Lanza-Kaduce, 1988).

Victimless Crime

A **victimless crime** is defined as the willing (hence "victimless") exchange among adults of strongly desired but illegal goods or services. As the term suggests, those who engage in victimless crimes are generally not preying on others. The list of victimless crimes includes gambling, illicit drug use, prostitution, loansharking, vagrancy, and public drunkenness.

Prostitutes, vagrants, and drunks are public eyesores who often draw police complaints. Arrests are frequent. In 1987, 6.4 percent of all arrests were for public drunkenness, with about 701,000 people arrested. There were also 811,000 arrests for drug abuse, 136,000 for (juveniles) running away from home, 101,000 for prostitution, and 76,000 for juvenile curfew violations and loitering (U.S. Bureau of the Census, *Statistical Abstract of the United States: 1989.* No. 293).

Defining the types of behavior just discussed as crimes has a couple of negative consequences. First, when highly desired goods and services are made illegal, black-market activities develop to supply users. If these operations are profitable enough, organized crime is likely to step in. It is hard to deny that in the 1920s the Volstead Act, which made the sale of alcoholic beverages illegal, helped organized crime to flourish and that the continuing illegal status of drugs, prostitution, and, to some extent, gambling have also strongly benefited organized crime. Second, the illegal status of these goods and services keeps prices high and quality questionable. For example, street-bought heroin varies markedly in its strength, and occasionally users take lethal or near-lethal overdoses because the strength of the drugs they have purchased exceeds expectations. With prescription drugs, in contrast, the strength and purity of the drugs are always guaranteed.

As we noted in the discussion of Merton's anomie theory, organized-crime leaders have been highly successful innovators, achieving great wealth and power through illegitimate channels when legitimate channels have been blocked for members of their particular ethnic group. The earliest organized-crime leadership was by WASPs ("White Anglo-Saxon Protestants") followed by Irish, Jewish, and currently Sicilian-Italian domination. As each successive ethnic group has found legitimate channels to achievement opening to them, they have moved into the middle class and out of organized crime. For Italian-Americans, who still are the most powerful group in organized crime, a middle-class base is now firmly established, and replacement by black and Hispanic personnel, who currently find limited opportunities through legitimate channels, seems likely (Ianni, 1973).

Organized crime activities fall roughly into three categories:

1. *Illegal activities,* such as gambling, prostitution, and narcotics. Public opinion varies widely on the morality of these different activities.
2. *Legitimate businesses,* such as the vending-machine and the solid-waste disposal industries, have been infiltrated by organized crime; such activities provide significant income and some measure of respectability to the participants.
3. *Racketeering,* which is the systematic extortion of funds over a period of time. For instance, if owners pay for "protection," their businesses will not be destroyed by the mob (Clinard and Quinney, 1973: 390).

The consequences of some of organized crime's activities have been devastating. For instance, organized crime has the cash to finance the heroin trade, which frequently employs expensive and elaborate equipment such as computers, processing laboratories powered by electric generators, and radar-equipped private planes.

What are the effects of organized crime's control of the heroin trade? For one thing this situation has created an army of muggers, who are estimated to initiate over half the violent crime in major cities. Courts and prisons are overloaded with addicts. Many billions of tax dollars are spent on efforts to combat and treat addiction. Furthermore government officials estimate that drug-related murders and overdoses account for some 15,000 deaths a year. Finally in order to keep law-enforcement officials from interfering in the heroin trade, organized crime has corrupted the police departments of many large cities (Newfield and Dubrul, 1979).

In recent years government officials have been making extensive efforts to fight organized crime. At times they have resorted to novel measures, including the confiscation of the attorney's fees for those defending accused organized-crime individuals. Prosecutors have argued that a person should be permitted to purchase neither a Rolls Royce nor a "Rolls Royce class of attorney" with the profits of criminal activity (Dombrink, Meeker, and Paik, 1988).

Certainly organized crime has produced tremendous profits. Estimates indicate that organized crime is the second largest business in the United States, with gross revenues of about $150 billion in 1978 compared to the automobile industry's $125 billion. White-collar crime produced about $100 billion (Fox, 1985: 252).

White-collar crime is crime committed by people of higher socioeconomic status in the course of their business activities. The list of white-collar crimes includes bribery, embezzlement, sale of dangerously defective cars, military equipment, and pharmaceuticals, criminal price-fixing, serious consumer fraud, Medicare theft, deliberate shipping of defective products to unsuspecting foreign markets, and systematic violation of safety and pollution-control standards. Consumer advocate Ralph Nader wrote, "By almost any measure, crime in the suites takes more money and produces far more casualties and diseases than crime in the streets—bad as that situation is (Nader, 1985: 3). According to Nader, corporations, like fish, rot from the head down. To attack white-collar crime in corporations, law-enforcement officials need to start at the top.

Some prosecution for white-collar crime has occurred, and those prosecuted experience highly varied impacts upon their careers. Professionals (lawyers, in particular), government workers, and people in licensed occupations (for instance, accountants) tend to suffer a negative response from their occupational group and frequently are barred from continued activity in their field. On the other hand, business people or employees of private business generally encounter few such negative responses (Benson, 1984).

Most Americans think of white-collar criminals as individuals or small groups involved in secretive, illegal money-making schemes. A broader outlook seems necessary, however. A prime case in point would be the Iran–*contra* affair, which became public in 1987: Members of the National Security Council engaged in several major illegal acts, selling arms to Iran and transferring funds from the sale to the *contra* rebel forces fighting the Sandinista government in Nicaragua; both of these acts were illegal because they occurred without congressional approval, which is required in each case. What makes such political examples of white-collar crime unusual is the ideological quality associated with the criminal acts. Some of the participants, in fact, claimed that while their activities were illegal, the behavior was justified because it represented the participants' willingness to do what the president felt was best for the country. Testifying before a Senate investigating committee, Lieutenant Colonel Oliver North became a hero to many Americans with statements like this one:

> This lieutenant colonel is not going to challenge a decision of the Commander in Chief for whom I still work, and I am proud to work for that Commander in Chief, and if the Commander in Chief tells this lieutenant colonel to go stand in the corner and sit on his head, I will do so.

(Draper, 1989: 40)

In the following Social Application, which examines illegal drugs in America, the role of

Even though Colonel Oliver North committed white-collar crimes, many Americans considered him a hero, fervently supporting his claim that the illegal acts in which he engaged were conducted in the country's best interest.

wealthy, powerful people is apparent. Because of the increasingly serious nature of the problem, the discussion is longer than normally found in these sections.

SOCIAL APPLICATION

Drugs in America

In 1989 the American government's war on drugs was in disarray. Involved in the war have been eleven federal departments and thirty-seven federal agencies, and Congress has seventy-four committees and subcommittees with jurisdiction over narcotics issues. To consider that a coordinated attack on the drug problem will occur soon requires courage that perhaps borders on the psychotic.

Nonetheless, at times governmental efforts have been valiant. In the longest, most expensive trial in American history, the U.S. attorney in New York City and his assistants presented evidence against twenty-two defendants indicating that they had conspired to import one-and-one-half tons of pure heroin into the United States and then had distributed it through pizzerias in the East and Midwest. In February 1987, after a trial that lasted nearly a year and one-half, the government was rewarded with convictions and long prison terms for all but two defendants. Drug trafficking was not affected, however.

The problem is that the traffickers are too well organized and powerful. They include individuals like the immensely successful Kojak (so called because of his shaved head), who runs a fleet of speedboats that travel at ninety miles an hour between remote islands in the Bahamas and drop-off points on the Florida coast. Because of the Coast Guard's limited resources, an elaborate radio network for warning his boatmen, and his intimate knowledge of the waters off Miami, about 98 percent of Kojak's shipments reach their destination. Another prominent participant has been Carlos Lehder, who took over a small Bahamian island with an airstrip, driving out the inhabitants with guns and dogs, and then hired a half-dozen pilots who flew to hidden airstrips in Columbia, loaded their planes with cocaine, refueled on Lehder's island, and under cover of darkness slipped into the United States.

The drug war is distinctly international, with govern-ment officials in the Bahamas, Cuba, Mexico, Nicaragua, and Panama accepting bribes for their participation. A study by the RAND Corporation concluded that even if the American government made a much greater commitment of personnel to stopping the entrance of illegal drugs, the effect would be no more than a 5 percent cutback on the current supply. Ten years ago cocaine was arriving a few kilos at a time; now the shipments are measured in *tonnage* — often three or four tons in size. Francis C. Hall, the former chief of the police department's narcotics division in New York City, explained, "There is so much cocaine in New York today, it is beyond measure. Beyond measure. When I look at 5000 pounds, I say to myself, how many more of these stash houses are there around?" (Hall, 1989: 9) But even if all supplies were cut off, synthetic cocaine and heroin, which are cheap and fairly easy to make, would be available in a few months. The problem, it seems, is less rooted in the supply of drugs than in the demand for them.

In 1988, for the first time, Congress seemed to accept the idea that cutting the drug supply should not be the only priority, allotting as much funding for treatment, prevention, education, and research as for restricting the supply. At the same time, the American public took a related stance, with 47 percent of a national sample indicat-ing that educating young people would be the best strategy for halting the drug epidemic and 35 percent choosing the option of making it harder for drugs to enter the country (George Gallup, Jr., *Gallup Report,* March 1988).

Educating young people might be a fine general goal, but how can program developers go about implementing it? To date most educational programs have emphasized that the best way of fighting drugs is to increase young people's knowledge of the subject. Very few data, however, indicate how successful drug-education and drug-treatment programs have been, and without such information experts have little basis for choosing how most effectively to use funds to restrict illegal drug use.

One good thing is now happening. Because of the current efforts to publicize the destructive effect of drugs, it appears that many middle-class young people are getting the message and cutting back or eliminating hard drug use. The problem is that drug addiction has increased dramatically among the young, urban poor, and the distinct possibility exists that if drug use is no longer a problem among middle-class youth, the governmental education and treatment efforts will decline or cease.

The result of the current trend will be massive destructive effects in poor, urban districts. Hall explained,

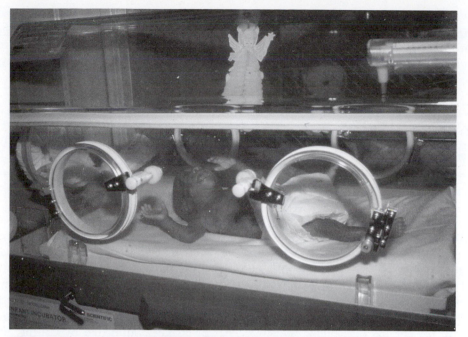

Victims of the modern drug problem include infants, such as this six-month-old boy who is suffering withdrawal symptoms produced by his mother's cocaine addiction.

"The social problems associated with drugs are mind-boggling — crack babies, babies born with AIDS. The death rate in Harlem among infants is as high as it gets in third world countries. It's outrageous, a national disgrace" (Hall, 1989: 9).

There will be other effects of drug increase among the poor. Individuals who use illegal drugs must pay for their supply, and those with little or no money will readily turn to crime. Examining the careers of male and female drug addicts, sociologists have found that increased involvement in property crime accompanies addiction.

Perhaps the most frightening legacy of the relationship between poverty and drugs is the distinct possibility of higher levels of violence, with crack, a fairly cheap, increasingly popular cocaine derivative playing a central role. A half-dozen sociologists doing research projects in East Harlem, an area where a young female jogger was raped and beaten by a gang of young adolescent boys in a highly publicized case in April 1989, all agreed that the district had changed dramatically in a few years. For decades heroin and cocaine had been prominent there, but, with the advent of crack, young adolescents and even children had become dealers. Their involvement in selling this prized commodity has meant a shift in power from adults to them;

along with this shift has come the feeling that a young person has the right to take anything he wants as long as he can get away with it. Furthermore, to be respected among his drug-selling peers, a young male frequently has to prove that he can be brutal. One of the sociologists explained, "There has been an extraordinary resurgence of violence since crack. Violence is up throughout the community and the types of crimes that are committed are more violent" (Kolata, 1989: C1).

When confronted with the relationship between drug use and poverty, and asked how education would help, Hall replied, "It's a damned good question." He didn't have an answer, and certainly as one looks at the vastness of the problem, it is hard to believe that education alone can have much impact. Programs that significantly restrict or even eliminate poverty would undoubtedly have a large effect. But precisely what kinds of programs should be implemented? And perhaps most fundamentally, are Americans willing to pay for such programs?

Sources: M. Douglas Anglin and Yih-ing Hser. "Addicted Women and Crime." *Criminology*. V. 25. May 1987, pp. 359–397; M. Douglas Anglin and George Speckart. "Narcotics Use and Crime: A Multisample, Multimethod Analysis." *Criminology*. V. 26. May 1988, pp. 197–233; George Gallup, Jr. *Gallup Report*. March 1988; Francis C. Hall. "Report from the Field on an Endless War." *New York Times*. March 12, 1989, p. 1+; Gina Kolata. "Grim Seeds of Park Rampage Found in East Harlem Streets." *New York Times*. May 2, 1989, p. C1+; Michael Massing. "Dealing with the Drug Horror." *New York Review of Books*. V. 36. March 30, 1989, pp. 22–26; David N. Nurco et al. "Differential Criminal Patterns of Narcotic Addicts over an Addiction Career." *Criminology*. V. 26. August 1988, pp. 407–423.

Who Commits Crime?

A number of years ago, I was speaking with a man who had spent fully half his life in prison. "You know, Chris," he said, "you and your friends grew up aware that you'd be going to college. For me and my friends the college we saw ahead was the slammer." Several of the theories we have discussed, most obviously the anomie and differential-association perspectives, support the conclusion that certain types of people are especially susceptible to becoming involved in crime. The speaker in the example just cited was black, male, of urban origin, as well as young when he started in crime. All these are factors associated with a high likelihood of being arrested. By no means, however, is it being suggested that the mere presence of these factors predestines a life of crime and arrest. We are simply addressing statistical probabilities here. Moreover, there may be biases involved in how crime statistics are compiled and also in arrest patterns.

Age

According to official statistics, people under twenty-five accounted for about 58.9 percent of all arrests for Part-I crimes in 1987. People in this age range were responsible for 52.8 percent of all arrests in 1987 (U.S. Bureau of the Census, *Statistical Abstract of the United States: 1989*. No. 293). Table 8.3 lists some relevant percentages. A number of factors contribute to this high rate of arrests among young people. For one thing the police are much more inclined to arrest those under twenty-five than they are to arrest older people. In addi-

tion, the rate of serious crime committed by those under twenty-five has apparently risen more sharply than has the rate for older persons (Cohen and Short, 1976: 59–60). Finally, until recent years, the number of young people had been increasing. This had meant an increase in the number of crimes committed by youths, whether or not their crime rate rose. Since the youthful group has begun to decline in size, it seems likely that the number of crimes committed by youths will start to decrease.

Sex

Men are considerably more likely to be arrested than are women. In 1987, 82.3 percent of the people charged were male, meaning that nearly five times as many men as women were arrested. Table 8.3 indicates that for serious crimes males are considerably more likely to be arrested than females. The only categories of crime in which men are arrested less frequently than women are prostitution and running away from home. However, the general trend over time has been for the female arrest rate to rise more rapidly than the male rate. In the past quarter-century, the ratio of males to females appearing before juvenile courts has dropped to 4 to 1, probably the lowest of any Western society. At the turn of the century, ratios of 50 to 60 to 1 prevailed. In the past two decades, arrests of females for property crime have increased more rapidly than arrests of males for property crime, but a similar trend has not occurred for violent crime. One fact that might help explain these findings is that women are generally socialized to restrain their emotions and especially

Table 8.3
Arrests for Serious (Part-I) Crimes: Males and Different Age Groups in 1987

	MALES	AGE GROUPS			
		UNDER 18	18–24	25–44	45 AND OVER
Murder and manslaughter	87.5%	9.5%	34.3%	47.1%	9.0%
Rape	98.8	15.7	29.2	48.4	6.6
Robbery	91.9	22.4	38.1	37.7	1.7
Larceny (theft)	68.9	30.9	27.6	33.2	8.3
Motor-vehicle theft	90.3	39.9	33.3	25.1	1.7
Arson	86.3	40.5	. 22.3	31.3	6.0

Source: U.S. Bureau of the Census. *Statistical Abstract of the United States: 1989.* No. 293.

Males and younger people are more inclined to be arrested for violent crimes than females and older individuals.

their violent tendencies much more effectively than are men. Furthermore women's inclination toward property crimes may be partially related to expectations associated with the contemporary female role, especially in difficult economic times —the female shopper becomes a shoplifter or the female casher of good checks turns into a passer of bad checks. It seems apparent that there are no simple, broad patterns of female criminality and that the variety of existing patterns will be most effectively revealed by detailed studies of the lives of women engaged in different criminal behaviors (Box and Hale, 1984; Simon, 1975; U.S. Bureau of the Census, *Statistical Abstract of the United States: 1989.* No. 293).

Ethnicity and Race

High ethnic crime rates can be explained in part by the recency of a group's immigration —for example, Puerto Ricans and other newly arrived Latin American groups currently display high crime rates —and, in part, by the amount of cultural conflict and deprivation each group has encountered—blacks and Native Americans are the most obvious cases. Some ethnic groups, such as the Jews and the Irish, were once very active in crime, but as they have gained some access to the legitimate channels that may be used to obtain economic success, they have tended to move out

of crime. On the other hand, certain Oriental groups, once relatively crime-free, have become more actively involved because of lessening economic opportunities and partial community disintegration.

Place of Residence

The extent to which an area is urbanized is definitely related to its arrest rate. Specifically, the larger the population of a community, the higher its arrest rate is likely to be. For instance, in 1987, cities of 50,000 or more had an arrest rate for violent crime that was over twice as high as that of cities with populations of under 50,000 and more than four times as high as the rate in rural areas (U.S. Bureau of the Census, *Statistical Abstract of the United States: 1989.* No. 278). Arrest rates are higher in more urbanized areas because larger cities are more likely to house high percentages of low-income people and to be characterized by physical deterioration and high population density. It is also possible that large cities, which tend to have professionalized police forces, place more emphasis on a high arrest rate than the police in small cities. Table 8.4 compares violent crime rates in selected American cities.

In order to combat crime and other forms of deviance, societies have various ways of maintaining social control.

Table 8.4
Violent Crime in Selected American Cities: 1987[1]

	TOTAL	MURDER	FORCIBLE RAPE	ROBBERY	AGGRAVATED ASSAULT
Baltimore	1869	29.5	78	976	785
Chicago	—	22.9	—	990	1133
Dallas	1989	32	125	900	932
Detroit	2545	62.8	130	1383	969
Houston	1090	18.6	67	557	447
Los Angeles	1910	24.3	65	784	1307
New York	2036	23	48	1083	882
Philadelphia	1055	20.5	67	564	404
San Francisco	1211	13.4	59	606	532
Washington, DC	1610	36.2	39	717	817

[1] Violent-crime arrests per 100,000 people of all ages.

Source: U.S. Bureau of the Census. *Statistical Abstract of the United States: 1989.* No. 280.

The Social Control of Deviance

A young child disobeys a parental command and is sent to his or her room. An adult breaks a law and must pay a fine or go to prison. Both individuals are punished by means of **social control**—the application of systematic behavioral restraints intended to motivate people to obey social expectations. Most people usually obey the rules because they have **internalized** cultural standards. This means that through socialization, social expectations have become part of the personality structure. People, therefore, feel guilty when they deviate. For some people in certain situations, however, these internalized standards are not sufficient to ensure conformity. In such situations informal or formal social control is necessary.

Informal Social Control

Most of the time people obey the norms, but sometimes the rules are violated, and informal social control is unleashed. **Informal social control** consists of unofficial pressure intended to convince potential deviants to conform to social norms. Consider a student who has recently transferred to a new college. He wants to be accepted by the other students in the dormitory, but he is too pushy. He jumps into conversations and then monopolizes them. When two close friends go out for a beer, he forces his company on them. Informal social control is soon applied. The new arrival gets the "cold shoulder." Everyone says, "I'll see you later" whenever he appears. Perhaps the newcomer will eventually realize his behavior is unacceptable, and he will tone down his efforts to gain acceptance. Perhaps he will fail to come to this realization and will continue to be shut out by the others.

Use of Informal Social Control

Most people are very responsive to informal social control. Few of us pick our noses publicly, make frequent obscene gestures, or speak loudly at weddings and funerals. We fear others' disapproval.

Informal social control is also commonly exercised in occupational settings. Numerous studies suggest that a certain kind of person is especially likely to be in business—the "organization man" (Whyte, 1956). Such people realize that the best way to get ahead and to escape the disapproval of their superiors is to be first and foremost a conformist. They subscribe to the organizational leadership's prevailing values and interests, displaying total loyalty to the organization and avoiding, at all costs, creative suggestions or pursuits. It is not just people's superiors who impose informal social control, however. One investigation concluded that informal social control initiated by one's coworkers can be a powerful deterrent to committing deviant acts on the job (Hollinger and Clark, 1982).

Effects of Ignoring Informal Social Control

Sometimes people risk a great deal when they ignore others' wishes. Loss of support from one's family and severed friendships are possible. Even bodily harm can result. A case in point is the "maverick," the person who, in many situations, stubbornly refuses to conform. Americans often have mixed feelings toward mavericks. Such people tend to be highly individualistic, a trait Americans widely admire. Yet their individualism, if uncontrolled, frequently triggers the disapproval of others and restricts their access to such highly valued items as wealth and power. Mavericks generally risk disapproval or even stronger reactions because they are unusually moral. They follow the dictates of their own internalized sense of right and wrong and not the external directives that bring material success. "Whistle-blowers" are a case in point — people who expose the existence of defective merchandise, cost overruns, client-harming bureaucratic policies, and safety and health violations in the companies or government agencies for which they work (Parmerlee, Near, and Jensen, 1982; Rosecrance, 1988). Common reactions to whistle-blowing include colleagues' and superiors' anger and hostility, dismissal, and even law suits. A study has suggested that whistle-blowers are more likely to suffer retaliation if they lack the support of supervisors and managers, if the wrongdoing is serious, and if they use channels outside the organization to blow the whistle (Near and Miceli, 1986). Not all whistle-blowers, however, suffer adverse effects. U.S. society offers fame and even fortune to the few mavericks whose accomplishments have made them nearly invulnerable to the effects of criticism and disapproval. Consumer-advocate Ralph Nader and columnist Jack Anderson have become household names as a result of their efforts to expose and eliminate governmental and business secrecy and corruption.

This discussion has suggested that there are many different ways to provide informal social control. The following Cross-Cultural Perspective describes a rather unusual example.

CROSS-CULTURAL PERSPECTIVE

Art Rides Shotgun on the Paris Subway

 We have noted that social control is the application of systematic behavioral restraints intended to motivate people to obey social expectations. Social control, in short, means the imposition of limits. The following situation demonstrates an innovative way that social control has been imposed and, at the same time, has created a situation providing some interesting new entertainment and experiences.

In the fall of 1982, the Paris Opera Ballet presented a benefit performance. That fact alone was hardly unusual. What was unusual was the setting — hundreds of feet below ground in the white-tiled corridors of the Opera subway stop. The Opera's performance of the ballet, "Massacre on Mac-Dougal Street," was the latest in a series of artistic activities sponsored by the Paris Transport Authority as part of a plan to use art to help fight crime. The program has included performances by thirteen theater troupes, 200 musicians, and a two-ton hippopotamus brought into the subway by elevator because it could not make it down the stairs.

Crime in the Paris subways is infrequent by American standards, but the number of muggings and thefts has more than tripled in a decade, reaching 1100 in 1981. In addition, acts of vandalism have been increasing by about 25 percent a year. Parisians were particularly shocked by two brutal murders in which an elderly woman was stabbed to death and a man was thrown in front of a moving train.

One of the reasons for this increase in crime is that machines have replaced the sharp-sighted attendants that punched subway tickets, increasing efficiency but leaving miles of corridors deserted and unprotected. Events such as the ballet are intended to support social control—to fight crime by restoring the human presence which was removed due to the introduction of modern technology. Claude Quin, the president of the Transport Authority, explained, "Criminals are bound to have a harder time if you have large numbers of people standing around listening to concerts and watching plays . . ." Although the crime rate has not dropped since the advent of the programs, Quin contended that it would have increased much faster without them. He said, "We estimate that 10,000 people are directly affected by every week-long program . . . There's no doubt that the activities are a deterrent."

Some of the more successful programs have attracted up to 3000 people. Several events, such as the ballet, have been held in the huge main hall of the Auber stop. Others, such as the Festival of French Song, were performed in twenty or thirty stations in order to reach more people. Not all of the activities involve theater, music, or dance. For one program, entitled "Vive le Cirque," trapezes were rigged at a major subway stop, and clowns and jugglers rode the trains, performing at different stations. During "Hobby Week" passengers learned how to paint porcelain, create Japanese flower arrangements, and make croissants in a baker's oven lowered into the subway for the occasion.

The most popular events are the Friday afternoon classical concerts held from July to September at the Auber stop. In the future Quin plans to expand the subway's offerings to include public-service activities, such as explanations of the intricacies of the social-service system and advice to the unemployed.

It will be interesting to learn whether the Paris subway program really does serve as a mechanism of social control. If, in fact, the program can demonstrate substantial success, perhaps other large cities may adopt similar strategies.

Source: *New York Times.* "Culture Rides Shotgun on the Paris Metro." November 30, 1982, p. C13.

Formal Social Control: The Criminal-Justice System

The American image of justice shows a woman blindfolded to ensure equal treatment for all people who appear before her. However, many feel that the blindfold must have holes in it, because in practice the American criminal-justice system is clearly biased. From arrest to sentencing, the likelihood of being ignored, released, or lightly treated improves as the accused person's affluence increases. This relationship will be apparent as we examine the different steps in the process: arrest, trial, and sentencing. We will also discuss prisons.

Arrest

For any particular crime, the poor are more likely than the affluent to be arrested. A study of 3475 delinquent boys in Philadelphia compared middle-class and lower-class boys with similar arrest records detained for equally serious offenses. It concluded that the police were considerably more likely to refer lower-class youth to juvenile court (Thornberry, 1973).

How can we explain these findings? A number of factors seem relevant. For one thing poor people have less privacy. More affluent people can engage in certain illegal activities—gambling or drug use, for example—in the seclusion of their homes. The poor, however, are more likely to be forced into the public arena, where they can be directly observed by the police or where the complaints of others are likely to draw the attention of law-enforcement officers. Second, in some cases the police are less likely to arrest affluent than poor youth because they believe that it is probable that middle-class parents will take a more active, effective role in disciplining their children. In addition, many researchers feel that police training and experience tend to make officers especially inclined to attribute criminality to certain groups — in particular, lower-class youth, blacks, Puerto Ricans, Mexicans, and Native Americans. Finally some evidence indicates that law-enforcement officers often are most willing to arrest those least able to bring political pressure to bear in their own behalf — in short, the poorest members of society (Reiman, 1979: 104).

Pretrial and Trial

Poor people usually have little hope of raising bail. Being in jail during the pretrial period means that defendants are unable to work actively for their own defense. Furthermore defendants out on bail are able to walk into court off the street, like anyone else. By contrast, defendants not released on bail are likely to be led into court from a nearby detention center and thus give the appear-

At each stage of the criminal-justice system, the wealthy and powerful have an advantage over poor or average-income people. In spite of such privilege, however, Leona Helmsly, an owner of serveral prominent luxury hotels charged with tax evasion, was ultimately convicted and sentenced to prison.

ance of being guilty, probably influencing juries and judges. Research indicates that among defendants accused of the same offenses, those who post bail are more likely to be acquitted than those who do not.

Besides bail another issue that can influence the outcome of a defendant's case is the quality of the legal assistance. Since the *Gideon* v. *Wainwright* decision in 1963, all defendants must be provided with a lawyer. The effectiveness of legal assistance varies considerably, however. The poor often receive "assembly-line" legal aid from a public defender or a private attorney assigned by the court. In both instances the lawyer's payment is likely to be modest, and public defenders' case loads are usually much larger than those of private criminal lawyers. Because of these facts, poor people's lawyers tend to be strongly motivated to bring cases to a quick conclusion. They may work out a deal with the prosecutor whereby the defendant pleads guilty to a somewhat reduced charge.

In business, time is money, and defendants without funds are normally unable to command more than a minimum of a lawyer's time. By contrast, wealthy, white-collar defendants are able to hire a battery of skilled lawyers with sufficient resources to make it in the prosecutor's interest to settle quickly and leniently out of court. When white-collar criminals appear before judges, they frequently find themselves in friendly surroundings. The judge often sees the defendant as someone whose style of dress and general behavior are much like his or her own — a prominent, wealthy individual who may well belong to the same country club and who is the kind of person whom the judge represented years before in private practice. One corporation lawyer explained that "it is best to find the judge's friend or [former] law partner to defend an antitrust client — which we have done" (Green, Moore, and Wasserstein, 1979: 543).

Sentencing

The poor experience a double bias when they appear before a judge for sentencing. First, as we noted, the crimes usually committed by poor people generally receive harsher penalties than do the "crimes in the suites" of the more affluent. For instance, a *New York Times* story on the fate of

twenty-one business executives found guilty of making illegal campaign donations during the Watergate scandal indicated that most of these men, including New York Yankees owner George Steinbrenner, are still presiding over their companies. Only two went to prison, serving no more than a few months each. Upper-class criminals, in short, were punished leniently for their attempts to undermine the independence of the electoral process and to endanger the basic vitality of our democratic form of government (Jensen, 1975).

Furthermore the poor are likely to be the objects of discrimination. They more frequently receive long prison terms than do more affluent people convicted of the same crimes. Research has suggested that even when equitable standards of sentencing are established and stressed, subtle ways to affect the lengths of sentences can be found. For instance, blacks are more readily charged than whites with the use of a weapon in the course of committing a crime (Miethe and Moore, 1985; Reiman, 1979).

A study of 504 cases eligible for capital punishment concluded that the victim, not the offender, was the critical factor affecting the sentence. Those killing whites were twice as likely to receive a death sentence as those killing blacks, regardless of the offender's race (Smith, 1987).

Prisons

What purposes are served by prisons? Retribution is certainly one of them. Prisons are supposed to make people suffer who have made the lives of other people unpleasant. A common interpretation of the Old Testament doctrine of "an eye for an eye and a tooth for a tooth" has often been the justification for putting people in prison.

Second, prison life is expected to act as a deterrent, encouraging individuals not to return to crime once they are released. Some research suggests, however, that the kinds of criminals generally incarcerated, such as drug addicts and sex offenders, are less likely to be deterred by prison sentences than are such criminal types as shoplifting homemakers and white-collar criminals who normally manage to avoid prison (Chambliss, 1969; Pittman and Gordon, 1968). There has also been the widespread belief that punishment can deter the noncriminal public from engaging in

Figure 8.1
Number of Federal and State Prison Inmates: 1987

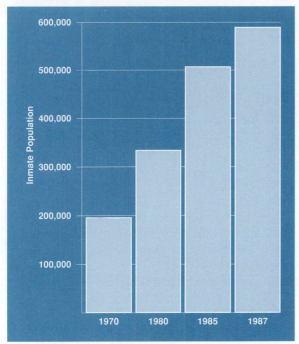

Over the past two decades, the American prison population has sharply increased. (Source: U.S. Bureau of the Census. Statistical Abstract of the United States, *1989. No. 322.)*

federal and state prisons nearly tripled in seventeen years — from 196,000 in 1970 to 581,609 in 1987 (U.S. Bureau of the Census, *Statistical Abstract of the United States: 1989.* No. 322). Many prisons are severely overcrowded, with inmates in them suffering high rates of hypertension, cardiovascular disease, mental disorders, and suicide. For whites, crowded prisons also offer the additional discomfort of being members of the minority group and, therefore, suffering the racial oppressions that nonwhites encounter in the outside world (Clayton, 1987; Leger, 1988).

Although the society's criminal population steadily increases, the amount of crime does not drop; in fact, as we noted earlier, it too increases. Considering this sorry situation, you might ask why strong support for continued prison construction exists. The following propositions offer a number of reasons:

1. The American tradition, in fact the tradition of all Western nations, is to put law-breakers in prison or to punish them some other way.
2. Politicians find such an approach useful, because the construction of new prisons gives the sense that something practical and tangible is being done to protect constituents' personal safety and property.
3. In line with the general approach of conflict theory, throwing people in prison is particularly easy to do if those people are different and can be considered inferior. Many politicians are white and affluent, and the majority of actual voters are white and somewhat more affluent than average; in federal and state prisons, the proportion of black inmates is four times greater than their proportion of the population, and they represent nearly half the total; whether nonwhite or white, prison inmates tend to come from low-income backgrounds.
4. In perceiving the prison system, both politicians and the general public are more concerned with short-term "solutions" — locking up those who are dangerous, or troublesome. They are less sensitive to the destructive impact prison can have on individuals or (as the processes described by both differential-association and labeling theory indicate) to the development of hardened criminals, which prison systems tend to produce.

crime. This might be an accurate claim, but there is limited research evidence to support it (Reid, 1985: 88).

Third, prisons are supposed to isolate criminals, thus protecting the law-abiding public. Incarceration does produce this effect for the period of time that the individual is imprisoned. An important question, however, is whether or not the person still pursues crime after being released. If so, the protection provided is only temporary.

The final purpose of prisons is rehabilitation, the effort to reform inmates so that they will become productive citizens and no longer commit crimes. Vocational education and psychotherapy have been used sporadically in attempts to rehabilitate inmates.

Prisons have quite successfully isolated and punished their inmates, but they have been much less effective at deterrence and rehabilitation.

The prison population has grown rapidly. As Figure 8.1 suggests, the number of people held in

The American prison system has serious problems, and it certainly is not reducing crime. With

220

these realizations in mind, I end this discussion with a difficult question. By what measures could crime be significantly reduced in this society? Systematic study and experimentation to answer this question seem to be activities worthy of major federal funding. Positive programs developed from these efforts would not only improve the lives of prospective victims and offenders, but in various ways all citizens would benefit. Do you agree or disagree with these ideas? You might discuss your reactions with classmates.

The chapter concludes with the third of five research sections; this one discusses research on rape.

RESEARCH IN SOCIOLOGY

Research on Rape: A Progressive Struggle

In the early and middle 1970s, social scientists' papers about rape were often strongly worded statements demanding greater societal concern with the issue. During the intervening years, as the modern women's movement has received stronger support, the issue of rape has become defined as a significant social problem worthy of scientific investigation. As a result the quality of research has steadily improved. However, research on rape is still in its infancy, and investigators face some special problems when they do studies on this topic.

To begin, let us consider the meaning of the statement that research on rape is in its infancy. For the most part, investigators have not yet approached the subject matter systematically. For instance, as we noted in Chapter 1, "Introduction," the relationship between research and sociological theory is an intimate one, with sociologists developing concepts and theory to guide research, and investigators, in turn, refining these tools based on their conclusions. For instance, investigators recognize that "date rape" and "stranger rape" differ in the conditions under which they occur, in responses produced by victims' friends and family members, and in the victim's own response, but they have not clearly distinguished the differences between the two types.

Besides the fact that researchers studying rape are charting new territory, they find themselves facing some special problems — in particular, bias in the reporting of rape and difficulties with studies of offenders.

Bias in Reporting Rapes

A significant problem with research on rape is that the victims studied represent a biased sample. In the United States, it is estimated that between 10 and 25 percent of rapes are reported. Thus a serious sampling problem exists. How do women who report rapes differ from those who do not? The troubling fact is that we really do not know. And, since we do not know, any generalizations made about rape victims based on those who report are biased in unknown ways.

Researchers of rape have been concerned about the sampling bias among victims and have tried to figure out who has reported and who has not. Studies have suggested that the victim's age, race, marital status, and relationship to the rapist are the factors that most strongly influence the eventual decision not to report the crime. However, until recently studies have produced inconsistent, seemingly unrelated information on the impact of different factors.

After a number of studies of rape victims had been published, sociologist Linda Williams did a systematic investigation, highlighting several steps in the research process discussed in Chapter 2, "Doing Research in Sociology." First, in the course of her literature review, she read the various studies on reporting rape and noted their different, often inconsistent conclusions. Then, based on the information obtained from those studies, she formulated a hypothesis, which

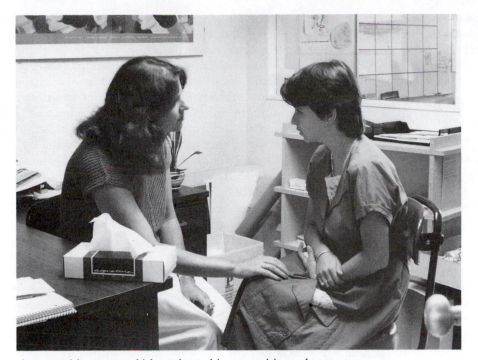

At rape crisis centers, which are located in many cities and towns throughout the country, victims receive counseling and support. Researchers on rape have sometimes obtained subjects from these centers.

seemed to resolve the major inconsistencies: A woman is more likely to report a rape if it approximated a classic rape than if it did not. What she meant by a "classic rape" was a situation in which a woman was raped in public by a stranger who threatened or used a high degree of force and frequently produced injury. After developing the hypothesis, Williams tested it. The results of systematic research paid off, generally supporting the hypothesis. In an article on the subject, Williams emphasized that the most significant factor related to reporting the crime was whether or not the victim had known the rapist.

If she had known him, Williams concluded, then the woman found herself in a difficult, self-blaming situation. Many women have been socialized to believe that they should control all female–male interaction. If such women are raped, then they are likely to believe that it is largely or wholly because they failed to control the situation. Williams wrote, "This study . . . shows that those circumstances in a classic rape which discourage the woman from blaming herself also increase the probability that she will report the crime to the police" (Williams, 1984: 265).

Another body of rape-vic-

tim research involves follow-up studies. Here, too, the conclusions that are drawn are affected by biased sampling; in this case the bias results not only from limited reporting but also because some subjects cannot be tracked down at a later date. For instance, Carol Nadelson and her associates initially interviewed 130 women in a general hospital emergency room after they had been raped. One to two-and-a-half years later, the investigators were only able to track down forty-one of those women — just 32 percent. Once more one does not know to what extent those interviewed in the follow-up were typical or not typical of the original set of respondents.

Difficulties with Research on Offenders

The limited reporting of rapes is a prominent reason why the samples of offenders in rape studies are biased. If only 10 to 25 percent of rapes are reported, then 75 to 90 percent of rapists are never caught. Furthermore, even when a rape is reported, a sizable percentage of offenders are not apprehended.

But wait! The sampling bias problem can be even greater than so far acknowledged. Consider, for instance, Diana Scully and Joseph Marolla's study of convicted rapists. In this study the researchers' subjects were drawn from the approximately 25 percent of rapists incarcerated in seven maximum- or medium-security prisons in Virginia who volunteered to be included in the investigation. Were the 25 percent who volunteered significantly different from the 75 percent who didn't? Again, we simply don't know.

The Scully and Marolla research also raises another research problem in rape-of-

fender studies—a question about validity. In Chapter 2 we briefly discussed validity—the condition in which a research item accurately measures what it claims to measure. In this case did the researchers receive valid answers to their questions? The authors did not examine this question, but they conceded that since the offenders talked more about their feelings and emotions when the interviewer was female, the interviewer's sex may have affected the information received. It is possible, for instance, that some of the harsh, brutal statements these men made about women could have been aroused by a woman's presence. On the other hand, one might argue that when the interviewer was a male, the offender might have been inclined to feel competitive with him and that he (the offender) might have asserted this competitiveness by demonstrating what he considered his mastery of women. While the researchers did not discuss the issue of the relationship between interviewer's sex and validity, they did acknowledge a general concern with validity, indicating that because prison inmates are known for "conning" outsiders, they had

taken the researcher's normal precaution of comparing the data from their interviews with pre-sentence reports on file at the prisons. For the most part, no significant discrepancies were found with rapists' earlier explanations of their crimes.

Conclusion

Several decades ago research on rape represented a small set of studies, but in recent years that situation has changed. As competent studies on this topic increase, some investigatory problems are likely to decline. For example, as research on rape helps publicize the issue, a higher proportion of women are likely to report the crime and decrease the sampling biases that currently exist. Eventually, based on modern research, a sophisticated body of theory will develop. It is hoped that from this theory there will emerge powerful insights for taking legal and social steps to curtail and, some day, eliminate this dreadful form of behavior.

Sources: Mary Beard Deming and Ali Eppy. "The Sociology of Rape." *Sociology and Social Research*. V. 65. July 1981, pp. 357–380; Mary P. Koss, Christine A. Gidycz, and Nadine Wisniewski. "The Scope of Rape: Incidence and Prevalence of Sexual Aggression and Victimization in a National Sample of Higher Education Students. *Journal of Consulting and Clinical Psychology* V. 55. April 1987, pp. 162–170; "Carol C. Nadelson et al. "A Follow-Up Study of Rape Victims." *American Journal of Psychiatry*. V. 139. October 1982, pp. 1266–1270; James D. Orcutt and Rebecca Faison. "Sex-Role Attitude Change and Reporting of Rape Victimization, 1973–1985." *Sociological Quarterly*. V. 29. Winter 1988, pp. 589–604; Diana Scully and Joseph Marolla. "Convicted Rapists' Vocabulary of Motive: Excuses and Justifications." *Social Problems*. V. 31. June 1984, pp. 530–544; Diana Scully and Joseph Marolla. "'Riding the Bull at Gilley's': Convicted Rapists Describe the Rewards of Rape." *Social Problems*. V. 32. February 1985, pp. 251–263; Linda S. Williams. "The Classic Rape: When Do Victims Report?" *Social Problems*. V. 31. April 1984, pp. 459–467.

STUDY GUIDE

Learning Objectives

After studying this chapter, you should be able to:

1. Define deviance and discuss changing definitions of deviance across time and space.
2. Define, discuss, and evaluate the anomie, differential-association, conflict, and labeling theories of deviance.
3. List and describe the limitations of criminal statistics.
4. Examine the following prominent types of crime: violent crime, property crime, victimless crime, and crimes by the powerful and affluent.
5. Determine who is likely to commit crimes and why by examining the following factors: age, sex, ethnicity and race, and place of residence.
6. Define informal social control, indicate how it is achieved, and describe the effects of ignoring it.
7. Identify and discuss the four steps of the criminal-justice process, examining the discriminations suffered by poor people at each stage.

Summary

1. Deviance is behavior that violates social norms considered sufficiently significant that the majority of a group or society responds negatively.

2. Sociology provides a number of theories of deviance. Merton's anomie perspective indicates that U.S. culture strongly emphasizes monetary success for all, without placing an equally strong emphasis on the legitimate means to achieve that success. The theory describes five individual adaptations, four of which are deviant.

The differential-association perspective claims that someone is likely to become a criminal if that person's values and the values of the influencing individuals show greater support for criminal activity than for noncriminal activity.

According to the conflict theory of deviance, a ruling class uses its strategic location to develop and maintain the legal standards the group desires, to the advantage of higher-class and the disadvantage of lower-class people.

Labeling theory contends that certain people are labeled as deviant by those powerful enough to impose their standards on society. The labeling process can be divided into two stages, which are designated as primary and secondary deviance.

4. Crime is simply an act that violates criminal law. Limitations to criminal statistics occur because many complaints are never reported, some victims refuse to cooperate, and administrative distortions happen. Among the different types of crimes are crime against people and property, victimless crime, and crimes by the powerful and affluent. People with certain social characteristics — the young, males, minority-group members, and city dwellers — are more likely to be arrested.

5. The social control of deviance is the application of systematic behavioral restraints intended to motivate people to obey social expectations. Both informal and formal means of social control exist. More affluent suspects fare better with the criminal-justice process at all stages — arrest, pretrial and trial activity, and sentencing. Prisons are supposed to serve the functions of retribution, deterrence, isolation, and rehabilitation. Prisons are seriously overcrowded, and the penal system, in general, needs major reform.

Key Terms

anomie the confusing situation produced when norms are either absent or conflicting

conformity a nondeviant adaptation in which individuals pursue legitimate goals and use the culturally accepted means to achieve them, even though it is likely they will not attain those goals

crime an act that violates criminal law

deviance behavior that violates social norms considered sufficiently significant that the majority of a group or society responds negatively

informal social control unofficial pressure intended to convince potential deviants to conform to social norms

innovation a deviant adaptation that develops when a person seeks legitimate goals but is blocked from effectively using culturally accepted means to achieve them

internalized through socialization, social expectations have become part of the personality structure

primary deviance violation of a social rule but the individuals in question are not labeled and so do not see themselves as deviant

rebellion a deviant adaptation displayed when a person decides that the existing society imposes barriers preventing the achievement of success goals. Therefore that individual strikes out against the society, seeking to change its goals and also the existing means for achieving them

retreatism a deviant adaptation in which an individual neither pursues the culturally prescribed goal of success nor uses the means for achieving this goal because of limited opportunities or a sense of personal inadequacy

ritualism a behavioral pattern that occurs when culturally prescribed success goals are no longer actively sought, but the legitimate means for achieving those goals are conscientiously pursued

secondary deviance violation of a social norm in which authorities label individuals deviants and the individuals accept the status of deviant

social control the application of systematic behavioral restraints intended to motivate people to obey social expectations

victimless crime the willing (hence "victimless") exchange among adults of strongly desired but illegal goods or services

white-collar crime crime committed by people of higher socioeconomic status in the course of their business activities

Tests

True–false Test

___F___ 1. The evaluation of what constitutes deviant behavior does not change across time and space.

___T___ 2. Robert Merton uses the concept of anomie to designate a discrepancy between a socially approved goal and the availability of means to achieve the goal.

___T___ 3. Using the differential-association theory, one can appreciate that prisons can serve as places where criminal practice can be learned.

___F___ 4. Labeling theory analyzes primary but not secondary deviance.

___T___ 5. It is possible to engage in behavior that is considered deviant but not criminal.

___F___ 6. A recent study concluded that the major factor determining the reporting and recording of crimes is offenders' personal characteristics.

   F   7. Studies done in the past decade clearly indicate that the return of the death penalty has reduced the murder rate in this country.

   T   8. The majority of people under correctional supervision are held for offenses against property.

   T   9. The Iran–*contra* affair can be considered a situation that involved white-collar crime.

   F   10. In the past decade, the construction of many new prisons has reduced the crime rate.

Multiple-choice Test

   D   1. According to anomie theory, the only nondeviant adaptation one can make to a condition of blocked opportunity is:
    a. innovation.
    b. ritualism.
    c. retreatism.
    d. conformity.

   d   2. Critics of the differential-association theory contend that it:
    a. fails to appreciate that criminal behavior is learned in interaction with others.
    b. can be used only to analyze juvenile gangs.
    c. overemphasizes criminals' involvement in violent activity.
    d. contains some vague terminology.

   A   3. Quinney's "social reality of crime" version of the conflict theory of deviance emphasizes:
    a. definitions of criminal activity by the ruling class.
    b. socialism as a cause of crime.
    c. that the social-class system has no relationship to criminal standards or behavior.
    d. learning criminal skills from peer associations.

   a   4. Labeling theory:
    a. is a form of symbolic interaction.
    b. analyzes causes of deviance.
    c. does not explain consequences of being labeled deviant.
    d. demonstrates how behavior distinguishes deviants from nondeviants.

   b   5. Biases exist in official crime statistics because:
    a. official reporting of misdemeanors is more likely than is reporting of felonies.
    b. of administrative distortions in reporting crimes.
    c. officers are more likely to report complaints made by low-income groups.
    d. of the widespread reporting of crimes when actually no crimes occurred.

   C   6. Which of the following statements is true of a Part-I offense?
    a. It is less serious than a Part-II offense.
    b. It does not have a uniform definition throughout the states.
    c. It is either a violent crime or a serious property crime.
    d. It is not likely to occur often enough to be statistically significant.

   D   7. Organized crime:
    a. is confined to illegitimate business activities.
    b. has not been attacked by the federal government.
    c. is no longer in the prostitution business.
    d. is involved in such illegal activities as gambling and narcotics, legitimate businesses, and racketeering.

_B_ 8. Arrest patterns indicate a greater likelihood of arrest for those who are:
  a. over twenty-five years of age.
  b. male.
  c. from small towns.
  d. white.

_A_ 9. Which of the following statements is true of the arrest process?
  a. The poor are more likely than the rich to be arrested.
  b. Since middle-class people have less privacy than do the poor, their crimes are more readily observed.
  c. There is no evidence suggesting that police officers arrest those least capable of exerting political pressures on their own behalf.
  d. Police are strongly inclined to arrest middle-class adolescents because they believe that their permissive unbringing has encouraged delinquent behavior.

_C_ 10. Prisons have successfully performed which purposes?
  a. inmates' rehabilitation
  b. prisoners' deterrence from further crimes
  c. inmates' punishment
  d. prisoners' improved health

Essay Test

1. What is deviance? Discuss the variations of standards of deviance across time and space.
2. Define, discuss, and evaluate two theories of deviance.
3. Is there bias in the reporting of criminal statistics? What factors seem to contribute most substantially to this bias?
4. Which categories of people are more likely to be arrested for crimes? Discuss.
5. Define informal social control and assess the effects of ignoring it.
6. By examining the four steps in the criminal-justice process, indicate whether or not this system truly provides justice.
7. Why is so much emphasis placed on building new prisons?

Suggested Readings

Barlow, Hugh D. 1987. *Introduction to Criminology.* Boston: Little, Brown and Company. Fourth edition. A well-written, thorough, up-to-date introduction to criminology, examining theories, types of crimes and criminals, and the administration of criminal justice.

Cockerham, William C. 1981. *Sociology of Mental Disorder.* Englewood Cliffs, NJ: Prentice-Hall. A sociological text examining the concepts, sources, social context, and treatment of mental illness.

DiIulio, John J. 1987. *Governing Prisons: A Comparative Study of Correctional Management.* New York: Free Press. A persuasive, optimistic analysis of modern prisons arguing that the key to prisons that rehabilitate inmates is effective management.

Erikson, Kai T. 1966. *Wayward Puritans.* New York: John Wiley and Sons. A study of deviance among Massachusetts Puritans. Erikson explained how the activities of the Puritan era contributed to the development of American standards of deviance and crime.

Green, Hannah. 1964. *I Never Promised You a Rose Garden.* New York: Signet. A beautifully written, fictionalized autobiography describing the thought patterns of a mentally ill girl as well as the frustrations and torments of life in a mental institution.

Kennedy, William. 1983. *Legs.* New York: Penguin Books. A powerfully written fictional account of the last years in the life of "Legs" Diamond, the famous gangster. The novel is particularly effective in conveying a sense of why many people have admired, even glorified major crimes figures.

Shoemaker, Donald J. 1984. *Theories of Delinquency: An Examination of Explanations of Delinquent Behavior.* New York: Oxford University Press. A text that effectively describes the principal bodies of theory seeking to interpret delinquent behavior.

Spiegel, Don, and Patricia Keith-Spiegel (eds.). 1973. *Outsiders USA.* San Francisco: Rinehart Press. Twenty-four, well-written, effectively documented analyses of different types of deviance.

Additional Assignments

1. The following list contains a combination of noncriminal deviant forms and criminal behaviors:
   a. alcoholism
   b. assault
   c. dependence on legally available drugs
   d. embezzlement
   e. behavior demonstrating mental illness
   f. murder
   g. nonviolent student protesting
   h. organized crime
   i. rape
   j. theft

   Ask five people (not in your sociology class) to rank these activities from 1 to 7, with 1 being the most serious. Compare and discuss your results with other students in the class. Is there strong consensus about the seriousness of the different activities? In particular, are the crimes always considered more serious violations than the noncriminal deviant activities?

2. Select an interesting prominent person, such as a celebrity, political figure, or religious leader. Prepare a short biography that outlines this person's well-known deviant and nondeviant activities. On the whole, can you conclude that this person's prominence occurred because of deviant or nondeviant behavior? Ask other students to name something famous this person did. Which did students name more frequently—deviant or nondeviant activities?

Answers to Objective Test Questions

True – false Test

1. f	4. f	7. f	9. t
2. t	5. t	8. t	10. f
3. t	6. f		

Multiple-choice Test

1. d	4. a	7. d	9. a
2. d	5. b	8. b	10. c
3. a	6. c		

PART III

Inequities in Modern Society

9
Social Stratification

10
Racial and Ethnic Groups

11
Emerging Minorities

9
SOCIAL STRATIFICATION

In July 1988, a national sample was asked which is more often to blame if a person is poor — lack of individual effort or circumstances beyond his or her control. Forty percent of the national sample indicated lack of effort, 37 percent circumstances, and 17 percent a combination of both factors. Four years earlier 33 percent of a sample had opted for lack of effort (George Gallup, Jr., *Gallup Poll,* September 1988). The rise is hardly surprising, considering that during the intervening years the country was exposed to the Reagan administration's fervent rhetoric emphasizing that people's failure or success is determined by individual effort.

Ronald Reagan and his associates, to be sure, were consistent with an American tradition that analyzes behavior in strictly individual terms and avoids consideration of the sociological perspective that social forces beyond individuals' control largely shape their opportunities and destiny. The sociological perspective might emphasize that a significant segment of unemployed poor people are able to get jobs and move out of poverty when government's fiscal policies encourage high employment; the problem is that these same policies also encourage a high rate of inflation, and neither government nor the public wants that situation. Therefore government tends to steer away from fiscal policies that make high employment a priority, and the result is that most of the time the unemployment rate is officially about 6 percent, with young people coming into the labor market, especially young minority-group members experiencing much higher rates (Jencks, 1988). The point is that individuals cannot control government policies that establish unemployment rates and thus help to determine poverty, but a sizable proportion of Americans, including many poor people, do not appreciate the existence of these social forces, instead placing the responsibility for individuals' poverty squarely on the individual's shoulders.

The social forces discussed here are part of the macro-order. Do you recall the distinction between the macro-order and the micro-order? If not, turn to p. 83 and p. 98 in Chapter 4, "Groups." When sociologists analyze social stratification, they appreciate that the social forces of the macro-order significantly affect people's lives.

Social stratification is the structured inequality of access to rewards, resources, and privileges that are scarce and desirable within a society. "Structured inequality" means that because of their roles and group memberships, some people have a better opportunity than others to obtain rewards, resources, and privileges. The sociological perspective emphasizes that social forces determine people's location within a social-stratification system. By contrast, the sociobiologists discussed on pp. 133–134 in Chapter 6, "Socialization," contend that through the evolutionary process some people have acquired biologically linked traits of aggressiveness, ruthlessness, and intelligence that make them the most likely candidates to seek and obtain highly valued rewards and privileges.

You undoubtedly realize that because of family income, parental connections, and other factors, some people have better opportunities to obtain these rewards and resources than others. At the same time, you probably are also aware that for most of us little of value simply drops into our laps. If you are going to obtain the benefits of the American stratification system, then you must plan your life and, in particular, your career. It is likely that you have decided that a college education will help you in this effort.

Throughout this chapter I emphasize the sociological perspective — that social forces largely beyond individuals' control help to determine their opportunities, successes, and failures. The next section examines three theories of social stratification. The following topic is the prominent dimensions of social stratification — wealth, power, and prestige. The next subject is the American social-class system, and in this discussion we see how stratification enters the everyday activities of Americans. The chapter closes with an examination of social mobility in American society.

Theories of Social Stratification

The conflict and structural-functional theories always offer different perspectives on a particular issue. In this instance conflict theory emphasizes that social classes emerge out of the production process, in which the rewards and privileges of social stratification are passed from one generation to the next. By contrast, the structural-functional theory focuses on the supposed contribution different jobs provide, contending that their respective contributions determine the rewards and privileges individuals receive but ignoring the advantages that well-placed parents can pass on to their children.

Marxist Conflict Theory

Karl Marx believed that the struggle between economic classes was the central feature in the development of societies. In his famous *Communist Manifesto,* he wrote, "The history of all hitherto existing society is the history of class struggles."

Marx was convinced that classes arise out of the productive system within a society. In an agricultural society, the principal positions are landowner and serf or tenant. In an industrial society, the principal positions are the **bourgeoisie** — the class of modern capitalists who own the means of economic production and employ wage labor — and the **proletariat** — the class of modern wage laborers who possess no means of production and thus must sell their own labor in order to survive.

According to Marx, the interests of the bourgeoisie and the proletariat are inevitably opposed. Those who own the means of economic production — the factories and the farms — are primarily interested in maximizing their profit, and the workers, in turn, invariably want to increase their wages and benefits. But capitalists' wealth gives them enormous power. Because of their economic prominence, the capitalists are able to exert political influence to control legislation, education, religion, the press, and the arts and also to prevent any organized expression of workers' discontent.

Marx contended that even though the members of the proletariat are disorganized and often unaware that they constitute a social class, they nonetheless share class membership because of two common experiences. First, they are all victims of the capitalist production process since they perform essential physical labor but receive minimal pay for their efforts. Second, all workers are powerless to confront the political strength of the state, which prevents them from expressing their discontent.

According to Marx, the proletariat gradually begins to develop **class consciousness**: recognition by the members of a class of the role they play in the production process. The workers' class consciousness involves an awareness of their relation to the bourgeoisie, especially a recognition of the

Marx believed that the interests of wage laborers, such as these factory workers, are in fundamental conflict with the interests of those who own the means of production.

owners' determination to prevent them from receiving a fair share of company profits. Marx believed that industrial conditions invariably encourage the development of class consciousness. He wrote:

> But with the development of industry the proletariat not only increases in number; it becomes concentrated in greater masses, its strength grows, and it feels that strength more. The various interests and conditions of life within the ranks of the proletariat are more and more equalized, in proportion as machinery obliterates all distinctions of labor and nearly everywhere reduces wages to the same low level . . . Thereupon the workers begin to form combinations [trade unions] against the bourgeois; they club [join] together in order to keep up the rate of wages. . .
>
> (Marx and Engels, 1959: 16)

Marx believed that in the final stage of class consciousness, the members of the proletariat recognize that the only way they will receive payment commensurate with their work efforts is to organize themselves into an army, overthrow the capitalists, and eliminate private ownership of the means of production.

Commentary

One point of contention involves Marx's claim that once a class of individuals recognizes its common interests and is willing to act on them in the public arena, it will always try to overthrow the existing system. This conclusion fails to recognize that most politically disenfranchised people usually want to become part of the system rather than to overthrow it. Prominent American cases in point have been the labor movement, a variety of racial and ethnic movements, and the women's movement. In the specific case of industrial workers, Marx underestimated the improving opportunities many of them have historically gained —in particular, good pay, pensions, social security, tenure and seniority, trade unionism, and the chance for some individuals, especially potential leaders, to move from lower- to higher-status positions. Thus, as one writer noted, were Marx to return to earth a century after his death, he would discover that "in the most advanced capitalist countries, the proletariat had gained in many

ways, despite the continuing exploitation against it, and that new middle classes had arisen, contrary to his expectation of class polarity" (Gurley, 1984: 112).

In addition, the Marxist scheme takes a highly oversimplified view of the human personality. For Marx, people seemed to be little more than the products of a uniform class experience, shifted around in large numbers in response to general social conditions. Thus Marx minimized the extent to which individuals are capable of making their own decisions (Beeghley, 1978: 22–24; Rossides, 1976:423–427).

One of the problems with Marx's insights is that since they were produced more than a century ago, they need updating. This has been a task Marxist scholars have either undertaken or advocated. Thus one pair of sociologists has been trying to determine to what extent Marx's social-class analysis applies to postindustrial society (Wright and Martin, 1987). Another team of researchers indicated that while Marx's prediction about the move toward classless societies in the socialist world has not proved accurate, the most effective way to update Marx in this regard would be to determine the size of the different social classes and the factors influencing their development in socialist nations (Resnick and Wolff, 1988).

Structural-Functional Theory

In 1945 Kingsley Davis and Wilbert Moore (1945) produced a structural-functional theory of stratification that attempts to explain the unequal distribution of rewards, resources, and privileges. Davis and Moore contended that all societies must face the problem of getting people to fill different positions and, once in those positions, to perform the duties associated with them. Some positions, however, are more critical to fill than others. The most critical jobs are those functionally important for the survival of society and those that require highly qualified personnel.

Davis and Moore suggested that functional importance alone will not assure job holders that they are well rewarded. Some positions make a major contribution, but their ranks are so easy to fill that high salaries are not necessary. Police, fire fighters, and sanitation workers are examples.

Other positions are both functionally important and require highly qualified personnel. The promise of rewards will increase the likelihood that a fairly large number of people will endure the long, costly training that will qualify them for these positions. The potential to be a physician, for example, probably falls within the mental capacity of most people, but the training is so expensive and demanding that it is unlikely that many individuals would seek to enter the profession without the promise of a high income.

Davis and Moore concluded that differences between one system of social stratification and another exist because of conditions affecting the two determinants of differential reward — namely, functional importance and scarcity of personnel. Doctors, for instance, would not receive a high income in a society in which the members do not believe that modern medical techniques will work or the training for medical personnel is fairly brief and inexpensive.

Commentary

Conflict theorists who have criticized Davis and Moore's theory have claimed that this perspective does not establish a convincing link between the rewards provided by the stratification system and the contributions people make. According to Davis and Moore, the people who fill all high-paid positions are making an important, even necessary contribution to the society. It seems impossible to argue, however, that such individuals as underworld crime leaders, baseball superstars, and corrupt but wealthy business people are performing essential, even important services. Furthermore many affluent individuals have neither special talents nor special training. Children of wealthy parents or people who marry the wealthy are cases in point. Melvin M. Tumin (1953) argued that the American stratification system restricts rather than facilitates the selection of talented people for prestigious, high-paying positions. The structural-functional theory provides a perspective that justifies, even praises a stable social order with sharp social-class distinctions, and while it does not explicitly praise the successful nor condemn the unsuccessful, it offers little insight into the social forces determining people's social stratification.

Lenski's Theory

Gerhard Lenski (1966) was convinced that neither conflict theory nor structural-functional theory offers a complete and effective analysis of social stratification. He borrowed from both approaches in developing his own theory. This theory is compatible with the open-minded approach of the previously cited, modern Marxist researchers.

Lenski noted that the structural-functionalists believe that people are generally self-serving — that when individuals must choose between their own group's interests and the interests of others, they almost always choose the former. By contrast, the conflict theorists are much more likely to conclude that many people, especially members of the proletariat, are "good," putting the interests of their entire class above their own and their family's interests. On this issue Lenski agreed with the structural-functionalists.

On the other hand, Lenski supported conflict theorists' observation that societies contain individuals and groups that constantly struggle to obtain precious, scarce goods. Lenski was critical of Davis and Moore's conclusion that "perfect" systems of social stratification develop in order to meet the precise needs of the societies in which they are located. He asserted that since

> there is no such thing as a perfect social system, we should stop spinning theories which postulate their existence and direct our energies toward the building of theories which explicitly assume that all human organizations are imperfect systems. Second, social theorists (and researchers too) should stop trying to find social utility in all the varied behavior patterns of men; they should recognize that many established patterns of action are thoroughly antisocial and contribute nothing to the general good.
>
> (Lenski, 1966: 34)

Lenski has suggested that on some issues the accuracy of the structural-functional or the conflict perspective varies with the type of society. For instance, structural-functionalists have contended that consensus (shared agreement) maintains social-stratification systems, and conflict theorists have concluded that coercion plays the dominant part. Lenski's analysis of societies led him to the conclusion that consensus is considerably more important in societies with little or no

236

economic surplus, while coercion is more significant in societies that possess a substantial economic surplus. Unlike the simpler societal forms, the latter kinds of societies have inevitably developed a small governing class that controls the political process and requires the people outside the elite to turn over most of their economic surplus; the use of force or the threat of its use has been the only way to insure such compliance.

Structural-functionalists are generally committed to the existing stratification system, and Lenski's analysis offers some evidence indicating that the current system works favorably for most American citizens. The United States and other major industrialized nations show somewhat more equitable distribution of power, privilege, and prestige than is apparent in less advanced industrial societies. On the other hand, Lenski's analysis has provided evidence in support of the

conflict theorists' criticism of the current stratification system. In particular, he noted that the gap between the wealthy and the poor nations has been growing since the beginning of industrialization. One expert has estimated that between 1860 and 1960, the wealthiest quarter of nations increased their share of the world's income from 58 to 72 percent; during the same period, the income of the poorest quarter dropped from 12.5 to 3.2 percent (Lenski and Lenski, 1982; Zimmerman, 1965: 38).

The chief difference between Lenski's theory and the other two is that Lenski's analysis does not take a firm ideological position into which facts are fitted. Instead basic theoretical conclusions are determined by available evidence. The Lenski theory, in short, is a more effective scientific endeavor than its predecessors.

Dimensions of Social Stratification

The focus now shifts from theories to the major dimensions of stratification systems. As you read this section, you might consider whether the facts you encounter are more consistent with structural-functional theory or with conflict theory.

Max Weber (Gerth and Mills, 1946: 180 – 195) emphasized that there are three dimensions of social stratification, which we will refer to as wealth, power, and prestige. The relationship among these dimensions is not self-evident. Sometimes they are highly interdependent. For instance, a person with great wealth might be able to exert considerable power in the political process by making substantial contributions to legislators' campaign funds. In other situations no apparent relationship exists. Members of long-time wealthy families in the locale of the wealthy individual just mentioned might feel that the person is low in prestige, lacking the education and social contacts that would make that individual an acceptable member of their set of friends.

Keep in mind that while we are analyzing these dimensions of social stratification as broad, somewhat abstract social forces, they profoundly affect individuals' lives.

Wealth and Income

The United States has about a half-million millionaires, or — in 1985 — about one in every 475 citizens. The largest number reside in big business centers — in New York, California, and Illinois — while Idaho, Maine, and North Dakota have the highest per capita ratio of millionaires. Historically the majority of millionaires have inherited wealth, but in the past two decades, that proportion has diminished, with entrepreneurs in such high-tech businesses as computer software, skilled professionals in fields like neurosurgery and the law, and corporate executives being among the most prominent new entries.

Wealth is people's economic assets — their cars, homes, stocks, bonds, and real estate — that can be converted into cash. A disproportionate share of economic assets belong to the wealthy. In 1984, 1.9 percent of American households (those with assets of $500,000 or more) possessed 63.3 percent of all economic assets, including 73.8 percent of stocks and mutual funds, 71.1 percent of business and professional ownership, and 60.5 percent of rental property (U.S. Bureau of the

Figure 9.1
Percentage of Full-time Workers in Different Income Categories: 1987

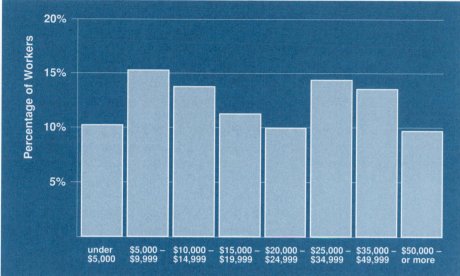

*The median income for all full-time workers was $19,305 in
1987. (Source: U.S. Bureau of the Census.* Statistical Abstract of
the United States: 1989. *No. 711.*)

Census, *Household Wealth and Asset Ownership:
1984.* Tables 1 and 3).

Data on **income,** which is people's earnings obtained through wages, salaries, business profits, stock dividends, and other means, are more accessible and easily measured than data on wealth. For this reason researchers study income more frequently than wealth. However, a study of income fails to acknowledge various sources that are not reported or are indirect, such as professors' research grants and business executives' use of company cars and recreational facilities. Figure 9.1 represents the distribution of income in the United States.

Absolute versus Relative Wealth and Income

Analysts often make a distinction between two types of wealth — absolute and relative. **Absolute wealth** is the cash value of an individual's economic assets. **Relative wealth** is the value of an individual's economic assets compared to the assets possessed by other citizens in that society.

Through most of American history, rising industrial productivity, the tax structure, and various supplemental income programs have produced an absolute increase in income for all classes. However, over time the relative inequality of class income has remained stable. One sociologist suggested that modern stratification systems are like "a fleet of ships in a harbor: an incoming tide —rising productivity and a rising standard of living— does not diminish the difference between rowboats, cabin cruisers, cargo vessels, and giant ocean liners" (Rossides, 1976: 112).

These two assessments of income distribution focus on different issues. For instance, absolute income figures suggest that until the mid-1970s people at all income levels were able to purchase increasing quantities of goods and services, thereby steadily improving their standard of living. Since the mid-1970s, however, the trend has reversed, and a growing proportion of Americans now find that their standard of living is declining. Absolute figures also make it clear that a significant number of Americans — about 32.5 million or 13.5 percent of the national population — have

238

insufficient income to provide a nutritionally adequate diet (U.S. Bureau of the Census, *Statistical Abstract of the United States: 1989.* No. 736).

Relative income figures highlight the fact that over time the distribution of income has changed little. Thus in 1947 the lowest fifth of the American population received 5 percent of all income, the highest fifth 43 percent, and the top 5 percent 17.5 percent. In 1983 the respective figures were 4.7 percent, 42.7 percent, and 15.8 percent (U.S. Bureau of the Census, *Current Population Reports,* Series P-60, *Money Income of Households, Families, and Persons in the United States: 1983,* 1984. Table 17).

Effect of Taxes

The tax structure is a prominent means by which unequal economic distribution is kept fairly stable. Certain taxes—those on property, sales, and on behalf of social security—are regressive, meaning that all people pay the same percentage of a product's value, regardless of their income. Therefore, if the state sales tax is 7 percent, any person making a purchase must pay an additional 7 percent beyond the cost of the item.

On the other hand, income taxes are supposedly progressive, apparently taking a greater percentage of people's income as it increases. If income taxes truly were progressive, then economic in-

While the income-tax system is technically progressive, the availability of loopholes increases as people's income rises. Wealthy individuals can afford to hire high-priced accountants, whose detailed knowledge of how to use the income-tax system to best advantage can save clients large sums of money.

equality might be significantly reduced. However, the tax system is progressive only for low-income and middle-income people. For those with high and very high income, a range of available tax loopholes permits them to keep significant portions of their income untaxed or taxed at sharply reduced rates. For example, people financially involved in the search for such exhaustible resources as oil or natural gas receive tax breaks because they are investing in the procurement of scarce but essential resources. In addition, people in various businesses and professions are able to "write off" a wide range of activities as business expenses. Sometimes these meals, travel costs, and rented cars, hotel rooms, and villas will represent legitimate business costs, and sometimes they will not.

Thus on the surface, the U.S. tax structure is progressive, but the more significant fact is that the number and size of tax loopholes increase as people's income increases. In 1972 a person with an income under $3000 a year averaged a $15 yearly benefit from tax loopholes, but at high income levels (over $500,000 per year) the savings provided by loopholes rose sharply, reaching an average of $726,198 for people with incomes over $1 million per year (Surrey, 1973: 71).

The instillation of tax loopholes is an example of the close relationship between wealth and power. As we see in Chapter 14, "The Political and Economic Institutions," interest groups attempt to influence politicians to pass favorable legislation, and wealthy interest groups tend to be more successful than their less affluent counterparts. In the last couple of decades, there has been a rising citizen dissatisfaction about the tax breaks available to the wealthy. For example, in 1969, Congress passed a seemingly major tax reform. However, in spite of the apparently sweeping changes that this law enacted, wealthy people continued to find multiple tax loopholes. Furthermore in 1971, after the furor over tax reform had died down, Congress passed a law restoring some of the loopholes plugged in 1969. Therefore wealthy people influence Congress through their interest groups, which act in a carefully planned series of maneuvers. A pair of sociologists noted, "Rarely is a frontal assault undertaken, lest the self-interest of the wealthy be exposed. Rather, the progressivity of the tax structure is eroded by a persistent series of skirmishes" (Turner and Starnes, 1976: 113).

Efforts to reform the income tax system continue. In September 1986, Congress passed a tax-reform bill, which enacted some important changes. About 6 million low-income people were removed from the tax rolls, and about 60 percent of taxpayers faced reduced payments. Many corporations taxed at or close to the maximum received a tax cut, while others, especially those benefiting from special tax subsidies that were repealed, were compelled to pay more. Overall it was estimated that business tax payments would increase by about $120 billion over six years to counterbalance an equivalent amount of tax cuts received by individuals (Egan, 1986; Koepp, 1986). Two years after the bill's passage, an expert's analysis indicated that while the new tax law created some greater equity among people at the same income level, the redistribution of the tax burden among different income groups remained almost unchanged (Herber, 1988).

The following American Controversy should encourage you to analyze an important issue related to wealth and income — inheritance.

AMERICAN CONTROVERSY

What Should Be Done about Inheritance?

Let me tell you about the very rich. They are different from you and me. They possess and enjoy early, and it does something to them, makes them soft where we are hard, and cynical where we are trustful, in a way that, unless you were born rich, it is difficult to understand. They think, deep in their hearts, that they are better than we are because we had to discover the compensations and refuges of life for ourselves. Even when they enter deep into our world or sink below us, they still think that they are better than we are. They are different.

F. Scott Fitzgerald

In this chapter we encounter some information backing Fitzgerald's position: that the wealthy not only have more valued material resources than others but they think of themselves as different, in significant ways superior. Should our society permit conditions encouraging people to maintain such a sense of superiority? A critical issue underlying this question is the subject of inheritance. After all, it is the opportunity to inherit that allows wealth to be passed from one generation to another. Let us consider different positions on inheritance.

A position in favor of inheritance: We live in a capitalist society, which rewards an individual's intelligence and perseverance. One of the most satisfying rewards that can be bestowed upon successful business people is the knowledge that their families will be able to inherit the wealth that they have accumulated. The existence of wealthy families serves as an incentive to others to produce similar achievements. Were inheritance eliminated or severely restricted, it is distinctly possible that many potentially excellent business ventures would not be pursued. Not only would individual families suffer but the society would not obtain the benefits provided by these enterprises. In particular, the diverse foundations wealthy individuals and families establish to assist various scientific, artistic, educational, and social programs would be eliminated, thereby restricting or ending numerous activities that have made a significant contribution to the enrichment of American society.

A position against inheritance: We live in a society that emphasizes equality. One of the most effective ways to achieve equality is to place a priority on economic equality, and the elimination of inheritance would be a significant step toward such an achievement. The government could use the enormous wealth that it obtained from taking over all inheritance to eliminate poverty, hunger, and disease and to reorganize and revamp a vast range of public structures and facilities, including the education system, health care, antiquated public buildings, highways, and other public works. It is unlikely that the elimination of inheritance will significantly discourage business people from pursuing commercial ventures: Immediate economic success and glory are considerably more important to those who engage in such activities than a consideration of their children's inheritance. Finally one might argue that for the wealthy, inheritance weakens or even kills the work ethic, a highly prized value in our society. Most of us work because we have no alternative means to purchase goods and services. Those born wealthy, however, have no such incentive.

What do you think? Do you strongly support one of the positions presented here, or do you find yourself somewhere in between? Discuss the issues in class or outside of class with several others in the course. In particular, try to assess the impact different policies would have on various groups, as well as on the society overall.

Power

Power is the ability of an individual or group to implement wishes or policies, with or without the cooperation of others. A young girl who forces a smaller child to bring her a cookie is exercising power. A special kind of power is **authority,** which is power that people generally recognize as rightfully maintained by those who use it. A college teacher who assigns two tests, three quizzes, and two short papers at scheduled intervals through the semester is exercising authority. However, it is in the realm of politics that sociologists most frequently study power, and we focus on the topic in Chapter 14, "The Political and Economic Institutions." At this time we briefly consider two sharply opposed theories on the operation of power in the American political process: the pluralist perspective and the power-elite approach.

The two theories differ in their assessment of whether or not political authority is concentrated. The pluralist perspective emphasizes that authority is not concentrated, that it is dispersed to different people who must represent their constituents' needs and interests or lose their access to political authority (Dahl, 1967). The pluralists contend that the only way elected officials can effectively represent their constituents' interests on different issues is to form a separate alliance on each issue. Thus a state legislator might be aligned with one set of politicians on a tax-reform bill and be working with an entirely different set on an antipollution measure. In both cases the legislator is seeking to promote constituents' interests.

The power-elite perspective popularized by C. Wright Mills (1956) opposes the pluralist approach. This theory claims that there is a group of high-status men who are well educated, often wealthy, socially prominent, and located in occupational positions where they can exert considerable power. Members of the elite control basic governmental policy in the political, economic, and military realms. If, in fact, Mills was correct, then our political system is not really a democracy. We, the people, might elect our political representatives, but these individuals are not attuned to the majority's interests; instead they are controlled by the power elite behind the scenes.

Mills visualized three levels of society. At the top is the power elite. Then there is a middle class of politically unorganized white-collar employees dominated by the corporations and government agencies for which they work. At the bottom are the masses, whose access to channels of power and influence is entirely cut off.

Overall neither the power-elite view nor the pluralist perspective provides a fully accurate picture of the role of authority in American society. The power-elite thesis probably exaggerates the extent to which upper-class people operate as a group with strongly shared interests. Competition sometimes exists among the rich and powerful for limited resources like government contracts or political offices. On the other hand, the pluralist thesis fails to recognize that exploitation, privilege, corruption, and powerlessness are deeply rooted in American politics. Both theories seem to provide a part of the truth.

Prestige

Prestige is the possession of attributes that elicit recognition, respect, and some degree of deference. Overall Americans tend to be fairly consistent in their assessments of prestige. A study found that two groups of respondents—one from the working class and the other from the middle class—were very similar in their prestige rankings for eighty-four Long Island communities (Logan and Collver, 1983). A similar consistency occurs with

occupations, which are frequently linked with prestige. Figure 9.2 shows the prestige ranking of selected white-collar occupations. In 1947 the National Opinion Research Center at the University of Chicago (NORC) used a national sample of 2920 respondents to rank ninety occupations in relation to each other, and across the nation there was remarkable consistency obtained from the subjects. The NORC study was repeated in 1963, and with minor variations the occupational rankings were strikingly similar (Hodge, Siegel, and Rossi, 1966). Research in other industrialized as well as nonindustrialized countries reveals a very similar pattern (Treiman, 1977).

The fact that Americans are highly consistent in the occupational rankings they provide suggests that for high-status jobs there is a nationally shared respect, which legitimates the performance of people in these positions. On the other hand, those ranked low are consistently valued in a negative way, an evaluation that tends to legitimate their economic failure and justify their placement at the bottom of the occupational prestige structure. Evidence suggests that the American public is particularly inclined to maintain generalized negative images of low-status occupational groups, not recognizing that such categories as farm workers contain people with diversified personal characteristics and lifestyles (Whitener, 1985).

People in low-status positions obviously feel the brunt of their prestige rankings. Taxi drivers, for example, do not possess an unusual or specialized skill. Sometimes drivers will try to convince their passengers that they do indeed have a special talent and "will resort to darting nimbly in and out of traffic, making neatly executed U-turns and leaping smartly ahead of other cars when the traffic light changes" (Davis, 1959: 160). Tenants generally believe that custodial work is low in prestige. Custodians usually recognize the tenants' estimations of their work and sometimes attempt to enhance their image by representing themselves as similar to professionals, especially doctors. Some custodians tell their tenants to call only during daylight hours except for emergencies, or like some doctors they charge their tenants on a sliding scale for any extra jobs that their tenants might request (Gold, 1952).

One of the major factors linked to prestige is sex.

Figure 9.2
Prestige of Selected White-Collar Occupations

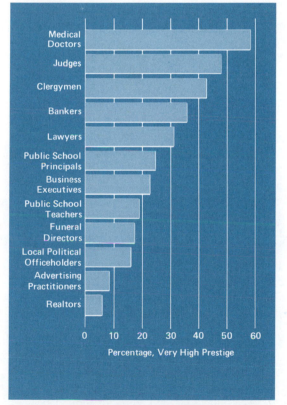

As this assessment of twelve occupations illustrates, Americans consider some white-collar positions much more prestigious than others. (Source: George Gallup. Gallup Poll. *October 7, 1981.*)

According to Tyree and Hicks (1988), women, especially homemakers, often receive little or no prestige for the work they do. One should not automatically assume that all statuses have prestige, Tyree and Hicks argued. They wrote, "A number of otherwise thoughtful sociologists seem to have forgotten this simple truth and have been trying to assign prestige scores to housewifery just because lawyering and plumbing and shoe polish-ing have prestige" (Tyree and Hicks, 1988: 1029).

In the first section, we looked at theories that consider why social stratification exists in socie-ties. We continued an analysis of the macro-order in this section, examining the distribution of wealth, power, and prestige throughout the soci-ety. Now the focus narrows, and we analyze the micro-order in the everyday lives of people be-longing to various social classes.

Social Class in America

A **social class** is a large category of people who are similar in income level, educational attain-ment, and occupational prestige-ranking. The members of a social class share a set of values and also similar opportunities to obtain desired goals and experiences.

Sometimes people speak about "the social-class structure" as if a single, distinct way of determin-ing an individual's social class placement exists. In reality a number of approaches have been used.

The **subjective definition of social class** is a measuring technique that requires people to indi-cate the social class to which they belong. In some cases the investigators provide a range of choices, and in other cases they do not. One problem with this approach is that research suggests that some people are not sure to which class they belong. One sociologist has reported that a substantial number of Americans have been unable to decide whether they are middle or working class (Kahl, 1957).

Research suggests that working women and men differ in their subjective definition of social class. Men's class identification tends to be based on whether they do manual or nonmanual work, while women's subjective view of social class is determined by whether or not they are self-em-ployed, work in a primarily female occupation, or have union membership. The two sets of results might have been produced by different work his-tories, with men's current work patterns develop-ing during industrial times and women's in the postindustrial, service-oriented era (Simpson, Stark, and Jackson, 1988).

The **reputational definition of social class** is a measuring technique in which researchers use resi-dent experts from the community — "judges" — to assess their neighbors' social-class position. This approach works well in residential areas that have a population that is sufficiently small and stable to permit the researchers to find judges who know all the local citizens well enough to place them in social classes. In the majority of modern American communities, the population is too large and physically mobile to make the use of this technique possible.

Finally the **objective definition of social class** is a measuring technique that uses certain quanti-fiable factors — income, occupational prestige level, or level of education, for example — as the basis for determining an individual's social-class position. Investigators sometimes employ a single factor, and in other cases they use a combination of several. Among sociologists the objective ap-proach is the most popular one, but what factors to use and how much weight each should receive are not issues on which unanimity exists. Table 9.1 summarizes the three approaches.

As we study social class, we should keep in mind that there is not unanimous agreement about how the American class system is structured. Most so-ciologists, however, would accept some approxi-mation of the following scheme:

1. A capitalist class, with considerable wealth, whose members, if working, maintain executive positions, have been educated at prestigious universities, possess a family income of about $475,000 a year, and represent about 1 percent of the population. (All the income figures presented in this discussion were calculated for the United States in 1988.)

2. The upper-middle class, containing people who are managers and professionals, have an annual income of about $47,000 or more, have

Table 9.1
Three Ways to Measure Social Class

THE APPROACH	WHO DETERMINES THE RESPONDENTS' SOCIAL CLASS?	A PROBLEM WITH THE APPROACH
Subjective definition	The respondents themselves	Some people's uncertainty about their own class membership
Reputational definition	Local "judges"	Modern, urbanized living making it impossible for any citizens to have sufficient knowledge of all fellow residents to serve as judges
Objective definition	Researchers using certain quantifiable factors, such as occupational evaluations, income, or educational level	Limited agreement about which factors to use or how much weight to provide each given factor

attended college, perhaps done postgraduate study, and constitute about 14 percent of the population.

3. The lower-middle class, with members who work as lower-level managers, semiprofessionals, salespeople, craft workers, and foremen, earn about $29,500 a year, have at least a high-school education, and comprise about 33 percent of the population.

4. The working class, who are operatives, clerical and sales workers, or low-paid craftspeople, receive about $21,000 a year, have graduated from high school, and represent about 32 percent of the population.

5. The working poor, employed as service workers, laborers, and low-paid operatives, have some high-school education, make below $14,000 a year, and are about 11 percent of the population.

6. The underclass, who are unemployed or underemployed and sometimes are maintained by welfare, tend to have a primary-school education, receive $10,500 a year or less, and comprise about 9 percent of the population (Gilbert and Kahl, 1982: 348).

People within a particular social class share a common sense of outlook and experience. Those in various social classes, for instance, have different opportunities and lifestyles (Tumin, 1967).

Opportunity and Social Class

Social classes offer different opportunities. The higher people's social class, the longer their life expectancy, the less likely they will suffer mental illness, the more effective their capacity to communicate, and the higher their self-esteem.

Life Expectancy

People can pay to lengthen their lives in a number of ways. In particular, the higher classes benefit from longer life expectancy in situations in which death is preventable since, because of income and other advantages, they have greater access than lower-class people to effective means of prevention. For example, when the *Titanic* was rammed by an iceberg and was sunk, sufficient lifeboats for everyone were not available. Only 4 of 150 women and children in first class (3 percent) went down with the ship compared to 13 of 117 in second class (11 percent) and 141 of 244 in third class (58 percent). It appears that third-class passengers suffered two distinct disadvantages — they were much more likely to be denied entrance to the life boats and their residential areas were much farther from the boat deck (Hall, 1986).

A variety of more general conditions promote greater life expectancy for people in higher social classes. For example:

Front-line troops have tended to come from the lower social classes. A researcher who studied combat soldiers in Vietnam found that about two-thirds of the soldiers in the units with which he stayed were from working-class backgrounds and the remainder

244

had lower-middle-class origins. Nearly two-thirds had graduated from high school, and most of the others were high school dropouts. Several had attended college, but none were college graduates (Moskos, 1969).

A study of four societies — Belize, Kenya, Nepal, and American Samoa — found that individuals given a high social-class ranking locally were two to four times more likely to be healthy than those given a low social-class ranking (Munroe and Munroe, 1984).

Evidence suggests that, in the past, coronary heart disease was disproportionately suffered by the affluent. With the development of mechanized transportation and a variety of labor-saving devices, emphasis on low cholesterol food among the educated, and the growing predominance of smoking among low-income citizens, heart disease has increasingly become a disease of the poor (Wing, 1988).

Mental Illness

Robert Faris and Warren Dunham (1939) examined over 30,000 people admitted to hospitals in Chicago for the treatment of mental illness. They found an inverse relationship between social-class position and the rate of mental illness. Another study, which assessed the psychiatric condition of a random sample of 1600 New Yorkers, reached a similar conclusion (Srole et al., 1962). Later research has produced consistent results, concluding that people in higher social classes have lower rates of schizophrenia, depression, unhappiness, and anxiety (Syme and Berkman, 1981).

We might wonder why. People in higher social classes generally have greater educational and occupational opportunities, which can promote a positive sense of self and decrease the likelihood of mental illness. Furthermore less affluent people's general life condition, in which most items that are highly prized are in short supply, is likely to encourage a negative, even fatalistic outlook on reality. Such an outlook makes it difficult to deal resourcefully with stress in the course of everyday life (Kessler and Cleary, 1980; Kohn, 1976). In addition, the perception of type of mental illness in different social classes is to some extent in the eye of the beholder. Growing evidence indicates that mental-health specialists develop preconceptions of the kinds of mental illness associated with various social classes (Landrine, 1987). They also might have preconceptions about frequency in different social classes.

Communication Effectiveness

The higher the social class of the family, the earlier and the more effectively speech will develop (Berelson and Steiner, 1964: 69). Leonard Schatzman and Anselm Strauss (1972) conducted 340 interviews with witnesses of tornados. They found that the social class (especially the amount of education) of the individuals involved in these disasters significantly influenced the effectiveness of the accounts they gave. In particular:

The working-class participants could see the events only through "their eyes." By contrast, the middle-class witnesses could also offer explanations from the point of view of another person or a group of other people.

The working-class respondents often did not anticipate what the listener who had not been present during the disaster knew about the course of events. The result was that the accounts from working-class people were often so undeveloped that they were hard to follow beyond the description of individuals' personal reactions. On the other hand, the middle-class person stood "between his own images and the hearer and [implicitly said], 'Let me introduce you to what I saw and know.'"

The working-class respondents could describe individuals, but they were not able to discuss effectively the activities of categories of people (the rich or the poor, the hurt or the unhurt) or organizations. Seemingly without effort middle-class people tended to analyze their perceptions in relation to these different categories and to convey information about them in an effective, coherent manner.

Self-Esteem

People who feel that individuals, including themselves, are responsible for their level of occupational achievement tend to believe that the social-class system and its inequalities are legitimate (Shepelak, 1987). Thus, if people feel high self-esteem because of occupational success or low self-esteem because of occupational failure, they consider the social-class system legitimate in both instances. On the other hand, if their sense of self-esteem is not linked to occupational success, then they are not especially attuned to the legitimacy of the social-class system. Because of the strong regard for individualism in American society, most citizens consider the inequalities of the American social-class system legitimate and use their own level of occupational success as a means of determining self-esteem.

A case in point is the "hidden injury" of class, the fact that working-class people are denied a sense of worth in the eyes of others and of themselves. This lack of esteem, Sennett and Cobb (1973) suggested, has two sources: first, the idea that class placement is the result of ability, and, second, the often futile pursuit of efforts to improve one's class position. Sennett and Cobb undertook a study in Boston, conducting 150 in-depth interviews of working-class men and women ranging in age from their late teens to their sixties. The study offered many illustrations of working-class people's low self-esteem.

For example, a respondent told the researchers about his sense of inferiority in the presence of middle-class people.

> Whenever I'm with educated people, you know, or people who aren't my own kind . . . um . . . I feel like I'm making a fool of myself if I just act natural, you know? See, it's not so much how people treat you, it's feeling like you don't know what to do.
>
> (Sennett and Cobb, 1973: 110)

The man went on to describe a time when he had appeared at a meeting of middle-class people and felt entirely out of place and isolated.

It seems that children's sense of relationship between their social-class position and self-esteem develops gradually. A study concluded that among children ranging from fifth- to eighth-graders, the perceived relationship between social class and self-esteem rose with age. Apparently as children become older, they pay more attention to social class, increasingly allowing their own position within the system to determine their self-image (Demo and Savin-Williams, 1983).

Lifestyle and Social Class

People demonstrate differences in lifestyle, as indicated in the following discussion of fertility, child-rearing patterns, sexual behavior, and clubs and friendships.

Research has indicated that some working-class people suffer the "hidden injury of class," but others, such as the men on the right side of this table, are able to take significant steps to overcome this problem. These men are factory workers who serve on the negotiating team for the local chapter of the United Auto Workers at Ford's Louisville assembly plant. The handshake signals that they have just completed negotiations with management for a new contract.

246

Fertility

In a chart that attempts to represent humorously the relationship between family life and social class, Simon and Gagnon (1972: 86 – 87) suggested that upper-class couples tend to have one child each by previous marriages — or as many as God provides; upper-middle-class couples produce 2.4 children; lower-middle-class couples usually have three children; and lower-class couples have as many as God provides.

In fact, this summary is somewhat accurate. An inverse relationship — in this case the higher the social class, the fewer the number of children — often exists between social class and family size. Blacks generally have more children than whites, and this pattern is apparently class-linked. When researchers compare black and white families of the same social class, the difference in family size disappears.

Several factors explain the statistical relationship between social class and family size. The higher the social class, the greater the tendency for women to be extensively educated and career-oriented and thus to want to control family size. Furthermore people in the middle or upper-middle class are more likely than lower-class individuals to plan their lives in accord with the dominant value patterns of the day as represented in the media, and having a modest number of children is such a prevailing value pattern (Duberman, 1976: 244 – 255; Reiss and Lee, 1988: 315; Wrong, 1966).

Approaches to Child Rearing

Middle-class and working-class parents' child-rearing techniques are similar in many respects. In the United States and several western European countries, however, some distinct differences are apparent: In particular, middle-class parents place more emphasis on self-direction and working-class parents on conformity to external authority. One factor that seems to contribute to the different child-rearing values is the influence of respective work environments. Working-class individuals' jobs are much more supervised and routinized than those of middle-class people, whose occupations involve more autonomy and task variety (Reiss and Lee, 1988; 328 – 330).

During the Vietnam War, different class attitudes toward raising children became a political issue. Vice-President Spiro Agnew, a man of working-class origin, made a number of speeches in which he sharply criticized the behavior of upper-middle-class antiwar activists. Agnew suggested that these young people were products of "permissive" child-rearing practices, practices that allowed or even encouraged the activists not to respect their parents and their political leaders.

Sexuality

Wardell Pomeroy (1972: 469) has suggested that by comparing adolescent boys' sexual histories, one can conclude which individuals will be more likely to attend college. For instance, one boy has intercourse with a number of girls, does not remove his clothes for sexual relations, disapproves of oral sex, masturbates less at eighteen than in his early teens, and has few "wet dreams." The sexual history of a second boy shows that if he has sexual intercourse, he has less than the other boy, engages in a great deal of petting and may try oral sex, and considers sexual activity more enjoyable in the nude. The first boy, according to Pomeroy, displays sexual behavior typical of a lower-class background; coming from this background, he is unlikely to attend college. On the other hand, the sexual behavior of the second boy is typically middle-class, and middle-class adolescents are likely to attend college.

Lower-class people tend to begin their sexual lives somewhat earlier, but their sexual activity tends to be less frequent and less fulfilling, especially for women (Howell, 1973). A study of low-status marriages in four places — the United States, Puerto Rico, Mexico, and England — suggests that the belief frequently exists that "sex is a man's pleasure and a woman's duty." This particular attitude seems to be a product of segregated gender roles, which permit a very limited sharing of interests and activities between women and men (Rainwater, 1964). On the other hand, middle-class or upper-class spouses are quite likely to share common interests and a sense of closeness, openly discussing their sexual relations and remaining sensitive to their partners' needs (Reiss, 1980: 275 – 285).

The modern era of sexual permissiveness can be

particularly confusing for working-class women. Like many modern men, most working-class men recognize the value placed on women's orgasms. Many of them now believe that unless their wives achieve orgasm, they have failed as lovers. The women, on the other hand, have often been raised by mothers who stress a "grin-and-bear-it" approach to sex, and they are unlikely to enjoy sex and achieve orgasm. (Rubin, 1983).

Among singles social-class position can serve as a basis of sexual exploitation. A study indicated that some male medical students use their rising social status to attract women into brief affairs, postponing long-term relationships and marriage until their careers are established (Townsend, 1987).

Friendships and Clubs

An upper-middle-class man spoke to a researcher about the prospect of having working-class friends. He said, "I am not a snob, but it is a fact of life that in most of those occupations we would have nothing in common" (Laumann, 1966: 28).

Many people would agree with this man. When classes are defined on the basis of occupation, people are more likely to choose friends from among their own or adjacent classes. In one study the pattern was most distinct at the extremes, with unskilled and semiskilled workers finding more than three-quarters of their friends close to their own class level and with the professional and business classes doing the same (Laumann, 1966: 65).

Recent research on the process of friendship development presented two notable findings. First, an investigation of 304 social and professional clubs from ten cities concluded that besides the members of these organizations sharing such social-class traits as occupational and educational background, friendship pairs are more inclined to share these traits with each other than with the general membership (McPherson and Smith-Lovin, 1987). But do they admit that these similarities exist? A second study involving seventy-

People are more likely to choose friendships and associations among their own class. Ethnic and racial similarities may also affect the choice of organizations and clubs people join.

five middle-class and upper-middle-class women indicated that while they do choose friends whose social traits are similar to their own, they are reluctant to acknowledge the relevance of these factors, preferring to emphasize friends' personality or other individual characteristics (Gouldner and Strong, 1987).

The members of different social classes tend to join certain kinds of organizations, and the prestige of the organizations depends on the prestige of the members. There are upper-class and upper-middle-class social clubs: athletic clubs, men's clubs, women's gardening clubs, and charitable organizations. These same classes support professionally oriented clubs: chambers of commerce, business and professional associations, and ser-

vice clubs. Such organizations can serve a variety of purposes for their members. Typically men's professional organizations provide the opportunity to make valuable contacts, to obtain useful information, and to engage in interesting, stimulating discussion. In contrast to men's clubs, women's organizations are more likely to be local than national. Upper-middle-class women usually belong to more clubs than their husbands and place greater emphasis on clubs as a source of status advancement (Hodges, 1964; Lerner, 1982).

Clubs and friendships can be effectively used to help people "get ahead." In the following section, we discuss Americans' efforts to improve their social-class position.

Social Mobility in American Society

At the end of the nineteenth century, Horatio Alger's novels about poor boys who rose from rags to riches through hard work sold more than thirty million copies. These novels underlined the American belief that the United States is an open society in which enormous opportunity for personal success exists and that people will receive rewards of wealth, power, and prestige in correspondence with the effort they make. Actually how open is the social-class system? To address this issue, we must first examine the concept of social mobility.

Social mobility is the movement of a person from one social class or status level to another, either upward or downward with accompanying gains or losses in wealth, power, and prestige. In the past couple of decades, there have been many studies of mobility processes (Kerckhoff, 1984; Smith, 1981) and also debates about how this complex topic should be conceptualized (Breiger and Jacobs, 1987; Snipp, 1987).

Sociologists generally study two kinds of social mobility. **Intergenerational mobility** is a comparison of a parent's and a child's social-class positions. This comparison indicates whether the child's social-class position is higher or lower than the parent's or has remained the same. Most prominent studies of intergenerational mobility have compared fathers' and sons' social-class position, using occupational status as its measure. An increasing number of intergenerational-mobility

studies on women seems inevitable as they enter the work world in rapidly increasing numbers. Recent research in sixteen countries concluded that in spite of some differences among the nations, their patterns of intergenerational mobility are basically similar (Grusky and Hauser, 1984).

Intragenerational mobility is an analysis of an individual's occupational changes in the course of a lifetime. Thus a researcher might observe that a particular woman started as a bank teller, advanced to management status, and eventually retired as the bank president. One recent study of intragenerational mobility in three countries—Austria, France, and the United States—found that because of different conditions governing the move from lower-status to higher-status jobs, the three cultures differed significantly in their intragenerational mobility patterns (Haller et al., 1985).

Let us consider current evidence of social mobility, the causes, some of the effects produced by it, and prospects for upward mobility.

Evidence

Perhaps you have participated in a conversation like the following. A group of friends are having lunch together. Jane says, "Last night I spoke with my grandfather, and all he talks about these days is how much things have changed. Yesterday he kept harping on the fact that you can't work your way up from the bottom anymore. The big corporations run the whole show, and they keep people pretty much locked in. If your family has got money and power it's one thing, but for the rest of us . . ." She shakes her head unhappily.

Ron smiles. "I don't agree. It seems to me that if you have a good idea and can market it, you can still make a pile and gain all the power and prestige that go with it. My mom and dad went to high school with Frank Trudeau. In his early twenties, he had a simple idea for a household device, and he turned it into a multimillion-dollar business."

Many Americans have bits and pieces of opinion and knowledge that suggest that U.S. society is either more or less open than it was in the past. We need to look beyond bits and pieces and see if we can detect a broad pattern. In the first place, we must be aware that it is difficult to make meaningful comparisons of social-mobility rates over long periods of time. It is misleading, perhaps impossible, to compare people in an agrarian society with those in an industrial one. If the grandson of a blacksmith who earned $500 a year becomes an automobile worker making $10,000 per year, he is likely to be downwardly mobile in a relative sense, in spite of a sizable increase in income. In this case "relative sense" means that the automobile worker will be proportionately lower in the modern stratification system. When agrarian societies become industrial, most people become "wealthier, healthier, more skilled, better educated, and the like than their forebears, but modern populations are just as unequal, relative to their own societies, as people were in the past" (Rossides, 1976: 99).

Comparisons over short periods of time involving a society with a fairly stable economic system are easier to understand. In 1962 sociologists Peter Blau and Otis Duncan (1967) conducted a study that David Featherman and Robert Hauser (1978) repeated a decade later. In both cases the investigators arranged with the Bureau of the Census to add two pages containing questions on career history and parental background to the regular monthly survey of employment and unemployment. Blau and Duncan received data on 20,000 fathers and sons, and Featherman and Hauser obtained information on 33,000 fathers and sons.

The researchers focused on their respondents'

occupations. They divided the men into five categories based on their type of job — white-collar, lower white-collar, upper manual, lower manual, and farm. In the 1978 study, Featherman and Hauser found that 49 percent of sons moved up, 32 percent stayed in the same general category, and 19 percent went down. The Blau and Duncan findings from eleven years earlier were just slightly different. The percentage of upward mobility was the same, but 2 percent more stayed the same, and thus 2 percent fewer went down.

Blau and Duncan examined findings from some older studies that allowed them to make comparisons back to 1947. They found that between 1947 and 1962 an increasing percentage of men moved from manual origins into white-collar jobs and that no corresponding downward move occurred. Furthermore in that fifteen-year span, an increasing proportion stayed at the same occupational level as their fathers (Blau and Duncan, 1967: 103).

Thus the American occupational structure has shown a trend toward upward mobility. However, some distinct limitations to that pattern occur.

Cases of Limited Access

In the first place, it is very difficult for lower-class people to move up. Many sociologists contend that millions of poor people are trapped in a **vicious cycle of poverty,** a pattern in which the parents' minimal income significantly limits the educational and occupational pursuits of the children, thereby keeping them locked into the same low economic status. Does such a circle of poverty actually occur? Bradley Shiller (1970) studied 1017 men who grew up in families receiving Aid to Families with Dependent Children. Sixty-three percent of the respondents were in some kind of unskilled jobs, and only 8 percent achieved a white-collar position. Therefore a few men did succeed in breaking the vicious cycle of poverty, but nearly two out of three remained in marginal job slots, leaving them likely candidates to carry the cycle into the next generation.

For decades governmental programs have tried to combat the cycle of poverty, but they have generally been unsuccessful. How could such programs be improved? An expert on the subject has suggested that all welfare programs seeking to

250

eliminate the cycle of poverty have had a common deficiency: These programs have not "sought to break the cycle of dependency and poverty by trying to improve the care and upbringing of young children on welfare. This task was left exclusively to the mother, often a teen-ager, completely disregarding her obvious limitations" (Bernstein, 1986: A35). Effective governmental intervention in the welfare family would insure good nutrition and health for infants, early childhood education, and the development of values that would encour-

age children to remain in school and to avoid activities that promote the cycle of poverty.

Meanwhile America's poor continue to become poorer. Recent figures indicate that between 1979 and 1987, the poorest fifth of American families suffered a 9-percent decline in their income's buying power, while the most affluent fifth experienced a 19-percent increase (Passell, 1989). The following Social Application demonstrates how the cycle of poverty can develop.

SOCIAL APPLICATION

The Vicious Cycle of Poverty: A Case Study

 The vicious cycle of poverty consists of the transmission of limited opportunity from one generation to the next. But how does the process actually occur? One concrete answer comes from looking at case studies of individuals, such as the life account of José Alvarez, who grew up in East Harlem, a Puerto Rican district of New York City. For José and other people caught in the cycle of poverty, the opportunity to obtain affluence, good jobs, and prestige has been remote.

At the time of the research, José was eighteen years old, a dropout from high school. He had a host of interests and talents, including photography, electrical gadgetry, and sports. His photographs were widely acclaimed by local residents and outsiders who saw them. After studying a stack of José's photos, one expert declared that the young man had a rare knack of "catching that special moment." José was also me-

chanically inclined; he could put together a television from spare parts or repair serious automotive problems without even a manual.

In spite of José's talents, a number of factors made his future bleak, beginning with his family. When José was young, his mother died and his father remarried. The new wife was not enthusiastic about raising her husband's son, and soon he was shipped to his grandmother. This small, white-haired woman, always dressed in black, had come to New York City before José was born. She survived on public assistance, living an almost reclusive existence, and she forced the same lifestyle on her grandson. José explained, "I never got to go downstairs and play outside like the kids now. So on the way home from school I'd sometimes stop at the library and pick up a book. All I ever did was read."

Although he read constantly, José generally did

not take school seriously. As a boy he failed to grasp its relation to occupational success. Neither his grandmother nor his counselors ever encouraged him to do anything but "just get by." He went to a vocational high school, but several of his friends explained to him that the best he could hope for in the future with a vocational degree was a job as a factory worker. As a result of this advice, he transferred to an academic high school, but then another hurdle appeared in front of him. He became involved with Maria Pagan.

Maria was divorced with two children, and soon after she and José started going together, she was pregnant again. José explained, "I quit school and got myself a job. Like the people say, when the woman gets pregnant you've got to forget about school and go to work!"

Several years later José returned to school, but his attendance was irregular, and he seldom did his homework.

I met José at this time, and he would speak enthusiastically about school, about the teachers who stimulated him, and about friends applying to college. The way he spoke made it clear that he felt that college and the good jobs that would come from higher education were fascinating but not attainable.

I told José that if he wanted to go on to college, he could. José pointed out to me that it was easy for me to say that. My life, after all, had been simple. I admitted that José had a point but still persisted. If José really wanted to go to college, he would be able to in spite of the difficulties involved. José laughed bitterly and gave me a paper he had written. One paragraph read in part:

POVERTY: WHO CAN KNOW WHAT IT REALLY IS?

You have to know from experience what it is like to be poor. You have to learn about a life where you can't afford to pay $1.25 for a hair cut. You have to get to know the smell of second-hand mattresses after too many babies have lain on them.

When I returned the paper to José, he told me that this was true, that you couldn't learn about poverty from books, only from experience. I agreed but added that José could still go to college. He stared blankly and said nothing.

Twenty years have passed, and José has had a long list of menial jobs, a lengthy involvement with hard drugs, a short jail sentence, two broken marriages, and five children. Not surprisingly he never went to college. Certainly there were economic and practical problems, but for José the cycle of poverty seems to have set its most vicious trap at the interpersonal level. As Cooley's looking-glass-self perspective suggests, we see ourselves as others see us. It appears that no one ever visualized José as a college student, or for that matter as any kind of consistent success. So he never visualized himself in any successful roles either, and his talents have simply gone to waste.

Source: Christopher Bates Doob. *The Development of Peer Group Relationships among Puerto Rican Boys in East Harlem.* Unpublished Ph.D. dissertation. Cornell University. 1967.

Blacks are another category of people who encounter special difficulties when they try to advance themselves in social-class position. On the average, blacks have certain distinct disadvantages compared to whites — poorer parents, fewer years of education, less sympathetic and thorough supervision early in their careers, and extensive discrimination. Yet, in spite of these disadvantages, the black community is no longer lower-class occupationally. Employed black males divide roughly into thirds, with one-third in the underclass or among the working poor, another third in working-class jobs, and the final third in some level of middle-class positions.

Let us consider some advancement problems blacks face. The black underclass continues to experience high unemployment rates, high welfare rates, and a decrease in movement out of poverty — in short, the vicious cycle of poverty. About 33.1 percent of blacks compared to 10.5 percent of whites — three times the proportion — are living in poverty (U.S. Bureau of the Census, *Statistical Abstract of the United States: 1989.* No. 736; Wilson, 1980). An editorial in the *Economist,* a British journal, offered a distinctly non-American viewpoint on the plight of the black underclass in the "land of opportunity," where upward mobility tends to be a dominant national concern. It was suggested that unlike Europeans, who are obsessed with the idea of people ending up relatively equal in wealth and income, Americans only want to ensure that people start out equal. Now, however, "with the emergence of a huge . . . largely black, underclass, that belief is now impossible to sustain" (*Economist,* March 15, 1986: 29). To many Americans black, middle-class people appear successful, but evidence suggests that they are concentrated in areas serving black consumers and communities and that in the 1980s the Reagan administration altered policies that had assisted middle-class blacks to rise (Collins, 1983).

Women also face special problems attaining upward mobility. One difficulty is the sex-typing of occupations. Traditionally people in occupations classified as "male" have considered women who tried to enter them as deviants and have placed obstacles in their paths. In the past two decades, however, women have managed to join many previously exclusive male professions. In certain high-status positions, they are still nearly absent, however—for instance, architecture, surgery, engineering, commercial piloting, and top business management.

Another difficulty is the informal, sex-linked "old boy" network that prevails in most professions. Like women, men often form a subculture. They talk about sports, about women, and about other "masculine" topics at lunch or over drinks in situations that implicitly or explicitly exclude women. This exclusion can be a serious problem for women, because career advancement often emerges out of these informal contexts. For the few women who possess the social skills to function in these male-oriented situations, however, this informal colleague system can prove to be an asset for career advancement.

Another problem women encounter is an outgrowth of the "old boy" network. In many situations men's occupational advancement results from the sponsorship of an established professional. The younger man serves an apprenticeship in which he "learns the ropes." Established professionals are less likely to develop such a relationship with women because they are often incapable of or unwilling to visualize women as their successors. Furthermore an apprentice relationship with a woman is likely to be awkward—to raise questions in people's minds about the possibility of a personal relationship between the two of them. Thus women frequently do not have the opportunity to participate effectively in male-dominated professional structures (Duberman, 1976; Epstein, 1970; Farr, 1988).

Causes

If one starts with the assumption that a society has a closed social-class system, in which children inevitably fill the same occupations as their parents, one can suggest four types of social mobility that would alter that static condition.

First, there is circulation mobility. Some people are downwardly mobile, opening up positions for others moving up.

Second, reproductive mobility can occur. As we noted earlier in the chapter, a relationship between social class and number of children exists

When poor immigrants, such as these nineteenth-century Irish people, arrived in the United States, they generally took low-paying, unskilled jobs, permitting the children of those previously occupying such positions to seek higher-status occupations.

—the higher the social class, the fewer the children. Before World War II, estimates indicated that professional men were not producing a sufficient number of sons to replace themselves — 870 sons to every 1000 professional fathers. Farmers, however, were averaging nearly double that number — 1520 sons to every 1000 farmers. Estimates suggest that if fathers of all status levels, including professionals, had produced families of equal size, then the upward mobility of blue-collar sons would have decreased by 7 percent.

Third, immigration mobility can encourage upward mobility. If immigrants fill a large number of the unskilled labor jobs, then opportunities increase for native-born citizens to move up the status ladder. For example, at the turn of the century, a strong demand existed for workers in the mines and factories. During those years the arriving immigrants provided a major source of unskilled and semiskilled labor, allowing native-born citizens, including the sons of foreign-born parents, to move into skilled manual and white-collar positions.

Finally a significant factor affecting upward mobility is occupational or structural mobility — a type of upward social mobility that occurs because technological innovation or organizational change creates more new jobs at the middle or upper levels of the occupational structure than at the lower levels. For instance, from 1940 to 1970, professional and technical jobs for men increased 192 percent, while jobs for farm laborers dropped by 75 percent (Gilbert and Kahl, 1982: 170–174).

Effects

Fifty million fans watch as the television coverage shifts to the locker room. The announcer moves through the crowd of players, coaches, and media personnel until he reaches the game's hero, whose hair and face are glistening with a combination of champagne and perspiration.

"How does it feel?" the announcer asks.

"I . . ." The player shakes his head. "I don't have the words to explain it. I've waited so long for this moment . . ."

Some semblance of this scene has occurred many times in American professional sport. The television camera catches the sporting hero at the moment of glory. Professional sport stars have been upwardly mobile — they have achieved wealth and prestige — and yet many have drug, alcohol, gambling, or other serious personal problems. Other upwardly mobile people do too.

Melvin Tumin (1957) has suggested that upward mobility can produce "diffusion of insecurity." The upwardly mobile have departed from their original social-class position and thus feel lost, no longer firmly grounded in a social-class tradition with its associated family, friends, and lifestyle. Other sociologists make a similar assessment (Ellis and Lane, 1967; Sorokin, 1927).

One study indicated that upwardly mobile people are more likely to show high levels of anxiety and psychosomatic illness than the socially stable, whereas downwardly mobile individuals exceed the average on serious forms of psychotic illness (Kessin, 1971). The last conclusion receives support from another investigation, where the major finding was that higher suicide rates occur among downwardly mobile men (Breed, 1963). Some social conditions can offset such tendencies. An investigation of upwardly mobile black families has concluded that the family (generally with the mother serving as a full-time homemaker) has played a significant role in blunting the impact of stress in members' lives (McAdoo, 1982).

In spite of the difficulties involved, a strong incentive exists for many Americans to improve their social-class position. Let us consider the current prospects for continuing upward mobility.

Prospects for Upward Mobility

Many Americans apparently believe that opportunities still exist to enter the higher social classes. Studies conducted in Boston and Kansas City indicate that Americans feel that getting ahead depends on four things: parental encouragement, an effective education, ambition to get ahead, and plenty of hard work. In particular, when the respondents in these studies talked about upward mobility "the phrases they most freely applied in explaining how it happened were 'pure effort,' 'perseverance,' 'just plain hard work,' 'sheer work,' 'work, work, and more work,' and 'he wasn't ever afraid of working'" (Coleman and Rainwater, 1978: 240). In addition, recent research has revealed a specific attribute that seems to contribute to upward mobility: the ability to keep one's emotions under control in situations that could easily provoke anger or irritation. This quality makes people easier to work with and more socially acceptable than individuals without it (Snarey and Vaillant, 1985).

Today if people are planning to move into the middle- or upper-middle class, they must be aware of the choices they are making. They must realize that in a slumping economy certain occupations offer prospects for affluence and others do not. People who have jobs in which salary advances have been running behind inflation include middle-level managers, secretaries and other office personnel, salespeople, retail clerks, college professors, public employees, construction laborers, and factory workers. Those who have stayed ahead include top-level managers, doctors, dentists, lawyers, and computer programmers.

In the past two decades, many people have not only found themselves entering occupations with receding incomes, but many others also discovered no work available. In the last decade, a third of male college graduates and two-thirds of female college graduates had to accept work outside their chosen field, often in jobs not requiring any college training.

Certain lifestyle choices are also likely to promote a middle-class affluence or to prevent it. The employment of wives can substantially increase family income. The decision to have one or two

children instead of three or more children will mean significant savings, particularly in an era when the cost of food, clothing, higher education, and many other goods and services paid for by parents has been skyrocketing. Finally the avoidance of divorce can be a decisive factor affecting family affluence. The capacity to support or partially support two families is simply beyond the economic scope of most modern citizens (Maloney, 1981).

Some Americans, including many college students, are in a situation that permits them to move from the working class into the middle class. For many Americans, however, upward mobility simply involves an escape from poverty or near poverty. For the 46 million families with incomes below $15,000, significant advance in their social position would probably not occur without some changes in federal policies.

Such changes would include a reallocation of federal spending to meet basic needs of the poor and near poor. Student loans or subsidies would seem particularly useful since educational opportunity could help people obtain jobs that would permit them to escape poverty.

In these closing paragraphs, we have been discussing practical steps to produce upward mobility for middle-class and lower-class people. Another line of thought, however — already anticipated by the brief discussion on the effects of social mobility — should also be mentioned.

Over the past two generations, the rate of depression, with symptoms of hopelessness, passivity, low self-esteem, and possible suicide, has risen about ten-fold. Frequently those who experience depression are upwardly mobile and, by income, education, and prestige measures, successful or very successful.

What observations can the sociological perspective offer on this widespread problem? At the core of the problem seems to be the rootlessness of modern American society, where support and direction provided by local communities, religion, and the family frequently no longer are effective.

Instead, for many people work is expected to supply meaning and direction, but major deficiencies exist here. First, while occupational success is emphasized in American society, what actually constitutes it is often unclear. High income and the conspicuous display of expensive consumer goods serve as the only fixed indicators of

Politics involves many upwardly mobile people, who often find themselves working hard while others are relaxing.

success, but their effectiveness in convincing people that they truly are successful is questionable. Generally individuals develop their own sense of what constitutes success, and then if they don't get the raise or promotion, the result is likely to be severe disappointment or depression. Second, when people become "career-oriented," the intrinsic worth of the job can become submerged in the quest for income, power, and prestige. Thus, while individuals might become "successful," their sense of self-esteem can still diminish if the job has lost value to them (Bellah et al., 1986: 148–150; Seligman, 1988).

In the past many Americans had more sources of support. They could go to church and hear that there was a power greater than themselves. Or, they could talk to members of their extended family or neighbors and receive friendly advice or encouragement. And, while all of their doubts and concerns might not have been removed, a sense of belonging and self-enhancement could have been produced.

With few emotional ties to kin, friends, and community, many modern people expect to obtain similar profound emotional meaning from work, and when the work fails in this regard, they have no place else to turn. It seems that as we move toward the twenty-first century, one of the great challenges will be to develop social systems on the job and elsewhere that encompass both people's need for meaning in their work and the need for support and belonging.

STUDY GUIDE

Learning Objectives

After studying this chapter, you should be able to:

1. Define social stratification and consider its significance in modern life.
2. Discuss and evaluate the three theories of social stratification examined in the text—Marxist conflict, structural-functional, and Lenski's.
3. Identify and analyze the three dimensions of social stratification.
4. Define social class, identify and define the three principal ways of measuring social class, and list and briefly discuss the American social-class structure.
5. Describe the impact of social class on people's opportunities and lifestyle.
6. Define social mobility, distinguish between intergenerational and intragenerational mobility, and summarize current evidence on the social-mobility issue, including cases of limited access.
7. Identify and discuss four causes of social mobility, examine its effects, and discuss prospects for upward mobility.

Summary

1. Social stratification is structured inequality of access to rewards, resources, and privileges that are scarce and desirable within a society.

2. The Marxist conflict and structural-functional theories take very different approaches. The conflict theory of social stratification emphasizes the inequity of the rewards which are passed from one generation to the next. The structural-functional theory of stratification does not consider the advantages parents pass to their children, focusing on the supposed relationship between the importance of people's jobs and the rewards they receive. Both theories have received extensive criticism, and Gerhard Lenski's theory is an effort to use their respective strengths and avoid their weaknesses.

3. Three prominent dimensions of social stratification are wealth, power, and prestige. Wealth is

people's economic assets that can be converted into money. Over time Americans have experienced an increase in absolute wealth, but relative wealth has remained fairly stable. The current tax system contributes to the sharp economic inequalities that persist in U.S. society.

Power is the ability of an individual or group to implement wishes or policies, with or without the cooperation of others. Authority is power that people generally recognize as rightfully maintained by those who use it. Sociologists have tended to use two approaches to examining power: the pluralist and the power-elite perspectives.

Finally prestige is the possession of attributes that elicit recognition, respect, and some degree of satisfaction. Survey research indicates that Americans show some consistency on ranking the prestige of a range of occupations.

4. A social class is a large number of people who are similar in income level, educational attainment, and occupational prestige-ranking. Sociologists have used a number of different approaches to measure social class. The members of different social classes vary in their life expectancy, mental illness, communication effectiveness, and self-esteem.

People from various social classes also differ in lifestyle. Fertility, approaches to child rearing, sexuality, and friendships and clubs are lifestyle activities that vary among the social classes.

5. The topic of social mobility, which is the movement of a person from one social class or social status to another, addresses the issue of the openness of the American social-class system. A comparison of two studies conducted a decade apart suggests that the amount of social mobility varied little at those two times. Certain people — the poor, blacks, and women — have below-average opportunities for upward mobility.

Upward mobility occurs because of circulation mobility, reproductive mobility, immigration mobility, and occupational or structural mobility. The effects of social mobility include the "diffusion of insecurity," anxiety, psychosomatic illness, and high rates of suicide.

In recent years upward mobility into the higher social classes is still possible, with the choice of profession and lifestyle serving as significant determinants. Changed governmental policies could help more people escape the poor or near-poor categories. In spite of the rewards upward mobility brings, serious psychological problems can accompany success.

Glossary

absolute wealth the cash value of an individual's economic assets

authority power that people generally recognize as rightfully maintained by those who use it

bourgeoisie the class of modern capitalists who own the means of economic production and employ wage labor

class consciousness recognition by the members of a class of the role they play in the production process

income people's earnings obtained through wages, salaries, business profits, stock dividends, and other means

intergenerational mobility a comparison of a parent's and a child's social-class positions

intragenerational mobility an analysis of an individual's occupational changes in the course of a lifetime

objective definition of social class a measuring technique that uses certain quantifiable factors — income, occupational prestige rank, or level of education, for example — as the basis for determining an individual's social-class position

power the ability of an individual or group to implement wishes or policies, with or without the cooperation of others

prestige possession of attributes that elicit recognition, respect, and some degree of deference

proletariat the class of modern wage laborers who possess no means of production and thus must sell their own labor in order to survive

relative wealth the value of an individual's economic assets compared to the assets possessed by other citizens in that society

reputational definition of social class a measuring technique in which researchers use batteries of resident experts from the community—judges—to assess their neighbors' social-class position

social class a large category of people who are similar in income level, educational attainment, and occupational prestige-ranking

social mobility the movement of a person from one social class or status level to another

social stratification structured inequality of access to rewards, resources, and privileges that are scarce and desirable within a society

subjective definition of social class a measuring technique that requires people to indicate the social class to which they belong

vicious cycle of poverty a pattern in which the parents' minimal income significantly limits the educational and occupational pursuits of the children, thereby keeping them locked into the same low economic status

wealth people's economic assets—their cars, homes, stocks, bonds, and real estate—that can be converted into cash

Tests

True–false Test

___F___ 1. Marx believed that in the final stage of class consciousness, members of the proletariat would be able to use negotiations to resolve their differences with capitalists.

___F___ 2. Evidence that many affluent people have neither special talents nor special training supports the structural-functional theory of social stratification.

___T___ 3. Gerhard Lenski's theory of social stratification accepts some ideas from both the structural-functional and the Marxist conflict theories.

___T___ 4. Relative income figures highlight the fact that over time the distribution of American income has changed little.

___F___ 5. The U.S. tax system is progressive only for high-income people.

___T___ 6. Women and men differ in their subjective definitions of social class.

___F___ 7. People who support the existing social-class system and its inequalities always have high self-esteem.

___T___ 8. The "hidden injury" of class is that working-class people are denied a sense of worth in the eyes of others and of themselves.

___F___ 9. A recent study of middle-class and upper-middle-class women's friendship patterns indicated that the subjects often bragged about their shared social-class membership.

___F-___ 10. Research done in sixteen countries has concluded that the patterns of intergenerational mobility are strikingly different.

Multiple-choice Test

___C___ 1. Marx suggested that the members of the proletariat share class membership because of the following characteristic:
   a. They are disorganized.
   b. They are unaware of their class position.

c. They are victims of the capitalist production process.

d. They are profit-oriented.

_B_   2. The theory of social stratification that emphasizes the need to fill jobs critical for the survival of society with highly qualified personnel was developed by:

a. Marx.

b. Davis and Moore.

c. Tumin.

d. Lenski.

_A_   3. Lenski's theory of social stratification is different from the structural-functional and conflict theories in which respect?

a. It is more scientific.

b. It is less scientific.

c. It emphasizes social mobility to a greater extent.

d. It demonstrates less commitment to the existing stratification system.

_B_   4. People's earnings obtained through wages, salaries, business profits, stock dividends, and other means are called:

a. wealth.

b. income.

c. relative income.

d. relative wealth.

_D_   5. In C. Wright Mills's power-elite theory, the politically unorganized white-collar employees of corporations and government agencies belong to the social class known as:

a. the power elite.

b. the pluralist class.

c. the proletariat.

d. the middle class.

_A_   6. When researchers use community judges to assess their neighbors' social-class position, the approach is called:

a. the reputational definition of social class.

b. the subjective definition of social class.

c. the power definition of social class.

d. the objective definition of social class.

_C_   7. The higher one's social class, the better one's chances are for:

a. mental illness.

b. communication problems.

c. long life.

d. low self-esteem.

_C_   8. Which statement about the relationship between social class and sexuality is true?

a. The statement that "sex is a man's pleasure and a woman's duty" has become increasingly applicable to upper-middle-class marriage in the last decade.

b. Working-class wives tend to enjoy sex and easily achieve orgasm.

c. Working-class boys tend to begin their sexual lives earlier than middle-class boys.

d. a and b

_B_   9. For middle-class blacks:

a. upward mobility has been an unqualified success.

b. employment is concentrated in areas serving black consumers and communities.

c. the vicious cycle of poverty is often a reality.

d. a and c

_D_   10. The situation in which some people are downwardly mobile, encouraging upward mobility for others, is called:
     a. occupational or structural mobility.
     b. immigration mobility.
     c. reproductive mobility.
     d. circulation mobility.

Essay Test

1. Define social stratification and discuss the general significance of social stratification in American society.
2. Summarize and evaluate the three theories of social stratification discussed in this chapter.
3. What are three major dimensions of social stratification? List and discuss them, focusing on recent evidence about each dimension.
4. Define social class and discuss two issues, citing social-class differences in opportunity and two issues indicating social-class differences in lifestyle. Use studies and examples described in the chapter.
5. What is social mobility? Discuss the causes and effects of social mobility, as well as prospects for and problems of upward mobility in the years ahead.

Suggested Readings

Berreman, Gerald D. (ed.). 1981. *Social Inequality: Comparative and Developmental Approaches*. New York: Academic Press. Anthropological studies examining the structured inequalities that exist in societies ranging from the primitive hunting-and-gathering type to the modern socialist variety. The papers share a conflict theoretical perspective.

Burris, Beverly H. 1983. *No Room at the Top: Underdevelopment and Alienation in the Corporation*. New York: Praeger. An interesting study of how underemployed clerical workers in a service corporation react to their jobs and why they react as they do.

Dreiser, Theodore. 1953. *An American Tragedy*. New York: Random House. Originally published in 1925. A gripping novel about a young man with aspirations to marry into the upper class. The sharp contrast between lower-middle-class and upper-class lifestyles appears throughout the book.

Gilbert, Dennis, and Joseph A. Kahl. 1987. *The American Class Structure: A New Synthesis*. Homewood, IL: Dorsey Press. Third edition. The newest edition of Kahl's leading sociological text on American social class published over thirty years ago. The current edition is fairly comprehensive and easy to read.

Gouldner, Helen, and Mary Symons Strong. 1987. *Speaking of Friendship: Middle-Class Women and Their Friends*. Westport, CT: Greenwood Press. A richly documented, readable discussion of a study about the development and maintenance of middle-class and upper-middle-class women's friendships.

Heller, Celia S. (ed.). 1987. *Structured Social Inequality*. New York: Macmillan. Second edition. A book of readings containing more than forty articles and covering a variety of issues on stratification, including theoretical contributions from Marx, Lenski, Weber, and Davis and Moore.

Rubin, Lillian Breslow. 1976. *World of Pain: Life in the Working-Class Family*. New York: Basic Books. A study based on intensive interviews with fifty blue-collar couples and a comparison group of twenty-five upper-middle-class couples. Rubin concluded that norms that originated in the upper-middle class are filtering to working-class people and are producing huge strains in their marriages.

Sennett, Richard, and Jonathan Cobb. 1973. *Hidden Injuries of Class*. New York: Vintage Books. An account of the pain, disappointment, and lack of confidence associated with American working-class life. This book is based on competent sociological research, and yet its poignant, well-written material makes readers feel they are caught up in a novel.

Warner, W. Lloyd, J. O. Low, Paul S. Lunt, and Leo Srole. 1963. *Yankee City*. New Haven: Yale University. A single, slim volume presenting the principal conclusions of the historic, five-volume Yankee City study, the earliest analysis of the American class structure.

Williams, Terry, and William Kornblum. 1985. *Growing Up Poor*. Lexington, MA: Lexington Books. Based on interviews conducted in four American cities, this study shows poor adolescents' everyday struggles with poverty.

Additional Assignments

1. Interview a dozen people with varied social characteristics — age, sex, race, and occupation. Ask them the following questions:
   a. Is there a difference in the contributions to the welfare of society made by people in high-status or low-status jobs?
   b. What substantial differences, if any, exist between people who are successful economically and socially and those who are not?
   c. Does class consciousness exist in the United States? Should it?
   d. Is America the "land of opportunity?" Explain.
   From the answers to these questions and perhaps others you might wish to add, try to construct a simple theory, or perhaps several theories of social stratification. What are the similarities to and differences from theories examined in this chapter?
2. From the local chamber of commerce or some other source, obtain a street map of the city or town in which your college or university is located. Then, choosing a sample of people who appear to be from varied social-class backgrounds, place them in the six social classes discussed on pp. 242–243, basing the placement on information about occupation, education level, and income level obtained from interviewing a selected number of people on every block or in every neighborhood. For an interesting comparison, it would be instructive to also ask people's subjective view of their class membership. Then, using different colors to designate different social classes, fill in the map. Did the two approaches to measuring social class produce similar or different results? Did some people refuse to answer all or some of the questions?

Answers to Objective Test Questions

True–false Test

1. f	4. t	7. f	9. f
2. f	5. f	8. t	10. f
3. t	6. t		

Multiple-choice Test

1. c	4. b	7. c	9. b
2. b	5. d	8. c	10. d
3. a	6. a		

10
RACIAL AND ETHNIC GROUPS

Racial, Ethnic, and Minority Groups

Racial Group
Ethnic Group
Minority Group

Prejudice and Discrimination: Producing Inequality

Sources
Effects

Majority and Minority Behavior Patterns

Dominant-Group Policies
Minority Responses

American Minority Groups

Black Americans
Hispanic-Americans
American Jews
Asian-Americans
Native Americans
White Ethnics

Moving toward the Twenty-First Century

Study Guide

Several decades ago a twelve-year-old black student named Jimmy was summoned to the headmaster's office of the well-known Eastern private school he attended.

According to his mother, Jimmy suspected nothing was wrong. Why should he have? He was one of the top students in his class, easily justifying the full scholarship that permitted him to attend the school.

When Jimmy arrived at the headmaster's office, however, he could instantly see that a problem existed. Instead of the usual easy smile, the man was biting his lower lip and tapping his wrist nervously. Without even a greeting, he said, "Look, we've got a tough one here."

"Yes, sir?" the boy replied.

"I'll have to be honest with you, Jimmy. I don't know how to resolve this situation. We're very pleased with your overall performance, and, besides, we're strong supporters of civil-rights activities, but," he continued, shaking his head, "this is a horrible mess."

The headmaster told Jimmy that he had just finished talking to the headmistress at the girl's school with which a joint glee-club performance was planned the following week. After the performance there would be dinner and a dance. "It's not as though you'd actually be dating each other," the headmaster went on, "but you will be paired off for the evening, and . . ." Embarrassed the man looked away from Jimmy, then blurted out, "They don't have any Negro girls."

The headmaster finally sat down behind his desk and looked hard at the boy. "Jimmy, there's no easy solution here. The way things stand, we'll have to cancel the concert if you plan on going. But it should be your decision."

"I'll stay."

"That's the best choice. I appreciate it." The headmaster reached across the desk, shook Jimmy's hand, and without another word Jimmy left the room.

After that exchange Jimmy's performance at school rapidly declined. He finished the year, then transferred to the local inner-city high school.

School, his mother explained later, never had much meaning to Jimmy after the glee-club episode. "He simply lost faith in the white man's world." Four years after high school, Jimmy joined the Black Panthers, a well-known black-power group, and shortly afterwards was killed when police broke into Panthers headquarters early one morning.

The racial incidents that receive headlines involve obvious violence — killings, beatings, rapes. As portrayed by this incident, however, on a quieter, seemingly more civilized level, millions of Americans have experienced incidents involving race or ethnicity that profoundly diminish their sense of self.

Undoubtedly you are aware that in U.S. society racial and ethnic issues often have a decisive, sober side. If you are the member of a racial or ethnic group that has been badly treated, then you have directly experienced the anger and frustration produced by discrimination in a country that appears to treat all its citizens equally. On the other hand, if you belong to the so-called dominant group, you also suffer the effects of American ra-

cial and ethnic problems. You are likely to feel confusion and fear — fear to talk seriously and honestly with members of certain groups, and fear to walk or drive through their neighborhoods.

Anger, frustration, and fear are certainly emotions that traditionally have been part of the American racial and ethnic picture. However, people of different heritages can also frequently have positive relations, and colleges and universities are places for such contacts. In these settings students of different backgrounds can meet on essentially neutral grounds, where the fears and prejudices they might have grown up with are likely to be muted. On campuses and elsewhere in many American communities, different ethnic and racial groups sometimes sponsor festivals, fairs, plays, dances, and other activities that can help make the American public aware of their particular cultural experiences. Quite possibly more of those kinds of activities occur in your locale than you realize. Local mass media on campus and in surrounding towns and cities, will reveal events that different groups sponsor.

In this chapter we consider a number of important issues involving racial and ethnic groups. The next two sections concern basic concepts — first, an analysis of racial, ethnic, and minority groups and then, in the second part, the important processes of prejudice and discrimination. In the following section, the discussion involves the diverse array of behavioral patterns that can emerge when different racial and ethnic groups encounter each other. The next subject is major American ethnic and racial groups. The chapter finishes with a brief analysis of future race and ethnic relations.

Throughout these discussions we should remain aware that while incidents involving racial and ethnic prejudice are ugly realities involving individuals and small groups, our principal task is not to focus on those individuals or small groups. Instead we aim to analyze the social forces producing both disruptive and harmonious ethnic and racial relations in American society.

Racial, Ethnic, and Minority Groups

In Chapter 3, "Culture," we examined the linguistic-relativity hypothesis, which emphasizes that language influences people's perceptions and behavior. (Check pp. 60–61 if you have not read about this concept or need to review it.) As far as the present topics are concerned, language allows people to place themselves and others in distinct categories that focus on differences considered significant.

Racial Group

The call reaches the patrol car from police headquarters. "Liquor store robbed at the corner of Hudson and Grove. The suspect is a . . ." Usually the next word is a reference to the person's race. Americans and the citizens of many other Western nations often use a person's race as a basic means of identification. Race and sex are the two most prominently used status characteristics for identification, but while people fall into either the male or female category, race does not divide as neatly.

Superficially a basis for classification of races seems to exist. Westerners designate three broad racial categories: Caucasoid, Mongoloid, and Negroid. The Caucasoids, who originally lived in western Europe, northern Africa, and western Asia, have light skin pigmentation, frequent male balding, prominent chins, and fairly long trunks. The Mongoloids, who first inhabited northern and eastern Asia, have brown to yellow skin, black hair, broad cheekbones, low-bridged noses, and eye folds, which produce the sense of slanting eyes. Negroids, the first residents of Africa, have dark pigmentation, low-bridged noses, and kinky or curly hair.

This three-part classification scheme is well-known, but many groups, including some large groups, do not fit easily into the categories. Specialists have developed nearly 200 categories to account for discrepancies such as the following. The Australian aborigines have Negroid skin but straight hair and are sometimes classified as a fourth race. Among Native Americans, who are a subrace of Mongoloids, there are great differences in height and head shape. The tallest people in the world, the Watusi, and the shortest, the Pygmy, are both in the Negroid category and live within a few miles of each other.

Racial classifications are imprecise, and their practical significance seems modest. Admittedly certain biological adaptations have probably been useful. The original inhabitants of areas with high solar radiation appear to have received protection from their dark skin, and Negroids apparently have developed a much greater resistance to malaria forms than the Caucasoids and Mongoloids arriving later in Africa. No evidence suggests, however, that one racial group is more intelligent, more creative, more athletic, more ferocious, in fact "more anything" involving brain power, personality, or capability than other groups. Sometimes the behavior of different racial groups suggests otherwise, but that is because one group receives better opportunities than another. Human beings are simply a single species, with all members possessing the same skeletal structure, the same complex nervous system, the same intricate sensory organs, and the same intellectual capacity.

If the classification of races has limited usefulness, one must wonder why racial distinctions are so important. In a sentence the answer is that race is significant because people consider it so. No matter what its biological meaning, therefore, race has social significance. Sociologically **race** refers to distinct physical characteristics, such as skin color and certain facial features, used to divide people into broad categories. Thus a **racial group** is a number of people with the particular physical characteristics that produce placement into a broad category.

Ethnic Group

An **ethnic group** is a category of people that is set apart by itself or by others because of distinct cultural or national qualities. Ethnic groups differ on such issues as values, religion, ideas, food habits, family patterns, sexual behavior, beauty standards, political outlook, work orientation, and recreational behavior. The culture of an ethnic group creates a sense of identity among the members. Outsiders recognize ethnic-group membership, and hostilities between different ethnic groups have been a major source of conflict in human history.

In U.S. society ethnicity is often synonymous with national group membership. Thus there are Chinese-Americans, Irish-Americans, Italian-Americans, Mexican-Americans, Polish-Americans, and other groups. Then there are linguistic groups that maintain their own cultural identity, such as the English-speaking Canadians and the French-speaking Canadians. Sometimes religious groups develop as ethnic groups — for instance, the Amish and Hutterite religious communities in the United States.

In many situations ethnic and racial groups have minority-group status, which is analyzed in the upcoming discussion.

Minority Group

A **minority group** is any category of people with recognizable racial or ethnic traits that place it in a position of inferior status so that its members suffer limited opportunities and rewards. The members of a minority group are inevitably aware of the unequal treatment they all share, and this awareness helps create a sense of belonging to the group. It is important to understand that minority status has no intrinsic relationship to group size. Sometimes a minority group is hundreds of times larger than the dominant group in the society. Such a situation existed when the European countries established colonies in Africa, Asia, and the Americas. In other cases — blacks in the United States, for instance — the minority group is smaller in numbers than the dominant group. Minority status is the result of a subordinate position in society, not the size of its membership.

All the racial and ethnic categories discussed in this chapter are minority groups. What are the processes that create minority status? The following section offers a response to this question.

Prejudice and Discrimination: Producing Inequality

"All people are created equal." As infants all human beings generally behave in accord with this principle. Yet in the course of socialization, many Americans learn to accept the belief that some groups are superior to others. They accept both prejudice and discrimination.

Prejudice is a highly negative judgment toward a group, focusing on one or more negative characteristics that are supposedly uniformly shared by all group members. If a person rigidly believes that all members of a racial or ethnic group are innately lazy, stupid, stubborn, and violent, then that person is prejudiced toward the group in question. Racial, ethnic, and religious prejudice are the most prominently discussed types. In general, prejudice is not easily reversible. The fact that prejudice is not easily reversible distinguishes it from a "misconception," in which someone supports an incorrect conclusion about a group but is willing, when confronted with facts, to change his or her opinion. The companion concept to prejudice is discrimination, which is the behavioral manifestation of prejudice. **Discrimination** is the behavior by which one group prevents or restricts another group's access to scarce resources.

Prejudice and discrimination are often a one–two punch: The behavior directly follows the judgment. The two situations do not always appear together, however. Discrimination sometimes takes place without prejudice. In the 1950s in Little Rock, Arkansas, many white ministers were not prejudiced toward black people (they wanted integrated congregations), but they continued to support discrimination against blacks. The ministers realized that a movement to integrate would have meant the disaffection of many affluent, white members who provided the major economic support for the churches (Campbell and Pettigrew, 1959). In other situations prejudice fails to evoke discrimination. From 1930 to 1932, a white social scientist traveled throughout the United States with a Chinese couple. They received courteous treatment at hotels, motels, and restaurants, and yet 90 percent of questionnaire responses later elicited from the establishments visited made it clear that Chinese would be unwelcome (LaPierce, 1934). The study does contain some problems — for instance, there is no assurance that the person answering the survey was the one who had served the researcher and the Chinese couple — and yet similar findings appear in later research (Kutner, Wilkins, and Yarrow, 1952). Thus in some situations, prejudice and discrimination do not occur in tandem.

It is possible to analyze prejudice as an ideology. An **ideology** is a system of beliefs and principles that presents an organized explanation of the justification for a group's outlooks and behavior. **Racism** is the ideology contending that actual or alleged differences between different racial groups assert the superiority of one racial group. Racism is a rationalization for political, economic, and social discrimination.

In a national survey, 55 percent of the sample indicated that, overall, American society is racist, while 37 percent said that it was not (Media General – Associated Press Poll, August 1988).

Two types of racism are individual racism and institutional racism. Whether practiced by one person or a group, **individual racism** is open, intentional racist behavior, for example, verbal or physical abuse. **Institutional racism** is the subordination of a race by means indirectly related to race instead of by race itself. The concept emphasizes that racism has been so profoundly imbedded in the structures of American society that destructive consequences for nonwhites are widespread. An example of institutional racism would be educational prerequisites for jobs having little or nothing to do with job performance but disproportionately screening out members of certain racial groups. For instance, if applicants to be truck drivers or custodians are required to be high-school graduates, this requirement is more likely to eliminate Native Americans, Puerto Ricans, and blacks than whites, whose educational level tends to be higher.

For most whites and some nonwhites, institutional racism is a difficult concept to grasp, because they have not consciously observed it. They do not realize that within many structures of American society — for instance, schools, work organizations, medical systems, and government agencies — the impact of institutional racism has dramatically limited nonwhites' chances for a comfortable, successful life.

When the members of one group have a racist outlook toward the members of a minority group, they develop stereotypes of those individuals. A **stereotype** is an exaggerated, oversimplified image, maintained by prejudiced people, of the characteristics of the group members against whom they are prejudiced. An early study of stereotypes discovered that respondents considered blacks superstitious, lazy, happy-go-lucky, ignorant, and musical, while Jews were designated shrewd, industrious, grasping, mercenary, intelligent, and ambitious (Katz and Braly, 1933).

Stereotypes often prove useful to those who maintain them. Their oversimplified conclusions offer a more orderly, straightforward analysis of a minority group than a nonstereotyped evaluation would provide. Furthermore stereotypes help to either confirm that a downtrodden group should remain in its lowly position or encourage members of the dominant group to push down minority-group individuals who are starting to achieve some economic and political success (Simpson and Yinger, 1985: 100–101).

One of the disturbing qualities of stereotypes is their self-fulfilling nature. A **self-fulfilling prophecy** is an incorrect definition of a situation that comes to pass because people accept the incorrect definition and act on it to make it become

268

true. For instance, if white teachers believe that black children are lazy, happy-go-lucky, and ignorant, then they are unlikely to make a sincere effort to help them learn. The students, in turn, will recognize the teachers' disinterest or contempt and will probably exert little effort in school. The teachers see "confirmation" of what they already "know"—that their black students are inferior. In reality what the teachers confirm is the process performed by the self-fulfilling prophecy.

With these concepts in mind, we can examine a number of explanations for prejudice, discrimination, and racism.

Sources

The old man nodded and smiled as she walked by, pushing the baby carriage. Her impulse was to hurry past the bench—he was unshaven, his clothes were threadbare, and the near-empty bottle leaning against his knee was no testimony to his sobriety—but she slowed down as he looked at the baby. And when he said, "Could I see her, ma'am?" she immediately pulled back the blanket. The old man's face relaxed and softened. "She's a beauty, ma'am, just a plain beauty! Look at her, laying there, peaceful and innocent. And she don't hate nobody. Black, white—it's all the same to her."

Like the old man, we make the assumption that prejudice and discrimination are learned forms of behavior. Social, economic, and psychological explanations all contribute to an understanding of the development of prejudice and discrimination.

Social Explanations

Language is a significant component of culture. Without the words "black," "white," "yellow," and "red," Americans would be unable to distinguish skin-color differences. Furthermore the words associated with "black" and "white" are often highly tinged with emotion. *Roget's Thesaurus* has about 120 synonyms for "blackness," most of which are negative—for instance, blot, blight, smut, evil, wickedness, and malignance. The 134 synonyms for "whiteness" have primarily favorable connotations. The list includes brightness, innocence, honor, purity, fairness,

and trust. Without language people would also not be able to produce such unflattering racial and ethnic designations as "frog," "honky," "kike," "kraut," "nigger," "slope," and "spic" or phrases like "lazy as a nigger" or "jew him down." Words also permit the development of stereotypes.

For instance, as we saw earlier, in U.S. society blacks have been traditionally stereotyped as superstitious, lazy, and so forth, while Jews are described as shrewd, mercenary, and so on. Countless jokes about blacks, Jews, and other minority groups elaborate these stereotypes. "What harm can a little joke be?" an observer might ask. "They're just meant to be funny, not to hurt anyone." The problem is that jokes directed at minority groups do emphasize the negative, distorted image represented by the stereotype. As a result people hearing the joke will perhaps more readily accept that members of the target groups are "that way." Furthermore while members of the dominant culture might see such humor as harmless, minority-group members are likely to be infuriated and offended.

The use of stereotypes demonstrates the existence of **social distance:** the feeling of separation between individuals or groups. In the 1920s Emory Bogardus developed a scale to measure social distance. The scale has become so widely known that social scientists simply call it *the Bogardus scale*. The scale asks people to indicate their willingness to interact with various racial and ethnic groups in certain social situations, which represent seven degrees of social distance. The seven items involve an increasing social distance as one moves down the list. Respondents must indicate whether they will accept members of the particular group:

To close kinship by marriage.

As a regular friend.

To the street as a neighbor.

To employment in one's occupation.

To citizenship in one's country.

As a visitor only to one's country.

Would exclude from one's country.

Over a forty-year period (from 1926 to 1966), research in the United States showed that white Americans and northern Europeans scored in the top third of the hierarchy, eastern and southern Europeans in the middle, and Asian minorities in the bottom third. The rankings stayed consistent over the forty-year period, and not just for whites. When Jewish-, Asian-, and black Americans took the test their results were similar to white Americans, with one exception — in each case their own group was placed at the top (Bogardus, 1968).

Social distance can be situational, operating more strongly in some contexts than in others. One study conducted in three British cities concluded that Asian residents' choice of whether to go to Asian- or white-run shops was strongly affected by the amount of contact required between customer and shopkeeper. When they patronized clothing stores and restaurants, where quite extensive contact between shopkeeper and customers was required (and thus social distance tended to be emphasized), Asians were more likely to go to Asian shops. When the shops sold newspapers, tobacco, and candy, and little contact between shopkeeper and patron was necessary, Asians were more willing to go to white-run shops (Aldrich et al., 1985).

One final point about social distance. To some extent social distance is self-fulfilling. A person says, "I can't stand that group. I don't even want them in my country." It is fairly certain that this person will avoid contacts with members of that group. It is very unlikely, therefore, that the unfavorable stereotypes will break down. The simplifications and exaggerations of stereotypes thrive on extensive social distance. In fact, it is likely that stereotypes cannot survive with frequent, relatively pleasant contacts among racial and ethnic groups. Figure 10.1 represents Americans' evaluations of different ethnic groups.

A number of social scientists have suggested that the dominant group within American society treats minority groups much as colonial nations have treated the inhabitants of their colonies, thus establishing a form of internal colonialism. These sociologists fall within the conflict-theory camp, emphasizing a power struggle for scarce rewards between the dominant group and exploited minorities. While the colonial model fails in certain regards, some similarities in cultural and structural patterns between colonial contexts and race relations in American society exist. The similarities include residential segregation, cultural stereotyping of minority-group members, incorpora-

Figure 10.1
Americans' Perception of Different Ethnic Groups

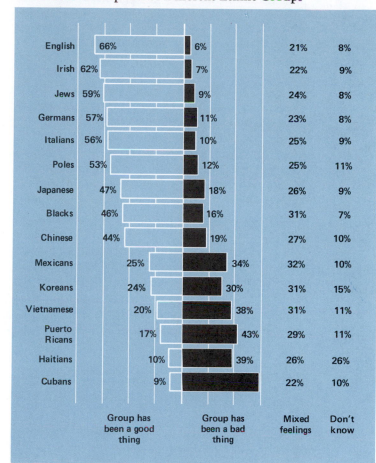

	Group has been a good thing	Group has been a bad thing	Mixed feelings	Don't know
English	66%	6%	21%	8%
Irish	62%	7%	22%	9%
Jews	59%	9%	24%	8%
Germans	57%	11%	23%	8%
Italians	56%	10%	25%	9%
Poles	53%	12%	25%	11%
Japanese	47%	18%	26%	9%
Blacks	46%	16%	31%	7%
Chinese	44%	19%	27%	10%
Mexicans	25%	34%	32%	10%
Koreans	24%	30%	31%	15%
Vietnamese	20%	38%	31%	11%
Puerto Ricans	17%	43%	29%	11%
Haitians	10%	39%	26%	26%
Cubans	9%		22%	10%

This figure suggests that the more recently an ethnic group has arrived in this country, the less favorable Americans' attitude toward that group tends to be. (Source: The Roper Organization. Roper Reports. May 1982.)

tion of minority-group individuals into the power structure to smoothe the way for control of the minority group, and the widespread exploitation of minority-group members in employment and level of material life (Feagin, 1989: 37–38). Let us discuss the economic point at greater length.

Economic Explanations

"Big bucks" in prejudice and discrimination? The immediate reaction might be to laugh at that idea, but a short reflection should produce a different response. In the United States and in other

270

countries, slavery developed because it was the cheapest form of labor. A study of American history shows that a strong economic incentive for the practice existed. The Northern states received little or no economic benefit from slavery, and they outlawed it soon after the Revolutionary War. Even in the South, slavery lost its popularity in the late 1700s, and many people saw it as a "necessary evil." By 1835, however, cotton had become the primary commodity of American foreign trade. At this point most white Southerners did not consider slavery a necessary evil but as a positive good that served as the foundation of a stable society and a prosperous economy (Lacy, 1972).

In some cases the economic factor is present but not readily apparent. In 1942 during World War II, the American government ordered the evacuation of 110,000 Japanese from the West Coast on the pretext that they were potential collaborators with the Japanese government. A major impetus behind the relocation was an organized effort by newspaper leaders, congressmen, and wealthy

The harsh reality of Japanese-American relocation during World War II is portrayed in this photo, which shows three family members tagged for shipment to a relocation center.

farmers to convince President Roosevelt of the necessity to undertake the endeavor. For the wealthy farmers, this was an unprecedented opportunity to divert less affluent, white farmers' attention from their own unpopular domination of agriculture and to redirect the small, white farmers' hostilities toward the Japanese. Other economic advantages were less subtle. At the time of the relocation, Japanese had to sell homes, farms, businesses, and personal possessions at a fraction of their real value. The official government estimate is that Japanese-Americans lost over $400 million (in 1940, preinflated dollars) (Berry and Tischler, 1978: 370–371). In 1988 Congress appropriated $1.3 billion in funds to the approximately 60,000 survivors of the relocation centers — $20,000 per person — and descendants of those who died were not eligible. One provision in the bill stated, "On behalf of the nation, the congress apologizes" (Willen, 1988: 1081).

Psychological Explanations

A number of psychological perspectives exist. One approach suggests that the acquisition of prejudice and discrimination is a three-stage process that occurs to children in the course of socialization. A girl of six runs home to her mother and says, "Mother, what is the name of the children I am supposed to hate?" This child is at the "first stage" in learning prejudice. She has not yet associated prejudicial attributes with the culturally supported target group. In fact, a study concluded that until children reach the age of eight, they do not have a clear, stable sense of people's ethnicity. The "second stage" in learning prejudice occurs when children connect prejudice with the culturally supported target group. In a social context in which racial or ethnic prejudice exists, children in the first and second grade often intermingle, but by the fifth grade they are usually more exclusive, choosing to stay with members of their own group. The "third stage" involves the ability to practice prejudice and discrimination subtly. In high school young people are able to express polite acceptance and tolerance toward members of other racial and ethnic groups, while rejecting those who are not members of their own group. This approach stands in sharp contrast to the behavior of eight-year-olds, who have learned

Since prejudice and discrimination must be learned, children of different races are not disposed to hate and fear each other. Such emotions, however, are often acquired in the course of socialization, and the modern resurgence of the Ku Klux Klan, an organization with a violent, anti-black tradition, offers ample evidence of this tendency.

the prejudicial categories and speak as if they completely reject people in different racial or ethnic groups, but their behavior is often nondiscriminatory (Aboud, 1984; Allport, 1954: 307–311).

An alternative psychological approach is the **scapegoat theory.** This explanation emphasizes that people blocked from achieving a goal will sometimes be unable or unwilling to take out their frustration on its source, and so they direct their aggression against an accessible individual or group. The displacement of the hostility from the real source of frustration to the scapegoat permits a release of tension called *catharsis.*

Three conditions make it likely that a racial or

ethnic group will become a scapegoat. First, the group must be easy to identify, whether by a skin color, a tattoo, or some insignia such as the Star of David, which the Nazis forced Jews to wear during World War II. Second, the ethnic group must be powerless enough so that it is unlikely to retaliate. Finally, in order to qualify as a scapegoat, a group must be accessible (Simpson and Yinger, 1985: 73–74).

In a pre-World War II experiment that tested the scapegoat theory, all three conditions existed. The subjects were white boys attending a summer camp. The first step was to give them a pretest assessing their prejudice toward Japanese-Americans and Mexican-Americans. Then the boys received a tedious paper-and-pencil test that lasted long enough to make them miss the weekly opportunity to go to town and see a movie. Finally the subjects were given a posttest to measure prejudice toward the two minority groups. This time the rate of prejudice increased significantly (Dollard et al., 1939: 43–44). The results support the scapegoat hypothesis, which contends that people (in this case white boys) are inclined to direct their hostility toward visible, vulnerable, and accessible minority groups (here Japanese- and Mexican-Americans) when the true source of their frustration (in this situation the adults administering the test) is too powerful to attack.

The economic factor encourages prejudice and discrimination, but the factor does not act alone. A person must have personal inclinations supporting these tendencies and must also receive cultural backing. Table 10.1 summarizes explanations of prejudice and discrimination.

Effects

A man named Eldridge Cleaver was in prison, and like many other prisoners put a pin-up girl — from the center of *Esquire* magazine — on the wall of his cell. One evening, however, when Cleaver returned to his cell, he was shocked and enraged to find his pin-up torn into little pieces and floating in the toilet. Cleaver said that "it was like seeing a dead body floating in a lake."

The next day he asked the guard why he had done it. There were rules against pin-ups, the guard said. Cleaver would not accept that reply. The rule was never enforced, he pointed out. The guard smiled, immediately making Cleaver wary. He would compromise, the guard said. If Cleaver would get himself a black pin-up, he would let it stay.

Cleaver was embarrassed. He called the guard two or three dirty names and walked away. He was disturbed by what the guard had revealed, however. Without realizing it, he, a black man, had chosen a picture of a white woman over the available pictures of black women. Was it true? Did he really prefer white to black women? The conclusion was inescapable. He did (Cleaver, 1970: 20–21).

Table 10.1
Explanations of Prejudice and Discrimination

APPROACH	CENTRAL IDEA	ILLUSTRATIONS
Social explanations	Different components of culture — language, values, and beliefs — contribute to the development of prejudice and discrimination.	The concepts "stereotype" and "social distance"
Economic explanations	The existence of prejudice and discrimination are economically beneficial for the dominant group.	The American slavery system or the relocation of Japanese-Americans during World War II
Psychological explanations	Prejudice and discrimination derive from individuals' socialization or frustrations felt toward a strong, inaccessible group.	Three-stage process of prejudice development or the scapegoat theory

Putting aside for the moment this serious sexism, we can link Cleaver's reaction to a widespread belief: that the members of minority groups tend to denigrate themselves and value majority-group status more highly.

Let us consider a large study that tested the issue of self-esteem with a random sample of 2625 Baltimore school children. Rosenberg and Simmons (1971) concluded that black children do not have lower self-esteem than white children. In fact, 46 percent of the black children interviewed had high self-esteem compared with 33 percent of the whites.

The researchers uncovered certain factors that affected black children's self-esteem. Blacks who did well in school and who came from higher social-class backgrounds tended to have high self-esteem. Black children who attended integrated schools were more likely to have low self-esteem. It seemed that these black children had many opportunities to compare themselves with high-achieving white children. Apparently integrated schools can improve black students' academic achievement and provide interracial friendships, but they do not raise their self-esteem.

Backed by other recent research, the Baltimore study makes it clear that black children do not usually hate themselves, idolize whites, and maintain low self-esteem. Further research on this topic, not only with blacks but also with other racial and ethnic groups, needs to consider the cautions previously indicated — in particular, the likelihood that such factors as social class, school performance, and the racial, ethnic, and class statuses of classmates have a significant effect on children's self-esteem, perhaps a more significant effect than their own race or ethnicity.

At the same time, it would be misleading to conclude that prejudice and discrimination do not produce negative effects upon people. On the subject of racism, one psychiatrist stressed that experiencing racism can be devastating to an individual's self-esteem and that effective therapy can help patients explore their coping mechanisms and develop more productive ways of dealing with the anxiety triggered by racism (Brantley, 1983). Furthermore a study using national survey data gathered between 1972 and 1985 found that when blacks and whites of similar socioeconomic background, age, and marital status were compared, blacks indicated lower life satisfaction, less trust in people, less general happiness, less marital happiness, and lower self-evaluated health (Thomas and Hughes, 1986). It appears that being black in American society does adversely affect one's outlook on life.

In addition, because of the structural disadvantages they have encountered, minority groups experience major deficiencies in the educational, occupational, and income areas. The section on American minority groups provides detailed information on these topics.

Majority and Minority Behavior Patterns

Some evidence suggests that over time Americans have become less inclined to support prejudice and discrimination. Consider the following two situations. In 1906 Mark Twain attended a banquet where a speaker received thunderous applause when he fervently told his audience of lawyers, bankers, and other middle-class professionals, "We are of the Anglo-Saxon race, and when the Anglo-Saxon wants a thing *he just takes it*" (Twain, 1973: 3). These respectable American citizens showed no inclination to support the rights of anyone besides their fellow Anglo-Saxons. Yet less than sixty years later in the fall of 1963, several hundred thousand black and white Americans marched in Washington, DC, on behalf of full civil rights for all Americans. Neither of these events was out of character with its time. Both were consistent with the dominant-group racial policies during the respective eras.

As we examine six dominant-group policies involving racial and ethnic relations, it should be kept in mind that each policy is also the product of its era. The same point emphatically applies to the various responses to minority-group status, which we also discuss.

Dominant-Group Policies

The first three patterns of dominant-group policies tend to maintain or increase social distance,

274

while the last three tend to decrease it (Simpson and Yinger, 1985: 15–21).

1. *Extermination.* The most extreme pattern is the elimination of the minority group. In the nineteenth century, the British decimated the Tasmanians, and the Dutch South Africans exterminated the Hottentots. In the effort to establish a "master race," the Nazis murdered six million Jews and thousands of Romany people, known as Gypsies. People of European heritage wiped out most of the native people of Hawaii and the continental United States.

2. *Continued subjugation.* Rather than choose to destroy a people, members of the dominant group can hold the minority group under complete control. In the United States, slavery was the outstanding example of this policy. The European colonial powers in Africa and Asia successfully maintained such an intergroup pattern in some countries until after World War II. As the following Cross-Cultural Perspective indicates, white South Africans currently maintain a policy of subjugation.

CROSS-CULTURAL PERSPECTIVE

South Africa and Its Apartheid *Policy*

The Republic of South Africa is a multinational state with four racial groups. In 1985 the population was 23.4 million people, with 15.2 million black Africans representing 64.8 percent, 4.6 million whites 19.5 percent, 2.8 million Coloreds (mixed black and white) 12.1 percent, and 820,000 Asians 3.5 percent.

Since it achieved independence in 1948, South Africa has maintained a pattern of subjugation for all nonwhite people. This policy poses a serious threat to the future stability of the country.

In 1795 the British acquired South Africa and controlled it until 1948. The British introduced Indians as sugar plantation workers and freed blacks who had been the slaves of Dutch farmers, known as Boers. The blacks also received most political and civil rights. The Boers were unhappy with these developments, and throughout the nineteenth century there

were violent confrontations with the increasing number of British colonists. The culmination was the Boer War, which the British won with the help of the blacks. Once in power, however, the British felt that the blacks' greater numbers posed a significant threat, and so the white leadership imposed limitations—for instance, property qualifications for voting were established and blacks' geographical movement was restricted.

In 1948 South Africa received its independence, and the Nationalist Party assumed governmental control. Afrikaners, the Boers' descendants, have dominated the Nationalist Party, and, under their leadership, white supremacy, which existed during the colonial period, has become more and more formalized by law. Most significantly the whites have established the *apartheid* policy to insure their

domination. In Afrikaans, the Afrikaners' language, *apartheid* means "separation" or "apartness"—a policy of compulsory segregation. Many blacks are forced to live in rural homelands, where few opportunities for a decent living exist. For the blacks and other nonwhites residing in cities, work opportunities are better, but these people are forced to live in townships outside the cities. While in the cities, nonwhites must use various separate facilities, including restaurants, taxis, restrooms, and staircases.

In South Africa today, blacks suffer second-class citizenship under *apartheid*. So far the government's strong military backing has prevented open civil war. However, other conditions encourage such an outbreak: In particular, in urban areas blacks' income is one-fifth that of whites, and in rural areas the ratio is worse; the blacks have few political rights and little prospects of receiving more; neighboring black-run nations might offer extensive support. In fact, some support is already apparent. Thousands of young, black South Africans are supposedly training outside the country, mainly in Angola. They can return home without weapons, because large caches of weapons are available, as those periodically discovered by the police demonstrate. Since the late 1970s, some black South Africans have launched increasingly skilled guerrilla attacks on police stations, banks, and industries. White leaders realize that the threat of extensive industrial sabotage can very seriously damage the climate for much-needed foreign business investment.

In the past decade, developments have discouraged those seeking an end to *apartheid*. For instance, when a group of progressive white South Africans trying to end *apartheid* peacefully met with members of the Af-

rican National Congress in July 1987, they were charged with high treason, because the African National Congress had been officially banned by the government. Then early in 1988, President P. W. Botha, fearing loss of support from extreme conservatives, outlawed seventeen anti*apartheid* organizations including the United Democratic Front, a broadly based antigovernment group with over two million members. Clearly the South African government has not effectively pursued peaceful solutions to its country's racial crisis.

It is uncertain whether a negotiated settlement between blacks and whites is still possible. Clearly any negotiations must recognize certain nonnegotiable positions. For blacks a solution must provide a genuine share in political power, and whites must receive assurance that because of their greater numbers blacks will not establish complete control. The hostility between blacks and whites impedes compromise. A black South

African union leader explained:

People talk about black and white consciousness. But it's not black consciousness, it's hatred. It's not white consciousness, it's hatred. Someone has said "To hell with the other person." What we need are ways and means of living together. We must recognize ourselves as humans because of our two feet, two hands, one head, and we must recognize that we are equal.

(Study Commission on U.S. Policy toward Southern Africa, 1981: 381)

Other industrialized nations have eradicated their most visible forms of racism, and many nations consider the *apartheid* policy a visible insult. Since 1947 motions to censure South Africa have been introduced each year in the United Nations. For over twenty years, regardless of ideological differences, most African states have voted as a bloc to isolate South Africa politically and economically. It seems inevitable that the *apartheid* policy will change. What is unclear is when and by what means.

Sources: Kai Crooks. "Peaceful Paths to Change Are Being Closed One by One." *Black Enterprise*. V. 18. May 1988, p. 36; Richard T. Schaefer. *Racial and Ethnic Groups*. Boston: Little, Brown and Company, 1979; South African Foundation. *1988 Information Digest*. Johannesburg, South Africa: South African Foundation. 1988; Study Commission on U.S. Policy toward Southern Africa. *South Africa: Time Running Out*. Berkeley and Los Angeles: University of California Press. 1981; *Time*. "Right of Way: A White Backlash Gathers Force." V. 131. March 14, 1988, p. 38.

3. *Population transfer.* Sometimes the leaders of the dominant group decide that the more desirable solution is the movement of an ethnic group from one locale to another. In some cases leaders force the minority members to leave the country. Idi Amin, the former president of Uganda, compelled all Indians to emigrate, even though most of them were natives of the country. American authorities

have also resorted to population transfers, forcing Native Americans to move to reservations. In the 1830s government officials ordered the Cherokee tribe to travel the thousand-mile "Trail of Tears" from the deep South to Oklahoma. Disease, starvation, and winter cold killed thousands along the way.

4. *Legal protection of minorities.* In some instances government officials recognize that to insure

the rights of minorities, they must pass special legislation. The Civil Rights Act of 1964 has been the most significant American legislative effort to eliminate discrimination. The act covers employment practices of all businesses with more than twenty-five employees, access to all public accommodations, such as hotels, motels, and restaurants, and the use of such federally supported organizations as colleges and hospitals. The Civil Rights Act of 1964 also includes voting, but other legislation focuses on this issue. The Voting Rights Act of 1965 has suspended the various qualifying tests for voter registration that many Southern states used. This act also authorized federal examiners to enter these states and register black voters. As a result of these actions, the opportunity for the registration of black voters has greatly increased.

5. *Cultural pluralism.* The policy of cultural pluralism emphasizes the existence of ethnic groups living peacefully but separately from one another. Switzerland, for example, has four separate ethnic areas, each with its own language—French, German, Italian, and Romansh. In U.S. society many Americans have retained a strong sense of ethnic identity, and successful politicians often find it necessary to acknowledge and support ethnic interests. Since the 1960s blacks and other minority groups have frequently focused on their racial or ethnic affiliation in the pursuit of political or economic goals that will benefit their particular group.

6. *Assimilation.* The use of assimilation assumes that the most productive course of action is to eliminate separate ethnic interests and develop a common identity. Assimilation can occur on a cultural level, on a racial level, or both. Brazil is a country that has been widely acclaimed for its assimilationist policies, including substantial interracial marriage. Recent research, however, has been instructive about such an undocumented claim, indicating that Brazilian nonwhites encounter substantial educational and occupational discrimination (Webster and Dwyer, 1988). In the United States, assimilation among people of northern European ancestry has been extensive. In general, though, Americans marry within the same broad religious and racial categories. The early twentieth-century concept of the "melting pot," in which ethnic identities would disappear through complete assimilation, has not come to pass, not even to the originally

proposed extent of eliminating all ethnicities of European origin.

Thus majority groups have established a number of different policies toward minority groups. Extermination, continued subjugation, and population transfer tend to maintain or increase social distance, while the legal protection of minorities, cultural pluralism, and assimilation tend to decrease it. The sociological perspective emphasizes that the policies established by majority groups are a significant social force influencing the responses of minority groups.

Minority Responses

Beginning with the Southern civil-rights activities in the late 1950s, blacks and eventually other ethnic groups began engaging in a range of protest activities in order to combat the discrimination and limited opportunities faced by their respective groups. Some Americans were frightened and surprised by this particular response to prejudice and discrimination. They were familiar with avoidance, acceptance, and assimilation—the other three responses—but now there was also aggression (Vander Zanden, 1972).

Avoidance

For many people avoidance is impossible. People have skin color or other physical characteristics that make their ethnic or racial status undeniable. In other cases an accent in speech or extensive involvement in the local community would make avoidance difficult. Many others have the opportunity, however. A study shows that during the 1920s in Washington, DC, many light-skinned blacks chose to "pass." Former associates took pains not to betray the people who slipped into white society, and if those who remained were envious, they did not reveal it. In those years so many people attempted to pass that the National Theatre hired a black doorman to locate and bounce passers whom whites could not detect (Green, 1967: 207–208). When Martin Luther King, Jr. was a graduate student at Boston University, he was keenly interested in the activities of a black student who was passing as white. Like the blacks at the National Theatre, he and his friends were careful to keep their distance, not wanting to be responsible for exposing her deception (Branch, 1988: 94).

Little research on passing exists, but some issues that studies could address come to mind. Does guilt often accompany the act? Certainly the possibility exists. People who deny their ethnic or racial status are cutting themselves off from family, friends, and heritage. What about the fear of discovery — the nagging thought that a former associate would inadvertently or perhaps even purposefully reveal the passer's identity?

For people who accept their ethnic status these problems do not develop.

Acceptance

The majority of people in an ethnic or racial category generally accept their minority status. The acceptance, however, does not mean that their self-esteem must suffer. Acceptors can take a number of productive steps to boost their self-esteem and pride. First, they can base their self-evaluations on comparisons with members of their own group, instead of the more advantageously situated majority-group members. Second, they can use traditional structures — family, neighborhood, and friends — to provide mutual support and self-enhancement. Finally those who accept their racial or ethnic status can establish special organizations, such as ethnic professional groups, study programs, or city-sponsored awareness projects to nurture ethnic and racial pride through the use of available mass media (Bahr, Chadwick, and Stauss, 1979: 329–336).

Several decades ago American cultural standards strongly supported "second-class citizenship" for many minority groups. Writing in the 1930s, a researcher described a black man who had lived his entire life in the South, where blacks faced a highly restrictive lifestyle. Once the man and his wife took a trip to the North. The experience was unsettling. The man was surprised to see only one entrance to the railroad station instead of two, and he was almost dumbfounded to sit with a white family at the dinner table, to sleep in their guest room, and to drive around and meet their friends.

As with other racial and ethnic groups, many members of the Puerto Rican community who accept their minority status have done so with great pride and self-respect, resisting pressures to assimilate themselves completely into the dominant culture.

The black man said that "it felt like 'being treated as a man'" (Dollard, 1937: 266).

After a lifetime of accepting a highly restricted minority status, the man found it difficult to adjust to a social situation in which assimilation had occurred.

Assimilation into the Majority

Minority-group members are pursuing assimilation when they attempt to eliminate their minority status and become socially and culturally unified with the dominant group.

Dominant-group policies play a significant part in determining the extent to which assimilation is possible. In American society European immigrants have been able to pursue this course of action successfully. Nonwhite groups, most notably blacks, have encountered severe difficulties.

Black executives serve as an illustration. Like all executives, they experience pressures, but, in addition, many feel they must face a special kind of stress — the effects of American racism. After interviewing many black executives, one writer noted that while they had encountered racism growing up,

> the strains of working in a white-dominated structure and the evidence of corporate racism, cloaked by a subtly worded memo or a promotion that never comes, are new and strangely disturbing. In a recent survey by *Black Enterprise* magazine on work, nearly 75 percent of those earning more than $35,000 a year reported discrimination on their jobs. The perception of many blacks is that whites-only signs still hang on the higher rungs of the corporate ladder.
>
> (Campbell, 1982: 37)

Outside of work the situation can be equally stressful. In interracial social situations, blacks often feel that they are being tested, with many whites inevitably considering them representatives of their entire race and grilling them on a variety of racial issues. When faced with this situation, an individual can use different strategies. One psychiatrist suggested, "Define the situation; devise a way of getting out of it very quickly. Develop some humorous responses or brush off the question and take charge by steering the conversation in another direction" (Williams, 1988: A15).

Historically situations that made blacks and other minority groups feel that assimilation was impossible have sometimes encouraged aggressive responses.

Aggression

What constitutes minority-group aggression varies sharply across time and space, sometimes existing only in the distorted perception of the majority-group beholder. In the 1930s some Southerners felt that blacks behaved aggressively if they held a prestigious job, owned a tract of land, or had a special talent. In some towns it was even considered an aggressive act for blacks to appear in public in formal attire during the week. The whites apparently wanted to see blacks in only one place: the fields (Dollard, 1937).

In the 1960s a new, much more aggressive approach became popular. Some blacks, along with some other minority-group members, became strong advocates of equal opportunity and justice for members of their respective groups. Most of this activity was nonviolent, but the threat of violence was often present, particularly as a response to whites who wanted to use violence to keep blacks in positions of inferiority.

In the 1970s and 1980s, the huge task of improving the lives of poor blacks was confronted by a variety of legal actions, close observation of government agencies' performance, and lobbying activities. While the overall goals of the earlier protests have not significantly changed, what were once militant, grass-roots activities have been channeled through more formal, more restrained procedures (Jenkins and Eckert, 1986).

At a given point in history, members of a minority group often pursue more than one response. All four responses appear in the following discussion of American minority groups.

American Minority Groups

An account of American minority groups is actually many accounts, one for each group. In this section we examine only the largest and most prominent American minority groups. Figure 10.2 indicates the size of each group and its percentage of the overall population.

Black Americans

Black slave labor existed in Virginia as early as 1619, but black slaves were more expensive than white servants in the short run, and their foreignness in appearance, language, and general behavior offended the ethnocentric English. Almost all these early colonists preferred white laborers. In 1640 there were only 150 blacks reported in Virginia. The figure rose to 300 in 1650, 3000 in 1680, and 10,000 by 1704. During the latter third of the seventeenth century, the plantation economy was developing, and an acute need for cheap labor arose. A new type of labor known as "chattel slavery" gradually took shape. The laws on which the system was based came from English property law. Thus blacks became property that could be bought and sold. They would serve their masters for life, and children automatically became the property of their masters. The only limits upon owners' treatment of slaves was their personal discretion.

Slavery ended in 1865, but the oppression of blacks did not cease. In the South the so-called *Jim Crow* laws legalized discrimination against blacks in all institutional areas. There were also lynchings, and in many Southern towns the Ku Klux Klan conducted terrorist raids. From 1880 to 1930, blacks often lived under very poor conditions. Rural Southern blacks frequently had substandard diets inferior to those received under slavery, and infectious diseases spread more rapidly because of poor diet. Gonorrhea and syphilis became prevalent among blacks during this period, and many pregnancies ended in stillbirths.

In the 1920s federal legislation restricted immigration, and as a result factories lost their chief source of cheap labor. Recruiters sought Southern blacks, and a migration of blacks from the South began. This migration stopped during the Great Depression of the 1930s, but it resumed when industrialization became revitalized with American involvement in World War II. The black migration to the North has continued, and by 1970 the states outside the South had about half the black population. Blacks migrating to the North usually experienced extensive discrimination in educational and occupational opportunities, in the availability of housing, and in the use of public facilities (bars, restaurants, grocery stores, buses, and trains, for example).

In the late 1950s and early 1960s, nonviolent demonstrations in the South protested discrimination against blacks. There were marches, pickets, and "sit-ins" at restaurants, on buses, and in other public facilities. During these years well-organized campaigns to register black voters occurred in Southern states so that blacks would be able to use the political machinery to improve their living conditions.

Gradually, imperceptibly at first, the tone of the protest efforts changed. Whites, who had taken a prominent role in much of the early protest activities, were told by black activists to devote themselves to eliminating racism in their own communities. In the black protest groups, a sense of black culture and consciousness began to appear: Afro

Figure 10.2

Prominent American Racial and Ethnic Groups[1]

Total Population: 226.5 million

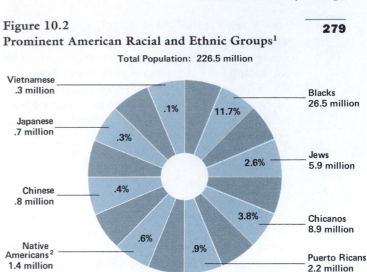

[1] Within the present figure, the representation of each group is the same size, not adjusted to its proportion of the total population.
[2] Includes Eskimos and Aleuts.

This figure indicates the size of most prominent minority groups in America and the percentage each represents in the overall population. (Sources: Adapted from U.S. Bureau of the Census. Statistical Abstract of the United States: 1982–83. No. 36; American Jewish Year Book, 1982. "Jewish Population in the United States, 1981.")

hair styles became fashionable, dashikis (African-style shirts) were worn, and black literature was widely read. A sense of black pride developed. "Black is beautiful" became a frequent slogan. The rhetoric and style of the black protest movement lost its nonviolent character. The young black leaders of the 1960s began advocating and predicting massive violence of blacks against whites if discrimination against blacks continued. On several occasions black protesters appeared carrying guns in public. For example, a group of armed Black Panthers marched through one of the state buildings in Sacramento, California, to announce their demands, and protesters emerged from a building occupation at Cornell University carrying rifles. No documented evidence has indicated, however, that blacks initiated violence during major protests.

On the other hand, blacks were often the victims of violence. The two most prominent black protest leaders of the 1960s — Malcolm X and Martin Luther King, Jr. — were assassinated. Other prominent blacks were killed, including a number of the most active, outspoken leaders of the militant Black Panther Party. Large segments of the white public were terrified of blacks revolting, and many whites were willing to accept if not condone the killings of black leaders. The only killing of a black leader that created widespread public sympathy among whites was the assassination of Martin Luther King, Jr., who had always advocated nonviolence in protest activity.

Situation of Blacks Today

An assessment of the situation of blacks in different institutional areas shows progress has occurred, and some of this progress took place during the protest years. In the 1896 case of *Plessy* v. *Ferguson*, the Supreme Court affirmed state court rulings that separate facilities for blacks and whites could exist as long as the facilities were equal. This segregationist standard survived largely unchallenged for nearly sixty years until 1954's landmark case of *Brown* v. *Board of Education*. At that time the Supreme Court declared that the segregation of public schools is illegal and that separate educational facilities are "inherently unequal." The same philosophy supported the Civil Rights Act of 1964, which legislated against discrimination in employment and the use of public facilities and threatened to withdraw federal funding from organizations practicing racial discrimination. In addition, during the mid-1960s, strong federal legislation assured equal rights for blacks and other minorities in voting and housing. Enforcement of the legislation, however, has been difficult because a limited number of government personnel have been available for the task, and their powers are often sharply restricted.

Blacks have tended to live in segregated, crowded, low-quality housing. The fact that blacks are usually poorer than whites is one reason why housing for blacks is relatively inferior. Other reasons also exist. Federal government housing policy supported segregation until the 1960s, and it has taken a limited role in opposing segregated housing since then.

Real estate agents have often cooperated with neighborhood associations and banks to keep blacks and other minorities out of all-white residential areas. Furthermore sometimes zoning restrictions exist, such as a minimum lot size, and in many cases local politicians will rigidly enforce restrictions on blacks but relax them for whites. In addition, many blacks are reluctant to leave inner-city areas, not wanting to destroy their community ties and feeling wary about possible hostile reactions from whites in a new neighborhood.

In spite of these problems, blacks sometimes do seek housing in all-white areas. A black woman with whom I spoke offered this reason: "Some whites believe I want to come into an all-white neighborhood as a status move. Nothing could be farther from the truth. The fact is that a white neighborhood is the only place I can hope to find a decent place to live."

As far as jobs, income, and education are concerned, improvements for blacks have occurred, but these must be kept in perspective. A gradual increase in the percentage of blacks in white-collar jobs and in skilled blue-collar jobs has taken place, but blacks still dominate in the low-skill, low-paid jobs. The fact that black income has remained about 60 percent of white income since 1966 serves as a reminder of that fact. It is noteworthy that the percentage gap was actually narrower before the 1954 Supreme Court decision against school desegregation, a decision supposed to be a major step in eliminating discrimination against blacks. The amount of education people receive influences their occupational and income opportunities. Thus it is noteworthy that on the average there is a gap of more than two years of schooling between blacks and whites. In addition, predominantly black schools are inferior to predominantly white schools in multiple respects — for example, in peer stimulation offered, in the age and condition of school buildings, and in the range and quality of facilities and supplies, such as science and language laboratories, textbooks, and libraries (Bailyn et al., 1977; Blackwell, 1975; Farley, 1977; Killian, 1975).

With financial austerity in the 1970s and 1980s, there has been a strong effort to cut back on programs that have benefited poor citizens, many of whom are black. One social scientist has suggested that the 1980s featured what he called "respectable racism," which we have considered under the term *institutional racism*. Code words such as "tax revolt," "competency based education," "merit," and "tuition tax credits" are polite yet effective means of discriminating against many black citizens, without ever bringing up the issue of race (Piliawsky, 1984).

The legacy of the disadvantages just discussed has been a host of problems for a substantial number of primarily poor blacks. A major study estimated that 27 percent of black inner-city males admitted to being involved in street crime during the previous year, believing that with their limited opportunities, they could earn much more money that way than at a legal job. Drug and alcohol problems are also widespread. In addition, the combination of intravenous drug use, sexual promiscuity, and homosexual activity has produced a high rate of AIDS among black inner-city youth. Not surprisingly national survey research has indicated that blacks tend to perceive whites as being hostile or indifferent to blacks' life situation. Sixty-nine percent of black respondents stated that they believed whites either want to keep blacks down or do not care about them, while 48 percent of whites assumed one of these two positions (Colasanto, 1988; Lex, 1987; Zinsmeister, 1988).

Hispanic-Americans

Hispanic-Americans, who are Americans of Spanish descent, number over 14.7 million and are classified separately from whites in the census records. About 8.9 million are Mexican-American

(also called Chicanos), 2.2 million are Puerto Ricans, and the remaining 3.6 million come primarily from Central America, South America, or Cuba. Table 10.2 offers a comparison of blacks, whites, and Hispanic-Americans.

Although Mexican-Americans and Puerto Ricans both speak Spanish, there are marked differences in historical experience and cultural tradition.

Mexican-Americans

The first serious colonization by the Spanish occurred north of Santa Fe, New Mexico, in 1598, more than twenty years before the Plymouth settlement in Massachusetts. Large-scale Mexican immigration to the United States, however, did not start until the social upheaval accompanying the Mexican Revolution of 1909. During the next two decades, migration was steady, and by the early 1930s there were nearly 1.5 million Chicanos. Migration declined during the war years when Mexican farming was prosperous, but since the 1950s, a steady flow of Mexicans has occurred. In the middle 1980s, worsening economic conditions in Mexico and Central America produced an

Table 10.2
Some Important Statistical Facts in the Lives of Whites, Blacks, and Hispanic-Americans

ISSUE	TOTAL POPULATION	WHITE	BLACK	HISPANIC
Median family income	$30,853	$32,274	$18,098	$20,306
Percent of persons below poverty line	13.6%	11%	31.1%	27.3%
Education[1]				
Four years of high school or more	75.7%	76.9%	63.5%	50.9%
Four years of college or more	19.9%	20.5%	10.7%	8.6%
Owner-occupied units	63.5%	66.8%	43.5%	39.5%

	TOTAL POPULATION	WHITES		NONWHITES	
		MALE	FEMALE	MALE	FEMALE
Life expectancy (in years)[2]	74.9	72.1	78.8	65.4	73.8

[1] All education figures are for people 25 years and older.
[2] The life expectancy figures compare whites with non-whites.
Source: U.S. Bureau of the Census. *Statistical Abstract of the United States: 1989.* No. 44, No. 106, No. 212, No. 721, No. 1243, and No. 1246.

Whites fare better than blacks and Hispanic-Americans on all these measures. Hispanic-Americans average higher income than blacks, while blacks tend to be better educated.

Although some individuals illegally entering the U.S. from Mexico are arrested and deported, illegal immigration from Mexico and its equally impoverished neighboring countries continues at a rapid rate.

tion has sought to obtain livable wages and benefits for its members. Among Chicano youth extensive political organizing has occurred in the past three decades. For instance, in the 1960s and 1970s, a Chicano political party called *La Raza Unida* developed. In the 1980s Mexican-Americans started voter-registration drives, thereby seeking to use their own voters to elect officials sensitive to their needs. Chicano political militancy, combined with extensions of the Voting Rights Act of 1965 and growing mainstream political activity, have helped win an increase in elected political positions. By the late 1980s, there were ninety Mexican-Americans in state legislatures. A number of well-organized interest groups present the Chicano or Hispanic cause, and since the "Viva Kennedy" campaign in 1960, both political parties have made efforts to gain the Mexican-American vote. Mexican-Americans, however, have tended to support the Democratic party (Feagin, 1989; Gonzalez, 1988; Moore and Pachou, 1976; Pachon and Moore, 1981; Shenon, 1986).

increase in illegal immigration. The number of illegal immigrants captured was 40 percent higher in 1986 than in the previous year. According to immigration officials, 1500 people a day were arriving by train at Mexicali, Mexico, and most were continuing by bus to Tijuana on the border. The combined impact of rapid immigration and a high fertility rate have made Mexican-Americans the fastest growing of all ethnic or racial groups in the United States.

Mexican-Americans are frequently poor and badly educated. The Chicano population aged fourteen or more averages nearly three years less schooling than whites and about $5000 less income per family in a given year. Most Mexican-Americans are blue-collar workers, primarily in service jobs. Only about 7 percent of men and about 3 percent of women do farm work, an occupation that many Americans associate closely with Chicanos.

One of the reasons for this association is the well-publicized and remarkably successful effort of Cesar Chavez and his associates to organize migrant Mexican-American workers into the National Farm Workers' Association. This organiza-

Puerto Ricans

In October 1898 Puerto Rico became an American possession, permitting people to move without restriction back and forth between the island and the mainland. By 1910 about 1500 Puerto Ricans had come to New York City, and their number rose to about 70,000 in 1940. Many of the early migrants were merchants who had lost their businesses when sugar became the dominant island crop. On the mainland, jobs were available because of restrictions in European immigration.

The major migration of Puerto Ricans started after World War II. Most of the new arrivals came in search of better-paying jobs. The majority of Puerto Ricans moving to the mainland still settle in New York City, but urban concentrations are developing in Chicago, Philadelphia, Jersey City, Newark, Los Angeles, Miami, and a number of other cities.

Economically and occupationally, Puerto Ricans have a difficult time in the United States. After Native Americans they are the poorest racial or ethnic group, with family income averaging less than half that of white families; over a third of

Puerto Ricans fall below the official poverty line. Occupationally Puerto-Rican men are heavily represented in lower-paying blue-collar jobs and women in low-level clerical and sales positions.

Because of nonrestrictive travel and the closeness of the island to the mainland, Puerto Ricans, unlike other migrants, often return to their ethnic homeland. Trips to the island are made in order to visit relatives or sometimes, if living on the mainland proves unsatisfactory, to resettle permanently. For many members of this ethnic group, adjustment to life in New York City and other cities has been difficult. Often language barriers increase the problem of finding a job. Then too there is a more pronounced color discrimination than exists in Puerto Rico.

On the other hand, Puerto Ricans choosing to return to the island encounter some distinct difficulties. In Puerto Rico the unemployment rate approaches 40 percent, with over half the islanders receiving food stamps. Wage levels are lower than in the United States. The alcoholism rate, the suicide rate, and the automobile-accident rate are much higher than in the United States. With such poor conditions on the island, it is not surprising that a study concluded that students who returned to Puerto Rico to live permanently had a less positive image of their teachers, schools, and themselves than a matched group of students who moved back and forth between Puerto Rico and the mainland (Fitzpatrick, 1975; Fitzpatrick and Parker, 1981; Lex, 1987; Mann and Smith, 1987; Prewitt-Diaz, 1984).

Puerto Ricans and other Spanish-Americans fall educationally and economically below American averages.

American Jews

It is not simple to determine the criteria that make a person a Jew. Certainly Jews are not a race. Among Jews one will find a wide variety of head and nose shapes, skin types, body builds, and hair colors. Jews also do not form a religious group. They include agnostics, atheists, and also converts to many different religions. Nor are Jews a nation. They come from many countries. It seems that the critical factor is "the consciousness of being a Jew." In short, Jews are people who think of themselves as Jews and are considered by others to be Jewish. Even in Israel, the reestablished homeland of Jews, uncertainty exists on this topic. Former Prime Minister Ben Gurion suggested that "being a Jew is so difficult that anyone professing to be one should be believed" (Berry and Tischler, 1978: 29–30). Recently a hot debate has revolved around the following question: While all Jews can automatically become Israeli citizens, should this privilege apply to non-Jews converted to Judaism?

The largest number of Jews reached the United States in the late nineteenth and early twentieth century from eastern Europe, where they had been poor, living in segregated villages or city ghettos. About 5.9 million Jews now live in the United States, forming about 2.6 percent of the American population. About three-quarters of American Jews live in large cities or their suburbs. Nearly half reside in the greater New York City area.

Jews often have been the target of hostile stereotypes and prejudices. **Anti-Semitism** is the complex of prejudicial attitudes toward Jews. The roots of this behavior lie in historical and economic conditions that go back many centuries in Asia and Europe. Anti-Semitism has also occurred in the United States. By the 1880s Jews appeared in newspaper and magazine cartoons that pictured them as "long-nosed, garishly dressed merchants speaking in broken English" or as revolutionaries trying to take over the American government. Industrialist Henry Ford contributed to anti-Semitism, financing a crusade against Jews in the 1920s. In the 1940s many Americans felt an intense hatred and fear of Jews, believing that American Jews were responsible for the outbreak of World War II. Since 1945 a gradual improvement in feelings toward Jews has occurred. Yet in 1989 the Anti-Defamation League of B'nai B'rith, which keeps a record of Anti-Semitic incidents, reported 1432 episodes, the greatest number since the organization started collecting these data in 1978. The Anti-Semitic incidents fall into two broad categories — vandalism, and harassment, threats, or assaults on individuals.

In spite of discrimination against them in the past, American Jews tended to be unusually successful in their occupational pursuits and income attainment. Success, however, often developed under trying circumstances. In the 1930s, for example, Jews were heavily represented in clothing,

284

textiles, films, and other industries on the edge of the mainstream economy and vulnerable to unusually high risk. In Carey McWilliams's phrase, Jews were "the ragpickers of American industry." In the 1950s American Jews showed a much higher proportion of men in white-collar employment than the national average. Yet from 1900 to 1950, Jews obtained few top-management positions, a fact suggesting that in this area Jews have also been the victims of discrimination.

For American Jews two significant trends have been occurring in the past twenty years. As Jews have divested themselves of their language and customs and moved into higher-status jobs, an increasing amount of intermarriage has taken place. At the same time, there has been a renewed interest in the survival of Jews as a distinct ethnic and religious group. Signs of this shift have been a revitalization of Jewish religious traditions, a greater focus of Jewish philanthropies exclusively on the needs of Jews, and a renewed emphasis on the importance of commemorating the Holocaust with courses, memorials, and museums.

American Jews have done well educationally and occupationally. Their level of education is considerably above the national standard, with Jews averaging nearly four more years of schooling than white Protestants. In the middle 1980s, a majority of Jewish families had incomes above white Americans' average, with Jews more heavily represented in professional and managerial positions than white Protestants (Brinkley, 1988; DeParle, 1990; Cohen and Fein, 1985; Feagin, 1989; Quigley and Glock, 1979; Sklare, 1971; Waxman, 1981).

Asian-Americans

There are about 2.5 million Asian-Americans in the United States. About 800,000 are of Chinese descent, 700,000 of Japanese, and 260,000 of Vietnamese descent. Although Asian-Americans reside in communities throughout the country, the West Coast, especially California, is where most live. In Hawaii Asian-Americans probably maintain greater economic and political prominence than in any other state. (Asian-American groups not discussed in this chapter include people of Bangladeshian, Cambodian, Indian, Korean, Pakistani, Philippine, and Thai heritage.)

Chinese-Americans

After 1850 Chinese arrived in the United States in substantial numbers and sought employment as laborers for mines and railroads. Within several decades the Chinese had become a source of fear to whites, who felt that they were a "yellow peril" that hated American institutions and maintained loyalty only to the homeland and their emperor. Motivated by fear, Congress passed the Chinese Exclusion Act of 1882, and the rate of immigration declined sharply.

Many Chinese-Americans have remained in ghettos ("Chinatowns") and have suffered from the problems that usually accompany depressed urban living. The Chinatowns of America are located in the most deteriorated parts of cities. In New York City's Chinatown, more than a third of the tenements have rats and three-quarters have roaches. In San Francisco two-thirds of Chinatown housing is substandard compared to one-fifth substandard for the rest of the city. The Chinatowns across the country have become seriously overcrowded because of recent immigration.

Overall, however, the Chinese have done well in basic achievement areas. They are well above the national average in high-school and college graduation rates, and they show the highest concentration of all Asian-American groups in white-collar jobs — 39 percent — which is well above the national average. The median family income is nearly $3000 over the national standard.

One reason for the success of the Chinese seems to have been their willingness to adjust to the standards of American life. For instance, immigrant parents generally do not try to restrict their children's career or marital choices. A factor contributing to Chinese-Americans' high income level has been the effective use of the "enclave" economy — family members and sometimes friends investing and working together to develop successful laundries, garment factories, and restaurants.

In spite of their success, the Chinese have often found evidence that they have not been accepted as full-fledged members of American society. As a college professor who was a third-generation American, a Korean War G.I., and a Stanford doctorate noted, it is infuriating to be frequently asked such questions as "How long have you been in the U.S.?" and "Where did you learn to speak English so well?" (Ikels, 1985; Kitano, 1981; Nee and Sanders, 1987; Wong, 1987).

Japanese-Americans

Japanese began arriving in the United States in the 1880s, at the time when restriction on Chinese immigration was occurring. About 28,000 Japanese settled in the United States between 1880 and 1900 and then over 213,000 in the next twenty years, as demand for low-wage agricultural workers grew on the West Coast. By the first decade of the twentieth century, the hostile, fearful images that had developed toward the Chinese started to become associated with the Japanese as well: "Now the Jap is a wily an' a crafty individual — more so than the Chink," warned one writer in the *Sacramento Bee* (Okimoto, 1971: 15).

In spite of discrimination, the West-Coast Japanese were industrious and successful as farmers, gardeners, and business people. In March of 1942, the *Los Angeles Times* revealed that Japanese agricultural products brought $40 million in sales annually. Japanese-Americans were growing 40 percent of the crops produced in California, specializing in those requiring intensive labor and capable of being grown profitably on small plots of marginal-quality land. As we have noted, this economic success did not protect Japanese-Americans during World War II. The American government ordered the forcible evacuation of 110,000 people of Japanese ancestry from the West Coast on the pretext that they might aid the Japanese war effort against the United States.

The forced migration was devastating to Japanese-American families. The average loss per family was about $10,000 in goods, property, income, and expenses (in 1940, preinflated dollars). Yet after World War II, Japanese-Americans were able to reestablish themselves in the American economy. Like the Chinese the Japanese have used education as a means of self-advancement. In recent years Japanese-Americans have had the highest college completion rate of any group in U.S. society, including majority groups, and have had an above-average placement in professional and management positions and in income. Nevertheless considering their high level of educational achievement, Japanese-Americans should be

doing even better occupationally; they continue to experience subtle discrimination in management and professional positions.

Japanese-Americans have been having an increasing amount of contact with other groups, and by 1985 over half of all new marriages of Japanese-Americans have involved a non-Japanese spouse. Reasons for the increase include the lessening of segregation and isolation, economic mobility, and the declining control imposed by the Japanese family (Feagin, 1989; Fugita and O'Brien, 1985; Jiobu, 1988; Kitano, 1981; Leighton, 1964; Taylor, 1986).

Vietnamese-Americans

The arrival of the Vietnamese in the United States has produced publicity out of proportion to their numbers. Some of the approximately 260,000 refugees arriving in the United States were "boat people" who left Vietnam, Laos, and Cambodia in small, often ill-equipped craft. Some died en route, but many others were picked up at sea, brought to temporary compounds, and then distributed to various countries. Other Vietnamese reaching the United States were war orphans adopted by American families, and a few children were American servicemen's offspring who joined their fathers. Understandably many newly arrived Vietnamese felt confused and alienated. In part, such a reaction occurred because of the disruptive conditions in Southeast Asia under which they departed, but it also took place because of the significance of what was left behind: a family network in which rights and duties were clearly specified and a sense of interdependence, support, and belonging were strongly emphasized. An article suggested that the conventional strategy of encouraging recently arrived Vietnamese children to become actively involved in American life as quickly as possible should be replaced by a policy emphasizing "grief work" — establishing a new identity after a significant loss. (In what context did we previously discuss grief work? If you do not remember or did not read the material, turn to Chapter 6, "Socialization," pp. 153–154.)

Compounding these immigrants' problems has been the fact that they arrived in the United States during a difficult economic era. Frequently they have found themselves pitted against American

As Vietnamese-Americans have become assimilated to American society, their new experiences have been diverse, including exposure to novel types of food.

citizens in the struggle to make a living. In Texas some people who fished for a living in the Gulf of Mexico have charged that since the arrival of the Vietnamese, certain areas have been fished out. To protest the increased competition, a local chapter of the Ku Klux Klan sponsored a fish fry during which the participants burned a fishing dinghy labeled the "U.S.S. Viet Cong." In Denver workers in a meat-packing plant were furious when they were dismissed and Vietnamese were hired at half the wage.

Because of their recent arrival, Vietnamese-Americans are well below other Asian-American groups and the American average in occupational and income level. A positive indication of future success, however, is the fact that their level of education is rising, with 62 percent high-school graduates and the average number of years of schooling scarcely below the national average (Eisenbruch, 1988; *New York Times,* 1981; Schmidt, 1981; Timberlake and Cook, 1984).

Native Americans

The number of Native Americans (also called American Indians) is about 1.4 million at present. When Columbus arrived in San Salvador in 1492, the figure was only slightly less, probably between 700,000 and a million. Experts believe that the number had declined to under 250,000 by the end of the nineteenth century, but the figure has increased steadily since then.

Native Americans treated early European settlers well. For example, most of the English people who landed at Plymouth in 1620 probably would have starved without gifts of corn and information about how to fish and grow corn. As more settlers arrived, they sought increasing amounts of land. The American government signed many treaties with Indian tribes, but when new arrivals needed more land, the government agreed that they could break the treaties. If the Native Americans resisted the invasion of their lands, then the military imposed compliance.

Eventually the Indians had to leave their lands and enter reservations. This policy weakened or destroyed their traditional economies (such as the buffalo-hunting lifestyle of Plains Indians), political systems, and religious systems. In addition, the requirement that children enter white schools undermined the family structure. Control of the reservations was fairly strict, and yet some rebellions did occur.

Perhaps the best-known rebellion was nonviolent. It was called the Ghost Dance, and in 1890 the practice of this dance spread quickly from tribe to tribe. The belief behind the dance was that some day all Indians, both the living and the dead, would unite on a new earth containing great herds of buffalo and wild horses and protected from death, disease, and misery. Those who performed the Ghost Dance would supposedly rise into the air and remain suspended until the new earth moved into place beneath them. Then they would come down onto this new earth without white people but containing all their ancestors.

Government and military personnel watched the development of the Ghost Dance warily. They acknowledged that it was nonviolent, but they were apprehensive about the enthusiasm for traditional customs and activities it generated. Then, when it seemed that the renowned Sioux warrior Sitting Bull was joining the movement, government officials became increasingly nervous. Officials ordered the arrest of Sitting Bull, and when he resisted, he was shot and killed. Two weeks after Sitting Bull's death, a Sioux chief named Big Foot was leading his people toward Pine Rock reservation, hoping to find protection from the army. At Wounded Knee, South Dakota, the cavalry stopped the march to check the men for weapons. Fighting broke out, and about 150 men, women, and children were killed. Many were wearing the fabled ghost shirts, which were supposed to protect the wearers from any harm, including bullets. With the Wounded Knee Massacre, the belief that Indians would be elevated to a better existence ceased to exist.

In modern times Native Americans retain less than 3 percent of the land area in the United States. Officials of the Bureau of Indian Affairs estimate that the quality of Indian land ranges from critically to slightly eroded. None of it is prime land for supporting crops or animals. Native Americans are the poorest ethnic group in the United States, with an unemployment rate double the national average, severely crowded living conditions, substandard water and sanitation facilities, and high disease and infant-mortality rates. Death from liver cirrhosis, which is primarily produced by alcoholism, is about three-and-a-half times the national rate, and among Indian adolescents the suicide rate is up to ten times greater than the national average.

Native Americans approach the future in different ways. Some believe that like all bad experiences, domination by the white majority will pass. Others have launched a legal battle to protect their rights and reclaim their lands. One significant activity has been the renewal of tribal traditions. Many tribes now emphasize teaching the younger generation tribal languages, craft skills, tribal histories, and religious ritual and ceremonies. Will these revitalized cultural traditions continue to develop, or will they be submerged by the continuing efforts to mainstream Native Americans in schools and jobs? Many modern Native Americans fear that the latter course of action will dominate (Brown, 1972; Davenport and Davenport, 1987; Deloria, 1981; Hodge, 1981; Lex, 1987; Robbins, 1984; Utley, 1963).

We have examined a variety of racial and ethnic groups. All of them are affected by affirmative action, which is discussed in the following American Controversy.

AMERICAN CONTROVERSY

Affirmative Action for Minority Groups

 Affirmative action is a government-supported directive requiring employers to develop timetables and goals for increasing the employment of women and members of minority groups. The roots of affirmative action can be traced to the Civil Rights Act of 1964, an executive order issued by President Johnson in 1965, and a Labor Department statement produced in 1970. Affirmative-action guidelines also include women, and they have been applied to educational as well as occupational opportunities.

In 1988, when a national sample of adult Americans was asked whether preference should be given to minorities in hiring and college admission, 79 percent opposed such efforts in hiring and 76 percent in college admissions. Let us consider some of the issues involved.

The Position Backing Affirmative Action

Those supporting affirmative action can stress that such an approach is traditionally American, representing our culture's emphasis on equal opportunity by helping to remedy the historical disadvantages suffered by minorities in educational, occupational, and income areas. Blacks and some other nonwhite groups are especially disadvantaged because, unlike many of the white immigrant groups arriving in the nineteenth and early twentieth century, they are seeking higher education and good jobs in a highly competitive situation against competitors whose chances for educational and occupational preparation have been better than theirs.

The problem of institutional racism is particularly relevant, the advocates emphasize. Employers can use such means as irrelevant educational credentials or past work history to screen out blacks and other members of minorities who are well qualified for jobs. It would be nice to think that subtle, "polite" racism does not occur in America, but it does.

A final point stressed by the advocates is that the goals and timetable for affirmative action are not rigid. Goals need not become quotas

specifying that in a given organization a precise number of minority-group members must fill certain job slots; affirmative-action procedures are flexible guidelines but nonetheless guidelines to be taken seriously.

The Position against Affirmative Action

The opponents of affirmative action might begin by stressing that theirs is the traditionally American position because it emphasizes that the individual must succeed in a competitive setting on his or her own without governmental intervention.

The major point the opponents make is that affirmative action represents reverse discrimination, with a division of modern society into two classes—those who benefit from this doctrine and those who do not. The problem, this group emphasizes, is that such a two-part division is impractical. Why, for instance, should Chinese-Americans and Japanese-Americans who, in spite of discrimination, have done

very well occupationally and economically in this country benefit from affirmative-action programs? On the other hand, what about poor, white males? They are judged solely on the basis of their ethnicity and sex, and the fact that they are victims of the "vicious cycle of poverty" (discussed in Chapter 9, "Social Stratification," pp. 249–251) is not considered.

Furthermore, the opponents conclude, goals might not start out as quotas, but over time they inevitably harden into them, and a quota system favoring minority occupational or educational candidates epitomizes reverse discrimination.

Conclusion

So these are two opposing positions on this complicated issue. Discuss your personal stances in a small group and, in particular, carefully examine the specific issues on which you disagree. Is there hope for effective compromise?

Source: Media General–Associated Press Poll. August 1988.

White Ethnics

White ethnics are primarily of Irish, Italian, Polish, Slavonic, and Greek origin. Most come from southern and eastern Europe and often have a Catholic heritage. They are usually blue-collar workers with incomes slightly below the national average. Part of the enormous popularity of the television program *All in the Family* was that Archie Bunker expressed the furies and frustrations

often attributed to white ethnics. Archie was an unabashed, devout conservative, suspicious of and hostile toward blacks, Puerto Ricans, and other nonwhite ethnics, contemptuous of people on welfare, and unyieldingly, unquestioningly patriotic. Others in public life have expressed the same fears and frustrations. During Nixon's first term, Vice-President Spiro Agnew gained great popularity speaking out for what he called the "Silent Majority" of hard-working, nonprotesting,

rchie Bunker, the central character in the popular television series "All in the Family," was portrayed as politically conservative and cist, but some research findings have opposed such a stereotype for hite ethnics.

patriotic Americans, many of whom were white ethnics.

Some evidence, however, disputes a conservative stereotype for white ethnics. A study suggested that white Catholics were more likely than white Protestants to have opposed the Vietnam War and to have supported such liberal causes as a guaranteed annual wage, governmental assistance for the poor, medicare, and the racial integration of public facilities (Greeley, 1977: Chapter 5).

Among the most traditional white ethnics are farmers, who sometimes lead quite isolated lives and, as a result, tend to maintain cultural patterns from other countries for many generations. Most white ethnics, however, have effectively moved into the economic and social mainstream. Since World War II, one of the most rapidly rising white-ethnic groups has been Italian-Americans, who are heavily represented in high-paying, prestigious occupations and now have higher income than their Irish-American counterparts.

For many white ethnics, especially those who move to suburban areas, the sense of ethnicity rapidly fades. Factors contributing to this loss of identity are sharp increases in intermarriage, geographical break-up of the extended family, decreasing influence of religious organizations, and integration into the local educational, occupational, and recreational structures (Alba, 1981; Fallows, 1979; Greeley, 1988; Novak, 1972; Salamon, 1985; *Wilson Quarterly,* 1988).

Our present discussion of racial and ethnic groups has provided us a background for some consideration of where American race relations are headed.

Moving toward the Twenty-First Century

During the presidential campaign of 1988, the Bush camp widely publicized information about the case of Willie Horton, a convicted black felon who raped a white woman while out of prison on a furlough program started by Governor Michael Dukakis, Bush's opponent. When asked to comment on why the Bush supporters were emphasizing this incident, Lee Atwater, Bush's campaign manager, said, "The Horton case is one of those gut issues that are values issues, particularly in the South, and if we hammer at these over and over, we are going to win" (Rosenthal, 1988: B5). So in politics, Atwater was saying, one should do whatever it takes to win, even if what it takes involved a major effort to inflame racial fears and hatred by suggesting that if Dukakis were elected president, white women's vulnerability to rape by black men would be increased.

Sociologist Troy Duster (1987) put this sort of issue, and race relations generally, in perspective. He suggested that while social scientists can analyze many issues involving race, a fundamental question emerges: "How and why has race been the persistent category of advantage and privilege throughout every generation of the nation's history?" (Duster, 1987: 12).

Such an analysis is consistent with a conflict-theory view, suggesting that nonwhites (and sometimes whites) have been submerged by dominant whites in the struggle for scarce resources. Duster's question also encourages analysts to specify the social forces establishing dominant whites' position of superiority.

Do you agree that Duster's question raises the fundamental issue about American race relations? Discuss this subject in class or outside of it.

290

STUDY GUIDE

Learning Objectives

After having studied this chapter, you should be able to:

1. Define and discuss racial group, ethnic group, and minority group.
2. Define prejudice, discrimination, ideology, racism, and institutional racism and distinguish between prejudice and discrimination, providing examples.
3. Identify and analyze the social, economic, and psychological explanations of prejudice and discrimination.
4. Discuss the effects of prejudice and discrimination.
5. List and describe the six dominant-group policies.
6. Examine the four minority responses to minority-group status.
7. Discuss the following large, prominent American minority groups: Blacks, Hispanic-Americans, Jews, Asian-Americans, Native Americans, and white ethnics.
8. State and analyze what may be the fundamental question involving American race relations.

Summary

1. Although all human beings are members of the same species, they are often more inclined to emphasize their racial and ethnic differences than their shared similarities.

2. Certain concepts divide the human species into different categories. Prominent among these are racial group, ethnic group, and minority group.

3. Prejudice and discrimination are the processes producing minority groups. Prejudice is a highly negative judgment toward a group, focusing on one or more negative characteristics that are supposedly uniformly shared by all group members. Discrimination is the behavior by which one group prevents or restricts another group's access to scarce resources. Prejudice and discrimination do not always occur in tandem, but they often do. Different explanations of prejudice and discrimination exist. Social explanations include the contributions of language to prejudice and discrimination, the part played by the social-distance factor, and the internal-colonialist version of conflict theory. Economic issues also encourage the development of prejudice and discrimination. Psychological perspectives involve a three-stage analysis of the development of prejudice and the scapegoat theory.

Studies have examined the effects of prejudice and discrimination. While one prominent study

found the self-esteem of black children higher than that of white children, negative effects of racism are numerous.

4. Dominant-group policies toward racial and ethnic groups include extermination, continued subjugation, population transfer, legal protection of minorities, cultural pluralism, and assimilation. Minority responses involve avoidance, acceptance, assimilation, and aggression.

5. The members of American racial and ethnic groups have distinct histories. Blacks are the largest group, with 26.5 million people representing 11.7 percent of the population. The original American blacks were slaves, and persecution of blacks has persisted since the freeing of the slaves. In the past several decades, some improvements in the economic, political, and social conditions of blacks' lives have occurred. However, in spite of these improvements, current living conditions for blacks still tend to be substantially inferior to the living conditions maintained by whites.

Over 14.7 million people of Spanish descent live in the United States. About 8.9 million are Mexican-Americans, 2.2 are Puerto Ricans, and about 3.6 million come from Central America, South America, or Cuba. They are frequently poor and badly educated, and the majority work in blue-collar jobs.

The United States has about 5.9 million Jews.

They come from many countries and are diversified in religion and biological characteristics. In spite of having been the target of vicious stereotypes and discrimination, Jews have traditionally done well in businesses that were on the edge of the mainstream economy. In recent years Jews have attained income and educational levels that are well above the national averages.

About 2.5 million Asian-Americans live in the United States. About 800,000 are of Chinese, 700,000 of Japanese, and 260,000 of Vietnamese descent. Chinese-Americans began arriving about 1850 and found jobs as laborers for mines and railroads. Many have remained in ghettos and have suffered the problems of depressed living, but, overall, their educational and income attainments exceed the national average. Japanese-Americans began arriving in this country in the 1880s, and, in spite of discrimination, they have become the most successful nonwhite ethnic group, both economically and educationally. The Vietnamese have primarily arrived in the past two decades. Like earlier ethnic groups, their willingness to work hard for low pay pits them against Americans in a variety of occupations.

At present U.S. society contains about 1.4 million Native Americans, slightly more than when Columbus reached San Salvador in 1492. The history of the relationship of white Americans with Native Americans includes a long string of broken treaties and wars that have forced Indians to inhabit increasingly smaller amounts of inferior land. Today Native Americans are the poorest ethnic group in the United States.

White ethnics are primarily of Irish, Italian, Polish, Slavonic, and Greek origin. They generally come from southern and eastern Europe and often have a Catholic heritage. White ethnics are sometimes stereotyped as very conservative, and yet some evidence disputes such a claim.

6. The fundamental question involving American race relations appears to be how and why race has been the persistently most important basis of advantage and privilege in American society.

Key Terms

anti-Semitism   the complex of prejudicial attitudes toward Jews

discrimination   the behavior by which one group prevents or restricts another group's access to scarce resources

ethnic group   a category of people that is set apart by itself or by others because of distinct cultural or national qualities

ideology   a system of beliefs and principles that presents an organized explanation of and the justification for a group's outlooks and behavior

individual racism   open, intentional racist behavior, for example, verbal or physical abuse

institutional racism   the subordination of members of a race by means indirectly related to race instead of by race itself

minority group   any category of people with recognizable racial or ethnic traits that place it in a position of inferior status so that its members suffer limited opportunities and rewards

prejudice   a highly negative judgment toward a group, focusing on one or more negative characteristics that are supposedly uniformly shared by all group members

race   distinct physical characteristics, such as skin color and certain facial features, used to divide people into broad categories

racial group   a number of people with the particular physical characteristics, such as skin color and certain facial features, that produce placement into a broad category

racism   the ideology contending that actual or alleged differences between different racial groups assert the superiority of one racial group. Racism is a rationalization for political, economic, and social discrimination

scapegoat theory   an explanation for prejudice emphasizing that people blocked from achieving a goal will sometimes be unable or unwilling to take out their frustration on its source, and so they direct their aggression against an accessible individual or group

self-fulfilling prophecy   an incorrect definition of a situation that comes to pass because

292

people accept the incorrect definition and act on it to make it become true

social distance　the feeling of separation between individuals or groups

stereotype　an exaggerated, oversimplified image, maintained by prejudiced people, of the characteristics of the group members against whom they are prejudiced

---

Tests

True–false Test

___T___　1. Racial classification often creates a self-fulfilling prophecy.

___F___　2. Prejudice and discrimination have exactly the same meaning.

___T___　3. The theory emphasizing that majority–minority relations in the United States can be analyzed as a form of internal colonialism has been rejected by all modern sociologists.

_____　4. A recent study of social distance conducted in three British cities concluded that when a particular kind of service required extensive contact between customers and shopkeepers, Asians were more likely to patronize white-owned shops.

_____　5. The economic factor played a significant role in the relocation of Japanese-Americans during World War II.

_____　6. As a minority response, assimilation means learning to live within the limitations of minority-group status.

_____　7. In the 1980s "respectable racism" has involved discrimination using measures referred to as "tax revolts," "competency based education," and "tuition tax credits."

_____　8. In the middle 1980s, the number of illegal immigrants from Mexico sharply decreased.

_____　9. Vietnamese immigrants have encountered hostility in the U.S. because they have been willing to work hard for low wages, thus competing with other workers for jobs.

_____　10. Native Americans are the poorest ethnic group in the U.S.

Multiple-Choice Test

___A___　1. Which of the following statements about race is true?
　a. Its classifications are imprecise.
　b. There are six categories of race.
　c. Members of different races vary considerably in intelligence, creativity, and athletic ability.
　d. It never creates a self-fulfilling prophecy.

_____　2. If a racial or ethnic group is easy to identify and weak, it may become the victim of aggression when groups are unable to direct hostility toward the real source of their frustration. This is the basic idea of:
　a. the authoritarian personality.
　b. the scapegoat theory.
　c. social distance.
　d. the stereotype.

_____ 3. *Apartheid* is:
  a. practiced widely in Brazil.
  b. a form of assimilation.
  c. a policy of compulsory segregation.
  d. a and c

_____ 4. A dominant-group policy that tends to decrease social distance is called:
  a. continued subjugation.
  b. legal protection of minorities.
  c. population transfer.
  d. extermination.

_____ 5. The decision of a light-skinned black person to "pass" into white society is an example of:
  a. acceptance.
  b. aggression.
  c. assimilation.
  d. avoidance.

_____ 6. The Supreme Court decision in the case of *Brown* v. *Board of Education* (1954):
  a. affirmed the doctrine of separate but equal facilities for blacks and whites.
  b. declared separate educational facilities to be inherently unequal.
  c. indicated that segregated restrooms are unconstitutional.
  d. stated that interracial dating would be unlawful.

_____ 7. Rapid immigration and a high fertility rate have made which group the fastest growing of all racial or ethnic groups in the United States?
  a. Vietnamese-Americans
  b. Puerto Ricans
  c. Chicanos
  d. Jews

_____ 8. Signs of a renewed interest in the survival of Jews as a distinct ethnic group include:
  a. a revitalization of Jewish religious traditions.
  b. a rapidly rising fertility rate.
  c. a sharp increase in the number of American Jews emigrating to Israel.
  d. a and c

_____ 9. Which statements best describes white ethnics?
  a. They are likely to be Protestant.
  b. They tend to be white-collar workers.
  c. They live only in urban areas.
  d. They have been stereotyped as patriotic and conservative.

_____ 10. Troy Duster's fundamental question about race relations:
  a. uses a structural-functional perspective.
  b. uses a conflict-theory approach.
  c. is concerned with racism in just the past ten years.
  d. relates only to Asian-Americans.

Essay Test

1. Define race and ethnicity and consider their sociological significance.
2. Define prejudice and discrimination and discuss in detail situations where both prejudice and discrimination exist as well as a situation where each exists without the other.

3. Summarize two explanations of prejudice and discrimination and analyze an event that illustrates each explanation.
4. What are the principal majority-group policies and minority-group responses? Discuss the relationship between the two sets of behavior, providing several examples. In other words how will a certain course of action taken by either a majority or minority group affect the other group(s) in question?
5. Summarize the history and current situation experienced by three minority groups examined in this chapter.
6. Discuss the extent to which people's race affects their advantage and privilege in modern society.

Suggested Readings

American Jewish Year Book. Philadelphia: Jewish Publication Society. The leading reference book on American Jews. This yearbook, which has been published annually since 1899, contains new articles in each edition as well as biographies, bibliographies, and statistics.

Brown, Dee. 1972. *Bury My Heart at Wounded Knee.* New York: Bantam Books. An eloquent, easily read history of the devastations suffered by Native Americans during their first 400 years of contact with whites.

Duster, Troy. 1987. "Purpose and Bias." *Society* 24 (January/February): 8–12. A short article that raises highly provocative, disturbing issues about race relations.

Erdrich, Louise. 1984. *Love Medicine.* New York: Holt, Rinehart and Winston. A vivid, often humorous series of first-person accounts representing modern Indians' hardships and tragedies as well as their spiritual resilience.

Feagin, Joe R. 1989. *Racial & Ethnic Relations.* Englewood Cliffs, NJ: Prentice-Hall. Third edition. A well-organized, effectively detailed account of American race and ethnic relations, including good summaries of theories and of the major racial and ethnic groups.

Grier, William H., and Price M. Cobbs. 1968. *Black Rage.* New York: Basic Books. Two black psychiatrists' analysis of the psychological effects of the oppression American blacks have suffered. The book contains considerable disturbing but thought-provoking case study material.

Helmreich, William B. 1982. *The Things They Say Behind Your Back: Stereotypes and the Myths Behind Them.* Garden City, NY: Doubleday. An informative, nicely written discussion about American ethnic and racial stereotypes.

Kitano, Harry H. L. 1976. *Japanese-Americans: The Evolution of a Subculture.* Englewood Cliffs, NJ: Prentice-Hall. Second edition. A sociological review of life among Japanese-Americans, including such issues as family, education, occupation, and cultural beliefs.

Mowat, Farley. 1965. *Never Cry Wolf.* New York: Dell. While observing a family of wolves, a biologist develops a clearer and deeper understanding of them. Although the terms never appear, prejudice and discrimination are central issues of this nicely written, sometimes humorous, and always compelling account.

Myrdal, Gunnar. 1944. *An American Dilemma.* New York: Harper & Row. A massive, influential study of a value clash many white Americans experience between their belief in the equality of all people and their prejudice and discrimination toward blacks.

Walker, Alice. 1982. *The Color Purple.* New York: Pocket Books. A powerful, often moving account of life for Southern blacks in the years before World War II.

Additional Assignments

1. Read television programming for one week. Tally the number of programs based on or including people belonging to an identifiable racial or ethnic group. Then watch as many programs as possible. What can you conclude, if anything, about the way television represents minority-group members as featured characters? Are minority-group members who are secondary characters represented differently from principal characters?

2. Have minority-group attitudes and behavior changed over time? One somewhat unusual way to answer this question is to read novels that represent the lives of people from various ethnic groups at different times. Form groups of six to eight students. Each group should choose one ethnic or racial group, and every member should read a novel about a different era. After reading his or her novel, each member of the group should be able to summarize the following issues:

   a. The lifestyle of the minority-group members described in the novel.

   b. Minority-group members' relationship with majority groups.

   c. How members' minority status affects their self-images.

   d. How, if at all, members of the minority group plan to change or improve their position in society.

   This information should provide basic material for a group report about how minority groups' attitudes and behavior have changed over time.

Answers to Objective Test Questions

True–false Test

1. t	4. f	7. t	9. t
2. f	5. t	8. f	10. t
3. f	6. f		

Multiple-choice Test

1. a	4. b	7. c	9. d
2. b	5. d	8. a	10. b
3. c	6. b		

11
EMERGING MINORITIES

The Emergence of Women

Sexism
The Women's Movement
The Future of Women's Rights

The Emergence of the Elderly

Ageism
The Elderly's Fight to Feel Useful and Satisfied

The Emergence of the Disabled

Prejudice and Discrimination Encountered by the Disabled
The Disability-Rights Movement

Study Guide

It was 1885, and Charlotte Perkins Stetson had recently given birth to a daughter, Katherine. She loved the child and referred to her as "a heavenly baby." Yet she was unhappy all the time, and when she nursed the child the tears ran down onto her breasts.

The doctor explained that she had "nervous prostration." In her words "a sort of gray fog [had] drifted across my mind, a cloud that grew and darkened" (Ehrenreich and English, 1980: 217). The fog never entirely left Charlotte Perkins Stetson (later Gilman). Years afterwards, in the midst of an active career as a feminist writer and lecturer, she would suddenly feel overwhelmed by the same sense of despair, unable to make even the smallest decision.

Charlotte Perkins Stetson was only twenty-five when depression struck her. Jane Addams, who became a well-known social reformer, was about the same age, scarcely twenty-one. Addams was affluent, well educated, and anxious to study medicine. Then in 1881 she fell into a "nervous depression" that immobilized her for seven years and continued to disturb her long after she had begun her work as a social reformer.

She was gripped by "a sense of futility, of misdirected energy" and was conscious of her estrangement from "the active, emotional life" within the family, which had automatically embraced earlier generations of women. "It was doubtless true," she later wrote of her depression "that I was 'Weary of myself and sick of asking what I am and what I ought to be.'"

(*Ehrenreich and English, 1980: 217–218*)

For women like Stetson and Addams, it was not clear what they ought to do. While they might have felt drawn to the "men's world" of business, politics, and science, that world was not ready to accept them. The domestic life, which their mothers and aunts had readily joined, was certainly available to them, but choosing that option meant turning their backs on the progress and opportunities late nineteenth-century society promised. These women felt they had no place to go. They were trapped, isolated, and, in their own perceptions, useless.

In this chapter we discuss three emerging minorities—women, elderly people, and disabled people. Each of these three minorities is "emerging" in the sense that it is starting to overcome the prejudice and discrimination imposed in the past.

About half of the readers of this text are women. If you are one, consider whether or not you have faced discrimination because you are a woman. Perhaps your parents have shown less concern for your education and job plans than they have for the efforts of your brothers or other male relatives. Sometimes you might feel that your boyfriend or husband treats you as little more than a sex object. Discriminatory treatment may represent a greater insult to you than it does to others.

On the other hand, about half of the readers of this text are men. If you are one, you might examine your approach to women. You might assess whether you value their advice and opinions as highly as you do men's. You might analyze your attitudes and behavior toward your girlfriend, wife, or other women with whom you come in contact in the course of a day.

In contrast to women, relatively few students belong to or have frequent contact with the other two emerging minorities we examine: the elderly and the disabled. The problems these two groups must face as minorities might seem less familiar to you, but we shall see that in many respects the prejudice and discrimination processes are similar for all three groups.

A chapter on emerging minorities could include some other minority groups: homosexuals, for instance. There is a discussion of this minority group in Chapter 7, "Gender Roles and Sexuality." In addition, if the space were available, we might also examine people with more than one emerging minority status: for instance, elderly women or the disabled elderly.

The Emergence of Women

Betty Friedan (1963) has called it "The problem that has no name." It was a "problem that lay buried, unspoken for many years in the minds of American women." It was a sense of dissatisfaction women suffered, and women struggled alone with it. Friedan suggested that as they made beds, bought groceries, or lay beside their husbands at night, homemakers had a sense of yearning and a fear that emerged as a silent question: "Is this all?" Each woman was alone, confronting a sense of dissatisfaction for which no label existed. In Chapter 7, "Gender Roles and Sexuality," we examined the development of male and female gender roles. In this section we focus on women's minority-group status. We examine the ideology of sexism and consider its costs. Then we shift the focus to the women's movement, the effort to curtail and eventually eliminate women's minority-group status. Finally we briefly discuss the future for women.

Important concepts in this section are "status," "role," and "role conflict." Can you define and illustrate all of them? If not, turn to Chapter 5, "Social Interaction," pp. 114–115.

Sexism

Any "ism" is an ideology, a system of beliefs and principles that presents an organized explanation of and justification for a group's outlooks and behavior. **Sexism** is an ideology emphasizing that actual or alleged differences between men and women establish the superiority of men. Sexism is a rationalization for political, economic, and social discriminations against women. Let us consider how the ideology of sexism has traditionally developed in American society.

First, unless observers can distinguish one group from another, then sexism or any other discriminatory behavior is impossible. Thus women's distinct visibility makes sexism possible.

Their secondary sex characteristics — breasts, absence of facial hair, fairly narrow shoulders, and relatively wide hips — and frequently distinctive manner of dress make them easily distinguishable from men. Even modern "unisex" styles of hair and dress seldom make the designation of a person's sex difficult.

Second, women have been attributed certain traits of inferiority. The sexist ideology has emphasized that women are less intelligent than men. At the emotional level, sexism claims that women are more likely to be irresponsible, inconsistent, and unstable.

Third, sexism involves rationalizations about women's status summed up by the following sentence: "Women's place is in the home." The title of Friedan's well-known book, *The Feminine Mystique,* is based on the elusive claim that the "occupation of housewife" will provide a glamorous, fulfilling role for modern women.

Fourth, sexism appears in the behavior patterns that women have traditionally learned. These patterns are accommodations to the attributed traits and rationalizations of status just described. Traditionally, in the presence of men, women have learned to hide their intelligence or to restrict its demonstration. Women have been expected to be ever-smiling, laughing, and helpless in appearance, thereby solidifying the conclusion that they are entirely content with their situation as long as men supply direction and control.

Finally discrimination is an aspect of sexism. In American society women have traditionally encountered more limitations on education than men. In the occupational area, women have suffered confinement to less prestigious jobs, with access to supervisory positions often prevented. In politics women have historically had almost no important roles. Women have also encountered multiple discriminations in everyday life, with men usually given much greater leeway in their sexual activity and general public behavior (Hacker, 1951).

Not surprisingly sexism has produced various costs for women.

Costs

Three prominent costs involve psychological, career, and physical issues.

PSYCHOLOGICAL COST   Americans believe that both men and women possess positive qualities, but those attributed to women have emphatically not been those for which society offers its highest rewards. The positive traits attributed to men include their tendency to be aggressive, independent, unemotional, competitive, skilled in business, self-centered, and capable of leadership. For women the list includes the capacity to be talkative, tactful, gentle, aware of the feelings of others, and interested in their own appearance (Cox, 1981; Freeman, 1975).

Historically the media have presented a narrow, stereotyped image of women. In 1974 an analysis of ten of the most popular children's television programs found dramatic differences between the treatment of male and female characters. Four of the programs had no regular female characters, and even with these four excluded, the male characters outnumbered the female two to one. Male characters appeared aggressive, constructive, and helpful, while female characters normally seemed passive and sometimes were punished if they were too aggressive (Sternglanz and Serbin, 1974). Similar gender-role stereotypes appeared in adult programming. In one study it was observed that prime-time TV presented about two male characters for every one female, and three-quarters of the leading characters were men. Most of the women did not have jobs, and the successful ones often had special or "magic" powers. For instance, Wonder Woman and the Bionic Woman helped popularize female TV characters, but it is noteworthy that when the heroics subsided, Wonder Woman worked as a secretary and the Bionic Woman taught elementary school (Schaffer, 1981: 115).

In recent years the portrayal of women on television has been changing. An analysis of four prime-time programs concerned with crime detection and featuring a male–female partnership found that viewers considered the male partner strongly representative of traditional male traits — aggres-

sive, emotionally restrained, resourceful, and independent — and the female partner demonstrating a similar set of characteristics (Dambrot, Reep, and Bell, 1988). While such representations are not sexist, one might conclude that they instruct young viewers that social relations should be played by both sexes as an aggressive, emotionless game. In another investigation involving television commercials shown over a fifteen-year period, the evidence indicated that a gradual increase in women's participation occurred and that by the middle 1980s, the sexes participated equally in prime-time commercials. While a lower percentage of women than men was represented as employed, an increasing proportion of men were being shown as spouses and parents, with no apparent occupation. Women continued to be more frequently shown in domestic situations and as product users. The most striking evidence suggesting women's continuing subordination was that in 90 percent of commercials, men were still the narrators. A female reporter recalled asking a male advertising executive representing a baby-care item about this situation. "So I ask 'Is a man a mother?' The answer: 'A man just knows what he's talking about. A man just has automatic credibility on TV'" (Bretl and Cantor, 1988: 607).

Looking beyond women's representation in the mass media, a study found that when women suffered depression, the positive attributes of both men's and women's traditional roles were absent from their lives. Their lives were without the ambition and self-confidence generally associated with men's roles; they tended to be submissive and dependent. Furthermore they lacked the sensitivity to others' needs and eagerness to soothe hurt feelings conventionally linked to women's roles (Landrine, 1988). These female victims of depression, in short, did not possess the positive attributes attached to either traditional gender role.

Therefore the psychological cost of sexism is that women have traditionally received negative or restricted images of themselves that tend to lock them into narrow roles offering little opportunity to achieve a high level of income, recognition, or personal satisfaction.

CAREER COST   If a woman feels fulfilled concentrating on housework, then she suffers no sense of career cost. However, many women do not feel fulfilled when limited to this work role. A study of British women, whose household tasks are basically similar to those of their American counterparts, indicated that 70 percent of the women expressed an overall dissatisfaction in their assessment of housework. The monotony of the work and its loneliness were other frequent complaints. This homemaker's statement sums up the most typical criticisms: "It's ridiculous to pretend that anyone actually likes cleaning floors and washing dishes — how can they? Housework is awful work. It's lonely and boring. There's nothing to show for it — it's all got to be done the next day. You don't get paid for it, either" (Oakley, 1974: 186).

Today many women extend themselves beyond the homemaker role. Women comprise over half the population and more than 40 percent of the labor force. Yet they are much less successful than men in the occupational realm.

Socialization is one contributing factor. As we saw in Chapter 7, "Gender Roles and Sexuality," traditional socialization has emphasized domestic tasks for women and breadwinning tasks for men. Many parents remain reluctant to give up the idea that boys are brighter, more talented, and better suited for valued jobs than girls. When asked about their children's ability and effort in math, parents with children of both sexes generally felt that their daughters made more effort but that their sons were more talented, even though the children's achievement-test scores and grades were about equal (Yee and Eccles, 1988). We might suspect that when such a differential perception is imposed on children, it will produce the imagined result. Recall our discussion of the self-fulfilling prophecy in Chapter 10, "Racial and Ethnic Groups," pp. 267 – 268.

Some evidence suggests that women with successful careers have often received a socialization that has made them feel particularly secure and certain about being successful. Margaret Hennig and Anne Jardim (1977) studied female presidents and vice-presidents of nationally recognized medium-to-large business firms and compared them with a group similar in age, education, and family background whose members had never risen beyond middle management. The basis for the achievement differences apparently lay in the family dynamics. Each high-achieving executive was either an only child or the first born of an all-girl family containing no more than three siblings. Both the mother and father simultaneously valued their daughter's femaleness and achievement and saw no contradiction to the enhancement of both. The parents wanted the girl to learn early to set her own goals and standards of excellence and to gain satisfaction from effectively performing any task she approached. One other distinctive quality about the families of top women executives was that both parents had strong relationships with their daughter. As one informant said:

> From my earliest recollections my parents and I were friends. . . . I always wanted to be just like my mother and just like my father, something which I am sure gave those hearing me say it no end of amusement! Yet in spite of this I think my parents really encouraged me to think through things very carefully and to venture my own opinion, even when I was very very young. I think they really trusted me and I them.
>
> (Hennig and Jardim, 1977: 84)

It appears that more than socialization accounts for most women's relatively limited career chances. For instance, the factor of socialization does not seem to account for the fact that between 1957 and 1987, mean earnings of women working full-time in relation to mean earnings of men working full-time remained virtually unchanged — going from $.64 to $.65 on the dollar (U.S. Bureau of the Census, *Statistical Abstract of the United States: 1959.* No. 419; U.S. Bureau of the Census, *Statistical Abstract of the United States: 1989.* No. 668). This almost stable earning gap seems to be the result of a couple of causes.

In the first place, when education, training, and work experience obtained by men and women are held constant, pay differences do occur. Thus to some extent women are the victims of "unequal pay for equal work."

However, a more significant factor helps explain sex differences in pay. Occupational segregation is widespread in the American job world. Women are more heavily concentrated in low-prestige, low-paying jobs. For whites to achieve occupational balance by sex, 61 percent of either women or men would need to change jobs. While there is a greater proportion of women than men in white-collar jobs, women are generally in nursing, elementary- and secondary-school teaching, social work, library service, and clerical and secretarial work — jobs that are fairly low in pay and prestige (Scarpitti and Andersen, 1989: 267–268).

Occupational segregation by sex is significant because it represents structural limits imposed on women's opportunities. An important implication of this point is that if we blame women's inability to reach higher occupational levels on personal shortcomings, then we are failing to use the sociological perspective to evaluate the influence of important social forces. As we noted in Chapter 9, "Social Stratification," traditional values and "old boys' networks" frequently hamper women's occupational advancement. Sometimes it is difficult to obtain a clear overall picture of women's occupational prospects. A team of researchers observed that the steadily increasing percentage of women in management and professional positions over the past two decades has produced "a politics of optimism"—a widely held belief that women are successfully moving in substantial numbers to high-paying, prestigious positions. The reality, however, is illustrated by the situation encountered by women in management, who are concentrated in lower levels, with fewer opportunities for advancement and lower pay than men. From 1960 to 1980, in fact, women in management experienced a slight salary decline in relation to men (Blum and Smith, 1988).

Table 11.1 offers some statistics that compare women and men on job types, income, and several other important issues.

PHYSICAL COST A study suggests that, roughly speaking, women agree on rankings of the hurtfulness of different kinds of violence against women (Leidig, 1981). At the least hurtful end of the continuum is "street hassling," which includes male verbal harassment, rude stares, and noises directed at women as they walk along the street. A more aggressive form of "hassling" is touching or grabbing a woman without her permission, including seemingly accidental physical contact with a woman's body in subways, elevators, or other crowded areas.

A stronger form of harrassment would be sexual harassment on the job or sexual abuse by male psychotherapists and other professionals; these acts can extend from patting a woman on her knee or bottom to more extensive sexual overtures. Pornography and prostitution also fall in this intermediate area of the continuum. Both activities

Table 11.1
Some Bread-and-Butter Issues: Men vs. Women

	WOMEN	MEN
Education for people 25 and over: 1987		
Four years of high school	41.6%	35.4%
One to three years of college	17.1%	17.1%
Four years of college or more	16.5%	23.6%
Occupation of people 25 to 64: 1988		
White-collar positions	71.8%	48.9%
Managerial/professional	28.6%	29.4%
Technical/sales/clerical	43.2%	19.5%
Blue-collar positions	28.2%	51.1%
Mean income of full-time workers 15 and over: 1987	$16,909	$26,008

Source: Adapted from U.S. Bureau of the Census. *Statistical Abstract of the United States: 1989.* No. 213, No. 644, No. 668, No. 729.

On bread-and-butter issues, women generally do not fare as well as men—for example, the 1987 woman's median salary was 65 percent of a man's median salary. Sometimes gender differences are deceptive at first glance. Thus women have a greater percentage of their workers in white-collar positions than do men, but about three-fifths of women's white-collar jobs are in technical/sales/clerical positions, which generally do not pay very well.

designate women as an object for male exploitation, with violence often intruding in fantasy or reality.

The continuum of violence reaches the extreme with outright, unadulterated violence: rape and physical abuse. Three prominent types of rape can occur: "date" rape, marital rape, and stranger-to-stranger rape. Police often receive reports of the third type but not of the other two. Nonetheless it is likely that marital rape occurs more often than stranger-to-stranger rape. Many overt acts of violence against women, such as wife-abuse, often contain both a sexual and physical component. An act of violence most people regard as extremely serious is girl-child incest, in which a trusted fam-

This photo shows Iranian women dressed in highly traditional chador robes doing something that is distinctly untraditional for women — shooting guns. These women are spending a month in a camp near Teheran, where they are trained to become members of a women's home guard that is supposed to help defend the nation from foreign invaders.

ily member, usually a father or stepfather, forces a girl to have sexual intercourse with him over a protracted period of time.

Certain trends appear among the violent acts against women. In the first place, nonreporting is a distinct pattern, whether the issue is indecent exposure, battering, girl-child abuse, or rape. Reasons for nonreporting include the expectation that nothing will be done, the belief that claims will receive ridicule, and the victims' fear of repercussions if they complain. Another trend has been that violence against women was not considered a serious problem until the advent of the women's movement in the late 1960s. Historically women have listened to jokes about wife-battering and rape and heard incest described as "the game the whole family can play." A third trend that appears in the acts of violence against women is the tendency to blame them for the acts perpetuated against them. When a man is robbed or assaulted,

police seldom ask if he provoked the crime, encouraged it, or dreamed about it. However, when a woman is physically or sexually assaulted, she traditionally has had to endure such questions from the police, therapists, physicians, and clergy. Now many police departments demonstrate increased sensitivity in interviewing rape victims; the growing use of female officers for this task has been particularly effective.

Closely linked to the blaming-the-victim trend has been a broad belief in "female masochism." A widespread and extremely harmful contention is that women not only do not mind pain and humiliation but that they also often like it — thus the common male claim that rape victims frequently "lie back and enjoy it" (Frieze, 1983; Leidig, 1981; Russell and Howell, 1983).

An idea that might prove useful in helping to understand sexual violence against women involves the perception that the sex offense is like an addiction in some respects. While alcoholism tends to flourish in cultures that do not allow children to learn safe drinking practices, exploitative sex may thrive in cultures not allowing children to learn easily and safely about sex (Herman, 1988).

Because of the costs of sexism, women have mobilized to combat the inequalities and brutalities imposed on them.

The Women's Movement

Through the centuries women have become increasingly aware of their position in society. Some prehistoric cave paintings appear to be women's first representation of their social organization. Ancient Sumerian and African mothers wrote poems about being women, and speeches attributed to medieval women condemned as witches have survived to the present. In the Middle Ages, some women lived in self-sufficient monastic communities in which insights and understanding about women's role in society developed (McLaughlin, 1989; Neel, 1989). Inevitably

women's recognition of their subordinate position has expanded during periods that stressed the importance of new ideas and influences, particularly the significance of individual rights. In the course of the eighteenth-century era called the Enlightenment, the importance of rational thought and the value of the individual man received an increasing recognition. In 1792 Mary Wollstonecraft was simply extending the Enlightenment tradition when she published *The Vindication of the Rights of Woman*. In this book she stated:

> My own sex, I hope, will excuse me, if I treat them like rational creatures, instead of flattering their fascinating graces, and viewing them as if they were in a state of perpetual childhood, unable to stand alone. . . . I wish to persuade women to endeavor to acquire strength, both of mind and body, and to convince them that the soft phrases, susceptibility of heart, delicacy of sentiment, and refinement of taste, are almost synonymous with epithets of weakness.
>
> (Wollstonecraft, 1980: 459)

In the early twentieth century, a new wave of enlightenment swept across western Europe and the United States: New ideas and new ways of

The first women's movement focused heavily on the right to vote. The modern movement, which evolved in the 1960s and continues today, has sought both broader and more profound changes and has drawn in women from a variety of racial and ethnic backgrounds. Over the past two decades, rallies on behalf of women's rights have become commonplace in the U.S.

doing things were supported by the spread of industrialism, the occurrence of World War I, the rise of Marxism, and the rapid development of the behavioral and social sciences. The most concrete accomplishment of this movement was the 1920 passage of the Nineteenth Amendment, which provided women the right to vote. After the passage of the Nineteenth Amendment, women's activities became less explicitly organized and involved less public fanfare. In the 1920s, however, various important women's organizations were formed: the League of Women Voters, the National Council of Women, and the International League for Peace and Freedom. After World War I, women increasingly entered the public work place, taking an active role in the trade-union movement and also producing such professional organizations as Business and Professional Women (BPW).

Like earlier women's consciousness efforts, the modern women's movement has been a product of its time. This movement has contained two separate sections. The first, which has been more traditional, received its impetus from the President's Commission on the Status of Women established by President Kennedy in 1961, the challenge to the status quo encouraged by Friedan's bestselling book, and the influence of a "sex" provision in the Civil Rights Act of 1964. In 1966 the National Organization for Women (NOW) was formed. Its members were primarily from the professions, labor, government, and communications and ranged in age from about twenty-five to forty-five. Its self-assigned task was to obtain equality and justice under the law, and its initial target was the executive branch, with the intention of bringing federal power to bear on behalf of women. In the intervening years, NOW's major activities have been in the economic and political spheres, most notably the narrowly defeated effort to seek passage of the Equal Rights Amendment.

The second section of the modern women's movement emerged from the 1960s civil-rights and antiwar movements, in which general human rights received extensive emphasis, but women's rights commanded little attention. The idea of women's "liberation" first appeared in a memo written in 1964 by two female members of Students for a Democratic Society (SDS); the women protested the fact that even in this activist student organization women were assigned menial office tasks, were not heeded at meetings, and were generally undervalued, and, as a result, undervalued themselves (Gitlin, 1989: 169). Three years later SDS women finally succeeded in passing a resolution calling for the full participation of women in SDS. Such early efforts brought no explicit resolution, but they did help create a "radical community" where women became increasingly aware of shared grievances and intentions. In such a context, five women's groups formed independently in 1967 and 1968 in five different cities: Chicago, Toronto, Seattle, Detroit, and Gainesville, Florida. The initial efforts to publicize a women's movement received an indifferent or hostile reaction from men (Freeman, 1980).

Throughout the 1970s, however, the women's movement expanded, affecting every aspect of human existence. Its growing influence becomes apparent upon examining the results of a national sample of Americans who were asked whether they favor or oppose most of the efforts to strengthen or change women's status in society today. The percentage favoring an improvement of status increased from a mere 42 percent in 1970 to 67 percent in 1981 (Louis Harris and Associates, *Harris Survey,* August 1981).

But what about the future of women's rights in the United States?

The Future of Women's Rights

Let us focus on the woman interested in the pursuit of full, equal rights. Such a woman believes and supports the pursuit of such rights because without them she feels trapped in a life deprived of meaning and power. But how is it possible for such a woman to establish intimate relations with men? One option emphasized in some women's groups has been to associate as little as possible with men: to avoid having them as lovers or spouses. To most women, however, such a course of action presents another type of deficiency: the denial of their deep-seated belief that heterosexual coupling is a highly desirable part of human existence. Women who maintain this belief and are simultaneously committed to women's rights often find themselves in a difficult position. What does such a woman do if she falls in love with a man who falls far short of her feminist ideals? Does she try to increase his awareness of her own values and needs? Does she grin and bear it? Does she pull out?

The result will vary depending on the people and the circumstances involved. Betty Friedan (1981) suggested that women and men would do well to cooperate more fully. Often compromise is possible, in the realm of couples' career and domestic responsibility, for example. According to preliminary research, Friedan reported, many equality-minded women are consciously and effectively implementing two ideologies that most people once considered contradictory. One ideology is the woman-as-individual, often enhanced through a career that women pursue part time or on different shifts from their husbands. The other ideology is woman-serving-her-family, and wives receive support in this area when husbands become more involved in domestic activities than they traditionally have been. Working out such problems seldom makes headlines, and yet the significance of this process for many modern women is enormous.

Compounding many women's difficulties has been the fact that American mothers have received relatively little federal help in the area of child care. In Sweden and Italy, women earn about 80 percent of the male wage, and in France, Germany, and Great Britain the figure is about 70 percent. By contrast, women in the United States earn about 64 percent of what men do. A major reason for women's greater earning power in European countries has been the various types of governmental economic assistance provided when they have children. In the 1970s and 1980s, American women pushed effectively for improved rights in the occupational, educational, and credit areas, but their European sisters have fought more effectively for assistance to working mothers (Hewlett, 1986). Admittedly it has probably been easier to secure those rights in countries with traditions that have more strongly emphasized governmental assistance to individuals and families than the United States has done.

While the majority of the elderly are women, both sexes frequently encounter patterns of prejudice and discrimination similar to those that develop when sexism occurs.

The Emergence of the Elderly

No one doubted that Alexander Freiheit was a first-rate college teacher. In lecture his breadth of vision gracefully combined with a vast store of anecdotal information about historical figures and events. Throughout the hour Professor Freiheit would pace quickly around the room, seemingly generated by the excitement of the ideas he was expressing. But what about possible signs of senility? When asked, most faculty members readily admitted that Professor Freiheit was considerably more intelligent, alert, and witty than many colleagues half his age. The problem he confronted was bureaucratic. As a publicly funded organization, the university was under the jurisdiction of state law, which required mandatory retirement at age seventy unless the employer—in this case the university president—strongly supported continuing employment. The vice-president, speaking for his superior, refused such support, indicating that the "planned configuration" for the next two decades emphasized the decline of the history department and an increase in other subject areas where student demand was greater. "But the man is irreplaceable," one of Professor Freiheit's supporters argued. "I'm afraid that ultimately everyone is replaceable," the vice-president replied.

A group of students and faculty formed an organization to keep Professor Freiheit employed at the university. They sought and received publicity from the school paper, a faculty newsletter, and the local newspaper as well as support from several local politicians. Finally they initiated a lawsuit, but the judge ruled against the teacher. Professor Freiheit was angry and discouraged. "The President of the United States is two years older than I am, and I could have gone to school with most of the Supreme Court Justices. It looks like you need to be prominent and powerful to avoid being put out to pasture."

Obviously Professor Freiheit was feeling that the laws involving retirement were meaningless and that he was powerless to do anything about them. In spite of recent change in this particular law, senior citizens frequently must face situations where they encounter discrimination—not an insignificant fact when we consider their numbers. As Figure 11.1 indicates, the American elderly—people aged sixty-five and older—are now about 25.3 million in number, representing 11.3 percent of the population (U.S. Bureau of the Census, *Statistical Abstract of the United States: 1989.* No. 45) and will increase in both numbers and percentage in the United States and other industrialized nations too. The elderly is the one minority group most of us can eventually expect to join.

In this section we discuss ageism and its costs, the reactions to ageism, and the future of the elderly as a minority group.

Ageism

Ageism is an ideology asserting the superiority of the young over the old. Ageism is a rationalization for economic, political, and social discrimination against the elderly. Like sexism, ageism is a process that is readily apparent in daily life.

First, like sexism, ageism could not occur without high social visibility. Senior citizens do possess such visibility. Their skin is wrinkled, and some of them walk slowly or stooped over. In addition, the elderly tend to dress more blandly than more youthful people. On this point they can face a dilemma. Colorless elderly styles mark people off as old, and yet if they wear bright, fashionable clothes, they are accused of "failing to act their age."

Second, the elderly have various negative qualities attributed to them. The prevailing stereotype of old people includes images of physical deterioration, passivity, dependency, rigidity, senility, inefficiency, and the loss of alertness and intelligence (Nuessel, 1982; Williamson, Munley, and Evans, 1980). When adolescent, middle-aged, and elderly people were asked to evaluate adults in these three age groups, the elderly received the lowest evaluation from all three groups (Luszcz and Fitzgerald, 1986).

Third, there is a rationalization of old people's status—the image of the "happy disengager," the picture of smiling, fulfilled elderly people reveling in their extensive free time and nearly endless opportunities to play with grandchildren. Life is not that simple, however. Research shows that adjustment to retirement depends on such factors as the

Figure 11.1
307

Percentage of Population 65 and More in the United States, West Germany, and Japan over Time.

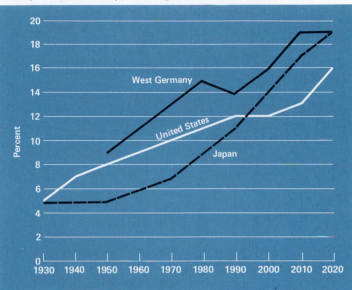

This graph illustrates that these three advanced industrial nations have a steadily increasing percentage of people in the elderly bracket. (Source: U.S. Bureau of the Census. Historical Statistics of the United States: Colonial Times to 1970. *Series A 119–134; U.S. Bureau of the Census.* Current Population Reports: Population Estimates and Projection, *No. 74. Tables 4 and 8.)*

availability of money, friends, and the capacity to make decisions for oneself (Atchley, 1976).

Like other minority groups, senior citizens make some accommodation to their status. This accommodation can appear as a graceful acceptance of retirement, in spite of personal reluctance, or a decision to give short, even truncated responses to an interviewer in order to avoid the slightest hint of being a rambling, senile old person.

Inevitably the elderly face discrimination, with retirement laws having been one of the most obvious illustrations. Thus it was a legislative landmark when congress in October 1986 passed a law eliminating mandatory retirement for nearly all employed Americans. The late Claude Pepper, an eighty-six-year-old congressman who was the chief sponsor of the bill, declared, "Abolishing age discrimination will offer new hope to older workers who are desperate to maintain their independence

308

and dignity . . . " (Noble, 1986: E6). The new retirement law, however, has not eliminated all work-associated problems for elderly people. Until age seventy a person cannot earn more than $6900 per year at a job, without receiving a reduction in social-security benefits. Above that amount a senior citizen is required to pay $1 for every $2 earned—a 50-percent tax rate. By contrast, the relatively affluent elderly who receive capital gains or interest on savings suffer no such tax penalty (Kornblum and Julian, 1989: 343–344).

The elderly's minority status also produces other costs.

Costs

In a study of 502 people aged forty-six to seventy-one, the respondents indicated that health was the principal factor contributing to life satisfaction, followed by participation in organizational or group activity, and sense of control over one's destiny (Palmore and Luikart, 1974). Let us consider some ways ageism asserts itself as a cost in each of these areas.

HEALTH AND MEDICAL-CARE COST Ageism appears to be a factor that influences health by affecting the quality of medical care. Several studies suggest that generally an inverse relationship exists between a person's age and the speed of emergency treatment—therefore, the older the patient, the more slowly he or she receives treatment (Simpson, 1976; Sudnow, 1967). Certain characteristics of senior citizens also can make them undesirable from a treatment point of view. Old people's illnesses are often chronic, tedious, uninteresting, and difficult to treat. Doctors frequently subscribe to the common sentiment that medical treatment should be immediately successful, not spoiled by situations that defy the doctor's ability to supply an instant cure. Furthermore, like the general public, physicians can be frightened by aging and death (Butler, 1975) and frustrated by family members, colleagues, and hospital administrators who want to prolong life in the inevitably vain hope that somehow a miracle will occur (Duff and Hollingshead, 1968).

The difficulties of treating the elderly are compounded if they also suffer a disability, because

they are forced to deal with two service agencies, neither one of which can address all of their needs. Agencies that are concerned with blindness, for instance, do not handle elderly people's problems, while organizations for the elderly cannot deal with issues related to blindness. Frequently the blind or visually impaired elderly feel caught between two agencies, neither of which can effectively respond to all their needs (Biegel et al., 1989).

Senior citizens seem to vary considerably in their ability to confront health problems. A study found that when urban elderly were involved in social networks composed of neighbors, friends, or kin, they tended to be healthier than old people without such networks (Cohen et al., 1985). Research on medical problems of black and white elderly women concluded that these two categories had some similar coping mechanisms but also

For many elderly people, a major cost of growing old is a state of disengagement in which isolation and loneliness dominate.

some differences. In particular, the black elderly had stronger support from friends, made more extensive use of prayer, and were more inclined to use nonprescription drugs (Conway, 1985).

GROUP-INVOLVEMENT COST Often senior citizens feel lonely, cut off from frequent, positive interaction with others. One reason some of them commit minor crimes, most notably shoplifting, is to draw attention to themselves. Arrest can lead to sessions with a counselor who can provide a reality-based relationship, or it might produce a renewed contact with a distant son or daughter who had ignored many plaintive invitations to visit. "The arrest becomes a reproach: See what you let happen to your father? And to get an extra bit of attention . . . many are arrested on their birthdays" (Gustaitis, 1980: 14). Research found that elderly who were married, healthy (according to their own perception), fairly affluent, socially active, and socially fulfilled tended to be less lonely. In this study the measurement of social fulfillment was compiled from three items — a person's sense of having or not having enough friends, sufficient activities to keep busy, and a sense of being needed — and was the factor that best predicted loneliness (Creecy, 1985).

With the introduction of the concept *disengagement,* researchers on aging have addressed the issue of the desirability of senior citizen's group involvements. **Disengagement** is a process of mutual withdrawal involving decreasing interaction between an elderly person and others in the social system to which he or she belongs (Cumming and Henry, 1961). Elaine Cumming and William Henry, who developed the concept, originally contended that disengagement was both functional for society, providing a process by which power can transfer from older to younger members and functional for individuals, initiating a less active and, therefore, more satisfying lifestyle. The early usage of the disengagement concept has received widespread criticism. At the very least, the original analysis was an oversimplification. A later study suggested that disengagement becomes a satisfying outcome only if the person voluntarily reduces role commitment and maintains high self-esteem in the process (Neugarten, Havighurst, and Tobin, 1968).

Perhaps more significant than disengagement is continuity. Most senior citizens are willing to make adaptive changes as they age if these changes permit a sense of continuity in self-image and personally significant activities (Atchley, 1989). For an elderly man, for instance, retirement might be fine so long as he can continue to have lunch twice a week with his long-time work buddies; for him the social side of the job had always been more meaningful than the job itself, and it is the social side of the job he wants to maintain.

The following Cross-Cultural Perspective describes activity that stands in bold contrast to most elderly Americans' experience.

CROSS-CULTURAL PERSPECTIVE

The Elderly in Abkhasia

Do the same conditions that encourage long life also discourage disengagement? That is a difficult question to answer. It is clear, however, that in Abkhasia the living situation experienced by the elderly does promote both results.

In the Soviet Republic of Abkhasia, an anthropologist raised a glass of wine to toast a man who looked no more than seventy. "May you live as long as Moses [120 years]," she said. The man was not pleased. He was 119.

No exact figures exist for the total number of aged people in Abkhasia. However, in the village of Dzhgerda, where this researcher did her study, 15 percent of the population was eighty-one and over. In 1954, the last year for which figures are available, 2.58 percent of the Abkhasians were over ninety. For the Soviet Union overall and the United States, the comparable figures were 0.1 and 0.4 percent respectively. Why the difference? We will see that the elderly Abkhasians experience a number of conditions very different from those encountered by their American counterparts.

First, the life of the Abkhasian elderly has a broad base of uniformity and certainty. Sexual behavior, for instance, occurs without any sense of guilt. It is a pleasurable activity to be regulated for the sake of one's health, like a good wine. The same outlook exists with work. From the beginning of life until the end, Abkhasians do the amount of work they feel capable of doing. Work, they believe, is vital to life, and the concept of retirement is unknown to them. As they become older, they gradually cut back. Observations on twenty-one men and seven women over the age of 100 showed that they averaged a four-hour workday. The men weeded and helped with the corn crop, and the women strung tobacco leaves. They worked at their own pace, moving evenly and without wasted motion, taking breaks on occasion. Both the Soviet medical doctors and the Abkhasian elderly feel that work habits have a lot to do with their long lives. The

doctors suggest that the work patterns allow the vital organs to function more efficiently. The Abkhasians say, "Without rest, a man cannot work; without work, the rest does not give you any benefit."

Like other elements in Abkhasian life, the diet is stable. Investigators have found that people who are 100 years and older have eaten the same foods throughout their lives. At each of their three meals, the Abkhasians have *abista,* a corn-meal mash cooked in water without salt. Other prominent foods include cheese, buttermilk, fresh fruits, especially grapes, and fresh vegetables, particularly green onions, tomatoes, cucumbers, and cabbage. Although they are the main suppliers of tobacco for the Soviet Union, few Abkhasians smoke. They drink neither coffee nor tea but do consume a local red wine of low alcohol content. At meals the food is cut into little pieces, and the people

take small bites, chewing their food very slowly. As a result effective digestion usually occurs.

One more special quality about Abkhasian culture is the highly integrated nature of life coupled with the respected role of the elderly. Abkhasians bear a close, interdependent relationship with a variety of kin, and these relationships tend to enhance the strong sense of security that underlies their existence. For the elderly that sense of security is further reinforced by the deep respect they receive. The elders preside at important ceremonies, mediate disputes, and offer their experience and knowledge about farming. Quite the opposite of burdens, they serve as valued resources. As one ninety-nine-year-old Abkhasian told his doctor, "It isn't time to die yet. I am needed by my children and grandchildren, and it isn't bad in this world — except that I can't turn the earth over and it has become difficult to climb trees."

Source: Sula Benet. "Why They Live to Be 100 or Even Older, in Abkhasia." *New York Times Magazine.* December 26, 1971, p. 3+.

COST OF LOSING CONTROL OVER ONE'S DESTINY   One of the problems senior citizens face is that they encounter many social norms that place highly limiting expectations upon them — in the sexual realm, for instance. As one elderly commentator pointed out, people do not "chide young people for being horny;" there is no such expression as a "dirty young man." The idea of "the dirty old man" is an accusation. The writer noted, "At the nonyouth time of life one has no business . . . being sexual. It is unwarranted, bizarre, if not obscene" (Neubeck, 1981: 314).

Relocation is another issue that can threaten old

people's sense of control over their destiny. Choice and predictability are important elements is this process. Older people who relocate voluntarily are likely to adapt better than those who relocate involuntarily. In addition, new environments that are comfortable because of their similarity to the old environment are generally easier to adapt to than those that are less similar — the issue of continuity for the elderly we discussed in the section on group-involvement cost (Bourestom and Pastalan, 1981; Schultz and Brenner, 1977).

Adaptation to nursing homes can be particularly difficult. A guiding principle of these organizations is that patients' social and psychological needs are less significant than the efficient performance of patient care. The rigid scheduling of meals and activities as well as movement en masse to entertainment, religious services, or therapy can be efficient practices, but they are highly disruptive activities for people who have lived a largely independent existence (Gubrium, 1975).

Recent research has emphasized the significance of the quality of care provided in nursing homes. Does the nursing staff maintain a rigid, highly controlled setting where communication between staff and patients and among patients is minimized, or do nurses establish a therapeutic environment where patients participate in decision making and meaningful social contacts are maximized? The quality of care is likely to have a significant influence on patients' quality of life in a nursing home (Bagshaw and Adams, 1986).

The elderly encounter ageism and other problems. What measures can they take to improve their situation?

The Elderly's Fight to Feel Useful and Satisfied

Maggie Kuhn, the founder of the Gray Panthers, an activist organization on behalf of the elderly, has said that three things please her about being old: She can speak her mind, she has succeeded in outliving most of her opposition, and she can reach out to others (Shapiro, 1982: 11). Maggie Kuhn has a useful, satisfying old age. Let us consider strategies people employ to produce such results at both an individual and a group level.

Some people focus at the individual level, finding that continuing to work produces a positive result. In a study of 4000 retired people who had held a variety of jobs, 73 percent of those who reported that work was a major source of satisfaction returned to work after retirement (Streib and Schneider, 1971). Others found satisfaction at the individual level in entirely different ways — foster grandparenting, for instance. Before entering such a program, one woman reported "[I] felt like I was dead but alive. I wasn't doing much." Her husband had died years earlier, and her children had long since left home. She heard on the radio that a local hospital wanted foster grandparents

In Japan, as in some other cultures, older people are regarded as vital contributors to society, both in their role as family members and, for many, as part of the work force.

for retarded children. The prospect frightened her, but she went anyway. She was brought to see a little boy. "They called him a mongoloid, but I couldn't tell. The first thing he did was hug me. He squeezed my legs so tight, I thought I'd fall over. We didn't talk much that day. We just sat and hugged. I felt warm all over" (Hultsch and Deutsch, 1981: 330). This woman eventually became the foster grandparent for five children, and she convinced one of her friends to enter the program.

At the individual level, senior citizens can find different ways to feel useful and satisfied. Can they, however, form a subculture at the community level to accomplish mutually sought goals? The answer, unequivocally, is yes. The inflationary pressures of recent years have provided a major impetus for the elderly to speak out and to act collectively on their own behalf. Like other minor-

While many elderly Americans choose to retire, others, like this 70-year-old man, prefer to keep working.

ity groups, they have started to realize that they will be much more successful if they visualize what they had once considered individual problems as group problems. Thousands of organizations composed of elderly citizens now lobby local government officials on behalf of old people's needs. Housing, medical care, tax relief, and the construction of senior centers are some of the issues dealt with. Many senior citizens have become highly politicized, recognizing that their power as a voting bloc is sufficiently strong to produce a sympathetic ear from many elected politicians. On the other hand, those who try to organize the elderly often find themselves frustrated. Maggie Kuhn has suggested that many old people "want to keep their lives as bland and as pleasant and as uncontroversial as possible. You don't talk about anything disagreeable" (Shapiro, 1982: 7). Certainly it is a common belief that old age should ideally be a happy time, free of significant worries, when a person can enjoy the fruits of toil well-earned during the earlier years. Organized efforts by the elderly to protest their common grievances hardly support such an image.

Over the past two decades, Canada has developed a national, government-financed program, which has encouraged elderly citizens to initiate projects for themselves and others. Since it began in 1972, the New Horizons program has helped establish 25,000 activities. At first efforts involved the development of social and recreational centers in towns or neighborhoods that previously had provided no place for the elderly to meet and do things. Senior citizens held bake sales, raffles, teas, and lotteries to raise a lot of the necessary funds.

In 1982 program officials began to encourage senior citizens to start community-service and mutual-help projects. One education center for the elderly began in two small classrooms and now enrolls over 1000 students. New Horizons sponsors leadership-training workshops, seniors' newspapers, and several national federations of seniors' groups. In one New Horizons report, it stated, "When they are not encumbered with society's prejudices, older people will continue to be active, creative, and productive members of their communities" (Novak, 1987: 353). Would it be desirable to establish a similar program in the United States?

As we move on to the disabled minorities and their problems, we see many parallels with the situation of elderly people.

The Emergence of the Disabled

There are about 36 million disabled Americans, and except for women they form the largest minority group (Meyerson, 1988). Disability is one minority status that shows no regard for age, race, sex, or class privilege. As one observer noted, "Anyone can become disabled. A skiing accident, a highway collision, a mistaken dose of medicine — it may take seconds or it may take years" (Bowe, 1978: viii).

In this section we examine the process of prejudice and discrimination encountered by the physically, mentally, and emotionally disabled. Then we look at the costs of being disabled and at the disability-rights movement.

"The disabled" is a large, diversified category of people that has existed in all societies across time and space (Scheer and Groce, 1988). The most general distinction is between those who are physically or mentally impaired, but within these two categories, there are often major differences in disability, lifestyle, and public response. With the space limitations of an introductory text, I can do little more than alert you to the complexity of the subject we are about to discuss.

Prejudice and Discrimination Encountered by the Disabled

There is no "ism" to describe the process, but the same steps that occur in the sexism and ageism processes occur for the disabled. In the first place, the disabled frequently have high social visibility. For physically disabled people, it can be dramatic. When a psychologist showed over a hundred students pictures of human faces lacking in noses or ears or partly caved in, they all expressed horror and disgust (Smith, 1973). In other cases social visibility is just as obvious but less startling — the physically disabled in wheelchairs, for instance.

Second, the disabled encounter a range of attributed characteristics that will vary with their disability. Like other minorities the disabled are generally considered both different and inferior. The stereotypes formed about the disabled frequently lack substantiating evidence. For instance, one woman who had been in a wheelchair ever since she had been hit by a car pointed out that often people falsely assumed she could not have sex (Bowe, 1978). This same assumption exists for other handicapped Americans. A frequent misperception about the disabled is that their central disability must be accompanied by other physical problems. Thus blind people often find that those addressing them will speak loudly, believing that they must also have a hearing problem. Many people readily classify physically handicapped people as mentally handicapped. In some situations a basis exists for such conclusions. Cerebral palsy and mental retardation are frequently present in the same person, and yet one does not cause the other — some cerebral palsied people are intellectually gifted, and many mentally handicapped people have no physical handicaps. It seems clear that accurate judgments about handicapped people require an evaluation of their individual characteristics and capabilities.

Third, a variety of rationalizations support prejudice and discrimination against the disabled. A number of studies indicate that people generally believe that they live in a "just universe." Given this condition, then why are some individuals suffering from serious handicaps? A number of people assume that one reason is that the disabled have done something wrong or that they are going to do something wrong. In short, the assumption goes, the disability represents a punishment for wrong-doing (Shaw and Skolnick, 1971). Another rationalization is that disabled people's problems are always inherited and of sufficient magnitude that little or nothing can be done to help them. Toward the end of the nineteenth and the beginning of the twentieth century, it was widely believed that mental retardation was an inherited condition that was largely responsible for crime, delinquency, vagrancy, poverty, and immorality. The so-called experts felt that it would be a waste of resources to allocate funds for training schools for mentally handicapped to improve their mental and physical functioning. Instead they were placed in institutions, where they received no more than custodial care (Katz, 1973).

Fourth, like other minorities, the disabled accommodate to the expectations or desires of the majority. The blind, for instance, frequently recognize that they are likely to receive greater acceptance if they consider the visual dimension when dealing with sighted people. Thus they learn to face others when talking to them instead of just turning an ear to the sound of their voice. Or they will teach themselves automatic use of such phrases as "I see" or "It looks like . . . " (Bowe, 1978: 51). One study of individuals with rheumatoid arthritis indicated that there was frequent "covering up," hiding the disability from others, and also "keeping up," pushing themselves to perform as if they were not suffering from the pain and swelling that interferes with normal activity (Wiener, 1975).

Finally the disabled encounter a range of discriminations: attitudinal, architectural, educa-tional, residential, occupational, and transportational. Perhaps U.S. society is less aware of and has taken fewer steps to confront discriminations toward the disabled than those toward other major minority groups.

The prejudice and discrimination process endured by the disabled thus involves the same five steps as sexism and ageism. Table 11.2 summarizes the three processes.

Costs

The prejudice and discrimination suffered by the disabled inevitably carry some heavy costs. We

Table 11.2
Prejudice and Discrimination against Emerging Minorities

COMPONENTS	SEXISM	AGEISM	PREJUDICE AND DISCRIMINATION AGAINST THE DISABLED
High social visibility	Secondary sex characteristics and distinctive clothing	Aging appearance — wrinkled skin, white hair, or stooped walk	Detectable physical disabilities or deformities
Attributed traits of inferiority	Less intelligent than men; irresponsible, inconsistent, and unstable	Images of passivity, dependency, rigidity, senility, and inefficiency	Unsubstantiated convictions, such as the widespread suspicion that blind people also have hearing problems
Rationalization of status	"Women's place is in the home"	Claims that the elderly are "happy disengagers"	Belief that handicaps are a punishment for wrong-doing or are so incapacitating that little or nothing can be done to help
Accommodating behavioral patterns	Hiding intelligence or acting helpless	Graceful acceptance of retirement in spite of deep-seated reluctance	Blind people's facing sighted speakers during conversations and using visually oriented phrases
Discriminations	In education, occupation, and political activity	In health care or in control over one's destiny	In attitudes, architecture, education, housing, occupation, and transportation

Adapted in part from Helen Mayer Hacker. "Women As a Minority Group." *Social Forces.* V. 30. October 1951, pp. 60–69.

consider three types of costs — the psychological, the physical, and the occupational.

PSYCHOLOGICAL COST   A labeling process often occurs with disabilities. For instance, a child not doing well in school receives a battery of diagnostic tests that educators themselves are likely to consider inadequate. If a disability is "discovered," then the officials involved can sigh with relief as they conclude, "No wonder Susie wasn't learning. She is learning-disabled." With the label placed, the school is now off the hook for the child's inability to learn. For the child, however, the problems are just starting. Once applied, labels are difficult to remove, even when observers demonstrate they are inappropriate. There are several reasons why. First, labels are concise designations that justify an organization or activity. "He wouldn't be in this mental hospital, would he, unless he were crazy as a loon?" Another reason labels remain is that they are self-fulfilling. A child is labeled "mildly retarded" and then receives less instruction to insure that she or he is not unduly burdened. When this child learns less than others who have been pushed harder, she or he "confirms" the original diagnosis (Bowe, 1978: 139).

Perhaps the most devastating psychological effect of disability for many people is the expectation of powerlessness they encounter. Those working on behalf of the rights of the disabled stress that many, perhaps most Americans believe that handicapped people are generally powerless to do anything significant for themselves — that being disabled means that an individual invariably must be helped and given social support (Fine and Asch, 1988). Sometimes highly publicized efforts to assist the handicapped receive such criticism. For instance, an organizer working to improve disabled people's civil rights made the following comment about the annual cerebral palsy telethon: "It's absolutely degrading. Watching those telethons one might think that all palsied adults are mentally retarded, pathetically trusting, asexual children" (Gliedman, 1979: 60).

Powerlessness is one debilitating condition the disabled have thrust upon them. They also frequently encounter another negative situation — isolation and aloneness. Many disabled people live an existence that sharply contrasts with that of other minorities. Ethnic groups, women, and the elderly can usually find others who share their experiences and problems, but people with major deformities, injuries, or other disabilities often have nobody nearby experiencing their same fate. In fact, the disabled often seek to avoid such a sense of community. Most of them view their minority status as more distinctly abnormal and undesirable than other groups view their respective minority statuses. A study of people with skin disease found that many reported shame and embarrassment and made largely unsuccessful efforts to hide evidence of their disease (Jowett and Ryan, 1985). And a little person said, "Didn't all of us, at the beginning, avoid little people because we didn't want to be identified with them? I didn't want to admit that I was little, too" (Smith, 1973: 125).

When we consider the problems and prejudices many disabled people must face, the following Social Application is instructive.

SOCIAL APPLICATION

The One-Handed Major-League Pitcher

In the spring of 1989, the weekly magazine *Baseball America* listed Jim Abbott second to Jackie Robinson as an "impact rookie" — a first-year player who would have a lasting effect on the game. In 1947 Robinson was the first black player to join major-league baseball. In 1989 Abbott was the first player with only one arm to play at the major-league level. Since Robinson there have been thousands of black ball players, but it is unlikely that a steady stream of disabled individuals will make major-league teams. Nonetheless, inspired by Abbott, others might try.

In the three months after he started spring training, Abbott received thousands of fan letters, many from children with only one arm or some other physical disability. The Angels' public-relations department always has helped Abbott answer the cards and letters; whenever there was a letter from someone with a disability, Abbott said what he wanted written and someone typed it for him. The public relations director said that Abbott "likes to say, 'Your handicap is a handicap only in the eyes of others.'"

In 1989 the Angels got off to a surprisingly good start, and Abbott's presence and personality were given con-

siderable credit. Teammates felt ashamed using alibis for mistakes when they had a one-armed teammate who, after he pitched, made a split-second switch of his glove from the stump that was his right hand to his left hand, in case the ball were to be hit back to him. Following a game in which Abbott pitched a four-hit shutout of the Boston Red Sox and defeated Roger Clemens, the two-time Cy Young Award winner (for pitcher-of-the-year honors), teammates cre-

ated a carpet of towels leading to his locker.

For Jim Abbott, however, the most emotional moment seemed to be when he won his first game, pitching six innings, giving up only four hits, and defeating the Baltimore Orioles 3 to 2. In his typical, low-key style, Abbott called his parents and brother in Flint, Michigan, and when they got on the phone all he said in a subdued voice was "I won." It was a special moment.

Source: Dave Anderson. "How Abbott Has Changed Baseball." *New York Times.* May 25, 1989, p. D23.

PHYSICAL COST Seriously disabled people, those in wheelchairs for example, frequently encounter both architectural and transportation barriers. Most buildings can be entered only after people climb steps or pass through narrow doorways. These buildings are inaccessible to people in wheelchairs.

Even though an increasing number of buildings are now constructed with accessibility in mind, no effective national policy controls either architectural or transportation barriers (Poister, 1982). This deficiency makes physical movement arduous for disabled people. They often find it difficult or impossible to enter buildings, and barriers are a major concern when planning trips, especially for people in wheelchairs. Are there any steps at the airline terminal? And what about the hotel? The management has assured a handicapped woman that she will be able to reach her fourth-floor room, but she knows that the building is old. So there are inevitable questions about the width of doors and accessibility to the elevator, not to mention that other everpresent problem: steps.

Some cities are becoming more receptive to the physical needs of disabled people. Atlanta is one, and Berkeley, California, is another. Two-thirds of the Berkeley intersections have either wheelchair ramps or curb cuts. In addition, the Bay Area Rapid Transit System, a modern bus and subway complex that connects Berkeley and San Francisco, is fully accessible to people in wheelchairs.

In addition, all buildings constructed in the last ten years are also accessible, and even the automated tellers at local banks are built at wheelchair height. One disabled resident explained, "It's easy to forget you're in a wheelchair here . . . But in most small towns where the disabled aren't as prevalent, it's not the same story" (Langway, 1982: 84).

OCCUPATIONAL COST A variety of barriers combine to produce an adverse effect on the work lives of many disabled people. Segregated and inferior schooling deprive millions of disabled people of the preparation they need to compete for well-paying jobs. Architectural barriers at job sites may deny entrance to the disabled. Transportation limitations may make it impossible to commute to and from work each day without paying exorbitant taxi fees. Employers' or prospective employers' attitudes can also be a problem. Many will resist hiring the disabled, mistakenly believing that they will be absent more often and generally prove less reliable. An experiment concluded that physically disabled people received a lower evaluation than nondisabled individuals for comparable task performances (Russell et al., 1985).

For the disabled the chance to work can provide an opportunity to attain considerable personal satisfaction, daily stimulation and challenge, ongoing contacts with a variety of people, and a sense of supporting oneself. By contrast, enforced idleness means the absence of all these opportunities, and it is a condition that readily stimulates self-hate and disgust (Bowe, 1978; Langway, 1982).

For some employed disabled people, the working situation can become almost intolerable once fellow workers are called upon to help them in a difficult situation involving their disability. If an epileptic has a seizure at work, other employees sometimes become overly watchful and wary in the future. One woman explained,

> You get to feel like a little baby after a while and you don't get treated the same. Every once in a while you'll see somebody coming in like to go to the bathroom on my floor when there's one on their floor . . . In a way it makes you feel kind of bad you can't operate on your own two feet.
>
> (Schneider, 1988: 73)

The present situation in which the disabled of America find themselves is not a particularly positive one. Analyzing the disability-rights movement, however, we see that there is now a tradition of working for disabled people's rights.

The Disability-Rights Movement

The first two American organizations concerned with the rights of disabled people developed between the two world wars, and each was involved with a specific category of people. The Disabled American Veterans was primarily seeking to expand government benefits for disabled veterans. The National Federation of the Blind became a militant supporter for blind people's rights, not only lobbying for some of the early civil-rights laws guaranteeing access to different facilities regardless of disability, but also establishing the use of the white cane and guide dogs. In the twenty years after World War II, major organizations for disabled people included the Paralyzed Veterans of America, the National Association of the Deaf, and the American Council of the Blind.

In the 1960s several factors converged to change many disabled people's prospects. First, medical and rehabilitative advances now made it possible for many individuals, such as polio victims of the last epidemics in the 1950s, to be much more active members of society than they could

Like this woman, who was paralyzed by spinal damage and uses a wand to punch computer keys, many disabled people must make much greater efforts than their able-bodied peers to perform effectively on the job.

have been in the past. Second, the social atmosphere was altering. Most middle-class children growing up in the 1950s and 1960s had parents who stressed self-confidence and achievement more strongly than counterparts a generation earlier, in many cases even if the children were disabled. Then came the protest years, featuring blacks' civil rights, opposition to the Vietnam War, and the assertion of women's rights. Some disabled people, who were veterans of other protests, began to visualize the need to respond to their disabilities in an equally militant way.

By the early 1970s, there were many local organizations seeking to improve disabled people's rights, but no coordinated effort to influence public policy existed. Then in 1974 the American Coalition of Citizens with Disabilities formed for that purpose. Increasingly the coalition and other organizations in the developing disability-rights movement became focused on the federal government.

During the 1970s the federal government helped the disability-rights movement in several ways. First, government became a major source of funding. Second, government programs helped the disability-rights movement organize itself more effectively, providing contracts for training and technical assistance and frequently seeking out disability-rights leaders for consultation, not only improving communication between the two camps but also facilitating lobbying activities. Finally during the 1970s, legislation established disabled people as a class of people whose rights were protected by federal laws and whose exclusion from federally financed programs and activities became illegal.

In some respects the 1980s was a less optimistic decade than its predecessor. The Reagan administration replaced a number of officials who had worked constructively with disability-rights organizations, and the federal government became more inclined to restrict disabled people's rights and diminish their funding than to support their efforts (Scotch, 1988).

What role will the federal government take toward the disability-rights movement in the future? At this writing there seems to be limited basis for optimism. Local disability-rights organizations probably will not be able to rely on significant federal-government support, but the fact that a tradition supporting disability rights has been established should help these organizations obtain resources and extend their social movement.

STUDY GUIDE

Learning Objectives

After studying this chapter, you should be able to:

1. Define sexism and summarize the five steps in the process.
2. Discuss the psychological, career, and physical costs of sexism.
3. Examine the modern women's movement and the future of women's rights.
4. Define ageism and summarize the five steps in the process.
5. Analyze the following effects of ageism — health and medical-care cost, group-involvement cost, and the cost of losing control over one's destiny.
6. Describe the strategies elderly people pursue to feel useful and satisfied.
7. Summarize the five steps in the process of prejudice and discrimination encountered by the disabled.
8. Examine the psychological, physical, and occupational costs of prejudice and discrimination suffered by the disabled.
9. Discuss the development of a disability-rights movement.

Summary

1. Women, the elderly, and the disabled are three prominent, emerging minorities. A similar process of prejudice and discrimination affects all three groups.

2. Sexism is an ideology emphasizing that actual or alleged differences between men and women establish the superiority of men. Sexism is a rationalization for political, economic, and social discrimination against women. In American society sexism has received extensive support. The sexist ideology has also produced a variety of costs. Psychological costs include the widespread belief that women possess a smaller quantity than men of the qualities considered desirable for a person. In addition, the media have traditionally presented a narrow, stereotyped image of women. Women have also suffered career costs. It has been widely believed that women can be fulfilled in the homemaker role, and yet it is clear that this often is not the case. Women in the work force have been less successful than men. Research shows that socialization patterns are one source of women's

disadvantage. Pay differences result from outright discrimination and the differing distribution of men and women into occupations. Women also encounter a variety of physical costs. Physical violence experienced by women ranges from "street hassling" to rape and physical abuse. Trends that appear among the violent acts against women include nonreporting, the failure to take the reports of violence seriously, and the tendency to blame the victim herself for the occurrence of the act.

In response to sexism, a modern women's movement has developed. Like earlier efforts by women to develop consciousness or to start a women's movement, the modern movement seems to be an outgrowth of the era in which it developed. The National Organization for Women (NOW) represents one source from which the modern women's movement originated. Another has been local women's groups that emerged from the 1960s civil-rights and anti-war movements.

How will women maximize their rights as individuals and at the same time associate with men? We discussed this question as we considered the future of women's rights.

3. Like women, the elderly are frequently victims of modern society. Ageism is an ideology emphasizing the superiority of the young over the old. Like sexism, ageism is a process that receives extensive support in daily life. One cost of ageism is health, which is adversely affected by the medical care some senior citizens receive. Another cost for some aging Americans involves the restricted organizational activity they experience. In addition, many senior citizens feel a limited control over their destiny. This sense of powerlessness appears quite frequently when old Americans face relocation, especially relocation to a nursing home.

We can speculate about the future of the elderly in America. One significant question to ponder is whether or not a strong political movement of the elderly will develop. At present mixed indications exist.

4. The 36 million disabled Americans often face prejudice and discrimination similar to that encountered by women and the elderly. In fact, the same steps that occur in sexism and ageism also occur for the disabled. Not surprisingly the costs of prejudice and discrimination are also similar. Psychological costs include the destructive effect of labeling. Unlike women and the elderly, disabled people who would like to share experiences with others suffering the same minority status often find it more difficult to locate such people or receive less cultural support for seeking out those with a shared experience. The physical costs of being disabled include limited access to buildings and to transportation. No systematic national policies exist in either area, making it difficult for wheelchair-bound people to be mobile. The occupational costs encountered by disabled Americans are the result of a variety of barriers—educational, architectural, transportational, and attitudinal.

Over the past couple of decades, a disability-rights movement has developed. At present this movement lacks the strong government support that it received in the 1970s.

Key Terms

ageism   an ideology asserting the superiority of the young over the old. Ageism is a rationalization for political, economic, and social discrimination against the elderly

disengagement   a process of mutual withdrawal involving decreasing interaction between an elderly person and others in the social system to which he or she belongs

sexism   an ideology emphasizing that actual or alleged differences between men and women establish the superiority of men. Sexism is a rationalization for political, economic, and social discrimination against women

Tests

True – false Test

_____ 1. In the 1980s sexism is no longer an ideology.

_____ 2. A recent study indicated that in television commercials women now serve as half the narrators.

_____ 3. For whites to achieve occupational balance by sex, 61 percent of either women or men would need to change jobs.

_____ 4. Women's recognition of their subordination expanded during periods stressing the importance of new ideas and influences, especially individual rights.

_____ 5. Like sexism, ageism could not occur without high social visibility.

_____ 6. Research has revealed that when urban elderly are involved in social networks of neighbors, friends, or kin, they tend to be less healthy than old people without such networks.

_____ 7. There are about 36 million disabled Americans.

_____ 8. One reason that labels on the disabled are hard to remove is that they are self-fulfilling.

_____ 9. An experiment found that physically disabled and nondisabled individuals received similar evaluations for comparable task performances.

_____ 10. During the 1970s the federal government severely restricted its earlier support of the disability-rights movement.

Multiple-choice Test

_____ 1. Which statement about sexism is true?
   a. Women's ability to perform, not their intelligence, has been questioned.
   b. In American society women have traditionally encountered more limitations on education than men.
   c. There are no rationalizations about women's traditional status.
   d. Women are the only minority group without social visibility.

_____ 2. A study found that when women suffered depression:
   a. they were too committed to personal success.
   b. the positive qualities of women's traditional roles were absent from their lives.
   c. they suffered from commitment to too many roles.
   d. the positive qualities of both men's and women's traditional roles were absent from their lives.

_____ 3. Margaret Hennig and Anne Jardim studied female presidents and vice-presidents of business firms and found that their achievement differences seemed to be produced by:
   a. family dynamics.
   b. work experience.
   c. training.
   d. social visibility.

_____ 4. The National Organization for Women:
   a. was organized by the more traditional, older segment of the modern women's movement.
   b. was developed by the younger, more radical section of the modern women's movement.
   c. still maintains close relations with different communist groups.
   d. is primarily concerned with developing the ideology of woman-serving-her-family.

_____ 5. Which statement is true of the elderly?
   a. They have low social visibility.
   b. They have negative qualities attributed to them.
   c. Disengagement no longer occurs.
   d. Most Americans will face mandatory retirement for the next couple of decades.

_____ 6. Compared with black female elderly, white female elderly are more inclined to:
   a. use prayer.
   b. use nonprescription drugs.
   c. have weak support from friends.
   d. a and b

_____ 7. Which of the following is a situation likely to threaten the elderly's sense of controlling their destiny?
   a. loss of the ability to vote
   b. religious conversion
   c. relocation
   d. sexual activity

_____ 8. Prejudice and discrimination against the disabled are supported by the rationalization that:
   a. their disabilities represent punishment for wrong-doing.
   b. there are not enough jobs for everyone.
   c. society cannot afford the cost of all the environmental modifications they need.
   d. they are being cared for effectively enough by the welfare system.

_____ 9. When fellow workers are called upon to help disabled people in a difficult situation involving the disability:
   a. relations between the disabled person and fellow workers usually improve.
   b. other employees may become overly watchful and wary.
   c. the disabled person is likely to be fired.
   d. there is no significant impact.

_____ 10. A city that has made impressive physical adjustments to meet the needs of the physically disabled is:
   a. Rome (Italy).
   b. New York City.
   c. New Delhi (India).
   d. Berkeley (California).

Essay Test

1. Define sexism and discuss the steps in the process, offering illustrations at each stage.
2. Discuss in detail three costs of sexism.
3. On what issue(s) is women's struggle for rights likely to focus in the future?

4. What is ageism? Discuss and illustrate stages in the process of ageism.
5. Discuss several significant costs of ageism.
6. Examine and illustrate the steps in the process of prejudice and discrimination against the disabled.
7. Describe the principal costs encountered by disabled Americans.
8. Discuss different ways that the disabled can confront and overcome their powerlessness.

Suggested Readings

Bowe, Frank. 1978. *Handicapping America*. New York: Harper & Row. A book for a general audience, describing the state of affairs for disabled people in modern America. The author, who is deaf, is a leading authority on and advocate for disabled people.

Cox, Harold G. 1988. *Later Life: The Realities of Aging*. Englewood Cliffs, NJ: Prentice-Hall. A highly detailed introduction to the study of aging, featuring current research in the social and biological sciences.

Cruzic, Kathleen. 1982. *Disabled? Yes. Defeated? No*. Englewood Cliffs, NJ: Prentice-Hall. A nurse's detailed account of the various resources available for the disabled, their families, friends, and therapists. The book's sixteen chapters offer detailed information on such issues as shortcuts in the kitchen, pursuit of new careers, tips for traveling, and aids for recreation.

Cumming, Elaine, and William Henry. 1961. *Growing Old: The Process of Disengagement*. New York: Basic Books. The study from which the disengagement theory originated. This work provides a look in depth at the development of this well-known, highly controversial perspective.

Fine, Michelle, and Adrienne Asch (eds.). 1988. *Journal of Social Issues*. Special issue on disability, with articles providing important historical information and recent research findings.

Foner, Anne. 1986. *Aging and Old Age*. Englewood Cliffs, NJ: Prentice-Hall. A concise, informative, wide-ranging, and up-to-date discussion of old age in modern society.

Friedan, Betty. 1963. *The Feminine Mystique*. New York: W. W. Norton and Company. The widely read treatise that helped initiate the modern women's movement in U.S. society. As you read this book, pretend that you are a woman of nearly three decades ago discovering suddenly that someone has articulated the feelings of confusion, uneasiness, and anger you experienced as a homemaker and mother.

Friedan, Betty. 1981. *The Second Stage*. New York: Summit Books. Friedan's thoughtful commentary on contemporary women's plight—seeking to fill both career, and wife and mother roles.

Hess, Beth B., and Myra Marx Ferree (eds.). 1987. *Analyzing Gender: A Handbook of Social Science Research*. Newbury Park, CA: Sage. A variety of feminist perspectives in the social sciences, featuring articles divided into sections involving gender and ideology, social control of female sexuality, gender stratification, and gender and the state.

Kahn-Hut, Rachel, Arlene Kaplan Daniels, and Richard Colvard (eds.). 1982. *Women and Work*. New York: Oxford University Press. A set of readings examining the effects produced at home and outside of it by growing numbers of women entering the work force.

Kesey, Ken. 1962. *One Flew over the Cuckoo's Nest*. New York: Signet Books. A chilling look at the alienated life of men living in the ward of a mental hospital. Kesey's novel makes it painfully clear how the process of controlling people's thoughts and actions is successfully conducted in this setting.

Murphy, Robert F. 1987. *The Body Silent*. New York: Henry Holt and Company. An anthropologist's detailed, highly insightful account of an anthropological experience he was compelled to witness — the transformation produced by a tumor in the spinal column changing him from a seemingly healthy individual in 1972 to a quadriplegic in 1986.

Stone, Deborah A. 1984. *The Disabled State*. Philadelphia: Temple University Press. An original, provocative analysis of the development of western nations' political definitions of disability.

Walker, Lenore E. 1984. *The Battered-Woman Syndrome*. New York: Springer. A detailed study of 435 battered women, examining their personalities and their inability to control the violence against them.

Additional Assignments

1. Find ten people, preferably five women and five men. Ask them to rank the following occupations from 1 (most prestigious) to 12 (least prestigious). How much agreement did you find regarding the prestige of each occupation? Did men and women rank them differently? Compare findings with other class members, and relate the trends you discover to information in this chapter, indicating, in particular, how much the sex typing of occupations appeared to affect rankings.

   The occupations

1.	Flight attendant	7.	Househusband
2.	Housewife	8.	Photographer
3.	Truck driver	9.	Doctor
4.	Waiter	10.	Waitress
5.	Fashion model	11.	Nurse
6.	Steward	12.	School-bus driver

   (Note: Occupations 2 and 10 are considered female occupations; occupations 4, 6, and 7 are considered male occupations. All other positions could have either male or female job holders, but we culturally identify women with occupations 1, 5, and 11 and men with 3, 8, and 9.)

2. Imagine yourself having a significant disability — being legally blind, wheelchair-bound, or hearing-impaired. Over a two-day period, keep a record of what you discover regarding the physical facilities you use on campus, such as stairs and doors. What conclusions can you draw about your ability as a disabled person to participate in campus activities? How could your school make improvements to assist disabled students?

Answers to Objective Test Questions

True–false Test

1. f	4. t	7. t	9. f
2. f	5. t	8. t	10. f
3. t	6. f		

Multiple-choice Test

1. b	4. a	7. c	9. b
2. d	5. b	8. a	10. d
3. a	6. c		

PART

The Institutions of American Society

12
FAMILY AND ALTERNATIVE LIFESTYLES

Selected Features of the Family

Some Functions of the Family
Kinship Terms

The Modern American Nuclear Family

Industrialization and the Nuclear Family
Declining Functions of the Nuclear Family

Changing Patterns of Love, Courtship, and Marriage

Living Together
Choice of Partners
Changing Marital Patterns

Divorce, Remarriage, and Alternatives to Marriage

Marital Failure
Remarriage
Alternatives to Conventional Marriage
Conclusion

Study Guide

On November 7, 1989, Diego Maradona and Claudia Villafañe were married in the enormous Luna Park arena in downtown Buenos Aires, Argentina. Maradona, widely considered the best soccer player in the world, flew more than two hundred teammates, former teammates, and friends to Buenos Aires from Italy, where he currently plays, and Spain, where he formerly played, on a chartered Boeing 747. He put up his friends in three of the best hotels in town. Maradona's management firm distributed an eight-page, full-color pamphlet containing details of the wedding, the food, and the clothing, including a description of the bride's floor-length dress of lace encrusted with over fifteen pounds of pearls and a train about ten feet long.

There is nothing rare about lavish weddings in the Western world. What made this wedding unusual was the circumstances that initiated it. Villafañe and Maradona, who have been together for at least twelve years, have two daughters. One day the older, who at the time was two-and-a-half, asked her parents to see their wedding photos. Not being able to comply with the request, Maradona and Villafañe decided to formalize their longtime relationship in both Roman Catholic and civil ceremonies.

At the top of the engraved wedding invitations were the daughters' names. It was stated that they and their grandparents invited the recipients to the marriage of their parents. Villafañe's father told a television interviewer that the family had been expecting this event for fourteen years. Other versions indicated that the romance had begun twelve years earlier on a dance floor (Christian, 1989).

In both the United States and many other countries, people are struggling with the traditional standards of marriage and the family. What is the best way to live? Sometimes, like Villafañe and Maradona, circumstances encourage an abrupt shift — in this instance seeking both religious and civil recognition for a family that already existed without these formal sanctions.

A **family** is traditionally defined as a social unit composed of two or more people who live together and are related by blood, marriage, or adoption. In the United States, the **nuclear family** has been the dominant form. This is a two-generation family that includes a father, a mother, and their children living separately from other relatives. In many other societies, however, the **extended family**, involving two or more generations of people related by blood and living together or close to each other, plays a more important role. The extended family has prevailed in rural settings. As societies have become increasingly industrialized and urbanized, however, the nuclear family has assumed a larger role.

The first section of this chapter discusses the functions of the family and also kinship terms. Next we analyze the development of the modern American nuclear family. The chapter then considers changing patterns of love, courtship, and marriage and closes with a look at divorce, remarriage, and contemporary alternatives to marriage.

Selected Features of the Family

In this section we examine functions of the family and also kinship terms. It becomes apparent that families share these features, even though the features often differ historically and cross-culturally.

Some Functions of the Family

Throughout human history families have provided basic food and shelter and emotional comfort for their members. They have also supplied status placement; Americans' sense of their location in the social-class system is provided by their family membership. In addition, families are the groups that are supposed to engage in reproduction, thereby supplying new citizens for the society. Families also perform the three functions we examine cross-culturally in this section: sexual regulation, economic activity, and socialization.

Sexual Regulation

People are likely to become nervous when contemplating the prospect of extreme sexual promiscuity. Most of us could not cope effectively with a society in which everyone was permitted to have sexual intercourse with everyone else. The universality of incest taboos demonstrates the importance that all cultures place on keeping sexual activity carefully controlled and limited.

THE INCEST TABOO   An **incest taboo** is a rule outlawing sexual relations between kin-group members believed to be too closely related as defined by the cultural standards of a given society. In all known societies, the incest taboo normally restricts marital relations within the nuclear family to the husband and wife. Throughout history the incest taboo has served several important functions. First, the rule eliminates the conflicts and jealousy that would result if there were sexual rivalry among members of the nuclear family. The taboo, in short, helps maximize cooperation within the family unit. Second, the incest taboo forces people to marry outside their own nuclear families, thus reducing isolation and encouraging families to cooperate with one another. These marital alliances increase the possibility that families will share inventions and discoveries, work together in the procurement or production of food and other valued commodities, and engage in mutual protection against enemies. Third, the taboo helps keep the roles of family members clearly defined. Without the incest taboo, a single individual could be simultaneously a wife and a daughter, or a brother and a husband, and so on. If this occurred, authority within the family would become confused, and the continued existence of the nuclear family as a functioning social unit would be seriously threatened (Murdock, 1949: 295–297). Given the fundamental importance of the family within societies and the critical part that

Extended families, like this one from the Aboure tribe on the Ivory Coast, remain the norm in many societies.

the incest taboo plays in maintaining the family, it is not surprising that the taboo exists universally.

Economic Activity

To be reputable members of a society or sometimes simply to survive, people must work. Often work has been gender-related. How often do we hear the phrase "That's women's work" or "That's a man's job"? These clichés reflect traditional gender-role definitions presently under heavy attack by many modern women and men. If we consider societies other than that of the United States, we will see that there are no tasks consistently categorized as "male" or "female" across cultures. For example, societies have existed where women were the warriors and others where men prepared the food. Societies have even existed in which men have "recovered" from childbirth while their wives went back to work. Although men's and women's family tasks often differ widely from one society to another, they all have gender-linked tasks. They also have age-linked tasks. Because of the complexity or danger associated with some important tasks, children must reach a certain level of growth before being allowed to undertake them. Hunting, warfare, and the manufacture of many intricate or important objects provide good examples.

330

In modern societies families generally no longer produce food, clothes, housing, and other basic subsistence items. Instead men and women work for organizations and buy with the money they earn the essential items formerly produced by the united activity of the family unit. As people become increasingly integrated into a modern industrial setting, they tend to break away from extended families, where the function of economic production is often important, and to reside in nuclear family units (Handwerker, 1973). As we see, the nuclear family is especially compatible with a modern, industrial setting.

Socialization

Social norms compel parents to provide socialization for their children, whether or not they wish to do so. However, within a given culture, socialization patterns often vary considerably (Leighton, 1984).

There are many different patterns of socialization cross-culturally. For example, anthropologist Margaret Mead (1963: 40–41) noted that women in Bali hold their children in a looser and more relaxed manner than do American parents. Mead suspected that because of this manner of being held, Balinese children retain much greater physical flexibility than do American children.

Research has also suggested that personality differences can be attributed in part to variations in socialization practices. Beatrice Whiting and John Whiting (1975: 172–185) studied the typical socialization patterns in six cultures; five were non-American and agricultural and one American, specifically a New England town. The children in two of the traditional societies tended to have unsociable, aggressive, and authoritarian (rigid, conformity-oriented, and excessively obedient to authority) personalities, while the children in the New England town were relatively sociable and less aggressive. The children with aggressive, authoritarian personalities came from societies with extended families in which an adult male was the most powerful individual. With many relatives living together, often amid numerous conflicting interests, family interaction tended to be controlled by clear, sharp commands from the dominant male. By contrast, a much more casual, intimate set-up is possible in the nuclear family characteristic of American towns, and this pattern

is similarly reflected in the American children's personalities. The Whitings concluded that by the age of six, children have assimilated the respective values of their cultures, and their personality structures are basically established.

A study of eighty-two families concluded that parents and children attributed to each other greater similarity in values than they actually possessed (Whitbeck and Gecas, 1988). Perhaps this inaccurate perception is a carry-over from preindustrial times when parents and children shared greater experience and probably maintained more value similarity than at present.

In modern times socialization has been partially usurped from the family by the government and other structures. In the Soviet Union and the People's Republic of China, for example, children generally spend most of the day in a collective setting. Similarly the increase in the number of working mothers within U.S. society has meant that day-care facilities for infants and young children have been rapidly expanding. In the kibbutzim (collective settlements) scattered throughout Israel, communal living is emphasized; socialization is a communal enterprise with children of the same age living together entirely apart from their parents. Although the members of one kibbutz told a researcher that they were deliberately attempting to undermine the nuclear-family structure, ties between parents and children remained strong. Families came together two hours a day and also on Saturdays and holidays. An observer wrote, "The eagerness of parents to see their children is equalled only by the eagerness of the children to see their parents" (Spiro, 1970: 125).

Kinship Terms

A **kinship system** is a number of people related by common descent, marriage, or adoption. Cross-culturally kinship systems have several types of marriage, customs for marriage eligibility, residential rules for newly married couples, and patterns of power within the family.

Types of Marriage

Polygamy is a marriage practice in which a person has two or more spouses of the other sex. **Polygyny** is the form of polygamy in which a man

This photo shows a polygynous family living in the Northern Cameroons, in western Africa. Not all of this man's twelve wives and numerous children appear here.

has two or more wives. **Polyandry** is the form of polygamy in which a woman has two or more husbands. **Monogamy** is a marriage practice in which there is one husband and one wife. In the United States, polygamy is illegal. About 90 percent of societies permit some form of polygamy, but it is not widely practiced because of the cost of maintaining two or more households. Polygyny is a much more common form of polygamy than polyandry. Because there is a higher death rate among male infants and men's life expectancy is shorter, there are fewer men in most societies than women. When polyandry does occur, it is because some practice creates an artificial scarcity of women; for example, the Todas of India used to drown some of their newborn infant girls.

Customs for Marriage Eligibility

Endogamy is a custom requiring a person to marry within a specific social unit, such as a kinship group, religious organization, or social class. **Exogamy** is a custom compelling someone to marry outside a specific social unit. In the United States, most marriages involve individuals similar in social-class background, religion, and race. All states have laws prohibiting marriage between members of the immediate family as well as between first cousins; some states will not permit second cousins to marry. Other societies also impose endogamous and exogamous standards. In some traditional societies, endogamy helps strengthen a kinship group or community; thus people who refuse to obey this standard and marry within a particular unit are likely to suffer strong penalties.

Residential Rules for Newly Married People

Matrilocal residence involves settling with or near the wife's parents. **Patrilocal** residence requires settling with or near the husband's parents. **Neolocal** residence occurs when married people establish an independent place to live. The respective roles that men and women play in the society largely determine the residential patterns. Therefore, if men within a particular society have an especially important role in obtaining food, then a patrilocal residential pattern is likely to exist. This is even more likely if men own property that can be accumulated and if males are the heads of elaborate political systems. On the other hand, if women have the dominant role in the procurement of food and if the political organization is relatively simple, then matrilocal residence is likely to take place. Neolocal residence generally occurs in societies in which the nuclear family is economically independent. In the United States, where many people must be free to move where they can find jobs, neolocal residence predominates.

Patterns of Power within the Family

A **patriarchal** family is a family in which the husband–father is the formal head and the abso-

lute or nearly absolute source of power. A **matriarchal** family is a family in which the wife–mother is the formal head and the absolute or nearly absolute source of power. An **egalitarian** family is a family in which the wife–mother and husband–father share power and also permit their children to participate in the family decisions. In most societies the husband–father usually had the final say in most important matters. No societies qualify as true matriarchies. American families have traditionally been patriarchal, but a gradual movement toward the egalitarian form has been encouraged by women's steadily improving educational and occupational status in the society at large.

The Modern American Nuclear Family

The American nuclear family is fairly egalitarian, with neolocal residence and a monogamous marriage pattern. The dominant form is nuclear. In this section we consider how industrialization has encouraged the development of the nuclear family type and also examine the declining functions of the American nuclear family.

Industrialization and the Nuclear Family

Sociologist William Goode (1963) suggested that the industrial era has encouraged people to discard the extended family and live exclusively in the nuclear family. What specific features of industrialization have prompted such a shift?

The increased need for physical movement from one specific location to another is one factor. In an industrial setting, it is impractical to move an entire extended family in order to allow one person to take a desirable new job.

In addition, social mobility, prevalent in industrial societies, plays an important role. An emphasis on upward social mobility has supported the development of the nuclear family, which is relatively small and flexible and allows people to conform their lifestyles, dress, and speech to the standards of the successful mainstream without encountering extensive criticism from kin. Such adjustments can help people get jobs (or better

jobs) in an industrial context, thereby contributing to their advancement. Recall our discussion of social mobility in Chapter 9, "Social Stratification."

Third, a member of an extended family normally has time-consuming domestic obligations toward a variety of kin. For an individual to perform effectively in an industrial setting, these obligations need to be severely limited, and the isolated nuclear family radically reduces kinship obligations.

Finally industrial society requires a family that, like the nuclear family, can afford to support children during a lengthy period of education or training provided by such social organizations as schools, corporations, and the military. In the extended family, children were expected to begin making an economic contribution to the family's upkeep soon after they started walking; for the most part, children in these families received no formal education at all.

Thus, Goode declared, industry has streamlined the family. He has also noted that the relationship between the two structures has not always been smooth and harmonious (Goode, 1982: 181). Sociologist Richard Sennett (1974) has developed the last point, suggesting that the nuclear family type may be less supportive of its members' emotional and occupational growth than the extended family. He found that men living in nuclear families when they immigrated to Chicago in the late nineteenth century tended to be less occupationally successful than men who had also recently moved to the city but were still living in extended families. Sennett suspected that the latter group of men viewed their nuclear families as protection against the new and alien urban social life. These men were, in fact, quite isolated. There were no adult males with whom they could readily discuss their fears and aspirations. Such men tended to view their work defensively; they generally accepted modest positions and held on to them. Furthermore they passed the same introverted, self-protective attitudes on to their sons.

On the other hand, when male members of extended families arrived in Chicago, they tended to react to the city much less defensively because their family was more active and supportive. Work was frequently discussed with other men in the household, and sometimes friendly competition for jobs and occupational advancement would develop among them. The sons in extended families not only had a more optimistic, less tension-laden outlook on work but also tended to be more successful than their counterparts in nuclear families (Sennett, 1974).

Modern people often recognize the assets of extended families. A study conducted in a small city found that more than half the adults in a randomly selected sample indicated that among their relatives there was someone who could be considered a "kinkeeper"—usually a woman—who used telephoning, writing letters, visiting, and organizing or holding family gatherings to keep extended family members in contact with one another (Rosenthal, 1985).

Declining Functions of the Nuclear Family

The American nuclear family has lost a number of functions since the colonial era. Because of the Industrial Revolution, the economic–productive function has been transferred from the home and family to factories, businesses, and other organizations, where one or more family members work in order to meet the family's economic needs. Therefore the family is no longer both producer and consumer, just the latter. This limited role might seem entirely natural to Americans but not to most people of the past. In fact, many prein-

dustrial people—the Greeks and Romans, for instance—visualized production and consumption as so thoroughly fused into a single life-giving function that they even lacked a separate word for consumer.

Other functions have also been largely separated from the family. Recreation was once centered in the home or the church, but it has become increasingly specialized along age lines and is now located outside the home. Children's sport and artistic programs and facilities, motion picture theaters, and video arcades provide a few illustrations. In addition, the protective function is no longer handled by the family but rather is now the responsibility of the police, the fire department, and other community agencies. Health care too has moved out of the home, with the dominant role played by doctors and nurses, drug stores, hospitals, and health-care agencies. Religious training, once rooted in the home, is now restricted to certain times and places outside it. Finally dramatic institutional expansion and specialization have occurred in education. Today the law makes it impossible to do what most parents routinely did two hundred years ago: educate their children in the home. From the age of four or five onward, children are now removed from home for thirty to forty hours a week (Adams, 1980: 87–88).

Consequences

As we have noted, Richard Sennett believed that extended families were healthier places for the development of nineteenth-century American men than were nuclear families. The French historian Phillipe Ariès (1962) broadened this argument to include women and children. Ariès contended that before the industrial era, women and children often encountered far fewer restrictions than they do today. The expectations that family members should constantly display mutual affection and that parents were obliged to ensure their children's maximum social and intellectual development simply did not exist. Once their household duties were completed, women and children were relatively free to do what they wanted. By contrast, Ariès described the modern nuclear family as a "prison of love."

Arlene Skolnick (1987) made a similar point.

334 She suggested that the nuclear family is characterized by "built-in strains." Men are freed from most obligations to the extended kinship unit, but they are compelled to support their wives and children in "the style to which they aspire to become accustomed." Skolnick has contended that women's plight is sometimes "obscured by the myth that women are the main beneficiaries of marriage." While women today have been released from their role obligations in extended family units, they now find themselves living in isolated households, often with extensive domestic duties. Skolnick pointed out that while labor-saving devices can facilitate the completion of specific tasks, they do not necessarily reduce the total number of work hours. It is possible that these devices simply raise the standards for meal preparation, house cleaning, and child care. Furthermore women now comprise nearly half of the labor force, and working wives and mothers tend to bear the burden of domestic responsibilities, even when the husband – father is vocally supportive of his wife's career and expresses a willingness to make a substantial contribution to the domestic chores.

Changing Patterns of Love, Courtship, and Marriage

The modern American family is the product of an industrialized, urbanized age. That same social context has produced some new developments in living arrangements. In this section we examine living together, choice of partners, and changing marital patterns.

Living Together

I always say we never got married, because we bought our own toaster.

Danny DeVito, actor

When he made this statement, Mr. DeVito had been living with the same woman for over ten years; this fact suggests that this particular couple belonged to a distinct numerical minority. Ira Reiss (1980: 106) has identified two types of cohabitation: courtship cohabitation, in which no desire for a lifelong union exists, and nonlegal marital cohabitation, DeVito's type, in which a desire for a lifelong union and possibly children has developed. The majority of people living together, Reiss contended, fall into the first category. Saxton (1980: 300) designated five types of cohabitation arrangements:

1. Temporary, casual cohabitation, with a man and a woman sharing the same living quarters chiefly out of short-term convenience
2. Affectionate cohabitation, which continues only so long as both partners remain pleased by it
3. Trial marriage, whereby a couple deliberately examines and tests their relationship before making a formal commitment
4. Cohabitation as a temporary alternative to marriage, with each partner committed to a permanent relationship but waiting, because of financial, legal, or other reasons, until that condition becomes more feasible
5. Cohabitation as a permanent alternative to marriage, a situation in which a long-term commitment exists

Most cohabitation arrangements meet the participants' needs at a particular point in time. Until recent years most of these relationships did not serve as trial marriages. A study, however, has concluded that in the modern era, in which premarital sex has become widely acceptable, a new stage in the courtship process might be emerging, with many couples using premarital cohabitation as an intermediate step between dating and marriage (Gwartney-Gibbs, 1986).

Table 12.1 shows that over time college freshmen have become increasingly supportive of the practice of cohabitation.

Who Engages in Cohabitation?

Cohabitation has sharply increased in recent years. Among student the relaxation of college rules and increased opportunities to live off-campus have encouraged this trend. Furthermore changing sexual attitudes — a general increase in

Table 12.1
College Freshmen's Positive Feelings about People Living Together before Marriage

	1974	1987
All	45%	52%
Men	51	58
Women	39	47

Source: Adapted from Richard G. Braungart and Margaret M. Braungart. "From Yippies to Yuppies: Twenty Years of Freshman Attitudes." *Public Opinion.* V. 11. September/October 1988, pp. 53–56.

Data from national surveys conducted with large samples of college freshmen at two points in time thirteen years apart indicated that over time students became more positive about living together, with men remaining somewhat more supportive of the practice than women.

sexual permissiveness and openness — have occurred among young people. Living together has also been encouraged by some people's disenchantment with marriage and by the belief that cohabitation can help to develop interpersonal skills that will be useful when people marry at a later date (Gagnon and Greenblat, 1978: 174–179). By 1987 there were over 2.3 million unmarried couples, nearly four-and-a-half times as many as in 1970 (U.S. Bureau of the Census, *Statistical Abstract of the United States: 1989.* No 56).

Overall the similarities between cohabitants and the general public appear to be more striking than their differences. In fact, among students opportunity may be the most significant factor differentiating between those who do and those who do not cohabit, although the participants must also possess sufficient interpersonal skills and personal attractiveness to be able to initiate a relationship.

Some research indicates that cohabiting women are more likely to consider themselves aggressive, competitive, independent, and managerial than are noncohabiting women. On the other hand, cohabiting men are more likely to regard themselves as warmer, less managerial, less competitive, and more emotionally supportive than are their noncohabiting counterparts. Both male and female cohabitants are more politically liberal, perceive themselves to be more androgynous (possessing a blend of both traditionally masculine

and feminine traits), and more liberated in terms of traditional gender-role expectations. Cohabitants also seem more inclined to major in the arts and in social sciences than in engineering or physical sciences (Macklin, 1983).

In addition, people who marry more than once are particularly likely to live together. A large study of cohabiting couples found that 60 percent of those who remarried between 1980 and 1987 lived with someone, usually the eventual spouse, beforehand (Barringer, 1989).

Consequences

In the legal realm, there are some decisive consequences of living together. A child born to a cohabiting couple is considered illegitimate and is subject to a variety of legal and social difficulties. Cohabiting people deny themselves some of the protections provided by the law to married couples. In some states merchants and landlords may legally refuse to sell or rent to a cohabiting couple.

One interesting trend revealed by research is that within ten years of the wedding, 38 percent of those who had cohabited had split up, compared with 27 percent of those who married without living together. One should not simply jump to the conclusion, however, that cohabitation encourages divorce. It appears that those who cohabit often have higher expectations for the emotional and sexual rewards of marriage (Barringer, 1989). In fact, people who have cohabited value the experience, arguing that it added to their personal growth and maturity and usually feeling that they would not marry a person without first living together (Macklin, 1983).

Choice of Partners

Americans prize freedom of choice. It is easy to imagine someone saying, "I'll marry anyone I choose. After all, people are created equal, and so marriage should simply be a question of whom I love." Despite such attitudes, most Americans practice **homogamy,** marriage with a person having social characteristics similar to one's own. Why is this? In the first place, many of us desire mates whose values are similar to ours. Those who share our racial, religious, ethnic, and social-class

336

statuses are especially likely to also share our values. Furthermore opportunity plays a part in promoting homogamy. Our residential areas, schools, and work places are usually somewhat segregated on the basis of race, ethnicity, and class, and so in these areas we are often going to meet people whose social characteristics are similar to ours. Another important factor promoting homogamy is informal pressure from family and friends to marry one's "own kind." We sometimes do not clearly perceive that these forces have an impact upon our lives, but for most of us, they are definitely significant. The data on homogamy support this conclusion.

Recent research has revealed that when people marry, they tend to find partners who are similar in age, race, religion, ethnic background, intelligence, income level, educational attainment, overall physical attractiveness, and various personality characteristics (Buss, 1986; Knox, 1988: 150).

One of the striking conclusions drawn from re-search on happy marriages was that the spouses maintained many common outlooks. In a study of 351 couples married fifteen years or more, Jeanette Lauer and Robert Lauer (1989) found that 300 couples indicated that they were happily married. From a list of thirty-nine statements about marriage, the female and male spouses listed the same seven top reasons in order of frequency. They were:

1. My spouse is my best friend.
2. I like my spouse as a person.
3. Marriage is a long-term commitment.
4. Marriage is sacred.
5. We agree on aims and goals.
6. My spouse has grown more interesting.
7. I want the relationship to succeed.

Whether or not they are homogamous, most Americans who marry have certain common characteristics in their wedding ceremonies, as the following Cross-Cultural Perspective indicates.

CROSS-CULTURAL PERSPECTIVE

The American Marriage Ritual: Contributions from Other Cultures

Human societies frequently borrow practices from other cultures. The traditional American marriage ceremony contains elements that originated in a number of other places. A discussion of the origin of these elements provides some sense of their earliest meanings as well as their meanings in contemporary American life.

The wedding ring is probably the oldest and most widespread symbol of marriage. Some ancient people apparently broke a coin in half, and each partner took one of the halves. The use of rings appears to have evolved out of this practice. Ancient Romans, Greeks, and Egyptians all used wedding rings; in those times rings represented the highest form of trust and power. In the Middle Ages, men in many European cultures still wore engagement rings, but this practice seems to have declined as rings gradually lost their earlier meaning and became symbols of bondage and obedience. In recent years, however, the number of double ring ceremonies has increased, reflecting the growing emphasis on sharing and mutuality in modern marriage.

Throughout history, couples have generally tried to choose a lucky wedding day. Hindus consulted astrologers before setting the wedding date. The Romans believed that it was unlucky to marry during the time when religious ceremonies and holidays occurred. As a result marriages did not take place for about a third of the year. The English traditionally regarded Friday as a bad day to begin any enterprise, and so they normally considered it a poor choice for a wedding day. Most Americans seem to display few superstitions about the choice of when to marry.

In many cultures brides have worn veils. Christian, Hindu, Jewish, and Moslem brides have used them, and tradition has emphasized that veils protect brides from malicious spirits — from the "evil eye."

Through the ages candles or torches have enhanced weddings. By the time the wedding procession in ancient Greece or Rome got under way, it was usually dark. Thus the torchbearers both provided light for those in the procession and also carried the flame that symbolized the enduring spirit of marriage. In early Christian marriages, the wedding was supposed to occur in the presence of God, who was represented by a single large candle.

Flowers too have been prominent in wedding ceremonies. Wreaths of flowers represented the bride's virtue. In medieval Europe women decorated both the bride's and the groom's house with olive and laurel leaves in order to symbolize abundance and virtue. This practice probably served as a forerunner of the later custom of decorating church alters with flowers and greenery.

Sources: Barbara Jo Chesser. "Analysis of Wedding Rituals: An Attempt to Make Weddings More Meaningful." *Marriage and Family 82/83.* Guilford, CT: Dushkin Publishing Group. 1982, pp. 57–61.

Changing Marital Patterns

Several years ago a film called *The Turning Point* portrayed two women who had made decisive choices about their lives. One had opted to become a ballerina and was successful in her career but was also lonely, with nothing in her life except her career. The other woman had married, turned away from an equally promising career, and while still satisfactorily married was always painfully aware of the choice she had made. The film raised a difficult question: Do women have to make a choice between career and family?

Women's increasingly common pursuit of careers is one reason the birthrate has been declining in the past three decades. Improved methods of contraception, the relentlessly increasing cost of raising children, and a growing concern about population control are others. From 1920 to 1924, there were about 3.3 children per woman. The figure rose to 3.7 children per woman in 1955 to 1959 and then declined, reaching 1.8 children per woman in 1986 (U.S. Bureau of the Census, *Population Profile of the United States: 1981.* Table 5.1; U.S. Bureau of the Census, *Fertility of American Women: June 1983.* Table 2; U.S. Bureau of the Census, *Statistical Abstract of the United States: 1989.* No. 87).

Voluntary Childlessness

While most couples still want children, some do not. About 5 percent of all couples choose childlessness, emphasizing that one's adult status can be produced by means other than parenthood, especially through a career. This percentage appears to be slowly rising, primarily among well-educated women in higher-status occupations (Reiss and Lee, 1988: 322). Voluntarily childless couples emphasize that children drain away time and energy that could otherwise be devoted to one's career and other interests.

J. E. Veevers (1973) studied fifty-two voluntarily childless wives and found that many of the subjects came from unhappy homes in which the parents had supposedly stayed together for the sake of the children, thus passing on to their offspring a feeling that children generally can be a cause of strife in marriage. Some of the voluntarily childless wives were the oldest children in large families and had shouldered major responsibilities for the care of their younger brothers and sisters. These women grew up with a sharply focused awareness that motherhood can be a burdensome responsibility.

One investigation discovered that career success is often a priority for women who remain voluntarily childless (Silka and Kiesler, 1977). Another study concluded that childless couples have two features that set them apart from couples with children: a tendency to value more highly women's achievement and independence and an inclination for the spouses to interact more extensively with each other in such positive ways as exchanging ideas, working together on projects, and having sexual relations (Feldman, 1981).

About two-thirds of Veevers's subjects remained childless because of a series of decisions to put off childbearing until a later date. The other third had agreed not to have children as a part of an informal marriage contract (Veevers, 1973). Research has produced data related to the last point; compared with other couples who are deliberating about whether or not to have children, childless couples are more firmly decided against having children in the first place (Oakley, 1985).

Working Mothers

Working mothers are a prominent segment of the work force. As Table 12.2 indicates, there has been a tremendous increase in the proportion of married working mothers over the past three decades.

A recent study suggested that many young women have little understanding of the demands of the combination of full-time work and motherhood. Seventy-three percent of a sample of 250 college women indicated that they wanted a career and children, and few doubted their ability to perform both of these roles successfully. The source of this conviction seemed to be the widespread contemporary thinking favoring the "do-both syndrome" (Baber and Monaghan, 1988). For anyone who has actively participated in parenthood, it seems clear that these young women (and doubtless their male counterparts) are in for a revealing learning experience.

Families in which women work or want to work outside the home sometimes experience conflict

Table 12.2
Married Mothers in the Work Force

	1960	1988
With children under 6	18.6%	57.1%
With children 6 to 17	39%	72.5%

Source: U.S. Bureau of the Census. *Statistical Abstract of the United States: 1989*. No. 639.

In the nearly three decades between 1960 and 1988, the percentage of married women with children under six in the work force increased over three-fold. For children six to seventeen, the proportion also grew substantially, nearly doubling.

because such behavior clashes with traditional attitudes about women's proper roles. An extreme example is provided by the husband who says, "I'm the provider. You're the homemaker. Case closed." Or perhaps the wife works, and this produces severe strains on the family. Sometimes career-oriented wives find themselves forced out of their work and back in the home. Alternative resolutions include divorce, "commuter" marriage, both spouses' lowering their career aspirations (Regan and Roland, 1985), or working on different shifts. Research has found that in dual-earning households an increasing proportion of young spouses, especially wives, are working part- or full-time at night in order to be with the children in the day and avoid the cost of day care. While such an arrangement might enhance the children's welfare, some evidence indicates that it increases family conflict (Presser, 1988).

Despite some husbands' negative attitudes, many wives now work, partly because they may simply desire to do so, and partly because of the necessity for additional income. While many husbands are willing or even happy to accept this situation, the lion's share of the domestic responsibility still almost always falls on the woman's shoulders even though she may be working full-time. In fact, research indicated that many married working women find themselves required to increase their domestic labors when husbands' job stresses cause them to restrict their contribution at home (Bolger et al., 1989). Most experts emphasize that women who work and rear children cannot be expected to meet traditional expectations that they bear the sole or principal responsibility for child care. They must be able to use day care or some other arrangement to lessen the physical and emotional burdens placed on them by child care (Kamerman and Kahn, 1981; Lein and Blehar, 1983).

Contention may also arise over the issue of whether or not children suffer if their mothers work. Until a few years ago, it was widely believed that some harm was inevitable or likely. However, if the mother likes her work and if effective child care is available, most studies suggest that the children will not be harmed. In fact, the daughters of working mothers are much more likely to score high on tests of independence, achievement, and positive self-image than are the daughters of non-

Like this thirty-five-year-old attorney, many working mothers must find the time and energy to complete the multiple tasks required of them.

working mothers (Hoffman and Nye, 1974). Research also suggests that working women are less likely to be highly possessive of and overly ambitious for their sons, largely because they are actively seeking their own fulfillment, rather than living vicariously through the children (Holmstrom, 1972). Children's evaluation of their mothers' work will vary, depending on a number of circumstances. For example, one study found that children are more likely to have a positive outlook toward their mothers' work if they perceive that their mothers view it positively (Thimberger and MacLean, 1982). This finding suggests that if mothers can locate jobs that please them, their children will benefit.

The physical, mental, and emotional well-being of employed mothers is often better than that of their nonworking counterparts. Some concern and even guilt are frequently aroused by the effort to combine the roles of mother, wife, and worker, but this is normally not a major problem. Working women usually feel useful, valued, and competent, giving them higher self-esteem than nonworking mothers. Working mothers generally display greater enjoyment of their activities and relationships with their children and have more realistic expectations for their children and for themselves as mothers (Green, 1978: 171–173). All in all, if the working wife–mother is able to balance her time and energy between her family and work, she usually constitutes a healthy influence on the domestic scene.

340 Divorce, Remarriage, and Alternatives to Marriage

The previous section makes it clear that the norms that influence people's patterns of love, courtship, and marriage have become considerably more flexible in the past several decades. The same tendency is apparent when we examine divorce, remarriage, and alternatives to marriage.

Marital Failure

While jogging on the beach in Guam, Chris Willie found a bottle containing a love note that was several years old. The writer said he was dropping the bottle into the Pacific halfway between Hawaii and Seattle. Mr. Willie followed directions in the bottle and mailed the note to the writer's wife in Seattle. The envelope was returned, however, marked "No longer at this address," and so Mr. Willie sent it to the *Seattle Times*. A newspaper official reached the woman by

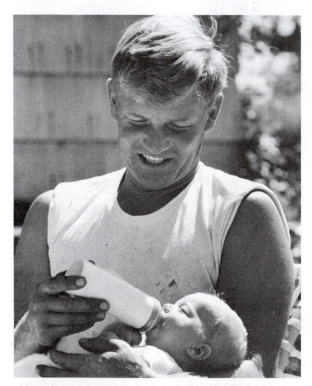

Changing patterns of marriage have affected the division of labor within many families. An increasing number of husbands, for example, share the responsibility for rearing and caring for their children.

phone, and she asked that the note be read to her. It said:

If, by the time this letter reaches you, I am old and gray, I know that our love will be as fresh as it is today. It may take a week, or it may take years for this note to find you. Whatever the case may be it shall have traveled by a strange and unpredictable route — the sea. If this should never reach you, it will still be written in my heart that I will go to extreme means to prove my love to you. Your husband, Bob.

The woman laughed and laughed, the newspaper reported. "We're divorced," she said and hung up the phone (Krebs and Thomas, 1981: 18).

Although surviving data are limited, research has concluded that in nineteenth-century America, there were fairly high rates of divorce, separation, and desertion (Schultz, 1984). Twentieth-century data are more thorough, however. As Figure 12.1 indicates, divorce has increased sharply in this century. In 1910 there were just 83,000 divorces, 385,000 in 1950, and about 1.1 million in 1987. The rate rose gradually, from .9 divorces per thousand people in 1910 to 4.8 per thousand in 1987. In 1940 there was one divorce for every six marriages. This figure rose to one divorce for every four marriages in 1950, and then rose to nearly one divorce for every two marriages in 1987 (U.S. Bureau of the Census, *Statistical Abstract of the United States: 1989*. No. 134). It appears that the divorce rate has now peaked (Norton and Moorman, 1987) and will probably begin to decline. By showing the 1987 divorce rate slightly lower than the 1980 divorce rate, Figure 12.1 indicates that this trend seems to be starting.

Some Factors Influencing the Divorce Rate

Three decades ago the divorced person, especially the divorced woman, was likely to receive the brunt of the blame when she was divorced. "There must be something wrong with her," unsympathetic observers often said. "She can't hold her man." Gradually, however, Americans have become more attuned to the sociological perspective, vaguely recognizing that social forces outside

Figure 12.1
Marriage and Divorce Rates: 1910 to 1987

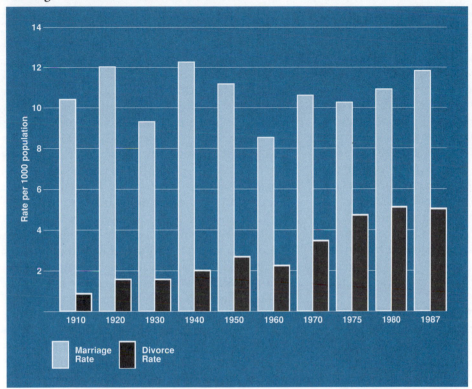

While the marriage rate has varied little over time, the divorce rate has risen steadily. In 1910 the marriage rate of 10.3 per 1000 people was more than eleven times the divorce rate of .9 per 1000. In 1987 the marriage rate of 9.9 per 1000 people was scarcely twice the divorce rate of 4.8 per 1000. (Source: Adapted from U.S. Bureau of the Census. Statistical Abstract of the United States: 1989. No. 134.)

the individual play a major role in the sharply increased rate of divorce over the past half-century.
INDUSTRIALIZATION   In preindustrial societies extended families play a major role in arranging and maintaining marriages. Modern industrialized nations, in contrast, are characterized by relatively independent courtship patterns, which permit love to become a critical criterion in mate selection. Love-based marriages tend to be especially unstable, frequently ending in divorce if the parties come to feel that love no longer endures. Consequently increasing levels of industrialization tend to mean higher divorce rates. The United States achieved a high degree of urban growth before 1930, and at that time its divorce

rate was running well ahead of those typical of European societies. Between 1930 and 1965, American divorce rates increased slowly, while the rates in many European countries, which were experiencing rapid industrialization, rose sharply (Reiss and Lee, 1988: 286–287).
AGE OF THE COUPLE   Age at the time of marriage is an important factor. Couples in their teens and early twenties are the least likely to have lasting marriages (Kunz and England, 1988) for several reasons. First, the young are often more likely than older people to grow apart over time in their values and personal interests. Second, young people are the most inclined to turn to marriage as a means of escaping from an unhappy home envi-

ronment, often failing in the process to realistically assess the chances of success. Third, young people are the most likely to decide to marry because of pregnancy, once again often without objectively assessing whether each partner is really ready to marry (Adams, 1980: 375–376).

CHANGING ROLE DEFINITIONS WITHIN MARRIAGE   But neither factor that we have analyzed explains why the divorce rate shot up in the late 1960s. One significant influence was that role definitions within marriage began to change. The social protests of the 1960s, the increasing proportion of women in the work force, and then the development of the women's movement all encouraged women to seize the opportunity to be more independent and assertive than they had been in the past. Freed of traditional economic and psychological dependence on their husbands, an increasing number of wives decided that they did not need to grit their teeth and accept unhappy marriages.

DECREASING LEGAL AND SOCIAL CONSTRAINTS   In 1970 California enacted the first no-fault divorce law in the United States, and forty-eight states have adopted this standard in some form. No-fault legislation simplifies divorce proceedings. For example, one spouse no longer needs to establish grounds for divorce, testifying to the other's adultery, cruelty, or desertion and bringing in witnesses to support his or her testimony. The wife and husband are no longer forced to be adversaries. With no-fault divorce, the legal focus becomes the partners' joint endeavor to end as quickly as possible a marriage that does not work (Weitzman and Dixon, 1983). In addition, many religious groups have become less critical of divorce, no longer seeing it in moral terms. Perhaps the factor underlying both of these changes is a value issue — a strong emphasis on freedom and happiness, with the feeling that marriage is an emotional more than a practical union and that it should be immediately discontinued if unhappy (Lamanna and Riedmann, 1988: 511–512).

Consequences

If someone's parents are divorced, he or she is said to come from a "broken home." This phrase calls to mind the image of a home in shambles, with everything — relationships, personalities,

and even furniture — in disarray or even destroyed. It seems obvious that the product of a "broken home" is likely to have psychological problems, perhaps serious ones. But is this true? What, in fact, happens to spouses and children after divorce?

CONSEQUENCES FOR THE COUPLE   Paul Bohannon (1970: 33) has suggested that, in a sense, divorce reverses the courtship process. Instead of having been "selected" out of the whole world, the former spouse feels "deselected." Not surprisingly research has concluded that following divorce people tend to become more depressed than they were before it occurred. The level of depression seems to be affected by the magnitude of one's economic problems, the availability of close, confiding relationships, and the extent to which one's former standard of living is maintained (Menaghan and Lieberman, 1986).

Economically women tend to suffer more from divorce than men do. In one study two-thirds of the women reported that their income following divorce was considerably lower than before, while only 19 percent of the males described such a situation. The researcher concluded that "the divorce experiences of males and of females are not the same. Although some of these differences lessened the negative consequences of divorce for women, most of them clearly favored the male" (Albrecht, 1980: 67).

Nonetheless, there are indications that in many cases men have a more difficult time adjusting to divorce than women. While the suicide rate for divorced women has been three times that of married women, four times more divorced men than married men have killed themselves (Moffett and Scherer, 1976). Furthermore evidence has indicated that men who have not remarried within six years after divorce have increased rates of car accidents, alcoholism, drug abuse, depression, and anxiety (Brody, 1983). Why do women seem to adjust more effectively to divorce? Women make more practical use of kin support, relying on them more extensively and seeing this reliance in a much more optimistic light than men do. In fact, following divorce, men who seek kin support tend to suffer a high level of depression, while women with such a reliance tend to be quite the opposite — more contented than most recently divorced people (Gerstel, 1988). Another factor operating here might be that men are more likely than women to lose custody of their children. Research concluded that some newly separated men's difficulties are compounded by their failure to accept the fact that the adaptation to their new existence will be greatly enhanced if they radically limit their interaction with their former spouse and also alter their relationship with their children (White and Bloom, 1981).

Age is another social characteristic that appears to affect people's adjustment to divorce. Morton Hunt and Bernice Hunt (1980) found that most childless people who divorce at a young age soon rejoin the never-married group, rapidly putting both the marriage and former spouse out of their minds. In contrast, people in mid-life who divorce after many years (Davis and Aron, 1988) or who divorce in old age (Weingarten, 1988) are likely to find the experience much more difficult and adjustment a lengthier process.

The unhappiness associated with most divorces does not mean that unhappily married people should stay married. A study indicated that individuals with unsatisfying marriages were more depressed, lonelier, and more socially isolated than were divorced people (Renne, 1974).

CONSEQUENCES FOR THE CHILDREN
One morning at the end of class, a student, accompanied by her twelve-year-old son, who was visiting the class, approached my desk. We had been discussing divorce, and our conversation continued on the same topic. After a few minutes, the mother said, "Ricky, tell Mr. Doob what you'd like to have happen."

Embarrassed, the boy replied, "You know." The mother then explained that ever since the divorce, which occurred when he was three, Ricky longed to be living again with both parents. The solution, he now believed, was to have his stepfather marry his father's wife, and then the way would be cleared for his parents' remarriage. "He doesn't think about the others involved," the mother said sadly. Certainly many children suffer because of divorce, but what is the overall picture? To begin, the number of children whose parents divorce has been increasing. Over the next few decades, about one-third of all children born in the United States are likely to experience parents' divorce (Levin, 1989). Following divorce, the relationship between children and the nonresident parent tends to change dramatically. One study concluded that in divorce situations, most children have little

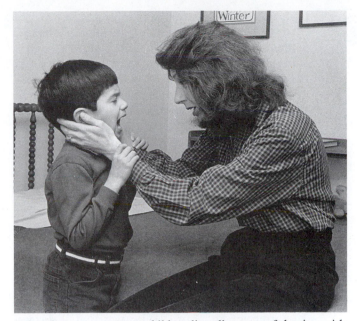

When divorce occurs, most children live all or most of the time with their mothers, who often must fulfill the diverse demands of parenthood by themselves.

contact with their nonresident parent, usually the father, and what contact occurs is fairly superficial, with the nonresident parent often acting more like a pal than a parent (Furstenberg and Nord, 1985).

A number of status factors seem to affect children's adjustment to divorce. Younger children usually find the experience more difficult than older children, with children under five suffering the strongest emotional reactions. Boys tend to have more difficulty adjusting to divorce than girls (Greene and Leslie, 1989; Lowery and Settle, 1985). Probably both younger children and boys adjust more slowly because of more limited social skills. In boys' case the more limited social skills might result because after divorce they are less likely than girls to have role models for learning appropriate gender-related behavior (Demo and Acock, 1988). Another factor affecting children's adjustment is the custodial parent's reaction to the divorce. Goode (1956: 317–321) found that the more trauma mothers experienced from their divorces, the more likely that they would describe their children as hard to handle following the split. Eighty-one percent of the mothers studied admitted that they were concerned about the impact of the divorce on their children. However, 55 percent encountered no increase in problems with their children afterward, and only 14 percent found that their children were more difficult to deal with in the months following the divorce.

Even though divorce is painful for children, research has found that they prefer the post-divorce period to the time when the family was still intact. An eleven-year-old boy indicated that while he missed his father, it was a relief to have no more fighting. He added, "The knots in my stomach were beginning to clear so things were much better" (Neugebauer, 1989: 158).

Remarriage

Several years ago the hostess at a party received a phone call that occupied her for nearly three quarters of an hour. "Who was that?" she was asked when she returned.

"Poor woman!" the hostess replied. "She's desperate. Several months back her husband divorced her, and tonight she feels trapped at home, alone on a Saturday night with no place to go and no one even to talk to. The funny thing is that I don't even know her very well and really don't like her much. She's very uptight. I invited her over, but she turned me down. So I just talked to her."

William Goode (1956) contended that the norms governing the behavior of divorced people are often unclear. Should they continue to socialize with their old married friends? Should they stay in the same town or move elsewhere? How should they deal with acute, even desperate loneliness such as that felt by the woman just described? One common course of action is to remarry.

As we have already noted, people tend to marry homogamously. This generalization also applies to divorced people. While over 90 percent of single men and women marry another single person, over half of divorced men and women remarry another divorced person. Among those who remarry, over 15 percent will do so within a few months of the completion of divorce proceedings and another 50 percent within three years. It takes an average of seven years for those who divorce to leave their first marriage but only three years for those who remarry to enter a second marriage (Reiss, 1980: 340–342). In 1970, 31.4 percent of all marriages were remarriages; the figure rose to

43.8 percent in 1980 and then 45.8 percent in 1985 (U.S. Bureau of the Census, *Statistical Abstract of the United States: 1989*. No. 129).

How satisfactory are remarriages? Glenn and Weaver (1977) claimed that divorce and remarriage are fairly effective mechanisms for replacing bad marriages with good ones — that second marriages that do not end quickly in divorce seem to be almost as successful as intact first marriages. In another study Albrecht (1979) asked his subjects to evaluate how happy their remarriages were compared with their first marriages and also how well each of their marriages compared with their acquaintances' marriages and with the level of happiness which they expected to find in marriage. The second marriages came out ahead on all these counts. When second marriages produce problems, therapists can work with clients to help them sort out unresolved issues, sometimes suggesting legal help to overcome the economic confusions and complexities remarried families often face (Bernstein and Collins, 1985).

For children remarriages are also confusing as they are left wondering which people qualify as fellow family members. Is it the mother's family, the father's, or some combination? One study, in fact, indicated children in remarriages provided five different designations of what constituted the family unit, including the immediate household, the biological family, and the combined biological and stepfamily (Hobart, 1988; Klee, Schmidt, and Johnson, 1989). Recall our discussion in Chapter 4, "Groups," that people's sense of self is shaped by primary-group or reference-group participation. Family membership qualifies in both regards. However, if your sense of family membership is confused, then your identity is also likely to be adversely affected.

Alternatives to Conventional Marriage

In the past two decades, a number of factors have made people feel freer to choose various alternatives to conventional monogamous marriage. These include a sharp decrease in social pressure to have children, vast improvements in the availability of effective methods of contraception for women, increased economic self-sufficiency among many single people, and rapid improvements in the communication of new ideas (Ramey, 1978: 3–5).

In the following pages we examine single-parent households, voluntary singlehood, gay relationships, and communes.

Single-Parent Households

The number of children under eighteen living in single-parent households rose from 8.2 million in 1970 to 15.1 million in 1987, as Figure 12.2 indicates, representing an increase from 12 to 24 percent of the total of American households containing children under eighteen (U.S. Bureau of the Census, *Marital Status and Living Arrangements: March 1982.* Table E; U.S. Bureau of the Census, *Statistical Abstract of the United States: 1989.* No. 71). Although the distinct majority of single-parent families are headed by women, an increasing number of men are also running families by themselves. Single-parent families tend to have modest incomes, with father–child families possessing incomes that are more than twice those of mother–child families. While about 24 percent of all children are living below the poverty level, the figure is 57 percent for one-parent families (Norton and Glick, 1986).

Single parents face some other significant prob-lems. Probably the most frequently expressed complaint is the overload of role commitments. Single parents must be all things to their children, not only mother but father as well, the breadwin-ner, the cook, and the nurse. Work schedules often conflict with parental obligations. How can the parent drive a child to day care, a Little League game, or a recital during working hours? Another difficulty is that single parents often have no one who can validate how they are treating their chil-dren. In a two-parent household, a mother or fa-ther can seek feedback for decisions from the other spouse. When single parents are challenged by their children, they often have no one who can effectively provide this feedback. As a result many begin to compromise their definition of reality, doing such things as giving in to a child whose personality development might be much more ef-fectively nurtured if firm guidelines were estab-lished (Glenwick and Mowrey, 1986; Sanik and Mauldin, 1986; Turner and Smith, 1983).

The parent's sex does not seem to be a signifi-cant factor affecting single parents' effectiveness. Children reared by mothers show about the same levels of self-esteem, social competencies, and se-verity and frequency of behavioral problems as children brought up by fathers. This finding op-poses both the widely held belief that women inev-itably make more effective parents than men and

Figure 12.2
Living Arrangements of Children under 18 Years Old: 1970 to 1987

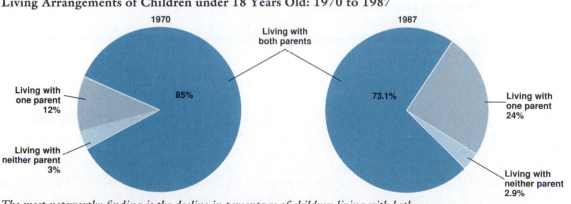

The most noteworthy finding is the decline in percentage of children living with both parents—from 85 percent in 1970 to 73.1 percent in 1987. The figure suggests that children increasingly experience parental divorce while growing up. (Source: Adapted from U.S. Bureau of the Census. Current Population Reports, *Series P–20,* Marital Status and Living Arrangements: *March 1982. Table E; U.S. Bureau of the Census.* Statistical Abstract of the United States: 1989. *No. 71.)*

346

also the tendency of many courts to more readily award children to mothers in a custody suit (Risman and Park, 1988; Schnayer and Orr, 1989).

Singlehood

Being single was frowned upon during the colonial era. Women were considered old maids if they were not married by the age of twenty-five, and bachelors were scorned, ridiculed, and sometimes even forced to pay a special tax. The Bible declares that people should be fruitful and multiply, and by not marrying and having children, single people were seen to be defying this command.

In modern times, however, a significant number of people have chosen to remain single. In 1960 about 32.8 percent of the adult population was unmarried. In 1987 about 38.2 million adults had never been married, while 13.2 million were widowed and 13.6 were divorced. This total of 65 million represented 34.5 percent, over one-third of the adult population (U.S. Bureau of the Census, *Statistical Abstract of the United States: 1989*. No. 50). It appears that the percentage of unmarried people will continue to increase; one specialist has predicted that among young people in their mid-twenties to early thirties, 12 percent of women and 10 percent of men will never marry — three times as high a proportion as in their parents' generation (Glick, 1986). Singles include recent college graduates who are on their own for the first time, as well as senior citizens who reside together in order to make the most of two social security checks. In between one finds millions of single people pursuing a diversity of lifestyles, including a host of single parents.

Currently many cities offer singles' apartment complexes as well as singles' bars, magazines, dating services, vacation packages, and resorts. However, the "swinging singles" side of singles' life has received widespread criticism. Many people believe that urban "body shops" — bars and clubs where sexual partners can be easily found — cater to men and degrade women.

The category of single people contains diverse outlooks and experiences. For instance, never-married people are much more likely than divorced singles to define singlehood as a permanent lifestyle, and marriage rates are higher for divorced than never-married singles (Cockrum and White, 1985). People who are voluntarily single are probably most strongly committed to this status. Peter Stein (1980) studied singles and found a number of "pushes away" from marriage as well as "pulls toward" being single. "Pushes away" from married life included the possible suffocation of a one-to-one relationship, sexual frustration, and, interestingly, fear of isolation and loneliness. "Pulls toward" singlehood involved the exciting lifestyle, self-sufficiency, and the availability of sexual variety.

A significant issue affecting both single and married people is the legalization of abortion. Americans feel strongly about this topic and have deeply divided opinions. Let us consider those opinions in the following American Controversy.

AMERICAN CONTROVERSY

Abortion: Pro-Life or Pro-Choice?

 On July 3, 1989, by a five to four decision, the U.S. Supreme Court expanded the powers of the states to regulate abortions, permitting them to decide such issues as where they can be performed and how many months into a pregnancy abortion is permissible. While this decision did not overturn the earlier *Roe* v. *Wade* decision, which had permitted unrestricted abortion, it did represent a significant victory for the opponents of legalized abortion and a set-back for its supporters. At that time it was clear that public discussion and debate about abortion would be a hot issue for years.

Pro-Life Position

The opponents of abortion often label themselves "pro-life." They believe that no matter when an abortion is performed, the life of a human being is taken. To emphasize this point, their advertisements frequently show pictures of fetuses, including fetuses in the first few weeks, to emphasize that in appearance they have the basic attributes of human beings.

How, the pro-life camp emphasizes, can one draw an arbitrary line saying that beyond one day, one month, three months, or whatever, the fetus becomes a living creature? Once conceived, a living creature exists, and that is the basic reality.

Under some circumstances it is reasonable for a person to give up her child for adoption. That, however, is no reason to kill him or her, the opponents conclude. Cherish the unborn child and then turn her or him over to the proper authorities, who will find a good home.

Pro-Choice Position

The supporters of abortion frequently refer to themselves as "pro-choice." Their emphasis is that a woman's body is her own—that she should be able to decide whether or not she wishes to have a child and that the state has no right to intervene on this issue.

If abortion becomes illegal, then women will lose this right. For all women that would be an injustice, but it would be particularly discriminatory against poor women. Middle-class and upper-middle-class women would be able to do what was done several decades ago—get a family doctor or a private clinic to perform an abortion for a sizable fee. For the poor, however, the options would be much more limited. They would either need to have an unwanted

child or would seek a cheap abortion, often with tragic injury or death the result.

Finally, while it might be nice to think that all unwanted children will find good homes, that simply has never been the case and would become considerably less likely if the illegalization of abortion led to more unwanted children. At present healthy, white children are usually placed for adoption, but nonwhites and children with physical or mental difficulties often must be raised in institutional settings, which puts them at enormous psychological and intellectual disadvantage in contrast to children brought up in effectively functioning families.

Discuss this difficult issue inside or outside of class. Is it possible to find some basis for compromise?

Homosexual "Marriages"

Donna Tanner (1978) found that lesbian relationships generally pass through three stages. First, there is the "trial phase," in which a regularized sexual association begins. Second, "insulation" occurs, with the couple living together covertly and attempting to develop a permanent commitment to each other. Finally "stabilization" takes place. At this point the couple lives together openly, though in a relationship that lacks legal validation, something like a cohabitational arrangement between a man and woman. The third stage is important because it is at this point that social recognition is conferred upon the relationship; for instance, the lesbian couple may be invited out to parties as a social unit.

Many homosexual couples, however, want more than the informal recognition of friends.

They would like a legally sanctioned marriage. In 1971, in the case of *Baker* v. *Nelson,* two men appealed to the Minnesota Supreme Court after a lower court ruled in favor of a county clerk who refused to grant them a marriage license. The couple contended that the state's statutes did not expressly forbid same-sex marriages. The court conceded that they were correct on this point but that marriage laws using such terms as *husband* and *wife* or *bride* and *groom* were meant to refer exclusively to a union between a man and a woman.

One reason many homosexuals want a legally sanctioned relationship is for psychological support. If a relationship is clearly regarded as a marriage in the eyes of other people, then the participants themselves are likely to feel more comfortable and secure in it. There are also practical reasons. Homosexual couples face problems with insurance, tax laws, and inheritance. Even some-

348 thing as simple as a hospital visit can pose difficulties. A report in the London *Times* told of a dying lesbian who could be visited only by her family and was therefore denied deathbed visits from her partner of twenty years (Scanzoni and Scanzoni, 1988: 186–187).

Communes

Communes are planned, intentional communities, bringing together biologically unrelated people in order to build a large, family-like group. Many, perhaps most, communes permit couples to maintain their social and sexual exclusiveness as a couple. There are over 1000 communes in the United States, Canada, and several other countries. The smallest contain as few as five or six people, while the largest is the Farm in Summertown, Tennessee, with over 1600 members (Knox, 1988: 176–178).

Rosabeth Moss Kanter (1968) studied thirty nineteenth-century American communes in order to determine which qualities increased or decreased the likelihood that a commune would survive. Nine of these communes were rated as successful, defined as lasting thirty-three years or more, and twenty-one were unsuccessful, enduring less than sixteen years and averaging a life span of just four years. The successful communes tended to build strong group commitment in a number of ways. They required significant personal sacrifices (ceasing sexual activity and alcohol and tobacco use, for instance) and also major investments of time, energy, money, and property. In addition, the more successful communes also created strong in-group feelings, often demanding that members give up all primary-group contacts with the outside world. Furthermore the participants' sense of individuality was largely eliminated; their identity was shaped and controlled by community standards.

The most comprehensive study of American communes to date is based on data derived from a sample of almost 700 men and women living in sixty urban communes in Los Angeles, Houston, Atlanta, Boston, New York, and Minneapolis. Some of the communes were intensely committed to certain religious positions or other values, while others were simply places where economic sharing occurred. Some were highly structured, and others were not. In a number of cases, children were present, but such groups were in the minority. Most of the participants were single, and all the communes included both men and women. In rank order the following were the primary reasons that members cited for joining the groups:

1. Financial advantages
2. Order and regularity
3. Friendship and support
4. A means of leaving home
5. A way to break from the past
6. A lifestyle that provided new and interesting experiences
7. A search for like-minded people
8. Companionship or community

The average participant stayed for two years, with some moving on to other communes, while others returned to more traditional lifestyles. A significant proportion of the commune members in the sample led otherwise fairly normal lives as students or as workers in conventional jobs (Zablocki, 1977).

Many Americans who are now living in communes do not fit 1960s stereotypes of long-haired hippies sitting around campfires in the evening singing folksongs. Often they lead quite ordinary middle-class lives, and instead of using the term *commune,* they speak of *intentional communities.* Such settlements have become one modern means of combatting food and heating bills, rising land prices, and high interest rates, while also serving as a way of restoring a sense of community frequently missing in modern life. In Florida, for instance, an intentional community of one hundred families has permitted participants to live comfortably on less than $10,000 per year. The members have pooled their resources in order to build houses and buy land and tools. Typically houses have been built by a combination of do-it-yourself efforts, house-building parties, and outside contracting. The residents have used each other's expertise through voluntary labor exchange. Families have controlled their own land, but the community members' cooperative efforts have created a positive situation in which to live — as one observer has phrased it, "an atmosphere where things are possible" (*Futurist,* 1985).

Conclusion

In 1980 a conference that originally had been called the White House Conference on the Family was renamed the White House Conference on Families. It might seem that changing one word in the title from the singular to the plural form was not significant, but it was. Sociologically speaking, the change represented an appreciation that the cultural standards shaping Americans' perception of the family have been altering—that it is now widely accepted that there is not one form of the modern American family but many (Berger and Berger, 1984: 59).

Until recently most Americans expected to grow up in nuclear families and develop this type of family themselves. While this option remains popular, it is just that—an option. Nowadays Americans have a variety of lifestyle choices, but they also find themselves encountering a great deal of confusion and uncertainty. In an era emphasizing individual choice and control, people, including members within families, frequently seem more on their own than in the past. Many modern parents, strong subscribers to the value position that individuals should control their own destiny, feel their obligations to their children should be distinctly limited. In *Habits of the Heart: Individualism and Commitment in American Life,* a therapist was asked if she was responsible for her children. She spoke hesitantly, "I . . . I would say I have a legal responsibility for them, but in a sense I think they in turn are responsible for their acts" (Bellah et al., 1986: 82). Do you agree with this position? Do you feel that American family members share sufficient values and activities? What differences, if any, would you like in the modern family?

STUDY GUIDE

Learning Objectives

After studying this chapter, you should be able to:

1. Define family and indicate why it is socially important.
2. Discuss with illustrations the three basic functions of the family examined in the text.
3. Identify and define kinship terms for marriage types, marriage-eligibility customs, residential rules, and family-power patterns.
4. Describe the effects of industrialization on the family and explain the nature and consequences of the nuclear family's loss of functions.
5. Discuss contemporary patterns of cohabitation, including the consequences of living together.
6. Examine the topics of voluntary childlessness and working mothers.
7. Identify and discuss the factors that influence the divorce rate.
8. Describe the consequences of divorce for the couple and for children.
9. Examine prominent alternatives to conventional marriage.

Summary

1. A family is traditionally defined as a social unit composed of two or more people who live together and are related by blood, marriage, or adoption. The family provides functions that are critical for its survival and also for the maintenance of society.

2. The functions of the family include sexual regulation, economic cooperation, and socializa-

350

tion. In other societies these functions are often performed in ways that differ sharply from those carried out by Americans. Prominent kinship terms involve the type of marriage, customs for marriage eligibility, residential rules for newly married people, and patterns of power within the family.

3. Like other institutional structures, the modern American nuclear family has been shaped by industrialization. In the course of the industrial era, the nuclear family has lost some of its preindustrial functions, with distinctly negative consequences for family members sometimes produced.

4. American society has experienced changing patterns of love, courtship, and marriage. Living together has become a widely practiced activity, with a number of social conditions contributing to the increased incidence. People tend to practice homogamy, marrying individuals whose social characteristics are similar to their own. Among the changing marital patterns are an increase in childlessness and in working mothers.

5. Divorce has increased sharply since the mid-1960s. Industrialization, age of the couple, changing role definitions within marriage, and decreasing social and legal constraints are factors affecting the divorce rate. There are significant, sometimes damaging effects of divorce for spouses and children. On the other hand, people's lives can become happier and more fulfilling once unhappy marriages are terminated. Frequently divorced people remarry, with second marriages often more satisfying than the first. Many Americans pursue alternatives to a conventional monogamous marriage. Among them are single-parent households, singlehood, gay "marriage," and communes.

Key Terms

commune a planned, intentional community, bringing together biologically unrelated people in order to build a large, family-like group

egalitarian a type of family in which the wife–mother and husband–father share power and also permit their children to participate in the family decisions

endogamy a custom requiring a person to marry within a specific social unit, such as a kinship group, religious organization, or social class

exogamy a custom compelling someone to marry outside a specific social unit

extended family a family involving two or more generations of people related by blood and living together or close to each other

family traditionally defined as a social unit composed of two or more people who live together and are related by blood, marriage, or adoption

homogamy marriage with a person having social characteristics similar to one's own

incest taboo a rule outlawing sexual relations between kin-group members believed to be too closely related as defined by the cultural standards of a given society

kinship system a number of people related by common descent, marriage, or adoption

matriarchal a type of family in which the wife–mother is the formal head and the absolute or nearly absolute source of power

matrilocal a type of residence that involves settling with or near the wife's parents

monogamy a marriage practice in which there is one husband and one wife

neolocal a type of residence that occurs when married people establish an independent place to live

nuclear family a two-generation family that includes a father, a mother, and their children living separately from other relatives

patriarchal a type of family in which the husband–father is the formal head and the absolute or nearly absolute source of power

patrilocal a type of residence that requires settling with or near the husband's parents

polyandry the form of polygamy in which a woman has two or more husbands

polygamy a marriage practice in which a person has two or more spouses of the other sex

polygyny the form of polygamy in which a man has two or more wives

Tests

True–false Test

_F_ 1. The incest taboo exists only in Western cultures.

_T_ 2. According to a recent study, parents and children tend to believe their values are more similar than they actually are.

_T_ 3. The nuclear family is compatible with a modern, industrial setting.

_F_ 4. Polyandry is a much more common form of polygamy than is polygyny.

_T_ 5. Richard Sennett's study of nineteenth-century Chicago families concluded that the nuclear-family type may be less supportive of male members' emotional and occupational development than the extended family.

_T_ 6. The French historian Ariès suggested that in the preindustrial era, women and children encountered fewer restrictions than today.

_F_ 7. Recent statistics indicated that people who live together before marriage are more likely to have long-lasting marriages than those who do not cohabit.

_T_ 8. Research concluded that children are more likely to have a positive outlook toward their mothers' work if they perceive that their mothers view the work positively.

_T_ 9. The divorce rate is roughly one divorce for every two marriages.

_F_ 10. Gay marriages are now legal in twenty-two states.

Multiple-choice Test

_D_ 1. Which of the following has NOT been recognized as a function of the incest taboo?
a. elimination of conflicts and jealousies produced by sexual rivalry
b. clear definitions of family roles
c. encouragement of alliances between families
d. accomplishment of age-linked tasks

_A_ 2. Compared to noncohabiting women, cohabiting women are more likely to consider themselves:
a. aggressive.
b. emotionally supportive.
c. politically conservative.
d. noncompetitive.

_B_ 3. Homogamy:
a. only involves gay couples.
b. involves both race and religion.
c. is not influenced by family and friends.
d. is not apparent in a study of successful marriages.

_B_ 4. The birth rate has been declining in recent years because of:
a. involuntary childlessness.
b. women's increasing pursuit of careers.

    c. increased fertility problems produced by environmental damage.
    d. reduced male willingness to be breadwinners.

_C_   5. Veevers's study of voluntary childlessness showed which of the following statements to be true?
    a. Women in the study tended to be youngest children and thus felt inadequate to provide child-care because of inexperience.
    b. Many of the women were neurotically dependent on others.
    c. Many of the informants came from unhappy homes in which parents had communicated to them the feeling that children generally cause strife in marriage.
    d. Most of the informants had tradition-oriented husbands.

_A_   6. Which of the following statements describes a condition affecting the divorce rate?
    a. People in their teens and early twenties are more likely than older individuals to get divorced.
    b. Love-based marriages tend to be particularly stable.
    c. No-fault divorce legislation has discouraged the occurrence of divorce.
    d. Changing role definitions within marriage have made modern marriages more stable.

_D_   7. Following divorce, women are more likely than men:
    a. to commit suicide.
    b. to have increased rates of car accidents, alcoholism, drug abuse, depression, and anxiety.
    c. to participate in clubs and organizations.
    d. to have financial problems.

_D_   8. Remarriages:
    a. seldom occur less than five years after divorce.
    b. tend to be unhappier than first marriages.
    c. do not pose confusion for children of previous marriages, who can readily figure out who are their fellow family members.
    d. represent an increasing percentage of all marriages.

_A_   9. Single-parent families:
    a. tend to be less affluent than most families.
    b. declined in numbers between 1970 and 1987.
    c. declined in their proportion of all families between 1970 and 1987.
    d. b and c

_D_   10. Voluntary singlehood:
    a. can be encouraged by "pushes away" from marriage.
    b. is likely to increase in the years ahead.
    c. is more likely to be defined as a permanent lifestyle by never-married individuals than by divorced people.
    d. a, b, and c

Essay Test

1. Define family. Discuss the relationship between industrialization and the nuclear family. Examine the declining functions of the nuclear family.
2. Analyze cohabitation, indicating who engages in this practice and also the consequences of living together.
3. Are modern Americans entirely free to choose their spouses? Use the concept homogamy in answering the question.

4. Examine three factors that significantly affect the divorce rate. Discuss in detail the consequences of divorce for both couples and children.
5. Describe two alternatives to conventional marriage, indicating why some people find these particular options either necessary or appealing in modern society.

Suggested Readings

Berger, Brigitte, and Peter L. Berger. 1984. *The War over the Family*. Garden City, NY: Anchor Books. A sociological analysis of both the American family and reactions to it, offering thought-provoking endorsement of the nuclear-family form.

Bozett, Frederick W. (ed.). 1987. *Gay and Lesbian Parents*. New York: Praeger. A collection of articles about gay families discussing such issues as types of family combinations, children's adjustment, and the impact of rearing children in a social world generally hostile to gays.

Cherlin, Andrew J. 1981. *Marriage, Divorce, Remarriage*. Cambridge: Harvard University Press. A description and analysis of recent trends in these three areas in which norms and behavioral patterns have been rapidly changing.

Goode, William J. 1982. *The Family*. Englewood Cliffs, NJ: Prentice-Hall. Second edition. A short, clearly written text, effectively introducing students to the sociological study of the family.

Hood, Jane C. 1983. *Becoming a Two-Job Family*. New York: Praeger. A study that follows sixteen couples over six years and indicates in detail the impact of women's working on the family. Previous research and theory is effectively incorporated into the analysis throughout the book.

McGrady, Mike. 1975. *The Kitchen Sink Papers*. Garden City, NY: Doubleday and Company. A journalist's often humorous, frequently revealing account of switching roles with his wife and becoming a househusband while his wife became the breadwinner.

Scanzoni, Letha Dawson, and John Scanzoni. 1988. *Men, Women, and Change*. New York: McGraw-Hill. Third edition. A nicely written, comprehensive, visually effective undergraduate text on marriage and the family.

Skolnick, Arlene S., and Jerome H. Skolnick (eds.). 1989. *Family in Transition*. Boston: Little, Brown, and Company. Sixth edition. Forty-three articles divided into eleven chapters on a variety of topics involving marriage, the family, and related issues. The book includes a good general introduction and effective part openers.

Stein, Peter J. (ed.). 1981. *Single Life: Unmarried Adults in Social Context*. New York: St. Martin's Press. Articles that examine some of the diverse types of unmarried people as well as singles' activities and problems.

Additional Assignments

1. Write a set of marriage vows that you believe acknowledges the important matters to be covered in a marriage relationship. If you are involved in a serious relationship, you might want to seek input from your partner. Compare the wording of your vows with the content of typical vows, containing such phrases as "to have and to hold," "to love and to cherish (or obey)," "in sickness and in health," and "until death do us part." Is the marriage your vows describe traditional or nontraditional? Compare your vows with classmates' efforts.

2. Using the text's list of alternatives to conventional marriage, including the option of cohabitation, ask at least ten people to rate the different choices on desirability—"1" would be a very low desirability and "10" would be the highest. For your informants seek a balance of males and females and also younger and older people. What explanations can you supply for your results? Discuss findings with other classmates.

Answers to Objective Test Questions

True–false Test

1. f	4. f	7. f	9. t
2. t	5. t	8. t	10. f
3. t	6. t		

Multiple-choice Test

1. d	4. b	7. d	9. a
2. a	5. c	8. d	10. d
3. b	6. a		

13
RELIGION AND EDUCATION

In December 1985 the U.S. Circuit Court of Appeals ruled by a vote of eight to seven that creationism (the Biblical story of the creation of the world and its inhabitants) need not receive as much attention in the schools as the teaching of evolution. The Louisiana Attorney General was not impressed by the vote. He vowed to take the case to the Supreme Court, declaring that the seven-vote dissent represented strong support for the creationist position (Lewin, 1986).

In California the creationism-evolution dispute appeared in another form. In September 1985 scientists successfully lobbied with the state Board of Education for a sophisticated, accurate treatment of evolution in school books. When the changes were made, however, many scientists were disappointed, feeling that the publishers were trying not to offend the creationists. One writer noted:

> Publishers have retreated to words such as "think" and "believe" in an attempt to be as vague as possible on the subject of evolution. At one hearing, . . . [a specialist] brandished a dinosaur bone to show how little the theory rests on belief and how much on substance.

(Marshall, 1986: 19)

The disputes continue. On both sides the feelings have been strong, because something important is at stake: the development of children's beliefs and values.

Religion and education are both personal forms of socialization. The discussion of creationism and evolutionism highlights the fact that in their socialization of individuals, participants in both institutions are concerned that the beliefs and values they support are passed on to children. When the risk develops that they will not be passed along, then people become agitated. Throughout this chapter it should be apparent that all issues addressed involve personal socialization in some way. Now let us consider the meanings of religion and education.

In sociology an analysis of religion is likely to begin with the concept of "the sacred." The **sacred** is anything that is superior in power, is set apart from the ordinary and practical, and creates a sense of awe. Something sacred is so special that it cannot be questioned. Members of a group or society accept sacred items or activities as representations of the fundamental meaning of life. That acceptance creates a sense of unity and common purpose among those people and serves as the basis for the formation of their religion. Thus what makes an item or idea sacred in a sociological sense is the way people regard it and the unifying effect it produces, not any quality inherent within it. The same wafers and wine that Catholics con-

sider to be sacred, representing the body and blood of Christ, would be regarded as ordinary food and drink by non-Catholics. In contrast to the sacred, those things that people consider ordinary and closely linked to practical demands are termed **profane.** Profane items do not create unity and a sense of common purpose the way sacred things do.

A **religion** may be defined as a unified system of beliefs and practices that focuses on sacred things and serves to create a community of worshippers (Durkheim, 1975: 123). Among other things religions may be analyzed as efforts to develop philosophical and spiritual insights that can be used in facing the stresses, confusions, and complexities of human existence. In this chapter we consider functions of religion and prominent trends in religion today.

Like religion, education is a type of personal socialization. **Education** is the transmission of knowledge, skills, and values by either formal or informal means. This transmission is critical for the survival of a culture. In modern societies the education process is in general highly formalized. We examine theoretical perspectives on education, reform in American education, as well as education and equality.

Many parents, like those of the children pictured here, choose to send their children to private schools which emphasize formal religious training.

Functions of Religion

Just as children must undergo socialization in order to become members of society, people must be socialized before they become members of a religious organization. Once socialized, people find that their religious organizations perform a number of functions. In this section we examine four functions of religion, three of which are associated with prominent sociological theories. We also discuss functional equivalents of religion.

Providing Social Cohesion

Émile Durkheim (1961; 1964) emphasized that as people in traditional societies performed religious rituals, they were focused on what was special and awe-inspiring—the sacred. Durkheim claimed that collective concentration on selected sacred ideas and activities helped create a sense of common purpose and unity.

The sense of common purpose and unity that religion provided assured preindustrial people's commitment to it, in part because of the demands it made upon them. Durkheim indicated that religion places

constraint upon the individual. It forces him into practices which subject him to small or large sacrifices which are painful to him. He must take from his goods the offerings that he is compelled to present to the divinity; he must take time from his work or play in which to observe rites; he must impose upon himself every sort of privation which is demanded of him, even to renounce life if the gods ordain.

(Durkheim, 1964: 92)

The deep commitment that preindustrial religion required of all worshippers strengthened their sense of involvement within the local community or society.

In preindustrial societies, then, religion generally served a cohesive function. With the advent of industrialism, however, secularization occurred. **Secularization** is the process by which religion loses influence within groups and societies.

Secularization involves the replacement of religious faith with belief in scientific principles, and, in addition, it leads to an increasing separation between the religious and nonreligious areas of life. Activities such as work, war, government, commerce, and learning and science become increasingly divorced from religion (Johnstone, 1975: 296; O'Dea, 1966: 81–86). An analysis of paintings contained in the Metropolitan Museum of Art in New York and ranging from the fourteenth to the twentieth centuries indicated that

Religion and religious rituals are an intimate part of the fabric of daily life for many people. This photo shows a Hassidic Jewish father and his son participating in a Bar Mitzvah, a ceremony in which the boy formally becomes a man and assumes all the religious duties of an adult member of the community.

over time the presence of religious themes has declined (Silverman, 1989).

Supporting and Maintaining Social Control

Many congregations include prominent, wealthy, and powerful members of the community. The clergy of such churches are likely to feel that they must support dominant standards of social control, no matter how their personal feelings differ, in order to retain these members' economic and social support. For instance, in the 1950s, white ministers in Little Rock, Arkansas, in spite of their personal inclinations, often publicly opposed the integration of their congregations because they feared that integration would drive out the wealthy and powerful white members (Campbell and Pettigrew, 1959).

Mark Twain, a strong opponent of organized religion, emphasized that churches backed domi-nant practices of social control with a vengeance. On the issue of slavery, Twain suggested, religious leaders originally focused on Biblical texts that supported the practice. In time, however, public opposition to slavery became widespread. "There was no place in the land where the seeker could not find some small budding sign of pity for the slave. No place in the land but one — the pulpit." Finally, Twain continued, organized religion eventually started opposing slavery. "It . . . did what it always does, joined the procession — at the tail end" (Twain, 1973: 109).

Karl Marx (1970: 131–132) also suggested that the primary function of religion is to support the status quo. Marx's analysis was centrally concerned with the class distinction between the exploited workers and the wealthy capitalists, who own the factories and farms where the workers labor. According to Marx, religion provides "illusory happiness" for workers, promising that the righteous will receive their just reward in heaven. In an often quoted Marxist phrase, religion is "the opium of the people." Thus Marx believed that religion has advanced the interests of the dominant capitalist class, providing a means by which capitalists could distract workers from their own immediate, pressing interests. Marx believed that in order for workers to perceive correctly the exploitation that they suffer, they must abandon religion. Once freed, they could start organizing to change their economic and political situation.

A review of Marx's writings suggested that were Marx to return to earth more than a century after his death, he would still find plenty of evidence supporting his conviction about the destructive effect of religion on workers (Gurley, 1984). Research using Marx's perspective on religion continues (Flynn and Kunkel, 1987).

Promoting Social Change

In the course of a major study of world religions, Max Weber suggested that religion has promoted social change by supporting the development of capitalism. Unlike Marx, who considered religion little more than a reflection of the economic system, Weber suggested that this institution has played an important role in the development of the economy. Weber conceded that capitalism has also influenced religion, but he basically reversed Marx's cause-and-effect relationship. That is, religion became the cause, and the economic system (capitalism) became the effect.

Weber (1958) developed his argument in *The Protestant Ethic and the Spirit of Capitalism*. He suggested that Calvinism is the theology that has had the strongest influence on the development of capitalism. In this Protestant denomination, God was originally thought of as an aloof, inscrutable being maintaining total control over the universe. Human beings existed solely for the glorification of God and were expected never to question God's decisions; they were supposed to accept them on faith. One critical article of faith involved the doctrine of predestination. This doctrine suggested that people were destined for either salvation or damnation before birth. While nothing could be done to earn salvation, God did provide certain signs that indicated whether or not particular individuals were likely to be among the minority who would be saved. In particular, if people dedicated themselves to their occupations and achieved wealth, then it was likely that they were destined for salvation.

Devout Calvinists, Weber contended, were thus given "a positive incentive to asceticism." They were driven to work hard, to save, and to invest what they had saved in order to become wealthy. Wealth itself had no spiritual value, but accumulated wealth gave evidence that people were fulfilling their calling, glorifying God. Furthermore they were proving both to themselves and to others that they were bound for salvation. Weber argued that precapitalist merchants were stimulated in their quest for material success by the competitive challenge — what we might call the joy of the hunt. By contrast, early Calvinist capitalists were under the influence of a religious standard for the conduct of life.

According to Weber, this drive to obtain wealth through thrift and hard work — in short, the spirit of capitalism — has endured despite the decline of Calvinism. As a case in point, Weber quoted Benjamin Franklin, who wrote in the eighteenth century. "Remember, that money is of the prolific, generating nature. Money can beget money, and its offspring can beget more, and so on. Five shillings turned is six, turned again it is seven and threepence, and so on, till it becomes a hundred pounds" (Weber, 1958: 49). Saving, investing, and building wealth might no longer be seen as providing proof of salvation in the next world, but Franklin's words suggest that these activities can become the key to the achievement of success in the present life. Thus the spirit of capitalism remains strong in the industrial era, even though its link to Calvinism was severed long ago.

It has been difficult to test Weber's conclusions in the United States. Numerous studies seeking to determine whether or not Protestant religion has influenced the development of capitalism have often been sharply criticized. One significant drawback to such research has been that comparisons of occupational success between Protestants and Catholics are probably invalidated by the fact that Catholics have tended to experience more discrimination, placing them at a distinct occupational disadvantage to Protestants. Some researchers have sought to broaden Weber's thesis, determining if there is a general relationship between religious values and business success. For instance, research concluded that Japanese immigrants' religious values have significantly contributed to their economic achievements in the United States (Woodrum, 1985). A scholar suggested that Weber's thesis will continue to provoke analysis and controversy (MacKinnon, 1988a; 1988b).

Making the World Comprehensible

The Biblical explanation of human creation is straightforward, concise, and complete. Like Christianity, many other religions also provide answers to such cosmic questions about how humanity originated and why people were created. Some religions, such as the Unitarian-Universalist Association, either deemphasize or deny belief in God and salvation, but they still believe that the pursuit of good works, such as continuing service to humanity, can make the world more comprehensible.

In 1986, 57 percent of the people interviewed in a national survey said that religion can provide answers for contemporary problems, while 23 percent said that religion is largely old-fashioned and out-of-date. In 1957, 81 percent of the public expressed faith in religion's ability to provide answers to contemporary problems, and only 7 percent considered it old-fashioned in this regard (George Gallup, Jr., *Gallup Poll*, April 1987). The

362

declining popular support for religion's function of making the world comprehensible is not surprising in a society that has been becoming increasingly secularized. It seems that Americans nowadays more frequently turn to a number of nonreligious specialists, including natural scientists, social scientists, and psychiatrists, for answers to contemporary problems.

Nonetheless religion continues to supply profound meaning for many individuals, especially in crises. Following devastating floods, ministers found that their greatest contribution was the use of rituals, readings, and sermons "to address the ultimate need of survivors to find meaning in their suffering" (Bradfield and Wylie, 1989: 404).

Table 13.1 summarizes the four functions of religion that we have discussed.

Functional Equivalents of Religion

Sometimes the functions normally provided by a particular structure are supplied by a different source. A **functional equivalent** is an organization or activity that provides service or assistance to an individual or group more commonly received from some other organization or activity. A number of organizations may be considered functional equivalents of religion. For example, Transcendental Meditation (TM) is a group that teaches meditation techniques claimed to promote physical, social, and spiritual well-being. Erhard Seminars Training (est) is a commercial program providing group workshops for the pursuit of increased self-understanding. Socialism is a political philosophy that many national governments have endorsed, beginning with the Soviet Union in 1917. In each case the leaders and members of these groups and movements deny that they are involved in religious activity. In a formal sense, they are correct. Their concerns focus on the immediate, empirical world, not on the supernatural level of existence. Like religions, however, each of these functional equivalents has a founding prophet, follows certain sacred or quasi-sacred texts, provides a world view that precludes or at least subordinates most other world views, and seeks to convert outsiders.

Furthermore functional equivalents can serve the same functions as religions. Soviet socialism has supported social change. A French visitor to

Table 13.1
Some Functions of Religion

THE FUNCTION	ILLUSTRATION
1. Providing social cohesion	1. Durkheim's contention that religion can support a common sense of purpose
2. Supporting and maintaining social control	2. Marx's conviction that religion is "the opium of the people"
3. Promoting social change	3. Weber's conclusion that Calvinism has served as an incentive for capitalist expansion
4. Making the world comprehensible	4. The belief, which is shared by the majority of Americans, that religion can provide answers to contemporary problems

The respective theoretical contributions of Durkheim, Marx, and Weber on religion can be visualized as illustrations of three separate functions of religion.

the Soviet Union in the 1930s was impressed by the changes that the leaders promised. He wrote, "Like many other visitors, I saw model factories, clubs, pleasure grounds, at which I marveled. I asked for nothing better than to be carried away with admiration and to convert others as well" (Crossman, 1952: 160). Soviet socialism has also fostered strong social cohesion; people have been unified by the hope that they have been building a better, more just world. The same French traveler observed a "a feeling of humanity, an immediate up-surge of brotherly love." Children were "well-fed, well-cared-for, cherished and happy. Their eyes were clear and full of confidence and hope" (Crossman, 1952: 159).

In the United States, functional equivalents of religion also exist. A prominent example is American civil religion. A **civil religion** is a shared, public faith in the nation, a faith linked to people's everyday life through a set of beliefs, symbols, and rituals that contain religious elements and overtones that are not formally affiliated with any particular religion. Common beliefs include statements made by American presidents ranging across time from Washington and Jefferson to Kennedy and Reagan and contending that the United States is on a divinely supported mission to fulfill God's will for humanity. Sacred symbols of the American civil religion include the flag, a Judeo-Christian god, the Declaration of Independence, the Bill of Rights, the eagle, and a host of buildings and structures such as the Capitol, the White House, the Washington Monument, the Lincoln and Jefferson Memorials, and many more. Major rituals of the American civil religion include Memorial Day, Veterans Day, Thanksgiving, and the Fourth of July, as well as the pledge of allegiance to the flag and the singing of the national anthem (Bellah, 1967).

During his presidency Ronald Reagan was a skilled spokesman for civil religion. An analysis of his speeches revealed that Reagan implicitly described a "genesis story" of American society in which a "golden age," where private initiative was prominent, existed before "the fall" — Franklin Roosevelt's New Deal, in which federal government involved itself extensively in people's lives by initiating social-welfare programs that supposedly destroyed private initiative. Reagan preached "a revival," which he felt would occur when the role of government in people's lives was reduced and as a result harmony between the individual and social good restored (Adams, 1987).

The flag is a prominent symbol of the American civil religion. Flag-burning incidents, like this one at the 1984 Republican Convention in Dallas, have enraged many citizens and prompted passage of a law making such actions illegal.

Prominent Trends in Religion Today

Many Americans have been socialized to make attendance at religious services a consistent practice. In 1939, 41 percent of a national sample had attended services at a church or synagogue in the past seven days. The figure rose to 49 percent in 1955 and 1958 and then dropped back to 40 percent in 1987 (George Gallup, Jr., *Gallup Poll*, April 1987).

In this section we examine religion from an organizational perspective. It is clear that membership is an important factor determining whether or not religious organizations survive. Modern religious groups have developed a number of ways of building membership. Of the modern religious movements, fundamentalism has had the greatest success in the area of membership growth.

Figure 13.1 presents the percentages of the adult American population affiliated with major religious groups.

The Declining Influence of Major Religions

Religion has sometimes been referred to as "a war for souls." If we think of religious activity in

Figure 13.1
American's Religious Preferences.

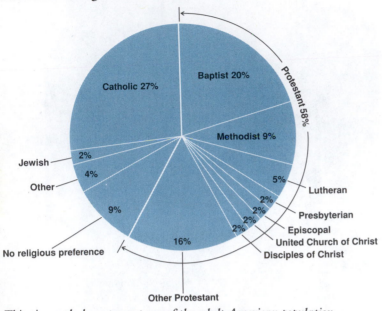

This pie graph shows percentages of the adult American population affiliated with major religious groups. (Source: Adapted from George Gallup, Jr. Gallup Poll. 1987.)

this way, then it seems as if the battleground has broadened in recent years. Many people display bumper stickers urging the unsaved to convert. Religious organizations purchase advertisements on radio and television. Various cults seek out young and confused people, offering them kindness and understanding and eventually imploring them to join their organizations.

Americans' feelings about the influence of religion have varied over time. In 1957, 69 percent of all Americans believed that the influence of religion was increasing, and only 14 percent felt that its power was decreasing. During the 1960s the percentage of the public that believed the influence of religion was increasing fell sharply, and then the figure gradually rose during the early 1970s until it reached 44 percent in 1976. After that it dropped again, registering 35 percent in 1980, but then it started rising once more, attaining 48 percent in 1986 (George Gallup, Jr., *Gallup Poll,* April 1987).

In the mid-1950s, popular ministers like Billy Graham and Norman Vincent Peale led a religious revival. The rapid increase in the size of the middle class and this group's widely held belief that attending church was "the thing to do" were also

contributing factors to the growth of religion during this era. The 1960s were characterized by widespread disillusionment regarding social institutions, especially among young people. The present era has represented a mild religious revival.

Fighting Back: Selling Organized Religion

The decline in interest in religion is a life-and-death matter for religious organizations. Consider some of the more dramatic shifts in membership. Since the mid-1960s, the leading Christian fundamentalist denominations — Southern Baptists, the Assembly of God, and the Seventh-Day Adventists — have increased their membership by at least 30 percent, while the leading, established, "main-line" Protestant denominations — the United Methodists, the Episcopalians, the Lutheran Church in America, and Presbyterian Church (U.S.A.) — have all lost membership (U.S. Bureau of the Census, *Statistical Abstract of the United States: 1966.* No. 45; U.S. Bureau of the Census, *Statistical Abstract of the United States: 1989.* No. 79). Many religious leaders have actively worked to reverse their organizations' declining influence. Three ways of maintaining and building religious membership deserve special attention.

1. *Adjusting organizational practices to meet members' changing requirements.* Since Israel's Six-Day War in 1967, many American Jews have been deeply concerned with Jewish survival. This preoccupation has supported such trends as the restoration of Hebrew to religious services and the establishment of many new religious schools (Cohen and Fein, 1985). Priest – sociologist Andrew Greeley has concluded that unless Catholic leaders become much more inclined to change traditional moral positions, such as the stance on birth control, there will be a profound alienation of lay Catholics and a continuing loss of members (McNamara, 1985). In Canada Buddhist temples with Japanese congregations have been finding it necessary to change some practices to accommodate their younger, Westernized members (Mullins, 1988).

2. *Using modern public-relations techniques.* A number of years ago, Catholic leaders in Michigan decided to conduct an intensive campaign to defeat a state referendum liberalizing abortion statutes. These leaders realized

that one benefit of winning such a campaign would be a renewal of their followers' faith that the Catholic Church remains a vigorous organization that can still defeat opponents' misguided efforts. The organizers hired an advertising and public-relations firm, and members of the Church carefully coordinated the campaign, regularly providing up-to-date details to local personnel throughout the state. In addition, the Church bought a great deal of television and radio time. Partly as a result, the antiabortion forces won on election day, despite being considerably behind (according to independent polls) less than a month earlier (Hinsberg, 1974).

3. *Developing sales skills*. Some clergy have become proficient salespeople in order to gain converts. This is not a new development. In December 1734, Jonathan Edwards initiated the first American revival, a recruiting drive to counteract poor attendance at church services. This campaign was known as "the Great Awakening." With "terrible vividness and earnestness," Edwards urged his listeners to flee the wrath of God and seek refuge in religion (Sweet, 1950: 130). One of the most celebrated modern salesmen of religion is the Reverend Robert Schuller, the founder of the first (and still the wealthiest) drive-in church in the world, located in southern California. His "Hour of Power" TV show is carried by eighty-eight stations, and he claims an audience of about thirty million people a week. According to Schuller, if a person continues to strive while putting his or her faith in God, success (material or otherwise) is inevitable. Schuller's supporters say that he provides hope and that he makes them feel good about their lives in a world where many people feel uprooted from traditional ties (Allman, 1976). During the late 1980s, however, a series of sexual and financial scandals led to a decline in support for television ministry. While 49 percent of a national sample admitted to watching religious programs sometimes on television, only 34 percent considered the ministers sincere or honest, 23 percent indicated that they were untrustworthy with money, and only 4 percent contributed money to them (George Gallup, Jr., *Gallup Poll*, April 1987).

Fundamentalism

While the influence of many religious organizations has declined in the United States, Christian fundamentalism has recently been very successful.

In his well-known novel *Elmer Gantry*, Sinclair Lewis wrote about a fictional fundamentalist minister and how he achieved popularity. For his first sermon in the town of Zenith, Gantry chose the topic "Can Strangers Find Haunts of Vice in Zenith?". He was gratified to see four hundred people turn out when his predecessor had had to settle for a hundred. In his sermon Gantry told how he had gone to a local beach and found — what a shock! — "mixed bathing." The minister titillated the men in the audience by describing the ladies' legs. Then he mentioned the two women who had tried to pick him up, the waiter who had offered to sell him liquor despite Prohibition, the illegal, all-night poker game he had discovered, and more. As he spoke, Gantry became increasingly emotional, chastising his congregation for tolerating such rampant vice: "We're lazy. We're not burning with a fever of righteousness. On your knees, you slothful, and pray God to forgive you and to aid you and me to form a brotherhood of helpful, joyous, fiercely righteous followers of every commandment of the Lord our God" (Lewis, 1970: 305). Gantry had let several newspaper reporters know that something special would be taking place in church that Sunday morning, and the papers reprinted almost the entire sermon. The next week 700 people turned out, and Gantry was solidly established as a local favorite.

It was during the period covered in *Elmer Gantry* — the post-World War I era — that the third of five Christian fundamentantalist revivals in the United States took place. The first revival occurred at the beginning of the nineteenth century; the fifth is taking place today. The five revivals have displayed six common themes:

1. *Individualism*. Fundamentalism focuses on personal woes and personal salvation, with supporters urged to examine their own private spirituality and to commit themselves to a personal relationship with Jesus Christ.
2. *Emotionalism*. Fundamentalism is a religion of the heart, not the head. Conversion is a highly emotional experience that remains almost unchanged since the early nineteenth-century revivals.
3. *Moralism*. Fundamentalism emphasizes living a Christian life. The path to salvation requires a recognition of one's own sinfulness and a determination to live righteously, resisting all temptations.

Jimmy Swaggart is one of the prominent fundamentalist ministers whose popularity has been sharply reduced by involvement in sexual or financial scandals.

4. *Conservatism.* People who embrace fundamentalism are generally suspicious of most social change.
5. *Nondenominationalism.* Fundamentalists maintain that no one church has a monopoly on the attainment of salvation. While revivalists do not dismiss established religious organizations, their primary focus is on a moral crusade against evil, a crusade that rests on a nondenominational basis.
6. *Evangelism.* Revivalism depends on evangelistic ministers who use oratory and personal magnetism to generate enthusiasm in revival campaigns. Evangelists are more likely to be prophets than messiahs, more interested in listeners than followers. Billy Graham, for instance, has characterized himself as "the Western Union Messenger of God" (Wilson, 1978: 67–68).

Beyond sharing these six themes, fundamentalists differ in some regards. For instance, followers of Pat Robertson emphasize speaking in tongues and faith healing and are fairly moderate politically. In contrast, Jerry Falwell's followers are more conservative politically and believe in Biblical infallibility (a literal acceptance of Biblical statements) (Guth and Green, 1988).

Fundamentalism seems to have become so popular in recent years because once individuals choose Christ as their personal savior, they are not only comforted but also spared the necessity of needing to personally struggle with interpretations of such complex modern issues as the possibility of nuclear war and the apparent end of economic growth (Hammond, 1985). Some prominent fundamentalist ministers, however, have lost public support because of well-publicized sexual or financial scandals. Between 1980 and 1987, the proportion of a national sample providing favorable ratings for the following fundamentalist ministers declined—from 58 percent to 23 percent for Jim Bakker, from 66 percent to 28 percent for Oral Roberts, and from 76 percent to 44 percent for Jimmy Swaggart. Of those included in the survey, only Billy Graham, whose name has remained free from scandal, kept a high rating; between 1980 and 1987 his favorable rating remained 76 percent (George Gallup, Jr., *Gallup Poll*, April 1987).

Some fundamentalists have been active politically. In 1980 Jerry Falwell and members of his Moral Majority launched a successful $1 million political campaign called "Target 80," during which television and radio spots and mailings of campaign literature strongly suggested that the primary intention was to give reasons why five prominent liberal Democratic senators should be defeated rather than why their opponents should be elected. The Moral Majority has worked with a large number of single-issue interest groups, such as those opposing abortion, gun control, the Equal Rights Amendment, and sex education in the schools, to achieve its political objectives (Ellerin and Kesten, 1981; Lienesch, 1982).

Until the 1980s fundamentalists were fairly inactive politically. If future efforts to mobilize them are even moderately effective, the outcomes of many elections might be affected (Smidt, 1988; 1989).

The following American Controversy discusses issues related to the role of religion in public life.

AMERICAN CONTROVERSY

Religion in the Public Arena

 Should religious leaders be permitted to participate extensively in public life? We will consider positions favoring and opposing this possibility.

The Position Favoring Religious Leaders' Involvement in Public Life

Initially it should be emphasized that the first amendment to the Constitution indicates not only that people have the freedoms of speech, press, and assembly but also that they have the freedom to establish and practice religion, without fear of intervention. Thus the Constitution supports religious leaders' right to involve themselves in public life.

Much more than a question of legality is involved, however. When religious spokespeople comment on public issues or even political candidates, Americans receive information and opinions from people who are unusually moral, people who are struggling to understand the meaning of life and the significance of our existence on earth. Who could possibly be a better choice to make a thoughtful, worthwhile commentary on such issues as prayer in the schools, creationism in the curriculum, and the moral character and godliness of different political candidates?

A final point for this posi-tion: In modern times people who criticize the right of religious officials' involvement in public life are, in reality, simply liberals who oppose conservative religious leaders' political philosophy. Such people would be happy enough if conservative clergy—in particular, Jerry Falwell and Pat Robertson—were banned from political participation, but they favor liberals' activities—for instance, Catholic bishops' calls for a reduction in nuclear weaponry and for a much more extensive government commitment to eliminating poverty in the United States.

The Position Restricting Religious Leaders' Involvement in Public Life

How much restriction should be imposed on religious leaders? Some, perhaps many critics of clergy's involvement in politics would say that there is quite a difference between a Jerry Falwell, who attempts to assess the religious quality of specific candidates, and people and groups that issue general pronouncements about social and political issues. The first activity means direct involvement in a political contest, while the second is usually no more than a general declaration of political and social opinions provided in sermons.

A topic of even greater concern exists, however. In its indisputable wisdom, the United States has preserved a separation of church and state. There is no official American religion. Were there a national religion, we would run the danger of a few unscrupulous people using the enormous influence that religion can generate to create a mass allegiance. The prospect of the United States becoming like Iran, which was controlled by a religious dictator and his team of Islamic officials until his death in 1989, might seem far-fetched to us. However, the analogy is thought-provoking. Consider the influence exercised by Reverend Moon of the Unification Church over thousands of young people or the power exercised by the deranged cult leader Jim Jones, who led a mass suicide of more than 900 Americans in 1978. No, the supporters of this position assert, it is safer and saner to have religious leaders removed from public issues.

Conclusion

So what do you think? Do you agree wholly with one position or the other? If you end up somewhere between the two positions, indicate precisely which points you support and oppose. Discuss these issues informally in small groups or examine them in class.

Our focus now shifts from religion to education. We have seen that religion involves socialization, that people involved in it concern themselves about the transmission of beliefs and values. As we have already noted, education also involves transmission — in this case knowledge, skills, and values by either formal or informal means.

The relationship between religion and education has shown itself throughout American history. In fact, the earliest American schools were run by churches. For instance, the Society of Friends (Quakers) opened a school in Philadelphia in 1689, and for the next century-and-a-quarter the only schools in Pennsylvania were run by churches (Binzen, 1970: 38). In 1636 Harvard College was created because the Puritans dreaded "to leave an illiterate ministry to the churches when our present ministers shall lie in the dust" (Bailyn et al., 1977: 159). In recent years there has been a revival of religious schools, increasing from several hundred in the 1960s to 13,000 in 1985. What is parents' primary motive for sending their children to such schools? Apparently they are seeking a Christian education for their children, an education which they feel has been denied in tax-supported schools since the Supreme Court's ban on school prayer in 1962. As one British observer noted, "They want the moral and religious instruction that publicly-financed schools cannot now provide without bumping up against the constitution" (*Economist*, 1985: 25). These parents, in short, want to control the kind of education their children receive. In both religion and education, control over the content of socialization is often a major concern for people involved.

Theories of Education

Among sociologists there exist different perspectives about the impact of education upon people. Does it provide socialization that permits people to fit smoothly and effectively into modern society? The structural-functional theory would answer in the affirmative, while conflict theory would respond negatively.

The Structural-Functional Theory

The structural-functional theory of education emphasizes that education contributes significantly to the stability and conflict-free existence of modern society. Even though structural-functional theorists are likely to suggest that individuals can use education to become socially mobile, they indicate that the education system basically helps maintain the existing distribution of wealth and power.

We examine six functions of education.

Cultural Transmission

For a society to survive, culture must be handed from one generation to the next. Once children in modern societies reach four or five, the schools begin to assume the burden of this task. American children must study such academic subjects as English, mathematics, geography, and history and also learn about such nonacademic topics as patriotism, culturally acceptable behavior, and morality.

The United States has been more inclined to stress patriotism in its schools than has England, perhaps because of the necessity of integrating a continuous flow of immigrants. High-school civics textbooks, for instance, have traditionally avoided virtually all unpleasant and controversial aspects of American life. A study concluded that American schools do a more effective job of molding loyal and obedient citizens than do those in the Soviet Union (Banks, 1976).

Social Control

"How'd you like school today, Joey?" a mother asks her young son when he gets home.

"Oh, it's all right, mommy, I guess." He pauses with a puzzled look on his face. "But the thing is, I feel much looser when I get home."

Although Joey would probably have trouble explaining it in detail, he seems to be quite aware of the **hidden curriculum:** a set of school rules that emphasizes blind obedience and that is seldom made explicit but is recognized as important by students. Pupils have traditionally been expected to sit only in assigned seats, to answer questions when called on to do so, to take tests when told to take tests, and to keep quiet the rest of the time. Many American teachers emphasize "repetition, redundancy, and ritualistic action" above all else (Jackson, 1968: 6). One article argued that part of the hidden curriculum in academically ambitious schools is the idea that cheating may be necessary because success is critical; moral sensibilities are numbed by the premium on getting good grades (Power and Kohlberg, 1987).

Exposure to the hidden curriculum begins in kindergarten. Children are expected to take part in a number of carefully supervised activities. Those who submit to the imposed discipline and eventually learn the habit of unthinking obedience tend to be evaluated by the school as good students. Those who accept the routines of the school but do not personally identify with them will probably find themselves in the category of adequate students. Finally children who refuse to accept the rules of the school will often receive the label of "problem children" or "bad students." In modern times schools frequently engage clinical psychologists or other therapists to help teachers deal with such children (Gracey, 1977).

Transmission of Knowledge and Academic Skills

Schools pass on critical knowledge and skills that make it possible for people to participate in the central activities of their society. Without the ability to read, write, and compute, Americans find themselves highly limited in the job market and are also unable to participate in a host of other activities that occur in daily life; they cannot calculate their own income tax, understand a street map, or keep a check book accurately.

Educators often find it difficult to justify studying the liberal arts beyond certain basic topics to students who insist that they are unwilling to devote attention to any topic that will not contribute directly to their future economic success. People who are concerned only about the immediate advantages of education will not appreciate the broader benefits that students can obtain from studying literature, social science, a foreign language, or calculus.

Sorting

Another critical function that the schools perform is the sorting of people into different occupational roles. Research strongly suggests that a person's occupational placement is determined largely before he or she completes elementary school. Teachers and principals evaluate students' elementary-school records and then use this evaluation as the primary basis for recommending whether or not particular students should be placed in a high track, which will qualify them for a college-preparatory program, or a low track, which will direct them toward vocational courses or some other program that is not college-bound. Sometimes the recommendation will change as a result of performance in junior-high school, but such changes are uncommon. Those who successfully complete college-preparatory programs then proceed to college. Ultimately successful completion and perhaps further schooling lead to the more prestigious and higher-paying jobs. The occupational prospects of even ten-year-olds, in short, are often quite determined (Parsons, 1968).

Development of Social Skills

"Sally, I don't know how you did it!"

"It was easy, Hank. Really!"

"But you presented the boss exactly the same proposal that I did. Nothing more and nothing less."

Sally smiles. "It's not what I said that was important, Hank. It's how I said it."

Sally is clearly aware of the importance of social skills. Tactfully (perhaps too tactfully for Hank to understand), she implies that his social skills could use some improvement. One of the functions of education is to help develop these abilities. Children who are evaluated as good students because they have learned to accept the rules that teachers emphasize also tend to develop the social skills that will help them behave appropriately in middle-class occupational spheres.

Research on successful management personnel has concluded that a high level of intelligence has been judged neither necessary nor desirable, and specialized or technical skills are of minor significance. The importance of managers' social skills is apparent when one realizes that corporate advancement often occurs when a manager becomes a member of a team or clique that provides assistance to a sponsoring higher executive. Failure in business can be largely explained by lack of social skills. A survey of seventy-six large corporations concluded that 90 percent of the managers fired from their jobs were believed to lack desirable personality traits (Collins, 1979: 32).

Advancement of Knowledge

The role expectations for faculty in colleges and universities vary considerably. In the elite schools, the basic principle is "publish or perish." Either faculty members produce a substantial quantity of high-quality publications (books, articles, or both), or they will be dismissed. Less elite colleges and universities favor publications and may require them for promotion or other forms of public recognition but do not consider them absolutely mandatory in order to keep a job.

There is no doubt that contributions to the advancement of knowledge are highly prized throughout the academic world. One's colleagues may respect first-rate teaching, but the only way to receive meaningful recognition, especially beyond the confines of one's own school, is to make a contribution to knowledge in one's field, normally in written form.

The process of advancing knowledge can bring new members into a discipline. When graduate students or undergraduate majors participate in a faculty-research project, they start to obtain the knowledge and skills that can make them productive members of that field and eventually contributors to its further advancement. Many academic departments provide courses that introduce students to the process of knowledge advancement in their field; the methods course in sociology is an example.

The Conflict Theory

While structural-functional theory emphasizes that education contributes to the stability and conflict-free existence of society, conflict theory makes the claim that education perpetuates existing inequalities among people. Conflict theorists will not accept the structural-functionalists' claim that social control in schools simply promotes an orderly society. The advocates of conflict theory emphasize that the current education system tends to produce unquestioning obedience to authority, like the frightening blind obedience Stanley Milgram created in the experiment reported in Chapter 2, "Doing Research in Sociology."

A Reexamination of Several Functions of Education

Conflict theory considers the functions we have just examined in a different light. While structural-functional theory emphasizes that education provides students information that encourages them to interact intelligently in modern society, the conflict approach is less optimistic; it claims that schools are simply trying to prepare students to become dull, conforming members of modern society by developing unthinking patriotism, good work habits, and good manners. Since American public education started, the schools have tended to stress the transmission of conservative values. As early as the 1840s, textbooks and teachers propagandized for the positive qualities of the American way of life, especially the capitalist economic system. In school immigrant children were told that if they simply worked hard and lived virtuously, they would eventually become successful, honored, and even wealthy. Educators emphasized this theme constantly, even including it in the arithmetic lessons. The following example illustrates how one test simultaneously taught subtraction and sermonized about drunkenness: "There were 7 farmers, 3 of whom drank rum and whiskey and became miserable. The rest drank water and were healthy and happy. How many drank water?" (quoted in Binzen, 1970: 43).

Like conflict theorists, West German educators have been deeply concerned about possible harmful effects of schools on children, as the following Cross-Cultural Perspective indicates.

Structural-functional and conflict theory agree on only one point about the issue of sorting: that it does take place. The structural-functional perspective claims that students are placed in tracks according to their abilities. Conflict theory, on the other hand, focuses on the fact that there is a distinct relationship between income and race, and students' tracks. Specifically, those who come from affluent families and are white are more

CROSS-CULTURAL PERSPECTIVE

Questioning Authority in German Schools

As an important agent of socialization, schools are a major source of children's values. With this fact in mind, West German educators have been systematically teaching their pupils to question all authority. If children challenge and even refuse to obey authority figures, they argue, then no Nazi-style dictatorship will ever again receive public support.

In 1973 Gerda Lederer, an American mathematics teacher, first learned what West German educators were trying to do. She had come to Germany as part of a group of twenty-three American teachers whose chief purpose was to discover why German students, like students in a number of other countries, did better than their American counterparts on math achievement tests. She found that the unlearning of blind obedience was a much more interesting topic, however. The subject seemed to come up almost continuously. For instance, Lederer and a German colleague were at a train station preparing to take a class on a day trip. Lederer suggested that they line up the students and count them. "Oh no! We never line them up!" exclaimed the German teacher. "That would be too authoritarian. We don't treat children like that."

"I felt like Alice in Wonderland," Lederer explained. Everything was the opposite of what she expected. When she returned to the United States, almost nobody would believe what she had found happening in the German schools. The results were simply too distant from stereotypes of blindly obedient Germans. After Lederer entered a doctoral program, she conducted a study comparing the values of German and American high-school students in the late 1970s with similar data from the two countries obtained in the 1940s.

Lederer found the following:

1. When asked whether a soldier in wartime would be justified in refusing to obey an order to shoot an innocent prisoner, 44 percent of German adolescents and 29 percent of American adolescents said no in 1945. By 1979 the figure had dropped to 7 percent for German adolescents, while for their American counterparts it had also fallen but not so far — to 12 percent.
2. In 1945, 30 percent of German adolescents and 29 percent of their American age peers felt that a boy who disobeys his elders was worse than a boy who beats up small children. In 1979, 12 percent of the Germans and 16 percent of the Americans agreed with this view.
3. German adolescents were inclined to disagree with a suggestion that children should feel a deep sense of obligation to act in accord with their parents' wishes. American adolescents, on the other hand, tended to support this suggestion.

Lederer's findings generally indicated that German adolescents are less inclined to be obedient to authority figures than are their American counterparts. Some observers, however, question how much the Germans have actually changed. Joseph Katz, professor of human development at Stony Brook, suggested that: "It looks like an ideological compliance with 'the right kind of thing to say' and does not necessarily reflect underlying feelings."

On the other hand, Lederer observed that the modern German effort to teach students not to obey authority figures does demonstrate the potential impact of education: "We, the teachers of the next generation, underestimate the influence that we have," says Lederer. "As a teacher it fascinates me — and terrifies me — to see what is in our hands."

Source: Maya Pines. "Unlearning Blind Obedience in German Schools." *Psychology Today.* V. 15. May 1981, pp. 59–60.

likely to be in college-preparatory tracks than those who are not from affluent families and are nonwhite. Furthermore track placement significantly affects future achievement: The academic track is more likely to encourage academic achievement and the educational and occupational rewards that accompany it than either a general or vocational track (Lee and Bryk, 1988; Natriello, Pallas, and Alexander, 1989). Thus, the conflict-theory argument goes, those who are children of the advantaged are assisted by tracking systems to maintain their advantages.

Structural-functional theory indicates that schooling will provide practical knowledge and skills that make it possible for people to participate in the central activities of the society. On the other hand, the conflict perspective, which focuses on the inequities existing in modern society, stresses that the knowledge that students obtain in school can make them aware of how and why injustices have developed in U.S. society. While structural-functionalists find it difficult to demonstrate the practical significance of a liberal education, the advocates of a conflict approach emphasize that students who have received an effective liberal education will be able to think clearly and independently, thereby equipping themselves to resist any tyrannies the elite might contemplate (Lichtenstein, 1985; Oestereicher, 1982).

Credentials and Social Skills

It has been widely recognized that a steadily increasing proportion of Americans are overeducated for their particular jobs (Clogg and Shockey, 1984). Conflict theorists have sharply criticized this situation, claiming that beyond the development of mass literacy, education is generally irrelevant to on-the-job productivity and sometimes even has a negative impact on it. Concrete vocational skills seem to be learned much more commonly through work experience than in school. Furthermore the findings of a series of studies indicate that there is little or no relationship between school grades and success in the occupational world (Collins, 1979). If in reality the educational system provides few skills relevant to effective job performance, then why is there such a widespread emphasis on academic credentials among employers?

Conflict theorists offer an answer. They claim that most occupations in modern society require a loyal and obedient work force that will perform work tasks that entail limited responsibility and minimal independent decision making. The advocates of the conflict approach contend that certificates of graduation from most high schools or colleges clearly indicate to employers that the young people in question have received training in school that has prepared them to serve effectively in the work world. As one recent study indicated, these certificates "get you in the door" (Bills, 1988). Elite high schools and colleges might place more emphasis on responsibility and self-direction, but, according to conflict theorists, the differences are only superficial. The graduates of elite schools are socialized to be just as unquestioningly loyal and obedient on the job as individuals who receive credentials from nonelite schools (Bowles and Gintis, 1976; Collins, 1979).

Prospects for Change

Conflict theorists contend that the current system of education will not change in any signifi-

While the law requires that free education be available to all children, those in less affluent areas generally have older, less effective facilities and equipment than their wealthier counterparts.

cant respects in the foreseeable future because the elite members of American society believe that their interests would suffer with any changes. According to the supporters of the conflict approach, the wealthy and powerful will usually tolerate and even encourage such innovations as open classrooms or newly developed teaching styles because they give the false impression that significant change is occurring, which might tone

down some critics' protests. Conflict theorists argue that the educational reforms that the elite will find threatening are those that will develop less readily obedient workers or open up elite status to large numbers of people in the nonelite classes.

Supporters of both theories are likely to agree that significant measures of educational reform need to be initiated in our society.

Educational Reform

On the football field, Dexter Manley has been recognized as big and bad—a towering, menacing defensive end for the Washington Redskins—but it was another story when Manley appeared before a Senate panel. Mumbling his words, Manley began to read a prepared statement; the sweat rolled down his cheeks, and tears filled his eyes. There was a long pause, then Wally (Famous) Amos, the cookie magnate and spokesman for Literacy Volunteers, approached the witness table, put his arm around Manley, and spoke to him. After Amos had returned to his seat, Paul Simon, chairman of the Senate Education Committee, turned to Manley and said, "Don't worry about that prepared statement. This takes more courage than anything you've done on the football field" (*New York Times*, 1989: B17). So Manley went on to explain how he had failed in school, or, more accurately, how the schools had failed him. Three years earlier, concerned about his future after football, he had started taking night classes and vastly improved his second-grade reading level.

Schools have failed and continue to fail many American children. When one assesses educational reform at either the national or local level, a number of issues need to be considered: They include understanding the problem, analyzing whose values are currently served by the present situation, seeking relevant information, and taking action (Sirotnik and Clark, 1988).

On the first point, a significant source of current problems is that schools are required to pursue two often conflicting goals. On the one hand, teachers are supposed to educate the individual, developing an interest in learning that must be sustained throughout life while, on the other hand, they are supposed to process masses of students through a series of complicated steps until

they receive a credential—the diploma (McNeil, 1988). Teachers find it difficult or impossible to meet both sets of goals simultaneously, and often learning loses out to the immediate demands of supplying credentials.

On the second issue, the outlook of conflict theory quickly comes to mind when the subject is raised of whose interests are served by the current educational situation. Is it true, however, that the wealthy and powerful will fight all significant reforms? Within individual school districts, investigators might find that there would be widespread support for selected educational reform.

The third subject involves seeking relevant information. In 1983 the National Commission on Excellence in Education issued its report on the state of American education. The commission indicated that unless significant educational reform occurred, the nation would be seriously endangered in the future. The report emphasized that throughout the world other nations are overtaking the once unchallenged American lead in science, technology, commerce, and industry. If the American system of education continues to deteriorate, then American world prominence will also keep declining.

The commission report, titled *A Nation at Risk*, paid tribute to "heroic" examples of educational excellence. Serious problems, however, were much more frequent. They include the following:

Some 23 million American adults are functionally illiterate—thus unable to read and write well enough to meet such practical demands of modern life as reading road signs or filling out an application for a home-insurance policy.

About 13 percent of American adolescents (and 40 percent of minority teenagers) are functionally illiterate.

Between 1963 and 1980, there was a steady decline in average scores on the Scholastic Aptitude Test (SAT). Furthermore during that time period, a significant decline occurred in the number of students who achieved superior scores on the SAT.

The number of remedial mathematics courses offered in public four-year colleges increased 72 percent between 1975 and 1980.

(Goldberg and Harvey, 1983)

Individual districts will vary in the extent to which they suffer these problems, with lower-income areas especially hard-hit.

Finally actions need to be taken. Once again the conflict perspective becomes relevant. Are wealthy and powerful citizens willing to accept significant education reform? At the final stage of this process, that will be determined.

Education and Equality

Frederick Douglass (1968), a well-known nineteenth-century black leader, published a book about his childhood experiences as a slave. He indicated that plantation owners were determined that their slaves should not learn how to read. The owners realized that literate slaves could obtain more extensive knowledge, and such knowledge could lead to discontentment with their situation and ultimately even encourage revolt. Douglass himself learned to read only by trading bread to poor white boys for "the more valuable bread of knowledge."

More recently black activists have consistently emphasized the importance of education. In the late 1930s and early 1940s, the National Association for the Advancement of Colored People (NAACP) and its allies began a concerted attack on segregated education, emphasizing that without equal educational opportunity, black people would forever be seriously handicapped in a highly competitive society. In the May 17, 1954 decision of *Brown* v. *The Topeka, Kansas Board of Education*, the United States Supreme Court ruled that segregated schools were inherently unequal. The years that followed saw widespread efforts to integrate America's public schools. The Coleman Report played a significant part in stimulating these efforts.

The Coleman Report and Busing

As part of the Civil Rights Act of 1964, Congress ordered the federal Commissioner of Education to conduct a study of the availability of educational opportunities for Americans of different races, religions, and national origins. The project was massive. About 600,000 children in more than 4000 schools across the country were tested. Some 60,000 teachers, several thousand principals, and several hundred school superintendents were also interviewed.

More than halfway through the research, sociologist James Coleman, who had been named to direct the project, predicted that the study's findings on the differing quality of the education available to the average white child and to the typical black child were "going to be striking" (Hodgson, 1973: 37). They were not. To Coleman's surprise the results of the study indicated that the physical facilities and the formal curricula in segregated schools attended by blacks and whites were roughly similar and that the test scores of black and white students were only marginally affected by physical facilities, formal curricula, and other measurable characteristics of schools.

Nevertheless, about 85 percent of the black students scored below the white students' average on the standardized tests administered by the researchers. The reason for this seemed to involve a combination of nonschool factors operating among blacks: in particular, poverty, nonsupportive community attitudes toward education, and the low education level achieved by most black parents. Coleman and his associates found that black children and other poor, primarily nonwhite children generally possess less effective educational skills at the time that they enter school and that the schools have been largely unable to overcome this disadvantage (Coleman et al., 1966).

While the Coleman Report has received criticism, many educators and social scientists have accepted its basic findings. One particular finding has had an especially significant effect on social policy: that students from poverty areas were frequently able to improve their academic performance substantially when they attended schools with students living in affluent areas. This conclusion led directly to the practice of busing.

Busing and Equality

Why has busing been used to promote school integration? To begin, recall that school districts normally serve only their immediate residential areas. Most of these areas are racially segregated, and in such situations the only way to bring affluent white children and poor black children into contact in the same schools is by physically moving them by means of busing. Busing in order to promote racial balance in the schools has provoked considerable controversy and even violence. Most white parents have not cited integrated classrooms as their reason for opposition. Instead they have claimed to be concerned about the supposed inferiority of inner-city schools, their unfamiliarity with the facilities, the lengthy days resulting from long-distance busing, the danger their children face by entering high-crime areas, and the destruction to community spirit produced by the loss of neighborhood schools (Armor, 1989: 26). One study concluded that nonracial factors, such as those just cited, were at least as important as the racial composition of schools in predicting white students' refusal to be bused to inner-city schools (Rossell, 1988).

Sixteen years after the Coleman Report was published, James Coleman wrote about busing, acknowledging "the general unpopularity of this policy, greatest among whites, but also true for Hispanics and blacks" (Coleman et al., 1982: 197). Coleman suggested that new ways of promoting equal opportunities in education need to be devised.

Specialists in the area of equality in education currently acknowledge that busing and other efforts to integrate schools have produced modest academic improvements for blacks and other non-whites (Jaynes and Williams, 1989: 373–374). It is also appreciated that other issues are at stake. In particular, an analysis of about a dozen major studies demonstrated that children who attend desegregated primary and secondary schools tend to continue segregation in college and their work lives. Thus desegregating schools is more than a question of teaching children to improve their reading or writing skills. More significantly it is a question of opening the gateway to mainstream opportunities (Braddock, Crain, and McPartland, 1984).

Equal Educational Opportunities in Development

During the 1970s there was extensive emphasis on equalization of educational opportunity. Several court rulings addressed the concern that heavy reliance on property taxes, which are levied by cities and towns as a prominent means of financing public education within their locales, tends to create sharp differences in the quality of education provided to children, with the richer districts characterized by better facilities and more highly qualified personnel. In the *Rodriguez* case, the U.S. Supreme Court urged the states to attempt to devise new ways of financing public education. During the 1970s about twenty-five states sought to equalize educational expenditures between rich and poor school districts. State legislatures, courts, and educational agencies became involved in this process. Nevertheless, true equalization of school funding is still a long way off.

There was also significant legislation during the 1970s on behalf of handicapped people. By the middle of the decade, about twenty state legislatures had passed bills mandating equal educational opportunities for handicapped people. Educators struggled to comply, complaining of a lack of special teachers, instructional materials, and funds. In response Congress passed the Education for All Handicapped Children Act in 1975. This was a massive effort, designed to provide individualized schooling for five to seventeen million physically, mentally, and emotionally handicapped children (Brodinsky, 1979). While efforts to weaken this legislation have been prevented, many school districts have failed to provide full compliance with the law (Scotch, 1988). Two educators suggested that the integration of severely handicapped children in public schools might benefit all students, making it possible for both handicapped and nonhandicapped children to learn from each other (Hanline and Murray, 1984).

Besides legislative remedies many steps can be taken to equalize educational opportunity. Edu-

This photo illustrates an increasingly popular, modern educational policy which emphasizes that all students will benefit if those with disabilities are integrated into school activities to the fullest extent possible.

cators have focused on such issues as the representation in history courses of the dramatic struggles of oppressed people around the globe as a means of encouraging minority students (Education for Democracy Project, 1987), the necessity to increase the proportion of blacks and Hispanic-Americans in graduate and professional schools (Mingle, 1988), and the importance of interracial friendships as a means of equalizing educational opportunity (Shrum, Cheek, and Hunter, 1988).

Commentary

In this chapter we have examined two types of personal socialization. When people initiate religious activity, they are transmitting values and beliefs. When people administer education, they are transmitting knowledge, skills, and values. In both institutional areas, many people feel strongly, and that is because they appreciate the processes that are unfolding: Members of society, especially children, can be significantly influenced by the content of either religion or education, and

the nature of the content and its extent of influence obviously are determined by those in control.

We have seen a significant difference between the types of socialization represented in this chapter and family-centered socialization discussed in Chapter 6. The activity in these two institutions is much more public, and in the case of education, in particular, it simply is not possible to eliminate public discussion and debate and the controversy that accompany them.

STUDY GUIDE

Learning Objectives

After studying this chapter, you should be able to:

1. Define religion and education and explain their significance in modern societies.
2. Identify and describe three major functions of religion.
3. Examine two prominent trends in religion today: the declining influence of major religious organizations and the prominence of fundamentalism.
4. Discuss the structural-functional and conflict theories of education.
5. Analyze recent developments in educational reform.
6. Examine education and equality, describing the Coleman Report, busing, and recent activities in this area.
7. Indicate why both religion and education are personal types of socialization.

Summary

1. A religion is a unified system of beliefs and practices that focuses on sacred things and serves to create a community of worshippers. The sacred is anything that is superior in power and dignity, set apart from the mundane and practical, and creates a sense of awe.

Education is the transmission of knowledge, skills, and values by either formal or informal means. Like religion, education is a type of personal socialization.

2. Religions serve a variety of functions, including providing social cohesion, supporting and maintaining social control, promoting social change, and making the world comprehensible. There are also functional equivalents of religion.

3. One trend in modern religion is the declining influence of major religions. In the past several decades, religious membership and attendance have also been declining. Nonetheless, established religious organizations have fought back with a number of strategies for selling religion. Fundamentalism is a strong modern religious movement. Its basic themes are individualism, emotionalism, moralism, conservatism, nondenominationalism, and evangelism.

4. The structural-functional theory of education is a prominent theoretical perspective on that subject. Cultural transmission, social control, transmission of knowledge and academic skills, sorting, development of social skills, and advancement of knowledge are six important functions of education.

The conflict theory of education focuses on the part that education plays in the perpetuation of inequalities among people. This theory provides a reexamination of the functions analyzed by structural-functional theory and also offers its own conclusions about credentials and social skills as well as the prospects for change.

5. Educational reform requires a systematic approach. Although one can outline such an approach, it is questionable whether powerful and wealthy individuals will support significant improvements in the educational system.

6. Attacks on inequality in American schools started in the 1930s. The Coleman Report concluded that the fact that black students on the average scored below whites on standardized tests was primarily because of nonschool factors. Findings in the Coleman Report promoted the initiation of busing. During the 1970s extensive emphasis on equalization of educational opportunity occurred.

Key Terms

civil religion   a shared, public faith in the nation, a faith linked to people's everyday life through a set of beliefs, symbols, and rituals that contain religious elements and overtones that are not formally affiliated with any particular religion

education   the transmission of knowledge, skills, and values by either formal or informal means

functional equivalent   an organization or activity that provides service or assistance to an individual or group more commonly received from some other organization or activity

hidden curriculum   a set of school rules that emphasizes blind obedience and that is seldom made explicit but is recognized as important by students

profane   anything that people consider ordinary and closely linked to practical demands

religion   a unified system of beliefs and practices that focuses on sacred things and serves to create a community of worshippers

sacred   anything that is superior in power, is set apart from the ordinary and practical, and creates a sense of awe

secularization   the process by which religion loses influence within groups and societies

Tests

True–false Test

_____T_____ 1. Profane items do not create unity and a sense of common purpose the way sacred things do.

_____T_____ 2. Both Weber and Marx regarded religion as no more than an effect of the economic system.

_____F_____ 3. As president, Ronald Reagan was a staunch opponent of civil religion.

_____T_____ 4. The text suggests that all major religious organizations have declined in membership in recent years.

_____T_____ 5. Modern fundamentalist groups have sometimes become involved in politics.

_____F_____ 6. The structural-functional theory of education suggests that the principal function of education is the pursuit of upward social mobility.

_____F_____ 7. Research evidence has strongly suggested that people's occupational placement is largely determined before they complete elementary school.

_____F_____ 8. Advocates of the conflict theory emphasize that the current educational system tends to encourage unquestioning obedience to authority.

_____T_____ 9. It is now clear that the busing program has been an unqualified success.

_____F_____ 10. According to the report issued by the National Commission on Excellence in Education, the United States still maintains an unchallenged lead over other nations in the quality of education provided to people preparing to work in the areas of science, technology, commerce, and industry.

Multiple-choice Test

_D_   1. According to Durkheim, secularization:
   a. is more prominent in preindustrial societies than in industrial societies.
   b. is more prominent in industrial societies than in preindustrial societies.
   c. declines as the influence of science increases.
   d. tends to promote cohesion in societies.

_C_   2. Marx's notion of "illusory happiness" relates to his view of religion as:
   a. the opium of the people.
   b. a support for slavery.
   c. a source of alienation for the wealthy and powerful.
   d. a Protestant ethic.

_____   3. Weber believed that the reason Calvinism encouraged the development of capitalism was because it:
   a. created a common purpose and unity in communities.
   b. raised morale by indicating that everyone would eventually enter heaven.
   c. condemned the ruling class.
   d. encouraged people to work hard, to save, and invest their savings.

_____   4. Prominent functions of religion discussed in the text include:
   a. making the world comprehensible.
   b. limiting social control.
   c. lessening social cohesion.
   d. slowing down social change.

_____   5. Which of the following is true of civil religion?
   a. It has declined sharply in importance since the Civil War.
   b. It is simply another term for religious fundamentalism.
   c. It is represented by socialism in the Soviet Union.
   d. It can be used by social movements and interest groups to promote their own interests.

_____   6. Religion and education:
   a. are personal types of socialization.
   b. have not changed in any significant ways in recent years.
   c. are topics of rapidly declining interest to most Americans.
   d. a and c

_____   7. The hidden curriculum in schools emphasizes:
   a. sorting.
   b. blind obedience to rules.
   c. a prohibition against students' cheating on tests.
   d. advancement of knowledge.

_____   8. The structural-functional theory of education supports the idea that:
   a. cultural transmission should not occur in schools.
   b. schools pass on critical knowledge and skills that permit people to participate in the central activities of their society.
   c. knowledge helps students understand how and why social injustices have developed in U.S. society.
   d. education is irrelevant to on-the-job productivity.

_____ 9. Conflict theorists believe that:
  a. the wealthy oppose the open-classroom concept.
  b. loyalty and obedience should be central values in the classroom.
  c. the elite will support innovations that create a false impression of significant change in education.
  d. elite high schools and colleges encourage considerably more independent thought and action than nonelite schools.

_____ 10. When assessing educational reform, one should:
  a. analyze whose values are served.
  b. understand the problem.
  c. seek relevant information.
  d. a, b, and c

Essay Test

1. Define religion and distinguish between the sacred and the profane.
2. Discuss three functions of religion, giving illustrations of how they are performed in modern American society.
3. Define functional equivalent of religion and provide examples from two countries.
4. Why are major religions declining in the United States? What are three techniques for selling established religions? Which of these techniques do you think would be the most effective and why?
5. Define education. Indicate why it is important in American society.
6. Evaluate the contributions that both the structural-functional and conflict theories make to understanding the role of education in modern America.
7. Discuss the steps that might be taken to initiate significant educational reform.
8. Summarize the relationship between education and equality, evaluating the busing program in the course of the analysis.

Suggested Readings

Bloom, Allan. 1987. *The Closing of the American Mind*. New York: Simon and Schuster. A controversial bestseller arguing that higher education fails to educate modern students effectively.

Caplow, Theodore, et al. 1983. *All Faithful People: Change and Continuity in Middletown's Religion*. Minneapolis: University of Minnesota Press. A volume comparing the impact that religion has had on the residents of a modern-day community with the effect it had on its local citizens in the 1920s and 1930s.

Durkheim, Émile. 1961. *The Elementary Forms of the Religious Life*. New York: Collier Books. Translated by Joseph Ward Swain. A classic work in the sociology of religion, demonstrating how religion contributes to social cohesion in technologically simple societies.

Farber, Jerry. 1970. *The Student as Nigger*. New York: Pocket Books. A series of sharp, humorous essays describing the repressive character of American higher education.

Goodlad, John I. 1983. *A Place Called School: Prospects for the Future*. New York: McGraw-Hill. Research based on observations of more than one thousand classes in grades one through twelve as well as surveys from about 27,000 parents, students, and teachers. Building from his findings, the author discusses the reforms that might provide students a fuller, more meaningful educational experience.

Herndon, James. 1972. *How to Survive in Your Native Land*. New York: Bantam Books. A junior-high-school teacher's irreverent, humorous, and thoughtful account of his successes and failures with students.

Johnstone, Ronald L. 1988. *Religion in Society: A Sociology of Religion*. Englewood Cliffs, NJ: Prentice-Hall. Second edition. A clearly written text introducing student readers in the sociology of religion to its history, theory, and currently significant issues, including such topics as fundamentalism and selling organized religion, which were discussed in this chapter.

Journal of the Scientific Study of Religion. The leading journal in the sociology of religion.

McGuire, Meredith B. 1981. *Religion: The Social Context*. Belmont, CA: Wadsworth. A highly readable textbook about the sociology of religion. Particularly appealing features are the effective integration of prominent sociologists' theoretical perspectives and the detailed analyses of contemporary religious movements and issues.

Parelius, Robert J., and Ann P. Parelius. 1987. *The Sociology of Education*. Englewood Cliffs, NJ: Prentice-Hall. A comprehensive introduction to the sociology of education, featuring the history of American education, prominent theories, and major modern issues and problems.

Phi Delta Kappan. A leading educational journal featuring historical essays, surveys, and evaluative studies. It is worth thumbing through if only to obtain a sense of the primary issues being analyzed and debated by American educators.

Roof, Wade Clark (ed.). 1985. "Religion in America Today." *Annals of the American Academy of Political and Social Science*. V. 480 (July). Thirteen recent articles offering detailed sociological commentary on contemporary American religion.

Sizer, Theodore R. 1984. *Horace's Compromise: The Dilemma of the American High School*. Boston: Houghton Mifflin. A detailed analysis of teaching, that includes vivid descriptions of real classroom activity based on the observations of an educator who visited more than fifty classrooms in recent years.

Sociology of Education. A contemporary sociological journal that specializes in sociological studies and essays addressing a range of educational topics.

Weber, Max. 1958. *The Protestant Ethic and the Spirit of Capitalism*. New York: Charles Scribner's Sons. Translated by Talcott Parsons. Original Parsons translation in 1930. Weber's best-known work in the sociology of religion. This challenging essay examines the relationship between the Calvinist ethic and the development of capitalism.

Additional Assignments

1. In your school library, go to the periodicals file. Select two periodicals from different religious organizations. Look through at least five recent issues of each periodical. List the topics covered in each issue. Do the interests reflected in the two periodicals seem similar or different? What conclusions can you draw about the two organizations' efforts to "sell" their religion? What about their respective interests in social issues and problems?
2. Talk to at least five people about their memories of the teacher they liked most and the teacher they liked least. What characteristics seem to have been most significant in shaping their good and bad opinions of teachers? Has the information you received suggested support or criticism for either the structural-functional theory or conflict theory? What insights, if any, have your discussions provided about teacher training and educational reform?

Answers to Objective Test Questions

True–false Test

1. t   4. f   7. t   9. f
2. f   5. t   8. t   10. f
3. f   6. f

Multiple-choice Test

1. b   4. a   7. b   9. c
2. a   5. c   8. b   10. d
3. d   6. a

14
THE POLITICAL AND ECONOMIC INSTITUTIONS

$\mathbf{A}$ bridge collapsed in Connecticut on a major highway, and Japan's Sony Corporation purchased CBS's record division. Are these two issues related to the arms race between the United States and the Soviet Union? One can argue that they are.

In Connecticut a bridge on the New England Thruway collapsed, and several people were killed. An investigation revealed that the bridge had significant defects and was badly in need of repairs. But because for almost the past half-century, federal spending priorities have been directed elsewhere — most notably toward an arms race with the Soviet Union — funds for repairing bridges, as well as federal subsidies for a variety of social, educational, and environmental programs, have been minimal.

Current lessening of tensions between the United States and the Soviet Union might produce a reduction in the arms race and an increase in federal funds for important domestic programs like bridge repair. This development could produce other outcomes as well, however.

For instance, a well-known economic and political analyst argued that Japan and West Germany have developed a delicately balanced relationship with the United States. In exchange for American military protection from the Soviet Union, those two countries have not exploited the huge capital and trade surpluses they have developed at Americans' expense (Rohatyn, 1988). But what if corporate leaders in these two countries feel that the Soviet threat has been largely eliminated? Will they then feel comfortable taking over major American corporations? Did Sony's purchase of CBS's record division in 1988 represent a sign of an increase in foreign acquisitions of American corporations in the future? These are difficult, troubling questions. They are meant to demonstrate that in the modern world, political and economic factors are related in a complex fashion.

There is an intimate relationship between the political and economic realms. Participants in both institutions are concerned with power. **Power** is the ability of an individual or group to implement wishes or policies, with or without the cooperation of others. Why study power? Power, it seems, is an integral element of social relationships. All of us live with it, and, to some extent, exercise it. A child demonstrates power when he or she makes choices about what clothes to wear, breakfast food to eat, or film to attend. The president of the United States exhibits power when exerting influence on behalf of a federal tax cut or increased military expenditure. Extensive power is often "heady stuff," providing those who possess it with the rare opportunity of having many others executing their wishes. Great power is sufficiently seductive that it often overshadows any associated distastefulness. Americans do not usually support organized crime and yet display widespread interest, even fascination, in the Mafia leader who can literally order an enemy's death with the flick of his fingers.

Authority is power that people generally recognize as rightfully maintained by those who use it. If a person with a gun forces a driver over to the side of the road, then that person has simply demonstrated power. On the other hand, police officers who flag down a motorist are employing their authority.

Power, authority, and politics are closely related. The **political institution** is the system of norms and roles that concerns the use and distribution of authority within a given society. Participants in the political process maintain social order and enact changes in the legal structure. The American political system is a democracy. A **democracy** is a government in which those in power are acting with the consent of the governed.

The **economic institution** is the system of norms and roles developed for the production, distribution, and consumption of goods and services. The economic institution meets the basic material needs and demands of the citizens within a society.

In the following section, we examine two prominent theories about the distribution of authority. The subsequent discussion deals with the three systems by which leaders obtain and exercise authority. Then the discussion shifts to American politics and its corruption. The next part examines modern economic systems, particularly the dominant role played by capitalism in our society. The chapter ends with an analysis of work in modern times.

Theories on the Concentration of Authority

The following discussion demonstrates that social scientists have developed varied conceptions about the role of authority in American society. The two theories discussed in this section provide such different perspectives that one might even begin to lose sight of the fact that their proponents are describing the same political system.

Pluralism

Pluralism is a theory which emphasizes that a dispersion of authority exists in American government. The supporters of this theory point out the existence of elected officials at the local, state, and national levels, all of whom are held accountable to constituents who in turn exercise authority with their votes. Proponents of pluralism believe that if authority is dispersed, then:

1. Authority will be controlled and limited to decent purposes because different centers will counterbalance each other. The evil, coercive use of power will remain at a minimum.
2. Minorities, who will have the authority to veto policies they strongly oppose, will be partners in the exercise of authority and therefore be more cooperative in the long run.
3. Constant negotiations among different centers of authority will be necessary to reach resolutions on political issues. The process of negotiations will provide those engaged in politics with opportunities for learning how to reach peaceful decisions beneficial to all parties in contention (Dahl, 1967).

A large body of research has found evidence supporting the existence of pluralism in many societies. For instance, recent studies have documented pluralist tendencies in the politics of East Central Europe (Arato, 1985), Latin America (Dealy, 1985), and France (Safran, 1985).

Some leading proponents of pluralism have acknowledged that American democracy has been plagued with serious problems — in particular, the abuse of authority by political leaders during the Vietnam War and the Watergate and Iran–*contra* scandals. They have also pointed to the failure to achieve the resolution to such social problems as the maldistribution of income and wealth, racial inequality, inadequate health care, and unemployment (Dahl, 1982; Lindblom, 1982). Although some leading pluralists have acknowledged various limitations to American democracy, they tend to be supporters of the political status quo. With this fact in mind, one critic has questioned whether pluralists are willing to advocate sufficient change in the political system to eliminate or even curtail the problems they now acknowledge (Manley, 1983).

Power-Elite Perspective

The power-elite theory, popularized in the work of C. Wright Mills (1959), opposes the pluralist approach. The **power-elite perspective** is a theory emphasizing that in American society a group of high-status people — well educated, often wealthy, and placed in high occupational positions — control the political process, including political authorities. The members of the power elite see themselves as an exalted group set apart from the other members of society. They "accept one another, understand one another, marry one another, tend to work and to think if not together at least alike" (Mills, 1959: 11). According to Mills, the power elite controls basic political, economic, and military policy. Mills vi-

388

sualized three levels of society in America. At the top is the increasingly unified power elite. Then there is a middle class of white-collar employees. The members of this class are "in no political way united or coherent." They are dominated by the corporations and the government agencies for which they work. They have, in short, little or no control over their own lives. At the bottom there is a mass society of people, whose lives lack purposeful direction and whose access to channels of authority and influence is entirely cut off (Mills, 1959).

G. William Domhoff (1978; 1983) provided evidence supporting the power-elite theory in the United States. He studied the upper class composed of about 0.5 percent of the population and measured by membership in the Social Register (restricted to families that consider themselves an economic and social elite — "high society"), attendance at elite private schools, membership in exclusive clubs, and wealth. He found that members of this class have disproportional representation in high positions in business, politics, and the military. Extensive evidence also indicated that

the American government has aggressively acted on behalf of powerful business interests, both nationally and internationally. Sometimes the government has even backed violent intervention in support of wealthy commercial interests. A number of years ago, a notable case was the participation of the Central Intelligence Agency (CIA) and International Telephone and Telegraph (ITT) in the unsuccessful effort to prevent the election of Salvador Allende to the presidency of Chile and then later their involvement in the successful effort to overthrow his socialist regime (Wise 1976; Wolfe, 1973). Domhoff concluded that the only possible way to adopt a pluralist perspective would be to ignore the privileged backgrounds, wealth, and diversified and interrelated activities and interests of people in the upper class.

A recent study of 243 corporations donating large sums of money to congressional candidates found considerable support for this theory's emphasis on a shared conservative ideology among power-elite members (Neustadtl and Clawson, 1988). Furthermore other studies have analyzed evidence of power elites in other countries, in-

Figure 14.1
Pluralist versus Power-Elite Perspectives on the Vietnam War Escalation

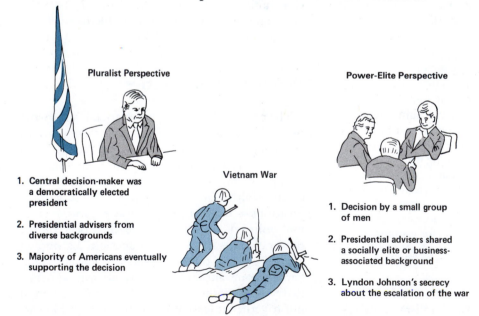

Pluralist Perspective

1. Central decision-maker was a democratically elected president

2. Presidential advisers from diverse backgrounds

3. Majority of Americans eventually supporting the decision

Vietnam War

Power-Elite Perspective

1. Decision by a small group of men

2. Presidential advisers shared a socially elite or business-associated background

3. Lyndon Johnson's secrecy about the escalation of the war

The facts people choose to emphasize in a given political situation often reflect the theoretical perspectives they support.

cluding Thailand (Anderson and London, 1985), Syria (Aziz-al Ahsan, 1984), and black Africa (Bradshaw, 1985).

A Combination of the Two Theoretical Perspectives

Domhoff dismissed the pluralist perspective. An alternative is to consider that the two theories emphasize different facts. We might examine, for instance, the escalation of the Vietnam War. Supporters of the pluralist thesis will stress that a democratically elected official — Lyndon Johnson — made the decision to escalate the war and that the president's key advisers came from diverse backgrounds and so clearly served the interests of different groups — specifically, business, academia, the military, and politicians. Besides, though the decision was initially unpopular, the majority of Americans eventually supported it.

In contrast, power-elite advocates will emphasize that a small number of people made the decision. These people shared a socially elite or business-associated background that may partially account for their willingness to have been more actively supportive of the escalation than the general public. In addition, in 1964, Johnson campaigned as a peace candidate opposed to escalation, but after his election he sought to keep the process of growing involvement in the war secret — very different from the pluralists' ideal of the elected official implementing constituents' interests (Garson, 1977: 146 – 147). Figure 14.1 demonstrates how the two theories apply to the escalation of the Vietnam War.

The pluralist and power-elite theories usually focus on different points. This condition suggests an important conclusion: Both theories can simultaneously apply. Or, to put it another way, Americans live within a less-than-perfect democracy. Certainly Americans elect their representatives, but these representatives and their associates often boost their own interests and desires ahead of those maintained by the general public.

We have examined two opposing theories involving the dispersion of authority. The upcoming section also focuses on authority, offering a theoretical analysis of three authority patterns.

Types of Authority

Max Weber (1947), the German sociologist, described three systems of authority that exist in political systems throughout the world. These systems of authority are ideal types, and as we saw in the discussion of bureaucracies in Chapter 4, "Groups," pp. 90 – 91, ideal types are simplifications of reality made to improve understanding. Actual political systems usually contain elements of two or even all three of Weber's authority systems. The United States is such a society, with the traditional, legal-rational, and the charismatic types all represented in the political structure.

Traditional System

A **traditional system of authority** is an authority system in which the standard of political leadership passes down from one generation to another. Weber said that within the traditional system inherited authority is believed "to have always existed." In this political context, the leaders' authority ranges widely because followers must fulfill almost unlimited obligations (Weber, 1947: 341 – 342). Yet within such a system, people's loyalty focuses on the position and not the incumbent, as the following declaration indicates: "The King is dead! Long live the King!"

Throughout American history citizens have demonstrated mixed reactions toward a traditional system of authority. During the first session of the Senate, Vice-President John Adams and others sought to make "His Highness" the title by which citizens would address the president. Adams and his associates lost out to the simpler title "Mr. President." Some of the most prominent leaders, including George Washington, James Madison, Alexander Hamilton, and John Adams, saw themselves as a natural aristocracy, "a gentlemanly elite to whom ordinary people, if they were only left alone, would naturally defer" (Bailyn et al., 1977: 359). In his farewell address, Washington contended that political parties were

While the United States has no traditional system of authority, its leaders often interact with royalty. In this photo President Bush and Prince Philip of England review the Scots Guards in the quadrangle of Buckingham Palace in London.

a mistake. Parties would readily become factions and thus sources of conflict.

Thomas Jefferson shared Washington's dislike of political parties, but he believed that they were necessary. Jefferson was disturbed by the extent to which early government leaders had consolidated authority. He also believed that these leaders were detached from ordinary citizens' interests. Jefferson led the movement to form the Democratic Republican Party (which later became the Democratic Party) in order to defeat the aristocratic interests of Washington, Adams, and other prominent leaders.

Although the American government has had some traditional tendencies, it more distinctly resembles Weber's second authority type.

Legal – Rational System

The **legal – rational system of authority** is an authority system based on laws enacted to pro-

duce rational behavior and the achievement of formally designated goals. The system depends on participants' competent performance. These people are "servants of the state" (nation), who work within government departments and agencies at the national, state, county, and local levels. Like bureaucrats generally, government officials must follow rationally determined rules and meet the formal qualifications of education and experience that will insure competent performance in their specific positions (Gerth and Mills, 1946: 79, 196 – 198).

Many Americans are generally critical of the legal-rational element in the government. People frequently claim that the federal government is too large and too encumbered with "red tape." For over half-a-century politicians have spoken about curtailing the size of the federal government, with a particular emphasis on the elimination of overlapping functions performed by different agencies. In the past three decades, most presidents have stressed that the best way to restrict the size of the federal government is to transfer increasing responsibility in education, transportation, community development, and social services to the states.

Within democracies ultimate authority, to be sure, rests in government officials' hands, but they are required to give somewhat free reign to the activities of other organizations. In a study of public-broadcasting corporations in four democracies — Australia, Britain, the Federal Republic of Germany, and Israel — Eva Etzioni-Halevy (1988) found that frequently disputes developed about reporting politically sensitive subjects that might either embarrass the government or reveal secret information. The key issue involved how much restriction the federal government should be permitted to impose on these organizations. No firm guidelines on this difficult issue were clearly established, but with an emphasis on efficiency and order, there was the constant potential that government bureaucrats would restrain the broadcasters.

Both the traditional and legal-rational systems tend to entrench themselves in societies, often persisting generation after generation no matter what individuals fill the leadership roles. As we see, the charismatic system is different in this respect.

Charismatic System

The **charismatic system of authority** is an authority system in which leadership develops because of the personal magnetism of an individual, whose followers believe that he or she possesses superhuman qualities. In Weber's phrase the charismatic leader maintains authority "by proving his strength in life." If followers decide to reject a charismatic leader's sense of mission, then the leadership collapses. Few things are ordinary or regularized about a charismatic leader: no career pattern, no formal training, and the rejection of conventional institutions and behavioral standards.

Charismatic leaders often arise when deep-seated problems exist within a society, and their mission usually involves an effort to change soci-

Table 14.1
Weber's Three Authority Systems

AUTHORITY SYSTEM	BASIS OF AUTHORITY	POSSESSORS OF AUTHORITY	CONTROVERSIAL APPEARANCE IN AMERICAN SOCIETY
Traditional	Standard of political leadership passed from one generation to another	Royalty or chieftains	Political orientation of the Federalists' "gentlemanly elite"
Legal-rational	Laws enacted to produce rational behavior and the achievement of formally designated goals	Government bureaucrats	Presidents' and other politicians' half-century effort to trim the size of the federal government
Charismatic	Followers' belief that a leader possesses special, even superhuman qualities	Individuals who appear at crisis times and promise to establish a better life for their followers	Political activities of leaders like Robert Kennedy and Malcolm X whose sense of mission primarily represented the dispossessed and conflicted with many Americans' economic and political priorities

Source: Adapted from Hans Gerth and C. Wright Mills (eds.). *From Max Weber.* Oxford University Press. 1946.

ety and eliminate social problems, thereby producing a better life for their followers. The behavior of charismatic leaders is often disruptive, opposing established policies and practices (Gerth and Mills, 1946: 245–250).

A number of prominent American politicians have been considered to possess charismatic qualities. One would be the late Senator Robert Kennedy. He was killed on the evening of his victory in the California presidential primary, when the road to the White House seemed unblockable. To Americans of wide-ranging political views, Robert Kennedy seemed to be the presidential candidate who could best move toward the resolution of the various social problems that helped create the dissensions and conflicts of the late 1960s. In this respect he was charismatic. In one Weberian respect, however, he did not qualify as a charismatic leader — he operated within the established political system.

Charismatic leaders are likely to appeal to the discontented, deprived members of society. By Weber's standard John Brown, Sitting Bull, Malcolm X, and Charles Manson qualify as charismatic. Outside the United States, Mao Zedong, Fidel Castro, Adolph Hitler, Joan of Arc, and Napoleon would qualify. Manson and Hitler were charismatic individuals who clearly illustrate the fact that the possession of charisma is not an attribute restricted to people most of us would consider "humanitarian" or "good." It is simply a question of whether a person performs the function of the charismatic leadership role, and someone who does qualifies as charismatic. (This chapter concludes with a research section about charismatic leadership.)

Thus the American political system has contained elements of Weber's three authority types. Table 14.1, on page 391, summarizes the previous discussion.

Let us now move beyond theory and consider the actual workings of the political system.

American Politics and Its Corruption

In the 1830s a young Frenchman named Alexis de Tocqueville (1966) visited American society and wrote about it. Some of his observations about the American political process remain accurate today. A pair of his insights summarize central themes of this section: the widespread desire of people to participate in the democratic process and the tendency of influential citizens to corrupt that process. You might note that the first idea is consistent with pluralism and the second with the power-elite perspective.

On the first point, de Tocqueville felt that a large amount of political activity occurred in America, with a wide range of groups mobilizing political action on behalf of their own interests. The Frenchman concluded that nothing was more important to Americans than discussion about their political involvement. According to de Tocqueville, Americans often became so involved in politics that they tended to speak as if addressing a meeting. In fact, Americans could become so excited with the subject that they would sometimes address an audience of one as "Gentlemen."

De Tocqueville claimed that many wealthy people appeared to support democracy. They tended to dress simply and to maintain a modest manner. If an affluent man met his shoemaker in the street, he would stop to talk with him, and most likely they would discuss politics. When they parted, they would inevitably shake hands as equals. If democracy were ever in peril, however, this same affluent man would be happy to help bring about its demise if his interests would benefit. Hence, while de Tocqueville saw authority widely dispersed in American society, he recognized the dangerous potential for the concentration of power in the hands of a few. As we will see, both these issues have been apparent in the American political process.

The Two-Party System

At the American Constitutional Convention of 1787, the delegates opposed "factions" because they feared that political parties would destroy the newly formed nation. Early advocates of political parties like Thomas Jefferson and James Madison believed that opposing, lasting differences of opinion, which political parties represent, are necessary in a free country, even if clashing party ambitions will sometimes endanger the existence of the country. Jefferson, Madison, and others felt that it would be impossible to support the basic freedoms of speech, press, and assembly and simultaneously oppose the development of political parties. The Constitutional decision to hold periodic elections among the people also favored the development of political parties (Dahl, 1976: 275–277).

Political parties provide a number of functions. First, they make the transfer of authority from one administration to another peaceful and smooth. When presidents, governors, or mayors leave office, the newly elected officials move in, bringing with them a slate of the party faithful who can fill government posts, judicial openings, or office staff positions. Thus for such transfers, parties can act as large personnel agencies. Second, parties are a major source of recruitment for government leaders. People who run for local, state, and federal offices have usually been active in party politics, where they display potential leadership qualities. Third, parties simplify voters' choices by providing party labels as a guideline. The majority of American citizens have limited knowledge about the wide array of candidates for whom they are entitled to vote, and so without the party labels to assist them, they would often be completely lost. Fourth, American parties supply a series of platforms and policies. These directives may be somewhat vague and are not always clearly differentiated between the two major parties, but they do broadly support the interests of different voter groups — more distinctly with some issues than others (Grant, 1979: 196–197).

Certainly the American political parties do not always meet their members' needs and interests. Yet the two parties have been successful enough to have dominated most of U.S. political history. Two parties have prevailed for several reasons. In the first place, in the United States, a broad consensus on political issues shared by both political parties exists. Whether Democrats or Republicans, Americans generally express a commitment to democracy, the Constitution, the free-enterprise economic system, universal free public education, and religious and racial tolerance. In contrast, in some other democratic countries, sharp disagreement on specific issues can be the basis for lasting political factions — for instance, Catholic

This display represents the leaders of France's major political parties and suggests that they should have a one-round free-for-all to decide which party dominates. An equivalent American display would present only two figures.

parties in Italy and the Netherlands, farmers' parties in the Scandinavian countries, and working-class parties throughout Europe. Second, the electoral process also encourages a two-party system. In the United States, a winner-take-all process prevails. For example, in congressional elections, each state is divided into districts, and within each district the person receiving the highest vote total obtains the seat. In a number of other democratic countries, on the other hand, there is a system of proportional representation, where each party receives the percentage of seats that corresponds with its total vote. Such a system encourages minority parties, which will receive little or no representation under the U.S. political system. Finally

394

another factor supporting the two-party system is the force of habit and tradition. For over a century, the current two parties have dominated politics. Many Americans receive their party loyalties and political positions from their parents and in turn transmit similar loyalties and positions to their own children (Dahl, 1976: 287–291).

In recent years the two-party system has worked more effectively for some Americans than for others. The Republican administration's tax and spending policies have benefited most Republicans and also affluent Democrats. On the other hand, low-income Democrats have either seen their tax burdens increase or have received the proportionately smallest tax reductions (Edsall, 1986). In many other political systems, there would be one or more political parties to represent this group's specific interests.

For over two centuries, the United States has maintained a stable political democracy. We are not directly aware of the problems a country must face as it moves from dictatorship to political democracy. Spain accomplished this shift in the late 1970s, as the following Cross-Cultural Perspective indicates.

CROSS-CULTURAL PERSPECTIVE

From Dictatorship to Democracy: The Spanish Case

The transition from dictatorship to democracy is a complex and ticklish process. Because of a combination of skillful national leadership and cooperative efforts from the major political parties involved, Spain successfully completed the transition in 1977.

On November 20, 1975, Francisco Franco, the dictator of Spain for thirty-six years, died. The new head of state was King Juan Carlos, who had been appointed by Franco as the individual most likely to perpetuate the standards and the structures of the Franco dictatorship. For a six-year period before Franco's death, Juan Carlos expressed public loyalty to the regime, but only his most intimate friends knew that he had strong sympathies for a democratic form of government.

Nonetheless Juan Carlos's first appointments were a disappointment to supporters of democratic rule.

In particular, legal restrictions made it impossible to choose a democratically oriented prime minister, and he picked Arias Novarro, a strong backer of Francoist policies. Arias held office for about six months. His refusal to support significant political and economic reform provoked strikes and major street demonstrations. Toward the end he even lost the support of his fellow Francoists, who were unwilling to make the most modest reforms to existing policies.

Arias resigned, and in his place King Juan Carlos appointed Adolfo Suárez. By all sensible criteria, Suárez seemed to be the finest choice as prime minister for the difficult period of transition to democracy. He was experienced politically, having held diverse posts in the Franco regime. He clearly saw that the remaining Franco supporters lacked the backing to maintain their system but that no opposition parties had the public support or the organizational unity and strength to assume the leadership. Suárez realized it was up to him to lead his nation gradually but relentlessly toward democratic rule. Besides knowledge and perceptiveness, Suárez had the right personal qualities for the task. He was flexible, self-disciplined, emotionally controlled, energetic at public relations, and above all, forceful.

During the late 1970s, Suárez maneuvered skillfully around the obstacles that opposed a transition to democratic rule. He worked carefully with his closest allies—King Juan Carlos and a number of other influential, progressively oriented individuals. He also managed to maintain effective relations with the army, enlisting senior officers' support behind his reformist program. A prominent reason these individuals and groups were willing to back Suárez was his determination to act entirely within the guidelines of the legal processes set down in the Francoist Constitution.

While the Prime Minister was courting the support of established individuals and groups, he was also determined to obtain backing from the developing political parties. The moderate opposition to Francoism—the Liberals, the Christian Democrats, and Social Democrats —readily approved his program. Even the rapidly growing Spanish Socialist Workers' Party recognized that Suárez's program for restoring democracy was in the best interest of the nation— that at times, as one leader said, "it's most revolutionary to be moderate."

Finally negotiations with the Communists were the only obstacle. Suárez was reluctant to cooperate with the Communists, whose support for his program seemed doubtful. Other moderates agreed that it would be better to keep the Communists out of the upcoming elections. The Communists were un-

happy with this prospect, and one of their most prominent leaders appeared openly in Madrid—a public challenge to Suárez's government since his party was still illegal. To maintain his authority, Suárez had no choice but to arrest this Communist leader. That action, in turn, endangered Suárez's entire program. Most of the moderates had no use for the Communists, but the arrest of their leader undermined the democratic credentials of Suárez and his administration. Suárez had no other option. He released the Communist leader and enlisted the help of King Juan Carlos and Vice-President Gutierrez Mellado to convince the military leaders, the staunchest opponents of Communism, that it was essential to permit the Communists to become a legal political party. Army leaders publicly expressed their dissatisfaction with this decision but said that out of patriotism they would cooperate. No military coup occurred. The Communist leaders, in turn, also made a number of significant concessions.

In this context of cooperation and compromise, a national vote on the government's political reform was held on December 15, 1976; 77.4 percent of the electorate went to the polls, and 94.2 percent of those voters supported the government's political reform, which featured elections in June 1977.

The elections were a triumph for an expanding democratic program. The Suárez coalition received 34.3 percent of the popular vote, and the Spanish Socialist Workers' Party was a highly respectable runner-up, with 28.5 percent. Both the remnants of Francoism and the Communists received only modest support. In 1982 the Socialist party won majority control in the national elections. Thus, within less than a decade, a modern European nation had used a democratic political process to move across the political spectrum: from a repressive, highly conservative dictatorship to an elected socialist government.

Sources: Raymond Carr and Juan Pablo Fusi Aizpurua. *Spain: Dictatorship to Democracy*. London: George Allen and Unwin. 1981. Second edition, pp. 207–258; Meir Serfaty. "Spanish Democracy: The End of the Transition." *Current History*. V. 80. May 1981, pp. 213–217+.

Interest Groups

Some efforts to influence politicians are illegal, but there is nothing inherently illegal about trying to influence politicians. In fact, interest groups are widespread in American society. An **interest group** is a group whose members seek to influence elected politicians or government bureaucrats to initiate the legislation or policies they want. In the American political system, there are thousands of organizations "representing or claiming to represent trade unionists, veterans, business people, industrialists, taxpayers, bankers, oil companies, copper importers, doctors, women's clubs, nature lovers, stream pollutionists, conservationists, foreign policy groups, old people" (Dahl, 1976: 482).

Some citizens' interest groups write letters to politicians, organize petition drives, or advertise in the media. Large, wealthy interest groups might advertise and write to politicians, but they are more likely than citizens' groups to engage extensively in lobbying activities. **Lobbying** is a face-to-face effort to persuade legislators and other government personnel to support the proposals of an interest group. Those proposals might involve the provision of tax loopholes that benefit various businesses, or lobbying might help produce legislation that protects the needs of organizations as diverse as the American Medical Association, the Associated Milk Producers, Inc., and United Aircraft. On the other hand, interest groups or their representatives might act to postpone legislation; the lobbying efforts of the National Rifle Association have prevented the passage of any effective gun-control legislation. Studies indicate that at the federal level, the amount of interest-group activity has sharply increased in recent years. In particular, political-action committees (PACs) started by large corporations have been making major contributions to conservative presidential

and congressional candidates, sometimes with the primary goal being the defeat of liberal candidates (Neustadtl and Clawson, 1988). Table 14.2 summarizes PAC contributions to candidates during the 1985–1986 congressional campaigns.

Why are interest groups so prevalent in U.S. society? A prominent reason is that the political system rests on the simple idea that government exists in order to protect people's rights. A well-known phrase states the condition widely believed by Americans to effectively protect these rights: The government governs best that governs least. John Locke expressed this political philosophy in his *Second Treatise on Civil Government,* and when Thomas Jefferson wrote the Declaration of Independence, he received much of his inspiration from Locke's book. In the more than two hundred years since the signing of the Declaration, Americans have generally accepted this political philosophy. As a result there has been much less government regulation in the lives of the American citizenry than in many other societies. Wealthy and powerful interests have been prominent beneficiaries of this clear absence of regulation (Roelofs, 1967: Chapter 6). When these groups have chosen to further their own interests at the expense of ordinary citizens, they have encountered

Table 14.2
PAC Contributions to Congressional Campaigns: 1985–1986[1]

	HOUSE OF REPRESENTATIVES		
	CORPORATIONS	TRADE ASSOCIATIONS[2]	LABOR
Democrats	12.9	12.3	21.1
Republicans	14	11.2	1.6
	SENATE		
	CORPORATIONS	TRADE ASSOCIATIONS	LABOR
Democrats	4.8	3.8	6.6
Republicans	14.4	5.7	.6

[1] In millions of dollars
[2] A variety of occupationally affiliated organizations
Source: U.S. Bureau of the Census. *Statistical Abstract of the United States: 1989.* No. 444.

Political-action committees (PACs) raise money to support the candidates of their choice. This table shows that Republican congressional candidates receive a greater share of corporate contributions, while their Democratic opponents receive major support from labor.

few if any limits or penalties. Through the late 1970s and into the early 1980s, the rapid rise in oil prices accompanied by a large increase in company profits was a case in point.

While interest groups and lobbying are legal, pay-offs to politicians obviously are not. The problem is where to draw the line. One could argue that even when lobbyists take politicians to dinner, they are actually offering them a low-level bribe: spending money on them in order to encourage action on behalf of their own interests. Evidence from the past fifteen years demonstrates that many prominent politicians have taken much more substantial bribes from lobbyists. On the list have been a president (Richard Nixon), a vice-president (Spiro Agnew), a Supreme Court justice who had been nominated for chief justice (Abe Fortas), and a long list of governors, congressmen, and mayors. In the 1980 Abscam scandal, a senator and a half-dozen congressmen accepted bribes from undercover FBI men pretending to act on behalf of Arab oil men seeking political favors. A team of historians claimed that these various scandals represent "the fall of the great men." Each new scandal "was more shocking than the last, and each set an historic precedent" (Bailyn et al., 1977: 1262). By 1989 so many investigations had been undertaken and so many politicians had been exposed for corrupt practices that, according to one Washington journalist, there was widespread anxiety among office holders and the feeling with each exposure that "there but for the grace of God go I" (Apple, 1989: Section 4, p. 1).

Not surprisingly Americans do not believe that politicians lead exemplary lives. While a national survey found that 66 percent of druggists and pharmacists and 60 percent of clergy were believed to have very high or high standards of ethics and honesty, only 19 percent of senators received such a rating (George Gallup, Jr., *Gallup Poll*, December 1988).

Corruption

George Washington Plunkitt, a prominent, corrupt nineteenth-century politician, once said: "Men ain't in politics for nothin', they want somethin' out of it" (Riordan, 1963: 37).

Candidates for political office would agree. If elected they will reward those who worked for their election. The distribution of favors to political supporters is called **patronage.** Sometimes patronage simply means giving jobs, which can be done in a legal manner, but it can also involve illegal activities: provision of construction contracts, defense contracts, banking and insurance funds, and specialized treatment by government agencies (Tolchin and Tolchin, 1972: 6). Favors such as these will establish the loyalty of one's supporters and thus help secure a politician in power.

In the United States, civil-service systems require that applicants for many government jobs be chosen under a merit, not a patronage system (Ranney, 1966: 468). However, the most powerful nonelected government jobs remain appointments, which are subject to the patronage system. Evidence suggests, for example, that patronage is a prominent factor influencing presidents' selection of their cabinet members (Burstein, 1977).

Political machines also use a patronage system.

Angelo Errichetti, a former mayor of Camden, New Jersey, was just one of many prominent people arrested and convicted for accepting bribes during the Abscam scandals.

398

A **political machine** is an organization established to control a city, county, or state government. At the head is a political boss, who seeks to dominate political activity within the machine's jurisdiction. In exchange for political control and perhaps pay-offs too, bosses and their associates provide certain advantages for different groups.

Robert Merton's (1968) well-known analysis of urban political machines in American cities argued that these arrangements emerged to satisfy a variety of local citizens' needs left unfulfilled by their city governments. Recently, however, a careful historical examination of the development of urban political machines revealed a critical factor about their emergence — that these structures only developed when the executive authority within a city was officially consolidated in the hands of one individual — the strong-mayor system — or in the hands of a few people — the commission form of government. Then, this argument went, that individual or group had the authority to control political patronage and with that control the means to establish and entrench the political machine (DiGaetano, 1988).

Throughout the discussion of the political institution, we have seen that in both its legitimate and illegitimate use, power is the politician's everyday companion. For business people, particularly big business people, we will see that power is also a tool quickly grasped.

From the earliest days of American history, a relationship between the political and economic institutions has existed. In 1629 John Winthrop, the first governor of Massachusetts, was a prosperous business man. Throughout American history the two institutions have shared an ideology emphasizing people's right to pursue an unrestricted existence: There is the Jeffersonian ideal that the politician who governs best governs least and Adam Smith's free-enterprise standard of the self-regulating market. At the same time, both politicians and business people are power brokers, affecting or controlling the destinies of thousands, in some cases millions of people.

The Corporate State

In his study of American society, Alexis de Tocqueville observed not only the American political process but successful American business enterprises as well. De Tocqueville claimed that the superiority of American businesses over their European counterparts was based on one factor: the ability to ship their goods more cheaply. But why? American ships cost as much as the European vessels, and the sailors received higher wages than their European counterparts. The reason, de Tocqueville concluded, was that the American sailors were willing to take more chances. Admittedly they were shipwrecked more frequently, but no one else crossed the ocean so quickly, and this timesaving saved money. For example, a captain would leave Boston and go to China to buy tea. He would arrive at Canton, stay a few days, and come back. In less than two years, he had gone around the world, and he had seen land only once. During an eight- to ten-month voyage, he had drunk brackish water and eaten only salted meat. The captain had fought the sea, disease, and boredom, but on his return he could sell tea a few pennies cheaper than his English competition. And that in a nutshell was what he was trying to do (de Tocqueville, 1966: 368–369).

In writing about what he called "the commercial greatness of the United States," de Tocqueville emphasized the daring of American sailors. A number of other factors, however, also encouraged the explosive development of the economic system — in particular, a range of rich natural resources, a large adult labor force arriving from Europe and Africa, isolation from the disruptive European wars, and, in particular, Adam Smith's revolutionary ideas about economic development.

The rest of this chapter examines the economic institution — the system of norms and roles developed for the production, distribution, and consumption of goods and services. Throughout the material on the political institution, we have frequently seen its relationship with the economic institution — in particular, in discussions indicating that many business people attempt to influence politicians to establish policies or pass laws that they want. The relationship between the two institutions remains apparent in the upcoming sections, especially in the analysis of how corporations exert influence in the political sphere.

Economic Ideologies: Capitalism versus Socialism

Perhaps we in the United States are more concerned than are the people of other nations with the threat of opposing values, beliefs, and activities. After all, we have a word for it: "un-American." The British or the French do not have a comparable word. Even our most powerful political rivals — the Soviets — do not classify any people's values, beliefs, and activities as "un-Soviet." We in this country are unique in this respect. In fact, at one time a congressional committee existed — the House Un-American Activities Committee — to investigate such matters. Such a classification presents a problem: It tends to preclude thoughtful analysis. Consider, for instance, the two economic systems we are about to examine. To many Americans capitalism is American – good, and socialism is un-American – bad. To some people there is no need to look further. We will.

To begin: Capitalism and socialism are economic systems, and therefore both concern themselves with the production and distribution of goods and services. The American system is capitalist. **Capital** is money, goods, or other forms of wealth invested to produce more wealth. **Capitalism** is an economic system where capital is controlled by private citizens who own the means of production and distribution of goods and services. **Socialism** is an economic system with collective ownership of the means of production and distribution of goods and services. Socialist measures range from limited steps advocating the public ownership of a few businesses to extensive control over economic planning and its implementation.

The Development of Capitalism

To Americans 1776 is renowned as the year when the Declaration of Independence was written and signed, and the nation officially began. To the rest of the Western world, however, 1776 has received more recognition as the year the Scottish philosopher Adam Smith (1723 – 1790) published *The Wealth of Nations*, in which he presented the first complete theory of economic behavior (Smith, 1930).

Smith began with the central idea that the great motivator of economic activity is all participants' powerful desire to better their own condition — in short, self-interest. Self-interest, Smith argued, produces the miracle of the capitalist system: the self-regulating market. If consumers are free to spend their money as they wish and if business people can compete equally for their patronage, then capital and labor certainly will be used where they are most needed. Thus if consumers want more shoes than are currently produced, they will pay high prices for shoes, and shoemakers will make a good profit. Those profits, in turn, will draw new investors into the shoe market. If more shoes are produced than consumers want, the price will fall, and investors will turn to other products — socks perhaps. In addition, competition wipes out the inefficient businesses, rewarding those who turn out the best products at the lowest prices and forcing even the successful people to invest in new products and procedures if they want to stay ahead of their competitors. Smith explained that this process keeps production rising, pulling up wages at the same time. The overall result is that while business people are seeking only their own profit, they become part of a market process that promotes the common good.

In Adam Smith's view, however, business people are likely to attempt to undermine the common good by trying to fix prices and keep down wages, efforts Smith believed could succeed only if government actively helps business. For this reason Smith strongly advocated that the economic system be "laissez-faire" (literally, let do), meaning that it should be allowed to function without government intervention.

By the early nineteenth century, many people had read *The Wealth of Nations,* and most Western governments accepted Smith's basic ideas. Open competition in the marketplace became the standard of the day, and the power of Adam Smith's theory seemed indisputable to many. Businessmen accumulated and reinvested capital in awesomely large amounts compared to the amounts of precapitalist times. For instance, the world production of pig iron rose from 10 million tons in

1867 to 357 million tons a century later. As recently as 1850, human muscle and animal power produced 94 percent of the energy used in American industry, whereas today these sources supply less than 1 percent.

Although capitalism created industrial expansion, it was also a disruptive force. The Industrial Revolution wiped out the rural cottage industries and forced workers to enter the new factory towns, where living conditions were crowded and squalid. Wages were low, and to help support their families, children as young as eight would work up to fourteen hours a day in factories and mines. At the same time, Andrew Carnegie, John D. Rockefeller, and other capitalists accumulated vast fortunes. In addition, there were depressions, which caused economic analysts to question whether the market could be self-regulating.

The Great Depression of the 1930s inspired the economic theory of John Maynard Keynes. Keynes, a British economist, argued that a government can generate an economic upsurge by using tax cuts, extensive government spending, and the outright creation of more money. Since World War II, capitalist governments have adopted Keynesian measures, and none of them would ever consider leaving a depression to right itself. Consequently widespread agreement now exists that a modern capitalist system cannot be entirely self-regulating; at least some government intervention appears periodically necessary (Greenberg, 1974; Samuelson, 1980).

Adam Smith provided the theory on which capitalism was based. For socialism Karl Marx supplied the basic perspective.

The Development of Socialism

In 1848, in *The Communist Manifesto,* Karl Marx described the conditions he believed would produce socialism from capitalism. Marx contended that within capitalism the interests of the capitalists and their workers are irreconcilably opposed. The capitalists' dominant interest is in increasing their profits. The workers' primary concern is increasing wages and improving job conditions. Since the owners are more powerful, however, their drive for profits will dominate. As a result certain developments will occur—in particular, the growing concentration of wealth in the hands of a few large businesses that absorb the small ones; the increasing use of machinery; the displacement of more and more workers, thereby creating widespread unemployment; and the recurrence of periodic, increasingly acute breakdowns in the economy.

At some point the workers will recognize that the economic system is the source of their problems and that these problems are shared by all workers. The workers will also see that since they represent the majority of the citizenry, they are potentially stronger than the owners. Eventually they will organize themselves into an army and will rise up and overthrow the owners. At this point the means of production and distribution will be in the hands of people—in short, socialism (Marx, 1932).

SOCIALIST PHILOSOPHY   Marx devoted his energy to the criticism of capitalism. He wrote little about the content of socialism and did not live to see the existence of a socialist nation.

A few elements distinctly characterize modern socialist philosophy. They include:

1. *Government ownership of productive resources.* Key industries such as railroads, coal, and steel are nationalized in the effort to downplay the role of private property.
2. *Planning.* Coordinated, centralized planning replaces the free play of the profit motive in a laissez-faire economy. There is an emphasis on "production for use rather than profit." Citizens are encouraged to develop craftsmanship and social services and to downplay the materialistic tendencies so strong in the Western "acquisitive societies."
3. *Redistribution of income.* Government taxing power sharply reduces inherited wealth. Social-security benefits and cradle-to-grave assistance programs will insure the well-being of previously poor people (Samuelson, 1980: 816–817).

The Soviet Union, the People's Republic of China, and Cuba practice socialism, and Sweden, Great Britain, Norway, Australia, and France have had governments with socialist platforms.

Americans have traditionally opposed socialism. In a 1942 survey, 25 percent of a national survey indicated that some form of socialism would be a good thing for the country, and 40 percent felt it would be a bad thing (Roper Organization, *Fortune Survey,* 1942). Thirty-four years later, only 10 percent of the respondents said they would support the introduction of socialism in the United States, whereas 62 percent opposed its introduction (*Cambridge Reports,* March 1976). These are not surprising findings when we consider the dominance of capitalist activities in U.S. society.

It should be emphasized that, like all ideologies, both capitalism and socialism seldom exist in absolutely pure form. Capitalist societies often contain some socialist elements: a range of governmental assistance programs in health care and income subsidy, for instance; some socialist nations, such as the Soviet Union, have been permitting increased foreign capitalist involvement as well as steady growth in domestic capitalist activity.

Capitalist Activity

Mark Twain once wrote that the leading capitalists live by the following gospel: "Get money. Get it quickly. Get it in abundance. Get it in prodigious abundance. Get it dishonestly if you can, honestly if you must" (Twain, 1973: 224). In Twain's day, especially at the end of the nineteenth century, the opponents of big business grew rapidly in number. Monopolies, which involve exclusive control by one or several corporations over the production of a commodity, were widely denounced as a conspiracy, evidence of greed, and a misallocation and underuse of resources (Bailyn et al., 1977: 843). The critics had little effect, however, upon the increasing concentration of corporate power and wealth.

Corporate Power and Wealth

A **corporation** is a legally designated organization that has powers and responsibilities separate from its workers and owners. For instance, in an unincorporated business, the owner may be forced to sell his or her home and possessions to settle business debts. Investors in corporations, however, have limited liability. No investor is responsible for more than the initial investment, and this limited liability attracts backers and serves as a primary basis for extensive capital accu-

mulation and massive growth in the size of some corporations.

In a given year, the 500 largest corporations account for over half — about 55 percent — of the Gross National Product, the sum total of the value of the goods and services produced in the United States in a year. The top hundred corporations have assets of over $1 billion each and yearly sales of more than $2.5 billion each. Corporations with over $250 million in assets account for nearly 75 percent of all corporate income.

The major corporations exert impressive political and social power through a number of sources. They include:

1. *Their wealth.* Because of their market domination, the business giants have enormous sums of money that their owners and managers can use the way they choose. They use these sums for continued market domination, especially for increased political and social power. For instance, vast expenditures on advertising support not only the sale of the particular products but also the company image and the legitimate use of the corporate system in general. With profits in mind, American corporations give about $3 billion to charity each year; these contributions frequently serve as an effective form of advertising when the contribution is publicized.

2. *Their accumulation of skilled and talented people.* No other modern organization has such a range of talented members, with the possible exception of the federal government. At a moment's notice, a giant corporation can mobilize scientists, social scientists, engineers, lawyers, accountants, management experts, and systems analysts to work together on a problem designated important by management, no matter what it may be — new product development, basic research, public relations, or overseas expansion.

3. *The linkage between citizen and corporate well-being.* Large corporations are massive organizations that employ hundreds of thousands of people, and each major corporation has numerous large companies to which it subcontracts its work. In the early 1970s, General Motors employed over 700,000 people, and in a single week in 1980 this largest American corporation laid off 155,000 workers, the population of a small city. In his campaign for a major government loan to stave off bankruptcy, Chrysler President Lee Iaccoca

frequently emphasized that if his company went bankrupt, hundreds of thousands of citizens would be forced out of work and into the already long unemployment lines.

4. *Commitment of all public officials to the existing economic and social system.* Liberals and conservatives or Republicans and Democrats might have somewhat different outlooks on the economic and social order, but they agree on one fundamental point: The basic principles of the current economic system should not be challenged. With rare exceptions public officials do not make such radical proposals as massive income distribution, restraints on corporate autonomy, or the establishment of public control over the production process. In fact, the relationship between prominent government personnel and corporate leadership is frequently intimate, especially in the realm of national defense and foreign policy. From 1940 to 1967, 77 percent of the individuals who directed the principal foreign-policy departments (Secretaries and Undersecretaries of State and Defense, the military-service Secretaries, the Chairmen of the Atomic Energy Commission, and Directors of the CIA) came from big business and high finance (Dugger, 1988; Gilpin, 1975; Greenberg, 1974; Navarro, 1988).

The power and influence of U.S. corporations extends well beyond the boundaries of our society. In the twenty-year period following World War II, the United States was dominant in productivity and in its ability to influence the world economy. In recent years its economic dominance has slackened as Japan and West Germany have surpassed the United States in the rate of economic development.

Multinationals

As American corporations helped establish their economic dominance by investing directly in the economies of other countries, multinationals have developed. A **multinational** is a large corporation with production plants and distribution centers in many countries. It draws its natural resources and labor supply and sells its products — as varied as autos, clothes, computers, and oil — around the world. About 200 American corporations are multinational. In 1988 the five largest multinationals were General Motors, Exxon,

Figure 14.2
Gross National Products Compared to Corporate Sales: Some Matchings[1]

Sales (billions of dollars)	Gross National Product (billions of dollars)
General Motors (1)[2] $101.8	Switzerland $96.1
Exxon (2) $76.4	Belgium $76.3
Ford Motor (3) $71.6	Denmark $72.2
IBM (4) $54.2	Finland $54.4
Mobil (5) $51.2	Algeria $51.9
Chrysler (10) $26.3	Iraq $27
Boeing (20) $15.4	Ireland $16
Johnson & Johnson (50) $8.0	Guatemala $9.1
Texas Instruments (75) $5.6	Kenya $5.7
Smithkline Beckman (100) $4.3	Luxembourg $4.7
Intel (200) $1.9	Jamaica $2.0
Allegheny Ludlum (350) $.9	Laos $.8
M.A. Hanna (500) $.5	Mauritania $.7

[1] The Gross National Product is the financial value of yearly goods and services in a national economy. In an economic sense, the GNP is comparable to corporate sales. Both represent the financial value of the products their respective units produce.
[2] The numbers in parentheses represent the U.S. corporate rank in sales for 1985.

This figure demonstrates the enormous wealth and associated power of some major U.S. corporations by comparing their corporate sales in 1988 with the gross national products of foreign countries in 1988. (Sources: The 1988 (Fortune) Directory of U.S. Corporations; 1988 Information Please Almanac.)

Ford, IBM, and Mobil Oil, all centered in the United States. It is an understatement to say that multinationals are large. Of the 100 largest economic structures in the world, exactly half are multinationals. The total sales revenue for General Motors in 1988 was greater than the sum of the Gross National Products for Finland, Iraq, Ireland, and Jamaica. Figure 14.2 matches the yearly sales revenues of various multinationals with the Gross National Products of different countries.

Massive corporations invest their capital in a number of ways. Some investments bring raw products to the United States for use domestically: for example, shipment of oil for refinement and use. Other investments involve the sale of American goods abroad. In some cases, such as the automobile industry, a corporation will open a factory abroad to manufacture products for local sale. Frequently, though, the products manufactured abroad are sold in the United States.

What conditions have encouraged the development of multinationals? In the first place, in many countries tariffs restrict the importation and sale of American products. Any locally manufactured goods, including those produced by multinationals, escape that restriction. Second, foreign labor is likely to be considerably cheaper than in the United States. Third, the shift of operations abroad allows multinationals to avoid some payments of taxes; thus a corporate division in a country with high taxes can avoid these taxes by transferring products to a division in a country with low taxes. Fourth, a multinational strategy seems consistent with a basic capitalist belief — the conviction that continuous growth is a desirable condition — and foreign markets obviously represent a massive growth opportunity. Finally, since World War II presidential administrations have encouraged large-scale foreign investment as a means of establishing American preeminence internationally (Gilpin, 1975; Greenberg, 1974; Salomon and Bernstein, 1982).

According to Immanuel Wallerstein (1974), the formation of multinationals represents the fourth and most recent stage of an international economy, which began to develop in the sixteenth century and was never limited by national boundaries. Following world-wide expansion of industrial activity during the century that ended in 1917, the leading capitalists began to consolidate enormous wealth, with multinationals establishing global political and economic control.

Multinationals' ability to cross national boundaries sometimes occurs in opposition to national policies, if profits seem promising. In 1938 ITT, using a German subsidiary, bought a company that produced military aircraft for the Nazis during World War II. After the war ITT sought and received government compensation for the damage American bombers did to its German plants. During an Arab boycott of the United States in the early 1970s, Exxon cooperated with the Arabs by refusing to sell to a U.S. Navy base in the Phillipines (Horton, Leslie, and Larson, 1988: 68–69).

The following American Controversy considers in greater detail some of the issues of modern capitalism that we have already examined.

Multinational corporations like Mobil sell their products and services around the world. The Mobil service station pictured here is in Thailand.

404 AMERICAN CONTROVERSY

Capitalism in America: Desirable or Undesirable?

In the early 1990s, capitalism seems to be experiencing a triumphant moment, as the Soviet Union and many other socialist nations have been increasingly receptive to it. Nonetheless the strengths and weaknesses of capitalism in this society are likely to be discussed and debated in the years ahead.

The Pro-Capitalist Position

Supporters of capitalism are likely to claim that theirs is the economic philosophy consistent with a democratic society, because it exists in a free market. Consumers are protected from maltreatment by sellers, because they can always turn to other sellers; employees are shielded from the tyranny of bosses, since they can always seek other jobs; and sellers are protected from consumers' exploitations, because they can hold out until less exploitative consumers appear. Thus economic activities are regulated by supply and demand. Basically no outside intervention is necessary; as Adam Smith indicated, the invisible hand of the marketplace acts for the common good.

Admittedly in complex modern economies, governments sometimes have had to play a role — to clarify the rules by which the economic game is played, such as preventing monopolies, and to serve as an umpire between disputing parties. Government's role, however, has and should remain minimal. What capitalist nations want to avoid is the situation that has developed in socialist countries, where government largely controls the economy and the options for both business people and consumers are highly limited. In the Soviet Union and other socialist nations, this deficiency has been appreciated, and increasing numbers of capitalist ventures are developing.

The Anti-Capitalist Position

In theory capitalist philosophy is appealing and consistent with the American emphasis on freedom and individualism. If the open-marketplace approach actually worked, many current opponents of capitalism would say, their opposition would decline or disappear. The problem is that it does not.

Instead of acting neutrally, government generally serves as an ally of big business. Consider, for instance, the relationship between the U.S. government and the major petroleum companies. Seeking to insure an independent supply of American oil, the federal government encouraged American companies' investment in the Middle East during World War II. Since then the government has used such measures as nearly eliminating corporate taxes to make certain that these organizations continuously received enormous profits. In addition, few restrictions were placed upon them. Occasionally, to be sure, even government officials were disturbed by the oil companies' practices. In 1973 the Federal Trade Commission charged the eight largest petroleum companies with monopolizing oil production — working together to inflate profits on crude oil and to drive independent companies out of business. The regulatory effort failed, however. In fact, later that same year, the oil companies retaliated, claiming that because of a boycott by oil-producing Arab nations, oil and gasoline were suddenly very scarce. Actually the United States had been importing only about 3 percent of its petroleum from Arab countries, and domestic supplies were greater than they had been a year earlier. Nonetheless the majority of the public accepted the false claim that the long lines at the gasoline pumps, the accelerated price for petroleum products, and the massive inflationary effect on the economy should be blamed on the Arabs.

The major point, the opponents of capitalism conclude, is that in modern times the invisible hand of the marketplace is not only invisible but nonexistent. Inevitably those who are wealthy use their wealth and associated power to unscrupulously promote their own economic interests, and all other interests, including those of needy people, are subordinated.

What do you believe? Review the specific points covered here and consider what would be the economic characteristics of your ideal society.

Material in this section has suggested that within our economic system, a small number of corporations have accumulated a lion's share of wealth and power and that their dominant concern is extension of their wealth and power. But what about workers' needs? This issue will be considered in the upcoming discussion.

Work in Modern Times

A staff member for a major management-consulting firm posed a question to American white-collar workers. "Do you really need an office as such at all?" He went on to suggest that by the 1990s two-way communication will be sufficiently advanced to encourage widespread working at home. At present many office workers perform tasks — entering data, typing, retrieving, and totaling columns of figures — that require few, if any face-to-face communications. In addition, many of the tasks performed by engineers, draftsmen, and other white-collar employees could be done more readily or as readily at home as at the office with often nothing more required than a computer terminal. Such a change would provide a greater work flexibility, an opportunity for more extensive family and community involvement, and a decisively lessened cost for transportation. Alvin Toffler has called this pattern of people increasingly working at home "the electronic cottage," a modern version of the preindustrial cottage industries, where workers performed their labors in their own homes (Toffler, 1981: Chapter 16).

Whether or not Toffler is correct, the scheme he proposed is consistent with the historical trend by which significant social eras create major changes in people's work patterns. The industrial age brought people into central places — factories and offices. Perhaps, as Toffler suggested, the postindustrial age will allow many people to do their work, or most of their work, in their homes. In this section we examine changing outlooks on work over time and the modern perception of work.

Changing Outlooks on Work over Time

People have attached as great a variety of meanings to work as they have to sex and to play. To the ancient Greeks, who had a slave-based economy, work was a curse. Homer claimed that the Gods hated humanity and therefore condemned people to work. Greek thinkers did consider the possibility that agriculture allowed independence and thus might be tolerable but that the mechanical arts were brutalizing to the mind. In general, the Greeks felt that work possessed two distinct attributes: It was humiliating and necessary.

The Hebrews shared the Greek outlook on work, and they believed that people had to engage in it as a punishment for Adam and Eve's fall from divine grace. By working, people could regain some of their lost dignity. In fact, early Jewish scholars emphasized that working, no matter how lowly the labor one faced, was never as repugnant as idleness.

Like the Greeks and the Hebrews, the early Christians gave little respect to work, but they also despised idleness. The early Christians believed that the most honorable labor in which people could engage was the contemplation of heavenly existence and that any other work served as a diversion from this noble task. From the eleventh to the fourteenth century, the Catholic Church became more involved in community activities, and religious leaders started to give more consideration to work. St. Thomas Aquinas took a position that closely resembles the current Catholic view: Work is a natural right and duty providing the foundation for property and profit, but it is always just a means to a higher spiritual goal.

In the sixteenth and seventeenth centuries, however, a sharply different outlook on work developed: The only effective way to serve God was through good work. During this period scientific and technological innovations provided the basis for the development of capitalism, and Protestant theology supported the emphasis on work, as we noted in Chapter 13, "Religion and Education." The Protestant-ethic focus on the importance, even sanctity of work was consistent with a number of positions that both preceded and followed it. Examples are the early Christians' disgust for idleness as well as the outlook on work, thrift, and success maintained by such prominent American capitalists as Carnegie, Rockefeller, and Ford (Wilensky, 1966: 119–123).

The modern American conception of work also has some distinct attributes.

Modern Perception of Work

Americans' feelings about work seem to be linked to four cultural values:

1. *The good-provider conception.* Traditionally men have been the breadwinners, and a "real" man is one who can take care of his family.
2. *The ability to maintain independence.* A paying job is the way to establish freedom and independence. Most adult Americans are uncomfortable if they are financially dependent on others.
3. *The emphasis on material success.* The higher people's wages or salaries, the more capable they will be to purchase the expensive homes, cars, clothes, and other material items that they enjoy and that are indicators to others of their occupational achievement.
4. *The importance of performing a good job.* For Americans, work is a source of self-respect, and so the people who do their job well have higher self-esteem than those who do not (Yankelovich, 1974).

Unemployed people are unable to attain any of these cultural standards. Therefore it is not surprising that the effects of unemployment on individuals can be serious. One long-term study has indicated that when the rate of national unemployment rises 1 percentage point, suicide increases 4.1 percent, homicide 5.7 percent, and stress-related disorders, such as heart disease, 1.9 percent (Riegle, 1982). While other factors besides the increase in unemployment might contribute to the rise in these problems, that increase has probably played a dominant role. Table 14.3 indicates how large a problem unemployment represents in modern times.

Job Satisfaction Today

In a journalistic study of Americans at work, Studs Terkel offered the following commentary about the significance of people's jobs.

During my three years of prospecting, I may have, on more occasions than I imagined, struck gold. I was constantly astonished by the extraordinary dreams of ordinary people. No matter how bewildering the times, no matter how dissembling the official language, those we call ordinary are aware of a sense of personal worth—or more often a lack of it—in the work they do.

(Terkel, 1974: xxiv)

Sociological studies have uncovered the following causes of job satisfaction or dissatisfaction:

1. *Monetary compensation.* Satisfied workers believe that they are paid well for their efforts. Besides wages or salary, such fringe benefits as medical care, retirement, and paid vacation time are important considerations.
2. *Control.* People generally are happier in jobs that give them some chance for control, especially over their own schedules. Recent research, in fact, has suggested that for many people this is the factor most strongly affecting job satisfaction.
3. *Location issues.* Workers are more satisfied in a place that is pleasant in a physical sense—not too hot or cold, too dirty, or too noisy, for instance—and that is not dangerous or crowded.
4. *Organizational amenities.* Desirable facilities include cafeterias, lounges, and gyms and such

features as training programs or promotion-from-within policies.

5. *Prevailing economic, political, and social conditions.* If prosperity exists within a society, then workers' outlook on their jobs will tend to be optimistic.

6. *Psychological satisfaction.* Employees are pleased when they have a chance to learn on the job, when the work relates to their particular abilities and preferences, and when it occurs in a nonconflictual atmosphere (Boffey, 1985; Morton, 1977; Oldham, 1988; Spector, Dwyer, and Jex, 1988).

WORK ALIENATION   Karl Marx noted that with the technological innovations of capitalism, the nature of work began to change. People's jobs were in factories, where the individual worker "becomes an appendage of the machine, and it is only the most simple, most monotonous and most easily acquired knack that is required of him" (Marx, 1932: 328).

Since Karl Marx's era, many studies have focused on the absence of job satisfaction. An analysis of Marx's writings reveals two prominent sources of work alienation:

1. *Control over the product.* Workers are unhappy because they produce commodities whose sale falls under the direction of the company owner.

2. *Control over the process of one's labors.* As the quotation from Marx indicates, the nature of work itself can be dissatisfying to workers.

Melvin Kohn (1976) interviewed 3101 men in a wide range of civilian occupations, and he learned that these informants were much more concerned about the work process than about control over the product. In assessing the literature on work alienation, Kohn concluded that three factors were intimately linked with satisfaction on the job: closeness of supervision, routinization, and substantive complexity. With Kohn's conclusions

Table 14.3
American Unemployment, Past and Present

UNEMPLOYMENT OVER TIME			RECENT FIGURES (SEPTEMBER 1989)	
	NUMBER (IN MILLIONS)	PERCENT OF LABOR FORCE		PERCENT OF LABOR FORCE
1950	3.3	5.2	Total (all civilian workers)	5.3
1955	2.9	4.3	Men, 20 years and over	4.8
1960	3.9	5.4	Women, 20 years and over	4.5
1965	3.4	4.4	Both sexes, 16–19	15.1
1970	4.1	4.8	White	4.5
1975	7.9	8.3	Black	11.6
1980	7.6	7.0	Hispanic	8.3
1985	8.3	7.1	Married men, spouse present	3.4
1988	6.7	5.4	Married women, spouse present	3.8
			Women who maintain families	7.6

Sources: Adapted from U.S. Department of Labor. *Employment and Earnings.* October 1989. Table A-1 and Table A-39.

This table demonstrates two general conclusions: first, that American unemployment has tended to rise in the past four decades and, second, that individuals with certain social characteristics are more likely to suffer unemployment. Such categories of people, by the way, are inclined to be in low-paying jobs that do not require extensive education or training.

In recent years an increasingly wide variety of occupational groups, including teachers, have concluded that demands for increased pay and other benefits are more likely to be granted if they militantly assert their demands by picketing or even going on strike.

in mind, one might propose the following definition. **Work alienation** is loss of control over the process of one's labor, with the resulting dissatisfaction primarily caused by overly close supervision, highly routine tasks, and an overall simplicity to one's job.

In recent years a number of occupational groups have become increasingly alienated on the job. In particular:

1. During the protest years of the 1960s, blacks and other minorities started to reject low-status jobs and demanded more work respectability, which training and higher education could produce.
2. Some teachers, government employees, social workers, and counselors have been demonstrating a growing discontent with their organizations' extensive bureaucratic regulations and limited job autonomy, conditions that often prevent advancement and the development of more refined job skills. Rapid unionization among these workers seems to have been one indication of their discontent.
3. A steadily increasing number of women have been rejecting the tradition that women's work

is in the home, doing housework and caring for children. In 1960, 30.5 percent of married women were in the labor force. In 1988, 56.5 percent of married women were working (U.S. Bureau of the Census, *Statistical Abstract of the United States: 1989.* No. 639).
4. Since the 1970s many factory workers have been openly responding in a negative way to their work. In 1972, at the General Motors plant in Lordstown, Ohio, factory workers went on strike, not for higher wages but in opposition to the alienating conditions of assembly-line work. The heart of the 1973 contract settlement between the Big 3 auto manufacturers and the United Auto Workers involved a reduction in work demands. Central issues were a restriction on compulsory overtime and the establishment of a full retirement plan for those with thirty years seniority. In recent years difficult economic conditions have reestablished the priority of financial factors, but such a shift, of course, does not eliminate the underlying discontent.
5. The American Management Association has indicated that some managers have expressed dissatisfaction with their work, that they feel "robbed by computers" of decision-making duties. In the last couple of decades, professionals, managers, and executives in their forties and fifties have frequently changed their careers (Gartner and Riessman, 1974).

Thus work alienation cuts across occupational types and class lines. In *Working* journalist Studs Terkel interviewed more than 130 people about a wide range of different jobs. An awareness of work alienation usually permeated the interviews. Many of the blue-collar workers made statements similar to this one expressed by a steelworker.

After forty years of workin' at the steel mill, I am just a number. I think I've been a pretty good worker. That job was just right for me. I had a minimum amount of education and a job using a micrometer and just a steel tape and your eyes — that's a job that was just made for me. . . . Bob [his son] worked in the mill a few months during a school vacation. He said, "I don't know how you done it all these years. I could never do it." I said, "I been tellin' you all your life never get into that mill." (Laughs.)

(Terkel, 1974: 557–558)

As new technologies make the workplace more automated, people are likely to feel less actively involved in the work process and become more alienated. Information obtained from telephone workers indicated that since 1980, increasing automation on the job has made them feel that their work is less autonomous and challenging (Vallas, 1988).

White-collar employees also indicate work alienation. For example, Terkel interviewed an audit-department head at a bank who described his job in the following way:

> The job is boring. It's a real repetitious thing . . . It's always the same. Nothing exciting ever happens.
>
> It's just the constant supervision of people. It's more or less like you have a factory full of robots working the machinery. You're there checking and making sure the machinery is constantly working . . . If they break down, replace them. You're just like a man who sits and watches computers all day. Same thing . . .
>
> A man should be treated as a human, not as a million-dollar piece of machinery. People aren't treated as good as an IBM machine is. Big corporations turn me off. I didn't know it until I became a supervisor and I realized the games you have to play.
>
> (Terkel, 1974: 400)

What can be said about job satisfaction in the years ahead? One point seems fairly obvious: As the structure of work changes, values will change, including people's sense of what is satisfying or dissatisfying work.

Computers have been becoming increasingly prominent in many jobs, and some observers believe that by the beginning of the twenty-first century, their prevalence in the work world will have a profound effect upon a variety of job holders. It has been suggested that working with computers supports an emphasis on personal freedom and self-expression on the job. One observer noted that the work force in the year 2000 might feature "young workers wearing sunglasses and having their ears plugged in to their own private music. The personal freedom they choose is having their inner consciousness free to roam" (Deutsch, 1985: 11).

Certainly this image will not represent the entire work force at the beginning of the next century. But if a large number of Americans seek computer-based jobs, several problems might develop. First, one might wonder whether there will be enough creative, computer-related work for all who are interested. If there is not—and certainly that seems to be a strong possibility—then those who have trained for it will be disappointed and easily become alienated if compelled to pursue what they perceive to be lower-quality jobs. Second, because of the autonomous, even solitary nature of many computer-based activities, it will be important and interesting to observe whether the holders of such jobs will be able to work smoothly with others in organizations. In the past people have been trained to function effectively in organizational settings, but perhaps the nature of computer-based work will undermine that capacity.

Conclusion

This chapter has examined both the political and economic institutions. The relationship between the two institutions has been apparent throughout. Both politicians and business people are prominent power brokers, whose decisions and activities can affect many people's lives. There are also numerous interrelationships between the two institutions. For instance, politicians often find that business people are a major source of financial support. Business people, in turn, can use either legal or illegal means to influence politicians. In particular, the great wealth of modern corporations permits them to exert enormous power.

Use the sociological perspective to consider the combined impact that these two institutions have on our daily lives. Imagine what it would be like not to live in a political democracy or in a capitalist economy. Would these two sets of changes significantly affect your life? If so, how?

The chapter concludes with the fourth of five Research in Sociology sections. This one involves studies about charisma.

410

RESEARCH IN SOCIOLOGY

The Case of Charisma: Research on an Elusive Concept

What is charisma? How do you define charismatic leadership? These words conjure up romantic notions, images of heroic, magnetic individuals arriving at crucial moments to lead their followers to victory or security. The charismatic individual makes the difference; it is the stuff of successful novels or films. Research analyzing the concept is fairly extensive. Sociologists have examined the resignation of a charismatic leader, the development of charisma in a mayoral election, and the relationship between personal charisma and both nonverbal skills and initial attraction by others.

In spite of this growing body of research, however, there has been a significant problem with investigations of the topic. Consider a point implied in the chapter — that charisma is a condition that is unusual, even rare in the real world. The rarity of true Weberian charisma has meant that individuals conducting studies of it have been compelled to follow one of two strategies: Either they revised Weber's definition or carefully chose research sites where something approximating Weber's definition could be claimed to exist. In the first instance, the definition had to be broad-ened to include modern leaders who did not actually meet the requirements of Weber's definition. In the second situation, investigators chose contexts that were either preindustrial or small, thus avoiding conventional modern political situations where Weber's conception of charismatic leadership could not legitimately be claimed to exist.

The material in this section is about the definition of a research concept and related matters. To some observers this might seem at first to be fairly insignificant stuff. It is not! As we saw in Chapter 2, "Doing Research in Sociol-

Mohandas Gandhi, shown here with Jawaharlal Nehru, was one of the most influential charismatic leaders of the twentieth century. Using the strategy of passive resistance, he helped hasten India's independence from British control.

ogy," good research builds on a series of distinct stages. How could we effectively study charismatic leadership without having a distinct sense of what charisma is? Actually it makes no more sense than sending a person out to buy bread or coffee when the person does not know what bread or coffee is. Fundamental issues such as this one should be addressed by researchers. The first reason to do so is that the investigation is made more rigorous and thus improved. Furthermore, if researchers do not effectively evaluate such concerns, it is likely that their critics *will,* sometimes to investigators' embarrassment in a book review or written comment in a professional journal on an article published earlier within that journal. As we noted in Chapter 2, people doing sociological studies sometimes move too rapidly through the early steps of the research process; the thrust of this discussion is that this is a fundamental error.

After discussions about broadening the definition of charisma and researching charisma in contexts where Weber's definition was preserved, we briefly consider the future of research on the concept.

Broadening Weber's Definition of Charismatic Leadership

Politicians, sports celebrities, actors and actresses, and many others appear to possess charisma. Is charisma actually widespread in our soci-

ety? No, not according to Max Weber's definition. Sociologists Joseph Bensman and Michael Givant have indicated that when Weber wrote of charisma, he was emphasizing three conditions: a personal relationship between leaders and followers, a radical or revolutionary situation, and irrationality (seeking followers not by an appeal to reason but by the magnetism of his or her personality).

Bensman and Givant have contended that most if not all modern uses of the term involve situations in which these conditions are absent. In politics the very size and impersonality of modern mass societies have prevented the personal appeals of Weber's kind of charismatic leaders; furthermore politicians' communications are highly rational, often carefully planned by media experts to produce the most potent impact upon the public. Bensman and Givant have concluded that instead of using the term *charisma,* it makes more sense to speak of *pseudocharisma,* the use of the appearance and imagery of charismatic leadership as a rational device to obtain or maintain power.

Arthur Schweitzer's *The Age of Charisma* is an example of a study of charisma that, in reality, examines pseudocharisma. Unlike Weber, Schweitzer claimed that charismatic leaders are not truly radical or revolutionary but are adaptable, seeking to ally themselves with established political parties, ideologies, armies,

and even state bureaucracies. Schweitzer examined fifty-five examples of twentieth-century charismatic leadership, including Churchill, DeGaulle, Hitler, John Kennedy, and Martin Luther King. Weber would not have considered any of these leaders charismatic, but then, as Bensman and Givant emphasized, Weber's definition of charismatic leadership is virtually nonapplicable to industrial societies.

Preserving Weber's Definition of Charisma

Since charisma as Weber defined it is so difficult to find in industrial societies, those interested in the concept can either broaden the definition as Schweitzer did, or they can keep Weber's definition and search out charisma in contexts where it conceivably can be found.

Richard Emerson, a sociologist, chose this second course of action, studying charismatic leadership in a preindustrial society. Emerson examined the formation of the state of Baltistan, a republic of Tibetan-speaking Islamic people in South Asia. His research included an analysis of the contribution of charismatic leadership, and his evidence came from somewhat unusual secondary sources. In Chapter 2, we learned that secondary sources are data banks produced by other individuals and organizations. Emerson's secondary sources were considerably more artistic than most — dances, songs, and other types of folklore. For instance, Emerson analyzed a long epic poem about King Kesar of the kingdom of Ling that has been passed on orally for over four centuries.

> [King Kesar] is a mythical charismatic warrior-king whose exploits and magical fighting powers are recounted in the saga at great length. But despite the supernatural powers of this warrior-ruler-deity, the vulnerability of his kingdom (Ling) is a major theme in the saga, symbolized by the frequent abduction of his wife, the queen Lomo Brugmo.
>
> *(Emerson, 1983: 429)*

Emerson concluded that this and other examples from Baltistan folklore reveal an important point about charismatic leadership and vulnerability. He suggested that unless people consider themselves vulnerable, they will not follow a charismatic leader. For instance, no matter how appealing and magnetic a personality, the leader of a powerful army facing modest opposition will not inspire the fervent loyalty charismatic leaders normally receive; in this situation people do not feel vulnerable, and thus the loyalty gladly given to a protecting leader is not inspired.

Emerson, in short, was suggesting that followers' perception of their own vulnerability significantly affects their willingness to follow someone they consider their charismatic leader. Is Emerson correct? Perhaps his conclusion is best viewed

as an hypothesis, which needs further testing.

Emerson's insights about charismatic leadership were based on information contained in ancient folklore. In contrast, Phyllis Day, a social researcher at Purdue University, obtained insights about charisma from investigating Roseland, a contemporary home for troubled girls. An unusual feature of Day's project was the fact that it was a study of charisma at an organizational level. Like Emerson, Day was not studying charisma in a modern, political context. Therefore, again like Emerson, she could approximate the characteristics of charismatic leadership emphasized by Weber. Remember what those characteristics are: a personal relationship between leaders and followers, a radical or revolutionary situation, and an appeal based on the magnetism of the leaders' personality.

Roseland possessed a leader with these three qualities. This woman, who was the director of an agency containing twenty-two residents and a staff of nine, had a powerful personal relationship with her followers and a magnetic impact on them. A staff members' statement suggested the existence of both conditions.

> She's always with us, and she always has time for the kids, too, even if it's only five minutes. Her door is never closed. She tunes in with the kids. She's involved in everything and involves us — I'm learn-

ing as much here as in any grad school.

> *(Day, 1980: 56)*

In addition, the leader's goal was widely considered controversial, even radical — namely the decision to shift the emphasis in the program from caring for pregnant girls to helping girls who were poor, emotionally disturbed, and frequently delinquent. After this shift in goal, Roseland was no longer a "nice" middle-class agency, and its support by the United Way and other established organizations was endangered.

Commentary on Future Research of Charismatic Leadership

We have learned that researchers who have studied charismatic leadership have been compelled to follow one of two options. Either they have needed to broaden Weber's definition of charisma to acknowledge political conditions in modern industrial societies, or they have had to seek either preindustrial or organizational contexts that approximated the conditions described in Weber's definition of the context.

But what about the future? Let us consider two possibilities. One option is to suspend all research on charismatic leadership, recognizing, as Bensman and Givant wrote, that industrial society eliminates the conditions that promote charisma as defined by Weber. Another, seemingly more interesting approach would be to pursue studies seeking to determine whether or not industrial and postindustrial societies can produce leadership which, though not always charismatic in the literal Weberian sense, contains interesting, provocative elements found in his description of charisma.

I would argue that one of the interesting ideas in Weber's discussion of charisma is its suggestion that followers are willing to follow such leaders without question. The director at Roseland possessed such an appeal, and I did a year-long study of a federally funded agency in which the director possessed a similar control over staff members. It is an impressive, yet frightening phenomenon to behold. In a recent paper on charisma, a psychiatrist indicated that in our society some charismatic, or perhaps we should say pseudocharismatic, people can be dangerous. "They offer *the* Answer, and promise purpose, meaning, and freedom from choice. It is the kind of intense charisma that especially needs to be explored" (Newman, 1983: 204).

What are your ideas about interesting directions for future research on charisma?

Sources: Joseph Bensman and Michael Givant. "Charisma and Modernity: The Use and Abuse of a Concept." *Social Research.* V. 42. Autumn 1975, pp. 570–614; Phyllis J. Day. "Charismatic Leadership in the Small Organization." *Human Organization.* V. 39. Spring 1980, pp. 50–58; Christopher Bates Doob. *How the War Was Lost.* Unpublished manuscript. 1970; Richard M. Emerson. "Charismatic Kingship: A Study of State-Formation and Authority in Baltistan." *Politics and Society.* V. 12. 1983, pp. 413–444; Howard S. Friedman, Ronald E. Riggio, and Daniel F. Casella. "Nonverbal Skill, Personal Charisma, and Initial Attraction." *Personality and Social Psychology Bulletin.* V. 14. March 1988, pp. 203–211; Hans Gerth and C. Wright Mills (eds.). *From Max Weber.* New York: Oxford University Press. 1946; Richard Ling. "The Production of Synthetic Charisma." *Journal of Political and Military Charisma.* V. 15. Fall 1987, pp. 157–170; Ruth G. Newman. "Thoughts on Superstars of Charisma: Pipers in Our Midst." *American Journal of Orthopsychiatry.* V. 53. April 1983, pp. 201–208; Susan J. Palmer. "Charisma and Abdication: A Study of the Leadership of Bhagwan Shree Rajneesh." *Sociological Analysis.* V. 49. Summer 1988, pp. 119–135; Arthur Schweitzer. *The Age of Charisma.* Chicago: Nelson-Hall. 1984.

STUDY GUIDE

Learning Objectives

After studying this chapter, you should be able to:

1. Define power, political institution, and economic institution and indicate the general functions performed by the two institutions.
2. Compare and contrast the pluralist and power-elite theories of authority.
3. Define authority and define and describe Weber's three types of authority—the traditional, legal-rational, and charismatic.
4. Discuss the American two-party political system and explain its dominance in the American political process.
5. Examine the influence of interest groups and lobbying in American politics.
6. Define patronage and political machine and briefly analyze both issues.
7. Define capitalism and socialism and discuss their respective economic ideologies.
8. Describe the political and social power of large American corporations and the conditions encouraging the development of multinationals.
9. Indicate how outlooks on work have changed over time.
10. Identify and discuss the cultural values associated with Americans' feelings about work.
11. List and examine the factors associated with workers' satisfaction or dissatisfaction on the job.

12. Define work alienation and discuss groups that have become increasingly alienated on the job in recent years.
13. Examine the relationship between the political and economic institutions.

Summary

1. Power is the ability of an individual or group to implement wishes or policies, with or without the cooperation of others. Authority is power that people generally recognize as rightfully maintained by those who use it. The political institution is the system of norms and roles that concerns the use and distribution of authority within a given society.

The economic institution is the system of norms and roles developed for the production, distribution, and consumption of goods and services.

2. The two leading theories on the concentration of authority are the pluralist and the power-elite perspectives. Pluralism focuses on the dispersion of authority in government, and the power-elite thesis claims that a privileged few control the political process. On a given issue, one finds that the two theories will focus on different facts, thus providing divergent insights into the political process.

3. Max Weber has designated three systems of authority — the traditional, the legal-rational, and the charismatic — and elements of each system appear in the American political process.

4. One of the prominent features of the American political process is the two-party system. In U.S. society this system dominates for a number of reasons, including the existence of a broad consensus on political issues, the winner-take-all quality of the American electoral process, and the force of habit and tradition. Another feature of the American political process is the existence of interest groups. While these structures are legal, many of the wealthier interest groups lobby illegally. Traditionally corruption has been widespread in American politics, with urban political machines playing a significant part.

5. In the United States, capitalism is the dominant economic system. It is an economic system where capital is controlled by private citizens who own the means of production and distribution of goods and services. In *The Wealth of Nations,* Adam Smith first described the theoretical workings of a capitalist system. He explained that self-interest would produce a self-regulating economy. In modern capitalist states, however, governments have found some regulation necessary. Socialism is an economic system in which collective ownership of the production and distribution of goods exists. Key elements in a socialist economy include government ownership of productive resources, coordinated, centralized planning, and a redistribution of income.

In the United States, the 500 largest corporations control about half of the Gross National Product in a given year. The major corporations exert political and social power through their wealth, their accumulation of skilled and talented people, the general support for business in the United States, citizens' link to corporate well-being, and the commitment of all public officials to the existing economic and social system. Multinationals, large corporations with production plants and distribution centers in many countries, are a major source of American corporate dominance.

6. Over time societal outlooks on work have been changing. The ancient Greeks and Hebrews shared a negative outlook on work, and whereas early Christians recognized that it might help insure the health of the body and soul, they too showed little respect for work. By the sixteenth and seventeenth century, a distinctly positive attitude toward work had developed: The only way to serve God effectively was through good work.

Americans' feelings about work appear to be linked to four cultural values: the good-provider conception, the ability to maintain independence, the emphasis on material success, and the importance of performing a good job. Satisfaction or dissatisfaction in one's occupation is the product of a number of causes. They include monetary compensation, control, location issues, organizational amenities, prevailing economic, political, and social conditions, and psychological satisfaction. Following the lead of Karl Marx, sociologists have studied work alienation, the loss of control over the process of one's labor. In recent years a number of conditions have encouraged work alienation. They include the protest tradition of the 1960s, white-collar workers' increased unhappiness with organizational bureaucracy and limited job autonomy, an increasing tendency for women to reject the traditional woman's role, factory workers' negative response to their work, and managers' dissatisfaction with their jobs.

Key Terms

authority   power that people generally recognize as rightfully maintained by those who use it

capital   money, goods, or other forms of wealth invested to produce more wealth

capitalism   an economic system where capital is controlled by private citizens who own the means of production and distribution of goods and services

charismatic system of authority   according to Weber, an authority system in which leadership develops because of the personal magnetism of an individual, whose followers believe that he or she possesses superhuman qualities

corporation   a legally designated organization that has power and responsibilities separate from its workers and owners

democracy   a government in which those in power are acting with the consent of the governed

economic institution   the system of norms and roles developed for the production, distribution, and consumption of goods and services

interest group   a group whose members seek to influence elected politicians or government bureaucrats to initiate the legislation or policies they want

legal–rational system of authority   according to Weber, a system of authority based on laws enacted to produce rational behavior and the achievement of formally designated goals

lobbying   a face-to-face effort to persuade legislators and other government personnel to support the proposals of an interest group

multinational   a large corporation with production plants and distribution centers in many countries

patronage   distribution of favors to political supporters

pluralism   a theory which emphasizes that a dispersion of authority exists in American government

political institution   the system of norms and roles that concerns the use and distribution of authority within a given society

political machine   an organization established to control a city, county, or state government

power   the ability of an individual or group to implement wishes or policies, with or without the cooperation of others

power-elite perspective   a theory emphasizing that in American society a group of high-status people — well-educated, often wealthy, and placed in high occupational positions — control the political process, including political authorities

socialism   an economic system with collective ownership of the means for the production and distribution of goods and services

traditional system of authority   according to Weber, an authority system in which the standard of political leadership passes down from one generation to another

work alienation   the loss of control over the process of one's labor, with the resulting dissatisfaction primarily caused by overly close supervision, highly routine tasks, and an overall simplicity to one's job

Tests

True – false Test

_____ 1. A police officer who flags down a motorist is using power and not authority.

_____ 2. As long as elections take place in a society, it can be considered a democracy.

_____ 3. Charismatic leaders are likely to appeal to the discontented, deprived members of society.

_____ 4. A two-party system has dominated political activity in all Western nations.

_____ 5. Generally a political machine did not develop in an American city until the executive authority was officially consolidated in the hands of one person or a few individuals.

_____ 6. Adam Smith suggested that as business people pursue self-interest in a capitalist system, they are promoting the common good.

_____ 7. Keynesian economic measures support the maintenance of a laissez-faire economy.

_____ 8. A major source of political and social power in corporations is the accumulation of skilled and talented people these organizations can mobilize.

_____ 9. Work alienation occurs when people lose control over the process of their labor.

_____ 10. According to the text, the political and economic institutions are completely independent of each other.

Multiple-choice Test

_____ 1. Pluralism emphasizes that:
   a. the evil, coercive use of power will be frequent.
   b. elected officials tend not to be accountable to voters.
   c. minorities will be without authority.
   d. constant negotiations among centers of authority will occur.

_____ 2. C. Wright Mills concluded that:
   a. a power elite no longer exists in the U.S.
   b. white-collar employees are dominated by the corporations and government agencies for which they work.
   c. pluralism is a more accurate theory in the 1980s than in the 1960s.
   d. a and c

_____ 3. The text indicated that escalation of the Vietnam War can be explained by:
   a. pluralism.
   b. the power-elite theory.
   c. a combination of the pluralist and power-elite theories.
   d. symbolic interactionism.

_____ 4. A study of public-broadcasting corporations in four countries found that the governments:
   a. exerted almost no control.
   b. tended to be highly controlling.
   c. had no clear policy of how much control to impose.
   d. sought American help with the problem.

_____ 5. Factors encouraging a two-party system in the U.S. include:
   a. the force of habit and tradition.
   b. the electoral process.
   c. a broad consensus on political issues.
   d. a, b, and c

_____ 6. Lobbying is primarily done by:
   a. charismatic leaders.
   b. elected officials.
   c. interest groups.
   d. alienated workers.

_____ 7. Adam Smith's theory of economics emphasizes the importance of:
   a. group interest rather than self-interest.
   b. government intervention to prevent depressions.
   c. socialism.
   d. self-interest.

_____ 8. Which of the following statements is true of capitalism?
   a. It has created industrial expansion.
   b. It has encouraged the equalization of wealth in industrial societies.
   c. It is an ideology that opposes the development of multinationals.
   d. It is very compatible with socialism.

_____ 9. A source of corporate political and social power is:
   a. job enrichment.
   b. wealth.
   c. socialist philosophy.
   d. union labor.

_____ 10. Research on charisma:
   a. has always used Weber's definition of the concept.
   b. has sometimes used Weber's definition of the concept and sometimes has not.
   c. has been discontinued because charismatic leadership is so difficult to find.
   d. has demonstrated that charisma cannot be found in organizations.

Essay Test

1. Define power, authority, political institution, and democracy and give examples of each.
2. Summarize the pluralist and power-elite theories and apply them to the American political process.
3. Define Weber's three systems of authority. Describe an episode or event in American history illustrating each type.
4. Would American democracy be significantly different without a two-party system or would it be essentially the same? Consider the alternatives of a single-party and a multiparty system.
5. What are interest groups? Evaluate their functions and dysfunctions in the American political process.
6. Why does corruption exist in the American political system? Discuss the development of political machines.
7. Define the economic institution. What are the similarities and differences between the capitalist and socialist economic systems?
8. How do major American corporations exert power and influence? Discuss various functions and dysfunctions of corporate activities.

9. What is a multinational? What conditions have encouraged their development?
10. Discuss the changing conceptions of work societies maintained through different historical periods.
11. What are five prominent factors that determine people's satisfactions and dissatisfactions toward their jobs? Indicate five occupational groups that have become more alienated from their work in recent years. Why have they become more alienated?

Suggested Readings

Breslin, Jimmy. 1976. *How the Good Guys Finally Won.* New York: Ballantine Books. A beautifully written, entertaining, sometimes humorous, always informative account of the congressional impeachment proceedings against Richard Nixon. In the course of the book, the reader learns a great deal about the workings of Washington politics.

Dahl, Robert. 1982. *Dilemmas of Pluralist Democracy.* New Haven: Yale University Press. An updated version of pluralism written by the most influential proponent of the theory.

Domhoff, G. William. 1983. *Who Rules America Now? A View for the Eighties.* Englewood Cliffs, NJ: Prentice-Hall. An updated version of Domhoff's analysis of modern American politics, offering a wealth of documented support for the power-elite theory.

Glassman, Ronald M., William H. Swatos, Jr., and Paul L. Rosen. 1987. *Bureaucracy against Democracy and Socialism.* Westport, CT: Greenwood Press. A set of eleven essays analyzing the destructive impact of bureaucracies on democratic and socialist systems. Weber's work is extensively examined.

Harvey, David. 1982. *The Limits to "Capital".* Chicago: University of Chicago Press. A very effective, updated critique of Karl Marx's historically significant analysis of capitalism.

Lerner, Max (ed.). 1948. *The Portable Veblen.* New York: Viking Press. The sharpest and most powerful writings of a well-known critic of American capitalism. Veblen lived and wrote at the end of the nineteenth and in the early twentieth century, the era when the great corporate monopolies were establishing themselves.

Lipset, Seymour Martin. 1981. *Political Man: The Social Bases of Politics.* Baltimore: John Hopkins University Press. Revised edition. An updated version of a widely read book on political behavior originally published in 1960. Most notably the author analyzes major studies in a variety of countries to determine why certain class and occupational groups take their respective positions and actions.

PS. 1982. "The Equal Rights Amendment: Anatomy of a Failure." V. 15 (Fall), pp. 572–591. Four articles by political scientists carefully analyzing the reasons the ERA failed to obtain passage and how such a failure might be avoided in the future.

Rothman, Robert A. 1987. *Working: Sociological Perspectives.* Englewood Cliffs, NJ: Prentice-Hall. A concise, well-written text, effectively using sociological theory and discussing currently significant issues, including unpaid housework. Vivid case studies are found in most chapters.

Schott, Kerry. 1984. *Power, Policy, and Order: The Persistence of Economic Problems in Capitalist States.* New Haven: Yale University Press. A thought-provoking effort to explain the performances of modern capitalist economies, integrating the ideas and data of a large body of modern literature on the political economy.

Terkel, Studs. 1974. *Working.* New York: Pantheon Books. A set of over 130 interviews showing how Americans in a wide range of occupations feel about their work. Terkel, a sensitive, perceptive writer, presents these detailed, insightful interviews as monologues—a form that increases the emotional power of people's commentary about their jobs.

Warren, Robert Penn. 1946. *All the King's Men*. New York: Harcourt, Brace and World. A fictionalized version of Huey Long's life, describing Governor Willie Stark's drive for power and privilege during the Depression years.

Wilensky, Harold. 1966. "Work As a Social Problem," pp. 117–166 in Howard S. Becker (ed.), *Social Problems: A Modern Approach*. New York: John Wiley and Sons. A sociologist's particularly effective analysis of work. The essay includes a historical examination of work as well as a detailed, penetrating study of work alienation.

Zurcher, Louis A., Jr. (ed.). 1981. "Citizen Participation in Public Policy," *Journal of Applied Behavioral Science*. V. 17 (Fall). Ten articles examining the role that citizens can play in affecting public policy on a variety of issues.

Additional Assignments

1. Talk to at least six Americans who are old enough to have voted in two presidential elections. (If you can find three Democrats and three Republicans, that will be useful for sensitizing you to some party differences in perception.) Ask them the following questions:

   a. What were the main issues in the presidential election of 19XX? (Fill in year of most recent election.)
   b. What were the differences in Democratic and Republican presidential candidates' views on each of these issues?
   c. Who were the vice-presidential candidates for each party? What did they say about the issues?
   d. What factor(s) made you choose a particular candidate?
   e. How did the issues in this presidential campaign differ from those in the previous campaign?

   On the basis of your findings, can you conclude that our two-party system does or does not encourage politicians' taking significantly different positions on issues? As you think about what your interviewees said, would you be optimistic or pessimistic about using the political process to produce changes you might advocate? Does the information you gathered stimulate any ideas about changing the American political process?

2. Without consulting the text, daydream for a few minutes about the occupation you are considering. Then make two lists — the positive and negative features you feel are associated with this occupation. Now consult the text material examining sources of job satisfaction and dissatisfaction. Are the factors listed there consistent with your perception of what is satisfying or dissatisfying about the job you are considering? How does your occupational choice rate using these criteria?

Answers to Objective Test Questions

True–false Test

1. f	4. f	7. f	9. t
2. f	5. t	8. t	10. f
3. t	6. t		

Multiple-choice Test

1. d	4. c	7. d	9. b
2. b	5. d	8. a	10. b
3. c	6. c		

15
SCIENCE, MEDICINE, AND HEALTH CARE

The Development of Science

The Rise of Science in the United States

Scientists and Scientific Work

The Practice of Scientific Norms
In the Throes of Controversy: DNA and Nuclear-Weapons Research

Disease and Death in the United States

Disease
Death

Health Care in the United States

Sickness in the System

Medical Careers

Physicians and Their Professional Activities
Nurses and Their Professional Development

Patient–Doctor Relations

Conceptual Perspectives
Special Features of Patient–Doctor Relations

Study Guide

In January 1986 the U.S. space program had its greatest tragedy. As many millions of Americans watched on television, the space shuttle *Challenger* exploded soon after taking off. The seven people aboard were killed.

Shortly after the disaster, a national poll was taken to reveal adults' and children's reactions. Americans of all ages were upset about the accident, but they also remained enthusiastic about the shuttle program. Eighty percent of adults and 84 percent of children said that the program should continue. Among the adults 68 percent said that an accident was bound to happen sooner or later.

Those interviewed were asked whether they would like to travel in space themselves. Forty-four percent of adults said that they would. Younger adults were more inclined to want to go than older people; 56 percent of those aged eighteen to twenty-nine indicated they would like to enter space. Children were even more enthusiastic about the prospect. For children aged nine to seventeen, 65 percent wanted to fly in space, and among twelve to fourteen-year-olds, the figure was 77 percent (Clymer, 1986).

The results of this survey seem typical of Americans' reactions to scientific endeavors. It is widely realized that some are dangerous — that there will be accidents, even deaths — but that chances must be taken if progress is to be made. The same outlook generally prevails in the area of medicine, where scientific procedures are used. Americans generally appreciate that medical advances are made at a price — that if progress is going to be made, then lives must be risked, even sometimes lost. Transplant operations and various new techniques for treating different forms of cancer are cases where such a perspective is maintained. Thus, as we will see in the pages ahead, Americans generally have a supportive, optimistic outlook on science and medicine. Let us consider what will be examined in this chapter.

Science is a systematic effort to develop general principles about a particular subject matter, based on actual observations and stated in a form that can be tested by any competent person. The body of knowledge that comprises a science represents the efforts of a scientific community, not simply the results of individual experience. In modern times scientific investigation has become the most widely accepted activity for accumulating knowledge, and it has taken over the role that religious specialists, astrologers, and philosophers usually had in preindustrial societies.

Science seldom existed in preindustrial societies. As we noted in Chapter 13, "Religion and Education," secularization occurred as societies industrialized: The belief in scientific principles replaced religious faith, and a new institution developed. In modern times theory and research based on the scientific method are located at the core of many different disciplines; the results of scientific endeavors diffuse through modern life, affecting such diverse subjects as prenatal care, childrearing techniques, nutrition and dieting, building and bridge construction, the refinement of clean-energy forms, the development of weapons systems, and health care. In the first half of this chapter, we discuss the development of science and also scientists and scientific work.

Medicine is the scientifically based practice concerned with the prevention and treatment of disease and the treatment of injury. Doctors and other medical personnel ideally use the most recent scientifically tested knowledge to treat illness and injury. Prevention has received more emphasis in the public-health movement than in traditional medical practice. The second half of this chapter is concerned with **medical sociology** — the study of the social settings in which health, sickness, and health care occur. This field, which has existed since the middle of the twentieth century, examines all subject matter involving health and health care but emphasizes disease and the medical professions. We discuss disease and death in the United States and then look briefly at American health care and the medical professions. The chapter closes with an analysis of patient–doctor relations.

In both institutional areas, we will see that over time knowledge has increased and technical skill has improved. We will also learn that in spite of such advancements, problems and controversy often develop in both areas.

The Development of Science

During most of human history, science and the scientist have had a negligible role in people's lives. Their potential to be important was always present, as science can always produce technological advances. For a number of reasons, however, science made very modest contributions to societies until modern times. The reasons include:

Limited range of practical tasks for science. In the realm of astronomy, for instance, ancient societies made certain practical advances through crude scientific investigation—in particular, the formation of a calendar, the establishment of dates for seasonal festivals, and the prediction of eclipses. After the early societies in Babylon, Egypt, Greece, India, and Mexico had mastered the technology necessary to complete these tasks, however, they visualized no practical reasons for further innovation. This was because innovation was motivated entirely by practical considerations and not by the modern scientific tradition emphasizing continuing research and development.

Little incentive to incorporate scientific analysis in most areas where technological development was occurring. In some preindustrial societies, technological advance was an on-going process, but progress was possible without contributions from science. Architecture and construction engineering are good cases in point. Ancient architects and engineers learned from working directly with their materials. They transmitted little knowledge in writing, and any drawings they used were simple and free of abstraction. Early buildings, bridges, and other structures were much more precise than they would have been if their developers had relied on contemporary scientific formulations.

Opposition to scientific inquiry. In some cases the use of science opposed a traditional system of belief. For example, if an ancient priest or priestess used religious ritual to determine when to hold a seasonal festival, he or she probably would have opposed the adoption of a scientifically derived calendar that would have eliminated a ritual that he or she both enjoyed performing and believed represented a significant religious activity.

In one ancient society—Greece—science did play a significant part. For about two hundred years (from the fourth to the second century B.C.), a flowering of pure science occurred in mathematics and physics, which both maintained a formal linkage with philosophy. However, the significance of these scientific disciplines declined when science and philosophy separated. With the separation many people turned to philosophy for answers to moral–religious and political problems. Science, widely considered little more than excess baggage, became the endeavor of a few learned men living an isolated existence in Alexandria. The most practical sciences—medicine and astronomy—continued to flourish until the second century A.D.

It was not until the seventeenth century in England that science received widespread acceptance. Two factors seem to have contributed to that development. In the first place, science gradually obtained a central part in the emerging conception of progress. Scientists and business people began to establish close relationships, with the production of better navigation techniques and instruments a particular concern. In England the mathematicians Robert Recorde and John Dee served as consultants to large trading companies. Henry Biggs, the first professor of mathematics at Gresham College in London, belonged to the London (later the Virginia) Company, which was the first commercial group to sail to the New World. Besides their common involvement in navigation, English scientists and business people showed mutual interest in machines, mining, lens grinding, and the construction of watches and other instruments.

A second factor that supported the rise of science to prominence in the seventeenth century was the contribution of Protestantism, which was much more inclined to permit individual believers to develop their own interpretations of the Bible than either Catholicism or Judaism. It was possible for Protestants to believe in good conscience

The spectacular advances of modern science could not have occurred without the contributions made by scientists in the past.

that God's will and scientific progress were in harmony. Not all Protestants, to be sure, supported the development of science. In some small, self-contained Protestant communities in Switzerland, Scotland, and Germany, the citizens regarded science with less tolerance than the people of Catholic countries. In England such religious control was not imposed, however, and the rise of science received early acceptance. It was similarly supported in America, where the Puritan settlers emphasized a regularized, pattern quality to all activity and readily accepted the conclusion that scientific investigation could provide human beings with extensive knowledge about the universe.

The Rise of Science in the United States

At the beginning of the twentieth century, the leaders of American industry began to recognize the potential contributions that a full-time professionalized scientific staff could make to the manufacture of new and more effective products. These industrial leaders encouraged the development of graduate programs where students could receive a Ph.D. in a variety of scientific fields. Within the U.S. system of professional education, degree recipients were expected to keep abreast of scientific advances, to initiate research, and to contribute generally to the advancement of science. One of the outgrowths of this research emphasis has been the extensive development of professional-scientific associations, which often sponsor journals as well as regional and national conventions. In addition, the belief in the significance of the professional researcher has meant a stronger support for increasingly complex and sophisticated types of organized research than in Europe, where research has traditionally been less professionalized.

At present large research units exist at universities and also in governmental and industrial settings. After World War II, a major impetus to government-sponsored research has been the interest of the national government in nuclear weapons and atomic energy. Scientists have become advocates and consumers of federal expenditure for research and also advisers and decision-makers in important areas of public policy. Figures indicate a steadily increasing federal governmental support for research. The federal expenditure for research and development activities rose (in current dollars) from $5.2 billion in 1953, to $26.1 billion in 1970, to about $117.9 billion in 1987. Within universities, government, and private industry, more than a half-million scientists and engineers are engaged in full-time research. Almost 100,000 scientific journals currently exist, and they publish more than 2 million scientific papers each year (Ben-David, 1971;

Figure 15.1
Twentieth-Century Nobel Prize Laureates in the Sciences:[1] Selected Countries

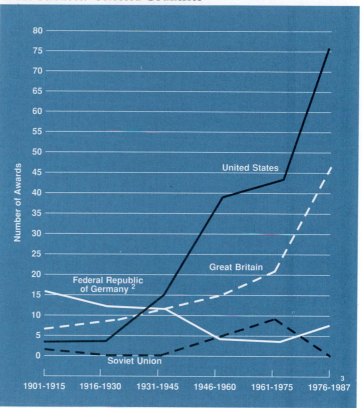

[1] Chemistry, physics, and physiology/medicine.
[2] Includes East Germany before 1946.
[3] The last span of time covers nine years compared to fifteen for all earlier spans. The number of American Nobel Laureates in science is actually proportionately higher in the nine-year period than in the previous fifteen-year span.

Winning a Nobel prize in science is an individual achievement, but as this graph suggests, some countries provide better contexts for encouraging this kind of scientific achievement than others do. In the United States, the professionalization of science, which has received the combined support of industry, higher education, and government, has helped produce a record of unparalleled success in this area of scientific achievement. (Source: Adapted from U.S. Bureau of the Census. Statistical Abstract of the United States: 1989. No. 990.)

Merton, 1973: 228–254; U.S. Bureau of the Census, *Statistical Abstract of the United States: 1984.* No. 1016; U.S. Bureau of the Census, *Statistical Abstract of the United States: 1989.* No. 970; Williams, 1970: 570–575; Wyngaarden, 1984). Figure 15.1 illustrates one result of the strong American scientific emphasis.

426

One of the most impressive developments in the history of science was Isaac Newton's *Principia,* in which he described the universe as guided by laws of motion harmonizing the forces of nature. Inspired by Newton's analysis, John Locke, Adam Smith, and James Madison supposedly discovered laws guiding and harmonizing human behavior. With scientific insight as a guide, it seemed that America would be able to move steadily in the direction of increased rationality, greater wealth, a more pleasant, civilized lifestyle — in short, unending progress.

In recent years, however, there has been a growing skepticism about such broad, scientifically linked claims, with increasing attention paid to the dangerous or destructive consequences of sci-entific developments — the immense destruction that could be created by nuclear weaponry, environmental pollution resulting from diverse by-products of the industrial world, death and injury caused by automobiles and other modern forms of technology, and the exploitation of poor countries by wealthy nations seeking resources and markets for their greater enrichment (Cleveland, 1988). The dangers of modern life and the growing public sense that science does not provide easy solutions is suggested by the following anonymous couplet.

Strange that man should make up lists of living things in danger.
Why he fails to list himself is really even stranger.

Scientists and Scientific Work

Ninety-three percent of Americans favor scientific endeavor. In one national survey, 74 percent felt that it is very important — and 19 percent that it is fairly important — that the United States be a leader in scientific growth and development (Roper Organization, *Roper Reports,* May 1979).

The public support for scientific endeavors is undoubtedly one factor that has provided scientists the freedom to conduct research without much concern for citizens' needs and interests. In this section the topics are the practice of scientific norms and two controversial areas of research.

Table 15.1 presents some significant characteristics of American scientists and engineers.

The Practice of Scientific Norms

Are scientists morally superior beings who lead exemplary professional lives? Some evidence disputes such a claim, indicating that scientists have their fair share of such uninspiring traits as driving personal ambition (Lee, 1985) and indifference to scientific advancement in their fields (Moravcsik, 1985). Robert Merton (1973: 268–278), in contrast, described four scientific norms that he suggested promote a high moral standard of scientific behavior:

1. *Universalism.* **Universalism** is a norm stating that all scientific claims of truth need to be evaluated by impersonal criteria consistent with existing knowledge in that field. Scientists will disregard such considerations as class, race, and national membership when they assess colleagues' work.

2. *Communism.* As a basic scientific norm, **communism** signifies that the substantive findings of science represent a common heritage, not the exclusive property of individual discoverers and their heirs. Thus Newton's famous remark — "If I have seen farther, it is by standing on the shoulders of giants" — both expresses indebtedness to the common heritage and acknowledges the expectation that all scientists will contribute to that heritage.

3. *Organized skepticism.* In scientific pursuits **organized skepticism** is the conclusion that no scientist's contribution to knowledge is acceptable without careful scrutiny. Sometimes this norm brings scientists into conflict with the members of other institutions — clergymen and politicians, for instance. A prominent controversy is the question of how humanity originated. Scientists' support for organized skepticism has simply made it impossible for them to accept the Biblical story of creation when archaeological evidence suggests the occurrence of an evolutionary process.

4. *Disinterestedness.* The fourth norm of **disinterestedness** is a requirement that scientists avoid the pursuit of work that is self-serving and self-interested. It is possible that science draws people with higher ideals than other occupations, but no evidence supports this position.

Table 15.1
Characteristics of American Scientists and Engineers: 1986

	PERCENT
SEX	
Male	84.9
Female	15.1
HIGHEST DEGREE	
Doctorate	13.3
Master's	23.6
Bachelor's	55.1
Other	8.0
TYPE OF EMPLOYER	
Business/industry	67.6
Educational institutions	13.6
Nonprofit organizations	3.6
Federal government	7.7
Military	.6
Another level of government	5.0
Other	1.6
SCIENTIFIC SPECIALTY	
Engineering	52.7
Life science	8.9
Computer science	12.2
Social science	9.3
Physical science	6.2
Psychology	5.5
Mathematics	2.8
Environmental science	2.4

Source: Adapted from U.S. Bureau of the Census. *Statistical Abstract of the United States: 1989.* No. 984.

More likely the emphasis on disinterestedness is the result of the public nature of scientists' work, which tends to encounter more rigorous policing than the work in many other professions.

A study of forty-two scientists associated with the Apollo lunar missions offered some evidence opposing Merton's four scientific norms. One scientist spoke against the claim of organized skepticism, saying, "It takes commitment to be a scientist. One thing that spurs a scientist on is competition, warding off attacks against what you've published" (Mitroff, 1974: 588).

All the scientists rejected the idea of the objective, emotionally disinterested scientist as naïve. One scientist noted, "The [emotionally] disinterested scientist is a myth. Even if there were such a being, he probably wouldn't be worth much as a scientist. I still think you can be objective in spite of having strong interests and biases" (Mitroff, 1974: 588).

A basic conclusion emerging from this research was that scientists were more likely to use the norms designated by Merton in situations where the problems were well-defined and clearly structured. On the other hand, the less clear and less settled a problem, the more frequently the scientists were inclined to develop intensely personal hypotheses and interpretations. Under these circumstances they often rejected the norms described by Merton for a set of "counter-norms," which the quotations above illustrate. Table 15.2 on p. 428 summarizes both Merton's scientific norms and the counter-norms.

In addition, one might consider the existence of a norm involving public service. In recent years there has been extensive writing emphasizing that one of scientists' most significant roles should involve publicizing scientific activities. If the citizenry is going to participate in an evaluation of scientific and technological issues — for instance, choosing between or among candidates for office who hold different priorities for environmental protection versus economic development — they need to be well informed. Countries that have a well-subsidized system of public television — Great Britain, the U.S.S.R., Australia, and the People's Republic of China — have developed programming that has popularized science and encouraged discussion and debate about the impact of scientific technological innovations; scientists have participated extensively in this activity (Daoyi, 1988; Kapitza, 1988). In American public television, such programs as *Discover, MacNeil/Lehrer News Hour, National Geographic,* and *Nova,* have had a similar effect; in this country too, scientists have played a significant role in the programming.

In the Throes of Controversy: DNA and Nuclear-Weapons Research

The richly funded areas of contemporary scientific research are the studies of DNA and of nu-

Table 15.2
Scientific Norms and Counter-Norms

MERTON'S SCIENTIFIC NORMS	COUNTER-NORMS
Universalism: that scientists use impersonal criteria to evaluate all claims to truth	Particularism: that scientists accept or reject claims primarily on the basis of colleagues' personal characteristics
Communism: that the substantive findings of science represent a common heritage	Solitariness or "miserism:" that scientists consider the disposition of their discoveries within the realm of property rights
Organized skepticism: that no scientists' contribution to knowledge is acceptable without careful scrutiny	Organized dogmatism: that scientists must have complete conviction about their own findings while doubting others' findings with all their worth
Disinterestedness: that scientists avoid the pursuit of work that is self-serving and self-interested	Interestedness: that scientists achieve self-satisfaction in work by serving special interest communities, such as their own research units

Adapted from Ian I. Mitroff. "Norms and Counter-Norms in a Select Group of the Apollo Moon Scientists: A Case Study of the Ambivalence of Scientists." *American Sociological Review.* V. 39. August 1974, pp. 579–595.

clear weapons. A discussion of these topics raises interesting and troubling questions about the conduct of scientific research. We turn now to a summary of the positions for and against each type of research and then consider the social conditions that permit these activities to continue unabated when they are so controversial.

DNA Research

The basis for these investigations is the relatively recent discovery that the combination of genetic material from one organism with genetic material from another can produce a new organism with entirely new properties.

Some supporters of this new technology claim that it will revolutionize health care by introducing new means of curing various diseases created by genetic deficiencies. Other advocates contend that DNA studies will help solve world food problems by producing huge crops of corn and wheat capable of supplying their own nitrogen fertilizer or that new organisms can be invented to perform critical tasks like cleaning up oil spills, producing valuable hormones such as insulin, or possibly even curing cancer.

On the other hand, the opponents of DNA research point out that this modern technology contains unknown, perhaps devastating potential for human destruction and that the possible costs considerably outweigh the possible gains. One of the critics' greatest fears is that the *E. coli* bacteria used in most DNA experiments might accidentally escape a laboratory and produce disastrous results. For instance, a lab technician might breathe or swallow a few particles containing *E. coli*. These organisms might then combine with the *E. coli* that already exists in the intestines of all human beings, and the result could be a particularly virulent virus that might eventually endanger or even destroy all humanity.

Nuclear-Weapons Research

Two laboratories at the University of California are entirely responsible for the conception, design, and testing of every nuclear warhead the United States has ever developed — from the first bomb dropped on Hiroshima to the most recent nuclear weaponry. The University of California has operated the labs from their beginning — Los Alamos since 1943 and Livermore since 1952. The Department of Energy has provided about $3.8 million yearly to fund Los Alamos and Livermore.

The proponents of nuclear-weapons research

contend that the only way to survive in the modern world is to maintain a superior military presence and that nuclear weaponry represents the most crucial component of that strength. Without a massive stockpile of nuclear weapons, the proponents state, the United States will be vulnerable to attack from the Soviet Union and perhaps lesser powers too. Nuclear weaponry, in short, represents a deterrent to World War III.

The opponents of nuclear-weapons research, however, contend that the idea of nuclear-weapons superiority is a fantasy — that both sides would be destroyed in a nuclear war and that there would be only losers, not winners. Nuclear-weapons research, the opponents contend, should cease. Instead of bolstering the nuclear arsenals, there should be an immediate curtailment of nuclear weaponry.

Both the scientific community and the American public are divided on these two research issues.

The Conduct of Controversial Research

Several conditions help to sustain the research on DNA and nuclear weaponry in spite of their controversial nature:

1. *Scientists' strong support for the research goals.* Scientists need to believe sufficiently strongly in what they are doing so that they can block out or at least significantly subordinate the issues raised by opponents.

   It seems likely that most, if not all, scientists involved in controversial studies must personally support the value positions underlying their research. For nuclear-weapons research, a commitment to the proponents' position on nuclear weaponry seems necessary. A team of writers noted:

   > Only by increasing the quantity and sophistication of our weapons, the proponents argue — improving their range, accuracy and maneuverability as well as total number of warheads — can we be sure they will not be used in warfare. Indeed, if this proposition is not true, in the context of today, there can be no point to weapons research: if it increases the chance of war, it is impossible to justify. As one Livermore Lab employee

has stated, "In order to work here, you have to believe in nuclear deterrence."

> (University of California Nuclear Weapons Labs Conversion Project, 1980: 96)

2. *Enthusiastic governmental sponsorship.* In order to conduct controversial research effectively, scientists need federal funding, governmental assistance in establishing favorable regulations, or both. In the case of DNA research, a number of the committee members who created the federal guidelines have had ties to the precise companies they have supposedly regulated. This situation has represented a blatant conflict of interest (Rifkin, 1980). In nuclear-weapons research, the process has been similar. For the Strategic Arms Limitation Talks (SALT) with the Soviet Union, a number of directors and former directors of both the Livermore and Los Alamos laboratories have served as technical experts and participants. It is difficult to believe that people committed to the development of more refined nuclear weaponry would seriously commit themselves to nuclear arms limitation. Once again, a conflict of interest seems apparent.

3. *Policy of secrecy.* People conducting controversial research often conclude that an effective way to avoid controversy is to keep their research hidden, thereby preventing the public from learning about the dangers that might be developing. Several years ago an interviewer asked the Attorney General of New Jersey, who was in charge of investigating DNA research in his state, whether he knew of any firms planning to do P-4 (maximum-risk) DNA studies in New Jersey. The Attorney General replied that he did not. The interviewer then explained that the Hoffman-LaRoche Company was constructing a P-4 facility in Nutley, New Jersey (Rifkin, 1980:151).

   Secrecy also prevails in the nuclear-research area, as Senator Stuart Symington learned during an inspection trip. Symington, who was a member of the Joint Committee on Atomic Energy and a former Secretary of the Air Force, was relatively well informed on nuclear matters. Yet he explained:

   > Not until I became a member of the Joint Committee and travelled to Europe with Sen. Pastore . . . in 1971, did I realize the military strength of the U.S. and become acquainted with the vast lethal power of our nuclear arsenal. I actually learned more about the true strength of the U.S. forces in Europe in those

six days than I had in some 18 years on the Armed Services Committee. One cannot help but consider the implication to our defense and foreign policies if these facts were known by the appropriate committees of Congress, as well as . . . by the American people.

(University of California Nuclear Weapons Labs Conversion Project, 1980: 101–102)

4. *An in-group for scientists.* Both kinds of controversial research are possible because of the primacy of the research goal, governmental support, and a context of secrecy. Another factor also seems to contribute, however. In the course of their work, individuals often need support and encouragement from others to perform effectively. Recall the concept of the "in-group" from Chapter 4, "Groups": An in-group is any group whose membership maintains a strong sense of identification and loyalty and a feeling of exclusiveness toward nonmembers.

In both DNA and nuclear-weapons research, scientists and technicians encourage each other's efforts, emphasizing the tremendous importance of what they are doing and dismissing outsiders' criticisms of their work as the ignorant chatter of the lay public.

Thus controversial scientific research, like all social activity, is fostered by certain social conditions. Our analysis of four conditions related to two types of controversial research reveals that these activities are strongly supported by a number of groups and practices.

Looking at the dangers posed by such scientific innovations as those we have been discussing, two prominent Hungarian engineers suggested that citizens of modern countries desperately need to use modern technology for worldwide communication that will develop a common set of ethical standards benefiting all humanity and subordinating the selfish goals of a privileged few (Bendzsel and Kiss, 1987). The idea has a distinctly conflict-theoretical flavor to it. How could it be implemented? An American specialist in public administration with a similar, if less global outlook proposed that officials who oversee the application of scientific innovations learn about them thoroughly, understand the implications of their use, and consult carefully with a wide range of experts in different fields before making decisions about their use (Cleveland, 1988). One of many challenges is to figure out some way to make certain that the bureaucracies that regulate scientific and technological innovations carry out their mandate fully and competently. For the past half-century, American regulatory agencies do not have a good track record in this regard.

The following American Controversy addresses a difficult, well-publicized issue involving the use of modern technology.

AMERICAN CONTROVERSY

Do We Want Nuclear Energy?

In April 1986 the worst nuclear accident in history occurred at the Chernobyl nuclear plant in Pripyat, a Soviet town. This serious accident revitalized the debate about whether or not the use of nuclear power should be continued.

One might consider such an issue within a structural-functional framework: One side emphasizes the dysfunctions of nuclear energy and the other its functions. Actu-

ally it is even more specific than that: One side emphasizes the *latent* dysfunctions of nuclear energy and the other its *manifest* functions. (If this distinction is unclear, check the meanings of these concepts in Chapter 1, "Introduction," pp. 13–15.)

Opponents of nuclear energy reading this chapter might be struck by the conclusions about controversial research discussed in the previous section. In particular,

they might emphasize that those employed in producing a particular type of technology are unlikely to assess the risks carefully because their own livelihood is dependent on that technology.

Opponents will also stress the problem of assessing the long-term impact of nuclear contamination. While nuclear proponents might say that the fallout from the Three Mile Island accident or the nuclear fire at Brown's

Ferry, the routine emissions occurring at all plants, and leaks from stored nuclear wastes have not proved harmful, optimism is premature. The impact of strontium 90, which can cause leukemia, is not detectable for up to five years, and some tumor malignancies can take twenty or even thirty years to appear. A particularly serious problem is the magnified effects of nuclear fallout in the food chain; some fish concentrate the impact of radiation up to 100,000 times its occurrence in the environment. Furthermore our water-treatment systems are not equipped to remove radioactive particles, and health departments cannot monitor all our food.

No, we are better off harnessing the wind, the sun, and the tides, the opponents conclude. We can burn municipal garbage, obtain methane from existing landfills, and mine coal safety and burn it cleanly as Australia does.

The proponents of nuclear power will say that opponents are exaggerating. They will point out that a large part of the cost of nuclear-power plants goes for insurance in the form of layer after layer of physical protection: fuel traps for radioactive gases, steel casings for uranium, and enormously strong concrete and steel containment buildings. Unfortunately the Soviets have not taken the same precautions that we have; the differences are tragically apparent when one compares the minimal impact produced by the Three Mile Island accident with the much more extensive damage created in the Soviet situation.

Nuclear power now lights about one out of every six bulbs in the United States. In France, which uses plants based on our designs, it is about three out of every four bulbs. It seems important to continue to develop this cheap, safe form of power as a means of insuring our energy independence from foreign energy sources.

What do you think? Certainly a problem in debating this issue is that more specialized information enters here than with most subjects analyzed in these American Controversies. For that reason perhaps it is tempting simply to let political leaders, with the advice of experts, resolve the issue. But can we trust them to make wise, balanced decisions that are truly in the American people's interest?

In discussing and debating the issue of nuclear energy, you might consider the reasons why people will take one side or the other on this issue. Evaluate not only experts but average citizens on this point.

Sources: Jeremy M. Hellman. "U.S. Plants Are Safe; Go Full Speed Ahead." *USA Today.* April 30, 1986, p. 12A; Jeanne Honicker. "To Save Ourselves, Stop Nuclear Pollution." *USA Today.* April 30, 1986, p. 12A.

We have just seen that science often involves itself with controversial subject matter; certainly medical activity often stirs controversy as well. This tendency is hardly surprising because medicine, even more frequently than science generally, is concerned with life-and-death issues. The fundamental relationship between the two institutions is emphasized by the fact that our definition of medicine contains a reference to science: Medicine is the scientifically based practice concerned with the prevention and treatment of disease and the treatment of injury.

Over the past three-and-a-half centuries, scientific advances have been the source of medicine's rapid advancement. For instance, in 1628 William Harvey provided the first description of the circulation of blood; in 1673 Anton Leewenhoek invented the microscope; in 1797 Edward Jenner discovered smallpox vaccine; in 1846 William Morton perfected ether as an anesthetic; in 1866 Joseph Lister first used antiseptic methods in surgery; in the 1880s Robert Koch discovered the causes of anthrax, cholera, and tuberculosis; in 1954 Jonas Salk discovered polio vaccine; in 1970 John Charnley made the first hip joint socket replacement (Coe, 1978: 188). In modern times many people simply take these advancements for granted. But what would life be like without them? Consider, for instance, a society periodically ravaged by smallpox, cholera, and tuberculosis, or major surgery performed without an anesthetic!

Disease and Death in the United States

Medicine is concerned with the treatment of **disease,** which is a condition of biological non-health. Microorganisms, which are either bacteria or viruses, invade human beings and other organisms and produce specific diseases. In this section we examine disease and the ultimate conqueror of all medical practice—death.

Disease

The United States Public Health Service (USPHS) has long recognized that an effective attack on disease requires knowledge of how many people have contracted various diseases and the extent to which different categories of individuals are vulnerable to particular diseases.

In the late 1950s and early 1960s, USPHS started three monthly surveys that collected a wealth of data on health and health care throughout the country.

The results of these surveys make it clear that some distinct trends in vulnerability to disease exist—in particular, in the likelihood that various groups will fall victim to acute or chronic disorders. Acute diseases, such as influenza, dysentery, and measles, are likely to be intense, even incapacitating, but short-term, whereas chronic diseases, such as heart conditions and arthritis, can usually be controlled but not cured.

One pattern is that the older people become, the more likely they are to develop chronic ailments and the less likely they are to come down with acute diseases. From a biological point of view, one would expect to find a higher rate of chronic disease among older people because such ailments are primarily the result of the degeneration of bodily tissue and the increasing ineffectiveness of various organs. On the other hand, younger people are less likely to have developed immunities through exposure to acute diseases than their elders have.

Women tend to have more acute and less chronic disease than do men. Once children pass the age of ten, females have a higher rate of acute disorders for the rest of their lives than males, and after the age of seventeen, males maintain a greater likelihood of developing chronic ailments than females. Several factors may account for men's greater susceptibility to chronic disease. It is possible that women are stronger physically than men—they do live longer—and therefore their bodies are more resistant to chronic disorders in old age. On the other hand, social conditions might play a significant part. Traditionally men have been more involved in the work world than women; perhaps work-related exposure to stress has made men more vulnerable to such chronic ailments as heart disease and ulcers.

There is also a relationship between income and disease. In general, the higher the income group, the lower the rate of disease. A number of factors are relevant. People in higher-income groups generally live in cleaner and more sanitary situations; they also tend to have better nutrition, more effective medical services, and greater knowledge about disease and illness (Coe, 1978: 61–64; Twaddle and Hessler, 1977: 59–62).

Disease prevention has drawn increasing attention from medical personnel, but it presents significant challenges. For example, should screening tests that indicate genetic vulnerabilities to heart disease, cancer, and stroke be used? The concern is that the results of such tests could unrealistically reassure low-risk individuals and unduly alarm high-risk people. This concern gains force when one consider that environmental factors and lifestyle play a much more significant role producing most diseases than genetic factors (Yankauer, 1988).

Death

Just as certain categories of people are more vulnerable to disease, some status groups are more susceptible to death.

Age is one important factor. During the first year of life, there is a high death rate; the likelihood of death then remains low until about the age of forty when physical deterioration and vulnerability to a number of serious chronic diseases cause the death rate to increase sharply.

At most ages males have a higher death rate than females. Working conditions, such as risk of injury and the likelihood of stress, are significant factors. As we have noted, it also seems possible that women are physically stronger than men, possessing, in particular, the capacity to resist more effectively a variety of diseases.

Married people tend to live longer than people who are not. Widowed individuals have higher death rates than married people, and the rates are the highest among those who have never been married. Perhaps part of the explanation for the relationship between marriage and long life is that married people are more likely to have an orderly existence and a range of relationships that will lessen the impact of stress.

Finally the higher an individual's social-class position, the lower the death rate. Some high-risk factors faced by individuals with low socioeconomic status include physically dangerous occupations, inadequate housing, poor nutrition, limited access to medical facilities, crowded living conditions, and exposure to a relatively high level of violence (Twaddle and Hessler, 1977: 78–84). Whites, whose social-class position tends to be considerably higher than blacks', average about six to seven years longer life expectancy (Keith and Smith, 1988).

A recent article concluded that since virtually all nations base cause-of-death statistics on information supplied on death certificates, it would be useful to researchers to know something about the quality of this information, particularly whether

Table 15.3
Death Rates for Different Diseases: 1986

DEATHS PER 100,000 AMERICANS	
Heart diseases	317.5
Cancer	194.7
Respiratory system	54.1
Digestive system	48.3
Genital organs	21.3
Breast	16.9
Cerebrovascular disease[1]	62.1
Pneumonia and influenza	29.0
Chronic liver disease and cirrhosis	10.9
Diabetes	15.4

[1]For instance, strokes.

Source: Adapted from U.S. Bureau of the Census. *Statistical Abstract of the United States: 1989*. No. 117.

some systematic biases occur in this area of reporting (Sirken et al., 1987). Table 15.3 lists the diseases that have been the leading causes of death over time.

No disease in modern times has created the attention and fear that AIDS has produced. The following Social Application uses historical information to reach some tentative conclusions about AIDS.

SOCIAL APPLICATION

What Does the History of Sexually Transmitted Diseases Reveal about AIDS?

In late 1988 sixty-nine percent of a national sample believed that it was likely AIDS would become an epidemic for the population at large. By the late 1980s, AIDS had already significantly disrupted health-care systems, creating an upsurge in tension and workload for many health-care personnel. By that time it was believed that five to ten million people in the world were infected.

In developing policies to combat the disease, one source is historical information. In the past half-century, American health-care officials have had little experience dealing with infectious, epidemic diseases, but in the 1930s they did, with the venereal (sexually transmitted) diseases of syphilis and gonorrhea causing debilitating symptoms and death and creating widespread fear.

While we must be careful generalizing from the impact of those diseases to that produced by AIDS, there are some parallels that can provide us with lessons.

Fear of the Disease Will Be Exaggerated and Influence Health–care Policy

Early in the twentieth century, the general public

tended to believe that syphilis could be transmitted by touching or using an infected person's pen, pencil, toothbrush, towel, or bed. During World War I, the U.S. Navy removed doorknobs from its battleships, fearing that they could prove a source of infection. How could concern with casual transmission be so strong, especially with increasingly conclusive medical evidence that syphilis could only be transmitted sexually? It appears that at the root of the fears was the Victorian moral order, which emphasized a rigidly disciplined lifestyle and the postponement of sex until marriage. Venereal disease represented a blatant threat to that order, at a time when the Victorian code was more subtly under attack from the growth of cities and their sophisticated lifestyle, the influx of large immigrant groups, whom many Victorians considered immoral, and the increasingly weakened family structure.

With AIDS there is also widespread, misplaced fear that the disease can be contracted by casual means. Many Americans fear exposure by public toilet seats, drinking glasses, or water fountains. Once again there is a concrete pattern to the sense of threat; this time it seems to be centered on the two categories of people most frequently stricken by the disease and widely considered deviants — male homosexuals and intravenous drug users. Homosexuals, in particular, have experienced increased hostility and provoked exaggerated fears. For instance, during a major protest by gays in 1989, New York City police at the scene wore surgical gloves. In addition, some medical personnel have refused to treat AIDS patients.

Education Will Have Limited Impact Controlling the Disease

Early in the twentieth century, many physicians, public-health officials, and social reformers attacked the Victorian code which declared that all discussion of sexuality and disease was unseemly. Only when the public understood the sources of venereal disease, these people argued, could it be fought effectively. While this idea was sensible, most of the campaigns promoted fear, with pamphlets and films describing and showing the most drastic

To combat AIDS effectively, ads should not simply try to create fear. Instead they should also emphasize that sex with condoms can be pleasurable.

cases of disfigured, blind, or insane victims. To avoid such a horrible outcome, young people were told to abstain from sexual activity. One prominent sex educator declared that fear is "the protective genius of the human body." It turned out to be untrue, however—the fear campaigns did not reduce the infection. Finally, during World War II, a different approach was used: Soldiers were urged to use condoms. As one medical official indicated, "It is difficult to make the sex act unpopular."

A similar approach appears necessary with AIDS. As we noted in the Social Application in Chapter 7, "Gender Roles and Sexuality," there is a growing recognition that the most effective advertisements advocating condom use are not the ones trying to frighten people but those emphasizing the pleasurable quality of sex with a condom.

Compulsory Health Measures Will Not Control the Disease

In 1906 the Wassermann test was developed, permitting the detection of syphilis by a simple blood analysis. As a result it became possible to test a large number of people quickly and easily, and, by the end of World War II, virtually all states required a Wassermann test for individuals getting married. This effort, however, has produced modest evidence of syphilis —in 1978, for example, turning up scarcely 1 percent of the cases of the disease detected that year. The problem is that premarital screening tests a low-risk group. Such testing, in fact, can be counterproductive, driving high-risk individuals away from treatment. In 1988 thirty-five states were considering screening applicants for marriage licenses for AIDS, but, as we have seen, this does not seem to be a productive step.

The AIDS Epidemic Will Not Quickly End with the Development of a Vaccine

In 1943 Dr. John S. Mahoney's penicillin injections of syphilis-infected rabbits were successful in eliminating the disease. After repeat-ing his experiment with human subjects, the massive production of penicillin began. Incidence of the disease fell from 72 cases per 100,000 population in 1943 to 4 per 100,000 in 1956, and gonorrhea was almost eliminated. In later years, however, as educational efforts and searching out affected individuals have been reduced, the rate has risen, reaching 13.3 per 100,000 population in 1987. Thus it is not simply a question of developing a vaccine for AIDS; it also must be delivered effectively.

Conclusion

This analysis has not been particularly optimistic, but there is no implication that the situation is hopeless. What the historical lessons teach is that there are certain obvious pitfalls to be avoided. Education, testing, and research are sources of hope for combatting this dread disease: They simply must be used under the most effective conditions.

Sources: Allan M. Brandt. "AIDS in Historical Perspective: Four Lessons from the History of Sexually Transmitted Diseases." *American Journal of Public Health.* V. 78. April 1988, pp. 367–371; George Gallup, Jr. *Gallup Report.* February 1989; Jonathan M. Mann. "AIDS: A Global Strategy for a Global Challenge." *Impact of Science on Society.* V. 38. 1988, pp. 159–167; Lawrence Shulman and Joanne E. Mantell. "The AIDS Crisis: A United States Health Care Perspective." *Social Science and Medicine.* V. 26. 1988, pp. 979–988.

Health Care in the United States

By seeking to avoid disease and death, people make these subjects significant issues in their lives. The significance is implied by the following state-ment: "Well, at least I've got my health." How many times have you heard people make such a statement? Fairly often, I suspect. Since people do

436

not like to be unhealthy, they usually take measures to restore their health. **Health care** is the variety of public and private organizations that support an individual's effective physical, mental, and social adaptation to his or her environment. Modern American health care has some significant problems, which we will review.

Sickness in the System

One prominent difficulty with modern health care is its cost. There has been a steady increase in the total expenditure, the per capita expenditure, and the percent of the Gross National Product. For instance, between 1960 and 1987, the total expenditure rose from $26.9 billion to $458.2 billion, increasing from $146 to $1772 per capita and from 5.3 to 10.1 percent of the Gross National Product (U.S. Bureau of the Census, *Statistical Abstract of the United States: 1989.* No. 136, No. 138, and No. 685).

Physicians' increasing fees have contributed to the rising cost of health care. Before World War II, medical doctors averaged about two-and-a-half times the income of all full-time workers. Now they average more than five times the national average, making them the highest paid occupational group in the country. The cost of specialization helps account for rising fees; six of seven practicing physicians are now specialists compared with about half in the early 1960s. Hospital costs, however, have made a more significant contribution to soaring health costs than doctors' fees. The increasing number of hospital workers, as well as their rising wages or salaries, have been contributing factors. A more significant influence on increasing costs has been the recent intensification of hospital care — the growing use of laboratory tests, X-rays, and such new and expensive advances as CAT-scanners and heart-bypass surgery.

Admittedly most people do not pay for most of their health care. About 83 percent of health care is paid by "third parties" — private health-insurance companies, company health plans, and government programs, especially Medicare and Medicaid. With the expansion of these third parties in the 1960s, a "fees for service" system was devised: the more services provided, the greater the payment. It is widely agreed that this system is the major culprit in spiraling health-care costs (Kornblum and Julian, 1989: 35).

Another major symptom of deficiency in American health care involves limited access to competent medical care. This difficulty is summed up by the sentence: "I can't find a doctor." The situation has two aspects. First, some people are unable to locate a physician qualified to treat their particular medical complaint. This is because throughout the country there are not enough doctors in certain medical areas — emergency care, home care, and care outside of regular working hours, in particular. Second, certain groups within the society face particular access problems. The poor, ethnic and racial minorities, and rural people are often deprived of effective medical care. The principal reason is that many members of these groups lack adequate incomes and insurance to pay for standard medical treatment. An additional factor operating here is that most physicians prefer to locate their offices in middle- or upper-income areas, and so the poor's access problem is also geographical (Wolinsky, 1980: 416–419).

Sickness in the American health-care system is apparent when one compares Americans' life-expectancy and infant-mortality rates with those of other major industrialized nations. In spite of the fact that Americans spend more per capita on health care than people in other countries, American life expectancy is lower than that of people in sixteen other nations. On infant mortality (death in the first year), fourteen countries have a lower rate than the United States (U.S. Bureau of the Census, *Statistical Abstract of the United States: 1989.* No. 1405).

How could American health care be improved? This country desperately needs a national health-care program that operates within a prescribed budget and makes comprehensive benefits universally available. The elimination or major reform of the fees-for-service system seems to be priority. One unfortunate development in recent years is that as health-care costs have skyrocketed, public attention has shifted from equitable treatment to cost containment (Bayer et al., 1988; Fein, 1988).

Let us consider the issue of equitable treatment. Whether capitalist or socialist, European nations supply all or most of citizens' medical coverage. Why, one might wonder, does the United States, which is wealthier than most of these nations, fail to provide comparable coverage? Certainly one significant factor is cultural — the American emphasis on autonomy and individualism. Each individual or family is widely felt responsible for meeting personal needs. Inability to do so represents a significant failure, and the government should not step in to bail out that person or family. In contrast, the sociological perspective emphasizes the social forces producing the vicious cycle of poverty (discussed in Chapter 9, "Social Stratification," pp. 249–251), putting poor people at a tremendous disadvantage to other Americans. As we saw in the opening of Chapter 9, survey data showed that the majority of Americans dismiss the sociological perspective here, holding the individual poor person responsible for his or her economic plight.

The focus now shifts from the health care-system to the central figures in that system — physicians and nurses.

Medical Careers

When Americans think of professions, medicine is at or near the top of the list. What is it that separates a profession from other occupational groups? Within their specialty area, the members of a profession have the exclusive right to "determine what the problem is, how the problem is to be dealt with, and what price is to be paid for dealing with it" (Freidson, 1970: 368–369).

The members of a profession, in short, have autonomy in their work, and they receive both cultural and legal backing in this regard. Physicians are the only people permitted to diagnose and treat disease and injury, and they also set the fees for their work. No outsiders may interfere; the policing of any irregularities is done by the members of the profession.

Physicians and
Their Professional Activities

What status characteristics do you associate with physicians? If "male" and "white" come to mind, then you are considering two prominent characteristics of most modern doctors. At present women and nonwhites are still underrepresented in medical schools. In addition, medical students tend to come from professional backgrounds and from families with above-average incomes. We see, in short, that a distinct selection exists for students entering medical school.

Socialization of Doctors

For the first two years, medical students' education is concentrated in the basic sciences associated with medicine: anatomy, biochemistry, biophysics, cellular biology, genetics, microbiology, pathology, pharmacology, and physiology. During those two years, students are expected to absorb a great deal of knowledge from these different specialties.

Medical students find themselves in an instructional environment that is generally much less structured than in college. At one medical school a directive to beginning students reads in part:

> We do not use the comfortable method of spoon-feeding . . . Limits are not fixed. Each field will be opened up somewhat sketchily . . . You will begin to paint a picture on a vast canvas but only the center of the picture will be worked in any detail. The periphery will gradually blur into the hazy background. And the more you work out the peripheral pattern, the more you will realize the vastness of that which stretches an unknown distance beyond.
>
> (Fox, 1978: 190)

During their first two years, medical students begin to distinguish three kinds of "vastness" stretching in front of them. The first type involves their imperfect mastery of current knowledge. The second type concerns the limitation to current knowledge; physicians presently do not possess answers to innumerable questions. A third type of "vastness" results from the inability to distinguish between the first two types. In the course of their schooling, medical students must be able to grasp the third uncertainty — to appreciate that grave consequences can result if they are unable to do so.

As women have become an increasing proportion of medical students, comparison between female and male students can be made. One recent

438

study found that while both sexes sought various forms of assistance from family members, school officials, and friends, women relied more extensively on friends and felt less mastery of their environment than men. In the beginning of medical training, the willingness to accept less mastery can be functional, since new students need to be quickly socialized to follow directions and orders as essential procedures in assimilating the wealth of new information (Grossman et al., 1987).

Doctors' Relations with Colleagues

"Harry, I'm worried." Dr. Finchlow stares straight ahead, lost in thought. "I've called you in for this consultation because Mary Perkins doesn't seem to be responding to treatment. I wanted to talk to you because you're our top person in neurosurgery. I'll give you a detailed rundown on her condition and treatment to date, and then you tell me what you think." Such scenes appear frequently in soap operas, but they do not seem to be a prominent part of medical activity.

Eliot Freidson (1978) has pointed out that many people believe that the mere existence of group practice will encourage a higher level of medical performance than if each doctor works alone. However, for group practice to have such an effect, doctors must be able to exercise some

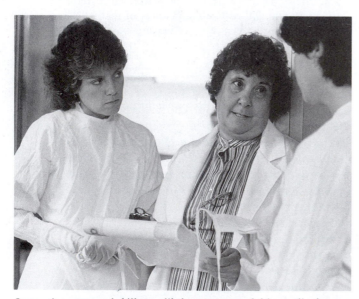

Strong interpersonal skills are likely to prove useful in medical consultations, such as the one involving these three doctors.

social control over each other's behavior, and such control is possible only with systematic and extensive exchange of information about patients by their physicians. Studying the subject, Freidson found that this process did not generally occur.

Doctors would frequently make referrals to other doctors in their group practice, but the information contained in the referral was often brief and superficial, thus providing the physician receiving the referral little information about the colleague's competence. In addition, within the group practice, no effort existed to make information available to all others about each physician's performance. For instance, pediatricians and internists worked at parallel services, seldom if ever referring to each other and so having little opportunity to learn about the competence of each other's work.

An important issue involved mistakes. Doctors were willing to discuss their own and colleagues' mistakes if they were relatively minor, not reflecting on their basic competence. With a clear blunder, however, they tended to be self-protective or protective. Freidson interviewed a surgeon who had recently examined a young girl. The girl had a cancerous thyroid, that, according to her chart, had only "blossomed" in the last few weeks. The surgeon spoke with the physician who had made the referral. This man admitted that the family doctor who had been treating the case for years had made a mistake, and the referring physician told the surgeon, "Look, the less said about it the better. The man who sent her to me feels horrible about it. He realizes now he missed something and he said, 'Forget it. Don't say anything about it.' He really feels badly about it, you see." The surgeon agreed with his colleague's comments about the family doctor. The surgeon said, "All right, he knows. What more can you do? After a man knows and he realizes, you are not going to go in and twist a knife in his back" (Freidson, 1978: 237).

Freidson concluded that while group practice does provide a fine opportunity to collect and share information and to evaluate colleagues' performances, such tasks are generally not pursued. In fact, it has been his observation that the benefits of group practice are no more than negligible.

Perhaps the most significant recent development affecting doctors' working relations is the steady increase in the proportion of organization-employed physicians. Organizational medicine is widely, if not necessarily accurately, felt to be a successful means of controlling spiraling medical costs; it also can employ the recent influx of young doctors; finally large organizations can afford to purchase the steady parade of new technology widely believed necessary for effective medical treatment. Evidence of this growth trend is the sudden surge in the size of multispecialty, group-practice organizations — increasing from an average of fifteen physicians in 1980 to twenty-seven just four years later (Madison and Konrad, 1988).

Nurses and Their Professional Development

In the latter half of the nineteenth century, the women who provided nursing care were either patients themselves, residents of nearby prisons, or women hired off the street. Physical strength, particularly a strong back, and a pleasing disposition were the major job requirements. Hiring was often a casual process. In one case the matron of a Boston Hospital wanted a nurse, but none of the applicants met her qualifications. So she had a recuperating patient become the laundress, and the laundress was promoted to nurse (Reverby, 1981: 221).

Certainly nursing has changed a great deal in the past century. The first three accredited nursing schools in the United States were founded in 1873. Hospitals were willing to finance the early training of nurses in exchange for their services in the hospital. The first nursing schools were sufficiently successful to encourage the formation of a number of new schools during the late 1800s and early 1900s. At present three distinct types of nursing education have emerged. In the hospital diploma programs, the student receives three years of practical training, with a strong emphasis on the nurse's readiness to follow doctor's orders without questioning them. The second type of nursing education is the baccalaureate program. There are now more than 430 baccalaureate programs in the United States, producing over a fifth of the new nurses each year. This training is less practical and more theoretical than the instruction received in the diploma program. The third type of nursing education — the associate degree program — is a "fence straddler." The students

receive a more theoretically oriented program than their colleagues at diploma schools — two years at a community college — but a less extensive professional emphasis than the baccalaureate candidates.

No matter which type of program they complete, registered nurses (RNs) comprise 58 percent of all active health-care professionals. In fact, the current nurse per-capita rate is 246 percent higher than the physician per-capita rate. Traditionally nurses have been lower-middle-class or

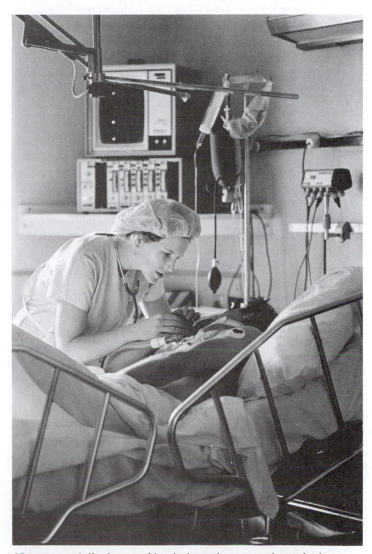

Nurses, especially those working in intensive care units and other special areas, are highly trained and skilled professionals. But the relatively low status and limited advancement opportunities compel many to change careers.

working-class women from small towns or rural areas. In recent years an increasing percentage have been coming from urban middle- to upper-middle-class families (Wolinsky, 1980: 315–340).

Nursing is taxing work. Nurses are not only expected to do their best to help patients get well, but they are also supposed to fill an emotional role, creating whenever possible a "therapeutic environment." Nurses interviewed in one study reported that they often felt badly equipped to do this, especially with critically ill patients (Gray-Toft and Anderson, 1981). An investigation of student nurses found that other major sources of stress include conflicts with other nurses and insecurity about professional skills (Parkes, 1985).

It is not surprising that student nurses feel this insecurity, because members of the profession face a number of basic problems. First, there is resistance to this field receiving the social prestige, monetary rewards, and deference normally associated with the major professions. The American public tends to view nursing with the limited respect accorded social work and elementary school teaching. One reason is that many people believe that nurses are no more than assistants to physicians. In addition, as a "female" occupation, nursing receives the brunt of many people's anti-feminist bias.

A second basic problem encountered by nurses involves the multiple demands they must satisfy. In particular, hospital nurses must face the dual pressure of serving in administrative capacities and also performing nursing services for patients. Both are difficult tasks that together can make overwhelming demands on a nurse's time and energy.

Finally a significant conflict often exists between the ideology of nursing and the realities of status advancement. Within the nursing profession, the conviction continues that the central activity should be the direct care of patients. However, in modern times the greatest tangible rewards—increased salary and promotions—come from administrative work (Coe, 1978: 246–248).

According to a prominent nursing administrator, nurses, like medical personnel generally, are likely to find themselves confronting increasingly sophisticated corporate, organizational, and individual purchasers, who will carefully and hard-headedly evaluate the contributions nurses make. To succeed when subjected to such analyses, nurses must make certain that the participation they specify in a given program is making a contribution that could not be made just as effectively by less trained, lower cost personnel, or in some cases they will find their services will be cut. On the other hand, when they clearly make effective contributions within current health-care systems, nurses should be duly rewarded. At present many hospitals have incentive plans for executives, but few of these plans include nurse administrators (McNerney, 1988; Navarre, 1988).

Patient–Doctor Relations

Portions of the two previous sections serve as effective background for the present one. Patient–doctor relations involve the problems of disease and death, and those relations are significantly affected by physicians' professional status.

Conceptual Perspectives

Talcott Parsons (1951) analyzed the sick role. Like any other role, this one has a distinct set of behaviors associated with it. First, if someone has a disease or injury, it is legitimate to consider oneself ill, to remain bedridden if necessary, and to be freed from one's normal obligations. Second, the sick person is expected to recognize that his or her disease or injury is undesirable and that it should be cured as quickly as possible. Third, sick people and the members of their families are aware that physicians supply the most effective treatment of disease and injury, and so they seek doctors when they become sick.

Parsons's conception of the sick role has been extensively criticized. It has been pointed out, in particular, that going to the doctor may be the end, not the beginning of a complex system of help-seeking behavior, which starts with informal consultations with family members and friends. In addition, Parsons's analysis of the sick role refers to acute rather than chronic illness, since the perspective assumes that the patient will improve. Finally Parsons's scheme implies standard treatment for all patients, failing to consider the likelihood that higher-income patients will receive longer, more thorough consultations (Turner, 1987: 45–48). In spite of limits to Parsons's perception of the sick role, however, the concept has been used extensively by sociologists studying health, disease, and sickness in modern American society (Wolinsky and Wolinsky, 1981).

Unlike Parsons, Szasz and Hollender (1956) acknowledged that patients play a significant role in the treatment process. They produced a classification of the kinds of relationships likely to develop between doctors and patients. Szasz and Hollender suggested that the nature of a disease or injury will strongly influence or determine the relationship between doctor and patient. Three types of relationships are proposed:

1. *Activity–passivity.* This type of relationship exists in medical emergencies when severe injury, delirium, coma, or blood loss makes the patient helpless. Treatment occurs whether or not the patient makes a contribution.
2. *Guidance-cooperation.* Such a relationship develops in less dangerous circumstances than those just described. When patients have acute, especially infectious disorders, they are likely to be very ill, but they are able to follow physicians' orders, respecting their doctors as experts who know the best way to produce a cure.
3. *Mutual participation.* This approach is often useful for the management of such chronic diseases as diabetes and hypertension, where the patient performs most of the treatment and only consults the physician occasionally. In this relationship doctors help patients to help themselves. The instructions that patients receive are often complex, and so unlike the other two kinds of doctor–patient relationships, children and mentally retarded or profoundly immature individuals will often be unable to participate. In his well-known *Love, Medicine & Miracles,* Bernie Siegel (1988) indicated that the most effective way to treat cancer patients is to establish "a healing partnership" between doctor and patient, with the emphasis on sharing and caring and a disregard or toning down of the doctor's expert status.

Special Features of Patient–Doctor Relations

Hank Johnson calls up the garage. "Charlie, I can't get the Ford started again. Do you think you could send a man over before noon?" Hank Johnson has just purchased a service. When most of us encounter doctors, we too are purchasing a service, a service that, to be sure, has some noteworthy features. In the first place, those who perform the service — doctors — are held in very high regard. As Table 15.4 indicates, 53 percent of a national sample assessed doctors as ranking very high or high in honesty and ethical standards.

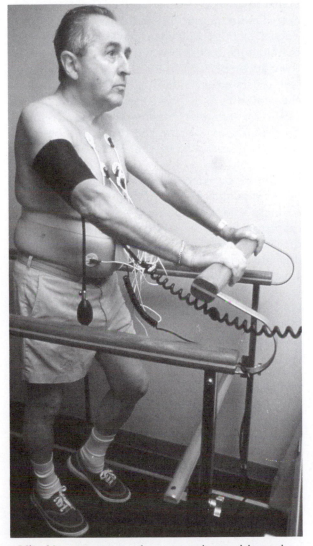

Like this man, many patients are active participants in their own treatment.

Table 15.4
The Medical Profession in Comparative Perspective

VERY HIGH OR HIGH STANDARDS OF
HONESTY AND ETHICAL STANDARDS

Druggists/pharmacists	66%
Clergy	60
College teachers	54
Medical doctors	53
Dentists	51
Engineers	48
Policemen	47
Bankers	26
TV reporters	22
Senators	19
Lawyers	18
Insurance salesmen	10
Car salesmen	6

Source: George Gallup, Jr. *Gallup Report*. December 1988.

The results of this survey demonstrate that doctors are well regarded compared to a variety of other occupational groups.

Only druggists and pharmacists at 66 percent, clergy at 60 percent, and college teachers at 54 percent scored better in the survey (George Gallup, Jr., *Gallup Report*, December 1988).

Another particular quality about medical service is that doctors will sometimes provide a less-than-complete summary of the patient's condition. One reason physicians withhold information is their belief that patients generally lack the expertise to assimilate the information they receive. Another reason is the nature of certain cases — cases of terminal illness, in particular. Doctors and nurses are likely to find such cases emotionally trying, and so they may frequently have as little as possible to do with such patients. In particular, contact with terminal patients reminds doctors that in these instances they are proving incapable of fulfilling their primary mission — to maintain life (Armstrong, 1987; Freidson, 1981: 189–190; Quint, 1978: 94).

Another important aspect of medical service is the fact that physicians' examinations of illness involve a variety of risks and costs in situations that can literally determine life and death. For instance, in trying to decide whether or not to continue an exploration of an illness without a clear diagnosis, a physician must weigh the following factors: the time and financial cost, the possible risks of medical tests, and the psychological distress for patients of continued investigation (Mechanic, 1978: 422–423). In recent years there have been many claims of unnecessary surgery. An analysis of the topic suggested that the best way to resolve questionable cases is close scrutiny by committees containing both medical and nonmedical personnel (Schacht and Pemberton, 1985).

A fourth noteworthy feature of medical services is that low-status people receive inferior medical care. One study, which involved research conducted in both Michigan and Australia, found that doctors in both places had particularly negative stereotypes of certain categories of patients who possessed characteristics negatively valued in their societies and/or were especially difficult to treat — in particular, patients who were alcoholic, unhygienic, angry, addicted to drugs, obese, or mentally disturbed (Najman, Klein, and Munro, 1982).

Millions of American are too poor to have health insurance or have limited and intermittent coverage, and as a result they receive inferior medical care (Bayer et al., 1988). Compared with middle-class citizens, the poor usually have greater difficulty gaining hospital admittance, receive less effectively coordinated treatment, and are much more likely to obtain the burden of care from "beginners" — medical students, interns, and residents. In addition, poor patients receive much more public care than their middle-class counterparts. One observer commented on the public treatment of the poor person: "Several staff members will congregate to examine him, and talk about him, callously and contemptuously ignoring him, talking over him, not to him" (Ryan, 1976: 168).

Old people are another category of low-status people who often receive inferior medical treatment. Elizabeth Markson (1971) examined the records of 174 elderly people admitted to Fairview State Hospital, a publicly funded mental hospital in New York City. Markson found evidence backing the frequent claim that elderly people are often sent to low-status institutions, especially mental hospitals, to die. She learned that the patients admitted to this hospital had a multiplicity of serious physical illnesses, especially heart and circulatory diseases. In fact, a full quarter of the sample died within a month of admission, especially those arriving incapacitated. This sociologist concluded that little effort was made to separate people with symptoms indicating serious physical disorder from those suffering old-age mental disabilities. The staff doctors apparently supported the idea that the Fairview geriatric patients should be provided little more than "a hiding place to die."

We have just seen that medical practice is often controversial, and this trend was also apparent when we discussed science, another topic that involves life-and-death matters. Besides both being controversial, we have also seen that the two institutional areas have changed rapidly over time, with progress a priority for each of them.

STUDY GUIDE

Learning Objectives

After studying this chapter, you should be able to:

1. Define science and medicine and discuss their social importance.
2. Examine the development of science in ancient societies, seventeenth-century England, and in the United States since the beginning of this century.
3. Identify and discuss the norms and counter-norms of scientific practice.
4. List and explain the factors that help sustain controversial scientific research.
5. Define disease and examine the trends on vulnerability to disease and death.
6. Examine sickness in the American health-care system.
7. Briefly discuss the socialization of doctors and their relations with colleagues.
8. Describe the development of nursing in the United States and examine nurses' basic problems.
9. Summarize Parsons's analysis of the sick role and Szasz and Hollender's classification of doctor–patient relationships and indicate differences between the two approaches.
10. Discuss the factors influencing patient–doctor relations.
11. Describe the relationship between the two institutions examined in this chapter—science and medicine.

Summary

1. A science is a systematic effort to develop general principles about a particular subject matter based on actual observations and stated in a form that can be tested by any competent individual. Medicine is the scientifically based practice concerned with the prevention and treatment of disease and the treatment of injury.

2. Until modern times science made modest contributions to societies. Reasons included limited breadth of practical tasks for science, little incentive to incorporate scientific analysis into technological development, and opposition to scientific inquiry. In ancient Greece science did play a fairly significant role for about 200 years. Science began to receive widespread acceptance in seventeenth-century England. Factors contributing to this acceptance included, first, the growing recognition of the part science played in the emerging conception of progress and, second, the contribution of Protestantism, which permitted supporters to believe that God's will and scientific activity were harmonious. In twentieth-century America, science received a boost when graduate schools started to develop professionally qualified

research workers. Since World War II, the American government has provided massive support for a wide range of scientific research. In recent years there has been a growing recognition of the problems associated with scientific innovations.

3. In examining scientists and scientific work, we have considered the practice of scientific norms. Robert Merton has suggested that four norms dominate scientific practice: universalism, communism, organized skepticism, and disinterestedness. A study of forty-two scientists associated with the Apollo lunar missions provided some evidence opposing Merton's set of norms. A set of "counter-norms" seems to exist.

Certain conditions help to sustain such controversial research projects as studies on DNA and nuclear weaponry. These conditions include the scientists' strong support of the research goals, effective governmental sponsorship, a policy of secrecy, and an active in-group for scientists.

4. Disease is a condition of biological nonhealth. Some distinct trends in vulnerability to disease exists. People's age, sex, and income are status characteristics that provide an indication of their likelihood of catching acute or chronic diseases. Just as certain categories of individuals are more vulnerable to disease, some status groups are more susceptible to death.

5. There is sickness in the American health-care system, including rapidly rising costs and, for many Americans, limited access to competent medical personnel. In some significant respects, health care in a number of other industrialized nations appears to be more effective.

6. Certain particularly significant elements exist in doctors' careers. Inevitably doctors' training involves a standardized socialization — attendance at medical school and postgraduate studies. During their schooling they must learn to work effectively in a context where they face three different kinds of "vastness." Most modern doctors tend to exchange a fairly limited amount of information about their respective practices. In general, peer review is not an effective mechanism.

Nurses represent the largest category of health-care personnel. Three different kinds of nursing programs are available. Nurses encounter a number of severe problems, including the difficulty of establishing nursing as a widely recognized profession, the necessity of satisfying multiple demands on the job, and the conflict between the ideology of nursing and the realities of advancement.

7. Parsons's analysis of the sick role focused on three distinct behavioral patterns. Szasz and Hollender produced a three-part classification of the kinds of relationships likely to develop between doctors and patients.

Four factors have a significant influence on doctors' relations with patients: the public's high regard for physicians, doctors' tendency to provide a less-than-complete summary of the patient's condition, life-and-death risks and costs involved in medical practice, and the provision of inferior medical treatment for low-status patients.

Key Terms

communism   according to Merton, a requirement that the substantive findings of science represent a common heritage, not the exclusive property of individual discoverers and their heirs

disease   a condition of biological nonhealth

disinterestedness   according to Merton, a standard that scientists avoid the pursuit of work that is self-serving and self-interested

health care   the variety of public and private organizations that support an individual's effective physical, mental, and social adaptation to his or her environment

medical sociology   the study of the social setting in which health, sickness, and health care occur

medicine   the scientifically based practice concerned with the prevention and treatment of disease and the treatment of injury

organized skepticism   according to Merton,

the conclusion that no scientist's contribution to knowledge can be accepted without careful scrutiny

science a systematic effort to develop general principles about a particular subject matter, based on actual observations and stated in a form that can be tested by any competent person

universalism according to Merton, a norm stating that all scientific claims of truth need to be evaluated by impersonal criteria consistent with existing knowledge in that field

Tests

True–false Test

_____ 1. In some preindustrial societies, technological advancement could occur without contributions from science.

_____ 2. Figures indicate steadily increasing federal governmental support for research.

_____ 3. In recent years there has been growing support for claims that scientific innovations exclusively produce continuous progress.

_____ 4. Robert Merton's set of four scientific norms is based on information obtained from a study of scientists associated with the Apollo lunar missions.

_____ 5. According to the text, DNA research is no longer considered controversial.

_____ 6. The existence of their own in-groups encourages scientists to pursue controversial research.

_____ 7. A study indicated that in medical school women relied more extensively on friends and felt less mastery of the environment than men.

_____ 8. Research has determined that the mere existence of group practice will encourage a higher level of medical performance than if each doctor works alone.

_____ 9. At one time the practice of nursing was so casual that patients, prison inmates, and women hired off the street were allowed to serve as nurses.

_____ 10. Parsons's analysis of the sick role has focused on the contribution patients make to the treatment process.

Multiple-choice Test

_____ 1. Which of the following statements is true about the relationship between science and Protestantism in the seventeenth century?
   a. Protestants violently opposed science.
   b. English Protestants supported science, but American Protestants did not.
   c. All early Protestants endorsed the development of science.
   d. In both England and America, Protestants backed science.

_____ 2. After World War II, a major impetus to government-sponsored research was the national government's interest in:
   a. nuclear weapons and nuclear energy.
   b. soil conservation.

    c. the development of synthetic chemicals.

    d. a greater range of cheap, high-quality consumer products.

3. Scientists' reluctance to accept creationism in the face of archeological evidence support-ing the occurrence of evolution in human beings and other animals illustrates which scientific norm?

    a. universalism

    b. communism

    c. organized skepticism

    d. disinterestedness

4. Which condition does NOT support controversial research?

    a. primacy of the research goal

    b. disinterestedness

    c. governmental support

    d. a policy of secrecy

5. Which statement is true?

    a. Younger people are more likely than the old to have developed immunities to illness.

    b. During the first year of life, there is a low death rate.

    c. Acute illnesses occur primarily because of the degeneration of bodily tissues.

    d. The higher the income level, the lower the rate of disease.

6. Historical lessons about AIDS suggest that:

    a. education will have limited impact controlling the disease.

    b. fear will not affect health-care policy.

    c. compulsory health measures will not control the disease.

    d. a and c

7. In the United States:

    a. the cost of health care leveled off in the past decade.

    b. doctors' fees are the principal reason why health care costs are high.

    c. the "fee for service" system is a major cause of spiraling health-care cost.

    d. there is the lowest infant mortality rate in the world.

8. One of the most significant recent developments affecting doctors' working relations is:

    a. the steady increase in the proportion of organization-employed physicians.

    b. the decline in group practice.

    c. the recent passage of a congressional bill providing comprehensive medical coverage for all citizens.

    d. a and b

9. Which statement is true of nurses?

    a. Their careers enjoy high status.

    b. The majority of all active professional nurses are RNs.

    c. Increased salary and promotions are most readily received by nurses working directly with patients.

    d. For women, nursing is the career with the least vulnerability to antifeminist bias.

10. The doctor–patient relationship analyzed by Szasz and Hollender that is best for the management of chronic diseases like diabetes and hypertension is:

    a. mutual participation.

    b. guidance–cooperation.

    c. activity–passivity.

    d. Parsons's perception of the sick role.

Essay Test

1. Define science. Discuss the conditions that encouraged the development of science in seventeenth-century England.
2. Why has the United States had such enormous growth in the scientific area during the twentieth century?
3. List and define Merton's four scientific norms. Summarize Mitroff's criticism of Merton's scheme.
4. What conditions encourage the continuance of controversial research? Use DNA and nuclear-weapons research to illustrate the different points made.
5. Define disease and summarize males' and females' disease and death patterns.
6. Evaluate American health care, focusing on major problems in the system.
7. Discuss doctors' socialization and their relations with colleagues, indicating the problems they face evaluating each other's work.
8. List and analyze three basic problems nurses must face.
9. Summarize the three types of doctor–patient relationships analyzed by Szasz and Hollender. Then discuss in detail two special features of the patient–doctor relationship.

Suggested Readings

Arditti, Rita, Pat Brennan, and Steve Cavrak (eds.). 1980. *Science and Liberation.* Boston: South End Press. A set of twenty-five articles analyzing significant problems that science and scientists help create and discussing areas in which a more liberated, humane science can develop.

Ben-David, Joseph. 1971. *The Scientist's Role in Society.* Englewood Cliffs, NJ: Prentice-Hall. A concise text on the sociology of science. The book is particularly effective in analyzing the developing role of science in societies from ancient to modern times.

Coe, Rodney M. 1978. *Sociology of Medicine.* New York: McGraw-Hill. Second edition. A nicely written comprehensive text on the sociology of medicine. Though covering a large, often complicated subject, the book is interesting and easy to read. The author has a flair for clear, thought-provoking sociological conceptualization.

Hingson, Ralph, et al. 1981. *In Sickness and in Health.* St. Louis: C. V. Mosby. A text covering the major issues in medical sociology. Perhaps the most notable contribution is the set of six chapters that examines the sequence of major steps patients seeking medical care must take.

Mechanic, David (ed.). 1983. *Handbook of Health, Health Care, and the Health Professions.* New York: Free Press. A fine general source for anyone seeking information about health, illness, and the provision of medical care in our society.

Merton, Robert K. 1973. *The Sociology of Science.* Chicago: University of Chicago Press. A series of twenty-two scholarly essays by the most prominent investigator of the sociology of science. The papers are divided into five chapters that address the sociology of knowledge, the sociology of scientific knowledge, the normative structure of science, the reward system of science, and the processes of evaluation of science.

Nelkin, Dorothy. 1987. *How the Press Covers Science and Technology.* New York: W. H. Freeman. A specialist on the topic mentioned in the title emphasizing that the mass media generally idealize major scientific and technological activities, favorably representing the positions of the more powerful scientific and technological interest groups.

Scully, Diana. 1980. *Men Who Control Women's Health: The Miseducation of Obstetrician–Gynecologists.* Boston: Houghton Mifflin. A three-year study of two obstetrician–gynecology training programs, concluding that physicians who specialize in pregnancy, childbirth, and the functioning of women's reproductive organs are socialized to pursue a number of practices that are not in their patients' best medical interest.

Siegel, Bernie S. 1988. *Love, Medicine & Miracles.* New York: Harper & Row. A surgeon's moving account of how cancer patients and doctors' cooperative efforts, using a wide range of approaches, including spiritual techniques, can prolong life or produce unexpected cures.

Simonton, Dean Keith. 1988. *A Psychology of Science.* Cambridge: Cambridge University Press. A thought-provoking, well-written book offering a theory and supporting evidence about the development of scientific genius.

Starr, Paul. 1982. *The Social Transformation of American Medicine.* New York: Basic Books. A Pulitzer-Prize-winning sociological analysis of how American medical practice has become increasingly subjected to corporate control over time.

Twaddle, Andrew C., and Richard M. Hessler. 1987. *A Sociology of Health.* New York: Macmillian. Second edition. A comprehensive, well-organized presentation of the major concepts, theories, and research findings available in this immense field.

Additional Assignments

1. We now have scientifically based technologies for both saving lives and artificially prolonging life. We can also alter the production of life through sperm banks, artificial transplants, and embryo transplants. Join with several other members of the class in a "brainstorming" session to develop a list of life–death technologies. Then produce for each technology a set of moral questions that the members of our society must face in evaluating these technologies and ultimately deciding whether to accept them or reject them.

2. For a week watch a soap opera that at least in part takes place in a medical setting. Keep notes on the interaction patterns of doctors–doctors, doctors–nurses, nurses–nurses, doctors–patients, and nurses–patients. Do the patterns you observed seem consistent with conclusions about these different interaction patterns presented in this chapter. If not, what are the primary inconsistencies?

Answers to Objective Test Questions

True–false Test

1. t	4. f	7. t	9. t
2. t	5. f	8. f	10. f
3. f	6. t		

Multiple-choice Test

1. d	4. b	7. c	9. b
2. a	5. d	8. a	10. a
3. c	6. d		

PART

The Rapidly Changing World

16
Urbanization, Population Growth, and Environmental Issues

17
Collective Behavior, Social Movements, and Social Change

16
URBANIZATION, POPULATION GROWTH, AND ENVIRONMENTAL ISSUES

On May 3, 1988, the Los Angeles City Council imposed the firmest restriction on growth in the city's history—an emergency-sewer ordinance cutting the construction of new buildings by almost 35 percent. The problem was that for the past five years rapid growth in Los Angeles had been increasing sewage by about 10 million gallons a day (mgd).

At that time the city pumped over 400 mgd of partially treated sewage into Santa Monica Bay—enough effluent every day to fill both the Rose Bowl and the Los Angeles Coliseum. Without the new ordinance, the fifty-five-year-old plant treating the sewage would soon have overflowed, and untreated sewage would have entered the bay, producing serious environmental problems and stiff state and federal fines.

The new ordinance was not popular. The construction industry complained about its drastic impact on business. On the other hand, a spokesperson for Heal the Bay, a local environmental group, called the ordinance "a Band-Aid approach to a serious problem" and said that what was needed was permanent growth management. The Environmental Protection Agency seemed to agree, pressuring city officials to build a second sewage-treatment plant at a cost of $2.3 billion and fining the city $625,000 for dragging its feet (Salvesen and Lassar, 1988).

This is a complex modern problem, and it involves all three issues discussed in this chapter. One of the factors influencing such problems in cities is population size—in the case of Los Angeles, continuous population growth. An increasingly prominent challenge for different levels of government and citizens' groups is environmental pollution: Can a growing urban population, with steadily increasing technological means for producing pollution, develop an environmentally healthy lifestyle? Thus the issues of cities, population, and the environment are interdependent.

Human ecology, the study of human beings' relationship with the environment, concerns itself with all three topics. Human populations build cities and they live in them. These cities are located in the natural environment, which develops pollution problems because of human beings' activities within it.

You might not have been especially aware that these three topics are interdependent, but certainly you are aware of their independent existence. Many of you live in cities, and those who do not probably visit them frequently. How do you feel about the city you know best? Do you like it, hate it, or have mixed feelings? Do you feel safe in it all the time, or do your feelings vary with where you are and when you are there? What about population problems? Certainly our society does not have the devastating population problems of many developing nations, but you still can find yourself adversely affected by the situation in the United States. Perhaps you have faced stiff competition for jobs from your age peers. Most likely you will face such a situation in the future. Consider the environmental issue. Twenty years ago most Americans paid little attention to environmental pollution, but now it is a "hot" topic. It should not be difficult to see how you are directly affected. Perhaps there is a river, pond, or bay that was a magnificent place to swim or fish forty years ago but now emits an odor that causes you to hold your breath as you drive by.

This chapter examines these three interrelated issues. The next section considers the development of cities, and then focus shifts to the problem of population growth. The final topic is environmental destruction.

Urbanization

Let us start with a pair of definitions. A **city** is a large, densely settled concentration of people permanently located within a relatively confined geographical area where nonagricultural occupations are pursued. **Urbanization** is the process by which a city forms and develops.

The earliest cities appeared about 5500 years ago, first along rivers in Mesopotamia (modern-day Iraq) and later in the Nile, Indus, and Yellow River Valleys. The growth of cities was slow until the Industrial Revolution was underway. By 1850 only 2 percent of the world population lived in cities of 100,000 people or more. Currently about 25 percent of people live in such cities, and by the year 2000 about 40 percent of the population will reside in cities of that size. Consequently, from a world perspective, we must recognize that cities are becoming the homes of an increasing percentage of people.

In this section we examine the development of cities, with special attention given to the growth of cities in the United States. Then we consider some of the problems and prospects of urban living.

The Development of Cities

We can begin by saying that human beings' adjustment to urban living has been remarkable. For over fifteen million years, the hominids, who were ancestors of human beings, and human beings themselves were "nomadic, small-group, wide-open-space creatures." Given this lengthy history, it is not surprising that people have trouble getting along in cities; what is notable is that they can do it at all, living "in the same place year round, enclosed in sharp-cornered and brightly-lit rectangular spaces, among noises, most of which are made by machines, within shouting distances of hundreds of other people" (Pfeiffer, 1989: 6). Keep in mind too that many Americans have much more living space than most people in other countries.

Considering that during most of human existence there was nothing resembling cities, one might wonder how they developed. Did a Mesopotamian leader awake one morning compelled

by a vision that he wanted to transform into reality? More than a mere vision was necessary for the building of the first city.

Early cities developed because three conditions were simultaneously favorable. First, there had to be an environment encouraging a large concentration of people — in particular, a climate and soil supporting an abundant growth of crops, an adequate supply of fresh water, and a location along a trade route, such as a river or a road, favoring contact between people of different cultures. Second, advances in technology were essential: the development and refinement of animal husbandry, irrigation works, metallurgy, the wheel, and especially the domestication of grains. These innovations freed a few members of the populace from the everyday tasks of producing food, clothes, and shelter and permitted them to govern the cities. Finally a well-developed social organization was essential. Techniques for the distribution of goods had to be produced, and an integration and coordination of the different occupational groups were necessary. An elite group developed to direct these tasks.

Once preindustrial cities evolved, they generally had certain characteristics. Populations of these cities were small, with most containing no more than 5000 or 10,000 people. In contrast with modern cities, these early settlements lacked the transportation and storage capacities necessary for maintaining large concentrations of people. Another quality of these cities was that the city center served as the focus of government and religious activity, as well as the location for elite housing, with lower-status residents pushed toward the outskirts. Thus the privileged people managed to avoid difficult and time-consuming commuting, which had to be accomplished on foot, by boat, on horseback, or in a carriage. In addition, preindustrial cities had a highly restrictive social-class system in which a small privileged group controlled power, wealth, religion, and education, basing their claims to authority on appeal to tradition and religious absolutes. Furthermore, within these early cities, economic growth was slow because of the ruling group's conservative commercial policies, the exclusiveness of the guilds (an early form of unions), the lack of standardized

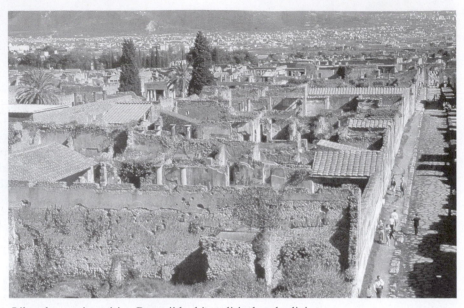

Like other ancient cities, Pompeii had its political and religious leadership living and working in the center of the city.

prices, currency, and measures, and few opportunities for credit and capital development.

In spite of their modest accomplishments, these early cities served a couple of important functions. First, they were founded at key locations along trade routes and so were able to control the most important commerce of their societies. In addition, preindustrial cities were important because they were the places where the elite lived and worked. The elite chose the cities because they could more readily protect themselves in urban areas, which tended to be walled enclosures, than in the open countryside. Another reason members of the elite resided in cities was that, concentrated in the central districts, they could efficiently work together to establish political, economic, and religious policies (Schwab, 1982: 108–109; Sjoberg, 1960: 27–31, 323–328).

When people took up residence in cities, their outlook and behavior started to change. In 1887 Ferdinand Tönnies wrote a book in which he discussed how urbanized, industrialized living altered people's lifestyle. Tönnies suggested that in small, homogeneous, preindustrial communities people generally spend their lives in the same locale. The social structure tends to be simple but rigid. People's position at birth determines where they belong, and few, if any, challenge the situation. Citizens strongly support the moral code and local conventions. In such simple communities, the basic social unit is the family, and an individual's life assumes meaning primarily in the context of family activity. The community itself, in fact, resembles a large family. Social relationships are personal and supportive. Privacy and individualism are minimal.

In modern urban society, Tönnies contended, self-interest prevails, with the accumulation of property becoming more important than personal ties. The use of a legal device—the contract—becomes the chief means to insure that both parties will fulfill an agreement. The family and the church gradually lose their influence. Individuals are freer to think and act as they please, but the danger exists that they will become isolated and alienated, feeling that life is meaningless and that they are powerless to do anything about it (Tönnies, 1957).

Tönnies's ideas certainly apply to American society. As the United States has urbanized, people's outlooks and social relationships have changed.

The Growth of American Cities

It seems useful to divide the history of American cities into four eras: the colonial period, the period of westward expansion, the period of metropolitan growth, and the modern period (Spates and Macionis, 1982: Chapter 7). Figure 16.1 shows that over time the United States has become increasingly urbanized.

COLONIAL PERIOD   During the colonial era, most American cities were small both in physical size and in population. None of the North American urban settlements had as many as 10,000 inhabitants until the eighteenth century, and, at the time of the Revolutionary War, Philadelphia, the largest American city, had only 40,000 people. These cities were not only small, but they also had little ethnic and religious diversity; the residents were primarily of northern European ancestry and Protestant. People shared a common lifestyle and outlook on life, with extensive contacts among neighbors and regular church attendance representing widely accepted patterns.

In spite of the fact that colonial cities seemed to be nothing more than small, intimate villages, they were important trading centers, whose residents sought profit and supported growth. As time passed, American merchants began to resent British directives that they serve as export centers for American raw products to be shipped to the mother country, and these colonial businessmen began to compete with the British, establishing their own trade agreements with the West Indies and even with European countries.

PERIOD OF WESTERN EXPANSION   Between 1800 and 1880, American cities grew at a faster rate than at any time before or since. It is worth noting that among the fifty largest cities in the United States, only seven were incorporated before 1816. Thirty-nine were incorporated between 1816 and 1876, and only four have been incorporated since then. At the beginning of the nineteenth century, business leaders began to recognize the tremendous economic potential of the rich westward lands and started to develop plans to link these new territories with eastern cities. Roads, canals, and later railroads provided the connections. By 1830 New York, Philadelphia, and Baltimore were the most prominent coastal cities, primarily because of their control over commercial relations with the Ohio Valley.

In the course of the nineteenth century, industrialization was also expanding. By the 1830s in the vicinity of Boston, for example, a proliferation of factory towns contained textile mills, paper mills, shoe factories, and iron foundries.

PERIOD OF METROPOLITAN GROWTH

Figure 16.1
187 Years of American Urban Growth

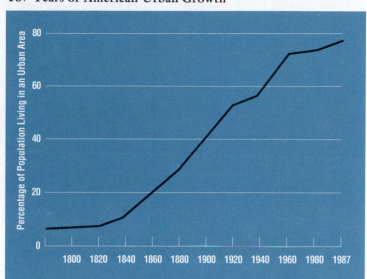

According to the Bureau of the Census, people live in an urban area if the place is incorporated and contains 2500 residents or more. By this definition the urban population, which rose steadily until 1960, has started to level off. (Source: U.S. Bureau of the Census. Current Population Report, Population Characteristics, *P–20, No. 374. Table 2–4; U.S. Bureau of the Census.* Statistical Abstract of the United States: 1989. *No. 32.)*

Between 1880 and 1940, U.S. cities reached the third phase: the period of metropolitan growth. A **metropolis** is a territorial unit composed of a large central city and the surrounding cities and towns.

During this era cities grew in size — explosively. Two factors appear to have been largely responsible for the accelerated population increase. First, a movement of people from rural areas into the cities occurred. Between 1880 and 1890, for example, almost 40 percent of the country's more than 25,000 townships actually lost population. Remarkably thousands of farms were simply abandoned as machinery made hand-powered labor obsolete and encouraged people to seek more lucrative jobs in the cities. Second, immigration was also an important factor in urban growth. By 1890 New York City possessed half as many Italians as Naples, as many Germans as Hamburg, twice as many Irish as Dublin, and two-and-a-half times the number of Jews as Warsaw. Between just 1901 and 1910, over 9 million immigrants came to the United States. The recent arrivals were

Street trolleys were an early response to the need for mass transit in increasingly populated cities.

packed into slums and offered the lowest-paying, most menial jobs. At the turn of the century, influential native-born Americans, primarily WASPS (white Anglo-Saxon Protestants), tended to blame the immigrants, many of whom were Catholics or Jews, for the sins of the city — slum housing, inferior health conditions, and crime, in particular. It was time, most of these powerful citizens agreed, to cut off immigration. Therefore in 1924 Congress established a quota system that severely restricted the number of immigrants from the southern and eastern European countries that had made the heaviest numerical contributions in the late nineteenth and early twentieth centuries.

This curtailment caused new problems, however. At that time industrial concerns needed a reliable source of cheap labor, which until then recent immigrants had supplied. Now industrialists started to recruit from within the country, and American cities received a new stream of immigrants, many of them Southern blacks. Between 1920 and 1929, over 600,000 blacks migrated to Northern cities from the South, and the ground for the racial tension that has characterized many American cities in recent years was established. As early as 1925, the rapid influx of blacks created not only an acute housing shortage but such strong tensions that in Detroit riots broke out.

Toward the end of this period in the history of American cities, another important event oc-

curred. The stock market crash of 1929 threw the country into financial chaos, and most cities were forced to face difficult economic times. In 1932 large numbers of urban residents voted for Franklin Roosevelt in the hope that he could help their cities. The following year the mayors of fifty cities met in Washington, DC and founded the U.S. Conference of Mayors, and the members of this organization then started to lobby the Roosevelt administration on behalf of the cities. They were very successful. The National Industrial Recovery Act appropriated $3.3 billion for important public works and housing operations, and later bills supplied billions more federal funding for housing, highway construction, and other projects that aided the cities. This policy, whereby cities depend on the federal government for extensive financial assistance, continued until the early 1980s, when federal aid to cities was sharply cut.

THE MODERN PERIOD   From 1940 to the present, two broad trends have dominated U.S. cities: decentralization and the growth of urban centers in the Sunbelt (the Southwest, Florida, and southern California). Decentralization means moving out of cities, often into suburbs. A **suburb** is a politically independent municipality that develops next to or in the vicinity of a city.

Why has the suburban movement occurred? Three reasons stand out. First, by about 1950, an increasing number of businesses, especially manufacturing concerns, were moving away from central city areas. Some assembly-line procedures needed more space than was readily available in the old central business districts. Growing crime rates, high taxes, and traffic congestion were other factors promoting a proliferation of "industrial parks" on the fringe of cities. As factories moved to the suburbs, workers often followed.

Second, technology has played an important part in the growth of suburbs. During the twentieth century, the use of electric power became widespread. Unlike its predecessor, steam power, electricity can be transmitted for long distances, thereby making it possible for both industries and residences to disperse throughout a large area. Automobiles and trucks have had a similar effect, permitting far greater flexibility and location than rail transportation, which had a dominant position during the latter half of the nineteenth and into twentieth century.

A third reason for suburban growth is that some people found city living distasteful. For example, at the end of World War II, millions of servicemen returned home to discover various conditions of their residential neighborhoods that they did not like — in particular, extensive physical deterioration because of urban-repair projects neglected during the war years and, in some cases (for whites), the proximity of black and other minority-group families. Many veterans took advantage of low-interest loans supplied by the Federal Housing Authority (FHA) and bought homes outside the center of the city or in the suburbs.

Looking back, we can easily see how this government policy contributed to urban deterioration. The policy encouraged white, middle-class people to leave cities, and their departure produced a substantial loss of tax revenue. This loss of revenue, in turn, meant the decline of local facilities and services. As police and fire protection, schools, and other facilities and services became more impoverished, people who could afford to leave cities often hastened to do so, further eroding the tax base.

In recent years American suburbs have changed. During the decade from 1970 to 1980, a prominent trend was the movement of urban black residents outward, often replacing suburban white inhabitants. While this pattern occurred in both the South and the North, blacks and whites in the South were more likely to share the same suburban

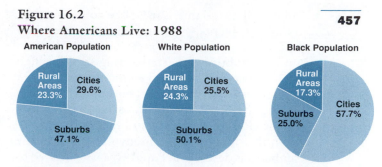

Figure 16.2
Where Americans Live: 1988

These figures demonstrate that Americans of various ethnic heritages tend to live in certain areas. Whites are overrepresented in the suburbs, while blacks, as well as other less affluent ethnic groups, are disproportionately located in cities. (Source: U.S. Bureau of the Census. Current Population Reports, Population Characteristics, P–20, No. 437. Table 2.)

locale (Stahura, 1988). Figure 16.2 shows Americans' distribution in cities, suburbs, and rural areas.

In recent years a dramatic urban change has been the growth of the Sunbelt cities. During the late 1970s and early 1980s, a shift of population and affluence from the industrial heartland of the Northeast to the fast-growing cities in Southern districts has occurred. The population of the fifteen Sunbelt states has grown from 61 million in 1970 (about a third of the nation's population) to 102 million in 1987 (about 42 percent of the total) and will expand to a projected 118 million inhabitants, representing 45 percent of the population, in the year 2000. We might readily wonder why.

The Sunbelt cities have had a series of distinct advantages over the historically prominent Northern cities. In many cases these Southern and Southwestern urban centers have industrialized only in recent years, and so they have been able to build modern, efficient plants. In addition, the recent development of the Sunbelt cities has meant that their superhighways most efficiently promote access to industrial parks. Furthermore, because their affluence has meant that they have not been pressed for cash, these new cities have been able to offer significant tax incentives to business executives who might want to relocate. Other advantages of the Sunbelt cities have included modern services, low energy costs, and limited unionization, which means lower labor costs. The prominent Northeastern cities have not

458

fared well in comparison. They contain aging, outmoded plants, superhighways providing limited access to industrial areas, few incentives to entice new business, deteriorating services, high energy costs, and extensive unionization. All in all, it is hardly surprising that businesses have been leaving the North by the thousands and heading for the cities of the South and the Southwest.

On the other hand, a cloudy side to life in the Sunbelt has developed. Rapid expansion has led to a massive, disorganized urban pattern, rising air pollution, and an overuse of the water and sewage systems. The influx of more than 10 million illegal aliens from Mexico and a number of other Latin American countries has heightened the problems. In many cases the immigrants are uneducated and unable to speak English. Those who have been able to find employment have taken the lowest-paying, most menial jobs. In a number of Southwestern cities, the immigrants' residential areas have begun to resemble the poverty-stricken slums of Third World countries (Palen, 1981: Chapter 3; Spates and Macionis, 1982: Chapter 7). In the middle 1980s, the loss of affluence in the oil industry had a distinctly negative impact on many Sunbelt cities, which started to suffer the economic woes long experienced in other parts of the country.

We have now briefly examined the history of American urban development, and in the course of this review, we have seen that a number of problems exist. In the following discussion, we focus on some of these problems and on possible solutions to them.

American Cities: Problems and Prospects

Daniel Boone, the frontiersman, apparently felt that the neighborhood was getting crowded when he could see the smoke from the nearest cabin. Mr. Boone would have had serious difficulty adjusting to modern, urbanized existence.

The massive movement of population and manufacturing from central cities to fringe areas has created "urban sprawl," where one metropolitan area frequently merges with the next. The resulting **megalopolis** is a string of closely bound metropolitan areas (Gottman, 1961). The largest American megalopolis runs from southern New

Hampshire to Prince William County, Virginia. It contains part or all of ten states and the cities of Boston, New York, Philadelphia, Baltimore, and Washington, DC. The population of "Bos Wash" exceeds 44 million people, representing about one-fifth of the American population. Megalopolitan growth is presently most rapid in the Sunbelt areas: the Southwest, Florida, and southern California.

As metropolitan areas expand and eventually form a megalopolis, serious urban problems often develop.

Urban Deterioration

Governmental proliferation, the influence of powerful political and economic interests, and financial limitations contribute significantly to the urban crisis.

GOVERNMENTAL PROLIFERATION At present there are about 80,000 governmental units in the United States, averaging nearly 1600 per state. This proliferation of governments makes it extraordinarily difficult to plan rationally. For instance, greater St. Louis is a typically "government-crowded" metropolis, where the participants are the federal government, two states, seven counties, 194 municipalities, and 615 special districts (concerned with such issues as water and sewage). Given such a massive number of organizations, it should be clear that coordinated policies will be difficult to achieve (Schwab, 1982).

POWERFUL POLITICAL AND ECONOMIC INTERESTS Lewis Mumford (1971), a well-known city planner, has claimed that throughout human history technological advances have generally been under the control of powerful economic and political groups whose primary goal has been to expand their own wealth and power. Therefore in modern cities, Mumford contended, businesspeople and politicians have cooperated to expand the number of highway miles, automobiles, and retail stores within their communities. As a result their own interests benefit, but the quality of city living for average inhabitants steadily deteriorates.

In the past American cities had "old machines," corrupt political organizations that ran cities by providing services and favors in exchange for citizens' political support. Modern cities are often controlled by "new machines," such as the Departments of Health, Fire, Police, Sanitation, Water, and Public Works. Frequently these organizations have been less corrupt than the old machines, but they can be equally irresponsible. They all help shape important public policies, but the leadership often refuses to accept the control of higher authorities (Lowi, 1981). In the late 1980s, one readily wondered whether the new machines, particularly at the federal level, are less corrupt. In the summer of 1989, for example, a congressional panel found that prominent politicians and government bureaucrats, including Housing and Urban Development (H.U.D.) officials, received illegal "consulting fees" — bribes actually — ranging up to $400,000 from developers seeking lucrative contracts for urban construction from H.U.D. As a commentary on his shady dealings, one official said, "I didn't invent it. Lobbying is probably the second oldest profession" (Shenon, 1989: A21).

FINANCIAL LIMITATIONS   American cities have been caught in a powerful financial squeeze, with affluent citizens' and businesses' outmigration, weak local economies, and inflationary pressures the major sources of the problem, according to an analysis of 234 American cities (Pagano, 1988). In the early 1980s, the federal government eliminated a range of social and public-works programs that benefit cities. At the same time, strict, local tax-cut measures were legislated in many states and cities. In 1982 in Massachusetts, for example, only .5 percent of the state budget was allotted for maintenance and repair — a policy that one expert on the state's budget called "pennywise and pothole foolish" (Beck, 1982: 12).

It has become impossible for cities to keep up with the deterioration of their public works: roads, bridges, government buildings, sewers, and mass-transit systems. At the current rate of repairs in New York City, for example, it would take 200 years to fix deteriorating streets and water mains and 300 years to replace the sewers (Palen, 1981: 261).

Politics compounds the financial problems. Elected officials seem to believe that they can convince their supporters that they are "doing something" in Washington if a new office building, dam, or highway is built in the district. The repair of old facilities would often be more beneficial for the local citizens, but such projects lack political appeal. As a H.U.D. official commented, "Have you ever seen a politician presiding over a ribbon-cutting for an old sewer line that was repaired?" (Beck, 1982: 13)

In the previous pages, it has been apparent that the problems of modern cities often have a profound, intimate impact on urban dwellers' lives. Let us continue to consider that idea.

The Urban Existence: Is Revitalization Possible?

During the late evening of April 19, 1989, an investment banker jogging through Central Park in New York City was brutally beaten and raped by an adolescent gang. Perhaps because the victim was white and the rapists were black, there were extensive angry outbursts. What was generally unrecognized by the public was that during the same week twenty-eight other women, primarily blacks and Hispanics, reported being raped in New York City (Terry, 1989). For many years sociologists have been analyzing the sources of such problems.

Georg Simmel (1950) examined the effect of city living on people's personalities. He observed that each individual encounters a great many people and experiences every day. Cities provide so much stimulation that serious mental disturbance can result. To protect themselves from overstimulation, urban residents must remain psychologically distant from most people. Otherwise they would be unable to cope with the pressures of daily living. Simmel wrote, "As a result of this reserve we frequently do not even know by sight those who have been our neighbors for years. And it is this reserve which in the eyes of the small-town people makes us appear to be cold and heartless" (Simmel, 1950: 415).

Louis Wirth (1938) shared Simmel's outlook on the city. Wirth believed that three factors — the size of cities, their densely populated neighborhoods, and continuous contact with strangers — produce deteriorating interpersonal relations in cities. The social significance of the family declines, neighborhood interaction disappears, and specialized outside agencies, such as the police, health agencies, and welfare organizations, assume tasks once handled by the family or community.

Sociologists like Simmel and Wirth have recog-

460

nized that the quality of urban life is often low. What are measures that might offer improvement?

EMPHASIS ON AN ACTIVE NEIGHBORHOOD LIFE   Recent research has concluded that metropolitan residents have distinct preferences about their neighborhoods. They tend to prefer them small rather than large and away from the inner-city instead of close to it (Dahmann, 1985).

Other factors also affect the quality of neighborhood life. Jane Jacobs, a well-known city planner, has contended that the best way to ensure neighborhood vitality is to combine a variety of land-use patterns in a given area. If neighborhoods contain a mixture of residences, small stores, schools, restaurants, bars, theaters, and parks, then there will be people on the streets from early morning until fairly late at night. Jacobs argued that a busy street life helps create a stimulating neighborhood and also makes it a relatively safe place, as the following account suggests.

One day Jacobs was watching an incident from her second-floor window. A struggle was going on between a little girl of eight or nine years and a man. The man was alternately trying to coax the girl to come with him and then ignoring her. The girl had made herself rigid against the wall of a building. She was determined not to move.

As Jacobs watched from her window and tried to decide whether or not to intervene, she saw that intervention would not be necessary. From the butcher shop, the owner came out with her arms folded and a determined look on her face. The man who ran the delicatessen across the street also emerged. Two men from the bar next to the butcher shop moved to the doorway and waited. On her own side of the street, Jacobs saw that the locksmith, the fruitman, and the laundry owner had all come out of their shops and were standing on the street. Other heads had appeared at windows. The man and the little girl were surrounded. Jacobs wrote, "Nobody was going to allow a little girl to be dragged off, even if nobody knew who she was. I am sorry—sorry purely for dramatic purposes—to have to report that the little girl turned out to be the man's daughter" (Jacobs, 1961: 39).

The protection offered by this city community turned out to be unnecessary. Nonetheless the incident offered evidence that a vital city neighborhood will help protect people, even strangers.

Neighborhood organizations are a proven means of helping to build strong neighborhoods, and the following Social Application examines this topic.

SOCIAL APPLICATION

Neighborhood Organizations: What Factors Can Make These Structures Strong?

It is the kind of stuff from which American heroic images are created: The people in a local neighborhood or community (the little guys) fight for what they believe to be their undeniable rights against the local political structure of a giant corporation (the big guys). TV news, magazine and newspaper articles, and films sometimes portray this situation.

But why are some of these organizations much more active and successful than others? The popular media are not likely to delve into such a topic. Let us consider some of the factors determining active, successful neighborhood organizations.

First, there is the issue of participants' characteristics. Abraham Wandersman and

his colleagues studied neighborhood organizations in Nashville. They concluded that people who join such groups are more likely to think highly of their own skills, to believe that their participation can produce change, to place a higher value on their local community, and to have a greater sense of citizen duty than those who do not join. Sociologist Pamela Oliver examined neighborhood organizations in Detroit and found that active members were better educated and, curiously, more pessimistic about their neighbors' willingness to make an active contribution than inactive members. On the last point, Oliver suggested that active participants are people who are convinced that if they do not join and participate actively in these structures, then nobody will; pessimism, in short, seems to encourage involvement.

Like active and inactive individuals, active and inactive neighborhood organizations differ in their characteristics. Compared to the inactive neighborhood organizations, those that are active tend to have leaders who are more experienced in organizational activity, are more likely to involve their members in the decision-making process, and are more capable of establishing high levels of cohesion and stability within the group. I spent over two years studying the development of neighborhood organizations. It was not difficult to separate those with leaders who had effective organizational skills from those without such leaders. Some relevant questions that will help draw the distinction: Does the leader enter meetings with a well-organized agenda? Does he or she have sufficient respect from members to hold their attention and generate enthusiasm? Do members

come to the meetings regularly? What, if any, organizational business is completed between meetings?

I also learned that active neighborhood organizations are more effective at pursuing tactics designed to produce physical and social improvements in the neighborhood area. In what often appears as a David versus Goliath contest, the members of local neighborhood groups can obtain a tremendous morale boost — and with it increased longevity for their organization — if the members can win a battle against the local power structure. Consider the following example.

In an upstate New York city, I was present the day after the leaders of city government agreed to the demands made by three local black-power leaders to tear down some old buildings that were considered dangerous temptations to children playing in the area. Local people spoke admiringly of the way the neighborhood organization leaders had handled themselves.

MRS. ALBRIGHT:
I think those guys handled themselves perfectly.
MRS. ROCHESTER:
Right!
MRS. ALBRIGHT:
The politicians won't do anything, because you who are reasonable go down to City Hall and request something. When the three guys from the neighborhood group went down to the mayor's office, they made it clear that if they

didn't get what they wanted, they were going to torch those buildings.
MRS. RICHETTE:
At City Hall they must have freaked out!
MRS. ALBRIGHT:
The threat was there. Certainly appearances helped get their point across. Those politicians took a look at Leroy's Afro, Carl's daishiki [African-style shirt] and beads, and. . .
MRS. ROCHESTER:
And Marcus's scar-covered face. . .
MRS. ALBRIGHT:
That's right! And then they started thinking of Detroit. [The worst riots of the 1960s occurred there in 1967.]

(Doob, 1970: 93–94)

Finally, active neighborhood organizations are more capable of accomplishing their goals, particularly their initial ones, than inactive groups. Saul Alinsky, a prominent organizer of community groups, believed that the way to build such organizations is much like training a prize fighter — that like the fighter, the neighborhood organization must be brought along slowly with progressively tougher opponents. Alinsky felt that in the beginning it is often helpful if those in charge set up what he called "a cinch fight," where the accomplishment of the goal is a certainty and thus assures that members' morale can be boosted for future, more difficult tasks. As an example Alinsky described a situation where he organized a demoralized neighborhood in Chicago to obtain infant welfare services. He knew that the services would be supplied the moment they were sought, but he did not tell the members. He wanted their apparent victory to serve as momentum for pursuing more difficult goals. Some people might say that Alinsky was deceptive, even dishonest. Most likely his reply would have been that in the harsh reality of city politics, one must use harsh methods to accomplish neighborhood organizations' goals.

Sources: Saul D. Alinsky. *Rules for Radicals.* New York: Vintage Books. 1971; Christopher Bates Doob. *How the War Was Lost.* Unpublished manuscript. 1970; Pamela Oliver. "'If You Don't Do It, Nobody Else Will': Active and Token Contributors to Local Collective Action." *American Sociological Review.* V. 49. October 1984, pp. 601–610; John E. Prestby and Abraham Wandersman. "An Empirical Exploration of a Framework of Organizational Viability: Maintaining Block Organizations." *Journal of Applied Behavioral Science.* V. 21. 1985, pp. 287–305; Abraham Wandersman. "Getting Together and Getting Things Done." *Psychology Today.* V. 19. November 1985, pp. 64–65+.

EXPERIMENTS WITH METROPOLITAN SOLUTIONS   As we have noted, a metropolis is composed of a central city and its surrounding cities and towns. The San Francisco Bay area, for instance, has eight counties, seventy-three cities, and eighty planning commissions. Small, local units could often efficiently promote their interests in the past. Today, however, such issues as mass transit, pollution control, civil defense, and water supply defy local solutions.

Many local governments have informally adopted metropolitan solutions to some problems. A survey of 6000 cities and towns indicated that many have joint service agreements that involve either one government purchasing services from another or a collaboration on projects.

Toronto, Canada, has used a two-level approach to the problem of metropolitan government. The first level is a metropolitan or regional government responsible for the issues common to the entire urban area. The second level of government is local, controlling such issues as police work, education, housing codes, and parks and recreation. This two-level approach seems promising. A serious drawback to all metropolitan plans, however, is that in spite of the fact that many urban problems require regional solutions, city and town officials are often unwilling to accept any loss of "home rule" (Campbell and Dollenmayer, 1975; Zimmerman, 1975).

EFFORTS TO BRING MIDDLE-CLASS PEOPLE BACK INTO CITIES, THEREBY BENEFITING THE AREAS ECONOMICALLY One trend has become so widespread in recent years that a concept has developed to describe it: **Gentrification** is the move of middle- and upper-middle-class people to formerly deteriorated, urban neighborhoods. A recent study concluded that characteristics of cities encouraging gentrification include the existence of a substantial segment of affluent, young adults not interested in having children but wanting to be "where the action is," the presence of corporate wealth that can subsidize redevelopment projects, and real-estate groups that can execute such projects (London et al., 1986). Extensive conversion of apartments to condominiums has already happened in many American cities. Middle-class people who purchase condominiums have the advantage of not only owning property that increases steadily in value but having the tax breaks that go with that ownership. Gentrification has helped transform the deteriorating centers of many American cities but usually at a significant cost: When old buildings are torn down and replaced or simply renovated, the former tenants are dispossessed. For many of them, this means hardship, but for the poor, who were barely surviving with modest rent rates, the result is often homelessness (Hopkins, 1989).

INCREASED FEDERAL AND STATE ASSISTANCE   As we have noted, since the New Deal, the federal government has provided major financial help to cities. Many financially troubled cities could benefit significantly from federal and state grants.

The recovery plan used in New York City can serve as a useful model. The gist of such a plan is to offer aid in exchange for financial reorganization. In 1975 the nation's largest city faced the threat of bankruptcy. City officials initiated tight management, local investment, and sharp controls on municipal workers' salaries in exchange for federal and state financial assistance. In the middle of

As this scene in Boston suggests, urban revitalization often involves not only the erection of new buildings but also the preservation of old ones.

1983, New York City had a substantial budget surplus, one of the few large American cities able to make such a claim. The New York City plan has been far from ideal — fiscal stability has been accompanied by a drastic cutback in local services

— and yet this situation shows that if realistic financial reorganization accompanies federal and state aid, some fiscal improvement is possible (Alpern, 1981).

Observers of American cities have some reason for optimism. Overall, though, the prospects are not positive. One specialist on urban affairs noted that

> the poor in cities have increased dramatically, the feminization of poverty has accelerated, the drop-out rate in high schools for blacks and hispanics is about 75%, unemployment for black youth is over 50%, teen-age births have reached new highs, infant mortality has increased, and deindustrialization has reduced the number of jobs in large cities.
>
> (Gittell, 1985: 19)

One means to halt the deterioration of American cities and the growing impoverishment of residents would be a federally funded program ensuring a guaranteed income for all citizens (Gittell, 1985). Such a program would certainly not eliminate all city problems, but it would probably represent a healthy start.

A recent study offered some interesting, if pessimistic insights into urban redevelopment. In the United States, local growth coalitions composed of real-estate entrepreneurs, politicians, and corporate officials were less subjected to regulation than their Japanese and Italian counterparts (Molotch and Vicari, 1988). Relatively unhampered by regulation, these wealthy and powerful groups seemed to be quite free to maximize personal economic and political interests and ignore or deemphasize other groups' interests, most emphatically those of poor citizens.

The Problem of Population Growth

The crowded, deteriorated sections of American cities illustrate that overpopulation exists in some places within U.S. society. The devastating population growth that many developing nations in Africa, Asia, and Latin America currently face, however, is a considerably more serious situation.

In the pages ahead, we consider the principal factors that affect population size. A **population** is all the people who live within a specified geographic area such as a nation, a region, or a city. **Demography** is the study of human populations. Demographers examine birth, death, and migration rates to understand population changes. This section introduces the basic concepts and theories

464

in demography and then examines the overpopulation issue in the developing and developed nations.

Basic Demographic Concepts and Theories

Rapid population growth is a new and distinctly frightening phenomenon. Since about 1750 the world population started to grow rapidly, and it has continued to do so. It took from the beginning of the Christian era to 1650 for the population to double, but with the current growth rate it will take only thirty-five years for the world's population to double to about 10 billion people. Why has this dramatic growth occurred? The central concept has been the death rate.

Before 1750 the primary reason for the low rate of population growth was the high death rate common in almost all societies. The most significant reason for this high death rate was a high infant mortality rate. In a given year, as many as one half of all infants would die before the age of one. For both adults and children, disease and famine were the major causes of the high death rate. The single most devastating disease in human history has been the bubonic plague, also known as the Black Death. A conservative estimate is that during the fourteenth century, 40 percent of all Europeans died of the disease. While the bubonic plague was the most devastating disease, others were also very destructive during the same period. Typhus, malaria, tuberculosis, and smallpox were at the top of the list. Famine has also helped limit population growth. Throughout history Asian famines have been more serious than the European ones, primarily because of the less predictable climate and rainfall of that continent. For example, a severe famine occurred in China in 1877 and 1878. In the course of the devastation, between 9 and 13 million people died of hunger, violence, and disease. Death was so prevalent that bodies were put in mass graves, which sometimes contained as many as 10,000 corpses (Petersen, 1975).

In the nineteenth century, the death rate started to drop in industrial nations, and the population began to rise, first in Western and later in non-Western countries. If we start by understanding a number of demographic concepts, then we can examine theories and problems of population growth.

The Factors in Population Growth

Demographers focus their attention on birth, death, migration, and growth rates, as they attempt to predict population trends around the world.

BIRTH RATE   The **crude birth rate** is the number of births per 1000 persons in society in a given year. This statistical measure is called "crude" because it does not provide specific information about the births. The crude birth rate, for instance, does not indicate the percentages of children born within different ethnic, racial, or class categories. The American crude birth rate of about 14 per thousand per year is scarcely one-third the rate in such developing nations as Bangladesh, Biafra, or Zaire.

A crude birth rate gives an indication of the fertility of women in a given society. The **fertility rate** is the number of actual births per 1000 women between the ages of fifteen and forty-four. That thirty-year span is the approximate length of time during which women are capable of giving birth. One must distinguish fertility from fecundity, the biological potential for reproduction. No society has ever approached its reproductive potential.

DEATH RATE   The **crude death rate** is the number of deaths per 1000 persons in a society in a given year. Once again, the designation "crude" means that the statistical measure provides no specific information, in this instance about death. It does not indicate, for instance, that in the United States the mortality rate (death rate for children during the first year) is 18 per 1000 black infants per year — double the figure of 9 per 1000 white infants per year (U.S. Bureau of the Census, *Statistical Abstract of the United States: 1989*. No. 113).

MIGRATION RATE   **Migration** is the flow of people in and out of a particular territory (city, region, or country). The **in-migration rate** is the number of people per 1000 members of the population moving into an area in a given year, and the **out-migration rate** is the number of people per 1000 members of the population moving out of an area in a given year. The **net migration rate** is the difference between the in-migration rate and the out-migration rate.

For several reasons data on migration are less effective than data on birth and death rates. In the first place, an individual's birth and death are more easily measured, occurring only once, while migration can and often does take place many times during a lifetime. In addition, demographers started to study migration rates much more recently than birth and death rates. Thus less extensive data are available on migration.

Migration can have a significant influence on a nation's population. The United States is certainly a case in point. Between 1919 and 1955, over forty million people immigrated to this country, with the peak years early in the twentieth century. In six of the eleven years from 1905 to 1915, more than a million immigrants per year reached American shores. Although restrictive legislation sharply limited the number of people who could arrive legally after 1924, significant numbers of immigrants have kept coming to the United States, and in recent years estimates indicate that as many illegal as legal migrants have entered the United States.

GROWTH RATE Immigration can significantly affect population growth, but birth and death tend to be the major influences. The **growth rate** is the crude birth rate minus the crude death rate. Colombia, for instance, has a crude birth rate of about 31 per 1000 people and a crude death rate of about 9 per 1000. Thus the crude growth rate is 22 per thousand or 2.2 percent growth per year. The American growth rate is much lower, about .7 percent per year (United Nations, *Demographic Yearbook, 1985*. Table 7).

A growth rate of 2.2 percent might seem relatively small at first glance, but the long-term result will be an enormous population increase. Consider, for instance, a nation of 10 million that increases 2.2 percent per year. After a year the population will be 10,220,000, and the following year it will total 10,444,840. Each year the population increases by an additional 2.2 percent, and as the population grows, that 2.2 percent represents a larger figure each year. In about thirty-two years, that population of 10 million will double.

Doubling time is the time span necessary for a population to double in size. A growth rate of 1 percent produces doubling in seventy years, a growth rate of 2 percent means twice the popula-

tion in thirty-five years, and a 3.5 percent rate leads to doubling in only twenty years.

The frightening fact is that the developing nations of Africa, Asia, and Latin America currently have a growth rate of about 2.1 percent, which means an average doubling time of only thirty-three years. Starvation and malnutrition are already widespread in many of these countries, and such rapid population growth will only worsen these tragic problems.

Two Significant Demographic Theories

The two theories that we now discuss both consider the disastrous effects that overpopulation can produce.

MALTHUSIAN THEORY In 1798 Thomas Robert Malthus published the *First Essay on Population*. In this essay the author, a minister, emphasized that humanity was guilty of original sin and, as a result, was destined to suffer. According to Malthus, God had established two conditions that would operate simultaneously to make continuous suffering inevitable: first, an unquenchable passion between the sexes ensuring rapid reproduction and, second, a limited capacity to produce food. Malthus contended that population growth occurs at a geometric rate (2, 4, 8, 16, . . .), whereas the food supply expands at a mere arithmetic rate (2, 3, 4, 5, . . .). Malthus wrote, "A slight acquaintance with numbers will shew [show] the immensity of the first power in comparison to the second" (Malthus, 1798: 14).

He believed that over time the scarcity of food would become increasingly alarming. While conceding that war, famine, and disease would hold population partially in check, Malthus thought that the future for most of the world population was bleak: bare subsistence at a very low level of material existence.

Malthus's first essay was an attack on the contemporary belief that large families among the poor are a blessing to be encouraged. The essay received extensive criticism, and five years later Malthus wrote a revision in which he emphasized that late marriage and fewer children could prevent a population disaster. Malthus advocated financial incentives as a means to restrict the number of children. He rejected birth control and abortion on religious grounds. The second essay was more popular in Malthus's day, but he is much better known for the earlier work.

Certainly Malthus's original essay has short-comings. In the first place, he did not anticipate significant improvements in agriculture that have made it possible to increase food production much more quickly than he had expected. Second, the industrial societies have not shared Malthus's distaste for birth-control methods. By using a variety of techniques, a number of nations have been able to limit population much more effectively than the pious minister anticipated.

Yet, in spite of these criticisms, Malthusian theory has turned out to be prophetic. As we see in the pages ahead, the population has outstripped the food supply in most developing countries. In addition, Malthus's theory applied to advanced industrial societies. In the West other resources besides food are rapidly running out — in particular, clean air, clean water, and energy sources. Several years ago a report to the House Committee on Agriculture included the following question: "Will Americans discover too late that Thomas Malthus is a 200-year-old alarmist whose time has finally arrived?" (Committee on Agriculture, 1976: 253)

DEMOGRAPHIC-TRANSITION THEORY

As Figure 16.3 indicates, the demographic-transition theory provides a three-stage analysis of population growth. The **preindustrial stage** existed before industrialization, and was characterized by a stable population, with both the birth and death rates remaining high. Overall a very slow rate of

population growth occurred, but as we have noted, disease or famine sometimes produced a population decline. The preindustrial stage finished somewhere between 1750 and 1850 for the majority of Western countries.

The **transition stage** was the second stage, in which a decline in the death rate and a continuing high birth rate produced a rapid growth in population. The transition stage happened at the beginning of the industrial age and was accompanied by significant advances in food production, sanitation, and health care.

The **industrial stage,** characterized by a low death rate and dropping birth rate, occurs as nations stabilize their populations in the course of industrialization. Eventually the birth and death rates are almost the same, and the population stabilizes.

Some modern demographers have also considered a postindustrial stage, where deaths steadily outnumber births and the population of society declines, eventually to the point that the society itself ceases to exist (Bouvier, 1984: 32). While this situation might occur in the future, no modern society presently seems an immediate candidate. Meanwhile, particularly in developing nations, high birth rates are a serious problems.

What conditions encourage a declining birth rate? The availability of contraception and family-planning information are contributing factors. A more significant factor, however, is the impact of the modern, urban lifestyle. Children no longer help earn the family living as in preindustrial times. In fact, they represent an economic liability. Furthermore, as women develop careers and other personal interests, they do not want to devote most of their energies to raising a family.

The industrial stage is nearly complete in Europe, the United States, and Canada. A number of eastern countries, or portions of countries, have been advancing rapidly into the third stage in recent years. Japan, the Republic of Korea, the major Chinese cities, and Chinese in east and southeast Asia have demonstrated sharply reduced fertility rates within marriage (Leete, 1987).

In contrast, most developing nations are in the transition stage. The introduction of Western technology — insecticides like DDT, improvements in food transportation and storage, and such modern health practices as inoculations against diseases — has sharply lowered the death

Figure 16.3
Demographic-Transition Theory

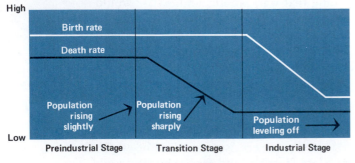

While the United States and other developed nations are attaining the population stability of the industrial stage, the developing nations are experiencing the rapid population expansion of the transition stage.

This rural Mexican family, with five children, is living in the transition stage of the demographic-transition theory. In contrast, the American family, with two children, is in the industrial stage.

rate. The birth rate, however, has remained high because the principal conditions of modern, urban life that would produce a decline in the birth rate do not exist.

A cruel irony is apparent. Western nations have introduced modern technology in order to reduce suffering and death; however, by rapidly expanding the population size of developing nations, those devices have increased suffering.

We will examine the effects of population problems in both developing nations and in the United States and also consider efforts to reduce overpopulation.

An Overview of World Population Problems

What are some of the results of massive population growth? In the first place, crowding happens. While people's perception of whether or not a sit-

uation is crowded varies according to their cultural standards, it seems safe to conclude that the more people, the more probable individuals will perceive a living situation as crowded. Some studies do suggest that as the number of people in a space increases, they are more inclined to experience nervous disorders and to engage in child abuse, incest, and suicide. Certainly the prospect of extreme crowding confronts us when we look at how rapid the population expansion in developing nations has been. In 1900 the population of the non-Western nations was about one billion. If present projections hold, the figure will reach about 5.5 billion by the end of the century— nearly a sixfold increase in 100 years.

Shortage of food is another serious problem produced by rapid population growth. In the past many famines were **distribution famines**—food shortages existing in certain provinces or regions of a country, not throughout the nation. Distribution famines usually result from inadequate trans-

Figure 16.4
Three Basic Population Pyramids — India, United States, and Sweden: ca. 1980

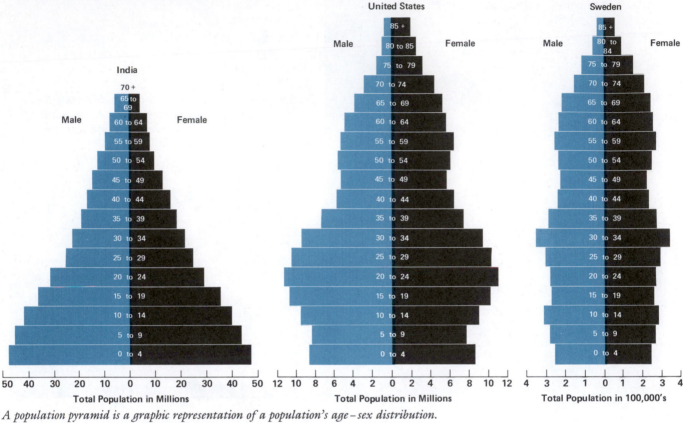

A population pyramid is a graphic representation of a population's age–sex distribution.
India, with a rapidly growing population, presents a bottom-heavy pyramid typical of
developing nations. A century ago the American population pyramid had a similar shape.
At present our age–sex distribution is gradually moving toward the Swedish pattern.
(Sources: U.S. Bureau of the Census. Current Population Reports, Population
Characteristics, *P–20, No. 374. Table 3–1; United Nations Publishing Service.*
Demographic Yearbook, 1985. Table 7.)

portation or the unwillingness of leaders in one region to help starving people in another. In contrast, **deficit famines** are situations in which no food supplies exist elsewhere in a nation sufficient to compensate for local inadequacies. In many developing nations, rapid population growth coupled with limited food supplies make the occurrence of deficit famines increasingly likely in the future (Sullivan et al., 1980: 111–117).

The future for many developing nations appears frightening. Figure 16.4 shows that a developing nation, such as India, generally has a disproportionately large young population, and, therefore, its prospect for continuing rapid growth seems excellent. A recent report issued by the National

Academy of Sciences has concluded that perhaps the greatest danger of excessive population growth is environmental destruction, particularly the pollution of air, water, and soil and the elimination of forests and various species of plants and animals (Silk, 1986). Developed nations, like the United States and Sweden have a much smaller proportion of young people, and so they are unlikely to have rapid growth in the years ahead.

The American Population Picture

Like other Western societies, the United States has passed through a phase of rapid population growth. Because of a steady flood of immigrants, the national population increased by about 30 percent each decade during the second half of the nineteenth century. Then in the 1920s, restrictions on immigration along with a declining birth rate slowed the rate of population growth. After World War II, the "baby boom" occurred, and in 1955 the birth rate reached its highest postwar figure. From that time the rate dropped steadily until 1975 before increasing slightly. The so-called "baby bust" of the past two decades has resulted because young people are having or plan to have fewer children than adults in the past.

To obtain **zero population growth**—a situation in which the population size stabilizes—American couples need to average about 2.1 children, slightly more than enough children to replace themselves in order to compensate for offspring who die and people who remain childless. In 1986 lifetime births expected for women aged eighteen to thirty-four was 1.836 children, lower than the figure needed for population stabilization (U.S. Bureau of the Census, *Statistical Abstract of the United States: 1989.* No. 87). It is apparent that unless the birth rate shoots up, the American prospects for zero population growth are good.

Yet the current American population situation contains some serious problems. First, while the overall fertility rate has been dropping, the proportion of births to unmarried mothers has been increasing. In 1986, 23.4 percent of all births were out of wedlock, nearly five times the percentage in 1960. Many of these children face distinct economic and social disadvantages in the years ahead (U.S. Bureau of the Census, *Statistical Abstract of the United States: 1989.* No. 89). Second, certain economic strains have developed. Insufficient jobs and housing currently exist to meet the needs of Americans. One of the reasons the crime rate is particularly high among young people seems to be that they are especially prone to unemployment. Third, a number of valuable resources are in increasingly short supply. A shortage of water already exists in the Southwest, and this problem will spread north and east in the years ahead. Food production could become a problem in American society, particularly if there is strict enforcement of the laws regulating the use of pesticides and various chemical fertilizers. With the average American using 450 pounds of wood and wood products each year, there will be continuing deterioration of the nation's lumber supply. Fourth, an increase in the population size will inevitably produce more pollution. In a highly developed country like the United States, the amount of water, air, and soil pollution is considerably greater per capita than in a developing country like India, Zaire, or Peru.

In spite of the difficulties just discussed, the American population problem seems to be quite effectively under control. In developing nations, however, overpopulation is an increasingly serious threat. What can be done to overcome this threat?

Attempts to Set Limits

How can we visualize the enormous number of people on this planet? In Robert Graves's (1962) historical novel *Claudius the God,* the Roman Emperor Claudius ordered a census taken of his kingdom, and the total number of Roman citizens was 5,984,072. On a page, Claudius admitted, the figure was not very impressive, but it was impressive if one considered it in human terms. Claudius explained, "If the whole Roman citizenry were to file past me at a brisk walk, toe to heel, it would be two whole years before the last one came in sight" (Graves, 1962: 479). Claudius ruled nearly 6 million people. The current population of the earth is about 5 billion people, about 836 times the population of Claudius's Rome, and growing by about 83 million a year. At the current growth rate, the planet gains another million people every four-and-a-half days, about 158 per minute. About 92 percent of the growth is concentrated in the developing nations of Africa, Asia (excluding Japan), and Latin America (*Population Today,* April 1986: 3).

It is easy to feel overwhelmed by the numbers and simply to believe that they are so large that nothing can be done to control overpopulation. Some practical measures do exist, however.

CONTRACEPTION   Many experts feel that the key to lowering the fertility rate and thus reducing population growth resides in technology: specifically, easy-to-use and effective means of contraception. Certainly the widespread use of contraceptives would curtail the population expansion. Some devices are more effective than others. Oral

470

contraceptives and intrauterine devices (IUDs) are the most effective methods. They are followed by the condom, diaphragm and spermicide, withdrawal, spermicide alone, rhythm, and douche in order of declining effectiveness.

Contraception can reduce the birth rate and curtail population growth, but a recent study indicated that its success is determined by two factors — the motivation for fertility regulation and the financial costs of that regulation (Ahmed, 1987).

FAMILY PLANNING **Family planning** is a program that encourages people to decide how many children they want, when they want them, and what contraceptives, if any, they wish to use to achieve their goals. Family-planning programs have helped to reduce the birth rate in such countries as Taiwan, Singapore, South Korea, and Hong Kong. Family planning alone, however, has not been able to halt population growth in any country. One difficulty is that many programs are poorly financed, thus permitting only a small number of people to use their services. The major problem, though, is that the family size a couple wants and the size that will be suitable for the welfare of a nation are often not the same. In many cases people turn to family planning after they have had large families, not before. Therefore a major challenge involves incentive — motivating people to accept small families.

INCENTIVES The most obvious incentives are financial, and several countries have experimented with paying cash for sterilization or the use of IUDs. Another possibility is to permit tax deductions for only the first two children or to impose a "child tax" on parents with more than a certain number of children. The chief problem with such proposals is that under them large, poor families would only encounter increased suffering. Some incentive plans are more far ranging, emphasizing the development of social and economic policies that would weaken social norms encouraging large families. Whereas couples would be free to decide the number of children, they would encounter pressure from family, friends, and government officials to keep that number low.

COERCION If family planning and incentives fail to lower the birth rate, some countries may be forced to impose limits on the number of children people are permitted to have. Such a policy, natu-

rally, would create an uproar in a country like the United States, where there has been a strong emphasis on the rights of individuals to conduct their private lives without government interference as long as they do not hurt anyone else. Of course, therein lies the problem. In many developing nations, if citizens continue to have large families, the current inadequacies of food and other resources will only worsen, and all, or at least many will suffer.

By what measures could a government administer a policy of coercive population control? One approach would be to issue a license to every woman of childbearing age permitting her to have the number of children that would be most suitable for that society's welfare. Another proposal would be to provide a chemical inhibitor for the entire population: some agent that would reduce fertility but not entirely eliminate childbirth. The goal of such an approach would be to regulate the chemical dosage so that the desired number of children would be produced each year. To Americans as well as to citizens of many other countries, such measures seem intolerable. And yet in the future, the governments of nations faced with explosive population growth might decide that no other approach will work.

A COMBINATION OF TECHNIQUES It turns out that some developing nations have been remarkably successful in limiting their population growth, and the greatest success seems to have resulted from a combination of techniques.

The People's Republic of China is a particularly significant case in point. In China large families have been a tradition for centuries. Within a ten-year span, however, China has cut its growth rate almost in half, to 1.2 percent a year. To attain this reduction, the government established a family-planning program designed to impress prospective parents with the importance of limiting population growth. Local paramedic teams, which always include at least one woman, pass out free contraceptives. Government officials seek the help of local organizations to establish and maintain birth quotas and to encourage late marriage. In addition, the government has supported strenuous efforts to enlist women in all aspects of local life, not just child rearing. Finally, in hopes of achieving the goal of zero population growth by the year 2000, the Chinese government is now considering proposals to provide child-care subsidies, priority in housing allocation and school placement, and generous pensions for families with only one child. The system has been successful, with particularly low fertility rates among highly educated people. While the results are impressive, many Americans are disturbed by the use of coercion, with governmental officials pressuring people on what Americans consider to be a private matter — their number of children (Davis, 1967; Freedman et al., 1988; Nam and Gustavus, 1976; Poston and Gu, 1987; Sullivan et al., 1980).

A study of thirty-eight developing nations found that formal schooling, which generates new knowledge, ideas, and outlooks, is a major social force encouraging a low fertility rate (Cleland and Rodriguez, 1988).

However, research in several Asian-Indian communities indicated that the reasons why different groups reduce their number of children are often linked to specific cultural traditions. In the city of Bombay, the Parsis, who form one cultural community, have reduced their number of children primarily in order to afford to establish and maintain Western-style homes and furnishings. In contrast, the Saraswats, members of another cultural community, have produced fewer children so that they will be able to invest heavily in their male children's education, which is a prerequisite for success in the highly competitive white-collar job market (Axelrod, 1988).

As the population of a nation grows, its environmental problems are likely to increase. The American case demonstrates, however, that other factors make a more prominent contribution.

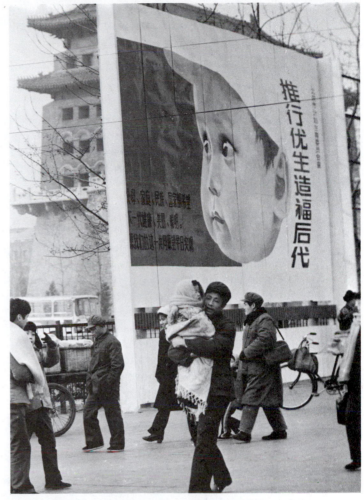

This billboard in Beijing, which says "practice birth control to benefit the next generation," is part of the one-child policy, which China has been promoting as a means of controlling the size of its already enormous population.

Environmental Issues

A riddle taught to French children asks the following question. If the number of lilies in a pond doubles each day and if the pond is entirely filled with lilies on the thirtieth day, when will the pond be half filled? The answer: on the twenty-ninth day (Brown, 1978). If the lilies represent the human population and the pond stands for the environment, is it reasonable to suspect that humanity is now in the twenty-ninth day?

The subject of this section is the **natural environment,** the combination of land, climate, water, air, mineral resources, and plant and animal life that together compose the physical world where people live. Ecologists point to the existence of a "web-of-life": an intimate, delicate relationship of plants and animals to each other and to the environment. With the development of mechanical sources of power, we human beings have assumed a dominant role in this community of interdependent living organisms and perhaps have brought ourselves to the eve of "the twenty-ninth day." Ecologists emphasize that many valuable resources are dangerously scarce and that environmental pollution has become increasingly serious.

Resource Depletion

Food supplies and natural resources are two major areas of resource depletion. Both pose significant difficulties that will become even more significant in the years ahead.

Food Supplies

In the developing nations, the average person consumes less than two-thirds as many calories as the individual in developed nations. In many cases the caloric consumption is even lower, especially in the developing African nations, where the majority of the population lives on roots, coarse grains, wild fruits, and vegetables—a diet generally low in both vitamins and proteins.

World hunger is an enormous problem today. An estimated 1.3 billion people are hungry all the time, and about 462 million people, over half of them small children, are starving. From an overall planetary perspective, the problem is not insufficient food. Each year farmers produce enough grain to provide every living person 3000 calories each day. Then why do so many people go hungry? A major problem is that countries where people are starving do not produce enough food or the kind of food they need. At least fifteen such nations grow more acres of food for export than acres of such staples as wheat, corn, rice, vegetables, and fruits that could sustain their own people. As a result they must import these staples, but seldom can they import enough to prevent famine.

Inadequate food supply is the primary problem in developing countries. In developed nations the greatest challenge involves natural resources.

Natural Resources

The most publicized concern in the area of natural resources is energy. Western nations depend on oil for almost half of their energy needs, and at present the world consumption level is awesome:

almost 30,000 gallons of oil every second. Estimates suggest that the available supplies of both oil and natural gas will run out within fifty to seventy-five years.

Water is another important, exhaustible resource. American society has required an ever increasing amount of water. In 1900 Americans used 40 billion gallons of water a year. By 1970 the figure had risen to 350 billion gallons. At the end of the century, estimates indicate that consumption will be between 700 and 1000 billion gallons.

Americans also employ a large proportion of various raw materials that are fast running out. We use over 60 percent of the planet's natural gas, more than 40 percent of the aluminum and coal, over 33 percent of the nickel, petroleum, platinum, and copper, and about 25 percent of the iron, gold, mercury, silver, tin, lead, zinc, and tungsten.

Technological advances now permit increased extraction of minerals from low-grade ore, but the associated activities—more mining, crushing, treating with chemicals, heating, cooling, and dumping—will greatly expand environmental pollution (Barnet, 1980; Meadows et al., 1972; Ridker and Watson, 1980).

Environmental Pollution

As we have noted, ecologists indicate that we human beings are a component in the "web of life." The pollution we create also enters this process. Barry Commoner (1972), an ecologist, described several principles of environmental pollution. First, he suggested that within the environment all the parts are interrelated and that a change in one part of the system causes changes in other parts. Second, nothing just disappears. Pollution will simply move from one place to another, or perhaps it will be transformed. Third, nature is enormously complicated. Commoner claimed that the environment is like a watch. If you close your eyes and poke a pencil into the works, the watch might run better, but the chances are it will be seriously damaged. The odds that "poking around" in the environment has been and will continue to be harmful are overwhelming. Commoner concluded that people have ignored these principles and violated the environ-

As Americans become increasingly aware of the environmental crisis, many are willing to take steps to reduce its destructive effects. Recycling bottles and cans is one modest effort.

ment for such a long period of time that the current pollution problems literally threaten the survival of humanity.

Americans are becoming increasingly aware of environmental problems. Table 16.1, which contains data from a nationally conducted survey, indicates the extent of public concern with major environmental problems as well as some measures respondents have taken to improve the environment. We will examine some major types of pollution in U.S. society.

In comparison to modern citizens, Native American groups seem to have had a nondestructive, healthy relationship to the environment.

Most of us know little about this subject, however, and so let us consider it in the following Cross-Cultural Perspective on pp. 474–475.

Air Pollution

When asked early in 1989 to express their concern about air pollution, 50 percent of a national sample said they were extremely concerned ("6" on a six-point scale ranging from 6 to 1) and another 23 percent opted for very concerned ("5" on the scale) (George Gallup, Jr., *Gallup Report,* January 1989).

There are four major sources of air pollution: transportation, power generation, industry, and waste incineration. Auto emissions represent the most serious contributor to air pollution. In the United States, 90 million cars release millions of tons of carbon monoxide, sulfur dioxide, hydrocarbons, and nitrogen oxides per year.

In recent years air pollution has been receiving extensive attention for two reasons. First, there has been growing international concern about destruction of the ozone layer, which protects the earth from ultraviolet radiation that is harmful to both animal and plant life. The major source of ozone destruction has been chlorofluorocarbons, which are versatile, low-cost chemicals used as coolants in refrigerators and air-conditioners, as propellants in aerosol spray cans, as solvents, and in foam insulation. Twelve European nations have agreed to cut production of chlorofluorocarbons by 85 percent as soon as possible and to ban their use by the end of the century. The U.S. Environmental Protection Agency (E.P.A.) regulations seek to reduce their production by 60 percent during the 1990s. However, it is widely believed that restoration of the ozone layer, particularly the hole in the layer that has opened up over Antarctica, will require a full ban (*Futurist,* 1989; Whitney, 1989).

The other significant recent concern related to air pollution has involved the impact of the "greenhouse effect" — the belief shared by many environmental scientists that over the next century a significant rise in the earth's temperature will occur, with a rising sea level, changing weather patterns, damage to forests and crops, and other possible destructive effects. The major culprit here is carbon-dioxide emissions from the

Table 16.1
Outlook toward Environmental Issues

EXTENT RESPONDENT WORRIES ABOUT SERIOUSNESS OF ENVIRONMENTAL PROBLEMS

	GREAT DEAL	FAIR AMOUNT
Ocean and beach pollution	60%	23%
Loss of habitat for wildlife	58	27
Contamination of soil and water by radioactive waste	54	24
Damage to the earth's ozone layer	51	26
Loss of tropical rain forest	42	25
Acid rain	41	27
Greenhouse effect or global warming	35	28

STEPS TAKEN BY RESPONDENT OR HOUSEHOLD MEMBER TO IMPROVE THE ENVIRONMENT

Voluntary recycling of newspapers, glass, aluminum, motor oil, or other items	78%
Cutting household use of energy by improving insulation or changing the heating or air-conditioning system	76
Replacing a "gas guzzling" automobile with one that is more fuel-efficient	66
Cutting household's use of water	65
Contributing money to an environmental, conservation, or wildlife preservation group	49
Cutting down on the use of a car by carpooling or taking public transportation	42
Boycotting a company's product because of its record on the environment	29
Working as a volunteer for an environmental, conservation, or wildlife preservation group	16
No steps taken	2

Source: George Gallup, Jr. *Gallup Report.* June 1989.

Recent survey data suggest that many Americans are concerned about major environmental problems and have taken modest steps to improve the environment.

CROSS-CULTURAL PERSPECTIVE

Native Americans' Relationship to the Environment

Frequently Americans have believed that Indians were simply another lower form of animal life, leaving little or no physical impact on the environment. Actually they often had an extensive impact. As we look at Native Americans' interaction with the environment, perhaps we will obtain some insights into our own troubled relationship with it.

As we noted, Native Americans often left their mark on the land. Many tribes used fire to clear forests and produce grasslands for hunting and fields for planting. Many times they overhunted animals, eliminating or at least greatly limiting the presence of different animal species within a locale. Historian Richard White commented, "One thing that has impressed me about Indians I've known is their realiza-

tion that this is a harsh planet, that they survive by the deaths of other creatures. There's no attempt to gloss over that or romanticize it" (Cronon and White, 1986: 20).

While the Native Americans' perception of the world should not be romanticized, it should be understood. One critical element in Indians' perception has been their belief that they exist in a social relationship with all other living creatures—something like Commoner's principle that all parts of the environment are related. If Indians killed an animal, for instance, they felt that they were under an obligation that needed to be repaid. This repayment might have taken the form of a prayer of sacrifice to the spirit of the departed animal.

Native Americans also maintained a careful relationship with the land itself. Unlike whites, Indians did not believe that they should seek maximum yield in food supplies but should simply try to obtain security. They tended to have a number of different ways of obtaining food, and these varied with the season. This diversification provided what might be considered "ecological safety nets." If one net failed —for example, a drought made growing corn unproductive in a given year— then the tribe still had other nets on which to rely, such as food gathering or hunting.

Native Americans tended to believe that their cycles of hunting, food gathering, and agriculture were profoundly interdependent. Most Americans failed to appreciate such a linkage. White described a conversation in the 1870s between a Pawnee Indian named Petalesharo and an Indian agent who was trying to persuade Petalesharo to stop hunting buffalo.

> Suddenly a cultural chasm . . . [opened] between them, because Petalesharo . . . [was] trying to explain that the corn will not grow without the buffalo hunt. Without buffalo to sacrifice at the ceremonies, corn will not come up and the Pawnee world will cease. You see them talking, but there . . . [was] no communication.
>
> *(Cronon and White, 1986: 21)*

Petalesharo's view makes little sense to modern Americans, but it must be appreciated as typical of Indians' beliefs about their relationship to the environment. Furthermore, whether or not one understands the Indians' perception, one can recognize its latent function: to establish a balanced, diversified cycle for obtaining food.

For many Native Americans the destruction of these cycles, not military conquest, became the chief means by which they were subjected to whites' control. In order to receive such valued items as textiles, alcohol, guns, and other metal goods, Indians had to exchange such products as furs and meat. Eventually these exchanges led to the devastation of beaver, buffalo, and deer. With traditional sources of subsistence destroyed, the Indians had to accept whites' means of obtaining food. These people, who had once been profoundly independent, became almost completely dependent.

There seems to be a lesson to learn from the Native Americans' tragic downfall. While differences exist between our current situation and theirs, we too are compelled to maintain a relationship with the environment and we too can find our environment sufficiently damaged to destroy our way of life.

Source: William Cronon and Richard White. "Indians in the Land." *American Heritage.* V. 37. August/September 1986, pp. 19–25. I am grateful to Shirley Varmette, a member of the Southern Connecticut State University sociology department, for supplying both the idea and source for this box.

---

extensive use of fossil fuels. While reduction in destructive emissions can lessen the greenhouse effect, many environmental scientists are convinced that invariably a significant impact will be produced (Shabecoff, 1988).

Water Pollution

In the famous 1960s film *Dr. Strangelove,* General Jack D. Ripper never drank water straight from the tap. He believed that only superdistilled H_2O would protect his "precious bodily fluids" from a "communist plot" to fluoridate U.S. water. While General Ripper's fear of fluoridation was unrealistic, people today are indeed anxious to protect themselves from the pollutants in the American water supply.

Several sources of water pollution exist. One prominent contributor is sewage. As towns and cities have grown, their sewage-treatment facilities have often failed to expand accordingly. In many

The pollutants in American waterways are sometimes so potent that they kill the fish inhabiting them.

areas septic tanks discharge their refuse into the same underground water supply that people use for drinking. In a public restroom along the upper Mississippi River, a statement scribbled on the wall read, "Flush the toilet. They need the water in St. Louis." This sarcastic bit of humor might contain more truth than St. Louis's citizenry would like to acknowledge. Another significant source of water pollution is industrial waste. Since the beginning of industrialization, American factories have been located near waterways, and manufacturers have long recognized that nothing works as well as a river to make one's own waste problems belong to someone else. As a result the major rivers of the U.S. contain large quantities of lead, sulfuric acid, hydrofluoric acid, ammonia, and dioxin, one of the most toxic chemicals known (Ehrlich, Ehrlich, and Holdren, 1977; Sun, 1983).

A well-known source of water pollution has been oil spills, the largest of which occurred when an Exxon tanker ran aground off the coast of Alaska in March 1989 and released 11 million gallons of crude oil into the water of Prince William Sound, polluting a virgin wilderness and killing vast numbers of wild animals, birds, and fish (Wald, 1989b).

While such publicized episodes occur, the destructive impact of many unheralded, systematic dumping activities is greater. A case in point involved the pharmaceutical company Ciba-Geigy, which ran a ten-mile pipeline from its dye and resin plants and dumped more than four million gallons per day of waste containing lead, chromium, and such extreme carcinogenic (cancer-producing) chemicals as POBs and nitrogen-bearing compounds into the ocean off New Jersey. The governor, both senators, other state politicians, and the E.P.A. were aware of the dumping for years, but no significant action to prevent it was taken (Cockburn, 1988).

Pesticide Residues

In 1981 the Mediterranean fruit fly damaged the fruit and vegetable crops in several sections of California. In order to prevent the further spread of the fruit fly, the governor reluctantly authorized the widespread spraying of insecticides. Shortly afterwards a survey firm asked a national sample of Americans whether they thought spraying the insecticides was the right or wrong thing to do. Seventy-two percent indicated it was the right thing, 8 percent felt it was wrong, and 20 percent had mixed feelings or did not know. However, after the fruit fly problem started, 41 percent of the respondents — more than two in five — changed their attitudes or behavior about buying California fruits and vegetables or noted that the stores in their area had made a change (Roper Organization, *Roper Reports,* November 1981). These survey items suggest that many Americans have a two-part attitude toward pesticides. Such people feel they are necessary but want to have as little personal contact with them as possible.

The pesticide issue is a difficult one. Farmers and consumers want to produce food as cheaply as possible, and pesticides help do this. In recent years, however, many consumers have become increasingly concerned that the food they buy is infected by carcinogenic pesticides. Florida and the South, which are particularly vulnerable to plant diseases and insects, would be hardest hit if pesticides were restricted or banned. A soil scientist said, "What we're seeing is a very real conflict in values out there. Some people say the only acceptable use of pesticides is no use. But the only way we can get high quality vegetables in Florida at the volumes we need and prices we expect is with pesticides" (Schneider, 1989: A14).

Radioactivity Effects

Soon after the Three Mile Island accident, a vice-president of the Metropolitan Edison Company, which operated the nuclear-power plant, said, "We didn't injure anybody, we didn't seriously contaminate anybody and we certainly didn't kill anybody (Matthews, 1979: 25).

It is still too soon, however, to make such a definite statement. Increasing evidence suggests that soldiers and civilians exposed to nuclear testing in the 1950s took many years, sometimes decades to show symptoms of cancer or leukemia.

Nuclear-power plants pose several significant dangers. The fallout from a major accident could produce the equivalent of that released by hundreds of Hiroshima-sized atomic bombs. Following the accident at the Chernobyl nuclear plant in the Soviet Union, heavy doses of radioactivity were detected in many European countries. Almost every plant in the United States has been shut down at some time because of an operating problem that could create a hazardous accident.

Another important problem produced by nuclear-power plants is their waste. Tiny quantities of this waste can cause cancer or birth defects. Large doses can kill people quickly. The major problem with radioactive waste concerns storage. Unfortunately much of the waste remains radioactive for hundreds, even thousands of years — in some instances as long as 300,000 years. Yet storage tanks are often not sufficiently sturdy to contain the waste for such long periods. The most troubling case in point involves the most lethal wastes: the strontium 90 and plutonium buried underground in concrete tanks, primarily in Richmond, Washington. This concentrated radioactive waste, which will remain deadly for thousands of years, has leaked at least sixteen times since 1968, releasing 115,000 gallons of radioactive liquid in 1974. The Nuclear Regulatory Commission is still seeking effective ways to dispose of nuclear wastes. The difficulties are as much political as technical. As one energy department official indicated, the problem is "deciding in which congressional district to put them."

In November 1989, after harsh criticism by a host of scientific experts, the Department of Energy abandoned a $500-million project for transporting highly radioactive nuclear waste from the nation's 110 civilian nuclear reactors to a single dump in the Nevada desert. As a result of this failure, a permanent location for the steadily growing supply of nuclear waste is unlikely to be available until at least 2010 (Wald, 1989c).

Finally, with the economical working lives of power plants about thirty years in duration, there is the eventual problem of dismantling such units. Unlike other kinds of discarded plants, nuclear facilities cannot just be leveled with a wrecking ball; contaminated parts and equipment must be isolated, sometimes for as long as thousands of years. Around the world more than twenty plants are already shut down; sixty-three more will probably be closed by the turn of the century and another 162 between 2000 and 2010 (Pollock, 1986; Robertson, 1980).

Ten years after the Three Mile Island accident, there were 111 nuclear-power plants in the United States, supplying nearly 20 percent of electrical needs. There had been no new orders for plants since 1978, and more than 110 plants ordered after 1973 had been canceled. In the future, nuclear plants will face stiff competition from efficient use of fossil fuels and from other technologies, like solar power (Wald, 1989a).

It seem reasonable to wonder why the Nuclear Regulatory Commission has continued a program that involves such extreme risks. The answer is that a variety of interests, including recent presidential administrations, major corporations, and many American citizens, believe that the United States must meet its growing energy requirements while decreasing reliance on foreign suppliers, regardless of the environmental impact.

What will happen in the future? Will we be able to survive the environmental challenge we currently face? Let us consider some measures that could help reduce the current environmental problems.

Restoration of a Healthy Environment

The issue of the damaged ozone layer suggests the well-known image of "spaceship earth" — a delicate vehicle hurtling through space. Political boundaries mean little; a hole in the ozone layer in Antarctica affects all of us. Using the sociological perspective throughout the text, we have seen that modern Americans often are isolated, with little sense of anything significant shared. Whether peo-

478

ple like it or not, however, the factors producing environmental pollution have made everyone share this major problem.

Americans are concerned about environmental pollution. As one researcher indicated, "Poll after poll confirms a deep and abiding popular concern for protecting the environment even at a considerable expense" (Reilly, 1982: 473).

But significant steps need to be taken to protect the environment. To date there has been no systematic effort to assess environmental risks across the board. Instead, both nationally and internationally, there have been piecemeal evaluations of specific problems as they crop up or receive public attention.

Hard-nosed, comprehensive planning is necessary, and, even more challenging, there needs to be tough, wide-ranging legislation that will force compliance from industrial giants. So far this simply has not happened. For instance, Congress appropriated over $10 billion for a "Superfund" to clean up about 1175 major pollution sites, but inefficiency and footdragging by both E.P.A. officials and industrialists, along with executive failure to review the program, meant that through the 1980s little effective cleaning up occurred (Alm, 1989; Miller, 1989; Russell, 1987).

A conflict-theoretical perspective based on material examined in this chapter suggests that wealthy and powerful business leaders play a major role in the pollution process. In the years ahead, it is distinctly possible that an upsurge of public concern about environmental issues will be manifest in political form—perhaps something like the West-German Green Party, which focuses on environmental issues and has received strong public support. It should be observed, however, that the American political system, as we noted in Chapter 14, most readily accommodates two political parties, and so it is questionable whether the present political structure would permit such a party to have the kind of impact it has produced in West Germany.

It is also likely that in the future an emphasis on restoring the environment will affect people's daily lives. We might need to keep our homes and offices less warm in the winter and less cool in the summer. We might need to pay more for electricity, fruit, and vegetables. But isn't it better to make small sacrifices than the ultimate one—the death of the planet and its inhabitants?

STUDY GUIDE

Learning Objectives

After studying this chapter, you should be able to:

1. Define human ecology and explain its social importance.
2. Define urbanization and describe the conditions encouraging the development of preindustrial cities.
3. List and discuss the four eras in the growth of American cities.
4. Analyze the primary causes of urban deterioration.
5. Discuss measures that could revitalize urban existence.
6. Define demography and discuss factors in population growth: birth rate, death rate, migration rate, and growth rate.
7. Examine in detail Malthusian theory and the demographic-transition theory.
8. Identify and explain the population problems of the United States and the world.
9. List and discuss the different measures for limiting population.
10. Discuss major resource-depletion problems.
11. Examine the major types of environmental pollution.

Summary

1. The three issues in this chapter — cities, population growth, and environmental problems — are interdependent. Human ecology concerns itself with all three issues.

2. A city is a large, densely settled concentration of people permanently located within a relatively confined geographical area where nonagricultural occupations are pursued. Urbanization is the process by which a city forms and develops.

Preindustrial cities generally had certain characteristics: small populations, limited transportation and storage facilities, a center serving as the focus of governmental and religious activity as well as elite housing, and a highly restrictive social-class system. We can distinguish four eras in the development of American cities: the colonial period, the period of westward expansion, the period of metropolitan growth, and the modern period. In the course of their development, American cities have undergone many changes, and in recent years the deterioration of urban facilities and services, as well as a steadily eroding tax base, have posed serious difficulties.

Central problems of modern cities are governmental proliferation, powerful political and economic interests, and financial limitations. Measures to revitalize American cities include an emphasis on an active neighborhood life, experiments with metropolitan solutions, efforts to bring middle-class people back into cities, and increased federal and state assistance.

3. A population is all the people who live within a specified geographic area such as a nation, a region, or a city. Demography is the statistical study of human populations. To determine population changes, demographers analyze birth, death, and migration rates. Prominent demographic theories include the Malthusian theory and the demographic-transition theory. In the developing nations, population growth now occurs at a rapid rate, and millions of people currently starve to death each year. In the United States, population growth has slowed down. Nonetheless, with the current population size, problems do exist — in particular, insufficient jobs and housing, a strain on the supply of natural resources, and significant levels of pollution. Attempts to set population limits throughout the world involve the use of contraception, family planning, incentives, coercion, and a combination of different techniques.

4. The natural environment is the complex of land, climate, water, air, mineral resources, and plant and animal life that together compose the physical world where people live. Resource depletion is a serious environmental problem. In developing nations the inadequacy of food supplies is the dominant issue related to this topic. In developed nations the chief difficulty is the declining supplies of major natural resources. In recent years Americans have become increasingly concerned about environmental pollution. Serious problems involve air pollution, water pollution, pesticide residues, and radioactivity effects. Currently there are signs that many Americans are willing to commit themselves to the restoration of a healthy environment.

Key Terms

city a large, densely settled concentration of people permanently located within a relatively confined geographical area where nonagricultural occupations are pursued

crude birth rate the number of births per 1000 persons in society in a given year

crude death rate the number of deaths per 1000 persons in society in a given year

deficit famine situation in which no food supplies exist elsewhere in a nation sufficient to compensate for local inadequacies

demography the study of human populations

distribution famine a food shortage existing in certain provinces or regions of a country, not throughout an entire country

doubling time the time span necessary for a population to double in size

480

family planning   a program that encourages people to decide how many children they want, when they want them, and what contraceptives, if any, they wish to use to achieve their goals

fertility rate   the number of actual births per 1000 women between the ages of fifteen and forty-four

gentrification   the move of middle- and upper-middle-class people to formerly deteriorated urban neighborhoods

growth rate   the crude birth rate minus the crude death rate

human ecology   the study of human beings' relationship with the environment

industrial stage (of the demographic-transition theory)   the third stage, characterized by a low death rate and dropping birth rate, which occurs as nations stabilize their populations in the course of industrialization

in-migration rate   the number of people per 1000 members of the population moving into an area in a given year

megalopolis   a string of closely bound metropolitan areas

metropolis   a territorial unit composed of a large central city and the surrounding cities and towns

migration   the flow of people in and out of a particular territory (city, region, or country)

natural environment   the combination of land, climate, water, air, mineral resources, and plant and animal life that together compose the physical world where people live

net migration rate   the difference between the in-migration rate and the out-migration rate

out-migration rate   the number of people per 1000 members of the population moving out of an area in a given year

population   all the people who live within a specified geographic area such as a nation, a region, or a city

preindustrial stage (of the demographic-transition theory)   the first stage, which existed before industrialization and was characterized by a stable population, with both birth and death rates remaining high

suburb   a politically independent municipality that develops next to or in the vicinity of a city

transition stage (of the demographic-transition theory)   The second stage, in which a decline in the death rate and a continuing high birth rate produced a rapid growth in population

urbanization   the process by which a city forms and develops

zero population growth   a situation in which the population size stabilizes

Tests

True–false Test

_____   1. In preindustrial cities the city center contained governmental and religious activities and also elite housing.

_____   2. Ferdinand Tönnies believed that when people took up residence in cities, their outlooks and behavior started to change.

_____   3. A metropolis is a preindustrial version of a megalopolis.

_____   4. Between 1970 and 1980, a prominent trend was the movement of urban black residents outward, often replacing suburban white inhabitants.

_____   5. Gentrification is the move of elderly people to inner-city areas.

_____   6. Fertility refers to the biological potential for reproduction.

_____   7. In most countries migration is the principal factor affecting population growth.

_____ 8. A study of thirty-eight developing nations indicated that formal schooling is the major social force encouraging a low fertility rate.

_____ 9. Each year farmers produce enough grain to provide every living person 3000 calories a day.

_____ 10. A variety of powerful interests, including presidential administrations and major corporations, have generally opposed the development of nuclear-power plants.

Multiple-choice Test

_____ 1. Which of the following qualities was characteristic of preindustrial cities?
   a. an open social-class system
   b. efficient transportation
   c. rapid economic growth
   d. elites' authority based on appeals to tradition and religious absolutes

_____ 2. Which of these factors did NOT contribute significantly to suburban development?
   a. widespread use of electric power
   b. movement of factories out of central cities
   c. unionization of workers in factories
   d. FHA loans to subsidize suburban housing

_____ 3. Jane Jacobs's ideas on improving the quality of urban life by combining land-use patterns in a given area illustrates which measure for improving urban life?
   a. experiments with metropolitan solutions
   b. emphasis on an active neighborhood life
   c. efforts to bring middle-class people back into cities
   d. increased federal and state assistance

_____ 4. The crude death rate:
   a. is determined by a combination of the fertility rate and the migration rate.
   b. provides no specific information about the characteristics of those who die.
   c. determines the growth rate.
   d. is the same as the infant-mortality rate.

_____ 5. A limitation of Malthusian population theory is that Malthus did not anticipate:
   a. people's distaste for birth-control methods.
   b. financial incentives as a means to restrict the number of children.
   c. significant improvements in agriculture that have increased the food supply.
   d. that a century after his death people would marry at a later age.

_____ 6. Which of the following factors contributes to declining birth rates in industrial societies?
   a. famine
   b. availability of medical facilities
   c. an urban lifestyle in which children are an economic liability
   d. advances in food production

_____ 7. Where no food supplies exist elsewhere in a nation sufficient to compensate for local inadequacies, there is a:
   a. Malthusian famine.
   b. distribution famine.
   c. chronic famine.
   d. deficit famine.

482 _____

8. Commoner suggested that all but one of the following statements about the environment is true. Which position was NOT asserted.
    a. The more things change, the more they stay the same.
    b. All parts of an environment are interrelated, with a change in one part affecting other parts.
    c. Nothing just disappears.
    d. Nature is enormously complicated.

_____ 9. Major air-pollution problems in recent years have included:
    a. the outhouse effect.
    b. the destruction of the ozone layer.
    c. the uncontrollable growth of the ozone layer.
    d. a and c

_____ 10. Serious problems with nuclear plants include:
    a. the disposal of nuclear wastes.
    b. nuclear fallout.
    c. dismantling of plants at the end of their working lives.
    d. a, b, and c

Essay Test

1. Define human ecology. Analyze the relationship among cities, human populations, and environmental problems. Provide an example that demonstrates their interdependence.
2. Discuss major trends of modern urban living, using studies and issues cited in the text to illustrate your conclusions.
3. Will American cities be significantly different in twenty years? What bits of evidence support your conclusion?
4. Discuss the Malthusian theory of population and the demographic-transition theory. What are their similarities and their differences?
5. Do you think rapidly growing developing nations can limit their population increase in the near future? What means will be most productive? Discuss.
6. Summarize the most serious environmental problems in American society.
7. If you were president of the United States, what steps, if any, would you take to combat resource depletion? What about environmental pollution?

Suggested Readings

Bogue, Donald J. 1985. *The Population of the United States: Historical Trends and Future Projections.* New York: Free Press. A demographer's view of the American population, examining its primary social and economic characteristics and also its patterns of change.

Duncan, E. R. (ed.). 1977. *Dimensions of World Food Problems.* Ames, IA: Iowa State University. A collection of articles that demonstrate the political and economic complexities of eliminating the serious food shortages existing in many developing nations.

Elliot, Jeffrey M. (ed.). 1989. *Urban Society.* Guilford, CT: Dushkin. Fourth edition. A series of readable, contemporary articles on urban issues and problems taken primarily from high-level newspapers, magazines, and popular journals.

Fischer, Claude S. 1984. *The Urban Experience*. San Diego: Harcourt Brace Jovanovich. Second edition. A short, ten-chapter text effectively covering the basics of urban sociology.

Fuller, R. Buckminster. 1970. *Operating Manual for Spaceship Earth*. New York: Pocket Books. A brief book filled with powerful ideas and expressing this well-known inventor's concern about environmental deterioration and his belief that a careful, imaginative use of technology can preserve our "spaceship earth."

Ghosh, Pradip K. (ed.). 1984. *Population, Environment and Resources, and Third World Development*. Westport, CT: Greenwood Press. Eighteen essays describing and analyzing the troubling, complicated interrelationship among rapid population increase, environmental deterioration, and slow economic growth in Third World nations.

Girouard, Mark. 1987. *Cities & People*. New Haven: Yale University Press. A nicely written and illustrated history of the development of European and American cities, examining across time and space such diverse issues as the economy, political structure, religion, city planning, urban lifestyle, architecture, and art.

Harris, Marvin, and Eric B. Ross. 1987. *Death, Sex, and Fertility: Population Regulation in Preindustrial and Developing Societies*. New York: Columbia University Press. An effective demographic analysis, arguing that reproductive practices are strongly affected by the production process and, most significantly, discussing the importance of this relationship in developing nations.

Heer, David M. 1975. *Society and Population*. Englewood Cliffs, NJ: Prentice-Hall. Second edition. A brief introduction to the field of demography, succinctly discussing the basic concepts, theories, and the problem of overpopulation.

Humphrey, Craig R., and Frederick R. Buttell. 1982. *Environment, Energy, and Society*. Belmont, CA: Wadsworth. A textbook that effectively examines issues of environment, energy, and population and includes "radical," "liberal," and "conservative" perspectives on most of the topics.

Jacobs, Jane. 1961. *The Death and Life of Great American Cities*. New York: Vintage Books. An analysis of the different factors that cause cities to be either healthy or unhealthy places to live. Jacobs's writing has been controversial, but whether or not you agree with her, you should find her thinking original and provocative.

Ophuls, William. 1977. *Ecology and the Politics of Scarcity*. San Francisco: W. H. Freeman. A focus on the scarcity of valuable resources. The author provides evidence to support his claims of resource depletion and argues that unless Americans limit economic growth, they will face tragic problems, including widespread starvation, when resources run out.

Sennett, Richard. 1974. *Families against the City*. New York: Vintage Books. A sociologist's analysis of how middle-class families adjusted to life in industrial Chicago in the late nineteenth century. Using census data, historical sources, and some sharp thinking, Sennett presented an interesting set of hypotheses.

Theodorson, George A. (ed.). 1982. *Urban Patterns: Studies in Human Ecology*. University Park: Pennsylvania State University Press. Revised edition. An updated edition of a well-known reader on the ecological patterns of cities, containing fifty-six articles and including a section devoted to the field of ecology.

Walker, Charles A., Leroy C. Gould, and Edward J. Woodhouse. 1983. *Too Hot to Handle?* New Haven: Yale University Press. A number of specialists writing about the political, economic, technological, and health issues associated with the disposal of radioactive wastes.

Wirth, Louis, 1938. "Urbanism As a Way of Life." *American Journal of Sociology* 44 (July): 3–24. In spite of its age, this widely read sociological article provides a useful introductory analysis of the dominant characteristics of urban life.

484

Additional Assignments

1. Using material from the text and library sources, outline two sets of population proposals, one for the United States and the other for the world. Include a discussion of the following issues:
   a. The dilemma of governmental intervention in family decision making: a limitation on personal freedom vs. the need to control population growth. (In addressing world population problems, consider the program initiated in the People's Republic of China.)
   b. The most effective/desirable forms of birth control
   c. The prospects for limiting population growth that your programs will produce
2. Urban areas are centers of high population density. It is a common theme for "disaster" literature and films to contemplate possible harm to large numbers of people. Pick a pollution problem and provide an account describing both the effects on people's lives produced by sudden drastic levels of pollution and the local resources needed to cope with the problem. Think about your own living area. Does it have the service organizations to handle your pollution "disaster"?

Answers to Objective Test Questions

True–false Test					**Multiple-choice Test**			
1. t	4. t	7. f	9. t		1. d	4. b	7. d	9. b
2. t	5. f	8. t	10. f		2. c	5. c	8. a	10. d
3. f	6. f				3. b	6. c		

17
COLLECTIVE BEHAVIOR, SOCIAL MOVEMENTS, AND SOCIAL CHANGE

Smelser's General Theory

Crowds

Characteristics
Crowd Theories
Violent Crowds
Frightened Crowds

Rumors

The Development of Rumors
Efforts to Stop Rumors

Social Movements

Theories of Social Movements

Sources of Social Change

Cultural Innovation
Population
The Environment
Social Movements

Research in Sociology: Prison Riots: Which Theory Can Explain Them?

Study Guide

$\mathbf{M}$arch 23, 1989, was a fairly quiet day on planet earth. The leading news stories indicated that the Afghan government suffered a major setback in its war with Muslim guerrillas; Congress and the White House had reached a tentative agreement to aid the Nicaraguan *contras*; and Fawn Hall testified in federal district court on behalf of her former boss, Oliver L. North.

Meanwhile, completely unobserved, an asteroid of about a half-mile in diameter hurtling through space at 46,000 miles an hour missed earth by about half-a-million miles, a near miss by astronomers' standards.

Had the asteroid struck earth, scientists estimated that the impact would have been as devastating as 20,000 one-megaton bombs. On land the asteroid would have left a crater five to ten miles wide and a mile deep; at sea the impact would have produced enormous tidal waves (Johnson, 1989).

What would have been the effect on people's social interaction? Obviously a major determining factor would have been where the collision occurred. It seems likely that if it had taken place in a populated area, the survivors' lives would have been seriously disrupted. Widespread floods, fires, and death, along with the distinct possibility of extensive disease and famine, would have threatened or destroyed the normal social patterns and have increased the likelihood of rumors, panic, mass hysteria, mobs, and riots — in short, forms of collective behavior.

Collective behavior is social activity that occurs under conditions that are temporarily unstructured and unstable because of the absence of clearly defined norms. The behavior itself is frequently emotional, often unpredictable, and episodic in occurrence. Collective behavior, in short, falls outside the confines of ordinary social activity. The lack of conventional structure, however, does not prevent the study of forms of collective behavior, although it can make this study difficult. As we will see, analysis reveals definite patterns to these activities.

Most of the time, norms, laws, and customs indicate the actions considered legitimate for specific roles or for people in general. Individuals usually receive rewards for conforming to the conventional expectations, and they normally suffer punishments for failing to conform. Collective behavior occurs when social conditions permit or encourage people to engage in activities that disregard normal expectations. Certainly, if an asteroid struck the earth, normal expectations would be suspended in the social disorder that followed.

All of us occasionally enter collective-behavior situations — in particular, when we mingle in crowds. Do crowds stimulate any special feeling? Have you ever considered how you would act if you were in a crowded movie theater and fire broke out? Let us consider another type of collective behavior — rumors. What is your response to rumors that you encounter? Do you willingly believe them and pass them on to others? Or are you careful to confirm information you receive before you transmit it to others? As we discuss the different forms of collective behavior, perhaps you will develop a clearer sense of how you would behave in each case. The difficulty in making such a prediction is that collective-behavior activities take us out of ordinary social situations and put us in relatively unusual, unstructured situations, where much of what happens, including our own behavior, is likely to be quite unpredictable.

Besides collective behavior we examine two other topics — social movements and social change. **Social movements** are organized, collective activities undertaken by people to promote or resist social change. Social movements — the women's or civil-rights movements, for instance — involve activities similar to collective behavior in the respect that to some extent they occur outside existing normative guidelines. However, social movements often are more stable and longer lasting than forms of collective behavior, and they can eventually become organizations, in which the normative standards and members' behavior are quite conventional.

Social movements and collective behavior often occur in situations where social change is taking place and, in turn, they frequently encourage its occurrence. **Social change** involves any modifications in culture, social organization, and social behavior. Generally the topic does not include changes that occur within a small group or organization. The focus of social change is alterations that take place within institutions or societies.

In the following section, we examine the best-known theory of collective behavior and social movements. Next the focus shifts to crowds; the discussion includes an examination of theories of crowd behavior and the analysis of several different kinds of crowd situations. The following topic is rumors, succeeded by social movements, and an analysis of different sources of social change. The chapter concludes with the final research section, which assesses the effectiveness of theory in analyzing studies of prison riots.

Smelser's General Theory

A section of George Orwell's *Animal Farm* can serve as an illustration of Neil Smelser's (1963) general theory of collective behavior and social movements.

One day the message filtered among the animals of Manor Farm that Old Major, a prize boar, had a strange dream the previous night and wanted to communicate it to the other animals. They regarded Old Major with such high regard that as soon as Mr. Jones had stumbled off to bed, drunk as usual, the animals all gathered in the barn to hear what the ancient boar had to say.

With the animals before him, Old Major cleared his throat and started to speak. He indicated that, indeed, he had had a strange dream the previous night, but before he discussed the dream, he needed to speak about something else: the abuse the animals experienced. Old Major spoke about how hard they worked and how little they were fed. He indicated that when each had reached the point where he or she was no longer useful, Mr. Jones would simply put an end to that animal's miserable life. All their problems, Old Major emphasized, were the result of human tyranny. It was clear that the only course of action was to get rid of their human overlords.

Then the old boar described his dream. It involved a time well into the future when humanity would have vanished from the earth. A dominant feature of the dream was a stirring song called "Beasts of England." The song described the glorious future when all animals would be free of human control and would be able to share earth's edible bounty among themselves. Old Major began singing the song, and almost before he had finished the animals joined in.

Three nights after his speech, Old Major died peacefully in his sleep. That was early in March. During the next three months, there was considerable secret activity. Old Major's speech provided the more intelligent animals with an entirely different outlook on life. They did not know when the rebellion would happen — perhaps it would not even take place in their lifetimes — but they all felt that it was their duty to prepare for it. Teaching and organizing were the principal preparatory activities. As the most intelligent animals on the farm, the pigs took a dominant leadership role. Two boars, named Snowball and Napoleon, elaborated Major's teachings into a complete system of thought, which they called Animalism. Several nights a week, after Mr. Jones had gone to sleep, they held meetings where they discussed principles of Animalism and convinced most of the animals that rebellion was in their interest.

It turned out that the rebellion occurred much sooner than anyone had expected. One Saturday in June, Mr. Jones went into town and got so drunk that he did not return until Sunday afternoon, when he immediately went to sleep on the drawing-room sofa with a newspaper over his face. The farm hands had milked the cows on Sunday morning, but, with their boss absent, they went out rabbit hunting, not even bothering to feed the animals. Evening arrived and the animals still had not been fed. Finally they could stand it no longer. One of the cows broke down the shed door with her horns, and all the animals started to help themselves from the bins.

At that point Mr. Jones awoke, and a few moments later he and the farm hands were in the shed with whips in their hands, lashing out wildly at the

When George Orwell's novel Animal Farm *was published, Joseph V. Stalin (second from the right) was the top political leader. In 1939, just before this photograph was taken, Stalin signed a nonaggression treaty with Nazi German leaders.* Animal Farm *is a thinly disguised indictment of the political corruption that occurred after the Communist Party took control of the Soviet Union.*

animals. That was more than the animals could endure. They attacked Jones and his men, butting and kicking them from all sides. The men were shocked. They had never seen animals behaving in this manner before, and this sudden uprising frightened them out of their wits. After no more than a moment of trying to defend themselves, they took to their heels with the animals in hot pursuit. The animals chased the men out of the barn and off the farm, slamming the five-barred gate behind them (Orwell, 1946: 17–22).

Let us suppose that the fleeing men ran into town, and someone asked one of them what had happened. The man might have replied, "It's that new grain we've been feeding the livestock. I told Jones it would bring him nothing but trouble."

People frequently offer one-factor explanations for the occurrence of collective-behavior episodes and social movements. In contrast, Smelser's theory outlines six elements necessary for the development of these activities. These elements develop in sequence, and as each one occurs, the likelihood of some alternate activity decreases. By the time the fifth element appears, collective action is inevitable.

1. *Structural conduciveness.* Smelser's first point involves basic conditions that permit or allow collective behavior or a social movement to emerge. The animals' ability to speak English, to assemble, and to organize themselves for an expected rebellion were conditions of structural conduciveness. Real farm animals, of course, lack the capacities just mentioned, and so they are unable to rebel.

2. *Structural strain.* Various immediate conditions, such as prejudice and discrimination, economic exploitation, and poor communication between groups or nations, can create a significant amount of tension or pressure for people. Structural strain can lessen people's willingness to stay within normal behavioral limits. Insufficient food, too much work, and death the moment they proved no longer useful were severe structural strains the animals experienced.

3. *Growth and spread of a generalized belief.* As collective behavior or a social movement

develops, an interpretation of the situation and how to respond to it will begin to emerge. The generalized belief supports a break with conventional behavior, emphasizing the current social strain and the rewards collective activity will produce. At the beginning of the account of *Animal Farm,* it is clear that the animals might have simply accepted harsh treatment for the rest of their lives—they could not imagine any other way of living. But then Old Major called them together and explained in painful detail how exploited they were and pointed out that, through rebellion, they could obtain another, much more desirable form of life. The song that he sang them and that they all readily learned summarized these ideas of freedom and equality in a powerful way. After Old Major's death, several pigs developed the doctrine of Animalism, producing an entire system of thought from Old Major's ideas.

4. *Precipitating factor.* Some incident or set of incidents must initiate collective behavior or a social movement. The first three elements of Smelser's theory create a situation that resembles a bone-dry forest vulnerable to devastation by fire. That destruction will not occur, however, unless a match falls unheeded on the forest floor. The precipitating factor is that match. In *Animal Farm* the precipitating factor was the fact that one day the animals were not fed.

5. *Mobilization for action.* At this point all that remains is the occurrence of collective activity.

At such a time, people typically find that the rewards and punishments promoting ordinary, everyday behavior are no longer present. The doctrine of Animalism had prepared the animals to understand and want to overthrow the unjust system under which they had been forced to live, and not being fed that Sunday was the outrage that finally produced rebellion against Jones's control.

6. *Social control.* Smelser's final stage concerns the various ways that people in authority act to encourage or discourage a particular incident of collective behavior. After the rebellion no authorities besides the animals remained. They chased Mr. Jones and his men off the farm, and then they slammed the gate, thereby locking out the men and ending the confrontation between beasts and human beings.

A significant limitation of Smelser's theory is that like other strain theories, it pays little attention to significant resources necessary to produce some forms of collective behavior and, in particular, social movements. As we see in the section on social movements, money, power, social networks, and other resources are often essential elements in the development of social movements.

Smelser's theory can analyze social movements and all types of collective behavior, including crowds, the topic of the following section.

Crowds

A **crowd** is a temporary gathering of individuals who share a common concern or interest and find themselves in close physical contact with one another. "Common concern or interest" and "close physical contact" suggest some similarities between crowds and groups. We will see, however, that crowd activity is not as responsive to established norms as group behavior. This section examines crowd characteristics, crowd theories, violent crowds, and frightened crowds.

Characteristics

Certainly crowds vary in their qualities and behavior. Some, such as ordinary street crowds, are composed of people sharing little or no common purpose; others, including the people gathered to hear a popular political candidate, possess a common interest. In many instances crowds are orderly (those attending an opera or a concert of classical music), and in other situations they are not (the participants in a mob or riot). In general, the members of crowds behave in distinct ways.

1. *Suggestibility.* People in crowds do not have the distinct guidelines for behavior that are normally available. They turn to their fellow crowd members for direction, literally "going along with the crowd."

2. *Anonymity and spontaneity.* Individuals in a crowd recognize that they are in a wilderness of strangers—that they are "lost in a crowd."

The sense of anonymity permits them to act more openly and freely than they normally would. They are likely to lose a sense of responsibility for any misdeeds. "Don't blame me," an individual might say after a riot. "Everyone was breaking things and stealing."

3. *Impersonality.* Since people in crowds are detached from their everyday normative guidelines, they often treat others in a more impersonal, harsh manner than they normally would. When fans at a baseball game yell "Kill the umpire," they are not stopping to consider that the object of their wrath is a human being. For many participants violent crowd activity would be difficult to perform without this element of impersonality.

Crowd Theories

Perhaps the brief discussion of crowd characteristics seems disturbing. You might have the impression that people in crowds can behave in much the same fashion as a herd of stampeding cattle. One of the theories we will consider makes such a claim. The other approach is more sophisticated.

Contagion Theory

At the end of the nineteenth century, Gustave Le Bon (1952) developed contagion theory. That era was a time of major upheaval characterized by the erosion of traditional religious, political, and social beliefs and their replacement by modern scientific and industrial standards. Le Bon suspected that disorder, even chaos lay ahead, and crowds would become an increasingly destructive force.

Contagion theory contends that the presence of a crowd encourages or compels people to think and act in a uniform manner.

Le Bon claimed that, when in a crowd, an individual inevitably becomes less civilized: "Isolated, he may be a cultivated individual; in a crowd, he is a barbarian — that is, a creature acting by instinct. He possesses the spontaneity, the violence, the ferocity, and also the enthusiasm and heroism of primitive beings" (Le Bon, 1952: 32).

Le Bon's work gives the impression that when people enter crowds, something both magical and

terrible happens. Herbert Blumer's (1975) analysis of contagion is more systematic. Blumer considered contagion a process where crowd members become increasingly preoccupied with each other's behavior, and outlooks and events that would normally concern them become insignificant. Eventually each crowd member becomes so focused on the others' activities that he or she loses self-consciousness, which usually is a "means of barricading oneself against the influence of others." At this point each individual will simply follow the crowd.

It is likely that anonymity also promotes contagion. A study of twenty-one cases in which crowds were present when people threatened to jump off a building, bridge, or tower suggested that certain conditions of anonymity would prompt members of the crowd to encourage individuals to jump: specifically membership in a large crowd, the protection of nighttime, and a considerable physical distance between the crowd and victim (Mann, 1981).

Contagion can also occur in less anonymous contexts. A recent study of two college sororities found that bulimia — an eating pattern where uncontrolled binge eating alternated with periods of fasting, strict dieting, or purging by forced vomiting — was linked to members' popularity. It appeared that the relevance of contagion was that women were drawn into the binging process as a means of establishing popularity. In one sorority the more one binged, the more popular one was; in the other, popularity was tied to being an average binger and thus neither doing it too much or too little (Crandall, 1988).

Emergent-Norm Theory

"As the fire spread, people were panicking all around us," the twelve-year-old boy explained. "My mom just stood there in the middle of the circus tent and gripped my hand tighter than ever before and looked around. Then after what seemed a century, she said, 'Over that way there's an exit.'" Hundreds were swept up in the contagion of panic, got trapped at the main entrance, and died in Hartford's tragic circus fire. In spite of the contagiousness of panic, however, this mother managed to avoid that response and maintained a calm, searching approach that permitted her to bring her son and herself to safety. In accord with this true incident, the proponents of emergent-norm theory reject the idea that the members of a crowd think and behave in the same way.

Emergent-norm theory analyzes the process by which a new social standard develops within a crowd — a standard that in reality receives a more enthusiastic acceptance from some crowd members than others, in spite of the fact that both crowd members and observers tend to perceive nearly unanimous support for it.

According to the emergent-norm theory, people in crowds often find themselves in a normative void — no clear standard of behavior exists. At this point some active people are inclined to take the initiative and present a new standard: an emergent norm, which could advocate such diverse activities as starting to throw rocks and bottles at the police or standing and clapping in appreciation at a graduation ceremony when the name of an especially beloved individual has been read off a list of retiring faculty members. Once the norm develops, the more assertive individuals in the crowd are likely to support behavior consistent with it and to oppose behavior against the norm. This helps to develop the impression that the crowd acts in unanimity.

There are important differences between contagion theory and emergent-norm theory. As we have noted, the emergent-norm perspective rejects the idea that crowd members possess a uniform mental state. Accounts of Nazi crowds attacking Jewish merchants often distorted the actual situation in which a few storm troopers harassed and beat the victims, while a disapproving crowd afraid to express dissent watched silently.

Another difference is that emergent-norm theory applies to a wider range of emotional situations. Contagion theory cannot effectively analyze crowds in a subdued state, but emergent-norm theory can. For example, there have been situations where late arrivals reaching the site of an automobile accident or airplane crash loudly exclaimed "What happened?" Disapproving looks and gestures from people in the crowd immediately prevented any further loud commentary. In this case the emergent norm required onlookers to speak quietly out of respect for the crash victims.

Finally, unlike contagion theory, the emergent-norm perspective does not attempt to analyze crowd behavior as separate from the rest of social behavior. In its use of the concept *norm,* emergent-norm theory makes a more concerted effort to extend conventional sociological thinking to an unconventional context — collective behavior (Brown and Goldin, 1973; Turner, 1964; Turner and Killian, 1972; Vander Zanden, 1981).

As you read the following Cross-Cultural Perspective, try to determine how the different theories we have discussed apply.

CROSS-CULTURAL PERSPECTIVE

Chinese Student Demonstrations

During the spring of 1989, hundreds of thousands of Chinese students demonstrated in favor of more democracy in The People's Republic of China. The demonstrations started in Beijing, spread to other major Chinese cities, and then to Taiwan, Hong Kong, Australia, and the United States. In some respects the protests were similar to the idealistic, light-hearted demonstrations launched by American students in the 1960s. Calling for universal freedom, Chinese students in Beijing's Tiananmen Square constructed a styrofoam goddess of liberty. They also popularized a mocking song calling for the resignation of China's top three leaders. In sharp contrast to China's much larger protests two decades earlier, the student demonstrations were largely nonviolent.

The government, however, did not respond nonviolently. After warnings against public demonstrations, troops moved into Tiananmen Square, where they opened fire on unarmed protesters, killing hundreds, perhaps even thousands, and arrested hundreds; a few of those arrested were executed while many of the others received long prison terms.

Like all social activity, collective behavior does not occur in a vacuum. So why did the demonstrations occur? At the root of the students' discontent seemed to be the economic-reform program initiated about a decade ago by Deng Xiaoping, the country's top leader, who wanted to replace central planning with market-oriented, capitalist incentives. This program produced a number of confusing, frustrating difficulties:

1. *Leaders' failure to acknowledge citizens' rights and interests.* Deng Xiaoping recognized that economic reform was impossible without some relaxation of political controls. This relaxation encouraged students and intellectuals to express their grievances, but they were frustrated because in China's nondemocratic setting, their statements and analyses went largely unreported in the mass media and thus were without impact. None of China's top leaders had any semblance of Gorbachev's understanding that citizens' support for the government would be increased if they felt its leaders were responsive to their rights and interests.
2. *The corruption of socialist ideals.* The political leadership undermined the country's forty-year socialist tradition, replacing

the once-honored ideal of "serve the people" with the position "to get rich is glorious." In a country where the passage of wealth and power from parents to children had been condemned, corruption became a widespread practice among the Communist Party's elite.
3. *The ineffectiveness of economic reforms.* A two-year freeze on price reform was declared, significant cuts in capital investment were made, and inflation, especially in rural areas, was a serious problem. By the beginning of 1989, three million (out of four million) workers in the private construction industry were out of jobs, and 20 million in unprofitable rural industries were at risk of losing theirs.

These were the factors precipitating student unrest—which took the form of largely orderly and peaceful demonstrations, even when troops were sent in to suppress them.

A significant problem, however, is that peaceful demonstrations, like any social activity, can be perceived in various ways by different sets of eyes. Undoubtedly the most important set of eyes observing the protests belonged to Deng Xiaoping. Deng had been a victim of the Red-Guard demonstrations, in which two decades earlier during what was known as the Cultural Revolution young people had hu-

miliated, beaten, and, in about a half-million cases, killed government officials or other established professionals whom they believed were involved in corrupt practices. Deng was treated quite leniently, being denounced in public and exiled to a menial job in south China, but one of his sons was thrown out of a window and crippled for life.

Even though the 1989 protests were peaceful, neither Deng nor his close advisor Yang Shangkun, who had also been dismissed from an important post during the Red-Guard era, saw a significant difference from the earlier demonstrations. In a country where Deng almost completely controlled basic policy, this represented a significant perception. In late April, as the demonstrations developed, Deng told colleagues, "What they are doing now is altogether the same stuff as what the rebels did during the Cultural Revolution. All they want is to create chaos under heaven" (MacFarquhar, 1989: 8).

So the demonstrations were repressively ended, and the students' demands for democratic reforms were silenced. What will happen in the future? One development is certain. Because of the fact that most of the senior leaders are old—Deng was eighty-four at this writing—they will soon be replaced. It seems almost as likely that without significant policy changes, students' grievances, as well as those maintained by other major groups, will not simply disappear. Will a new, more progressive leadership attuned to citizens' major needs and interests arise, or will the 1989 Tiananmen Square massacre prove to be the forerunner of further bloody confrontations between the Chinese government and its people?

Sources: Fox Butterfield. "Deng Reappears with a Chilling Lesson about Power in China." *New York Times.* June 11, 1989, section 4, p. 1; Roderick MacFarquhar. "The End of the Chinese Revolution." *New York Review of Books.* V. 36. July 20, 1989, pp. 8–10; Sheryl Wu Dunn. "Spies Learn Students Can Be Stern Teachers." *New York Times.* May 29, 1989, p. A7.

Violent Crowds

A typical scene from a cowboy film illustrates a contagion perspective on riots. Standing in front of the seething crowd, the grief-stricken ranch hand shouts, "Hal Smith was a good man who'd give a stranger the shirt off his back. Now he's lyin' dead in his coffin and them stinkin' townspeople are responsible. They ain't gettin' away with it. Let's tear up the town!" And a moment later they mount their horses and gallop down the main street, destroying everything in their path.

Mobs and riots are related phenomena, but we can draw a distinction between them. A **mob** is a crowd whose members engage in destructive and aggressive behavior in the pursuit of a short-term but valued goal. A mob, for instance, might want to catch a certain person and hang him or her or destroy a particular piece of property. A **riot**, however, is aggressive, destructive crowd behavior that is less focused or unified than mob activity. A crowd of angry, frustrated people might run through city streets indiscriminately looting and burning buildings.

The most costly racial riots of this century in the United States occurred between 1966 and 1968 in Los Angeles, Newark, Detroit, Washington, DC, Cleveland, and a host of other American cities. Table 17.1 lists some of these costs. The bloodiest racial violence happened in Detroit from July 23

Table 17.1
Ghetto Riots and Interracial Clashes

	NUMBER OF EVENTS IDENTIFIED[1]	ESTIMATED NUMBER OF PARTICIPANTS[2]	REPORTED DEATHS	REPORTED INJURIES	REPORTED ARRESTS
Period I (June 1963–December 1965)	48	100,000	56	1800	12,500
Period II (January 1966–June 1968)	200	150,000	140	6156	37,362
Period III (July 1968–December 1970)	256	100,000	42	1050	4,632

[1] The statistics reported here are based on a tally of newspaper accounts.
[2] Only private citizens are counted, not the police, National Guardsmen, and other officials involved in riot suppression.

Source: Adapted from Ted Robert Gurr. "Political Protest and Rebellion in the 1960s," pp. 49–76 in Hugh Davis Graham and Ted Robert Gurr (eds.), *Violence in America: Historical Perspectives.* Beverly Hills: Sage Publications. 1979, p. 54.

More riots occurred in Period III than in Period II, but participation, casualties, and arrests were much more extensive in the second period.

to July 28, 1967. Forty-three people were killed and over a thousand injured. The rioters destroyed more than 1300 buildings and sacked more than 700 businesses (Brown and Goldin, 1973).

Riots have also occurred in more recent years. In December 1982 a policeman killed a young black man in Overtown, a black section of Miami. The incident produced violent demonstrations in which nearly 200 enraged protesters ran through the streets throwing rocks and bottles, looting stores, and setting cars ablaze. After three days of rioting, twenty-six people were injured, thirty-eight were arrested, and a second black youth was killed by police, allegedly while trying to break into a store (Beck, 1983).

Smelser's theory can help analyze the development of the 1960s riots. First, there were certain structurally conducive conditions. The mass media played a significant part, spreading the news about the outbreaks of violence. A federal study identified "a chain reaction of racial violence" (National Advisory Commission on Civil Disorders, 1968: 206). Without radio, television, and newspapers, the information that initiated the "chain reaction" would not have been able to speed from city to city.

Structural strain was also apparent. The "blocked-opportunity" theory, which suggests that blocked opportunity represents a significant source of structural strain, claims that blacks who strongly resented racial discrimination were especially likely to join riots. Rioters were more bitter than local nonrioters, were less willing than nonrioters to fight for their country in a major war, and were more likely to express hatred toward whites (Caplan and Paige, 1968). A recent article reached a slightly different conclusion. While this analysis also accepted the blocked-opportunity theory, it did not focus on such emotional topics as bitterness and hatred but emphasized rioters' rationality. According to this argument, the major reason blacks in the 1960s engaged in riots was powerlessness: They clearly perceived their lack of economic and political power and saw no effective alternative to rioting for asserting their resistance to the devastating impact of racism (Davis, 1986).

During the 1960s there was growth of a generalized belief supporting protests and demonstrations, if not outright rioting. Many black and white civil-rights leaders clearly became more mil-

itant, emphasizing that patience was no longer desirable and that the rich and powerful would make necessary political and economic changes only if pressured to do so. The feeling that violence might be a productive course of action was widely discussed and debated during those years.

Local incidents, such as a black man's arrest or shooting by a white policeman, precipitated riots in different cities. One event of national significance helped initiate a large number of riots in 1968—the assassination of Martin Luther King, Jr.

Mobilization for action occurred because people suffering from "blocked opportunity" were not motivated to abide by conventional norms. Riots offered them a chance to strike out against the system and, more particularly, the groups and individuals that they believed were oppressing them. For instance, following riots in New York City (East Harlem) in 1968, one could observe a number of blocks where stores owned by outsiders had been burned, whereas locally owned stores remained intact.

Eventually police and/or National Guardsmen would occupy a riot area, imposing social control. Many of the deaths and injuries and all the arrests reported in Table 17.1 happened during the process of establishing social control. A recent study of those riots indicated that up to a point, the larger a city's police force, the greater the violence directed at the police. This relationship seemed to develop because as the proportion of police increased, there was greater likelihood of residents and police making contact. With hostility toward the police intense, greater contact simply raised the chances of violence against them. However, where police forces were very large relative to the local population, violence against the police during riots was decreased, probably because the unusually large number of police were able to prevent the residents forming large, uncontrollable crowds (Carter, 1987).

The emergent-norms perspective also helps us to understand the riots. One norm that developed during the riots was a standard supporting cooperative looting, with looters working in pairs or in small groups. Many rioters took goods openly, while others, including the police in some instances, watched (Quarantelli and Dynes, 1970).

It is noteworthy that while many riots occurred in the United States during the 1960s, other

Table 17.2
Rebellion[1] in Selected Countries, 1961–1970[2]

	PERSON DAYS OF REBELLION PER 100,000 CITIZENS	CONFLICT DEATHS PER 10 MILLION CITIZENS
Largest Western democracies (1970 population 50 million+)		
United States	250	18.3
West Germany	0	0.3
Britain	20	0.5
Italy	1,300	8.0
France	15,000	17.1
Some small Western democracies		
Canada	700	1.5
Australia	0.1	0
Sweden	0	0
Israel	70	11.8
Republic of Ireland	70	0
Northern Ireland	40,000	129.3
Other major nations of the world		
Europe: USSR	0.3	18
Poland	0	118
Spain	1,900	13
Middle East: Turkey	50	14
Egypt	40	9
Iran	10	76
Asia: India	4,700	42
Indonesia	100,000+	30,000+
Japan	0.5	0.1
Africa: Nigeria	150,000+	250,000+
South Africa	200	16
Latin America: Brazil	150	7
Mexico	9,000	26
Argentina	35,000	31

[1] An outbreak against those in authority
[2] Within each group countries are listed by descending population rank. The data are rounded to reflect their imprecision. Estimates of death are more accurate than estimates of person days. Estimates for Western countries are more accurate than those for Communist and Third World countries.

Source: Adapted from Ted Robert Gurr. "Political Protest and Rebellion in the 1960s," pp. 49–76 in Hugh Davis Graham and Ted Robert Gurr (eds.), *Violence in America: Historical Perspectives.* Beverly Hills: Sage Publications. 1979, p. 60.

During the 1960s a number of nations suffered a considerably higher proportion of death produced by rebellion and conflict than the United States did. Nigeria and Indonesia, which had devastating internal wars, were at the extreme.

countries had much more extensive rioting. Table 17.2 provides data that address this issue.

The research section at the end of the chapter examines the topic of prison riots.

Frightened Crowds

In panics and mass hysteria, the emotional level is high, just as in riots. Members of frightened

Two prominent types of crowds are violent crowds and frightened crowds.

crowds, however, seek to escape the source of shared concern.

Panics

A **panic** is a collective flight to safety. Panic occurs under specific circumstances. It takes place only if people believe that escape routes are available but limited or closing. It will not occur if people are convinced that there is no way to escape; under this condition they might experience terror or start behaving like children, but they usually do not panic (Smelser, 1963).

A recent study of 183 nonclinical respondents suggested that the occurrence of panic attacks is fairly common, with somewhere between 10 and 30 percent of the general population experiencing such an attack at some time and a smaller proportion, perhaps 10 percent, having them frequently (Kennedy and Shear, 1988).

One observer of a fire that started in a crowded theater in Chicago in 1903 and killed 602 people provided some evidence for contagion theory when he indicated that heel prints were apparent on many dead faces. The marks testified "to the cruel fact that human animals stricken by terror are as mad and ruthless as stampeding cattle" (Foy and Harlow, in Turner and Killian, 1957: 96–97).

Experimental studies involving panic suggest that its occurrence depends primarily on the availability of information about the amount of danger involved, people's perception of opportunities to escape, and their sense of whether or not those present will help each other (Brown and Goldin, 1973). On the last point, the quality of leadership can make a significant difference. In the course of experiments with 144 college-aged males, Klein (1976) offered his subjects financial rewards if they could escape from handcuffs and threatened an electric shock if they could not. Klein found that effective leadership could reduce the likelihood of panic by countering the lack of coordination that "can make a minor crisis a major tragedy." Marshall (1947: 130) indicated that if an army unit is under attack and the leader says, "Let's get out of here!" then panic is quite possible. However, if the leader simply tells his troops to follow him to a nearby destination, then the chances of panic sharply decrease. Both studies suggest that the effectiveness of an emergent norm established by leaders in an anxiety-laden situation will significantly influence the likelihood of panic.

Mass Hysteria

Mass hysteria is a type of panic that occurs when people are scattered over a wide geographical area. Often the mass media play a significant role in promoting these incidents. More than 180 reports have been published describing a variety of ailments for which no medical source can be located. A modern case was "the mysterious gas poisoning" that affected over 900 people, mainly schoolgirls, in the Jordan West Bank region (Hefez, 1985).

A celebrated example of mass hysteria occurred on Halloween, October 30, 1938. Millions of Americans found themselves listening to a broadcast on CBS radio. It was entitled "The War of the Worlds," an adaptation of H. G. Wells's novel of the same title. At the beginning of the radio play, Orson Welles, the narrator, explained that what followed was, in fact, fiction, but many who tuned in late never heard the statement, and some who listened from the beginning were swept along by the drama and simply forgot what Welles had said.

The play told how Martians had invaded the United States. They landed in New Jersey, then headed north toward New York City, killing hundreds of troops sent to stop them as well as large numbers of civilians. Hadley Cantril (1940), who studied this incident of mass hysteria, wrote:

> Long before the broadcast had ended, people all over the United States were praying, crying, fleeing frantically to escape death from Martians. Some ran to rescue loved ones. Others telephoned farewells or warnings, hurried to inform neighbors, sought information from newspapers or radio stations, summoned ambulances and police cars. At least six million people heard the broadcast. At least a million of them were frightened or disturbed.
>
> (Cantril, 1940: 47)

Cantril conducted 130 detailed interviews soon after the event. He found some people who thought that the invasion had been no more than a story, whereas others were convinced it was true. Several different characteristics, Cantril found, made some people more inclined to believe that an invasion was occurring. In particular, the idea of an invasion fitted better with some people's preconceptions than with those of others'. Some respondents had been expecting a foreign invasion from the Germans or Japanese, and for these people the threat of a Martian attack was a concrete illustration of their war-related dread. Apparently invaders were simply invaders, whether from across the ocean or from outer space. Other people questioned whether they were sufficiently competent to pit their judgment against that of the announcers, scientists, and government authorities supposedly being presented on the program. Uneducated people, in particular, lost confidence in their own judgment (Cantril, 1940).

As this incident suggests, mass hysteria may happen when people suddenly believe that they face serious, rapidly approaching danger. The conventional guidelines no longer seem fully applicable, and terror-stricken people grapple for

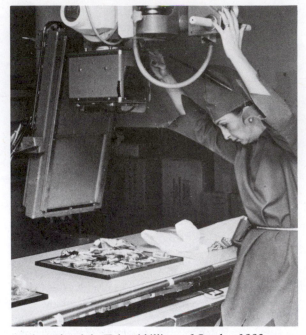

In the wake of the Tylenol killings of October 1982, steps taken to prevent possible injury to children eating Halloween candy included the use of x-rays to scan candy for razor blades or other metal objects.

some way to save themselves. In contrast, if they have an opportunity to prepare for the approaching danger, the conventional norms are likely to remain intact, and mass hysteria is much less likely to occur.

A case in point happened again at Halloween time, forty-four years after the "War of the Worlds" incident. In October 1982 widespread concern developed about the poisoning of Halloween candy, following seven nationally publicized deaths involving cyanide-contaminated Extra Strength Tylenol capsules. As the mayor of Vineland, a New Jersey city of 53,000 residents, explained, "I got scared thinking what an opportunity this was for some nut to do something" (Barron, 1982: 81).

That mayor banned trick or treating. In other towns or cities, officials employed a variety of measures. Police chiefs urged parents to limit their children's Halloween visits, school officials promised prizes to children who stayed home, and hospitals offered to scan candy with the same sort of x-ray devices used on luggage at airports. There were no serious injuries that Halloween, nor any panic or mass hysteria.

Rumors

As part of the breakdown in normative guidelines that occurs in crowd situations, established channels of communication are either out of order or are unable to supply sufficiently thorough, explicit, and up-to-date information. Rumors are likely to develop.

A **rumor** is a report transmitted informally (often by word of mouth) and concerned with subject matter difficult to verify. Rumors involve information that is important to people, and in this respect they differ from gossip. Frequently rumors provide false information, but that is not necessarily the case.

A recent analysis suggested that four conditions predict the likelihood of rumor development and transmission. They are more likely to develop and spread when the following conditions exist:

1. *The topic is important to people* — for instance, the rumor involves a life-threatening situation to loved ones and thus encourages the individ-

ual to determine the rumor's accuracy, an activity making it more widely known.
2. *There is general uncertainty suggested by the rumor.* Under this condition one is likely to look for information about the rumor, thereby helping to publicize it.
3. *The rumor produces a high level of personal anxiety.* The more concerned people are about a rumored subject, the more likely they will present it to others, seeking comfort, support, or some other gratification and, once again, helping to make others aware of the rumor.
4. *One's belief in the rumor is strong.* The more firmly people believe a rumor, the more inclined they are to discuss it with others as a means of sharing and perhaps lessening their discomfort (Rosnow, 1988).

The Development of Rumors

The content of a rumor is likely to change over time, with the amount of change strongly affected by the emotional reaction the rumor creates. The greater the capacity to excite emotion, the more extensive the changes in content are likely to be. Those who transmit the rumor tend to eliminate some details and, in turn, to emphasize others. The changes in detail generally reflect the fears, prejudices, hopes, and other prominent feelings of the people who pass on the rumor.

The transmission of a rumor is a collective process in which individuals can play a number of roles. Some people are messengers, relaying the information. Others act as skeptics, expressing doubt about what they hear. Individuals can also be interpreters, trying to figure out what is happening. Finally there are likely to be decision-makers, who initiate action in response to the news the rumor brings (Shibutani, 1966).

The "shortage" of bathroom tissue was an incident that illustrates how rumors can develop. On December 11, 1973, Harold V. Froehlich, a Wisconsin congressman, issued a statement after many complaints from people in his district about what they perceived as a rapidly developing paper shortage. Mr. Froehlich said, "The United States may face a serious shortage of toilet paper within a few months. . . . I hope we don't have to ration toilet tissue. . . . A toilet paper shortage is no laughing matter. It is a problem that will touch every American" (Malcolm, 1980: 497).

Froehlich and his staff were amazed at how much attention the news release received. This was an era when members of the mass media and the public were becoming increasingly aware of and concerned about shortages. A shortage of toilet tissue seemed as likely as short supplies of gasoline, heating oil, coffee, sugar, and a number of other commodities. As the rumor spread, the message became clear and decisive in line with people's expectations and fears. Qualifying words like "potential" disappeared.

Certain individuals played important roles in the transmission of this rumor. One celebrity became a messenger. "You know, we've got all sorts of shortages these days," Johnny Carson told his late-night television audience. "But have you heard the latest? I'm not kidding. I saw it in the paper. There's a shortage of toilet paper" (Malcolm, 1980: 497). The day after these comments, a toilet-paper-buying binge began nationally. Some shoppers—we can consider them "decision-makers"—went to local stores and

bought huge supplies of toilet tissue. Other people remained skeptics, proving correct in their analysis that the rumor of a shortage was false.

Like Carson with the bathroom-tissue rumor, other celebrities sometimes underestimate their impact as messengers. During the "Stupid Pet Tricks" segment of his late-night show, David Letterman presented a poodle that walked upright on its hind legs while balancing a glass of water on an upside-down Frisbee. As the dazzled audience watched, Letterman said, "The only thing that kind of detracts from that [the animal act] is I know that the woman has performed intricate spinal surgery on the dog and that's illegal and she'll end up doing time. But as far as the trick goes it's a 10" (*New Haven Register,* July 26, 1986: 14). Letterman only meant to be humorous. However, there were some immediate negative effects when that segment of his show was rebroadcast at an early evening hour to an audience unused to his off-beat humor. The owner's pet grooming business rapidly lost customers, and the dog's budding show business career—modeling, performances at birthday parties, and even some commercials—was seriously damaged. The owner sued Letterman for $1 million.

Efforts to Stop Rumors

Rumors can be troublesome and persistent. Can individuals or organizations take steps to terminate them?

A number of years ago the rumor started that McDonald's was selling hamburgers with worms in them. In some areas sales dropped 30 percent, in spite of the company's advertisements emphasizing that McDonald's sold only "100 percent pure beef" or suggesting that at $5 to $8 a pound for worms, it would be crazy to put them in hamburgers.

Soon after the incident, market researchers at Northwestern University conducted a study. The subjects were sixty-four graduate students, divided into four- to six-member groups. The researchers told the students that they would participate in an experiment evaluating their reaction to violence. Each group watched a typical evening television show containing three commercials for McDonald's. After the third commercial, a young man who, unknown to the students, was working

502

for the researchers casually indicated that the commercials reminded him that McDonald's had worm meat in their hamburgers.

When the television show was over, the investigators treated various groups in different ways. A couple of groups received no additional information from the research team. In several other groups, a researcher repeated a statement similar to McDonald's own advertisements—that a Food and Drug Administration study had concluded that the company's beef was 100 percent pure and that, besides, worms were simply too expensive to be used in hamburgers. In other groups the researcher asked the students about their own experiences with McDonald's—where and how often they went and whether the franchises they visited had indoor seating. The object of these questions was to stimulate neutral or positive thoughts that would counter the rumors. In a third collection of groups, one of the researchers tried to create a positive attitude toward worms in the students' minds. He told these groups of students that he had taken his mother-in-law to Chez Paul, an expensive Chicago restaurant, where they had eaten a very tasty sauce made out of worms.

At the end of the experiment, the students rated the quality of McDonald's food as well as their likelihood of eating there. The results:

1. The least favorable ratings came from those who simply heard the worm rumor and had no follow-up experience. This outcome occurred in spite of the fact that in a separate test most of these students indicated that they did not believe the worm story.
2. The ratings from those who heard the worm rumor and the same denials that McDonald's had presented in their own advertisements were almost as low as those of the first group of students.
3. The students who had the opportunity to discuss their own experiences with McDonald's gave significantly higher ratings. Their ratings, in fact, were as high as those that came from people who had not heard any rumors.
4. The students who heard about the worm sauce at Chez Paul gave equally high ratings (Rice, 1981).

The rumor of worms in McDonald's hamburgers created structural strain for the students. The most effective means to combat the strain was to shift the students' attention to conventional social situations, where structural strain was absent: either their memories of worm-free meals at McDonald's or the situation at Chez Paul, where a worm sauce was considered a delicacy.

The following Social Application examines another situation in which collective behavior occurs.

SOCIAL APPLICATION

The 1989 California Earthquake

Sociologists interested in collective behavior have studied a variety of disasters, including explosions, fires, floods, hurricanes, tornadoes, and earthquakes. Perhaps you can see why disasters qualify as contexts in which collective behavior occurs. Like other activities we have been examining in this chapter, disasters generally produce situations in which conditions are unstructured and behavior unstable and unpredictable.

Certainly the earthquake that occurred in northern California in the late afternoon of October 17, 1989, is a case in point. By analyzing this situation, we consider some of the topics addressed by sociologists who study disasters.

Survivors' Responses

When a disaster occurs, people are often dazed and bewildered. For instance, in Sunnyvale, a suburb of San Francisco, Neta Lott felt her house shaking and rolling, and when she tried to stand up, she fell onto the floor. "I sat under the desk and thought I would be buried," she said. "I thought, 'This is it. I'm going to die'" (Magnuson, 1989: 32). At Candlestick Park, just before the start of the third game in the World Series, reporter Dennis Wyss explained, "The stadium kept swaying faster and faster. I thought, how much more can it take before it caves in? I felt utterly helpless. Then it stopped" (Miller, 1989: 28).

Sociologists say that individuals are suffering from a "disaster syndrome" when following a disaster they are not only dazed and bewildered but docile and indecisive, and temporarily unable to respond effectively to circumstances. Such a reaction seems to have been fairly unusual in the California earthquake. Perhaps this was because, as Wyss suggested, after the fifteen-second tremor, the shaking and rolling stopped, and most people found themselves unhurt in an environment that was not significantly damaged.

In disasters generous, even heroic deeds are fairly common. When Dr. James Betts crawled into the rubble of Oakland's collapsed Nimitz Freeway, he had no reason to believe that he would be able to come out alive, especially when he noticed that the remains of the two-deck highway were shaking in the aftershocks. Yet Betts and several others crawled through a narrow gap until they reached six-year-old Julio Berumen, who was trapped by the corpse of his mother's friend. The corpse had to be dismembered with a chain saw and the child's leg amputated at the knee, and yet in spite of the combined danger and horror, Betts indicated that he never once thought about leaving.

Elsewhere, over 100 private pilots flew in 250,000 pounds of food and supplies to the rural community of Watsonville, one of the most seriously devastated areas. In a uniquely California style, 200 masseuses donated massage therapy to exhausted, very sore fire fighters, police, and rescue workers.

Besides individuals' heroic and generous acts, groups and organizations made significant contributions. In

In disasters, such as the California earthquake of 1989, many people go to extraordinary lengths to rescue those who are trapped or injured.

downtown San Francisco, newly homeless people were allowed to sleep in hotel lobbies, and some restaurants served free food to anyone who wanted it.

Organizational Response

When a disaster occurs, many people are going to experience physical and emotional upheaval. The California earthquake damaged or destroyed about 100,000 buildings. The city of Oakland, which already had a serious homelessness problem, suffered an additional displacement of 2500 citizens. Many people were forced to enter Red Cross shelters or live in tents. Seeking assistance, individuals often felt overwhelmed by long lines, the seemingly endless numbers of forms that needed to be filled out, and the delays. With her children in an Oakland shelter, where she felt unprotected, Betty Pitts complained, "I need a safe place now, not next week" (Magnuson, 1989: 40).

In San Francisco, Mayor Art Agnos was widely praised for spending every waking moment consoling and listening to residents in the Marina district, which was the city's most damaged area. At the same time, some frustrated citizens suggested that city officials prematurely destroyed buildings that could have been saved. The mayor took the brunt of the criticism. Rebecca Pride, a financial counselor, said, "He may have been here last week, but he wasn't here crying with me as I watched my apartment destroyed by the wreckers" (Salholz et al., 1989: 37).

Overall, though, police, medical personnel, rescue workers, and private citizens were widely praised. As a result of the 1989 experience, they are probably better prepared than before for other, possibly stronger earthquakes in the future.

What's Ahead?

Sixty-three people were killed, 14,000 individuals were displaced, and 100,000 buildings were seriously damaged or destroyed in the California earthquake of 1989. It could have been much worse.

According to the United States Geological Survey, in the next thirty years, there is a 60 percent chance of a much stronger earthquake in the Los Angeles area and a 50 percent likelihood of a similar earthquake in the San Francisco environs.

In the 1989 earthquake, a portion of the Bay Bridge and a section of the Nimitz Freeway in Oakland collapsed and fatalities resulted. In a stronger earthquake, similar or worse damage would occur widely and produce thousands, even hundreds of thousands of deaths and injuries. It is now clear that current building codes are either too lenient or insufficiently enforced.

A significant problem is the cost of needed improvements. California simply lacks the funds to repair crumbling highways and bridges. Will the citizens be willing to pay the bills?

Sources: Timothy Egan. "Building Codes: Designs for Last Quake, Not Next." *New York Times.* October 22, 1989, p. 26; Ed Magnuson. "Earthquake." *Time.* V. 134. October 30, 1989, pp. 32–40; Robert L. Miller. "From the Publisher." *Time.* V. 134. October 30, 1989, p. 28; Joseph B. Perry, Jr., and M. D. Pugh. *Collective Behavior.* St. Paul: West Publishing. 1978; Robert Reinhold. "California Struggles with the Other Side of the Dream." *New York Times.* October 22, 1989, section 4, p. 1; Eloise Salholz et al. "Recovery by the Bay." *Newsweek.* V. 114. November 6, 1989, pp. 37+.

Both collective behavior and social movements involve behavior that occurs to some extent outside existing normative guidelines. Social movements, however, are somewhat more conventionally structured, with the distinct possibility that they will eventually become part of established society. Table 17.3 provides some comparisons among violent crowds, social movements, and organizations.

Table 17.3
Some General Comparisons among Violent Crowds, Social Movements, and Organizations

	VIOLENT CROWD	SOCIAL MOVEMENT	ORGANIZATION
Leadership	Informal	Increasingly formalized over time	Formal
Duration	Minutes or hours	From a few months to many years, depending on the movement	Many years frequently
Normative guidelines	Informal and emergent	Increasingly formalized over time	Formal
Structural strain on members	Excessive	Considerable when individuals join but generally declining as the movement ages	Variable, depending on the nature of people's tasks

With the passage of time, the characteristics of social movements become increasingly like those of organizations.

Social Movements

As we have noted, a social movement is an organized, collective activity undertaken by people to promote or resist social change. The members of a social movement share:

1. An ideology justifying their actions.
2. A sense of unity.
3. A set of norms prescribing followers' behavior.
4. Some division of labor between leaders and followers and among the different categories of followers (Killian, 1964).

Smelser (1963) outlined a distinction between norm-oriented and value-oriented social movements. The goal of a norm-oriented social movement is to create new norms or occasionally to restore old ones. Examples would be a reform movement agitating for a local park or for more police protection, a group of workers seeking to establish their own independent union, or groups mobilizing at the state or national level for tax reform, nuclear disarmament, or lower gasoline prices. The goal of a value-oriented social movement, however, is to change a society's values, which are the basic principles upon which social behavior is based. Value-oriented social movements often involve efforts to make revolutionary change. They tend to be more demanding of members' time, energy, and emotional commitment than are norm-oriented social movements. Political revolutionaries, religious "cult" members, and people in utopian communities may be considered members of social movements advocating new values.

In the upcoming discussion, we examine two theoretical approaches to social movements.

Theories of Social Movements

Strain theories dominated the analysis of social movements until the early 1970s. Since then resource-mobilization theory has assumed a more prominent role (Hannigan, 1985; Kerbo and Shaffer, 1986; Klandermans, 1984; Nielsen, 1985).

Strain Theory

As we noted in the discussion of the second stage of Smelser's theory, a number of social conditions can create structural strain, which is a significant amount of tension or pressure for people,

506

and this strain lessens their willingness to stay within normal behavioral limits.

James Davies (1962) developed a strain theory. He studied historical accounts of the French and Russian revolutions, gathering evidence that revolutions occur when social conditions improve. Davies concluded that during such periods people's expectations inevitably rise, outstripping their capacity to achieve expectations. As long as the gap between expectations and the capacity to achieve expectations remains fairly small, strain will be minimal, and no revolution will occur. The strain, however, becomes great if people's actual capacity to achieve need satisfaction levels off (somewhat like the partially inverted curve of the letter "j" as represented in Figure 17.1), while the expected need satisfaction continues to rise. As Figure 17.1 suggests, an intolerable gap then exists between what people want and what they can get. This gap sets the stage for revolution.

Consider the application of strain theory to the modern women's movement, which we discussed briefly in Chapter 11, "Emerging Minorities." In 1963 Betty Friedan published *The Feminine Mystique,* which attempted to analyze the plight of modern women. Friedan was referring to strain when she summarized women's situation as something seldom discussed or understood — "the problem that has no name." In 1966 Friedan and others founded the National Organization for Women (NOW) when the federal government did not take any action to improve women's second-class status. Only a few years later, another large group of women became interested in women's rights. These women, who were generally younger than the members of NOW, had participated in civil-rights and antiwar activities and had begun to feel that they faced the contradiction (a specific type of strain) of working in freedom movements and finding themselves restricted to traditional women's roles that permitted almost no use of creative skills and leadership capacities.

Strain appears to have been a factor in the development of the modern women's movement, and one might argue that it plays a role in the development of most social movements. In recent years, however, many social scientists have become increasingly convinced that the explanatory capacity of strain theories is quite limited and that the resource-mobilization perspective makes a more valuable contribution to understanding how social movements have developed (Gurney and Tierney, 1982; Kerbo, 1982).

Figure 17.1
The J-Curve: Strain and Revolution

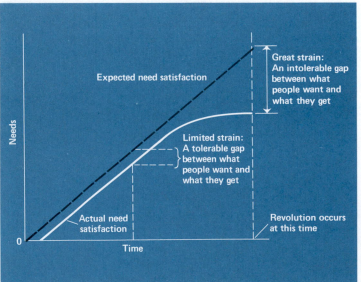

Davies's theory of revolution suggests that revolutions occur when an intolerable gap develops between people's actual need satisfaction and their expected need satisfaction. (Source: Adapted from James C. Davies. "Toward a Theory of Revolution." American Sociological Review. *V. 27. February 1962, p. 6.)*

Resource-Mobilization Theory

Resource-mobilization theory focuses on the process by which the members of social movements acquire and use certain resources necessary to accomplish their collective goals. The supporters of this theory agree that strain can encourage people to join social movements but that social movements will not develop until the members have access to such necessary resources as money, goods, power, members' commitment of time and energy, votes, or communication techniques (Allen, 1987; Gamson, 1975; Tilly, 1978).

Successful social movements do not simply seek to recruit large numbers of people. Their priority is the recruitment of politically experienced and well-adjusted groups and individuals (Oberschall, 1973).

Resource-mobilization theory helps explain the development of the modern women's movement. For instance, one resource that encouraged the creation of NOW was a citizen's advisory council on women's issues established in the early 1960s. This organization provided a communications network through which women could discuss their common grievances and decide what actions to take. Once NOW existed, it broadened and deepened those channels of communications.

The younger segment of the women's movement acquired its own, informal communications resource: the discussion group. These groups engaged in a process known as "consciousness-raising." Women came together in groups of five to fifteen members and discussed their feelings, experiences, problems, and concerns. The participants soon realized that what they had considered personal problems were usually the result of limited opportunities imposed on all of them since birth. They started to understand that the women's movement represented a very effective vehicle for reaching a solution. Jo Freeman, a sociologist, concluded:

Once women have gone through such a resocialization, their views of themselves and the world are never the same again even if they stop participating actively in the movement. Those who do drop out rarely do so without spreading feminist ideas among

Women's consciousness raising has developed in settings where they have been able to be open with each other about their feelings, experiences, goals, and problems.

their own friends and colleagues. All who undergo consciousness-raising feel compelled themselves to seek out other women with whom to share the experience.

(Freeman, 1979: 562)

Sources of Social Change

Collective behavior and social movements are produced by social change and also cause it to take place. In fact, in the following discussion of the sources of social change, social movements is one of the four factors examined. The others are cultural innovation, population, and environment.

Cultural Innovation

A **cultural innovation** is the recognition or development of new material or nonmaterial elements in a culture. There are three prominent means by which cultural innovation occurs: discovery, invention, and diffusion.

Discovery

Discovery is the perception of something that already exists but that had not been previously recognized. A discovery can be a material item (another continent or a new "wonder" drug) or a nonmaterial item (the principle of gravity).

A discovery often takes place because of chance. Random strikes of lightning undoubtedly played an important part in the process by which people first learned about fire. It is likely that it took many chance encounters before early humanity began to appreciate the potential contribution that fire could make for cooking food and providing warmth, and it is also probable that efforts to

508 control fire began only after these potentials were recognized and appreciated.

Something that is discovered does not have an effect on social change until it is used widely. In ancient Alexandria, Greece, the residents discovered how to use steam power, and they even employed steam power as a means of hauling firewood to the top of the lighthouse on the nearby island of Pharos. However, it was not until about 1700 years later that the use of steam to power boats and trains revolutionized transportation and produced significant social and economic change in Western societies (Linton, 1973).

Invention

An **invention** is a combination of known components to produce something new. The invention of the airplane involved the combination of such elements as the wings of a glider, an internal-combustion engine from an automobile, and the adaptation of a ship's propeller. Though less well known, nonmaterial inventions are also common. The city-manager plan, for instance, represents the transfer of business-management techniques to city government (Murdock, 1956).

It is important to recognize that, like any other cultural element, an invention is a piece in a cultural puzzle, not a disconnected event. Because of this interrelation, the development of an innovation is likely to generate pressure for change in other parts of social life. Thus the invention and production of the automobile, for instance, has stimulated the formation of an entire new body of law. Television led to further innovations in dozens of areas, including advertising, regulatory law, political campaign styles, family life, and even diet (e.g., TV dinners).

All inventions do not produce an equally strong impetus for change. A new method of painting, for instance, might have no apparent effect beyond a small circle of artists and critics. A new religious doctrine might arouse interest and support only among a highly select group of followers. An invention that affects the way people obtain the material necessities of life, however, will produce extensive changes in a society. The spear, which permitted early hunters to kill animals for food at a much greater distance than had previously been possible, and the automobile,

which allowed people to travel distances much more quickly and easily than they could before its introduction, are cases (Lenski and Lenski, 1982). Without very much thought, you can probably figure out how the existence of the automobile has affected all five major institutional structures.

In recent years it has become widely recognized that the impact of inventions can be a mixed blessing. The explosion of the space shuttle *Challenger* and the Chernobyl nuclear disaster are prominent recent events emphasizing that inventions leading to technological advances have a potentially destructive as well as a progressive side. At present many people agree that there needs to be an ethical dimension to invention — that innovations introduced into our modern world should be assessed carefully by a range of experts for all the impacts they produce (Bendzsel and Kiss, 1987).

Diffusion

Diffusion is the process by which cultural traits move either from one culture to another or from one part of a culture to another. Some scholars believe that about 90 percent of all cultural development results from diffusion. To illustrate this point, Ralph Linton wrote a well-known essay, which, with tongue-in-cheek, he entitled "One Hundred Percent American." He began, "There can be no question about the average American's Americanism or his desire to preserve this precious heritage at all costs" (Linton, 1982: 58). Then Linton indicated that unfortunately some "insidious foreign ideas" have managed to enter American civilization. He went on to reveal that virtually all material objects average Americans encounter in their homes — their pajamas, clocks, toothbrushes, razors, coffee, waffles, newspapers, and so on — are innovations that originated in other cultures.

The diffusion process displays certain distinctive characteristics. First, some cultural elements diffuse more readily than others. Material objects and technology generally spread more easily than do belief systems and forms of social organization.

Second, innovations that diffuse are often adapted in modified form by the receiving culture. For example, the Africans who were brought to Brazil as slaves carried their religion with them.

Whereas their descendants became Catholics, they retained certain modified elements of their tribal religion. These descendants linked particular African gods with different saints, and they developed some interesting mixed beliefs: for example, that a hollow-log drum must receive spiritual control through baptism, or it will fail to call the appropriate deities to a religious ceremony.

A third significant point about diffusion is that it is often a two-way process. Films, novels, history books, and even sociology texts have strongly emphasized the diffusion of culture traits from whites to Native Americans: horses, guns, alcohol, clothing, religion, schooling, and eventually all major elements of the modern American lifestyle. Much less attention has focused on the cultural contributions that Native Americans have given to white Americans and also to the members of other countries. A few of the better-known Native-American plants include corn, beans, squash, sweet potatoes, and the so-called "Irish" potatoes. Prominent modern drugs well-known among Native-American cultures include coca (the source of cocaine and novocaine), curare (an anesthetic), cinchona bark that produces quinine, and cascara used in laxatives. Furthermore Native-American music has had a significant impact on a number of American composers, who borrowed melodies and themes from Native Americans (Lauer, 1977).

Finally, within a single culture, conditions can produce the diffusion of a particular cultural trait more readily to certain areas or groups than to others. For example, in the United States, automobiles and telephones were most quickly adopted in urban areas with extensive commercial activity and in more affluent rural areas (Fischer and Carroll, 1988). Table 17.4 on p. 510 lists products that have diffused to American culture.

Population

At the extremes population size can have a profound effect on a society. If the population becomes small enough, a society will cease to exist. Disease, famine, and annihilation can produce such a result. The American Indian population was probably between about 700,000 and one million when Columbus reached the New World. It dropped to about 250,000 at the end of the

nineteenth century, and a substantial number of tribes simply disappeared. Most historians agree that more Indians died of white people's diseases than died in warfare. Unlike the whites the Indians had not developed any immunities to smallpox, typhoid, yellow fever, and the other diseases brought over from Europe, and in some areas the effects were devastating, killing 90 percent of the indigenous population (Farley, 1982: 111–112).

On the other hand, rapid population growth can also lead to destructive social change. Many overpopulated developing nations suffer from hunger, poor housing, crowding, poverty, political conflict, and inadequate health services—a complex of conditions producing a distinctly deprived life by Western standards (Brown, McGrath, and Stokes, 1982).

A change in the size of particular segments of the population can also promote social change. For instance, the American baby boom of 1946–1965 led to a period of growth for schools and colleges until the early 1970s. However, the past two decades, in which the youthful population has declined, has featured teacher layoffs and also the elimination of some schools in many districts. In addition, the baby boom had contributed to intensified job competition and to unemployment in many job areas.

More generally it appears that if prospective parents are part of a large generation, then they will probably find themselves caught in a highly competitive job situation. They will take a fairly long time to establish themselves occupationally, and they will therefore be likely to start having children relatively late in life and to produce a small number of offspring. On the other hand, as members of a small generation, these children will find it somewhat easier to establish themselves occupationally. Thus they will be able to start having children at a younger age and will therefore be likely to produce more of them. Census data indicate that these two patterns have alternated with each other since the 1890s (Ryder, 1980).

The Environment

At present Americans find themselves confronting two contradictory priorities—one emphasizing a clean environment and the other stressing the significance of low energy costs or other eco-

Table 17.4
A Variety of Products That Diffused to Modern American Culture

FOOD AND DRINK	PLACE OF ORIGIN
Alcoholic beverages	Near East (Syria, Lebanon, and Israel)
Bananas	South Asia
Beans	Eastern United States (Indians)
Butter	Near East
Chocolate	Mexico
Coffee	Abyssinia (Ethiopia)[1]
Corn	Eastern United States (Indians)
Eggs	Southern Asia
Grains	Near East
Milk	Asia Minor (Turkey)
Squash	Eastern United States (Indians)
Sugar	India
Sweet potatoes	Eastern United States (Indians)
Tea	China

OTHER MATERIAL PRODUCTS FOR EVERYDAY USE	PLACE OF ORIGIN
Bathtub	Rome (Italy)
Bed	Persia (Iran) or Asia Minor (Turkey)
Checks	Persia (Iran)
Cigar	Brazil
Cigarette	Mexico (A.D. 400 to 1400)
Clock	Medieval Europe
Coins	Lydia (Turkey)
Cotton	India
Fork	Italy
Glass	Egypt
Linen	Near East
Paper	China
Paper money	China
Printing	China
Shoes	Greece
Soap	Gaul (France)
Spoon	Rome (Italy)
Toilet	Rome (Italy)

IMPORTANT NONMATERIAL PRODUCTS	PLACE OF ORIGIN
Alphabet	Phoenicia (Syria and Lebanon)
Banking (credits, loans, discounts, and mortgages)	Babylonia (Iraq) and later influences of Italy and England
Family organization	Medieval Europe
Language	England
Numerical system	India[2]
System of real-property ownership[3]	Medieval Europe

[1] If the product first appeared in a country with an ancient name, the modern name appears in parentheses.
[2] The numerical system originated in India, diffused to the Middle East, and then eventually reached Europe.
[3] Ownership of such fixed, immovable things as land and buildings

Sources: Ruth Benedict. "The Growth of Culture," pp. 182–195 in Harry L. Shapiro (ed.), *Man, Culture, and Society.* New York: Oxford University Press. 1956; Ralph Linton. "One Hundred Percent American." *American Mercury.* V. 40. April 1937. pp. 427–430; George Peter Murdock. "How Culture Changes," pp. 247–260 in Harry L. Shapiro (ed.), *Man, Culture, and Society.* New York: Oxford University Press.

In at least one American town, citizens appear to have made a firm choice about the dangers and benefits of nuclear industrial production. The helmets of the high-school football team (known as The Bombers) are adorned with a mushroom cloud, symbolizing the town's commitment to an industry that employs or supports about three-fourths of the area residents.

nomic issues. National survey data suggest that Americans split quite evenly on whether they should underscore the development of new energy sources or environmental protection. In September 1981, 39 percent of a national sample indicated that they believed that progress depends on maintaining an adequate supply of energy. On the other hand, 40 percent believed that environmental protection was more important — that it is better to risk not having enough energy than to spoil the environment. Some fluctuations had occurred in these figures since 1973, but they were minor; in that year the respective numbers were 37 percent and 37 percent (Roper Organization, *Roper Reports,* November 1981).

Controlling and reducing environmental pollution is difficult, even if a consensus exists on the necessity to act. Air pollution is a case in point. What represents a reasonable goal in this area? Is it enough to remove all pollutants detectable by the human senses, or should we be concerned with impurities identifiable only by scientific instruments? In the late 1940s in Pittsburgh, industrial leaders, politicians, and the public agreed that air pollution was a serious problem, but the different groups could never accept a single comprehensive

plan for air-pollution control. The restrictions eventually placed on air pollution were limited, concerned only with solving the immediate, observable problem (Stiefel, 1982).

Social Movements

As we noted earlier in the chapter, two broad types of social movements exist. Norm-oriented social movements maintain a narrow focus, seeking to change a specific law or practice. Value-oriented social movements, which attempt to alter or replace existing values, are much more ambitious. Effective value-oriented movements can significantly change people's values, beliefs, and behavior.

Four conditions seem to play an especially important role in the development of effective social movements. First, a sense of strain must exist among a large number of people — a clearly shared awareness of the disparity between existing conditions and the ideal state of affairs. Second, developing social movements require close interaction and communication among members. Without such contacts people's perceptions of the strains that they are encountering are apt to be less clear, and they are considerably less likely to develop coherent ideologies. Third, social movements are more likely to grow if the members share prominent statuses — for instance, women, students, blacks, or the elderly — and thus possess common outlooks, experiences, and grievances. Fourth, the existence of previous social-movement activity is usually important. Unless the members see actual evidence indicating that large-scale social change is possible, then they are unlikely to believe that their own movement will succeed (Morrison, 1973). The more developed these factors, the more successful the social movement is likely to be, at least initially, and successful social movements have the ability to produce significant social change.

What kind of social movements are most likely to succeed? A study of a sample of fifty-three American social movements that developed between 1800 and 1945 found that groups that used violence had a greater likelihood of achieving some of their goals than did social movements that totally rejected forceful means. However, the absolute number of social movements in the sam-

512

ple that did engage in violence was small, and thus all conclusions from this study must be tentative (Gamson, 1975).

Social movements can "fail" — cease to exist — and yet still have a long-term effect on society. For instance, twenty years after the Garvey Movement of the 1920s, many scholars had simply dismissed it as an extreme expression of black racial consciousness and pride that flowered temporarily during the social upheaval that occurred in black America during and after World War I. By the 1950s, however, the Black Muslims or Nation of Islam had formed a large social movement that promoted essentially the same goals as Garveyism,

and Elijah Muhammed, the founder of the Black Muslims, acknowledged that Marcus Garvey was a spiritual ancestor of his own movement. In American politics "third party" movements usually fail to put their candidates into office. In some instances, however, they do succeed in making segments of the electorate sympathetic to their positions, ultimately forcing the major parties to adopt modified versions of their own programs (Killian, 1964).

The chapter concludes with the fifth of five Research in Sociology sections: "Prison Riots: Which Theory Can Explain Them?"

RESEARCH IN SOCIOLOGY

Prison Riots: Which Theory Can Explain Them?

 If a sociological theory contains clear, thought-provoking statements, has it managed to establish the accuracy of its claims? The answer is a resounding "NO." As we noted in the first two chapters, scientists' work must encounter colleagues' critical review. A sociological theory can be subjected to such a review by determining whether or not it can explain relevant data.

In Chapter 17 we saw that both the strain theory and resource-mobilization theory can be applied to social movements. They also can be used to analyze prison riots. Does one theory succeed in explaining why prison riots occur, while the other one fails? That does not seem to be the case. It appears that in the late 1960s and early 1970s, the causes of prison riots were consistent with resource-mobilization theory, while in the 1980s the factors

encouraging riots have fitted better with the strain theory. To illustrate this shift, we will examine a study of the Attica riot, the most devastating prison rebellion of the 1970s, and then analyze research involving the New Mexico riot of 1980. Then we will be able to understand more thoroughly the relationship between theory and research.

The Attica and New Mexico Riots

Between September 9 and September 13, 1971, forty-three citizens of New York State were killed in the correctional facility at Attica, New York. Thirty-nine of the deaths occurred during the fifteen minutes it took the state police to recapture the prison, which had been controlled by inmates. The total number of deaths was the highest produced in this cen-

tury from any violent encounter limited to Americans.

Shortly after the Attica riot, the governor of New York asked the five justices of the state's Appellate Division to appoint a citizens' committee — the New York State Special Commission on Attica — to lead an investigation that would try to explain what happened, and why, and also make recommendations to prevent such violence in the future. This nine-person commission hired a staff, which then conducted the investigation. These people interviewed most of the inmates who had been at Attica during the riot — about 1600 men — as well as the majority of the corrections officers and state police who were present during the conflict. It would be helpful to know just what questions were asked or if the researchers had a standard interview for each category of people examined. Unfortunately this information was not made public.

While it is possible to have reservations about how the data for the report were gathered, its presentation is straightforward and clear and its findings consistent with those produced by other investigators of the Attica riot. And what are those findings? Most basically the investigators found that the Attica rioters were products of their social era, a time when protest against inequality and oppression was popular.

Could one argue that conditions in the prison were poor and deteriorating, thus creating strain for inmates? No, the commission concluded. Prison conditions, in fact, were improving under the new state Commissioner of Corrections. The root of the problem was the tone of the times. According to the report, those who participated actively in the riot were

. . . part of a new breed of younger, more aware inmates, largely black, who came to prison full of deep feelings of alienation and hostility against the established institutions of law and government, enhanced self-esteem, racial pride, and political awareness, and an unwillingness to accept the petty humiliations and racism that characterize prison life.

(New York State Special Commission on Attica, 1972: 105)

Using the resource-mobilization perspective, one can consider these angry young men a potential resource encouraging the development of a riot. "Potential" is an important word here. As we saw in the section on riots, anger and pride are not enough to generate a riot; there must be mobilization. Thus the resource must be developed to contribute to collective action — in this case a riot. The Attica report indicated that, indeed, this did happen. About a month before the riot occurred, the three major militant organizations among the inmates — the Black Panthers, the Young Lords, and the Nation of Islam — reached an accord where they were in sufficient agreement to override their differences and recognize their common grievances against the power structure of the prison. In addition, these common grievances were solidified by the death of George Jackson, a prominent black radical, in a California prison under conditions that made the inmates believe the guards had either cooperated or actually killed the man.

The Attica report concluded that the riot was unplanned, that it began following a confrontation between guards and inmates. Because a central gate failed to function and the communications system within the prison was outmoded, the inmates were able to take over large sections of the prison quickly.

It seems that a resource-mobilization perspective can also be applied to the time period after the take-over. Supporters of this theory would point out that while the inmates lacked the resource of a full-fledged organization at the time of the take-over, they had a fairly united group of like-minded participants whose common grievances allowed them to be welded into a fairly cohesive unit once the outbreak took place. About an hour after the riot occurred, one of the "inmate lawyers" — a man who, though lacking formal training, was sufficiently knowledgeable of the law to help fellow inmates prepare legal petitions — took a bullhorn and spoke. This man was greatly respected, and when he said that they needed to organize themselves effectively, the others listened. A definite tone was set. The report stated:

Now, inmate after inmate jumped up on the table and took the bullhorn, extolling brotherhood among inmates and calling for the presentation of demands for reform. The speakers were principally those men to whom other inmates naturally turn for guidance and advice: outstanding athletes, leaders of political groups, and, or course, the "inmate lawyers."

(New York State Special Commission on Attica, 1972: p. 297)

Because of the resource of angry, united inmates, the mobilization of a fairly well-organized group was easily accomplished.

The New Mexico riot of 1980 was a different situa-

514

tion, however. The political outlook and rhetoric of the 1960s and the early 1970s had lessened or disappeared. Within the prison itself, conditions were not improving as at Attica—they were becoming worse. In this era and particularly within this prison, the strain theory seems to offer a more effective explanation than the resource-mobilization perspective.

The data on the New Mexico riot come from two articles based, in turn, on two sources—the official investigation by the Attorney General's office conducted shortly after the riot and sociologist Bert Useem's interviews in 1985 with the remaining thirty-six inmates who had been present during the riot.

When interviewed, inmates mentioned problems that are compatible with strain theory. Perhaps most significantly they often indicated that the turning point toward worse prison conditions occurred in 1975, when the deputy warden was fired and the warden, named Felix Rodriguez, was transferred. One inmate explained that the new warden

came in like a real maniac. People can say what they want about Rodriguez, and maybe he did have his finger in the pie, but all I know, man, all I know empirically, when he was warden here, you didn't have guys stabbing each other in wholesale numbers, you didn't have guys breaking out and running up the fence 15 or 20 at a time because it was

too heavy for them to do time here. . . . It was a mellow, laid-back place under Rodriguez.

(Useem, 1985: 683)

According to Useem's data analysis, inmates compared the conditions under different wardens 181 times; 160 of those comparisons favored the Rodriguez administration.

The change in administrations created strain throughout the entire prison system. Inmates related to each other differently after Rodriguez left; robbery and violence were more widespread and trust rarer. Perhaps the new administration's most decisive means of producing strain was its establishment of a system of inmate informants. "Snitching" became the order of the day, and most of the inmates despised the snitches.

When the New Mexico riot occurred, it did not closely resemble the one at Attica. While this outbreak was also unplanned, the inmates behaved differently, reflecting the dissimilar factors behind the violence. The New Mexico riot lacked the resource of inmates capable of being rapidly organized to make demands for reform. Instead these men were wild and uncontrollable, undone by the destructive prison system that had been imposed on them; strain, in short, appears to have been the primary factor igniting this riot. And victims of that strain—the rioters—took out their fury and frustration on those

they considered responsible. The twelve guards held as hostages were repeatedly beaten, sodomized, and threatened with death, though none were actually killed. Most of the thirty-three inmates killed were informers, and they were killed with incredible brutality: beaten, raped, mutilated, and tortured to death with acetylene torches.

Perhaps no point indicates the difference between the two riots as sharply as the respective role played by blacks. At Attica aroused young blacks were the largest group in the prison and at the focus of the riot. In contrast, the New Mexico uprising occurred during a politically more apathetic era, and black inmates represented only 9 percent of the prison population. These men formed a group for their mutual protection and stayed away from the violence. Thus they mobilized themselves for inaction, quite the opposite of what was done by many black inmates at Attica.

Comment on the Relationship of Theory and Research

As we learned in Chapter 2, "Doing Research in Sociology," theory and research need to go hand-in-hand, supporting each other. Effective theory must fit the facts studies provide.

What theoretical contributions will occur in the next few years? While this section strongly implies that it would be difficult to produce a general theory of prison riots, such a theory would be a formidable contribution. Can a theory be developed that more effectively predicts prison outbreaks than intelligent officials or inmates who are on-the-scene? That would be quite an accomplishment. We never know what's ahead. Perhaps at this very moment, some sociologist is preparing to publish a paper or a book that will significantly improve this body of theory. With prison riots a frequent reality, practical insights offered by such a theory would be useful.

Sources: Burton M. Atkins and Henry R. Glick (eds.). *Prisons, Protests and Politics.* Englewood Cliffs, NJ: Prentice-Hall. 1972; Mark Colvin. "The 1980 New Mexico Prison Riot." *Social Problems.* V. 29. June 1982, pp. 449–463; J. R. Johnson and Joseph S. Petrovsky. "Lessons Learned after the Riots." *Corrections Today.* V. 50. June 1988, pp. 16–18+; New York State Special Commission on Attica. *Attica: The Official Report of the New York State Special Commission on Attica.* New York: Bantam Books. 1972; John Pallas and Bob Barker. "From Riot to Revolution." *Issues in Criminology.* V. 7. 1972, pp. 1–19; Bert Useem. "Disorganization and the New Mexico Prison Riot." *American Sociological Review.* V. 50. October 1985, pp. 677–688; Ann Yurkanin. "Inmate Uprising at Riker's Island." *Corrections Today.* V. 50. April 1988, p. 204.

STUDY GUIDE

Learning Objectives

After studying this chapter, you should be able to:

1. Define collective behavior and social movements and discuss their occurrence in daily life.
2. Discuss and illustrate Smelser's general theory of collective behavior and social movements.
3. Define crowds and discuss their characteristics.
4. Examine the contagion and emergent-norm theories of crowds, defining and illustrating them.
5. Define mobs and riots and analyze riots with different crowd theories.
6. Discuss panics and mass hysteria, defining and illustrating them.
7. Define rumors, examine their development, and describe efforts to stop them.
8. Summarize the major conclusions of strain theory and resource-mobilization theory.
9. Discuss prominent sources of social change.

Summary

1. Collective behavior is social activity that occurs under conditions that are temporarily unstructured and unstable.

2. Smelser's general theory of collective behavior and social movements contains six stages — structural conduciveness, structural strain, growth and spread of a generalized belief, the precipitating factor, mobilization for action, and social control.

3. A crowd is a temporary gathering of individuals who share a common concern or interest and find themselves in close physical contact with each other. Crowd characteristics include suggestibility, anonymity and spontaneity, and impersonality. Crowd theories include contagion theory and emergent-norm theory.

Mobs and riots occur in violent crowds. A mob is a crowd whose members engage in destructive and aggressive behavior in the pursuit of a short-term but valued goal. A riot is aggressive, destructive crowd behavior that is less focused or unified than mob activity. The most costly riots of this century in the United States occurred between 1966 and 1968. Smelser's theory and the emergent-norm perspective are useful in their analysis.

Panics and mass hysteria involve frightened

crowds. A panic is a collective flight to safety. Mass hysteria is a type of panic that occurs when people are scattered over a wide geographical area. As "The War of the Worlds" situation demonstrated, some people are more prone to mass hysteria than others. Some measures can be taken to reduce the likelihood of mass hysteria.

4. A rumor is a report transmitted informally (often by word of mouth) and concerns subject matter difficult to verify. The content of a rumor is likely to change over time, with the elimination of some details and the emphasis of others. The transmission of a rumor is a collective process in which individuals can play a number of roles. A study of a rumor claiming that McDonald's hamburgers had worms in them examined different ways to limit the impact of rumors.

5. A social movement is an organized, collective activity undertaken by people to promote or resist social change. Smelser outlined a distinction between norm-oriented and value-oriented social movements.

One theory has indicated that the tension and pressure of structural strain are the chief reasons social movements develop. On the other hand, resource-mobilization theory focuses on the process by which the members of a social movement acquire and use certain resources necessary to accomplish their collective goals.

6. Prominent sources of social change include cultural innovation, population, environment, and social movements. Discovery, invention, and diffusion are three means by which cultural innovation occurs. Some scholars believe that about 90 percent of all cultural development results from diffusion.

A massive increase in population can produce a number of negative changes in societies. In the United States, the size of different age groups will help determine their effect on society.

For Americans two contradictory priorities face them on environmental issues. One places a priority on a clean environment, and the other emphasizes low energy costs and other economic issues. Even where support for the first priority is strong, it is difficult to accomplish substantial social change.

Social movements are another source of social change. A study of fifty-three American social movements has suggested that groups engaged in violence were somewhat more likely to gain advantages than nonusers of violence. The impact of social movements is not always readily apparent. A social movement that "fails" may produce a significant impact years later.

Key Terms

collective behavior   social activity that occurs under conditions that are temporarily unstructured and unstable because of the absence of clearly defined norms

contagion theory   a perspective emphasizing that the presence of a crowd encourages or compels people to think and act in a uniform manner

crowd   a temporary gathering of individuals who share a common concern or interest and find themselves in close physical contact with one another

cultural innovation   the recognition or development of new material or nonmaterial elements in a culture

diffusion   the process by which cultural traits move either from one culture to another or from one part of a culture to another

discovery   the perception of something that already exists but that had not been previously recognized

emergent-norm theory   a perspective analyzing the process by which a new social standard develops within a crowd—a standard that in reality receives a more enthusiastic acceptance from some crowd members than others

invention   a combination of known components to produce something new

mass hysteria   a type of panic that occurs when people are scattered over a wide geographical area

mob   a crowd whose members engage in destructive and aggressive behavior in the pursuit of a short-term but valued goal

panic   a collective flight to safety

resource-mobilization theory   a perspective that focuses on the process by which the members of social movements acquire and use certain resources necessary to accomplish their collective goals

riot   aggressive, destructive crowd behavior that is less focused or unified than mob activity

rumor   a report transmitted informally (often by word of mouth) and concerned with subject matter difficult to verify

social change   modifications in culture, social organization, and social behavior

social movement   an organized, collective activity undertaken by people to promote or resist social change

Tests

True–false Test

_____ 1. Collective behavior is rare in modern societies.

_____ 2. Smelser's general theory can be used to analyze collective-behavior activities but not social movements.

_____ 3. Le Bon, who developed contagion theory, believed that when in a crowd, an individual inevitably becomes less civilized.

_____ 4. The emergent-norm theory rejects the idea that crowd members contain a united mental state.

_____ 5. Panic rarely occurs in the general American population.

_____ 6. Mass hysteria is a type of panic that occurs when people are scattered over a wide geographical area.

_____ 7. The rumor of a toilet-paper shortage was simply a joke that nobody took seriously.

_____ 8. Resource-mobilization theorists would suggest that the consciousness-raising group was an important resource in the development of the modern women's movement.

_____ 9. Discoveries always involve material, not nonmaterial items.

_____ 10. In the United States, the diffusion of automobiles and telephones most readily occurred to urban areas with extensive commercial activity and to more affluent rural areas.

Multiple-choice Test

_____ 1. In Smelser's general theory, basic conditions that permit or allow collective behavior or a social movement to emerge are termed:
    a. structural conduciveness.
    b. structural strain.
    c. growth and spread of a generalized belief.
    d. a precipitating factor.

_____ 2. Blumer suggested that contagion occurs in crowds when:
    a. anonymity decreases.
    b. crowd members lose awareness of each other's activities.

c. key crowd members establish norms for each other.

d. crowd members become increasingly preoccupied with each other's activities.

_____ 3. Which of the following statements about crowd theories is true?

a. Contagion theory is useful for analyzing crowds in subdued states.

b. Emergent-norm theory applies to a wider range of crowd types than contagion theory.

c. Emergent-norm theory analyzes collective behavior as separate from the rest of social behavior.

d. Emergent-norm theory supports the idea that all crowds are destructive forces.

_____ 4. People who oppose the policies of a certain organization overturn a bus belonging to that organization, smash its windows, and then disperse. These people have been participating in:

a. a mob.

b. a riot.

c. mass hysteria.

d. panic.

_____ 5. The reaction to the radio broadcast of H. G. Wells's "War of the Worlds" was an example of:

a. a riot.

b. panic.

c. a rumor.

d. mass hysteria.

_____ 6. Rumors are more likely to spread when:

a. the topic produces a high level of personal anxiety.

b. the issue is unimportant to people.

c. one's belief in the rumor is strong.

d. a and c

_____ 7. Compared to violent crowds, social movements:

a. last longer.

b. have a more informal leadership.

c. have more informal normative guidelines.

d. a, b, and c

_____ 8. Strain theory:

a. makes the analysis of resource mobilization a priority.

b. was used by James Davies to analyze the French and Russian revolutions.

c. cannot analyze such modern social movements as the women's movement.

d. only examines norm-oriented social movements.

_____ 9. Cultural innovation occurs through all of the following means EXCEPT:

a. discovery.

b. invention.

c. diffusion.

d. displacement.

_____ 10. Which of the following situations occurs during diffusion?

a. Belief systems change more rapidly than material elements.

b. Innovations that diffuse are often adopted in a modified form.

c. Diffusion is always a one-way process.

d. A new cultural trait gains equal acceptance from all groups within the receiving culture.

Essay Test

1. Define collective behavior and indicate how it differs from other social behavior.
2. Apply the six-stage Smelser theory to a collective-behavior situation that you choose.
3. Evaluate the effectiveness of the contagion and emergent-norm theories for analyzing crowd behavior, providing examples whenever possible.
4. Use one of the crowd theories to examine the occurrence of a riot.
5. Define panic and mass hysteria and discuss the conditions encouraging these activities of frightened crowds.
6. Recall a rumor you heard recently, or make up a rumor. Then examine the development of the rumor and also possible efforts to stop the rumor.
7. What is a social movement? Choose a prominent modern social movement (not the women's movement) and use both strain theory and resource-mobilization theory to analyze its development.
8. What are four prominent sources of social change? Give an example of each.

Suggested Readings

Blumberg, Rhoda Louis. 1984. *The 1960s Freedom Struggle.* Boston: Twayne. A well-written, thorough discussion of the 1960s protests, including an appendix on the use of social-movement theories to analyze those protests.

Branch, Taylor. 1988. *Parting the Waters: America in the King Years 1954–63.* New York: Simon and Schuster. A highly detailed, beautifully written account of the development of civil-rights protests, with Martin Luther King, Jr.'s activities central to the presentation.

Chirot, Daniel. 1986. *Social Change in the Modern Era.* San Diego: Harcourt Brace Jovanovich. A broad, effective review of social change in the past, present, and future and in both capitalist and socialist nations.

Cohen, Jean L. (ed.). 1985. *Social Research.* V. 52 (Winter). Six somewhat technical but thought-provoking papers on recent developments in theory and analysis of social movements.

Erikson, Kai. 1976. *Everything in Its Path: Destruction of Community in the Buffalo Creek Flood.* New York: Simon and Schuster. Along with the death and physical damage they bring, disasters also destroy social networks, leaving little worthwhile in people's lives. This well-written book provides a painfully detailed account of how a flood devastated a mining community in West Virginia.

Gamson, William. 1975. *The Strategy of Social Protest.* Homewood, IL: Dorsey Press. A study of several hundred protest groups that challenged the American political structure between 1800 and 1945.

Levine, Adeline Gordon. 1982. *Love Canal: Science, Politics, and People.* Lexington, MA: Lexington Books. A study of one of the nation's most publicized environmental crises, showing how local people eventually were able to organize a social movement that forced concessions from the federal government and a major chemical company.

Miller, David L. 1985. *Introduction to Collective Behavior.* Belmont, CA: Wadsworth. An effective discussion of both collective behavior and social movements. Each chapter presents case studies, which are analyzed with four theoretical perspectives.

Orwell, George. 1946. *Animal Farm.* New York: Harcourt, Brace and World. A short, simply written novel that describes the life of a social movement as it progressed from a pure beginning to complete corruption.

520 Perry, Joseph B., Jr., and M. D. Pugh. 1978. *Collective Behavior*. St. Paul, MN: West. A clearly written, short overview of collective-behavior theory, disaster research, crowd violence, and social movements. This book has done a particularly good job of blending theoretical analyses with modern and historical illustrations.

Rose, Jerry D. 1982. *Outbreaks: The Sociology of Collective Behavior*. New York: The Free Press. A detailed analysis and categorization of different forms of collective behavior, examining the background, membership, process, and consequences of each type.

Schneider, Louis. 1976. *Classical Theories of Social Change*. Morristown, NJ: General Learning Press. A short summary and analysis of fourteen major theoretical contributions to the topic of social change. With no more than a couple of hours of fairly easy reading, a student can develop a basic understanding of these classical theories of social change.

Additional Assignments

1. Play the following, well-known children's game with about a half-dozen classmates. The first person whispers a fairly elaborate story to the next person, who then whispers it to the next in line, and so on. At the end of the game, the last person will tell the story to everyone. What changes in content occurred along the way? With everyone's help try to reconstruct where information was lost or altered. What insights have you obtained about the transmission of rumors? How would a high-stress situation affect the ability to transmit information accurately?

2. Get back issues of newspapers, news magazines (such as *Time* or *Newsweek*), or watch the evening network news for a week, and list items covered that would be considered either (a) collective behavior or (b) social movements. Do some activities get more or different coverage than others? Is coverage of some activities more dramatic than others? What reactions to or commentaries about the different topics are found in the media? From your observations what collective activity is "news"? How might an awareness of what serves as "news" affect how people behave collectively to gain their objectives?

Answers to Objective Test Questions

True–false Test

1. f	4. t	7. f	9. f
2. f	5. f	8. t	10. t
3. t	6. t		

Multiple-choice Test

1. a	4. a	7. a	9. d
2. d	5. d	8. b	10. b
3. b	6. d		

GLOSSARY

absolute wealth the cash value of an individual's economic assets

abstinence total restraint from sex

ageism an ideology asserting the superiority of the young over the old. Ageism is a rationalization for political, economic, and social discrimination against the elderly

aggregate two or more people who share physical space but lack the interaction maintained by group members

androgynous possessing a definite blend of both traditionally masculine and traditionally feminine traits

anomie the confusing situation produced when norms are either absent or conflicting

anticipatory socialization the acceptance of a group's standards preparatory to becoming a member of the group

anti-Semitism the complex of prejudicial attitudes toward Jews

authoritarian leader a leader who controls all aspects of group activity yet stays somewhat aloof from the group

authority power that people generally recognize as rightfully maintained by those who use it

backstage the physical area or region where people construct the illusions and impressions they will use in a performance

belief a statement about reality that people accept as true

biosocial position a recently developed perspective that acknowledges the significance of both biology and social experience in the development of gender roles and that emphasizes their interplay, contending that the independent significance of each factor is impossible to assess since they never exist in isolation from each other

bourgeoisie the class of modern capitalists who own the means of economic production and employ wage labor

bureaucracy a formal organization's administrative section that has the task of controlling its operation

bureaucratic personality a type of personality that emphasizes rules and procedures and tends to lose track of organizational goals

capital money, goods, or other forms of wealth invested to produce more wealth

capitalism an economic system where capital is controlled by private citizens who own the means of production and distribution of goods and services

causation a situation in which one variable can produce the occurrence of another

charismatic system of authority according to Weber, an authority system in which leadership develops because of the personal magnetism of an individual, whose followers believe that he or she possesses superhuman qualities

city a large, densely settled concentration of people permanently located within a relatively confined geographical area where nonagricultural occupations are pursued

civil religion a shared, public faith in the nation, a faith linked to people's everyday life through a set of beliefs, symbols, and rituals that contain religious elements and overtones that are not formally affiliated with any particular religion

class consciousness recognition by the members of a class of the role they play in the production process

cognitive ability the capacity to use perception, thought, memory, and other mental processes to acquire knowledge

collective behavior social activity that occurs under conditions that are temporarily unstructured and unstable because of the absence of clearly defined norms

commune a planned, intentional community, bringing together biologically unrelated people in order to build a large, family-like group

communism according to Merton, a requirement that the substantive findings of science represent a common heritage, not the exclusive property of individual discoverers and their heirs

community a settlement of people living in a specific geographical area and maintaining a system of interrelationships that satisfies many of the people's physical and social needs

conflict theory a theory contending that the struggle for power and wealth in society should be the central concern of sociology

conformity an individual's behavior in line with the relevant social norms

conformity according to Merton, a nondeviant adaptation in which individuals pursue legitimate goals and use the culturally accepted means to achieve them, even though it is likely they will not attain those goals

contagion theory a perspective emphasizing that the presence of a crowd encourages or compels people to think and act in a uniform manner

corporation a legally designated organization that has power and responsibilities separate from its workers and owners

correlation a statistical description of the relationship between variables

counterculture a subculture whose members consciously and often proudly reject some of the most important cultural standards of the mainstream society

crime an act that violates criminal law

crowd a temporary gathering of individuals who share a common concern or interest and find themselves in close physical contact with one another

crude birth rate the number of births per 1000 persons in a society in a given year

crude death rate the number of deaths per 1000 persons in a society in a given year

cultural innovation the recognition or development of new material or nonmaterial elements in a culture

cultural relativism the principle that a culture should be evaluated by its own standards and not by those of any other culture

cultural universals traits believed to exist in all cultures

culture all the humanmade products associated with a society

culture shock the psychological and social maladjustment many people suffer when they visit or live in another culture

deficit famine situation in which no food supplies exist elsewhere in a nation sufficient to compensate for local inadequacies

democracy a government in which those in power are acting with the consent of the governed

democratic leader a leader who permits group members to determine many policies and take an active role in discussion

demography the study of human populations

dependent variable a variable that is the consequence of some cause

deviance behavior that violates social norms considered sufficiently significant that the majority of a group or society responds negatively

diffusion the process by which cultural traits move either from one culture to another or from one part of a culture to another

discovery the perception of something that already exists but that had not been previously recognized

discrimination the behavior by which one group prevents or restricts another group's access to scarce resources

disease a condition of biological nonhealth

disengagement a process of mutual withdrawal involving decreasing interaction between an elderly person and others in the social system to which he or she belongs

disinterestedness according to Merton, a standard that scientists avoid the pursuit of work that is self-serving and self-interested

distribution famine a food shortage existing in certain provinces or regions of a country, not throughout an entire country

double standard a position asserting that men may engage in premarital sex but women may not

doubling time the time span necessary for a population to double in size

dramaturgic sociology a theoretical approach that analyzes social interaction as if the participants were actors in a play

dysfunction a disruptive or destabilizing consequence produced by an item, individual, or group and affecting a particular group or society

economic institution the system of norms and roles developed for the production, distribution, and consumption of goods and services

education the transmission of knowledge, skills, and values by either formal or informal means

egalitarian a type of family in which the wife–mother and husband–father share power and also permit their children to participate in the family decisions

ego Sigmund Freud's conception of the self that must cope with pressures from three often contradictory forces

emergent-norm theory a perspective analyzing the process by which a new social standard develops within a crowd—a standard that in reality receives a more enthusiastic acceptance from some crowd members than others

endogamy a custom requiring a person to marry within a specific social unit, such as a kinship group, religious organization, or social class

ethnic group a category of people that is set apart by itself or by others because of distinct cultural or national qualities

ethnocentrism the automatic tendency to evaluate other cultures by the standards of one's own

ethnomethodology the study of the sometimes recognized, often unrecognized social order, the set of underlying shared norms and expectations that promote harmony in most everyday social interactions

exogamy a custom compelling someone to marry outside a specific social unit

experiment a research technique in which the investigator manipulates conditions so that the effects produced by one independent variable can be isolated and observed

explicit norm a standard that is out in the open

expressive concerned with emotional or social issues

extended family a family involving two or more generations of people related by blood and living together or close to each other

family traditionally defined as a social unit composed of two or more people who live together and are related by blood, marriage, or adoption

family planning a program that encourages people to decide how many children they want, when they want them, and what contraceptives, if any, they wish to use to achieve their goals

fertility rate the number of actual births per 1000 women between the ages of fifteen and forty-four

folkway a norm that specifies the way things are customarily done—folkways are concerned with standards of behavior that are socially approved but not considered morally significant

formal organization a group characterized by formally stated rules, clearly defined members' roles, and distinct objectives

frontstage the physical area or region where people present a performance

function an adjustive or stabilizing consequence produced by an item, individual, or group and affecting a particular group or society

functional equivalent an organization or activity that provides service or assistance to an individual or group more commonly received from some other organization or activity

game according to George Herbert Mead, a group activity in which each participant's role requires interaction with two or more individuals

gender the general behavioral standards that distinguish males and females in a given culture

gender role a set of specific behavioral patterns associated with either the female or male gender

generalized other an image of the role expectations for all the game participants with whom a person must interact

gentrification the move of middle- and upper-middle-class people to formerly deteriorated urban neighborhoods

grief work the process by which people attempt to establish a new identity after the death of a loved one

group two or more interacting people who share certain expectations and goals

growth rate the crude birth rate minus the crude death rate

health care the variety of public and private organizations that support an individual's effective physical, mental, and social adaptation to his or her environment

hidden curriculum a set of school rules that emphasizes blind obedience and that is seldom made explicit but is recognized as important by students

homogamy marriage with a person having social characteristics similar to one's own

human ecology the study of human beings' relationship with the environment

hypothesis a scientifically researchable suggestion about the relationship between two or more variables

id according to Sigmund Freud, the part of the personality that is unconscious, primitive, and constantly pleasure-seeking

ideal norm a standard requiring strict obedience to the guidelines provided

ideal type a simplified description of some phenomenon based on an analysis of concrete examples, emphasizing those characteristics that best help us to understand its essential nature

identification a process by which an individual incorporates another person's values, standards, and expectations into his or her own behavior and sense of self

ideology a system of beliefs and principles that presents an organized explanation of and the justification for a group's outlooks and behavior

implicit norm a standard that normally is not discussed and is not easily stated

impression management the attempt to control others' evaluations by presenting oneself in the most favorable light

incest taboo a rule outlawing sexual relations between kin-group members believed to be too closely related as defined by the cultural standards of a given society

income people's earnings obtained through wages, salaries, business profits, stock dividends, and other means

independent variable a variable that influences another variable — the dependent variable

individual racism open, intentional racist behavior — for example, verbal or physical abuse

industrial stage (of the demographic-transition theory) the third stage, characterized by a low death rate and dropping birth rate, which occurs as nations stabilize their populations in the course of industrialization

informal social control unofficial pressure intended to convince potential deviants to conform to social norms

in-group any group characterized by a strong sense of identification and loyalty and by the exclusion of nonmembers

in-migration rate the number of people per 1000 members of the population moving into an area in a given year

innovation according to Merton, a deviant adaptation that develops when a person seeks legitimate goals but is blocked from effectively using culturally accepted means to achieve them

instincts unalterable behavior complexes that parents transmit genetically to their children

institution a system of statuses, roles, groups, and behavioral patterns that satisfies a basic human need and is necessary for the survival of a society

institutional racism the subordination of members of a race by means indirectly related to race instead of by race itself

instrumental intended to promote the pursuit of group goals

interest group a group whose members seek to influence elected politicians or government bureaucrats to initiate the legislation or policies they want

intergenerational mobility a comparison of a parent's and a child's social-class positions

internalized through socialization, social expectations that become part of the personality structure

interview a type of survey composed of questions that are delivered face-to-face or over the telephone

intragenerational mobility an analysis of an individual's occupational changes in the course of a lifetime

invention a combination of known components to produce something new

kinship system a number of people related by common descent, marriage, or adoption

laissez-faire leader a leader who does not take an active role in group discussions, leaving group members free to reach individual or group decisions

language a system of symbolic communication that uses words, which are sound patterns that have standardized meanings

latent function a function that is not intended and that often goes unrecognized by members of the group producing it

law a norm that is recorded by political authorities and supported by police or other enforcement officials

leadership the exercise of influence or authority within a group by one or more members

legal-rational system of authority according

to Weber, a system of authority based on laws enacted to produce rational behavior and the achievement of formally designated goals

linguistic-relativity hypothesis the contention that the unique grammatical forms of a language actually shape the thoughts and perceptions of its users

lobbying a face-to-face effort to persuade legislators and other government personnel to support the proposals of an interest group

looking-glass self according to Charles Cooley, our understanding of what sort of person we are is based on how we imagine we appear to other people

macro-order the large-scale structures and activities that exist within societies and even between one society and another

manifest function a function that is intended and openly recognized by members of the group producing it

mass hysteria a type of panic that occurs when people are scattered over a wide geographical area

mass media the instruments of communication that reach a large audience without any personal contact between the senders and the receivers

matriarchal a type of family in which the wife–mother is the formal head and the absolute or nearly absolute source of power

matrilocal a type of residence that involves settling with or near the wife's parents

medical sociology the study of the social setting in which health, sickness, and health care occur

medicine the scientifically based practice concerned with the prevention and treatment of disease and the treatment of injury

megalopolis a string of closely bound metropolitan areas

membership group a group to which an individual belongs

methodology the set of principles and procedures that guides sociological research

metropolis a territorial unit composed of a large central city and the surrounding cities and towns

micro-order the structure and activity of small groups

migration the flow of people in and out of a particular territory (city, region, or country)

minority group any category of people with recognizable racial or ethnic traits that place it in a position of inferior status so that its members suffer limited opportunities and rewards

mob a crowd whose members engage in destructive and aggressive behavior in the pursuit of a short-term but valued goal

monogamy a marriage practice in which there is one husband and one wife

mores norms people consider vital

mortification process a series of degradations and humiliations of inhabitants systematically carried out by staff members of total institutions

multinational a large corporation with production plants and distribution centers in many countries

natural environment the combination of land, climate, water, air, mineral resources, and plant and animal life that together compose the physical world where people live

natural sciences older sciences such as astronomy, biology, chemistry, and physics that study the physical world

nature inborn biological characteristics or heredity

neolocal a type of residence that occurs when married people establish an independent place to live

net migration rate the difference between the in-migration rate and the out-migration rate

nonparticipant observation a method of observation in which an investigator examines a group process without taking part in the group activities

norm a standard of desirable behavior; the rules people are expected to follow in their relations with each other.

nuclear family a two-generation family that includes a father, a mother, and their children living separately from other relatives

nurture socialization

object permanence according to Jean Piaget, the childhood recognition that specific objects still exist after they are removed from one's line of vision.

objective definition of social class a measuring technique that uses certain quantifiable factors — income, occupational prestige rank, or level of education, for example — as the basis for determining an individual's social-class position

objectivity   the ability to evaluate reality without using personal opinions and biases

organized skepticism   according to Merton, the conclusion that no scientist's contribution to knowledge can be accepted without careful scrutiny

out-group   people who do not belong to an in-group; outsiders who are viewed with hostility and even contempt by the in-group members

out-migration rate   the number of people per 1000 members of the population moving out of an area in a given year

panic   a collective flight to safety

participant observation   a method of observation in which an investigator becomes involved in the activities of the group being studied

patriarchal   a type of family in which the husband – father is the formal head and the absolute or nearly absolute source of power

patrilocal   a type of residence that requires settling with or near the husband's parents

patronage   distribution of favors to political supporters

permissiveness with affection   a standard arguing that men and women who love each other and have a stable relationship have the right to express their feelings sexually

permissiveness without affection   a position contending that women and men should feel free to have sexual relations whether or not there is commitment or affection between them

play   according to George Herbert Mead, the process of taking the role of specific individuals and thereby starting to learn the rights and obligations their particular roles entail

pluralism   a theory which emphasizes that a dispersion of authority exists in American government

political institution   the system of norms and roles that concerns the use and distribution of authority within a given society

political machine   an organization established to control a city, county, or state government

polyandry   the form of polygamy in which a woman has two or more husbands

polygamy   a marriage practice in which a person has two or more spouses of the other sex

polygyny   the form of polygamy in which a man has two or more wives

population (for research)   the entire category of people possessing the characteristics that interest a researcher undertaking a particular study

population (people)   all the people who live within a specified geographic area — such as a nation, a region, or a city

power   the ability of an individual or group to implement wishes or policies, with or without the cooperation of others

power-elite perspective   a theory emphasizing that in American society a group of high-status people — well-educated, often wealthy, and placed in high occupational positions — control the political process, including political authorities

preindustrial stage (of the demographic-transition theory)   the first stage, which existed before industrialization and was characterized by a stable population, with both birth and death rates remaining high

prejudice   a highly negative judgment toward a group, focusing on one or more negative characteristics that are supposedly uniformly shared by all group members

prestige   possession of attributes that elicit recognition, respect, and some degree of deference

primary deviance   violation of a social rule but the individuals in question are not labeled and so do not see themselves as deviant

primary group   a group in which relationships are usually stable over long periods of time, members are able to expose many facets of their personality, and a strong sense of affection and identity develops

principle of *verstehen*   Max Weber's concept that involves an effort to grasp the relationship between individuals' feelings and thoughts, and their actions

privilege system   a framework for inmates' resocialization

profane   anything that people consider ordinary and closely linked to practical demands

proletariat   the class of modern wage laborers who possess no means of production and thus must sell their own labor in order to survive

questionnaire   a type of survey in which a respondent writes the answers to a list of questions

race   distinct physical characteristics, such as skin color and certain facial features, used to divide people into broad categories

racial group   a number of people with the particular physical characteristics, such as skin color and certain facial features, that produce placement into a broad category

racism   the ideology contending that actual or alleged differences between different racial groups assert the superiority of one racial group; a rationalization for political, economic, and social discrimination

random sample   a sample drawn from a population by a process that assures that every individual in that population has an equal probability of being included

real norm   an adjusted standard reflecting the practical conditions of living

rebellion   according to Merton, a deviant adaptation displayed when a person decides that the existing society imposes barriers preventing the achievement of success goals. Therefore that individual strikes out against the society, seeking to change its goals and also the existing means for achieving them

reference group   a group whose standards a person uses to help shape his or her own values, beliefs, and behavior

relative wealth   the value of an individual's economic assets compared to the assets possessed by other citizens in that society

reliability   consistency in measurement

religion   a unified system of beliefs and practices that focuses on sacred things and serves to create a community of worshippers

replication   a repetition or near-repetition of an earlier study to determine the accuracy of its findings

reputational definition of social class   a measuring technique in which researchers use batteries of resident experts from the community to assess their neighbors' social-class position

resource-mobilization theory   a perspective that focuses on the process by which the members of social movements acquire and use certain resources necessary to accomplish their collective goals

retreatism   according to Merton, a deviant adaptation in which an individual neither pursues the culturally prescribed goal of success nor uses the means for achieving this goal because of limited opportunities or a sense of personal inadequacy

riot   aggressive, destructive crowd behavior that is less focused or unified than mob activity

ritualism   according to Merton, a behavioral pattern that occurs when culturally prescribed success goals are no longer actively sought, but the legitimate means for achieving those goals are conscientiously pursued

role   a set of expected behaviors associated with a particular status

role conflict   an incompatibility between two or more roles associated with different statuses

role strain   an incompatibility between two or more roles associated with the same status

rumor   a report transmitted informally (often by word of mouth) and concerned with subject matter difficult to verify

sacred   anything that is superior in power, is set apart from the ordinary and practical, and creates a sense of awe

sample   a limited number of individuals chosen from a population for the purpose of conducting research

scapegoat theory   an explanation for prejudice emphasizing that people blocked from achieving a goal will sometimes be unable or unwilling to take out their frustration on its source, and so they direct their aggression against an accessible individual or group

science   a systematic effort to develop general principles about a particular subject matter, based on actual observations and stated in a form that can be tested by any competent person

secondary analysis   a study using data banks available to researchers but produced by other individuals and organizations for their own purposes

secondary deviance   violation of a social norm in which authorities label individuals deviants and the individuals accept the status of deviant

secondary group   a group of people who cooperate with each other for specific, practical reasons and maintain few, if any, strong emotional ties within the group

secularization   the process by which religion loses influence within groups and societies

self   one's perception of his or her own person, formed as a result of other people's response in the course of socialization

self-fulfilling prophecy   an incorrect definition

of a situation that comes to pass because people accept the incorrect definition and act on it to make it become true

sex the division of a variety of animals forms, including human beings, into the biological categories of male and female

sexism an ideology emphasizing that actual or alleged differences between men and women establish the superiority of men. Sexism is a rationalization for political, economic, and social discrimination against women

sign an object or event that stands for something else

social category a number of people who have one or more social characteristics in common

social change modifications in culture, social organization, and social behavior

social class a large category of people who are similar in income level, educational attainment, and occupational prestige-ranking

social control the application of systematic behavioral restraints intended to motivate people to obey social expectations

social distance the feeling of separation between individuals or groups

social interaction the basic process through which two or more people use language and gestures to affect each other's thoughts, expectations, and behavior

social mobility the movement of a person from one social class or status level to another

social movement an organized, collective activity undertaken by people to promote or resist social change

social sciences the sciences that focus on various aspects of human behavior

social stratification structured inequality of access to rewards, resources, and privileges that are scarce and desirable within a society

socialism an economic system with collective ownership of the means for the production and distribution of goods and services

socialization the process by which a person becomes a social being, learning the necessary cultural content and behavior to become a member of a group or society

society the interacting people who share a culture

sociobiology a field in which the proponents contend that through the evolutionary process, human beings have acquired tendencies that determine much of their behavior

sociological theory a combination of observations and insights that offers a systematic explanation of social life

sociology the scientific study of human behavior in groups and of the social forces that influence that behavior

status a position that indicates where a person fits into a group or society and how that person should relate to others in the structure

stereotype an exaggerated, oversimplified image, maintained by prejudiced people, of the characteristics of the group members against whom they are prejudiced

structural-functional theory a theory suggesting that groups in interaction tend to influence and adjust to one another in a fairly stable, conflict-free pattern

subculture the culture of a specific segment of people within a society, differing from the dominant culture in some significant respects

subjective definition of social class a measuring technique that requires people to indicate the social class to which they belong

suburb a politically independent municipality that develops next to or in the vicinity of a city

superego according to Sigmund Freud, the part of the personality that has internalized standards of right and wrong; a conscience

survey a research technique that uses carefully constructed questions to obtain a variety of facts about people's thoughts and behavior

symbol an object or event whose meaning is fixed not by the nature of the item to which it is attached but by the agreement of the people who use it in communication

symbolic-interaction theory a theory that emphasizes the importance of symbolic communication—the use of gestures and above all language—in the development of the individual, group, and society

technology any repeated operation people use to manipulate the environment to achieve some practical goals

total institution a place of residence where inhabitants experience nearly complete restriction of their physical freedom in order to be effectively resocialized into a radically new identity and behavioral pattern

traditional system of authority according to Weber, an authority system in which the standard of political leadership passes down from one generation to another

transition stage (of the demographic-transition theory) the second stage, in which a decline in the death rate and a continuing high birth rate produced a rapid growth in population

universalism according to Merton, a norm stating that all scientific claims of truth need to be evaluated by impersonal criteria consistent with existing knowledge in that field

urbanization the process by which a city forms and develops

validity the condition in which a research item accurately measures what it claims to measure

value a general conviction about what is good or bad, right or wrong, appropriate or inappropriate

variable a factor that has two or more categories or measurable conditions

vicious cycle of poverty a pattern in which the parents' minimal income significantly limits the educational and occupational pursuits of the children, thereby keeping them locked into the same low economic status

victimless crime the willing (hence "victimless") exchange among adults of strongly desired but illegal goods or services

wealth people's economic assets—their cars, homes, stocks, bonds, and real estate—that can be converted into cash

white-collar crime crime committed by people of higher socioeconomic status in the course of their business activities

work alienation the loss of control over the process of one's labor, with the resulting dissatisfaction primarily caused by overly close supervision, highly routine tasks, and an overall simplicity to one's job

zero population growth a situation in which the population size stabilizes

REFERENCES

Chapter 1

Allen, Michael Patrick, and Philip Broyles. 1989. "Class Hegemony and Political Finance." *American Sociological Review* 54 (April): 275–287.

Bernstein, Richard. 1988. "Sociology Branches Out But is Left in Splinters." *New York Times* (August 30): A14.

Blumer, Herbert. 1969. *Symbolic Interactionism: Perspective and Method*. Englewood Cliffs, NJ: Prentice-Hall.

Butterfield, Fox. 1989. "A Boy Who Killed Coldly Is Now a 'Prison Monster.'" *New York Times* (March 22): A1+.

Chass, Murray. 1989. "Clubs Dip into Minor Leagues in Search for Good Starters." *New York Times* (June 11): Sec. 8, p. 3.

Dahrendorf, Ralf. 1959. *Class and Class Conflict in Industrial Society*. Stanford, CA: Stanford University Press.

Friedrich, Otto. 1983. "The Computer Moves In." *Time* 121 (January 3): 14–18+.

Gans, Herbert J. 1989. "Sociology in America: The Discipline and the Public." *American Sociological Review* 54 (February): 1–16.

Gouldner, Alvin. 1970. *The Coming Crisis of Western Sociology*. New York: Equinox Books.

Hallinan, Maureen T., and Richard A. Williams. 1989. "Interracial Friendship Choices in Secondary Schools." *American Sociological Review* 54 (February): 67–78.

Horowitz, Irving Louis (ed.). 1964. *The New Sociology*. New York: Oxford University Press.

Lyman, Stanford M. 1988. "Symbolic Interactionism and Macrosociology." *Sociological Forum* 3 (Spring): 295–301.

Merton, Robert K. 1968. *Social Theory and Social Structure*. New York: The Free Press. Third edition.

Mills, C. Wright. 1956. *The Power Elite*. New York: Oxford University Press.

Mills, C. Wright. 1959. *The Sociological Imagination*. New York: Oxford University Press.

Schell, Jonathan. 1982. *The Fate of the Earth*. New York: Alfred A. Knopf.

Toffler, Alvin. 1981. *The Third Wave*. New York: Bantam Books.

Whyte, William Foote. 1955. *Street Corner Society*. Chicago: University of Chicago Press. Revised edition.

Chapter 2

Bandura, Albert, et al. 1963. "Imitation of Film-Mediated Aggressive Models." *Journal of Abnormal and Social Psychology* 66: 3–11.

Baumrind, Diana. 1964. "Some Thoughts on Ethics of Research: After Reading Milgram's 'Behavioral Study of Obedience.'" *American Psychologist* 19 (June): 421–423.

Berg, Ellen. 1986. "Sociological Perspectives on AIDS. *Footnotes* 14 (December): 8–9.

Berg, Ellen. 1988. "Reach Out and Touch Someone: A Report on AIDS." *Footnotes* 16 (April): 4.

Card, Josefina J. 1989. "Facilitating Data Sharing." *Footnotes* 17 (January): 8.

Cole, Stephen. 1980. *The Sociological Method*. Chicago: Rand McNally. Third edition.

Doob, Christopher Bates. 1970. "Family Background and Peer Group Development in a Puerto Rican District." *Sociological Quarterly* 11 (Fall): 523–532.

Footnotes. 1989. "NIAAA Funds Sociologists, Seeks Proposals on Alcohol and AIDS." 17 (February): 5.

Freeman, Derek. 1983. *Margaret Mead and Samoa*. Cambridge, MA: Harvard University Press.

Gallup, George. 1972. *The Sophisticated Poll Watcher's Guide*. Princeton: Princeton Opinion Press.

Hallowell, Lyle. 1985. "The Outcome of the Brajuha Case: Legal Implications for Sociologists." *Footnotes* 13 (December): 1+.

Humphrey, Ronald. 1985. "How Work Roles Influence Perception: Structural-Cognitive Processes and Organizational Behavior." *American Sociological Review* 50 (April): 242–252.

Melton, Gary B., and Joni N. Gray. 1988. "Ethical Dilemmas in AIDS Research." *American Psychologist* 43 (January): 60–64.

Leo, John. 1983. "Bursting the South Sea Bubble." *Time* 121 (February 14): 68–70.

Marshall, Eliot. 1983. "A Controversy on Samoa Comes of Age." *Science* 219 (March): 1042–1045.

Milgram, Stanley. 1963. "Behavioral Study of Obedience." *Journal of Abnormal and Social Psychology* 67: 371–378.

Milgram, Stanley. 1974. *Obedience to Authority*. New York: Harper & Row.

Okraku, Ishmael O. 1987. "Age and Attitudes toward Multigenerational Residence, 1973 to 1983." *Journal of Gerontology* 42 (May): 280–287.

Rank, Mark R. 1989. "Fertility among Women on

Welfare: Incidence and Determinants." *American Sociological Review* 54 (April): 296–304.

Sennett, Richard. 1974. *Families against the City.* New York: Vintage Books.

Sieber, Joan E., and Barbara Stanley. 1988. "Ethical and Professional Dimensions of Socially Sensitive Research." *American Psychologist* 43 (January): 49–55.

Wilford, John Noble. 1983. "Customs Check: Leave Your Ideological Baggage Behind." *New York Times* (February 6): Section 4, p. 8.

Chapter 3

Baumeister, Roy F. 1984. "Choking under Pressure: Self-Consciousness and Paradoxical Effects of Incentives on Skillful Performance." *Journal of Personality and Social Psychology* 46 (March): 610–620.

Bellah, Robert N., Richard Madsen, William M. Sullivan, Ann Swidler, and Steven M. Tipton. 1986. *Habits of the Heart: Individualism and Commitment in American Life.* New York: Harper & Row.

Block, Jeanne Humphrey. 1973. "Conceptions of Sex Role: Some Cross-Cultural and Longitudinal Perspectives." *American Psychologist* 28 (June): 512–526.

Bohannon, Laura. 1975. "Hamlet and the Tiv." *Psychology Today* 9 (July): 62–66.

Brand, Stewart. 1987. *The Media Lab: Inventing the Future at MIT.* New York: Viking Penguin.

Braungart, Richard G., and Margaret M. Braungart. 1988. "From Yippies to Yuppies: Twenty Years of Freshman Attitudes." *Public Opinion* 11 (September/October): 53–56.

Chagnon, Napoleon A. 1977. *Yanamamö: The Fierce People.* New York: Holt, Rinehart and Winston. Second edition.

Devine, John. 1985. "The Versatility of Human Locomotion." *American Anthropologist* 87 (September): 550–574.

Geer, Blanche. 1964. "First Days in the Field," pp. 322–345 in Phillip E. Hammond (ed.), *Sociologists at Work.* New York: Basic Books.

Gitlin, Todd, and Ruth Rosen. 1987. "Give the 60's Generation a Break." *New York Times* (November 14): 27.

Harris, Marvin. 1974. *Cows, Pigs, Wars and Witches.* New York: Random House.

Hoffman, Curt, Ivy Lau, and David Randy Johnson. 1986. "The Linguistic Relativity of Person Cognition: An English–Chinese Comparison." *Journal of Personality and Social Psychology* 51 (December): 1097–1105.

Malinowski, Bronislaw. 1922. *Argonauts of the Western Pacific.* London: Routledge & Kegan Paul.

Molotch, Harvey, and Serena Vicari. 1988. "Three Ways to Build the Development Process in the United States, Japan, and Italy." *Urban Affairs Quarterly* 24 (December): 188–214.

Morgan, Lewis H. 1964. *Ancient Society.* Cambridge, MA: Belknap Press. Originally published in 1877.

Murdock, George P. 1965. *Culture and Society.* Pittsburgh, PA: University of Pittsburgh Press.

Popkin, Samuel. 1988. "Optimism, Pessimism, and Policy." *Public Opinion* 11 (November/December): 51–55.

Rimer, Sara. 1985. "Poll Sees Landslide for Santa: Of U.S. Children, 87% Believe." *New York Times* (December 24): 1+.

Ryan, William. 1976. *Blaming the Victim.* New York: Vintage Books. Revised edition.

Sapir, Edward. 1921. *Language: An Introduction to the Study of Speech.* New York: Harcourt, Brace and World.

Sapir, Edward. 1929. "The Status of Linguistics As a Science." *Language* 5:207–214.

Shannon, William V. 1966. *The American Irish.* New York: Macmillan. Revised edition.

Slomczynski, Kazimierz, et al. 1981. "Stratification, Work, and Values: A Polish–American Comparison." *American Sociological Review* 46 (December): 720–744.

Waegel, William B. 1984. "How Police Justify the Use of Deadly Force." *Social Problems* 32 (December): 144–155.

Weisskopf, Michael. 1982. "French Wine Venture in China in a Ferment. *International Herald Tribune* (June 1): 6.

Weissman, Diane, and Adrian Furnham. 1987. "The Expectations and Experiences of a Sojourning Temporary Resident Abroad: A Preliminary Study." *Human Relations* 40 (May): 313–326.

Whorf, Benjamin L. 1956. *Language, Thought, and Reality.* New York: John Wiley and Sons.

Whyte, William Foote. 1955. *The Organization Man* Chicago: University of Chicago Press. Revised edition.

Williams, Robin M., Jr. 1970. *American Society.* New York: Alfred A. Knopf. Third edition.

Xinhua News Service. 1987. "Joint Wine Venture Extends Contract." June.

Chapter 4

Abramovitch, Rona, et al. 1986. "Sibling and Peer Interaction: A Final Follow-up and a Comparison." *Child Development* 57 (February): 217–229.

Applebaum, Herbert A. 1982. "Traditional versus Bureaucratic Methods." *Anthropological Quarterly* 55 (October): 224–234.

Barrett, Mark E., D. Dwayne Simpson, and Wayne E. K. Lehman. 1988. "Behavioral Changes of Adolescents in Drug Abuse Intervention Programs." *Journal of Clinical Psychology* 44 (May): 461–473.

532

Bellah, Robert N., et al. 1986. *Habits of the Heart: Individualism and Commitment in American Life.* New York: Harper & Row.

Blau, Peter M., and W. Richard Scott. 1963. *Formal Organizations.* London: Routledge & Kegan Paul.

Bluth, B. J. 1985. "Pilots of Outer Space." *Society* 21 (January): 31–36.

Braungart, Richard G., and Margaret M. Braungart. 1988. "From Yippies to Yuppies: Twenty Years of Freshman Attitudes." *Public Opinion* 11 (September/October: 53–56.

Burns, Tom. 1980. "Sovereignty, Interests and Bureaucracy in the Modern State." *British Journal of Sociology* 31 (December): 491–506.

Byron, Christopher. 1981. "How Japan Does It." *Time* 117 (March 30): 54–60.

Cooley, Charles Horton. 1962. *Social Organization.* New York: Schocken Books. Originally published in New York: Charles Scribner's Sons, 1909.

Coutu, D. L. 1981. "Consensus in San Diego." *Time* 117 (March 30): 58.

Dyer, Gwynne. 1985. *War.* New York: Crown Publishers.

Gerth, Hans, and C. Wright Mills (eds.). 1946. *From Max Weber: Essays in Sociology.* New York: Oxford University Press.

Gilbert, Richard Karmen. 1988. "The Dynamics of Inaction: Psychological Factors Inhibiting Arms Control Activism." *American Psychologist* 43 (October): 755–764.

Granberg, Donald, N. Lyneel Jefferson, Edward E. Brent, Jr. and Michael King. 1981. "Membership Group, Reference Group, and the Attribution of Attitudes to Groups." *Journal of Personality and Social Psychology* 41 (October): 833–842.

Grey, Andrew. 1988. "Bureaucracy and Political Power." *Political Studies* 36 (March): 131–134.

Halloran, Richard. 1988. "Skipper Defended." *New York Times* (July 4): A1+.

Janis, Irving L. 1972. *Victims of Groupthink.* Boston: Houghton Mifflin Company.

Kohn, Melvin L. 1971. "Bureaucratic Man: A Portrait and an Interpretation." *American Sociological Review* 36 (June): 461–474.

Krause, Elliot. 1980. *Why Study Sociology?* New York: Random House.

Leonard, Wilbert Marcellus. 1980. *A Sociological Perspective of Sport.* Minneapolis: Burgess Publishing.

Liddell, Christine, S. Peter Henzi, and Merrill Drew. 1987. "Mothers, Fathers, and Children in an Urban Park Playground: A Comparison of Dyads and Triads." *Developmental Psychology* 23 (March): 262–266.

Mann, Thomas. 1955. *Confessions of Felix Krull, Confidence Man.* New York: Alfred A. Knopf.

Meindl, James R., and Melvin J. Lerner. 1984. "Exacerbation of Extreme Responses to an Out-Group." *Journal of Personality and Social Psychology* 47 (July): 71–84.

Merton, Robert K. 1968. *Social Theory and Social Structure.* New York: Free Press. Third edition.

Michener, James A. 1976. *Sports in America.* New York: Random House.

Mosbach, Peter, and Howard Leventhal. 1988. "Peer Group Identification and Smoking: Implications for Intervention." *Journal of Abnormal Psychology* 97 (May): 238–245.

Mowat, Farley. 1965. *Never Cry Wolf.* New York: Dell.

Newcomb, Theodore M., et al. 1967. *Persistence and Change: Bennington College and Its Students after 25 Years.* New York: Wiley.

Ng, Sik Hung, and Fiona Cram. 1988. "Intergroup Bias by Defensive and Offensive Groups in Majority and Minority Conditions." *Journal of Personality and Social Psychology* 55 (November): 749–757.

Ouchi, William. 1981. *Theory Z: How American Business Can Meet the Japanese Challenge.* Reading, MA: Addison-Wesley.

Pagan, Rafael D., Jr. 1989. "A New Era of Activism." *Futurist* 23 (May/June): 12–16.

Peter, Lawrence J., and Raymond Hull. 1969. *The Peter Principle.* New York: William Morrow.

Roethlisberger, Fritz J., and William J. Dickson. 1939. *Management and the Worker.* Cambridge, MA: Harvard University Press.

Scott, William A., and Ruth Scott. 1981. "Intercorrelations among Structural Properties of Primary Groups." *Journal of Personality and Social Psychology* 41 (April): 279–292.

Sherif, Muzafer, and Carolyn W. Sherif. 1956. *An Outline of Social Psychology.* New York: Harper & Brothers. Revised edition.

Sjoberg, Gideon, Ted R. Vaughan, and Norma Williams. 1984. "Bureaucracy As a Moral Issue." *Journal of Applied Behavioral Science* 20: 441–453.

Slater, Philip. 1976. *The Pursuit of Loneliness.* Boston: Beacon Press. Revised edition.

Smith, Douglas A., and Craig D. Uchida. 1988. "The Social Organization of Self-Help: A Study of Defensive Weapon Ownership." *American Sociological Review* 53 (February): 94–102.

Stasser, Garold, and William Titus. 1985. "Pooling of Unshared Information in Group Decision Making: Biased Information Sampling during Discussion." *Journal of Personality and Social Psychology* 48 (June): 1467–1478.

Stouffer, Samuel A., et al. 1949. *The American Soldier: Combat and Its Aftermath.* Volume II. Princeton: Princeton University Press.

Sumner, William Graham. 1906. *Folkways.* Boston: Ginn and Company.

Suzuki, Takahiro. 1988. "A Hollow Future for Japan?" *Futurist* 22 (May/June): 33.

Warren, Mark. 1988. "Max Weber's Liberalism for a Nietzchean World." *American Political Science Review* 82 (March): 31–50.

Werner, Carol, and Pat Parmelee. 1979. "Similarity of Activity Preferences among Friends: Those Who Play Together Stay Together." *Social Psychology Quarterly* 42 (March): 62–66.

Wood, B. Dan. 1988. "Principals, Bureaucrats, and Responsiveness in Clean Air Enforcements." *American Political Science Review* 82 (March): 213–234.

Wright, Sara E., and Paul C. Rosenblatt. 1987. "Isolation and Farm Loss: Why Neighbors May Not Be Supportive." *Family Relations* 36 (October): 391–395.

Chapter 5

American Broadcasting Company. 1988. "Remembering Marilyn" (a television program): May 8.

Asch, Solomon E. 1963. "Effects of Group Pressure upon the Modification and Distortion of Judgments," pp. 177–190 in Harold Geutzkow (ed.), *Group, Leadership and Men.* New York: Russell and Russell.

Bales, Robert F. 1953. "The Equilibrium Problem in Small Groups," pp. 111–161 in Talcott Parsons, Robert Bales, and Edward A. Shils (eds.), *Working Papers in the Theory of Action.* Glencoe, IL: Free Press.

Bales, Robert F., and Philip E. Slater. 1955. "Role Differentiation in Small Decision-Making Groups," pp. 259–306 in Talcott Parsons, Robert F. Bales, et al., *Family, Socialization and Interaction Process.* Glencoe, IL: Free Press.

Bales, Robert F., and Fred L. Strodtbeck. 1968. "Phases in Group Problem-Solving," pp. 389–398 in Dorwin Cartwright and Alvin Zander (eds.), *Group Dynamics.* New York: Harper & Row.

Berkowitz, Leonard. 1980. *A Survey of Social Psychology.* New York: Holt, Rinehart and Winston. Second edition.

Bettelheim, Bruno. 1958. "Individual and Mass Behavior in Extreme Situations," pp. 300–310 in Eleanor E. Maccoby, Theodore M. Newcomb, and Eugene L. Hartley (eds.), *Readings in Social Psychology.* New York: Holt, Rinehart and Winston. Third edition.

Beutell, Nicholas J., and Marianne M. O'Hare. 1987. "Coping with Role Conflict among Returning Students: Professional versus Nonprofessional Women." *Journal of College Student Personnel* 28 (March): 141–145.

Bialer, Seweryn. 1988. "Gorbachev's Program of Change: Sources, Significance, Prospects." *Political Science Quarterly* 103 (Fall): 403–460.

Blumer, Herbert. 1969. *Symbolic Interactionism: Perspective and Method.* Englewood Cliffs, NJ: Prentice-Hall.

Brosius, J. Peter. 1988. "Significance and Social Being in Ifugao Agricultural Production." *Ethnology* 27 (January): 97–110.

Brown, Clifton. 1989. "Changing Team Chemistry Adds Risk to Equation." *New York Times* (March 5): Section 8, p. 1+.

Bruce, Steve, and Roy Wallis. 1983. "Rescuing Motives." *British Journal of Sociology* 34 (March): 61–70.

Bryman, Alan, et al. 1988. "Qualitative Research and the Study of Leadership." *Human Relations* 41 (January): 13–29.

Burden, Dianne S. 1986. "Single Parents and Work Setting: The Impact of Multiple Job and Homelife Responsibilities." *Family Relations* 35 (January): 37–43.

Caton, Steven C. 1985. "The Poetic Construction of Self." *Anthropological Quarterly* 58 (October): 141–151.

Cohen, Michele, and Jean-Yves Jaffray. 1988. "Is Savage's Axiom a Universal Rationality Principle?" *Behavioral Science* 33 (January): 38–47.

de Vries, Manfred F. R. Kets. 1988. "Prisoners of Leadership." *Human Relations* 41 (March): 261–280.

Dowd, Maureen. 1988. "The Star Is a Smash in the Street Scenes." *New York Times* (December 8): A1+.

Farber, R. S. 1988. "Integrated Treatment of the Dual-Career Couple." *American Journal of Family Therapy* 16 (Spring): 46–57.

Fiedler, Fred E. 1967. *A Theory of Leadership Effectiveness.* New York: McGraw-Hill.

Fort, Karen Orendurff. 1989. "Bringing Up Father," pp. 79–82 in Kurt Finsterbusch (ed.), *Sociology 89/90.* Guilford, CT: Dushkin.

Frankl, Viktor E. 1959. *Man's Search for Meaning.* Boston: Beacon Press. Translated by Ilse Lasch.

Frost, Dean E., Fred E. Fiedler, and Jeff W. Anderson. 1983. "The Role of Personal Risk-Taking in Effective Leadership." *Human Relations* 36 (February): 185–202.

Garfinkel, Harold. 1967. *Studies in Ethnomethodology.* Englewood Cliffs, NJ: Prentice-Hall.

Garfinkel, Harold. 1988. "Evidence for Locally Produced, Naturally Accountable Phenomena of Order, Logic, Reason, Meaning, Method, etc., in and as of the Essential Quiddity of Immortal Ordinary Society (I of IV): *An Announcement of Studies.*" *Sociological Theory* 6 (Spring): 103–109.

Gedye, G. E. 1939. *Fallen Bastions.* London: Victor Gollancz.

Goffman, Erving. 1959. *The Presentation of Self in Everyday Life.* New York: Doubleday.

Goffman, Erving. 1961. *Encounters.* Indianapolis: Bobbs-Merrill.

Hockenberry, Stewart L., and Robert E. Billingham. 1987. "Sexual Orientation and Boyhood Gender Conformity: Development of the Boyhood Gender Conformity Scale." *Archives of Sexual Behavior* 16 (December): 475–492.

534

Hoffman, L. Richard. 1979. "Applying Experimental Research on Group Problem Solving to Organizations." *Journal of Applied Behavioral Science* 15 (3): 375–391.

Holloway, David. 1989. "Gorbachev's New Thinking." *Foreign Affairs* 68 (1): 66–81.

Hughes, Everett C. 1968. "Good People and Dirty Work," pp. 596–607 in Robert Perrucci and Marc Pilisuk (eds.), *The Triple Revolution*. Boston: Little, Brown and Company.

Hurley, John D., and Susan R. Meminger. 1987. "The Relationship among Negative Attributions, Conformity, and Modeling Behavior." *Journal of Clinical Psychology* 43 (July): 360–365.

Jennings, Luther B., and Stephen G. George. 1984. "Group-Induced Distortion of Visually Perceived Linear Extent: The Asch Effect Revisited." *Psychological Record* 34 (Winter): 133–148.

Kelly, Robert F., and Patricia Voydanoff. 1985. "Work/Family Role Strain among Employed Parents." *Family Relations* 34 (July): 367–374.

McGlashan, Charles Fayette. 1879. *History of the Donner Party*. Truckee, CA: Crowley and McGlashan.

McLaughlin, Mike, et al. 1988. "Relation between Coping Strategies and Distress, Stress, and Marital Adjustment of Multiple-Role Women." *Journal of Counseling Psychology* 35 (April): 187–193.

Manz, Charles C., and Henry P. Sims, Jr. 1984. "Searching for the 'Unleader': Organizational Member Views on Leading Self-Managed Groups." *Human Relations* 37 (May): 409–424.

Orwell, George. 1959. *Down and Out in London and Paris*. New York: Berkley Medallion Books. Originally published in 1933.

Ravlin, Elizabeth C., and Bruce M. Meglino. 1987. "Effect of Values on Perception and Decision Making: A Study of Alternative Work Value Measures." *Journal of Applied Psychology* 72 (November): 666–673.

Riedmann, Agnes. 1988. "Ex-Wife at the Funeral: Keyed Anti-Structure." *Free Inquiry in Creative Sociology* 16 (May): 123–129.

Russell, Joyce E. A., Michael C. Rush, and Ann M. Herd. 1988. "An Exploration of Women's Expectations of Effective Male and Female Leadership." *Sex Roles* 18 (March): 279–287.

Schachter, Stanley. 1959. *The Psychology of Affiliation*. Stanford, CA: Stanford University Press.

Schafer, Robert B., and Patricia M. Keith. 1985. "A Causal Model Approach to the Symbolic Interactionist View of the Self-Concept." *Journal of Personality and Social Psychology* 48 (April): 963–969.

Scheff, Thomas J. 1988. "Shame and Conformity: The Difference-Emotion System." *American Sociological Review* 53 (June): 395–406.

Schofield Michael. 1989. "Exercises in Diplomacy." *Futurist* 23 (March/April): 8–11.

Sharrock, W. W., and D. R. Watson. 1984. "What's the Point of 'Rescuing Motives'?" *British Journal of Sociology* 35 (September): 435–451.

Smircich, Linda, and Gareth Morgan. 1982. "Leadership: The Management of Meaning." *Journal of Applied Behavioral Science* 18 (3): 257–273.

Soros, George. 1989. "The Gorbachev Prospect." *New York Review of Books* 36 (June 1): 16–18+.

Stolte, John F. 1987. "The Formation of Justice Norms." *American Sociological Review* 52 (December): 774–784.

Stoner, J. A. F. 1961. "A Comparison of Individual and Group Decisions Involving Risk." Unpublished master's thesis, Massachusetts Institute of Technology.

Tjosvold, Dean. 1988. "Effect of Shared Responsibility and Goal Interdependence on Controversy and Decisionmaking between Departments." *Journal of Social Psychology* 128 (February): 7–18.

Wiley, Donna L. 1987. "The Relationship between Work/Nonwork Role Conflict and Job-Related Outcomes: Some Unanticipated Findings." *Journal of Management* 13 (Fall): 467–472.

Chapter 6

Ariès, Phillipe. 1962. *Centuries of Childhood: A Social History of Family Life*. New York: Vintage Books. Translated by Robert Baldick.

Axline, Virginia M. 1968. *Dibs: In Search of Self*. New York: Ballantine Books.

Azmitia, Margarita. 1988. "Peer Interaction and Problem Solving: When Are Two Heads Better than One?" *Child Development* 59 (February): 87–96.

Balkin, Joseph. 1987. "Contributions of Friends to Women's Fear of Success in College." *Psychological Reports* 61 (August): 39–42.

Baron, James N., and Peter C. Reiss. 1985. "Mass Media and Violent Behavior." *American Sociological Review* 50 (June): 347–363.

Baron, Pierre, and Elisabeth Joly. 1988. "Sex Differences in the Expression of Depression in Adolescents." *Sex Roles* 18 (January): 1–7.

Barrett, Mark E., D. Dwayne Simpson, and Wayne E. K. Lehman. 1988. "Behavioral Changes of Adolescents in Drug Abuse Intervention Programs." *Journal of Clinical Psychology* 44 (May): 461–473.

Berger, Brigitte, and Peter L. Berger. 1984. *The War over the Family*. Garden City, NY: Anchor Books.

Berman, William H. 1988. "The Role of Attachment in the Post-Divorce Experience." *Journal of Personality and Social Psychology* 54 (March): 496–503.

Bohannon, Paul (ed.). 1970. *Divorce and After*. Garden City, NY: Doubleday.

Bronfenbrenner, Urie. 1970. *Two Worlds of Childhood*. New York: Russell Sage Foundation.

Cherlin, Andrew. 1983. "Remarriage as an Incomplete Institution," pp. 388–402 in Arlene Skolnick and Jerome H. Skolnick (eds.), *Family in Transition.* Boston: Little, Brown and Company. Fourth Edition.

Coleman, James. 1961. *The Adolescent Society.* New York: Doubleday.

Cooley, Charles Horton. 1964. *Human Nature and the Social Order.* New York: Schocken Books. Originally published in 1902.

Costos, Daryl. 1986. "Sex Role Identity in Young Adults: Its Parental Antecedents and Relation to Ego Development." *Journal of Personality and Social Psychology* 50 (March): 602–611.

Counts, Robert M., and Anita Sacks. 1985. "The Need for Crisis Intervention during Marital Separation." *Social Work* 30 (March/April): 151–158.

Davies, James C. 1987. "Aggression: Some Definition and Some Physiology." *Politics and the Life Sciences* 6 (August): 27–42.

Davis, Kingsley. 1948. *Human Society.* New York: Macmillan.

Davison, Peter, and Jane Davison. 1979. "Coming of Age in America," pp. 52–55 in Phillip Whitten (ed.), *Readings in Sociology.* New York: Harper & Row.

Ellis, Margaret McMahon, and William N. Ellis. 1989. "Cultures in Transition: What the West Can Learn from Developing Countries." *Futurist* 23 (March/April): 22–25.

Flacks, Richard. 1979. "Growing Up Confused," pp. 21–32 in Peter I. Rose (ed.), *Socialization and the Life Cycle.* New York: St. Martin's Press.

Freud, Sigmund. 1952. *A General Introduction to Psychoanalysis.* New York: Washington Square Press. Originally published in 1920. Translated by Joan Riviere.

Gallup, Alec M., and Stanley M. Elam. 1988. "The 20th Annual Gallup Poll of the Public's Attitudes toward Public Schools." *Phi Delta Kappan* 69 (September): 33–46.

Goffman, Erving. 1961. *Asylums.* Garden City, NY: Anchor Books.

Goleman, Daniel. 1987. "Teen-Age Risk-Taking: Rise in Death Prompts New Research Effort." *New York Times* (November 24): C1+.

Gracey, Harry L. 1977. "Learning the Student Role: Kindergarten As Academic Boot Camp," pp. 215–226 in Dennis H. Wrong and Harry L. Gracey (eds.), *Readings in Introductory Sociology.* New York: Macmillan. Third edition.

Halebsky, Mark. 1987. "Adolescent Alcohol and Substance Abuse: Parent and Peer Effects." *Adolescence* 22 (Winter): 961–967.

Harlow, Harry F., and Margaret K. Harlow. 1962. "Social Deprivation in Monkeys." *Scientific American* 207 (November): 137–147.

Harlow, Harry F., and R. R. Zimmerman. 1959. "Affectional Responses in the Infant Monkey." *Science* 130: 421–423.

Hiebert, Ray Eldon, Donald F. Ungurait, and Thomas W. Bohn. 1974. *Mass Media.* New York: David McKay Company.

Hiltz, Starr Roxanne. 1980. "Widowhood: A Roleless Role," pp. 237–253 in Arlene Skolnick and Jerome H. Skolnick (eds.), *Family in Transition.* Boston: Little, Brown and Company. Third edition.

Howes, Carollee. 1988. "Relations between Early Child Care and Schooling." *Developmental Psychology* 24 (January): 53–57.

Hultsch, David F., and Francine Deutsch. 1981. *Adult Development and Aging.* New York: McGraw-Hill.

Iversen, Lars, and Svend Sabroe. 1988. "Psychological Well-Being Among Unemployed and Employed People after a Company Closedown: A Longitudinal Study." *Journal of Social Issues* 44: 141–152.

Kagan, Jerome. 1983. "The Psychological Requirements for Human Development," pp. 409–420 in Arlene Skolnick and Jerome H. Skolnick (eds.), *Family in Transition.* Boston: Little, Brown and Company. Fourth edition.

Kemper, Theodore. 1987. "How Many Emotions Are There? Wedding the Social and Autonomic Components." *American Journal of Sociology* 93 (September): 263–289.

Kessler, Ronald C., J. Blake Turner, and James S. House. 1988. "Effects of Unemployment on Health in a Community Survey: Main, Modifying, and Mediating Effects." *Journal of Social Issues* 44: 69–85.

Kirkendall, Lester. 1968. "Understanding the Problems of the Male Virgin," pp. 123–129 in Isadore Rubin and Lester Kirkendall (eds.), *Sex in the Adolescent Years.* New York: Association.

Kopec, Joseph A. 1984. "The Big Chill." *Vital Speeches* 50 (June 1): 528–530.

Liebert, Robert, and Rita W. Poulos. 1972. "TV for Kiddies—Truth, Goodness, Beauty, and a Little Bit of Brainwash." *Psychology Today* 6 (November): 122–124.

Loether, Herman J. 1975. *Problems of Aging.* Encino, CA: Dickenson. Second edition.

Lopata, Helena Znaniecka. 1988. "Support Systems of American Urban Widowhood." *Journal of Social Issues* 44: 113–128.

McCrae, Robert R., and Paul T. Costa, Jr. 1988. "Psychological Resilience among Widowed Men and Women: A 10-Year Follow-up of a National Sample." *Journal of Social Issues* 44: 129–142.

Main, Mary, and Carol George. 1985. "Responses of Abused and Disadvantaged Toddlers to Distress in Agemates: A Study in the Day Care Setting." *Developmental Psychology* 21 (May): 407–412.

Marcuse, Herbert. 1964. *The One-Dimensional Man.* Boston: Beacon Press.

Marmar, Charles R., et al. 1988. "A Controlled Trial

of Brief Psychotherapy and Mutual-Help Group Treatment of Conjugal Bereavement." *American Journal of Psychiatry* 145 (February): 203–209.

Mavreas, V. G. 1987. "Greece: The Transition to Community Care." *International Journal of Social Psychiatry* 33 (Summer): 154–164.

Mead, George Herbert. 1930. "Cooley's Contribution to American Social Thought." *American Journal of Sociology* 35 (March): 693–706.

Mead, George Herbert. 1934. *Mind, Self and Society.* Chicago: University of Chicago Press.

Mechanic, David. 1987. "Correcting Misconceptions in Mental Health Policy: Strategies for Improved Care of the Seriously Mentally Ill." *Milbank Quarterly* 65: 203–230.

Metcalf, Kaaren, and Eugene L. Gaier. 1987. "Pattern of Middle-Class Parenting and Adolescent Underachievement." *Adolescence* 22 (Winter): 919–928.

Mills, Marlene Christine. 1983. "Adolescents' Self-Disclosure in Individual and Group Theme-Centered Modeling, Reflecting, and Probing Interviews." *Psychological Reports* 53 (December): 691–701.

Molotch, Harvey, and Marilyn Lester. 1975. "Accidental News: The Great Oil Spill As Local Occurrence and National Event." *American Journal of Sociology* (September): 235–260.

Montgomery, Reid H., Jr., and Ellis MacDougall. 1986. "Curing Criminals: The High-Tech Prisons of Tomorrow." *Futurist* 20 (January/February): 36–37.

Moore, Beverly, Charles W. Show, and Michael Poteat. 1988. "Effects of Variant Types of Child Care Experience on the Adaptive Behavior of Kindergarten Children." *American Journal of Orthopsychiatry* 58 (April): 297–303.

Mulder, Monique Borgerhoff. 1987. "On Cultural and Reproductive Success: Kipsigis Evidence." *American Anthropologist* 89 (September): 617–634.

National Commission on the Causes and Prevention of Violence. 1969. *Violence in America: Historical and Comparative Perspectives.* Washington, DC: U.S. Government Printing Office.

Offer, Daniel. 1969. *The Psychological World of the Teenager.* New York: Basic Books.

Papirno, Elissa. 1976. "Life on Hectic Fringe Led to Girl's Death Try." *Hartford Courant* (August 25): 1+.

Parenti, Michael. 1983. "The Moneyed Media." *Economic Notes* 51 (October): 7–12.

Patten, Sylvia B., et al. 1989. "Posttraumatic Stress Disorder and the Treatment of Sexual Abuse." *Social Work* 34 (May): 197–203.

Payne, Roy. 1988. "A Longitudinal Study of the Psychological Well-Being of Unemployed Men and the Mediating Effect of Neuroticism." *Human Relations* 41 (February): 119–138.

Phillips, David P., and Lundie L. Carstensen. 1988.

"The Effect of Suicide Stories on Various Demographic Groups, 1968–1985." *Suicide and Life-Threatening Behavior* (Spring): 100–114.

Phillips, John L., Jr. 1969. *The Origins of Intellect.* San Francisco: W. H. Freeman and Company.

Piaget, Jean. 1970. "Piaget's Theory," pp. 707–732 in Paul H. Mussen (ed.), *Carmichael's Manual of Child Psychology.* New York: John Wiley and Sons. Third edition. Translation of the Piaget article by Guy Gellerier.

Pirella, Agostino. 1987. "The Implementation of the Italian Psychiatric Reform in a Large Conurbation." *International Journal of Social Psychiatry* 33 (Summer): 119–131.

Powell, Douglas H., and Paul F. Driscoll. 1979. "Middle-class Professionals Face Unemployment," pp. 309–319 in Peter I. Rose (ed.), *Socialization and the Life Cycle.* New York: St. Martin's Press.

Rushton, J. Philippe, and Ian R. Nicholson. 1988. "Genetic Similarity Theory, Intelligence, and Human Mate Choice." *Ethnology and Sociobiology* 9 (January): 45–58.

Simmons, Roberta G., Florence Rosenberg, and Morris Rosenberg. 1973. "Disturbance in the Self-Image at Adolescence." *American Sociological Review* 38 (October): 553–568.

Skinner, B. F. 1972. *Beyond Freedom and Dignity.* New York: Alfred A. Knopf.

Slater, Philip E. 1976. *The Pursuit of Loneliness.* Boston: Beacon. Revised edition.

Spitz, René. 1945. "Hospitalism." *The Psychoanalytic Study of the Child* 1: 53–72.

Stroebe, Wolfgang, Margaret S. Stroebe, and Gunther Domittner. 1988. "Individual and Situational Differences in Recovery from Bereavement: A Risk Group Identified." *Journal of Social Issues* 44: 143–158.

Szilard, Leo. 1961. *The Voice of the Dolphins and Other Stories.* New York: Simon and Schuster.

Thomas, L. Eugene, Robert C. DiGiulio, and Nancy W. Sheehan. 1988. "Identity Loss and Psychological Crisis in Widowhood: A Re-evaluation." *International Journal of Aging and Human Development* 26: 225–239.

Thompson, Larry W., et al. 1984. "Effects of Bereavement on Self-Perceptions of Physical Health in Elderly Widows and Widowers." *Journal of Gerontology* 39 (May): 309–314.

Turnbull, Colin M. 1979. "The Mountain People," pp. 19–26 in Phillip Whitten (ed.), *Readings in Sociology: Contemporary Perspectives.* New York: Harper & Row. Second edition.

U.S. News and World Report. 1984. "America: Glued to the Tube." 96 (February 6): 9.

Vachon, Mary L. S., and Stanley K. Stylianos. 1988. "The Role of Social Support in Bereavement." *Journal of Social Issues* 44: 175–190.

Watson, John B. 1924. *Behavior.* New York: W. W. Norton and Company.

Weidner, Gerdi, et al. 1988. "Type A Behavior in Children, Adolescents, and Their Parents." *Developmental Psychology* 24 (January): 118–121.

Wilhelm, Mari S., and Carol A. Ridley. 1988. "Stress and Unemployment in Rural Nonfarm Couples: A Study of Hardships and Coping Resources." *Family Relations* 37 (January): 50–54.

Wilson, Edward O. 1978. *On Human Nature*. Cambridge, MA: Harvard University Press.

Chapter 7

Arnoff, Joel, and William D. Crano. 1975. "A Re-examination of the Cross-Cultural Principles of Task Segregation and Sex Role Differentiation in the Family." *American Sociological Review* 40 (February): 12–20.

Barry, Herbert, III, and Alice Schlegel. 1984. "Measurements of Adolescent Sexual Behavior in the Standard Sample of Societies." *Ethnology* 23 (October): 315–329.

Bell, Robert R., and Norman M. Lobsenz. 1977. "Married Sex: How Uninhibited Can a Woman Dare to Be?" pp. 112–118 in John H. Gagnon (ed.), *Human Sexuality in Today's World*. Boston: Little, Brown and Company.

Bem, Sandra L. 1975. "Sex-Role Adaptability: One Consequence of Psychological Androgeny." *Journal of Personality and Social Psychology* 31 (April): 634–643.

Berger, Brigitte, and Peter L. Berger. 1984. *The War over the Family*. New York: Anchor Books.

Berger, Raymond M. 1983. "What Is a Homosexual? A Definitional Model." *Social Work* 28 (March/April): 132–135.

Block, Jeanne Humphrey. 1973. "Conceptions of Sex Role: Some Cross-Cultural and Longitudinal Perspectives." *American Psychologist* 28 (June): 512–526.

Blumstein, Philip, and Pepper Schwartz. 1983. *American Couples*. New York: William Morrow and Company.

Braungart, Richard G., and Margaret M. Braungart. 1988. "From Yippies to Yuppies: Twenty Years of Freshman Attitudes." *Public Opinion* 11 (September/October): 53–56.

Brecher, Edward M. 1969. *The Sex Researchers*. Boston: Little, Brown and Company.

Bretschneider, Judy G., and Norma L. McCoy. 1988. "Sexual Interest and Behavior in Healthy 80- to 102-Year-Olds." *Archives of Sexual Behavior* 17 (April): 109–129.

Cann, Arnie, and William D. Siegfield, Jr. 1987. "Sex Stereotypes and the Leadership Role." *Sex Roles* 17 (October): 401–408.

Christopher, F. Scott, and Rodney M. Cate. 1985. "Anticipated Influences on Sexual Decision-Making for First Intercourse." *Family Relations* 34 (April): 265–270.

Collins, Randall. 1971. "A Conflict Theory of Sexual Stratification." *Social Problems* 19 (Summer): 3–21.

Collins, Randall. 1974. *Conflict Sociology: Toward an Explanatory Science*. New York: Academic Press.

Crano, William D., and Joel Arnoff. 1978. "A Cross-Cultural Study of Expressive and Instrumental Role Complementarity in the Family." *American Sociological Review* 43 (August): 463–471.

Cuber, John F., and Peggy B. Harroff. 1972. "Other Involvements," pp. 115–129 in Robert R. Bell and Michael Gordon (eds.), *The Social Dimension of Sexuality*. Boston: Little, Brown and Company.

Deaux, Kay, and Laurie L. Lewis. 1984. "Structure of Gender Stereotypes: Interrelationships among Components and Gender Label." *Journal of Personality and Social Psychology* 46 (May): 991–1004.

England, Eileen M. 1988. "College Student Stereotypes of Female Behavior: Maternal Professional Women and Assertive Housewives." *Sex Roles* 19 (September): 365–385.

Ford, Clellan S., and Frank A Beach. 1951. *Patterns of Sexual Behavior*. New York: Harper & Row.

Friedan, Betty. 1981. "Feminism's Next Step." *New York Times Magazine* (July 5): 12–15.

Gagnon, John H., and Cathy S. Greenblatt. 1978. *Life Designs: Individuals, Marriages, and Families*. Glenview, IL: Scott, Foresman and Company.

Gagnon, John H., and William Simon. 1973. *Sexual Conduct*. Chicago: Aldine.

Goleman, Daniel. 1978. "Special Abilities of the Sexes: Do They Begin in the Brain?" *Psychology Today* 12 (November): 48–49+.

Green, Richard. 1978. "Sexual Identity of 37 Children Raised by Homosexual or Transsexual Parents." *American Journal of Psychiatry* 135 (June): 692–697.

Hunt, Morton. 1974. *Sexual Behavior in the 1970s*. Chicago: Playboy Press.

Hunt, Morton. 1983. "Marital Sex," pp. 219–234 in Arlene Skolnick and Jerome H. Skolnick (eds.), *Family in Transition*. Boston: Little, Brown, and Company. Fourth edition.

Keller, James F., Stephen S. Elliott, and Edwin Gunberg. 1982. "Premarital Sexual Intercourse among Single College Students: A Discriminant Analysis." *Sex Roles* 8 (January): 21–32.

Kohlberg, Lawrence. 1966. "A Cognitive-Development Analysis of Children's Sex-Role Concepts and Attitudes," pp. 82–172 in Eleanor E. Maccoby (ed.), *The Development of Sex Differences*. Palo Alto, CA: Stanford University Press.

Kurdek, Lawrence A. 1988. "Relationship Quality of Gay and Lesbian Cohabiting Couples." *Journal of Homosexuality* 15: 93–118.

Lance, Larry M. 1987. "The Effects of Interaction with Gay Persons on Attitudes toward Homosexuality." *Human Relations* 40 (June): 329–336.

Maccoby, Eleanor Emmons, and Carol Nagy Jacklin. 1974. *The Psychology of Sex Differences*. Palo Alto, CA: Stanford University Press.

Mead, George Herbert. 1934. *Mind, Self and Society*. Chicago: University of Chicago Press.

Mead, Margaret. 1963. *Sex and Temperament in Three Primitive Societies*. New York: William Morrow and Company.

Millett, Kate. 1970. *Sexual Politics*. Garden City, NY: Doubleday & Company.

Molm, Linda D. 1986. "Gender, Power, and Legitimation: A Test of Three Theories." *American Journal of Sociology* 91 (May): 1356–1386.

Money, John. 1987. "Sin, Sickness or Status?: Homosexual Gender Identity and Psychoneuroendocrinology." *American Psychologist* 42 (April): 384–399.

Money, John, and Anke E. Ehrhardt. 1972. *Man and Women, Boy and Girl*. Baltimore: Johns Hopkins Press.

Money, John, and Bernard F. Norman. 1987. "Gender Identity and Gender Transportation." *Journal of Sex and Marital Therapy* 13 (Summer): 79–92.

Moore, Suzanne. 1988. "Condom Culture." *New Statesman* 115 (February 19): 24–25.

Parsons, Talcott, and Robert F. Bales. 1955. *Family, Socialization and Interaction Process*. Glencoe, IL: Free Press.

Peplau, Letitia Anne, Zick Rubin, and Charles T. Hill. 1977. "Sex and Intimacy in Dating Relationships." *Journal of Social Issues* 33 (Spring): 86–109.

Pomeroy, Wardell B. 1982. *Dr. Kinsey and the Institute for Sex Research*. New Haven, CT: Yale University Press. Revised edition.

Rainwater, Lee. 1972. "Marital Sexuality in Four Cultures of Poverty," pp. 79–94 in Robert R. Bell and Michael Gordon (eds.), *The Social Dimension of Human Sexuality*. Boston: Little, Brown and Company.

Reiss, Ira L. 1960. *Premarital Sexual Standards in America*. New York: The Free Press.

Reynolds, Janet. 1989. "The DINS Dilemma: Double Income, No Sex," p. 114 in Ollie Pocs (ed.), *Marriage and Family 89/90*. Guilford, CT: Dushkin.

Richardson, Laurel. 1988. "Secrecy and Status: The Social Construction of Forbidden Relationships." *American Sociological Review* 53 (April): 209–219.

Robinson, Bryan E., Patsy Skeen, Carol Flake Hobson, and Margaret Herrman. 1982. "Gay Men's and Women's Perceptions of Early Family Life and Their Relationships with Parents." *Family Relations* 31 (January): 79–83.

Roscoe, Will. 1988. "Making History: The Challenge of Gay and Lesbian Studies." *Journal of Homosexuality* 15: 1–40.

Rosen, David H. 1974. *Lesbianism*. Springfield, IL: Charles C. Thomas.

Rossi, Alice S. 1984. "American Sociological Association, 1983 Presidential Address." *American Sociological Review* 49 (February): 1–19.

Rubenstein, Carin. 1989. "Is There Sex after Baby?" pp. 115–116 in Ollie Pocs (ed.), *Marriage and Family 89/90*. Guilford, CT: Dushkin.

Rubin, Lillian Breslow. 1983. "Blue-Collar Marriage and the Sexual Revolution," pp. 234–250 in Arlene Skolnick and Jerome H. Skolnick (eds.), *Family in Transition*. Boston: Little, Brown and Company. Fourth edition.

Rubin, Zick. 1980. "The Love Research," pp. 279–285 in Arlene Skolnick and Jerome H. Skolnick (eds.), *Family in Transition*. Boston: Little, Brown and Company. Third edition.

Saghir, M. R., and E. Robins. 1971. "Male and Female Homosexuality: Natural History." *Comparative Psychiatry* 12: 503–510.

Saunders, Janice Miller, and John N. Edwards. 1984. "Extramarital Sexuality: A Predictive Model of Permissive Attitudes." *Journal of Marriage and the Family* 46 (November): 825–835.

Scanzoni, Letha Dawson, and John Scanzoni. 1988. *Men, Women, and Change*. New York: McGraw-Hill. Third edition.

Scarpitti, Frank R., and Margaret L. Andersen. 1989. *Social Problems*. New York: Harper & Row.

Schmidt, William E. 1988. "Nebraska's First Man Enjoys the Last Laughs." *New York Times* (October 21): A14.

Segal, Marian. 1989. "AIDS Education," pp. 229–233 in Ollie Pocs (ed.), *Marriage and Family 89/90*. Guilford, CT: Dushkin.

Segell, Michael. 1989. "Of Human Bonding." *Parenting* 3 (May): 58–62.

Shernoff, Michael. 1988. "Integrating Safer-Sex Counseling into Social Work Practice." *Social Casework* 69 (June): 334–339.

Siegelman, M. 1974. "Parental Background of Male Homosexuals and Heterosexuals." *Archives of Sexual Behavior* 3: 3–18.

Simon, William, A. S. Berger, and John H. Gagnon. 1972. "Beyond Anxiety and Fantasy: The Coital Experiences of College Youth." *Journal of Youth and Adolescence* 1: 203–222.

Smith, Hendrick. 1976. *The Russians*. New York: Quadrangle.

South, Scott J., and Katherine Trent. 1988. "Sex Ratios and Women's Roles: A Cross-National Analysis." *American Journal of Sociology* 93 (March): 1096–1115.

Stacey, J. 1975. "When Patriarchy Kowtows: The Significance of the Chinese Revolution for Feminist Theory." *Feminist Studies* 2: 64–112.

Tavris, Carol. 1984. *The Longest War: Understanding Sex Differences*. New York: Harcourt Brace Jovanovich. Second edition.

Vance, Carole S. 1983. "Gender Systems, Ideology, and Sex Research," pp. 371–384 in Ann Snitow et al., *Powers of Desire: The Politics of Sexuality*. New York: Monthly Review Press.

Vicinus, Martha. 1982. "Sexuality and Power: A Review of Current Work in the History of Sexuality." *Feminist Studies* 8 (Spring): 133–156.

Weis, David L., and Joan Jurich. 1985. "Size of Community of Residence As a Predictor of Attitudes toward Extramarital Sexual Relations." *Journal of Marriage and the Family* 47 (February): 173–178.

Whitehurst, Robert N. 1972. "Extramarital Sex: Alienation or Extension of Normal Behavior?" pp. 236–248 in John N. Edwards *(ed.), Sex and Society*. Chicago: Markham.

Chapter 8

Agnew, Robert. 1985. "A Revised Strain Theory of Delinquency." *Social Forces* 64 (September): 151–167.

Alter, Jonathan. 1983. "Sex and Pages on Capitol Hill." *Newsweek* 102 (July 25): 16–17.

Anglin, M. Douglas, and Yih-ing Hser. 1987. "Addicted Women and Crime." *Criminology* 25 (May): 359–397.

Anglin, M. Douglas, and George Speckart. 1988. "Narcotics Use and Crime: A Multisample, Multi-Method Analysis." *Criminology* 26 (May): 197–233.

Bacon, Donald C. 1979. "Ripoffs: New American Way of Life," pp. 283–290 in Leonard Cargan and Jeanne Ballantine (eds.), *Sociological Footprints*. Boston: Houghton Mifflin Company.

Bell, Daniel. 1962. *The End of Ideology*. New York: The Free Press.

Benson, Michael L. 1984. "The Fall from Grace." *Criminology* 22 (November): 573–593.

Box, Steven, and Chris Hale. 1984. "Liberation/Emancipation, Economic Marginalization, or Less Chivalry." *Criminology* 22 (November): 473–497.

Broad, William J. 1983. "Rising Use of Computer Networks Raises Issues of Security and Law." *New York Times* (August 26): 1+.

Chambliss, William J. 1969. *Crime and the Legal Process*. New York: McGraw-Hill.

Chambliss, William. 1973. "The Saints and the Roughnecks." *Society* 11 (December): 24–31.

Chambliss, William J., and Robert B. Seidman. 1971. *Law, Order, and Power*. Reading, MA: Addison-Wesley.

Cheatwood, Derral. 1988. "Is There a Season for Homicide?" *Criminology* 26 (May): 287–306.

Clayton, Obie, Jr. 1987. "An Empirical Assessment of the Effects of Prison Crowding upon Recidivism Utilizing Aggregate Level Data." *Journal of Criminal Justice* 15: 201–210.

Clinard, Marshall B. 1974. *Sociology of Deviant Behavior*. New York: Holt, Rinehart and Winston. Fourth edition.

Clinard, Marshall B., and Richard Quinney. 1973. *Criminal Behavior Systems: A Typology*. New York: Holt, Rinehart and Winston. Second edition.

Cohen, Albert K. 1966. *Deviance and Control*. Englewood Cliffs, NJ: Prentice-Hall.

Cohen, Albert K., and James F. Short, Jr. 1976. "Crime and Juvenile Delinquency," pp. 47–100 in Robert K. Merton and Robert Nisbet (eds.), *Contemporary Social Problems*. New York: Harcourt Brace Jovanovich. Fourth edition.

Covington, Jeanette. 1984. "Insulation from Labelling." *Criminology* 22 (November): 619–643.

Deming, Mary Beard, and Ali Eppy. 1981. "The Sociology of Rape." *Sociology and Social Research* 65 (July): 357–380.

Dombrink, John, James W. Meeker, and Julie Paik. 1988. "Fighting for Fees—Drug Trafficking and the Forfeiture of Attorney's Fees." *Journal of Drug Issues* 18 (Summer): 421–436.

Dotter, Daniel L., and Julian B. Roebuck. 1988. "The Labeling Approach Reexamined: Interactionism and the Components of Deviance." *Deviant Behavior* 9: 19–32.

Draper, Theodore. 1989. "The Oliver North Library." *New York Review of Books* 35 (January 19): 38–45.

Foote, C. 1954. "Compelling Appearances in Court-Administration of Bail in Philadelphia." *University of Pennsylvania Law Review* 102: 1031–1079.

Fox, Vernon. 1985. *Introduction to Criminology*. Englewood Cliffs, NJ: Prentice-Hall. Second edition.

Gibbons, Don C. 1977. *Society, Crime and Criminal Careers: An Introduction to Criminology*. Englewood Cliffs, NJ: Prentice-Hall.

Gove, Walter R., et al. 1985. "Are Uniform Crime Reports a Valid Indicator of the Index Crimes? An Affirmative Answer with Minor Qualifications." *Criminology* 23 (August): 451–491.

Green, Mark J., Beverly C. Moore, and Bruce Wasserstein. 1979. "Criminal Law and Corporate Disorder," pp. 527–547 in Jerome H. Skolnick and Elliot Currie (eds.), *Crisis in American Institutions*. Boston: Little, Brown and Company. Fourth Edition.

Hall, Francis C. 1989. "Report from the Field on an Endless War." *New York Times* (March 12): 1+.

Haskell, Martin R., and Lewis Yablonsky. 1974. *Crime and Delinquency*. Chicago: Rand McNally. Second edition.

Hollinger, Richard C., and John P. Clark. 1982. "Formal and Informal Social Controls of Employee Deviance." *Sociological Quarterly* 23 (Summer): 333–343.

Hollinger, Richard C., and Lonn Lanza-Kaduce. 1988. "The Process of Criminalization: The Case of Computer Crime Laws." *Criminology* 26 (February): 101–126.

Hunt, Morton M. 1961. "How Does It Come to Be So?" *New Yorker* 36 (January 28): 39–40+.

Ianni, Francis A. J. 1973. *Ethnic Succession in Organized Crime*. Washington, DC: Government Printing Office.

Jackson, Patrick G. 1988. "Assessing the Validity of

540

Official Data on Arson." *Criminology* 26 (February): 181–195.

Jensen, Michael C. 1975. "Watergate Donors Still Riding High." *New York Times* (August 24): Section 3, p. 1+.

Kolata, Gina. 1989. "Grim Seeds of Park Rampage Found in East Harlem Streets." *New York Times* (May 2): C1+.

Koss, Mary P., Christine A. Gidycz, and Nadine Wisniewski. 1988. "The Scope of Rape: Incidence and Prevalence of Sexual Aggression and Victimization in a National Sample of Higher Education Students." *Journal of Consulting and Clinical Psychology* 55 (April): 162–170.

LeBeau, James L. 1988. "Statute Revision and the Reporting of Rape." *Sociology and Social Research* 72 (April): 201–207.

Leger, Robert G. 1988. "Perception of Crowding, Racial Antagonism, and Aggression in a Custodial Prison." *Journal of Criminal Justice* 16: 167–181.

Lemert, Edwin M. 1951. *Social Pathology.* New York: McGraw-Hill.

Massing, Michael. 1989. "Dealing with the Drug Horror." *New York Review of Books* 36 (March 30): 22–26.

McCarthy, Sarah J. 1981. "Pornography, Rape, and the Cult of Macho," pp. 82–90 in *Social Problems 81/82.* Guilford, CT: Dushkin.

Merton, Robert K. 1968. "Social Structure and Anomie," pp. 175–214 in Robert K. Merton, *Social Theory and Social Structure.* New York: The Free Press. Third edition.

Merton, Robert K. 1976. "Introduction: The Sociology of Social Problems," pp. 3–43 in Robert K. Merton and Robert Nisbet (eds.), *Contemporary Social Problems.* New York: Harcourt Brace Jovanovich. Fourth edition.

Messner, Steven F. 1988. "Merton's 'Social Structure and Anomie': The Road Not Taken." *Deviant Behavior* 9: 33–53.

Messner, Steven F., and Kenneth Tardiff. 1985. "The Social Ecology of Urban Homicide: An Application of the 'Routine Activities' Approach." *Criminology* 23 (May): 241–267.

Miethe, Terance D., and Charles A. Moore. 1985. "Socioeconomic Disparities under Determinate Sentencing Systems: A Comparison of Preguideline and Postguideline Practices in Minnesota." *Criminology* 23 (May): 337–363.

Nadelson, Carol C., et al. 1982. "A Follow-up Study on Rape Victims." *American Journal of Psychiatry* 139 (October): 1266–1270.

Nader, Ralph. 1985. "America's Crime without Criminals." *New York Times* (May 19): III:3.

Near, Janet P., and Marcia P. Miceli. 1986. "Retaliation against Whistle Blowers: Predictors and Effects." *Journal of Applied Psychology* 71 (February): 137–145.

New York Times. 1982. "Culture Rides Shotgun on the Paris Metro." (November 30): C13.

Newfield, Jack, and Paul Dubrul. 1979. "The Political Economy of Organized Crime," pp. 414–427 in Jerome H. Skolnick and Elliot Currie (eds.), *Crisis in American Institutions.* Boston: Little, Brown and Company. Fourth edition.

Nurco, David, et al. 1988. "Differential Criminal Patterns of Narcotic Addicts over an Addiction Career." *Criminology* 26 (August): 407–423.

Orcutt, James D., and Rebecca Faison. 1988. "Sex Role Attitude Change and Reporting of Rape Victimization, 1973–1985." *Sociological Quarterly* 29 (Winter): 589–604.

Palamara, Frances. 1986. "The Effect of Police and Mental Health Intervention on Juvenile Deviance: Specifying Contingencies in the Impact of Formal Reaction." *Journal of Health and Social Behavior* 27 (March): 90–105.

Parmerlee, Marcia A., Janet P. Near, and Tamila C. Jensen. 1982. "Correlates of Whistle-Blowers' Perception of Organizational Retaliation." *Administrative Science Quarterly* 27: 17–34.

Peterson, Ruth D., and William C. Bailey. 1988. "Murder and Capital Punishment in the Evolving Context of the Post-*Furman* Era." *Social Forces* 66 (March): 774–807.

Pittman, David J., and C. Wayne Gordon. 1968. *Revolving Door.* New York: The Free Press.

Proctor, Robert N. 1988. *Medicine under the Nazis.* Cambridge, MA: Harvard University Press.

Quinney, Richard. 1974. *Critique of Legal Order: Crime Control in Capitalist Society.* Boston: Little, Brown and Company.

Quinney, Richard. 1975. *Criminology.* Boston: Little, Brown and Company.

Reid, Sue Titus. 1982. *Crime and Criminology.* New York: Holt, Rinehart and Winston. Third edition.

Reid, Sue Titus. 1985. *Crime and Criminology.* New York: Holt, Rinehart and Winston. Fourth edition.

Reiman, Jeffrey H. 1979. *The Rich Get Rich and the Poor Get Prison.* New York: John Wiley & Sons.

Roberts, Steven V. 1983. "House Censures Crane and Studds for Sexual Relations with Pages." *New York Times* (July 21): 1+.

Rosecrance, John. 1988. "Whistleblowing in Probation Departments." *Journal of Criminal Justice* 16: 99–109.

Scully, Diana, and Joseph Marolla. 1984. "Convicted Rapists' Vocabulary of Motive: Excuses and Justifications." *Social Problems* 31 (June): 530–544.

Scully, Diana, and Joseph Marolla. 1985. "'Riding the Bull at Gilley's': Convicted Rapists Describe the Rewards of Rape." *Social Problems* 32 (February): 251–263.

Shaw, Clifford R., and Henry D. McKay. 1942. *Juvenile Delinquency and Urban Areas.* Chicago: University of Chicago Press.

Simon, Rita James. 1975. *Women and Crime.* Lexington, MA: D. C. Heath.

Smith, M. Dwayne. 1987. "Patterns of Discrimination in Assessments of the Death Penalty: The

Case of Louisiana." *Journal of Criminal Justice* 15: 279–286.

Sutherland, Edwin H., and Donald R. Cressey. 1978. *Criminology.* Philadelphia: J. B. Lippincott. Tenth edition.

Taylor, Ian, Paul Walton, and Jock Young. 1973. *The New Criminology.* London: Routledge & Kegan Paul.

Thio, Alex. 1978. *Deviant Behavior.* Boston: Houghton Mifflin.

Thoits, Peggy A. 1985. "Self-Labeling Process in Mental Illness: The Role of Emotional Deviance." *American Journal of Sociology* 91 (September): 221–249.

Thornberry, Terence P. 1973. "Race, Socioeconomic Status and Sentencing in the Juvenile Justice System." *Journal of Criminal Law and Criminology* 64: 90–98.

Thrasher, Frederic M. 1926. *The Gang.* Chicago: University of Chicago Press.

Tittle, Charles R. 1988. "Two Empirical Regulations (Maybe) in Search of an Explanation: Commentary on the Age/Crime Debate." *Criminology* 26 (February): 75–85.

U. S. Bureau of the Census. 1989. *Statistical Abstract of the United States: 1989.* Washington, DC: U.S. Government Printing Office. 109th edition.

Whyte, William H. 1956. *The Organization Man.* New York: Simon & Schuster.

Williams, Linda S. 1984. "The Classic Rape: When Do Victims Report?" *Social Problems* 31 (April): 459–467.

Wolfgang, Marvin E. 1967. "A Sociological Analysis of Criminal Homicide." pp. 15–28 in Marvin E. Wolfgang (ed.), *Studies in Homicide.* New York: Harper & Row.

Zeisel, Hans. 1973. "FBI Statistics: A Detective Story." *American Bar Association Journal* 59 (May): 510.

Chapter 9

Beeghley, Leonard. 1978. *Social Stratification in America: A Critical Analysis of Theory and Research.* Santa Monica, CA: Goodyear.

Bellah, Robert N., et al. 1986. *Habits of the Heart: Individualism and Commitment in American Life.* New York: Harper & Row.

Berelson, Bernard, and Gary A. Steiner. 1964. *Human Behavior.* New York: Harcourt, Brace and World.

Bernstein, Blanche. 1986. "A Way to Break the Welfare Cycle." *New York Times* (October 31): A35.

Blau, Peter M., and Otis Dudley Duncan. 1967. *The American Occupational Structure.* New York: John Wiley & Sons.

Breed, Warren. 1963. "Occupational Mobility and Suicide among White Males." *American Sociological Review* 28 (April): 179–188.

Breiger, Ronald L., and Jerry A. Jacobs. 1987. "On

Occupational Mobility and Social Class." *American Sociological Review* 52 (June): 413–416.

Coleman, Richard P., and Lee Rainwater, with Kent A. McClelland. 1978. *Social Standing in America: New Dimensions of Class.* New York: Basic Books.

Collins, Sharon M. 1983. "The Making of the Black Middle Class." *Social Problems* 30 (April): 369–382.

Dahl, Robert A. 1967. *Pluralist Democracy in the United States.* Chicago: Rand McNally.

Davis, Fred. 1959. "The Cabdriver and His Fare: Facets of a Fleeting Relationship." *American Journal of Sociology* 65 (September): 158–165.

Davis, Kingsley, and William E. Moore. 1945. "Some Principles of Stratification." *American Sociological Review* 10 (April): 242–249.

Demo, David H., and Ritch C. Savin-Williams. 1983. "Early Adolescent Self-Esteem As a Function of Social Class: Rosenberg and Pearlin Revisited." *American Journal of Sociology* 88 (January): 763–774.

Doob, Christopher Bates. 1967. *The Development of Peer Group Relationships among Puerto Rican Boys in East Harlem.* Unpublished Ph.D. dissertation. Cornell University.

Duberman, Lucille. 1976. *Social Inequality: Class and Caste in America.* Philadelphia: J. B. Lippincott Company.

Economist. 1986. "America's Underclass." (March 15): 29–32.

Egan, Jack. 1986. "Changing Course." *U.S. News and World Report* 101 (October 6): 46–47.

Ellis, Robert A., and W. Clayton Lane. 1967. "Social Mobility and Social Isolation." *American Sociological Review* 32 (April): 237–253.

Epstein, Cynthia F. 1970. "Encountering the Male Establishment: Sex-Status Limits on Women's Careers in the Professions." *American Journal of Sociology* 75 (May): 965–982.

Faris, Robert E. L., and H. Warren Dunham. 1939. *Mental Disorders in Urban Areas.* Chicago: University of Chicago Press.

Farr, Kathryn Ann. 1988. "Dominance Bonding through the Good Old Boys' Sociability Group." *Sex Roles* 18 (March): 259–277.

Featherman, David L., and Robert M. Hauser. 1978. *Opportunity and Change.* New York: Academic Press.

Gerth, H. H., and C. Wright Mills (eds.). 1946. *From Max Weber: Essays in Sociology.* New York: Oxford University Press.

Gilbert, Dennis, and Joseph A. Kahl. 1982. *The American Class Structure.* Homewood, IL: The Dorsey Press. Revised edition.

Gold, Ray. 1952. "Janitors versus Tenants: A Status–Income Dilemma." *American Journal of Sociology* 57 (March): 486–493.

Gouldner, Helen, and Mary Symons Strong. 1987. *Speaking of Friendship: Middle-Class Women and Their Friends.* Westport, CT: Greenwood Press.

Grusky, David B., and Robert H. Hauser. 1984.

"Comparative Social Mobility Revisited: Models of Convergence and Divergence in 16 Countries." *American Sociological Review* 49 (February): 19–38.

Gurley, John G. 1984. "Marx's Contributions and Their Relevance Today." *American Economic Review* 74 (May): 110–115.

Hall, Wayne. 1986. "Social Class and Survival on the S.S. *Titanic*." *Social Science and Medicine* 22: 687–690.

Haller, Max, et al. 1985. "Patterns of Career Mobility and Structural Positions in Advanced Capitalist Societies: A Comparison of Men in Austria, France, and the United States." *American Sociological Review* 50 (October): 579–603.

Herber, Bernard P. 1988. "Federal Income Tax Reform in the United States." *American Journal of Economics and Sociology* 47 (October): 391–408.

Hodge, Robert W., Paul M. Siegel, and Peter H. Rossi. 1966. "Occupational Prestige in the United States: 1925–1963," pp. 322–334 in Reinhard Bendix and Seymore Martin Lipset (eds.), *Class, Status, and Power.* New York: The Free Press.

Hodges, Harold M. 1964. *Social Stratification.* Cambridge, MA: Schenkman.

Howell, Joseph T. 1973. *Hard Living on Clay Street.* Garden City, NY: Doubleday.

Jencks, Christopher. 1988. "Deadly Neighborhoods." *New Republic* 198 (June 13): 23–32.

Kahl, Joseph A. 1957. *The American Class Structure.* New York: Rinehart Press.

Kerckhoff, Alan C. 1984. "The Current State of Social Mobility Research." *Sociological Quarterly* 25 (Spring): 139–153.

Kessin, Kenneth. 1971. "Social and Psychological Consequences of Intergenerational Occupational Mobility." *American Journal of Sociology* 77 (July): 1–18.

Kessler, Ronald C., and Paul D. Cleary. 1980. "Social Class and Psychological Distress." *American Sociological Review* 45 (June): 463–478.

Koepp, Stephen. 1986. "Playing the New Tax Game." *Time* 128 (October 13): 66–67.

Kohn, Melvin L. 1976. "Interaction of Social Class and Other Factors in the Etiology of Schizophrenia." *American Journal of Psychiatry* 133: 179–180.

Landrine, Hope. 1987. "On the Politics of Madness: A Preliminary Analysis of the Relationships between Social Roles and Psychotherapy." *Genetic, Social, & General Psychology Monographs* 113 (August): 341–406.

Laumann, Edward O. 1966. *Prestige and Association in an Urban Community.* Indianapolis: Bobbs-Merrill.

Lenski, Gerhard E. 1966. *Power and Privilege.* New York: McGraw-Hill.

Lenski, Gerhard E., and Jean Lenski. 1982. *Human Societies.* New York: McGraw-Hill. Fourth edition.

Lerner, Michael A. 1982. "The Elite Meet in Retreat." *Newsweek* 100 (August 2): 21–22.

Logan, John R., and O. Andrew Collver. 1983. "Residents' Perceptions of Suburban Community Differences." *American Sociological Review* 48 (June): 428–433.

Maloney, Lawrence. 1981. "America's New Middle Class." *U.S. News and World Report* 90 (March 30): 39–41+.

Marx, Karl, and Friedrich Engels. 1959. "Manifesto of the Communist Party," pp. 6–41 in Lewis S. Feuer (ed.), *Marx and Engels: Basic Writings on Politics and Philosophy.* Garden City, NY: Anchor Books. Translated by N. I. Stone.

McAdoo, Harriette P. 1982. "Stress Absorbing Systems in Black Families." *Family Relations* 31 (October): 479–488.

McPherson, J. Miller, and Lynn Smith-Lovin. 1987. "Homophily in Voluntary Organizations: Status Distance and the Composition of Face-to-Face Groups." *American Sociological Review* 52 (June): 370–379.

Mills, C. Wright. 1956. *The Power Elite.* New York: Oxford University Press.

Moskos, Charles C. 1969. "Why Men Fight." *Trans-action* 7 (November): 13–23.

Munroe, Robert L., and Ruth H. Munroe. 1984. "Health and Wealth in Four Societies." *Journal of Social Psychology* 123 (June): 135–136.

Passell, Peter. 1989. "Forces in Society, and Reaganism, Helped Dig Deeper Hole for Poor." *New York Times* (July 16): 1+.

Pomeroy, Wardell B. 1972. *Dr. Kinsey and the Institute for Sex Research.* New York: Harper & Row.

Rainwater, Lee. 1964. "Marital Sexuality in Four Cultures of Poverty." *Journal of Marriage and the Family* 26 (November): 457–466.

Reiss, Ira L. 1980. *Family Systems in America.* New York: Holt, Rinehart and Winston. Third edition.

Reiss, Ira L., and Gary R. Lee. 1988. *Family Systems in America.* New York: Holt, Rinehart and Winston. Fourth edition.

Resnick, Stephen, and Richard Wolff. 1988. "Communism: Between Class and Classless." *Rethinking Marxism* 1 (Spring): 14–42.

Rossides, Daniel W. 1976. *The American Class System.* Boston: Houghton Mifflin Company.

Rubin, Lillian Breslow. 1983. "Blue-Collar Marriage and the Sexual Revolution," pp. 234–250 in Arlene Skolnick and Jerome H. Skolnick (eds.), *Family in Transition.* Boston: Little, Brown and Company. Fourth edition.

Schatzman, Leonard, and Anselm Strauss. 1972. "Social Class and Modes of Communication," pp. 48–60 in Saul D. Feldman and Gerald W. Thiebar (eds.), *Life Styles: Diversity in American Society.* Boston: Little, Brown and Company.

Seligman, Martin E. P. 1988. "Boomer Blues." *Psychology Today* 22 (October): 50–55.

Sennett, Richard, and Jonathan Cobb. 1973. *The*

Hidden Injuries of Class. New York: Vintage Books.

Shepelak, Norma J. 1987. "The Role of Self-Explanations and Self-Evaluations in Legitimating Inequality." *American Sociological Review* 52 (August): 495–503.

Shiller, Bradley R. 1970. "Stratified Opportunities: The Essence of 'The Vicious Circle.'" *American Journal of Sociology* 76 (November): 426–441.

Simon, William, and John Gagnon. 1972. "Sex, Marriage, and Social Class," pp. 86–88 in Saul D. Feldman and Gerald W. Thielbar (eds.), *Life Styles: Diversity in American Society.* Boston: Little, Brown and Company.

Simpson, Ida Harper, David Stark, and Robert A. Jackson. 1988. "Class Identification Processes of Married, Working Men and Women." *American Sociological Review* 53 (April): 284–293.

Smith, Kevin B. 1981. "Class Structure and Intergenerational Mobility from a Marxian Perspective." *Sociological Quarterly* 22 (Summer): 385–401.

Snarey, John R., and George E. Vaillant. 1985. "How Lower- and Working-Class Youth Become Middle-Class Adults: The Association between Ego Defense Mechanisms and Upward Social Mobility." *Child Development* 56 (August): 899–910.

Snipp, C. Matthew. 1987. "More on Occupational Mobility and Social Class." *American Sociological Review* 52 (June): 416–418.

Sorokin, Pitrim A. 1927. *Social Mobility.* New York: Harper & Brothers.

Srole, Leo, Thomas S. Langner, Stanley T. Michael, Marvin K. Opler, and Thomas A. C. Rennie. 1962. *Mental Health in the Metropolis.* New York: McGraw-Hill.

Surrey, Stanley A. 1973. *Pathways to Tax Reform.* Cambridge, MA: Harvard University Press.

Syme, S. Leonard, and Lisa F. Berkman. 1981. "Social Class, Susceptibility, and Sickness," pp. 35–44 in Peter Conrad and Rochelle Kern (eds.), *The Sociology of Health and Illness.* New York: St. Martin's Press.

Townsend, John Marshall. 1987. "Sex Differences in Sexuality among Medical Students: Effects of Increasing Socioeconomic Status." *Archives of Sexual Behavior* 16 (October): 425–444.

Treiman, Donald J. 1977. *Occupational Prestige in Comparative Perspective.* New York: Academic Press.

Tumin, Melvin M. 1953. "Some Principles of Stratification: A Critical Analysis." *American Sociological Review* 18 (August): 387–394.

Tumin, Melvin M. 1957. "Some Unapplauded Consequences of Social Mobility in a Mass Society." *Social Forces* 36 (October): 32–36.

Tumin, Melvin M. 1967. *Social Stratification.* Englewood Cliffs, NJ: Prentice-Hall.

Turner, Jonathan H., and Charles E. Starnes. 1976.

Inequality: Privilege and Poverty in America. Pacific Palisades, CA: Goodyear.

Tyree, Andrea, and Rebecca Hicks. 1988. "Sex and the Second Moment of Prestige Distributions." *Social Forces* 66 (June): 1028–1037.

U. S. Bureau of the Census. 1984. *Current Population Reports,* Series P-60, *Money Income of Households, Families and Persons in the United States: 1983.* Washington, DC: U. S. Government Printing Office.

U. S. Bureau of the Census. 1989. *Statistical Abstract of the United States: 1989.* Washington, DC: U. S. Government Printing Office. 109th edition.

Whitener, Leslie A. 1985. "The Migrant Farm Work Force: Differences in Attachment to Farmwork." *Rural Sociology* 50 (Summer): 163–180.

Wilson, William J. 1980. *The Declining Significance of Race.* Chicago: University of Chicago Press. Second edition.

Wing, Steve. 1988. "Social Inequalities in the Decline of Coronary Mortality." *American Journal of Public Health* 78 (November): 1415–1416.

Wright, Erik Olin, and Bill Martin. 1987. "The Transformation of the American Class Structure, 1960–1980." *American Journal of Sociology* 93 (July): 1–29.

Wrong, Dennis H. 1966. "Trends in Class Fertility in Western Nations," pp. 353–361 in Reinhard Bendix and Seymour Martin Lipset (eds.), *Class, Status, and Power.* New York: Free Press. Second edition.

Zimmerman, L. J. 1965. *Poor Lands, Rich Lands: The Widening Gap.* New York: Random House.

Chapter 10

Aboud, Frances E. 1984. "Social and Cognitive Bases of Ethnic Identity Constancy." *Journal of Genetic Psychology* 145 (December): 217–230.

Alba, Richard D. 1981. "The Twilight of Ethnicity among American Catholics of European Ancestry." *Annals of the American Academy of Political and Social Science* 454 (March): 86–97.

Aldrich, Howard, et al. 1985. "Ethnic Residential Concentration and the Protected Market Hypothesis." *Social Forces* 63 (June): 996–1009.

Allport, Gordon W. 1954. *The Nature of Prejudice.* Cambridge, MA: Addison-Wesley.

Bahr, Howard M., Bruce A. Chadwick, and Joseph H. Stauss. 1979. *American Ethnicity.* Lexington, MA: D.C. Heath.

Bailyn, Bernard, et al. 1977. *The Great Republic.* Lexington, MA: D. C. Heath.

Berry, Brewton, and Henry L. Tischler. 1978. *Race and Ethnic Relations.* Boston: Houghton Mifflin. Fourth edition.

Blackwell, James E. 1975. *The Black Community: Diversity and Unity.* New York: Harper & Row.

Bogardus, Emory. 1968. "Comparing Racial Distance in Ethiopia, South Africa, and the United

States." *Sociology and Social Research* 52 (January): 149–156.

Branch, Taylor. 1988. *Parting the Waters: America in the King Years, 1954–63.* New York: Simon and Schuster.

Brantley, Thomas. 1983. "Racism and Its Impact on Psychotherapy." *American Journal of Psychiatry* 140 (December): 1605–1608.

Brinkley, Joel. 1988. "Angry American Jews Press Shamir on 'Who Is a Jew' Law." *New York Times* (November 19): 1+.

Brown, Dee. 1972. *Bury My Heart at Wounded Knee.* New York: Bantam Books.

Campbell, Bebe Moore. 1982. "Black Executives and Corporate Stress." *New York Times Magazine* (December 12): 36–39+.

Campbell, Ernest Q., and Thomas Pettigrew. 1959. *Christians in Racial Crisis.* Washington, DC: Public Affairs Press.

Cleaver, Eldridge. 1970. *Soul on Ice.* New York: Dell.

Cohen, Steven M., and Leonard J. Fein. 1985. "From Integration to Survival: American Jewish Anxieties in Transition." *Annals of the American Academy of Political and Social Science* 480 (July): 75–88.

Colasanto, Diane. 1988. "Black Attitudes." *Public Opinion* 10 (January/February): 45–49.

Crooks, Kai. 1988. "Peaceful Paths to Change Are Being Closed One by One." *Black Enterprise* 18 (May): 36.

Davenport, Judith A., and Joseph Davenport, III. 1987. "Native American Suicide: A Durkheimian Analysis." *Social Casework* 68 (November): 533–539.

Deloria, Vine, Jr. 1981. "Native Americans: The American Indian Today." *Annals of the American Academy of Political and Social Science* 454 (March): 139–149.

De Parle, Jason. 1990. "1989 Surge in Anti-Semitic Acts Is Reported by B'nai B'rith. *New York Times* (January 20): 10.

Dollard, John. 1937. *Caste and Class in a Southern Town.* New Haven: Yale University Press.

Dollard, John, Leonard Doob, Neal E. Miller, O. H. Mowrer, and R. R. Sears. 1939. *Frustration and Aggression.* New Haven: Yale University Press.

Duster, Troy. 1987. "Purpose and Bias." *Society* 24 (January/February): 8–12.

Eisenbruch, Maurice. 1988. "The Mental Health of Refugee Children and Their Cultural Development." *International Migration Review* 22 (Summer): 282–300.

Fallows, Majorie R. 1979. *Irish Americans: Identity and Assimilation.* Englewood Cliffs, NJ: Prentice-Hall.

Farley, Reynolds. 1977. "Trends in Racial Inequalities: Have the Gains of the 1960s Disappeared in the 1970s?" *American Sociological Review* 42 (April): 189–207.

Feagin, Joe R. 1989. *Racial & Ethnic Relations.* Englewood Cliffs, NJ: Prentice-Hall. Third edition.

Fitzpatrick, Joseph P. 1975. "Puerto Ricans in Perspective: The Meaning of Migration to the Mainland," pp. 297–304 in Norman R. Yetman and C. Hoy Steele (eds.), *Majority and Minority.* Boston: Allyn and Bacon. Second edition.

Fitzpatrick, Joseph P., and Lourdes Travieso Parker. 1981. "Hispanic-Americans in the Eastern United States." *Annals of the American Academy of Political and Social Science* 454 (March): 98–110.

Fugita, Stephen S., and David J. O'Brien. 1985. "Structural Assimilation, Ethnic Group Membership, and Political Participation among Japanese Americans: A Research Note." *Social Forces* 63 (June): 986–995.

Gonzalez, Judith Teresa. 1988. "Dilemmas of the High-Achieving Chicana: The Double-Bind Factor in Male/Female Relationships." *Sex Roles* 18 (April): 367–380.

Greeley, Andrew. 1977. *The American Catholic.* New York: Basic Books.

Greeley, Andrew. 1988. "The Success and Assimilation of Irish Protestants and Irish Catholics in the United States." *Sociology and Social Research* 72 (July): 229–236.

Green, Constance McLaughlin, 1967. *The Secret City: A History of Race Relations in the Nation's Capital.* Princeton: Princeton University Press.

Hodge, William. 1981. *The First Americans: Then and Now.* New York: Holt, Rinehart and Winston.

Ikels, Charlotte. 1985. "Parental Perspectives on the Significance of Marriage." *Journal of Marriage and the Family* 47 (May): 253–264.

Jenkins, J. Craig, and Craig M. Eckert. 1986. "Channeling Black Insurgency: Elite Patronage and Professional Social Movement Organizations in the Development of the Black Movement." *American Sociological Review* 51 (December): 812–829.

Jiobu, Robert M. 1988. "Ethnic Hegemony and the Japanese of California." *American Sociological Review* 53 (June): 353–367.

Katz, David, and Kenneth Braly. 1933. "Racial Stereotypes of One Hundred College Students." *Journal of Abnormal and Social Psychology* 28 (October): 280–290.

Killian, Lewis M. 1975. *The Impossible Revolution, Phase 2: Black Power and the American Dream.* New York: Random House.

Kitano, Harry H. L. 1981. "Asian-Americans: The Chinese, Japanese, Koreans, Philippinos, and Southeast Asians." *Annals of the American Academy of Political and Social Science* 454 (March): 125–138.

Kutner, Bernard, Carol Wilkins, and P. R. Yarrow. 1952. "Verbal Attitudes and Overt Behavior involving Racial Prejudice." *Journal of Abnormal and Social Psychology* 47 (July): 649–652.

Lacy, Dan. 1972. *The White Use of Blacks in America.* New York: McGraw-Hill.

LaPierce, Richard T. 1934. "Attitudes vs. Actions." *Social Forces* 13 (October): 230–237.

Leighton, Alexander H. 1964. *The Governing of Men.* New York: Octagon Books. Originally published in Princeton: Princeton University Press, 1945.

Lex, Barbara W. 1987. "Review of Alcohol Problems in Ethnic Minority Groups." *Journal of Consulting and Clinical Psychology* 55 (June): 293–300.

Mann, Arthur J., and Robert Smith. 1987. "Public Transfers, Family Socioeconomic Traits, and the Job Search Behavior of the Unemployed: Evidence from Puerto Rico." *World Development* 15 (June): 831–840.

Moore, John W., and Harry Pachon. 1976. *Mexican Americans.* Englewood Cliffs, NJ: Prentice-Hall. Second edition.

Nee, Victor, and Jimy Sanders. 1987. "On Testing the Enclave-Economy Hypothesis." *American Sociological Review* 52 (December): 771–773.

New York Times. 1981. "750 Attend Klan Rally for Fishermen in Texas." (February 26): 36.

Novak, Michael. 1972. *The Rise of the Unmeltable Ethnics.* New York: Macmillan.

Okimoto, Daniel I. 1971. *American in Disguise.* New York: John Weatherhill.

Pachon, Harry P., and John W. Moore. 1981. "Mexican Americans." *Annals of the American Academy of Political and Social Science* 454 (March): 111–124.

Piliawsky, Monte. 1984. "Racial Equality in the United States: From Institutionalized Racism to 'Respectable' Racism." *Phylon* 45 (June): 135–143.

Prewitt-Diaz, Joseph O. 1984. "Migrant Students' Perceptions of Teachers, School and Self." *Perceptual and Motor Skills* 58 (April): 391–394.

Quigley, Harold E., and Charles Y. Glock. 1979. *Anti-Semitism in America.* New York: The Free Press.

Robbins, Susan P. 1984. "Anglo Concepts and Indian Reality: A Study of Juvenile Delinquency." *Social Casework* 65 (April): 235–241.

Rosenberg, Morris, and Roberta G. Simmons. 1971. *Black and White Self-Esteem: The Urban School Child.* Washington, DC: American Sociological Association.

Rosenthal, Andrew. 1988. "Foes Accuse Bush Campaign of Inflaming Racial Tension." *New York Times* (October 24): A1+.

Salamon, Sonya. 1985. "Ethnic Communities and the Structure of Agriculture." *Rural Sociology* 50 (Fall): 323–340.

Schaefer, Richard T. 1979. *Racial and Ethnic Groups.* Boston: Little, Brown and Company.

Schmidt, William E. 1981. "Dismissed Workers Call Meat Plant Sale a 'Shame.'" *New York Times* (November 7): 7.

Shenon, Philip. 1986. "'Startling' Surge Is Reported in Illegal Aliens from Mexico." *New York Times* (February 21): A15+.

Simpson, George Eaton, and J. Milton Yinger.

1985. *Racial and Cultural Minorities: An Analysis of Prejudice and Discrimination.* New York: Plenum Press. Fifth edition.

Sklare, Marshall. 1971. *America's Jews.* New York: Random House.

South African Foundation. 1988. *1988 Information Please Digest.* Johannesburg, South Africa: South African Foundation.

Study Commission on U.S. Policy toward Southern Africa. 1981. *South Africa: Time Running Out.* Berkeley and Los Angeles, CA: University of California Press.

Taylor, Stuart, Jr. 1986. "Justices to Hear Plea on Internment of Japanese-Americans." *New York Times* (November 18): A26.

Thomas, Melvin E., and Michael Hughes. 1986. "The Continuing Significance of Race: A Study of Race, Class, and Quality of Life in America, 1972–1985." *American Sociological Review* 51 (December): 830–841.

Timberlake, Elizabeth M., and Kim Oanh Cook. 1984. "Social Work and the Vietnamese Refugee." *Social Work* 29 (March/April): 108–113.

Time 1988. "Right of Way: A White Backlash Gathers Force." 131 (March 14): 38.

Twain, Mark. 1973. *Mark Twain and the Three R's.* Maxwell Geismar (ed.). Indianapolis: Bobbs-Merrill.

Utley, Robert M. 1963. *The Last Days of the Sioux Nation.* New Haven: Yale University Press.

Vander Zanden, James W. 1972. *American Minority Relations.* New York: Ronald Press. Second edition.

Waxman, Chaim I. 1981. "The Fourth Generation Grows Up: The Contemporary American Jewish Community." *Annals of American Political and Social Science* 454 (March): 70–85.

Webster, Peggy Lovell, and Jeffrey W. Dwyer. 1988. "The Cost of Being Nonwhite in Brazil." *Sociology and Social Research* 72 (January): 136–138.

Willen, Mark. 1988. "World War II Internees to Get Cash, Apology." *Congressional Quarterly* 46 (April 23): 1081.

Williams, Lena. 1988. "Uneasy Mingling: When Small Talk at Parties Tackles Large Racial Issues." *New York Times* (October 21): A15.

Wilson Quarterly. 1988. "The Italian-Americans." 12 (Spring): 109.

Wong, Bernard. 1987. "The Role of Ethnicity in Enclave Enterprises: A Study of the Chinese Garment Factories in New York City." *Human Organization* 46 (Summer): 120–130.

Zinsmeister, Karl. 1988. "Black Demographics." *Public Opinion* 10 (January/February): 41–44.

Chapter 11

Anderson, Dave. 1989. "How Abbott Has Changed Baseball." *New York Times* (May 25): D23.

546

Atchley, Robert C. 1976. *The Sociology of Retirement.* Cambridge, MA: Schenkman.

Atchley, Robert C. 1989. "A Continuity Theory of Normal Aging." *Gerontology* 29 (April): 183–190.

Bagshaw, Margaret, and Mary Adams. 1986. "Nursing Home Nurses' Attitudes, Empathy, and Ideologic Orientation." *International Journal of Aging and Human Development* 22: 235–246.

Benet, Sula. 1971. "Why They Live to Be 100 or Even Older, in Abkhasia." *New York Times Magazine* (December 26): p. 3+.

Biegel, David E., et al. 1989. "Unmet Needs and Barriers to Service Delivery for the Blind and Visually Impaired Elderly." *Gerontologist* 29 (February): 86–91.

Blum, Linda, and Vicki Smith. 1988. "Women's Mobility in the Corporation: A Critique of the Politics of Optimism." *Signs* 13 (Spring): 528–545.

Bourestom, Norman, and Leon Pastalan. 1981. "The Effects of Relocation on the Elderly." *Gerontologist* 21 (February): 4–7.

Bowe, Frank. 1978. *Handicapping America.* New York: Harper & Row.

Bretl, Daniel J., and Joanne Cantor. 1988. "The Portrayal of Men and Women in U.S. Television Commercials: A Recent Content Analysis and Trends over 15 Years." *Sex Roles* 18 (May): 595–609.

Butler, Robert N. 1975. *Why Survive? Being Old in America.* New York: Harper & Row.

Cohen, Carl I., et al. 1985. "Social Networks, Stress, and Physical Health: A Longitudinal Study of an Inner-City Elderly Population." *Journal of Gerontology* 40 (July): 478–486.

Conway, Katherine. 1985. "Coping with the Stress of Medical Problems among Black and White Elderly." *International Journal of Aging and Human Development* 21: 39–48.

Cox, Sue. 1981. *Female Psychology.* New York: St. Martin's Press. Second edition.

Creecy, Robert F. 1985. "Loneliness among the Elderly: A Causal Approach." *Journal of Gerontology* 40 (July): 487–493.

Cumming, Elaine, and William Henry. 1961. *Growing Old: The Process of Disengagement.* New York: Basic Books.

Dambrot, Faye H., Diana C. Reep, and Daniel Bell. 1988. "Television Sex Roles in the 1980s: Do Viewers' Sex and Sex Role Orientation Change the Picture?" *Sex Roles* 19 (September): 387–401.

Duff, Raymond S., and August B. Hollingshead. 1968. *Sickness and Society.* New York: Harper & Row.

Ehrenreich, Barbara, and Deirdre English. 1980. "Reflections on the 'Woman Question,'" pp. 217–231 in Arlene Skolnick and Jerome H. Skolnick (eds.), *Family in Transition.* Boston: Little, Brown and Company. Third edition.

Fine, Michelle, and Adrienne Asch. 1988. "Disability beyond Stigma: Social Interaction, Discrimination, and Activism." *Journal of Social Issues* 44: 3–21.

Freeman, Jo. 1975. *The Politics of Women's Liberation.* New York: David McKay Company.

Freeman, Jo. 1980. "The Roots of Revolt," pp. 511–524 in Sheila Ruth (ed.), *Issues in Feminism.* Boston: Houghton Mifflin.

Friedan, Betty. 1963. *The Feminine Mystique.* New York: W. W. Norton and Company.

Friedan, Betty. 1981. "Feminism's Next Step." *New York Times Magazine* (July 5): 12–15+.

Frieze, Irene Hanson. 1983. "Investigating the Causes and Consequences of Marital Rape." *Signs* 8 (Spring): 532–553.

Gitlin, Todd. 1989. *The Sixties: Years of Hope, Days of Rage.* New York: Bantam Books.

Gliedman, John. 1979. "The Wheelchair Rebellion." *Psychology Today* 13 (August): 59–60+.

Gubrium, Jaber F. 1975. *Living and Dying at Murray Manor.* New York: St. Martin's Press.

Gustaitis, Rasa. 1980. "Old vs. Young in Florida: Preview of an Aging America." *Saturday Review* 7 (February 16): 10–12+.

Hacker, Helen Mayer. 1951. "Women As a Minority Group." *Social Forces* 30 (October): 60–69.

Hennig, Margaret, and Anne Jardim. 1977. *The Managerial Woman.* Garden City, NY: Anchor Press.

Herman, Judith Lewis. 1988. "Considering Sex Offenders: A Model of Addiction." *Signs* 13 (Summer): 695–724.

Hewlett, Sylvia Ann. 1986. "Feminism's Next Challenge: Support for Motherhood." *New York Times* (June 17): A27.

Hultsch, David F., and Francine Deutsch. 1981. *Adult Development and Aging.* New York: McGraw-Hill.

Jowett, Sandra, and Terence Ryan. 1985. "Skin Disease and Handicap: An Analysis of the Impact of Skin Conditions." *Social Science and Medicine* 20: 425–429.

Katz, Elias. 1973. "The Mentally Retarded," pp. 132–153 in Don Spiegel and Patricia Keith-Spiegel (eds.), *Outsiders USA.* San Francisco: Rinehart Press.

Kornblum, William, and Joseph Julian. 1989. *Social Problems.* Englewood Cliffs, NJ: Prentice-Hall. Sixth edition.

Landrine, Hope. 1988. "Depression and Stereotypes of Women: Preliminary Analyses of the Gender-Role Hypothesis." *Sex Roles* 19 (October): 527–541.

Langway, Lynn. 1982. "A Bad Year for the Disabled." *Newsweek* 99 (February): 82+.

Leidig, Margorie Whittaker. 1981. "Violence against Women: A Feminist-Psychological Analysis," pp. 190–205 in Sue Cox (ed.), *Female Psychology.* New York: St. Martin's Press. Second edition.

Luszcz, Mary A., and Karen M. Fitzgerald. 1986.

"Understanding Cohort Differences in Cross-Generational, Self, and Peer Perceptions." *Journal of Gerontology* 41 (March): 234–240.

McLaughlin, Mary Martin. 1989. "Creating and Re-creating Communities of Women: The Case of Corpus Domini, Ferrara, 1406–1452." *Signs* 14 (Winter): 293–320.

Meyerson, Lee. 1988. "The Social Psychology of Physical Disability: 1948 and 1988." *Journal of Social Issues* 44: 173–188.

Neel, Carol. 1989. "The Origins of the Beguines." *Signs* 14 (Winter): 321–341.

Neubeck, G. 1981. "Getting Older in My Family: A Personal Reflection," pp. 313–315 in David F. Hultsch and Francine Deutsch, *Adult Development and Aging*. New York: McGraw-Hill.

Neugarten, Bernice L., Robert J. Havighurst, and Sheldon S. Tobin. 1968. "Personality and Patterns of Aging," pp. 173–177 in Bernice L. Neugarten (ed.), *Middle Age and Aging: A Reader in Social Psychology*. Chicago: University of Chicago Press.

Noble, Kenneth B. 1986. "End of Forced Retirement Means a Lot to a Few." *New York Times* (October 26): E5+.

Novak, Mark. 1987. "The Canadian New Horizons Program." *Gerontologist* 27 (June): 353–355.

Nuessel, Frank H. 1982. "The Language of Ageism." *Gerontologist* 22 (June): 273–276.

Oakley, Ann. 1974. *The Sociology of Housework*. London: Martin Robertson.

Palmore, Erdman. 1975. *The Honorable Elders: A Cross-Cultural Analysis of Aging in Japan*. Durham, NC: Duke University Press.

Palmore, Erdman, and C. Luikart. 1974. "Health and Social Factors Related to Life Satisfaction." In Erdman Palmore (ed.), *Normal Aging II: Reports from the Duke Longitudinal Studies 1970–1973*. Durham, NC: Duke University Press.

Poister, Theodore H. 1982. "Federal Transportation Policy for the Elderly and Handicapped: Responsive to Real Needs?" *Public Administration Review* 42 (January/February): 6–14.

Russell, Dan, et al. 1985. "Evaluating the Physically Disabled: An Attributional Analysis." *Personality and Social Psychology Bulletin* 11 (March): 23–31.

Russell, Diana E. H., and Nancy Howell. 1983. "The Prevalence of Rape in the United States Revisited." *Signs* 8 (Summer): 688–695.

Scarpitti, Frank R., and Margaret L. Andersen. 1989. *Social Problems*. New York: Harper & Row.

Schaffer, Kay F. 1981. *Sex Roles and Human Behavior*. Cambridge, MA: Winthrop.

Scheer, Jessica, and Nora Groce. 1988. "Impairment As a Human Constant: Cross-Cultural and Historical Perspectives on Variation." *Journal of Social Issues* 44:23–37.

Schneider, Joseph W. 1988. "Disability As Moral Experience: Epilepsy and Self in Routine Relationships." *Journal of Social Issues* 44: 63–78.

Schultz, Richard, and G. Brenner. 1977. "Reloca-tion of the Aged: A Review and Theoretical Analysis." *Journal of Gerontology* 32: 323–333.

Scotch, Richard K. 1988. "Disability As the Basis for a Social Movement: Advocacy and the Politics of Definition." *Journal of Social Issues* 44: 159–172.

Shapiro, Bruce. 1982. "Wrinkled Radical." *New Haven Advocate* (July 28): 6–7+.

Shaw, J. I., and P. Skolnick. 1971. "Attribution of Responsibility for a Happy Accident." *Journal of Personality and Social Psychology* 18: 380–383.

Simpson, Michael A. 1976. "Brought in Dead." *Omega* 7: 243–248.

Smith, Richard W. 1973. "The Physically Deviant," pp. 99–115 in Don Spiegel and Patricia Keith-Spiegel (eds.), *Outsiders USA*. San Francisco: Rinehart Press.

Sternglanz, S., and L. Serbin. 1974. "Sex Role Stereotyping in Children's Television Programs." *Developmental Psychology* 10: 710–715.

Streib, Gordon F., and C. J. Schneider. 1971. *Retirement in American Society: Impact and Process*. Ithaca, NY: Cornell University Press.

Sudnow, David. 1967. *Passing On: The Social Organization of Dying*. Englewood Cliffs, NJ: Prentice-Hall.

U.S. Bureau of the Census. 1959. *Statistical Abstract of the United States: 1959*. Washington, DC: U.S. Government Printing Office. 80th edition.

U.S. Bureau of the Census. 1989. *Statistical Abstract of the United States: 1989*. Washington, DC: U.S. Government Printing Office. 109th edition.

Wiener, C. 1975. "The Burden of Rheumatoid Arthritis: Tolerating the Uncertainty." *Social Science and Medicine* 9: 97–104.

Williamson, John B., Anne Munley, and Linda Evans. 1980. *Aging and Society*. New York: Holt, Rinehart and Winston.

Wollstonecraft, Mary. 1980. "A Vindication of the Rights of Women," pp. 457–463 in Sheila Ruth (ed.), *Issues in Feminism*. Boston: Houghton Mifflin. Originally published in 1792.

Yee, Doris K., and Jacquelynne S. Eccles. 1988. "Parent Perceptions and Attributions for Children's Math Achievement." *Sex Roles* 19 (September): 317–333.

Chapter 12

Adams, Bert N. 1980. *The American Family*. Chicago: Rand McNally. Third edition.

Albrecht, Stan L. 1979. "Correlates of Marital Happiness among the Remarried." *Journal of Marriage and the Family* 41: 857–867.

Albrecht, Stan L. 1980. "Reactions and Adjustments to Divorce: Differences in the Experiences of Males and Females." *Family Relations* 29 (January): 59–68.

Ariès, Phillipe. 1962. *Centuries of Childhood*. New York: Vintage Books.

Baber, Kristine M., and Patricia Monaghan. 1988.

"College Women's Career and Motherhood Expectations: New Options, Old Dilemmas." *Sex Roles* 19 (August): 189–203.

Barringer, Felicity. 1989. "Doubt on 'Trial Marriage' Raised by Divorce Rates." *New York Times* (June 9): A1+.

Bellah, Robert N., et al. 1986. *Habits of the Heart: Individualism and Commitment in American Life.* New York: Harper & Row.

Berger, Brigitte, and Peter L. Berger. 1984. *The War over the Family.* Garden City, NY: Anchor Books.

Bernstein, Barton E., and Sheila K. Collins. 1985. "Remarriage Counseling: Lawyer and Therapist's Help with the Second Time Around." *Family Relations* 34 (July): 387–391.

Bohannon, Paul (ed.). 1970. *Divorce and After.* Garden City, NY: Doubleday.

Bolger, Niall, et al. 1989. "The Contagion of Stress across Multiple Roles." *Journal of Marriage and the Family* 51 (February): 175–183.

Braungart, Richard G., and Margaret M. Braungart. 1988. "From Yippies to Yuppies: Twenty Years of Freshman Attitudes." *Public Opinion* 11 (September/October): 53–56.

Brody, Jane E. 1983. "Divorce's Stress Exacts Long-Term Health Toll." *New York Times* (December 13): C1+.

Buss, David M. 1986. "Human Mate Selection," pp. 60–65 in *Marriage and Family, 86/87.* Guilford, CT: Dushkin.

Chesser, Barbara Jo. 1982. "Analysis of Wedding Rituals: An Attempt to Make Weddings More Meaningful." *Marriage and Family 82/83.* Guilford, CT: Dushkin.

Christian, Shirley. 1989. "Million-Dollar Player Weds in Millionaire Style." *New York Times* (November 9): B25+.

Cockrum, Janet, and Priscilla White. 1985. "Influences on the Life Satisfaction of Never-Married Men and Women." *Family Relations* 34 (October): 551–556.

Davis, Bea, and Arthur Aron. 1988. "Perceived Causes of Divorce and Postdivorce Adjustment among Recently Divorced Midlife Women." *Journal of Divorce* 12: 41–55.

Demo, David H., and Alan C. Acock. 1988. "The Impact of Divorce on Children." *Journal of Marriage and the Family* 50 (August): 619–648.

Feldman, Harold. 1981. "A Comparison of Intentional Parents and Intentionally Childless Couples." *Journal of Marriage and the Family* 43 (August): 593–600.

Furstenberg, Frank F., Jr., and Christine Winquist Nord. 1985. "Parenting Apart: Patterns of Childrearing after Marital Disruption." *Journal of Marriage and the Family* 47 (November): 893–904.

Futurist. 1985. "Land Co-op." 19 (April): 62+.

Gagnon, John H., and Cathy S. Greenblat. 1978. *Life Designs: Individuals, Marriages, and Families.* Glenview, IL: Scott, Foresman and Company.

Gerstel, Naomi. 1988. "Divorce and Kin Ties: The Importance of Gender." *Journal of Marriage and the Family* 50 (February): 209–219.

Glenn, Norval D., and Charles Weaver. 1977. "The Marital Happiness of Remarried Divorced Persons." *Journal of Marriage And the Family* 39 (May): 331–337.

Glenwick, David S., and Joel D. Mowrey. 1986. "When Parent Becomes Peer: Loss of Intergenerational Boundaries in Single-Parent Families." *Family Relations* 35 (January): 57–62.

Glick, Paul C. 1986. "How American Families Are Changing," pp. 23–26 in *Marriage and Family 86/87.* Guilford, CT: Dushkin.

Goode, William J. 1956. *After Divorce.* New York: The Free Press.

Goode, William J. 1963. *World Revolution and Family Patterns.* New York: The Free Press.

Goode, William J. 1982. *The Family.* Englewood Cliffs, NJ: Prentice-Hall. Second edition.

Green, Ernest J. 1978. *Personal Relationships.* New York: McGraw-Hill.

Greene, Robert M., and Leigh A. Leslie. 1989. "Mothers' Behavior and Sons' Adjustment Following Divorce." *Journal of Divorce* 12: 235–251.

Gwartney-Gibbs, Patricia A. 1986. "The Institutionalization of Premarital Cohabitation: Estimates from Marriage License Applications, 1970 and 1980." *Journal of Marriage and the Family* 48 (May): 423–434.

Handwerker, W. Penn. 1973. "Technology and Household Configuration in Urban Africa: The Bassa of Monrovia." *American Sociological Review* 38 (April): 182–197.

Hobart, Charles. 1988. "The Family System in Remarriage: An Exploratory Study." *Journal of Marriage and the Family* 50 (August): 649–661.

Hoffman, Lois Wladis, and F. Ivan Nye. 1974. *Working Mothers.* San Francisco: Jossey-Bass.

Holmstrom, Lynda Lytle. 1972. *The Two-Career Family.* Cambridge, MA: Schenkman.

Hunt, Morton, and Bernice Hunt. 1980. "Another World, Another Life," pp. 340–354 in Arlene Skolnick and Jerome H. Skolnick (eds.), *Family in Transition.* Boston: Little, Brown and Company. Third edition.

Kamerman, Sheila B., and Alfred J. Kahn. 1981. *Child Care, Family Benefits, and Working Parents.* New York: Columbia University Press.

Kanter, Rosabeth M. 1968. "Commitment and Social Organization: A Study of Commitment Mechanisms in Utopian Communities." *American Sociological Review* 33 (August): 499–517.

Klee, Linnea, Catherine Schmidt, and Colleen Johnson. 1989. "Children's Definitions of Family Following Divorce of Their Parents." *Journal of Divorce* 12: 109–127.

Knox, David. 1988. *Choices in Relationships.* St. Paul: West. Second edition.

Krebs, Albin, and Robert M. Thomas, Jr. 1981. "A

Message of Love Travels in High Seas." *New York Times* (August 28): 18.

Kunz, Phillip R., and J. Lynn England. 1988. "Age-Specific Divorce Rates." *Journal of Divorce* 12: 113–126.

Lamanna, Mary Ann, and Agnes Riedmann. 1988. *Marriages & Families*. Belmont, CA: Wadsworth. Third edition.

Lauer, Jeanette, and Robert Lauer. 1989. "Marriages Made to Last," pp. 85–88 in Ollie Pocs (ed.), *Marriage and Family 89/90*. Guilford, CT: Dushkin.

Leighton, Alexander H. 1984. "Then and Now: Some Notes on the Interaction of Person and Social Environment." *Human Organization* 43 (Fall): 189–197.

Lein, Laura, and Mary C. Blehar. 1983. "Working Couples As Parents," pp. 420–437 in Arlene S. Skolnick and Jerome H. Skolnick (eds.), *Family in Transition*. Boston: Little, Brown, and Company. Fourth edition.

Levin, Martin L. 1989. "Sequelae to Marital Disruption in Children." *Journal of Divorce* 12: 25–80.

Lowery, Carol S., and Shirley A. Settle. 1985. "Effects of Divorce on Children: Differential Impact of Custody and Visitation Patterns." *Family Relations* 34 (October): 455–463.

Macklin, Eleanor. 1983. "Nonmarital Heterosexual Cohabitation," pp. 264–285 in Arlene Skolnick and Jerome H. Skolnick (eds.), *Family in Transition*. Boston: Little, Brown and Company. Fourth edition.

Mead, Margaret. 1963. "Children and Ritual in Bali," pp. 40–51 in Margaret Mead and Martha Wolfenstein (eds.), *Childhood in Contemporary Cultures*. Chicago: Phoenix Books. Originally published in Chicago: University of Chicago Press, 1955.

Menaghan, Elizabeth G., and Morton A. Lieberman. 1986. "Changes in Depression Following Divorce: A Panel Study." *Journal of Marriage and the Family* 48 (May): 319–328.

Moffett, Robert K., and Jack F. Scherer. 1976. *Dealing with Divorce*. Boston: Little, Brown and Company.

Murdock, George Peter. 1949. *Social Structure*. New York: Macmillan.

Neugebauer, R. 1989. "Divorce, Custody, and Visitation: The Child's Point of View." *Journal of Divorce* 12: 153–168.

Norton, Arthur J., and Paul C. Glick. 1986. "One Parent Families: A Social and Economic Profile." *Family Relations* 35 (January): 9–17.

Norton, Arthur J., and Jeanne E. Moorman. 1987. "Current Trends in Marriage and Divorce among American Women." *Journal of Marriage and the Family* 49 (February): 3–14.

Oakley, Deborah. 1985. "Premarital Childbearing Decision-Making." *Family Relations* 34 (October): 561–563.

Presser, Harriet B. 1988. "Shift Work and Child Care among Young Dual-Earner American Parents." *Journal of Marriage and the Family* 50 (February): 133–148.

Ramey, James. 1978. "Experimental Family Forms —the Family of the Future." *Marriage and Family Review* 1 (January/February): 1–9.

Regan, Mary C., and Helen E. Roland. 1985. "Rearranging Family and Career Priorities: Professional Women and Men of the Eighties." *Journal of Marriage and the Family* 47 (November): 985–992.

Reiss, Ira L. 1980. *Family Systems in America*. New York: Holt, Rinehart and Winston. Third edition.

Reiss, Ira L., and Gary R. Lee. 1988. *Family Systems in America*. New York: Holt, Rinehart and Winston. Fourth edition.

Renne, Karen S. 1974. "Correlates of Dissatisfaction in Marriage," in Robert Winch and Graham Spanier (eds.), *Selected Studies in the Family*. New York: Holt, Rinehart and Winston. Fourth edition.

Risman, Barbara J., and Kyung Park. 1988. "Just the Two of Us: Parent–Child Relationships in Single-Parent Homes." *Journal of Marriage and the Family* 50 (November): 1049–1062.

Rosenthal, Carolyn J. 1985. "Kinkeeping in the Familial Division of Labor." *Journal of Marriage and the Family* 47 (November): 965–974.

Sanik, Margaret M., and Teresa Mauldin. 1986. "Single versus Two Parent Families: A Comparison of Mothers' Time." *Family Relations* 35 (January): 53–56.

Saxton, Lloyd. 1980. *The Individual, Marriage, and Family*. Belmont, CA: Wadsworth. Fourth edition.

Scanzoni, Letha Dawson, and John Scanzoni. 1988. *Men, Women, and Change*. New York: McGraw-Hill. Third edition.

Schnayer, Reuben, and R. Robert Orr. 1989. "A Comparison of Children Living in Single-Mother and Single-Father Families." *Journal of Divorce* 12: 171–184.

Schultz, Martin. 1984. "Divorce in Early America: Origins and Patterns in Three North Central States." *Sociological Quarterly* 25 (Autumn): 511–526.

Sennett, Richard. 1974. *Families against the City*. New York: Vintage Books. Originally published in 1970.

Silka, Linda, and Sara Kiesler. 1977. "Couples Who Choose to Remain Childless." *Family Planning Perspectives* 9 (January/February): 16–25.

Singer, Barry. 1982. "Conversation with Robert McGinley." *Alternative Lifestyles* 5 (Winter): 69–77.

Skolnick, Arlene. 1987. *Intimate Environment*. Glenview, IL: Scott, Foresman. Fourth edition.

Spiro, Melford E. 1970. *Kibbutz*. New York: Schocken Books. Second edition.

Stein, Peter J. 1980. "Singlehood: An Alternative to Marriage," pp. 517–536 in Arlene Skolnick and Jerome H. Skolnick (eds.), *Family in Transition.* Boston: Little, Brown, and Company. Third edition.

Tanner, Donna. 1978. *The Lesbian Couple.* Lexington, MA: Lexington Books.

Thimberger, Rosemary, and Michael J. MacLean. 1982. "Maternal Employment: The Child's Perspective." *Journal of Marriage and the Family* 44 (May): 469–475.

Turner, Pauline H., and Richard M. Smith. 1983. "Single Parents and Day Care." *Family Relations* 32 (April): 215–226.

U.S. Bureau of the Census. 1982. *Population Profile of the United States: 1981.* Washington, DC: U.S. Government Printing Office.

U.S. Bureau of the Census. 1983. *Current Population Reports,* Series P-20, *Marital Status and Living Arrangements: March 1982.* Washington, DC: U.S. Government Printing Office.

U.S. Bureau of the Census. 1984. *Fertility of American Women: June 1983.* Washington, DC: U.S. Government Printing Office.

U.S. Bureau of the Census. 1989. *Statistical Abstract of the United States: 1989.* Washington, DC: U.S. Government Printing Office. 109th edition.

Veevers, J. E. 1973. "Voluntarily Childless Wives: An Exploratory Study." *Sociology and Social Research* 57 (April): 356–366.

Weingarten, Helen R. 1988. "The Impact of Late Life Divorce: A Conceptual and Empirical Study." *Journal of Divorce* 12: 21–39.

Weitzman, Lenore J., and Ruth B. Dixon. 1983. "The Transformation of Legal Marriage through No-Fault Divorce," pp. 353–366 in Arlene Skolnick and Jerome H. Skolnick (eds.), *Family in Transition.* Boston: Little, Brown, and Company. Fourth edition.

Whitbeck, Les B., and Viktor Gecas. 1988. "Value Attributions and Value Transmission between Parents and Children." *Journal of Marriage and the Family* 50 (August): 829–840.

White, Stephen W., and Bernard L. Bloom. 1981. "Factors Related to the Adjustment of Divorcing Men." *Family Relations* 30 (July): 349–360.

Whiting, Beatrice, and John W. M. Whiting. 1975. *Children of Six Cultures: A Psycho-Cultural Analysis.* Cambridge, MA: Harvard University Press.

Zablocki, Ben. 1977. *Alienation and Investment in the Urban Commune.* New York: Center for Policy Research.

Chapter 13

Adams, David S. 1987. "Ronald Reagan's 'Revival': Voluntarism As a Theme in Reagan's Civil Religion." *Sociological Analysis* 48 (Spring): 17–29.

Allman, T. D. 1976. "Jesus in Tomorrowland." *New Republic* 177 (November 27): 6–9.

Armor, David J. 1989. "After Busing: Education and Choice." *Public Interest* 23 (Spring): 24–37.

Bailyn, Bernard, et al. 1977. *The Great Republic.* Lexington, MA: D. C. Heath.

Banks, Olive. 1976. *The Sociology of Education.* New York: Schocken Books. Revised edition.

Bellah, Robert N. 1967. "Civil Religion in America." *Daedalus* 96 (Winter): 1–21.

Bills, David B. 1988. "Educational Credentials and Promotions: Does Schooling Do More than Get You in the Door?" *Sociology of Education* 61 (January): 52–60.

Binzen, Peter. 1970. *Whitetown, USA.* New York: Random House.

Bowles, Samuel, and Herbert Gintis. 1976. *Schooling in Capitalist America: Educational Reform and the Contradictions of Economic Life.* New York: Basic.

Braddock, Jomills Henry, II, Robert L. Crain, and James S. McPartland. 1984. "A Long-Term View of School Desegregation: Some Recent Studies of Graduates As Adults." *Phi Delta Kappan* 66 (December): 259–264.

Bradfield, Cecil, and Mary Lou Wylie. 1989. "After the Flood: The Response of Ministers to a Natural Disaster." *Sociological Analysis* 49 (Winter): 397–407.

Brodinsky, Ben. 1979. "Something Happened: Education in the Seventies." *Phi Dela Kappan* 61 (December): 238–241.

Campbell, Ernest Q., and Thomas Pettigrew. 1959. *Christians in Racial Crisis.* Washington, DC: Public Affairs Press.

Clogg, Clifford C., and James W. Shockey. 1984. "Mismatch between Occupation and Schooling: A Prevalence Measure, Recent Trends and Demographic Analysis." *Demography* 21 (May): 235–257.

Cohen, Steven M., and Leonard J. Fein. 1985. "From Integration to Survival: American Jewish Anxieties in Transition." *Annals of the American Academy of Political and Social Science* 483 (July): 75–88.

Coleman, James S., et al. 1966. *Equality of Educational Opportunity.* Washington, DC: U.S. Government Printing Office.

Coleman, James S., et al. 1982. *High School Achievement.* New York: Basic.

Collins, Randall. 1979. *The Credential Society.* New York: Academic.

Crossman, Richard (ed.). 1952. *The God That Failed.* New York: Bantam Books.

Douglass, Frederick. 1968. *Narrative of the Life of Frederick Douglass.* New York: Signet Books. Originally published in 1845.

Durkheim, Émile, 1961. *The Elementary Forms of the Religious Life.* New York: Collier Books. Translated by Joseph Ward Swain.

Durkheim, Émile. 1964. *The Division of Labor in Society.* New York: The Free Press. Translated by

George Simpson. The Simpson translation originally published in New York: The Macmillan Company, 1933.

Durkheim, Émile. 1975. *Durkheim on Religion.* London: Routledge Kegan Paul. Edited by W. S. F. Pickering and translated by Jacqueline Gedding and W. S. F. Pickering.

Economist. 1985. "Religious Schools: Dividing and Multiplying." 294 (February 23): 25.

Education for Democracy Project. 1987. "Education for Democracy: The Changes We Need to Make." *Education Digest* 53 (October): 10–13.

Ellerin, Milton, and Alisa Kesten. 1981. "The New Right: What Is It?" *Social Policy* 11 (March/April): 54–62.

Flynn, Charles P., and Suzanne R. Kunkel. 1987. "Deprivation, Compensation, and Conceptions of an Afterlife." *Sociological Analysis* 48 (Spring): 58–72.

Goldberg, Milton, and James Harvey. 1983. "A Nation at Risk: The Report of the National Commission on Excellence in Education." *Phi Delta Kappan* 65 (September): 14–18.

Gracey, Harry L. 1977. "Learning the Student Role: Kindergarten as Academic Boot Camp," pp. 215–226 in Dennis H. Wrong and Harry L. Gracey (eds.), *Readings in Introductory Sociology.* New York: Macmillan. Third edition.

Gurley, John G. 1984. "Marx's Contributions and Their Relevance Today." *American Economic Review* 74 (May): 110–123.

Guth, James L., and John C. Green. 1988. "Grand Old Deity." *Psychology Today* 22 (April): 20+.

Hammond, Phillip E. 1985. "The Curious Path of Conservative Protestantism." *Annals of the American Academy of Political and Social Science* 480 (July): 53–62.

Hanline, Mary Frances, and Carola Murray. 1984. "Integrating Severely Handicapped Children into Regular Public Schools." *Phi Delta Kappan* 66 (December): 273–276.

Hinsberg, Thomas F. 1974. "The Church: Agent of Social Change." *Journal of Applied Behavioral Science* 10 (Summer): 432–437.

Hodgson, Godfrey. 1973. "Do Schools Made a Difference?" *Atlantic* 231 (March): 35–46.

Jackson, Philip. 1968. *Life in Classrooms.* New York: Holt, Rinehart and Winston.

Jaynes, Gerald David, and Robin M. Williams (eds.). 1989. *A Common Destiny: Blacks and American Society.* Washington, DC: National Academy Press.

Johnstone, Ronald L. 1975. *Religion and Society in Interaction.* Englewood Cliffs, NJ: Prentice-Hall.

Lee, Valerie E., and Anthony S. Bryk. 1988. "Curriculum Tracking As Mediating the Social Distribution of High School Achievement." *Sociology of Education* 61 (April): 78–94.

Lewin, Roger. 1986. "Creationism Downed Again in Louisiana." *Science* 231 (January 10): 112.

Lewis, Sinclair. 1970. *Elmer Gantry.* New York: Signet Classics. Originally published in New York: Harcourt, Brace and Company, 1927.

Lichtenstein, Peter M. 1985. "Radical Liberalism and Radical Education: A Synthesis and Critical Evaluation of Illich, Freire, and Dewey." *American Journal of Economics and Sociology* 44 (January): 39–54.

Lienesch, Michael. 1982. "Right-Wing Religion: Christian Conservatism As a Political Movement." *Political Science Quarterly* 97 (Fall): 403–425.

MacKinnon, Malcolm H. 1988a. "Part I: Calvinism and the Infallible Assurance of Grace: The Weber Thesis Reconsidered." *British Journal of Sociology* 39 (June): 143–177.

MacKinnon, Malcolm, H. 1988b. "Part II: Weber's Exploration of Calvinism: The Undiscovered Provenance of Calvinism." *British Journal of Sociology* 39 (June): 178–210.

McNamara, Patrick H. 1985. "American Catholicism in the Mid-Eighties: Pluralism and Conflict in a Changing Church." *Annals of the American Academy of Political and Social Science* 480 (July): 63–74.

McNeil, Linda M. 1988. "Contradictions of Control, Part 1: Administrators and Teachers." *Phi Delta Kappan* 69 (January): 333–339.

Marshall, Eliot. 1986. "Dinosaurs Ruffle Some Feathers in California." *Science* 231 (January 3): 18–19.

Marx, Karl. 1970. *Critique of Hegel's "Philosophy of Right."* London: Cambridge University Press. Translated by Annette Jolin and Joseph O'Malley.

Mingle, James R. 1988. "Minorities in Higher Education." *Education Digest* 53 (February): 18–20.

Mullins, Mark R. 1988. "The Organizational Dilemmas of Ethnic Churches: A Case Study of Japanese Buddhism in Canada." *Sociological Analysis* 49 (Fall): 217–233.

Natriello, Gary, Aaron M. Pallas, and Karl Alexander. 1989. "On the Right Track?: Curriculum and Academic Achievement." *Sociology of Education* 62 (April): 109–118.

New York Times. 1989. "Senate Panel Hears Manley Tell of Learning Disability." (May 19): B17.

O'Dea, Thomas F. 1966. *The Sociology of Religion.* Englewood Cliffs, NJ: Prentice-Hall.

Oestereicher, Emil. 1982. "The Depoliticization of the Liberal Arts." *Social Research* 49 (Winter): 1004–1012.

Parsons, Talcott. 1968. "The School Class As a Social System: Some of Its Functions in American Society," pp. 199–218 in Robert R. Bell and Holger R. Stub (eds.), *The Sociology of Education.* Homewood, IL: Dorsey Press. Revised edition.

Pines, Maya. 1981. "Unlearning Blind Obedience in German Schools." *Psychology Today* 15 (May): 59–60.

Power, Clark, and Lawrence Kohlberg. 1987. "Using a Hidden Curriculum for Moral Education." *Education Digest* 52 (May): 10–13.

Rossell, Christine H. 1988. "Is It Busing or the Blacks?" *Urban Affairs Quarterly* 24 (September): 138–148.

Scotch, Richard K. 1988. "Disability As the Basis for a Social Movement: Advocacy and the Politics of Definition." *Journal of Social Issues* 44: 159–172.

Shrum, Wesley, Neil H. Cheek, Jr., and Saundra MacD. Hunter. 1988. "Friendship in School: Gender and Racial Homophily." *Sociology of Education* 61 (October): 227–239.

Silverman, William. 1989. "Images of the Sacred: An Empirical Study." *Sociological Analysis* 49 (Winter): 440–444.

Sirotnik, Kenneth A., and Richard W. Clark. 1988. "School-Centered Decision Making and Renewal." *Phi Delta Kappan* 69 (May): 660–664.

Smidt, Corwin. 1988. "Evangelicals within Contemporary American Politics: Differentiating between Fundamentalists and Non-Fundamentalist Evangelicals." *Western Political Quarterly* 41 (September): 601–620.

Smidt, Corwin. 1989. " 'Praise the Lord' Politics: A Comparative Analysis of the Social Characteristics and Political Views of American Evangelical and Charismatic Christians." *Sociological Analysis* 50 (Spring): 53–72.

Sweet, William Warren. 1950. *Story of Religion in America*. New York: Harper & Company.

Twain, Mark. 1973. "Bible Teaching and Religious Practice," pp. 106–110 in Maxwell Geismar (ed.), *Mark Twain and the Three R's*. Indianapolis: Bobbs-Merrill.

U. S. Bureau of the Census. 1966. *Statistical Abstract of the United States: 1966*. Washington, DC: U.S. Government Printing Office. 87th edition.

U. S. Bureau of the Census. 1989. *Statistical Abstract of the United States: 1989*. Washington, DC: U. S. Government Printing Office. 109th edition.

Weber, Max. 1958. *The Protestant Ethic and the Spirit of Capitalism*. New York: Charles Scribner's Sons. Translated by Talcott Parsons. Original Parsons translation in 1930.

Wilson, John. 1978. *Religion in American Society*. Englewood Cliffs, NJ: Prentice-Hall.

Woodrum, Eric. 1985. "Religion and Economics among Japanese Americans: A Weberian Study." *Social Forces* 64 (September): 191–204.

Chapter 14

Anderson, Kristine L., and Bruce London. 1985. "Modernization, Elites, and the Distribution of Educational Resources in Thailand." *Social Forces* 63 (March): 775–794.

Apple, R. W., Jr. 1989. "Washington's New Wave of Ethics Anxiety." *New York Times* (April 23): Section 4, p. 1.

Arato, Andrew. 1985. "Some Perspectives of Democratization in East Central Europe." *Journal of International Affairs* 38 (Winter): 321–335.

Aziz-al Ahsan, S. 1984. "Economic Policy and Class Structure in Syria: 1958–1980." *International Journal of Middle East Studies* 16 (August): 301–323.

Bailyn, Bernard, et al. 1977. *The Great Republic*. Lexington, MA: Heath.

Bensman, Joseph, and Michael Givant. 1975. "Charisma and Modernity: The Use and Abuse of a Concept." *Social Research* 42 (Autumn): 570–614.

Boffey, Philip M. 1985. "Satisfaction on the Job: Autonomy Ranks First." *New York Times* (May 28): 28.

Bradshaw, York W. 1985. "Dependent Development in Black Africa: A Cross-National Study." *American Sociological Review* 50 (April): 195–207.

Burstein, Paul. 1977. "Political Elites and Labor Markets: Selection of American Cabinet Members, 1932–72." *Social Forces* 56 (September): 189–201.

Carr, Raymond, and Juan Pablo Fusi Aizpurua. 1981. *Spain: Dictatorship to Democracy*. London: George Allen and Unwin. Second edition.

Dahl, Robert A. 1967. *Pluralist Democracy in the United States: Conflict and Consent*. Chicago: Rand McNally.

Dahl, Robert A. 1976. *Democracy in the United States: Promise and Performance*. Chicago: Rand McNally. Third edition.

Dahl, Robert A. 1982. *Dilemmas of Pluralist Democracy*. New Haven: Yale University Press.

Day, Phyllis J. 1980. "Charismatic Leadership in the Small Organization." *Human Organization* 39 (Spring): 50–58.

Dealy, Glen C. 1985. "The Pluralistic Latins." *Foreign Policy* (Winter): 108–127.

Deutsch, R. Eden. 1985. "Tomorrow's Work Force." *Futurist* 19 (December): 8–11.

DiGaetano, Alan. 1988. "The Rise and Development of Urban Political Machines: An Alternative to Merton's Functional Analysis." *Urban Affairs Quarterly* 24 (December): 242–267.

Domhoff, G. William. 1978. *The Powers That Be*. New York: Random House.

Domhoff, G. William. 1983. *Who Rules America Now?: A View for the Eighties*. Englewood Cliffs, NJ: Prentice-Hall.

Doob, Christopher Bates. 1970. *How the War Was Lost*. Unpublished manuscript.

Dugger, William M. 1988. "An Institutional Analysis of Corporate Power." *Journal of Economic Issues* (March): 79–111.

Edsall, Thomas Byrne. 1986. "Republican America." *New York Review of Books* (April 24): 3–4+.

Emerson, Richard M. 1983. "Charismatic Kingship: A Study of State-Formation and Authority in Baltistan." *Politics and Society* 12: 413–444.

Etzioni-Halevy, Eva. 1988. "Inherent Contradictions of Democracy: Illustrations from National Broadcasting Corporations." *Comparative Politics* 20 (April): 325–340.

Friedman, Howard S., Ronald E. Riggio, and Daniel F. Casella. 1988. "Nonverbal Skill, Personal Charisma, and Initial Attraction." *Personality and Social Psychology Bulletin* 14 (March): 203–211.

Garson, G. David. 1977. *Power and Politics in the United States*. Lexington, MA: Heath.

Gartner, Alan, and Frank Riessman. 1974. "Is There a Work Ethic?" *American Journal of Orthopsychiatry* 44 (July): 563–567.

Gerth, Hans, and C. Wright Mills (eds.). 1946. *From Max Weber: Essays in Sociology*. New York: Oxford University Press.

Gilpin, Robert. 1975. *U.S. Power and the Multinational Corporation: The Political Economy of Foreign Direct Investment*. New York: Basic Books.

Grant, Alan R. 1979. *The American Political Process*. London: Heinemann.

Greenberg, Edward S. 1974. *Serving the Few*. New York: John Wiley & Sons.

Horton, Paul B., Gerald R. Leslie, and Richard F. Larson. 1988. *The Sociology of Social Problems*. Englewood Cliffs, NJ: Prentice-Hall Ninth Edition.

Kohn, Melvin L. 1976. "Occupational Structure and Alienation." *American Journal of Sociology* 82 (July): 111–130.

Lindblom, Charles E. 1982. "Another State of Mind." *American Political Science Review* 76 (March): 9–21.

Ling, Richard. 1987. "The Production of Synthetic Charisma." *Journal of Political and Military Charisma* 15 (Fall): 157–170.

Manley, John F. 1983. "Neo-Pluralism: A Class Analysis of Pluralism I and Pluralism II." *American Political Science Review* 77 (June): 368–383.

Marx, Karl. 1932. "Manifesto of the Communist Party," pp. 315–355 in Marx, *Capital, the Communist Manifesto and Other Writings*. New York: The Modern Library. Translated by Stephen L. Trask.

Merton, Robert K. 1968. "Manifest and Latent Functions," pp. 73–138 in Merton, *Social Theory and Social Structure*. New York: Free Press. Third edition.

Mills, C. Wright. 1959. *The Power Elite*. New York: Oxford University Press.

Morton, Herbert C. 1977. "A Look at Factors Affecting the Quality of Working Life." *Monthly Labor Review* (October): 64–65.

Navarro, Peter. 1988. "Why Do Corporations Give to Charity?" *Journal of Business* 61 (January): 65–93.

Neustadtl, Alan, and Dan Clawson. 1988. "Corporate Political Groupings: Does Ideology Unify Business Political Behavior?" *American Sociological Review* 53 (April): 172–190.

Newman, Ruth G. 1983. "Thoughts on Superstars of Charisma: Pipers in Our Midst." *American Journal of Orthopsychiatry* 53 (April): 201–208.

Oldham, Greg R. 1988. "Effects of Changes in Workspace Partitions and Spatial Density on Employee Reactions: A Quasi-Experiment." *Journal of Applied Psychology* 73 (May): 253–258.

Palmer, Susan J. 1988. "Charisma and Abdication: A Study of the Leadership of Bhagwan Shree Rajneesh." *Sociological Analysis* 49 (Summer): 119–135.

Ranney, Austin. 1966. *The Governing of Men*. New York: Holt, Rinehart and Winston.

Riegle, Donald W., Jr. 1982. "The Psychological and Social Effects of Unemployment." *American Psychologist* 37 (October): 1113–1115.

Riordan, William L. 1963. *Plunkitt of Tammany Hall*. New York: E. P. Dutton and Company.

Roelofs, H. Mark. 1967. *The Language of Modern Politics*. Homewood, IL: Dorsey Press.

Rohatyn, Felix. 1988. "Restoring American Independence." *New York Review of Books* 35 (February 18): 8–10.

Safran, William. 1985. "The Mitterand Regime and Its Policies of Ethnocultural Accommodation." *Comparative Politics* 18 (October): 41–63.

Salomon, David, and Jules Bernstein. 1982. "The Corporate Thrust in American Politics," pp. 176–179 in Leonard Cargan and Jeanne H. Ballantine (eds.), *Sociological Footprints*. Belmont, CA: Wadsworth. Second edition.

Samuelson, Paul A. 1980. *Economics*. New York: McGraw-Hill. Eleventh edition.

Schweitzer, Arthur. 1984. *The Age of Charisma*. Chicago: Nelson-Hall.

Serfaty, Meir. 1981. "Spanish Democracy: The End of the Transition." *Current History* 80 (May): 213–217+.

Smith, Adam. 1930. *Inquiry into the Nature and Causes of the Wealth of Nations*. London: Methuen and Company. Originally published in 1776.

Spector, Paul E., Daniel J. Dwyer, and Steve M. Jex. 1988. "Relation of Job Stressors to Affective, Health, and Performance Outcomes: A Comparison of Multiple Data Sources." *Journal of Applied Psychology* 73 (February): 11–19.

Terkel, Studs. 1974. *Working*. New York: Pantheon Books.

Tocqueville, Alexis de. 1966. *Democracy in America*. New York: Harper & Row. Translated by George Lawrence. Originally published in 1835.

Toffler, Alvin. 1981. *The Third Wave*. New York: Bantam Books.

Tolchin, Martin, and Susan Tolchin. 1972. *To the Victor. . . .* New York: Vintage Books.

Twain, Mark. 1973. *Mark Twain and the Three R's*. Indianapolis: Bobbs-Merrill.

U.S. Bureau of the Census. *Statistical Abstract of the United States: 1989*. Washington, DC: U.S. Government Printing Office. 109th edition.

Vallas, Steven Peter. 1988. "New Technology, Job Content, and Worker Alienation: A Test of Two Rival Perspectives." *Work and Occupations* 15 (May): 148–178.

Wallerstein, Immanuel. 1974. *The Modern World-System: Capitalist Agriculture and the Origins of the European World-Economy in the Sixteenth Century*. New York: Academic Press.

Weber, Max. 1947. *The Theory of Social and Economic*

Organization. New York: The Free Press. Translated by A. M. Henderson and Talcott Parsons.

Wilensky, Harold L. 1966. "Work As a Social Problem," pp. 117–166 in Howard S. Becker (ed.), *Social Problems: A Modern Approach.* New York: John Wiley & Sons.

Wise, David. 1976. "Cloak and Dagger Operations: An Overview," pp. 88–101 in Jerome H. Skolnick and Elliot Currie (eds.), *Crisis in American Institutions.* Boston: Little, Brown and Company. Third edition.

Wolfe, Alan. 1973. *The Seamy Side of Democracy.* New York: David McKay Company.

Yankelovich, Daniel. 1974. "The Meaning of Work," pp. 19–47 in J. M. Rosow (ed.), *The Worker and the Job.* Englewood Cliffs, NJ: Prentice-Hall.

Chapter 15

Armstrong, David. 1987. "Silence and Truth in Death and Dying." *Social Science and Medicine* 24: 651–657.

Bayer, Ronald, et al. 1988. "Toward Justice in Health Care." *American Journal of Public Health* 78 (May): 583–588.

Ben-David, Joseph. 1971. *The Scientist's Role in Society.* Englewood Cliffs, NJ: Prentice-Hall.

Bendzsel, Miklós, and István Kiss. "The Socio-ethical Dimension of Invention. *Impact of Science on Society* 37: 233–240.

Brandt, Allan M. 1988. "AIDS in Historical Perspective: Four Lessons from the History of Sexually Transmitted Diseases." *American Journal of Public Health* 78 (April): 367–371.

Cleveland, Harlan. 1988. "Theses of a New Reformation: The Social Fallout of Science 300 Years after Newton." *Public Administration Review* 48 (May/June): 681–686.

Clymer, Adam. 1986. "Poll Finds Children Remain Enthusiastic on Spaceflight." *New York Times* (February 2): 1+.

Coe, Rodney M. 1978. *Sociology of Medicine.* New York: McGraw-Hill. Second edition.

Daoyi, Zhang. 1988. "Fostering Understanding between Scientists and the Public." *Impact of Science on Society* 38: 355–362.

Fein, Rashi. 1988. "Toward Adequate Health Care." *Dissent* 35 (Winter): 98–104.

Fox, Renee C. 1978. "Training for Uncertainty," pp. 189–202 in Howard D. Schwartz and Cary S. Kart (eds.), *Dominant Issues in Medical Sociology.* Reading, MA: Addison-Wesley.

Freidson, Eliot. 1970. *Profession of Medicine.* New York: Harper & Row.

Freidson, Eliot. 1978. "Colleague Relationships among Physicians," pp. 228–237 in Howard D. Schwartz and Cary S. Kart (eds.), *Dominant Issues in Medical Sociology.* Reading, MA: Addison-Wesley.

Freidson, Eliot. 1981. "Professional Dominance and the Ordering of Health Services: Some Consequences," pp. 184–197 in Peter Conrad and Rochelle Kern (eds.), *The Sociology of Health and Illness.* New York: St. Martin's Press.

Gray-Toft, Pamela, and James G. Anderson. 1981. "Stress among Hospital Nursing Staff: Its Causes and Effects." *Social Science and Medicine* 15 (September): 639–647.

Grossman, Hildreth Y., et al. 1987. "Coping Resources and Health Responses among Men and Women Medical Students." *Social Science and Medicine* 25: 1057–1062.

Hellman, Jeremy M. 1986. "U. S. Plants Are Safe; Go Full Speed Ahead." *USA Today* (April 30): 12A.

Honicker, Jeanne. 1986. "To Save Ourselves, Stop Nuclear Pollution." *USA Today* (April 30): 12A.

Kapitza, Sergei P. 1988. "Issues in the Popularization of Science." *Impact of Science on Society* 38: 317–326.

Keith, Verna M., and David P. Smith. 1988. "The Current Differential in Black and White Life Expectancy." *Demography* 25 (November): 625–632.

Kornblum, William, and Joseph Julian. 1989. *Social Problems.* Englewood Cliffs, NJ: Prentice-Hall. Sixth edition.

Lee, Vicki L. 1985. "Scientific Knowledge As Rules That Guide Behavior." *Psychological Record* 35 (Spring): 183–192.

McNerney, Walter J. 1988. "Nursing's Vision in a Competitive Environment." *Nursing Outlook* 36 (May/June): 126–129.

Madison, Donald L., and Thomas R. Konrad. 1988. "Large Medical Group-practice Organizations and Employed Physicians: A Relationship in Transition." *Milbank Quarterly* 66: 240–282.

Mann, Jonathan M. 1988. "AIDS: A Global Strategy for a Global Challenge." *Impact of Science on Society* 38: 159–167.

Markson, Elizabeth. 1971. "A Hiding Place to Die." *Trans-action* 9 (November/December): 48–54.

Mechanic, David. 1978. *Medical Sociology.* New York: Free Press. Second edition.

Merton, Robert K. 1973. *The Sociology of Science.* Chicago: University of Chicago Press.

Mitroff, Ian. 1974. "Norms and Counter-Norms in a Select Group of the Apollo Moon Scientists: A Case Study of the Ambivalence of Scientists." *American Sociological Review* 39 (August): 579–595.

Moravcsik, Michael. 1985. "The Ultimate Scientific Plateau." *Futurist* 19 (October): 28–30.

Najman, J. M., D. Klein, and C. Munro. 1982. "Patient Characteristics Negatively Stereotyped by Doctors." *Social Science and Medicine* 16: 1781–1789.

Navarre, Bonnie Puckett. 1988. "Incentive Plans Needed for Nurse Administrators." *Nursing Management* 19 (October): 60–64.

Parkes, Katherine R. 1985. "Stressful Episodes Reported by First-Year Student Nurses: A Descriptive Account." *Social Science and Medicine* 20: 945–953.

Parsons, Talcott. 1951. *The Social System.* New York: The Free Press.

Quint, Jeanne C. 1978. "Institutionalized Practices of Information Control," pp. 87–99 in Howard D. Schwartz and Cary S. Kart (eds.), *Dominant Issues in Medical Sociology.* Reading, MA: Addison-Wesley.

Reverby, Susan. 1981. "Re-forming the Hospital Nurse: The Management of American Nursing," pp. 220–233 in Peter Conrad and Rochelle Kern (eds.), *The Sociology of Health and Illness.* New York: St. Martin's Press.

Rifkin, Jeremy. 1980. "Recombinant DNA," pp. 145–156 in Rita Arditti, Pat Brennan, and Steve Cavrak (eds.), *Science and Liberation.* Boston: South End Press.

Ryan, William. 1976. *Blaming the Victim.* New York: Vintage Books. Second edition.

Schacht, Paul J., and Alec Pemberton. 1985. "What is Unnecessary Surgery? Who Shall Decide? Issues of Consumer Sovereignty, Conflict and Self-Regulation." *Social Science and Medicine* 20: 199–206.

Shulman, Lawrence, and Joanne E. Mantell. 1988. "The AIDS Crisis: A United States Health Care Perspective." *Social Science and Medicine* 26: 979–988.

Siegel, Bernie S. 1988. *Love, Medicine and Miracles.* New York: Harper & Row.

Sirken, Monroe G., et al. 1987. "The Quality of Cause-of-Death Statistics." *American Journal of Public Health* 77 (February): 137–139.

Szasz, Thomas S., and Marc H. Hollender. 1956. "A Contribution to the Philosophy of Medicine: The Basic Models of the Doctor–Patient Relationship." *A.M.A. Archives of Internal Medicine* 97 (May): 585–592.

Turner, Bryan S. 1987. *Medical Power and Social Knowledge.* London: Sage Publications.

Twaddle, Andrew C., and Richard M. Hessler, 1977. *A Sociology of Health.* St. Louis: C. V. Mosby Company.

University of California Nuclear Weapons Labs Conversion Project. 1980. "Livermore and Los Alamos Scientific Laboratories," pp. 93–112 in Rita Arditti, Pat Brennan, and Steve Cavrak (eds.), *Science and Liberation.* Boston: South End Press.

U.S. Bureau of the Census. 1984. *Statistical Abstract of the United States: 1984.* Washington, DC: U.S. Government Printing Office. 104th edition.

U.S. Bureau of the Census. *Statistical Abstract of the United States: 1989.* Washington, DC: U.S. Government Printing Office. 109th edition.

Williams, Robin M., Jr. 1970. *American Society.* New York: Alfred A. Knopf. Third edition.

Wolinsky, Frederic D. 1980. *The Sociology of Health.* Boston: Little, Brown and Company.

Wolinsky, Frederic D., and Sally R. Wolinsky. 1981. "Expecting Sick-Role Legitimation and Getting It." *Journal of Health and Social Behavior* 22 (September): 229–242.

Wyngaarden, James B. 1984. "Science and Government: A Federal Agency Perspective." *American Psychologist* 9 (September): 1053–1055.

Yankauer, Alfred. 1988. "Disease Prevention: Still a Long Way to Go." *American Journal of Public Health* 78 (October): 1277–1278.

Chapter 16

Ahmed, Bashir. 1987. "Determinants of Contraceptive Use in Rural Bangladesh: The Demand for Children, Supply of Children, and Costs of Fertility Regulation." *Demography* 24 (August): 361–373.

Alinsky, Saul D. 1971. *Rules for Radicals.* New York: Vintage Books.

Alm, Alvin L. 1989. "Setting Environmental Priorities." *Environmental Science and Technology* 23 (April): 397.

Alpern, David M. 1981. "Mr. Fixit for the Cities." *Newsweek* 98 (May 4): 26–30.

Axelrod, Paul. 1988. "Natality and Family Planning in Three Bombay Communities." *Human Organization* 47 (Spring): 36–47.

Barnet, Richard J. 1980. *The Lean Years: Politics in the Age of Scarcity.* New York: Simon & Schuster.

Beck, Melinda. 1982. "The Decaying of America." *Newsweek* 99 (August 2): 12–17.

Bouvier, Leon F. 1984. "Planet Earth 1984–2034: A Demographic Vision." *Population Bulletin* 39 (February): 3–39.

Brown, Lester R. 1978. *The Twenty-Ninth Day.* New York: W. W. Norton and Company.

Brown, M. 1980. *Laying Waste: The Poisoning Of America by Toxic Chemicals.* New York: Pantheon.

Campbell, A. K., and J. A. Dollenmayer. 1975. "Governance in a Metropolitan Society," pp. 355–396 in A. H. Hawley and V. P. Rock (eds.), *Metropolitan America in Contemporary Perspective.* New York: John Wiley & Sons.

Cleland, John, and German Rodriguez. 1988. "The Effects of Parental Education on Marital Fertility in Developing Countries." *Population Studies* 42 (November): 419–442.

Cockburn, Alexander. 1988. "Chemical Reaction." *Environment and Society* 1 (August): 18–19.

Committee on Agriculture, House of Representatives. 1976. "Malthus and America (1974)," pp. 253–256 in Phillip Appleman (ed.), *Thomas Robert Malthus: An Essay on the Principle of Population.* New York: W. W. Norton and Company.

Commoner, Barry. 1972. *The Closing Circle: Nature, Man and Technology.* New York: Bantam Books.

Cronon, William, and Richard White. 1986. "Indians in the Land." *American Heritage* 37 (August/September): 19–25.

Dahmann, Donald C. 1985. "Assessments of Neighborhood Quality in Metropolitan America." *Urban Affairs Quarterly* 20 (June): 511–535.

Davis, Kingsley. 1967. "Population Policy: Will Current Programs Succeed?" *Science* 157 (November 10): 730–739.

Doob, Christopher Bates. 1970. *How The War Was Lost.* Unpublished manuscript.

Ehrlich, Paul R., Anne H. Ehrlich, and John P. Holdren. 1977. *Ecoscience: Population, Resources, Environment.* San Francisco: W. H. Freeman.

Freedman, Ronald, et al. 1988. "Local Area Variations in Reproductive Behavior in the People's Republic of China, 1973–1982." *Population Studies* 42 (March): 39–57.

Futurist. 1989. "Economics of Preserving the Ozone Layer." 23 (January/February): 40–41.

Gittell, Marilyn. 1985. "The American City: A National Priority or an Expendable Population?" *Urban Affairs Quarterly* 21 (September): 13–19.

Gottman, Jean. 1961. *Megalopolis: The Urbanized Northeastern Seaboard of the United States.* Cambridge, MA: M.I.T. Press.

Graves, Robert. 1962. *Claudius the God.* New York: Vintage Books. Originally published in New York: Harrison Smith and Robert Haas. 1935.

Hopkins, Ellen. 1989. "The Dispossessed," pp. 82–87 in Jeffrey M. Elliot (ed.), *Urban Society.* Guilford, CT: Dushkin. Fourth edition.

Jacobs, Jane. 1961. *The Death and Life of Great American Cities.* New York: Vintage Books.

Leete, Richard. 1987. "The Post-demographic Transition in East and South East Asia: Similarities and Contrasts with Europe." *Population Studies* 41 (July): 187–206.

London, Bruce, et al. 1986. "The Determinants of Gentrification in the United States: A City-Level Analysis." *Urban Affairs Quarterly* 21 (March): 369–387.

Lowi, Theodore J. 1981. "Machine Politics—Old and New," pp. 214–217 in J. John Palen (ed.), *City Scenes.* Boston: Little, Brown and Company. Second edition.

Malthus, Thomas Robert. 1798. *First Essay on Population: 1798.* London: Printed for J. Johnson in St. Paul's Churchyard.

Matthews, Tom. 1979. "Nuclear Accident." *Newsweek* 93 (April 9): 24–26+.

Meadows, Donella H., et al. 1972. *The Limits to Growth: A Report on the Club of Rome's Project on the Predicament of Mankind.* New York: Signet Books.

Miller, Stanton S. 1989. "Superfund: An Environmental Boondoggle." *Environmental Science and Technology* 23 (April): 394.

Molotch, Harvey, and Serena Vicari. 1988. "Three Ways to Build the Development Process in the United States, Japan, and Italy." *Urban Affairs Quarterly* 24 (December): 188–214.

Mumford, Lewis. 1971. "Statement of Lewis Mumford, Author. Hearings before the U.S. Senate, Subcommittee on Executive Reorganization, Committee on Government Operations, April 21, 1967," pp. 431–456 in Ted Venetoulis and Ward Eisenhauer (eds.), *Up against the Urban Wall.* Englewood Cliffs, NJ: Prentice-Hall.

Nam, Charles B., and Susan O. Gustavus. 1976. *Population: The Dynamics of Demographic Change.* Boston: Houghton Mifflin.

Oliver, Pamela. 1984. "'If You Don't Do It, Nobody Else Will': Active and Token Contributors to Local Collective Action." *American Sociological Review* 49 (October): 601–610.

Pagano, Michael A. 1988. "Fiscal Disruptions and City Responses: Stability, Equilibrium, and City Capital Budgeting." *Urban Affairs Quarterly* 24 (September): 118–137.

Palen, J. John. 1981. *The Urban World.* New York: McGraw-Hill. Second edition.

Petersen, William. 1975. *Population.* New York: Macmillan. Third edition.

Pfeiffer, John. 1989. "How Man Invented Cities," pp. 6–11 in Jeffrey M. Elliot (ed.), *Urban Society.* Guilford, CT: Dushkin. Fourth edition.

Pollock, Cynthia. 1986. "The Closing Act: Decommissioning Nuclear Power Plants." *Environment* 28 (March): 10–15+.

Population Today. 1986. "Population Momentum Is the Key." 14 (April): 3+.

Poston, Dudley L., Jr., and Baochang Gu. 1987. "Socioeconomic Development, Family Planning, and Fertility in China." *Demography* 24 (November): 531–551.

Prestby, John E., and Abraham Wandersman. 1985. "An Empirical Exploration of a Framework of Organizational Viability: Maintaining Block Organizations." *Journal of Applied Behavioral Science* 21: 287–305.

Reilly, William K. 1982. "Reconciling Mineral Development and Environmental Quality." *Vital Speeches* 48 (May 1): 471–475.

Ridker, Ronald G., and W. D. Watson. 1980. *To Choose a Future: Resources and Environmental Problems of the United States.* Baltimore: Johns Hopkins Press.

Robertson, Ian. 1980. *Social Problems.* New York: Random House. Second edition.

Russell, Milton. 1987. "Environmental Protection for the 1990s and Beyond." *Environment* 29 (September): 12–15+.

Salvesen, David, and Terry Jill Lassar. 1988. "L.A.'s Sewer Moratorium Curbs Growth." *Urban Land* 47 (August): 36–37.

Schneider, Keith. 1989. "Fears of Pesticides Threaten American Way of Farming." *New York Times* (May 1): A1+.

Schwab, William A. 1982. *Urban Sociology.* Reading, MA: Addison-Wesley.

Shabecoff, Philip. 1988. "Major 'Greenhouse' Impact Is Unavoidable, Experts Say." *New York Times* (July 19): C1+.

Shenon, Philip. 1989. "Former Florida G.O.P. Chief Got $500,000 for Lobbying of H.U.D." *New York Times* (July 25): A1+.

Silk, Leonard. 1986. "Modern Views of Population." *New York Times* (July 9): D2.

Simmel, Georg. 1950. *The Sociology of Georg Simmel.* Glencoe, IL: Free Press. Translated by Kurt H. Wolff.

Sjoberg, Gideon. 1960. *The Preindustrial City: Past and Present.* Glencoe, IL: The Free Press.

Spates, James L., and John J. Macionis. 1982. *The Sociology of Cities.* New York: St. Martin's Press.

Stahura, John M. 1988. "Changing Patterns of Suburban Racial Composition, 1970–1980." *Urban Affairs Quarterly* 23 (March): 448–460.

Sullivan, Thomas, et al. 1980. *Social Problems.* New York: John Wiley & Sons.

Sun, Marjorie. 1983. "Missouri's Costly Dioxin Lesson." *Science* 219 (January 28): 367–369.

Terry, Don. 1989. "In Week of an Infamous Rape, 28 Other Victims Suffer." *New York Times* (May 29): 25.

Tönnies, Ferdinand. 1957. *Community and Society.* New York: Harper & Company.

United Nations. 1985. *Demographic Yearbook, 1985.* New York: United Nations Publishing Service.

U.S. Bureau of the Census. *Statistical Abstract of the United States: 1989.* Washington, DC: U.S. Government Printing Office. 109th edition.

Wald, Matthew L. 1989a. "10 Years after Three Mile Island." *New York Times* (March 23): D1+.

Wald, Matthew L. 1989b. "Exxon Estimating $1.28 Billion Cost for Spill Cleanup." *New York Times* (July 25): A1+.

Wald, Matthew L. 1989c. "U.S. Will Start over on Planning for Nevada Waste Dump." *New York Times* (November 29): A1+.

Wandersman, Abraham. 1985. "Getting Together and Getting Things Done." *Psychology Today* 19 (November): 64–65.

Whitney, Craig R. 1989. "12 European Nations to Ban Chemicals that Harm Ozone." *New York Times* (March 3): A1+.

Wirth, Louis, 1938. "Urbanism As a Way of Life." *American Journal of Sociology* 44 (July): 3–24.

Zimmerman, J. F. 1975. "The Patchwork Approach: Adaptive Responses to Increasing Urbanism," pp. 431–473 in A. H. Hawley and V. P. Roch (eds.), *Metropolitan America in Contemporary Perspective.* New York: John Wiley & Sons.

Chapter 17

Allen, James R. 1987. "The Use of Strategic Techniques in Large Systems: Mohandas K. Gandhi and the Indian Independence Movement." *Jour-nal of Strategic & Systematic Therapies* 6 (Fall): 57–64.

Atkins, Burton M., and Henry R. Glick (eds.). 1972. *Prisons, Protests and Politics.* Englewood Cliffs, NJ: Prentice-Hall.

Barron, James. 1982. "Poison Worries Lead to Precautions for Halloween." *New York Times* (October 28): B1.

Beck, Melinda. 1983. "A Racial Outburst in Miami." *Newsweek* 101 (January 10): 23.

Bendzsel, Miklós, and István Kiss. 1987. "The Socio-ethical Dimension of Invention." *Impact of Science on Society* 37: 233–240.

Blumer, Herbert. 1975. "Outline of Collective Behavior," pp. 22–45 in Robert Evans (ed.), *Readings in Collective Behavior.* Chicago: Rand McNally. Second edition.

Brown, Lester R., Patricia L. McGrath, and Bruce Stokes. 1982. "The Population Problem in 22 Dimensions," pp. 262–269 in Leonard Cargan and Jeanne H. Ballantine (eds.), *Sociological Footprints.* Belmont, CA: Wadsworth. Second edition.

Brown, Michael, and Amy Goldin. 1973. *Collective Behavior.* Pacific Palisades, CA: Goodyear.

Butterfield, Fox. 1989. "Deng Reappears with a Chilling Lesson about Power in China." *New York Times* (June 11): section 4, p. 1.

Cantril, Hadley. 1940. *The Invasion from Mars.* Princeton: Princeton University Press.

Caplan, Nathan S., and Jeffrey M. Paige. 1968. "A Study of Ghetto Rioters." *Scientific American* 219 (August): 15–21.

Carter, Gregg Lee. 1987. "Police Force Size and the Severity of the 1960s Black Rioting." *Journal of Conflict Resolution* 31 (December): 601–614.

Colvin, Mark. 1982. "The 1980 New Mexico Prison Riot." *Social Problems* 29 (June): 449–463.

Crandall, Christian S. 1988. "Social Contagion of Binge Eating." *Journal of Personality and Social Psychology* 55 (October): 588–598.

Davies, James C. 1962. "Toward a Theory of Revolution." *American Sociological Review* 27 (February): 5–19.

Davis, Terry. 1986. "The Forms of Collective Racial Violence." *Political Studies* 34 (March): 40–60.

Egan, Timothy. 1989. "Building Codes: Designs for Last Quake, Not Next." *New York Times* (October 22): 26.

Farley, John E. 1982. *Majority–Minority Relations.* Englewood Cliffs, NJ: Prentice-Hall.

Fischer, Claude S., and Glenn R. Carroll. 1988. "Telephone and Automobile Diffusion in the United States, 1902–1937." *American Journal of Sociology* 93 (March): 1153–1178.

Foy, Eddie, and Alvin F. Harlow. 1957. *Clowning through Life.* New York: E. P. Dutton and Company. Originally published in 1928. Pp. 104–113, excerpted in Ralph H. Turner and Lewis M. Killian, *Collective Behavior.* Englewood Cliffs, NJ: Prentice-Hall.

558

Freeman, Jo. 1979. "The Woman's Liberation Movement: Its Origins, Organizations, Activities, and Ideas," pp. 557–574 in Jo Freeman (ed.), *Women: A Feminist Perspective*. Palo Alto, CA: Mayfield.

Gamson, William. 1975. *The Strategy of Social Protest*. Homewood, IL: Dorsey Press.

Gurney, Joan Neff, and Kathleen J. Tierney. 1982. "Relative Deprivation and Social Movements: A Critical Look at Twenty Years of Theory and Research." *Sociological Quarterly* 23 (Winter): 33–47.

Gurr, Ted Robert. 1979. "Political Protest and Rebellion in the 1960s," pp. 49–76 in Hugh Davis Graham and Ted Robert Gurr (eds.), *Violence in America: Historical Perspectives*. Beverly Hills: Sage.

Hannigan, John A. 1985. "Alain Touraine, Manuel Castells and Social Movement Theory: A Critical Appraisal." *Sociological Quarterly* 26 (Winter): 435–454.

Hefez, Albert. 1985. "The Role of the Press and the Medical Community in the Epidemic of 'Mysterious Gas Poisoning' in the Jordan West Bank." *American Journal of Psychiatry* 142 (July): 833–837.

Johnson, George. 1989. "Scientists Try to Handicap the Odds of a Great Celestial Smashup." *New York Times* (April 23): section 4, p. 7.

Johnson, J. R., and Joseph S. Petrovsky. 1988. "Lessons Learned after the Riots." *Corrections Today* 50 (June): 16–18.

Kennedy, Sara L., and M. Katherine Shear. 1988. "Prevalence of Panic Attacks in a Nonclinical Sample." *American Journal of Psychiatry* 145 (March): 384–385.

Kerbo, Harold R. 1982. "Movements of 'Crisis' and Movements of 'Affluence.'" *Journal of Conflict Resolution* 26 (December): 645–663.

Kerbo, Harold R., and Richard A. Shaffer. 1986. "Unemployment and Protest in the United States, 1890–1940: A Methodological Critique and Research Note." *Social Forces* 64 (June): 1046–1056.

Killian, Lewis M. 1964. "Social Movements," pp. 426–455 in Robert E. L. Faris (ed.), *Handbook of Modern Sociology*. Chicago: Rand McNally.

Klandermans, Bert. 1984. "Mobilization and Participation: Social–Psychological Expansion of Resource Mobilization Theory." *American Sociological Review* 49 (October): 583–600.

Klein, Andrew L. 1976. "Changes in Leadership Appraisal As a Function of the Stress of a Simulated Panic Situation." *Journal of Personality and Social Psychology* 34 (December): 1143–1154.

Lauer, Robert H. 1977. *Perspective on Social Change*. Boston: Allyn and Bacon. Second edition.

Le Bon, Gustave. 1952. *The Crowd*. London: Ernest Benn Limited. Originally published in 1896.

Lenski, Gerhard, and Jean Lenski. 1982. *Human Societies*. New York: McGraw-Hill. Fourth edition.

Linton, Ralph. 1973. "Discovery, Invention, and Their Cultural Setting," pp. 451–456 in Amitai Etzioni and Eva Etzioni-Halevy (eds.), *Social Change*. New York: Basic Books. Second edition.

Linton, Ralph. 1982. "One Hundred Percent American," pp. 58–59 in Leonard Cargan and Jeanne H. Ballantine (eds.), *Sociological Footprints*. Belmont, CA: Wadsworth. Second edition.

MacFarquhar, Roderick. 1989. "The End of the Chinese Revolution." *New York Review of Books* 36 (July 20): 8–10.

Magnuson, Ed. 1989. "Earthquake." *Time* 134 (October 30): 32–40.

Malcolm, Andrew H. 1980. "The 'Shortage' of Bathroom Tissue," pp. 497–498 in Reece McGee et al., *Sociology*. New York: Holt, Rinehart and Winston. Second edition.

Mann, Leon. 1981. "The Baiting Crowd in Episodes of Threatened Suicide." *Journal of Personality and Social Psychology* 41 (October): 703–709.

Marshall, S. L. A. 1947. *Men under Fire*. New York: William Morrow and Company.

Miller, Robert L. 1989. "From the Publisher." *Time* 134 (October 30): 28.

Morrison, Denton E. 1973. "Some Notes toward Theory on Relative Deprivation, Social Movements, and Social Changes," pp. 103–116 in Robert R. Evans (ed.), *Social Movements*. Chicago: Rand McNally.

Murdock, George Peter. 1956. "How Culture Changes," pp. 247–260 in Harry L. Shapiro (ed.), *Man, Culture, and Society*. New York: Oxford University Press.

National Advisory Commission on Civil Disorders. 1968. *Report of the National Advisory Commission on Civil Disorders*. New York: Bantam Books.

New Haven Register. 1986. "Letterman's Flip Remark Prompts $1 Million Suit." (July 26): 14.

New York State Special Commission on Attica. 1972. *Attica: The Official Report of the New York State Special Commission on Attica*. New York: Bantam Books.

Nielsen, François. 1985. "Toward a Theory of Ethnic Solidarity in Modern Societies." *American Sociological Review* 50 (April): 133–149.

Oberschall, Anthony. 1973. *Social Conflict and Social Movements*. Englewood Cliffs, NJ: Prentice-Hall.

Orwell, George. 1946. *Animal Farm*. New York: Harcourt, Brace and World.

Pallas, John, and Bob Barker. 1972. "From Riot to Revolution." *Issues in Criminology* 7: 1–19.

Perry, Joseph B., Jr., and M. D. Pugh. 1978. *Collective Behavior*. St. Paul, MN: West.

Quarantelli, E. L., and Russell R. Dynes. 1970. "Property Norms and Looting: Their Patterns in Community Crises." *Phylon* 31 (Summer): 168–182.

Reinhold, Robert. 1989. "California Struggles with the Other Side of the Dream." *New York Times* (October 22): section 4, p. 1.

Rice, Berkeley. 1981. "Gourmet Worms: Antidote to a Rumor." *Psychology Today* 15 (August): 20+.

Rosnow, Ralph L. 1988. "Rumor As Communication: A Contextualist Approach." *Journal of Communication* 38 (Winter): 12–28.

Ryder, Norman B. 1980. "The Future of American Fertility," pp. 51–66 in Arlene Skolnick and Jerome H. Skolnick (eds.), *Family in Transition*. Boston: Little, Brown, and Company. Third edition.

Salholz, Eloise, et al. 1989. "Recovery by the Bay." *Newsweek* 114 (November 6): 37+.

Shibutani, Tamotsu. 1966. *Improvised News: A Sociological Study of Rumor*. Indianapolis: Bobbs-Merrill.

Smelser, Neil J. 1963. *Theory of Collective Behavior*. New York: Free Press.

Stiefel, Michael. 1982. "Soft and Hard Energy Paths: The Roads Not Taken," pp. 49–50 in John Allen (ed.), *Environment 82/83*. Guilford, CT: Dushkin.

Tilly, Charles. 1978. *From Mobilization to Revolution*. Reading, MA: Addison-Wesley.

Turner, Ralph H. 1964. "Collective Behavior," pp. 382–426 in Robert E. L. Faris (ed.), *Handbook of Modern Sociology*. Chicago: Rand McNally.

Turner, Ralph H., and Lewis M. Killian. 1972. *Collective Behavior*. Englewood Cliffs, NJ: Prentice-Hall. Second edition.

Useem, Bert. 1985. "Disorganization and the New Mexico Prison Riot." *American Sociological Review* 50 (October): 677–688.

Vander Zanden, James W. 1981. *Social Psychology*. New York: Random House. Second edition.

Wu Dunn, Sheryl. 1989. "Spies Learn Students Can Be Stern Teachers." *New York Times* (May 29): A7.

Yurkanin, Ann. 1988. "Inmate Uprising at Riker's Island." *Corrections Today* 50 (April): 204.

LITERARY CREDITS

Table 2.1. Adapted from Roper Reports, May 1981. Used by permission.

Table 3.1. From The New York Times Poll of December 24, 1985. Copyright © 1985 by The New York Times Company. Reprinted by permission.

Table 3.4, Table 4.1. Data From Richard G. Braungart and Margaret M. Braungart. "From Yippies to Yuppies: Twenty Years of Freshman Attitudes." *Public Opinion II* (September/October 1988): 53–56.

Figure 6.1. From Roper Reports, April 1982. Used by permission.

Table 6.2. From Alec M. Gallup and Stanley M. Elam, "The 20th Annual Gallup Poll of the Public's Attitudes Toward Public Schools," *Phi Delta Kappan 69* (1988): 33–46. Used by permission.

Figure 7.1. Adapted from Joel Aronoff and William D. Crano, "A Cross-Cultural Study of Expressive and Instrumental Role Complementarity in the Family," *American Sociological Review 43* (1978), tables 1 and 2. Used by permission.

Table 7.2. From Gallup Poll, April 12, 1985. Used by permission.

Table 7.3. Adaptation of Fig. 27 in *American Couples* by Philip Blumstein and Pepper W. Schwartz. Copyright © 1983 by Philip Blumstein and Pepper W. Schwartz. Adapted by permission of William Morrow & Company.

Table 7.4. From Gallup Poll, November 11, 1985. Used by permission.

Table 7.5. From Gallup Poll, May 1, 1985. Used by permission.

Figure 8.1. U.S. Bureau of the Census.

Table 8.1. Adapted with permission of The Free Press, a division of Macmillan, Inc., from *Social Theory and Social Structure*, revised edition, by Robert K. Merton. Copyright © 1968, 1967 by Robert K. Merton.

Table 8.3, Table 8.4; Figure 9.1. U.S. Bureau of the Census.

Figure 9.2. From Gallup Poll, "Prestige of Selected White Collar Occupations," October 7, 1981. Used by permission.

Figure 9.3. Adapted from Lawrence Maloney, "America's New Middle Class," *U.S. News and World Report*, March 30, 1981, p. 40. Used by permission.

Figure 10.1. From Roper Reports, May 1982. Used by permission.

Figure 10.2, Table 10.2; Figure 11.1, Table 11.1. U.S. Bureau of the Census.

Table 11.1. U.S. Bureau of the Census.

Table 11.2. Based on Helen Mayer Hacker, "Women as a Minority Group," *Social Forces* (October 1951), 60–69.

Table 12.1. Adapted from Richard G. Braungart and Margaret M. Braungart. "From Yippies to Yuppies: Twenty Years of Freshman Attitudes." *Public Opinion II* (September/October 1988): 53–56.

Table 12.2; Figure 12.1, Figure 12.2. U.S. Bureau of the Census.

Figure 13.1. Adapted from the Gallup Report "Religion in America" (June–July 1982). Used by permission.

Figure 14.2. Data from *Fortune Directory* (1988) and *Information Please Almanac* (1988).

Table 14.1. Data from *From Max Weber*, edited by Hans Gerth and C. Wright Mills (New York: Oxford University Press, 1946).

Table 14.2. U.S. Bureau of the Census.

Table 14.3. U.S. Department of Labor.

Table 15.1, Figure 15.1. U.S. Bureau of the Census.

Table 15.2. From Ian Mitroff, "Norms and Counter-Norms in a Select Group of

562
Apollo Moon Scientists: A Case Study of the Ambivalence of Scientists," *American Sociological Review 39* (1974), table 4, p. 592.

Table 15.3. U.S. Bureau of the Census.

Table 15.4. From Gallup Poll, December 1988. Used by permission.

Table 16.1. From Gallup Report, June 1899. Used by permission.

Figure 16.1, Figure 16.2, Figure 16.4. U.S. Bureau of the Census.

Figure 16.5. From Roper Reports, November 1981. Used by permission.

Table 17.1, Table 17.2. Adapted from Ted Robert Gurr, "Political Protest and Rebellion in the 1960s," in *Violence in America: Historical Perspectives*, edited by Hugh Davis Graham and Ted Robert Gurr (Newbury Park, Calif.: Sage Publications, 1979), pp. 54, 60. Used by permission.

Figure 17.1. Adapted from James C. Davies, "Toward a Theory of Revolution," *American Sociological Review 27* (1962), 6: the J-curve. Used with permission.

Photo Credits

Chapter 1 Opener: Steve Krongard/Image Bank; Page 6, Elizabeth Crews; Page 12, AP/Wide World Photos; Page 14, David Campione/Taurus; Page 17, Susan Meiselas/Magnum; **Chapter 2** Opener: Ted Kawalerski/Image Bank; Page 29, Gale Zucker/Stock, Boston; Jerry Berndt/Stock, Boston; Page 32, Elizabeth Crews; Page 42, © 1965 by Stanley Miligram. From the film *Obedience*, distributed by the New York University Film and Video Library and the Pennsylvania State University, PCR. **Chapter 3** Opener: Vince Compagnone/Jeroboam; Page 53 (top left), Jean-Claude Lejeune/Stock, Boston; Page 53 (top right), Ira Kirshenbaum/Stock, Boston; (bottom left) Ken Gaghan/Jeroboam; Page 55, UPI/Bettmann Newsphotos; Page 57, Victor Englebert/Photo Researchers, Inc.; Page 59, AP/Wide World Photos; Page 63, P. Spadavecchia/Image Works; Page 65, AP/Wide World Photos; Page 68, Don Hogan Charles/NYT Pictures. **Chapter 4** Opener: Carolyn McKeone/FPG; Page 84, Joel Gordon; Page 85, AP/Wide World Photos; Page 87, AP/Wide World Photos; Page 89, AP/Wide World Photos; Page 94, Owen Frank/Stock, Boston; Page 97, Edna Douthat/Photo Researchers, Inc.; **Chapter 5** Opener: Jean-Claude Lejeune/Stock, Boston; Page 109, Elizabeth Crews/Stock, Boston; Page 112, Jerry Berndt/Stock, Boston; Page 118, Irene Bayer/Monkmeyer Press Photos; Page 119, AP/Wide World Photos; **Chapter 6** Opener: Bob Daemmrich/Stock, Boston; Page 135, Museum of Modern Art/Film Stills Archive; Page 138, Elizabeth Crews; Page 139, Elizabeth Crews; Page 143, Michael Weisbrot/Stock, Boston; Page 149, Nina Berman/SIPA Press; Page 152, UPI/Bettmann Newsphotos. **Chapter 7** Opener: Kent Reno/Jeroboam; Page 165, David Strickler/Monkmeyer Press Photos; Page 167, Abigail Heyman/Picture Project; Page 167, Jean-Claude Lejeune/Stock, Boston; Page 173, Joel Gordon; Page 183, Robert George Gaylord/Jeroboam; Page 185, AP/Wide World Photos. **Chapter 8** Opener: Doug Milner; Page 200, Jean Pierre Laffont/Sygma; Page 205, AP/Wide World Photos; Page 209, AP/Wide World Photos; Page 211, SIPA Press; Page 217 (left), AP/Wide World Photos; Page 217 (right), Leonard Freed/Magnum; Page 221, Suzanne Arms Wimberly/Jeroboam. **Chapter 9** Opener: Fredrik Bodin/Stock, Boston; Page 233, UPI/Bettmann Newsphotos; Page 245, Michael Hayman/Photo Researchers, Inc.; Page 247, Costa Manos/Magnum; Page 252, Byron Collection/Museum of the City of New York; Page 254, Elizabeth Hamlin/Stock, Boston. **Chapter 10** Opener: Alice Kandell/Photo Researchers, Inc.; Page 270, Bob Adelman/Magnum; Page 271 (left), Dan Walsh/Picture Cube; Page 271 (right), AP/Wide World Photos; Page 277, Jason Laure/Woodfin Camp & Associates; Page 282, Alex Webb/Magnum; Page 286, Ira Berger/Woodfin Camp & Associates; Page 289, © ELP Communications. All rights reserved. Courtesy of Columbia Pictures. Television. **Chapter 11** Opener: California Angels; Page 303, Jean Gaumy/Magnum; Page 304 (left), Culver Pictures; Page 304 (right), Bettye Lane/Photo Researchers, Inc.; Page 308, Emilio Mercado/Jeroboam; Page 311, Martine Franck/Magnum; Page 312, Alan Carey/Image Works; Page 317, Dan Ford Connolly. **Chapter 12** Opener: Ben Mitchell/The Image Bank; Page 329, Marc & Evelyn Bernheim/Woodfin Camp & Associates; Page 331, Kay Lawson/Jeroboam; Page 339, Elizabeth Crews; Page 340, Christa Armstrong/Photo Researchers, Inc.; Page 343, Paul Fortin/Stock, Boston. **Chapter 13** Opener: Bruce Flynn/Stock, Boston; Page 359, David Strickler/Picture Cube; Page 360, Eugene Gordon/Photo Researchers, Inc.; Page 363, Doug Milner; Page 366, AP/Wide World Photos; Page 372, George Gardner/Stock, Boston; Page 376, Bob Daemmrich, Stock, Boston. **Chapter 14** Opener: Dan Bryant Photos; Page 390, AP/Wide World Photos; Page 393, Joseph Koudelka/Magnum; Page 397, AP/Wide World Photos; Page 403, Barbara Alper/Stock, Boston; Page 408, Mimi Forsyth/Monkmeyer Press Photos; Page 410, AP/Wide World Photos. **Chapter 15** Opener: Michael Melford/Image Bank; Page 424, Mary Evans Picture Library/Photo Researchers, Inc.; Lynn McLaren/Photo Researchers, Inc.; Page 435, AP/Wide World Photos; Page 438, Susan Lapides/Design Conceptions; Page 439, Suzie Fitzhugh/Stock, Boston; Page 441, © Martin/Custom Medical Stock Photo. **Chapter 16** Opener: Stuart Rosner/Stock, Boston; Page 454, Peter Menzel/Stock, Boston; Page 456, Culver Pictures; Page 463, Alan Carey/Image Works; Page 467, Harry Crosby/Photo Researchers, Inc.; John Coletti/Stock, Boston; Page 471, AP/Wide World Photos; Page 473, Rose Skytta/Jeroboam; Page 476, Daniel Brody/Stock, Boston. **Chapter 17** Opener: AP/Wide World Photos; Page 490, AP/Wide World Photos; Page 498 (left), Owen Frank/Stock, Boston; Page 498 (right), AP/Wide World Photos; Page 500, AP/Wide World Photos; Page 503, Damon Burris; Page 507, Hazel Hankin/Stock, Boston; Page 511, UPI/Bettmann Newsphotos.

Name Index

565

Subject Index

Terms written in **boldface** type are defined in the running glossary, usually on the first text page listed in the index.

575